1. Sloane-fifty

IN
THE
TWENTIES

By

HARRY KESSLER

with an Introduction by Otto Friedrich
Translated by Charles Kessler

HOLT, RINEHART AND WINSTON
New York   Chicago   San Francisco

IN
THE
TWENTIES

THE DIARIES
OF HARRY KESSLER

First published in Germany under the title
Harry Graf Kessler, Tagebücher 1918–1937
© Insel Verlag, Frankfurt am Main, 1961

English Translation © 1971 by Weidenfeld & Nicolson Ltd., London.

Published in England under the title *The Diaries of a Cosmopolitan, Count Harry Kessler, 1918–1937*

Published simultaneously in Canada by Holt, Rinehart and Winston of Canada, Limited.
Library of Congress Catalog Card Number: 76–117264
First Edition

ISBN: 0–03–072630–1
Printed in the United States of America

Contents

Illustrations

The publishers are grateful to the following copyright-holders for their permission to reproduce the illustrations on the pages shown: Methuen & Co. Ltd., pages 188 and 234; Angelica Garnett and the Hogarth Press, page 362; Editions Stock, pages 146, 208, 298, 356; The Mansell Collection, page 162; Bildarchiv der Österreich Nationalbibliothek, pages 3, 37, 75, 109, 129, 156, 369 and 488; The Estate of George Grosz, Princeton, New Jersey, other illustrations by George Grosz; Mrs Renée Hague, illustrations by Eric Gill.

INTRODUCTION

There is no chance, we like to reassure ourselves, that what happened in Germany during the darkest years of this century could ever happen here. Unlike the Germans, we are democrats; we do not persecute minorities or wage wars of aggression. And because we have mastered our economic system, we will not have a devastating inflation, or armies of unemployed men skulking in the streets, or riotous confrontations between extremists of the right and left. We do not have alienated students and intellectuals engaging in fierce denunciations of what the Germans of the 1920s called "The System." We will never, in short, let our disagreements reach such a state of crisis that we will vote power to a new dictator. Or will we?

Because we do not wholly trust our reassuring declarations that it can't happen again, there have been signs, in this country, of an increasing fascination with the Germany of the pre-Hitler years. This was, of course, a period of immense cultural vitality, a period that brought forth the novels of Thomas Mann and Hermann Hesse, the new music of Schoenberg and Hindemith, the pioneering films of Lang and Murnau, the experimental designs of the Bauhaus. But our fascination is not wholly cultural. It began, as far as one can determine, with a mysterious interest in half-disguised theatrical portraits of the period. The astringent plays of Bertolt Brecht, which had received little attention during the poet's years in exile here, gradually began appearing in college theaters in the Midwest, and when the long-ignored Brecht-Weill *Three-Penny Opera* opened in a little theater in Greenwich Village, it became the longest-running hit in Off-Broadway history. Mac the Knife again became what he had been a generation earlier, a folk figure of nihilism and destruction. Even more symptomatic was the transformation of Christopher Isherwood's modest *Berlin Stories* into the successful play and movie, *I Am a Camera* and, with the addition of some rather undistinguished songs, the even more successful musical, *Cabaret*.

The success of *Cabaret* illustrates, to some extent, what the Germany of the 1920s has come to mean to us. For in the course of the changes from novel to play to musical, the elegiac quality of Isherwood's stories gave way to a night-club tone of noisy frivolity. The Nazis, who remained a shadowy menace in Isherwood, were brought onstage and made to shout. What fascinates us about pre-Hitler Germany, then, is not just cultural vitality but also a combination of licentiousness and impending violence, a sense that this brittle and hysterical society will soon succumb, with the

ix

inevitability that we always ascribe to past events, to the perverse brutality of Nazism.

Fascinated by the cynical spirit of doomed Berlin, we necessarily come back to political questions. How did the disaster happen, and why, and are we ourselves really immune to the disease? From American university presses nowadays there pours a stream of books, morbidly analyzing and documenting the tragedy—but this is all, in every sense of the word, academic. What we really want, in this age of TV journalism, is the testimony of eyewitnesses, of someone who was there, watching, listening, and recording. There have been, to be sure, a good many official auto-biographies from this period, but they generally suffer from a need for self-justification, a need to explain rather than to tell. It is safe to say that no other autobiographical account of these times has the immediacy, the richness, and the variety of the diaries of Count Harry Kessler.

The reasons are simple. For one thing, Kessler was a writer of sharp perception and boundless curiosity. For another, he wrote everything down as it happened, and he never had the time to go back and tamper with his own record, to suppress the mistakes and misjudgments that are themselves part of his story. The most important reason, though, is that Kessler's restless and inquiring spirit brought him into contact with every aspect of German political and cultural life. He was a skilled diplomat, and something of an intriguer, but he was also a dedicated collector and patron of art; he was a distinguished publisher, but he was also an able writer, whose work ranged from a biography of Walther Rathenau to a ballet scenario for Richard Strauss. And he knew everyone, from Einstein to the Kaiser to Josephine Baker to Bernard Shaw to the now-forgotten countesses who ornamented the best salons of Berlin, Paris, and London.

Count Kessler was of unusual origins. Born in Paris, on May 23, 1868, he was the son of a Hamburg banker who had been ennobled by Kaiser Wilhelm I. His mother was a famous Irish beauty, the former Alice Bosse-Lynch, and there were rumors that the Kaiser took a discreet interest in her during the summers that both families spent at the resort of Ems. Mrs. Kessler named her daughter Wilma, and old Kaiser Wilhelm served as the child's godfather. Kessler himself was aware of these rumors, and even late in his life, he treated them somewhat ambiguously. A luncheon guest "spoke frankly about the 'legends' . . . relating to my origins. I am generally thought to be a Hohenzollern, son of the Emperor Wilhelm I, and therefore 'uncle' to Wilhelm II. . . . The matter can very easily be pinned down for the nonsense that it is, I replied. My poor mother was not introduced to the old Emperor until subsequent to my birth. True, he agreed, but she was in fact the old gentleman's last love. Maybe, I countered, but in the same way as Marianne was the last love of Goethe in his old age."

It is difficult to imagine what it must have felt like to be rumored the illegitimate uncle of a reigning monarch, but Kessler carried it off with aristocratic swagger. Edvard Munch's portrait shows him to be a tall, slim figure with calmly penetrating eyes, a bushy moustache and enough self-possession to wear a broad-brimmed canary-yellow hat. Later portraits show Kessler without the moustache, his long thin mouth turning down at the corners, his eyes still coolly appraising. Surveying the shambles of the royal palace after the revolution of 1918, Kessler noted the looting of the Empress's wardrobe, the scattering of glass trinkets and powder boxes, but then he added: "These private apartments, the furniture, the articles of everyday use . . . are so insipid and tasteless, so Philistine, that it is difficult to feel much indignation against the pilferers. Only astonishment that the wretched, timid, unimaginative creatures who liked this trash and frittered away their life in this precious palatial haven, amidst lackeys and sycophants, could ever make any impact on history. Out of this atmosphere was born the World War. . . ."

Educated partly in France, partly in England, and finally at the universities of Bonn and Leipzig, where he absorbed the revolutionary new ideas of Marx, Ibsen, Wagner, and Nietzsche, Count Kessler was in England when war became imminent, and he returned to France on the same channel steamer as Auguste Rodin. (The sculptor, on being offered some lunch, said, "No, I'm not hungry. I'm looking at nature; nature nourishes me.") Kessler continued on to Germany and became an officer of the Uhlan Guards. He fought in Belgium, then on the eastern front, and finally was sent to Switzerland, where he took part in the negotiations that led to Lenin's sealed-train trip across Germany to the Finland Station in St. Petersburg. Toward the end of the war, Kessler also came to know General Pilsudski, the military leader of reborn Poland. So it was natural that the new German government, seeking to establish cordial relations with the fractious regime to its east, asked Kessler to escort Pilsudski back home from internment in Germany, and then to serve as the first German minister to Warsaw. His assignment was to oversee the peaceful withdrawal of more than 100,000 German troops from the eastern front. It is this brief and unsuccessful mission, highlighted by Polish mobs chasing Kessler from hotel to hotel, that begins the present diary.

The diary improves as it goes on, for what we really seek in old memoirs is not the explication of relatively minor political crises but rather a sense of intimacy and revelation, a sense of the past brought back to life. Kessler is remarkably skillful in sketching his characters in a few words. He deflates the intrigues of Chancellor Franz von Papen, for instance, by describing him as having "the air of an irritable billy-goat trying to adopt dignity [by wearing] a silk-lined black jacket." Regarding Lenin's special envoy, Karl Radek, he sees "a mask of youthful ardor. From behind it, and his flashing spectacles, there suddenly crept into his face an expression [of] a wolf and at the same time having something of the look of a street urchin after a particularly successful prank." Even people he dislikes—and he is often malicious—Kessler is able to judge sharply. Thus, listening to a speech by the ambitious Catholic Center Party leader Matthias Erzberger: "I had a full view of his badly made, flat-soled boots, his comic trousers rising via corkscrew crinkles to his full-moon bottom, his broad and thick-set peasant shoulders. . . . I could see every clumsy move of his clumsy body, every change of color in his chubby cheeks, every drop of sweat on his greasy forehead. But gradually this comic, uncouth figure grew into a personality enunciating the most frightful of indictments. . . ."

Kessler not only creates vivid portraits; he also tells splendid stories about his social wanderings. There was the dinner, for example, at which Einstein and Gerhart Hauptmann got into a fierce argument about astrology. And the night when someone telephoned Kessler to come to see Josephine Baker dance in someone's apartment, where most of the men turned out to be in evening clothes and most of the women naked. "Miss Baker was also naked except for a pink muslin apron, and the little Landshof girl . . . was dressed up as a boy in a dinner-jacket. Miss Baker was dancing a solo with brilliant artistic mimicry. . . . Apparently she does this for hours on end. . . ." Then there was the story of the Marchesa Casati, who telephoned the Archbishop of Paris at three in the morning because she wanted to talk to him. The priest sent by the Archbishop arrived to find the Marchesa standing stark naked in the doorway of her mansion, a candelabra in each hand. . . .

Of all Kessler's tales, none is so sad, so funny, and so completely bizarre as the story of his flight from France to Germany with the 69-year-old Aristide Maillol and his 20-year-old model, Lucile Passavant. Maillol's wife was so jealous that the sculptor often had to model his statues on pictures from magazines, but she liked Mademoiselle Passavant, until the modeling began. Then she pursued her husband like a fury, peering through keyholes, inspecting his sketches for evidence of deception. "My wife," the old man snuffled to Kessler, "makes me sicker than my cold." Kessler himself rather liked Mademoiselle Passavant—"I find her quite appealing, but she belongs to that type of lower middle class, plumpish, made-up Parisiennes"—and so he agreed to Maillol's plan to bring her secretly on a trip to Germany. Madame Maillol suspected what was happening and, in a fit of rage, tore up all of Maillol's drawings of Mademoiselle Passavant, then turned dark red and fell in a faint. But once Maillol got to Germany, after all this, he spent his time pottering around at the public swimming pools, admiring the nudists, while Mademoiselle Passavant appeared sullen and red-eyed at the breakfast table. "In short," Kessler noted, "we have here the old tragicomedy of the aging man and the hot-blooded girl. . . . Madame Maillol is avenged!"

It would be a mistake, of course, to portray Kessler simply as a purveyor of good gossip. He was also an intensely serious political figure. The monarchists called him "the Red Count," which was probably intended as an insult, but one suspects that Kessler rather prided himself on the title. He was not by any means a Communist, to be sure, but his loathing of the Kaiser helped to make him a supporter of the Republic, which, in the eyes of many aristocrats, was almost the same thing. Now that monarchism has ceased to be a political issue, it is a little hard to realize here how important it once was, and to realize how few genuine republicans there were among the ruling classes of the Weimar Republic. The army, the judiciary, the civil service, the industrialists, and even the intelligentsia had very little fondness for the idea of being ruled by politicians from the working class. The Social Democratic leaders, notably President Friedrich Ebert, were deeply aware of this hostility, and they moved with great caution, probably too much caution, in trying to liberalize the monarchical establishment. They thought the greatest danger came from the revolutionary left, and they willingly used armed force to suppress it. To the intellectual left, which traditionally shares the monarchical disdain for ordinary politicians, this seemed a grievously mistaken policy, and Count Kessler, like a number of his artistic and literary friends, wrote indignantly of the Socialists' "betrayal" of the Republic.

Kessler's political judgments were somewhat mercurial, however. He started with a lordly disdain for both the Kaiser and the Socialists, but he also scorned such moderates as Chancellor Josef Wirth, whom he first called a "typical *Boche*" but later praised. "He is someone after all." Similarly, he first dreaded the election of Marshal Hindenburg as president, then came to see some good in it. Kessler's own political career was equally ambiguous. He was one of the founders of the Democratic Party, an influential but never very powerful group of liberals and intellectuals, and he hoped at one point to enter the Reichstag, but his candidacy came to nothing. There also were rumors that he might become foreign minister, but Kessler himself denied them. He did serve on diplomatic missions, however, to the Genoa conference of 1922, and to some secret negotiations with the British in the following year. Both a patriot and a pacifist, Kessler was dismayed to see the victorious allies building a League of Nations based on the same old national power structures. He drafted and published a constitution for a League made up of international collectivities—labor unions, churches, professional groups, and so on—and, as president of the German Peace Society, he lectured widely in favor of his doomed plan.

What makes Kessler's political activity interesting, however, is not so much his theories, but his role of witness to his time. Every time a shot was fired in the streets of Berlin—and a great many shots were fired—Kessler set out to find what was happening, and to record it in his diaries. Though he had no press function whatever, he was a talented and tireless reporter. Apparently oblivious to machine-gun fire and the explosions of hand-grenades, he wandered through the panicky crowds, observing and questioning, noting down not only the bloodstains on the sidewalks but also the sound of barrel-organs still playing throughout the battles. Nor was he simply an objective observer. On one splendid occasion, after seeing some government troops beat their prisoners, he marched into army headquarters, demanded to see the officer in command, and swore out a formal complaint against the assailants.

As a witness to his times, Kessler roamed far and wide. The death of his father in 1895 had given him a fairly substantial private income, and, free to do whatever he wanted, he devoted himself to the service of art. In his youth, he had taken part in the founding of an influential avant-garde quarterly named *Pan*. He had met Maillol and bought his work long before the war; indeed, the two of them went on a trip to Greece in 1908, along with the poet Hugo von Hoffmansthal. Appointed director of the art museum in Weimar, Kessler came under the influence of the Belgian architect Henri Van de Velde, who founded in Weimar the State School of Arts and Crafts that ultimately developed into the Bauhaus. Van de Velde was an ardent champion of the new art form known as *Jugendstil* (the German equivalent of France's *Art nouveau*), an attempt to replace the fustiness of turn-of-the-century design with a more flowing, more abstract, and more airy elegance. As the Bauhaus of Walter Gropius was to demonstrate, the reintegration of "pure" art and everyday living meant that the artist must master the new technology; it meant the creation of a new style not just in building but in furniture, clothing, and even jewelry. Working out his theories, Van de Velde designed the whole interior of Kessler's apartment in Berlin and his house on the Cranach Strasse in Weimar. And it was under Van de Velde's influence that Kessler found his vocation in the creation of the Cranach Press.

Kessler had been fascinated by the technical possibilities of publishing ever since his childhood days in England. There, he had helped to found the weekly *St. George's Gazette* for the edification of his schoolmates, who included Winston Churchill. But the Cranach Press that Kessler established in Weimar in 1913 was conceived on a somewhat grander scale. His goal was to publish only masterpieces, superbly translated, superbly illustrated, and superbly printed. He even started a mill in France solely to provide the finest quality of paper, some of it made largely from raw silk. His first project was Virgil's *Eclogues*, with woodcuts by Maillol; he got Gerhart Hauptmann to translate *Hamlet*, with illustrations by Edward

Gordon-Craig; Victoria and Edward Sackville-West translated Rilke's *Duino Elegies*, with wood-engraved initials by Eric Gill. The printings were infinitesimal, usually only a few hundred copies, and sometimes the special editions on vellum or Imperial Japan were limited to a dozen copies or less; one expert has cited Kessler's books as "among the great printing achievements of the twentieth century."

There is little of this in the diaries, since Kessler was not writing his autobiography, but his life as a publisher led to much of his restless wandering through Europe. It took him to the remote mountains of Wales, for instance, where his driver got lost in the narrow byways and Kessler finally set out on foot to find the bearded, monk-robed Eric Gill living in a secluded monastery. His wandering took him repeatedly to Paris for interviews with Gide and Valéry and Cocteau, and it took him, of course, into the preposterous private life of Aristide Maillol. And on his voyages —during one year alone, the diary includes entries in Rome, Munich, Berlin, Genoa, Paris, Capri, The Hague, and London—he kept managing to find himself in the middle of contemporary life. In Berlin, he heard Toscanini's *Falstaff*, and the breathtaking debut of the young Yehudi Menuhin; in Rome, he stood in St. Peter's Square with the mob awaiting the smoke signal that would mark the election of a new Pope. "If the crowd were to be swayed by any strength of emotion or even Christian love, it would be irresistible," he observed. "But it only gazes toward the stovepipe."

Yet we keep re-examining the 1920s not just because of the exuberance and vitality of the period itself, but because we know that all of its creativity was soon to be engulfed. In America, we date that devastation from the great stock-market crash of 1929. In Europe, the American crash had its immediate effects, but the date of doomsday is January 30, 1933. Like many Germans, Kessler found it difficult to believe that the whole machinery of government would really be turned over to the little demagogue whom Hindenburg had recently ridiculed as "that Bohemian corporal." Just two days before Hitler's appointment as chancellor, Kessler complained of the possibility that Hindenburg might once again hand over the chancellery to his favorite, Von Papen. When Kessler finally heard the real outcome, he noted, "I was astounded. I did not anticipate this turn of events." Within a month, Kessler learned of his own fate from one of his servants, who informed him, "pale as a sheet," that he was quitting because "there will shortly be 'unpleasantness' in my household." Kessler needed to leave anyway on a short business trip to Paris—a departure that was not difficult in those early days—and it was only in Paris that he learned that he could never return home again. A lonely exile in his native France, Kessler died there on December 4, 1937, at the age of 69, a few weeks after the final diary entry.

Count Kessler kept his diaries for 35 years, apparently assuming from the beginning that the events of his time would be worth recording. Late in life, he used the journals of his first twenty years to write a memoir of his youth, *Faces and Times,* but when it appeared in 1935, Kessler himself was a half-forgotten refugee, and the book attracted little attention in a world preparing for war. More than two decades passed before a German scholar unearthed the remaining diaries—23 notebooks, all handwritten and neatly bound in morocco leather. They contained not only Kessler's own notations but news clippings, visiting cards, and theater programs. As soon as they were published in Germany, they were recognized for what they are: a major document of a nation in crisis.

They do not, of course, answer our questions. What was the fundamental sickness of Germany in the 1920s that led so inexorably to the horrors of Nazism? Various ideologists have offered explanations based on the wickedness of monopoly capitalism, or the inherent evil of the German national character, or, more generally, on the demoralization of all modern society. But Kessler was not an ideologist, any more than he was a leader and mover of men. He was an observer and a recorder. He saw the dangerous vacuum in German society, more clearly than many, and if he failed to realize the violence of the hatred that would fill that vacuum, it was not because he lacked perception but because he was simply too decent to imagine the depths of human depravity. He was a man of character and intelligence and principle, and it was part of the tragedy of Weimar Germany that there were too few men with such qualities. But if the rarity of those qualities proved fatal a generation ago, who can say that we have them in abundance today?

MAY 1971   OTTO FRIEDRICH
LOCUST VALLEY, N.Y.

Translator's Note

The Diaries of Harry, Count Kessler were edited for the original German edition with the consent of the owner of Kessler's papers, the Marquis de Brion. The English edition has been somewhat cut from the published German version, to exclude matter unlikely to be of interest to an international public and, in some places, to avoid repetitions of purely business or administrative detail. Persons named in the Diaries can be identified by reference to the Index.

The identity of name between the writer of these Diaries and the present translator is pure co-incidence: there is no family connection.

C.K.

1918

At eight in the morning a telephone call from Hatzfeldt. Last night the Cabinet did after all reach a decision about Pilsudski.[1] Groener and Hoffmann concurred, though the Chancellor was not there and, the meeting over, everyone standing ready to leave. He is to be released, but is first to sign a statement drafted by General Hoffmann. I am to go to Magdeburg and induce him to agree to this text.

With Hatzfeldt to the Chancellery, but the Chancellor not available. Spoke to Groener for only a moment and without mention of Pilsudski. Then Haeften took matters in hand officially. Mann, the Navy State Secretary, was meanwhile conferring with Ebert,[2] the Social Democrat, at a small table in the imposing Congress Hall. Haeften was in a hurry because

Phillip Scheidemann (Kursell)

he had to see Hermann Müller into an aeroplane for Hamburg, with which communications are severed. Scheidemann,[3] in conversation with another 'statesman', stalked majestically through the apartments. Oberndorff, whom I met on the stairs, called across to me that at five o'clock he leaves with Erzberger for French headquarters to hear the armistice conditions from

Foch. The débâcle, capitulation and revolution is complete and in these surroundings, sacred to the memory of Bismarck since the days of the Congress of Berlin, as gripping as the Imperial coronation[4] at Versailles fifty years ago. At the War Ministry we were told that the naval mutineers have seized Hamburg, Lübeck, and Cuxhaven as well as Kiel. At Hamburg the soldiers have joined the sailors, forming a Red government. Reds are streaming with every train from Hamburg to Berlin. An uprising is expected here tonight. This morning the Russian Embassy was raided like a disreputable pot-house and Joffe,[5] with his staff, deported. That puts paid to the Bolshevik centre in Berlin. But perhaps we shall yet call these people back.

Thursday, 7 November 1918   *Magdeburg*

This morning Schloessmann, the officer in charge of Pilsudski, came to me in great excitement because the Commanding Officer had sent him orders for the garrison to stand by. He thought – probably correctly – that this would simply upset the troops and render them the more likely to mutiny. He asked me to intervene. My mission, I replied, gives me not the slightest right to interfere with military measures. If, however, the Commanding Officer should want my private opinion, I would advise against taking any conspicuous precaution that is not absolutely necessary. Just then a call came through from Command Headquarters; the Commanding Officer wished to talk to me. I drove out there and heard that Hanover had fallen to the Reds. They have arrested the Commanding Officer and occupied the Headquarters. This afternoon a deputation of Red sailors is expected to reach Magdeburg, but Headquarters hopes to intercept them at the station. Though work continues, there is unrest at Krupp's.

The Commanding Officer, a cavalry general, fat, tired, back from the Front and not up to local conditions, sat slumped behind his desk. He had already rescinded his stand-by order at the suggestion of the chief of police. How, he inquired, do they handle these matters at Berlin? So far as I know, I said, by using as far as possible the workers themselves, in the form of the trade union and Social Democrat organizations, to maintain order. Pushing the workers forward is his intention too, he commented wearily, at the same time hinting that he will not be surprised to find himself under arrest by the revolutionaries before the day is out. Obviously neither he nor any of his officers to whom I have spoken has real confidence in the troops. As he has nothing at his disposal, he remarked dejectedly, with what is he supposed to crush an uprising? I could not help thinking of Liège in August 1914 when we also had nothing at our disposal and insurrection, followed by gruesome suppression, did occur. We must hope that we don't now face that in Germany! Events at Kiel, Lübeck, Altona, Hamburg and Hanover have as yet passed off fairly bloodlessly. That is the way all revolutions start. The thirst for blood grows gradually with the strains involved in setting up the new order.

The soldiers in the streets here salute promptly and smartly. Their discipline has not so far suffered in public.

The shape of the revolution is becoming clear: progressive encroachment, as by a patch of oil, by the mutinous sailors from the coast to the interior. Berlin is being isolated and will soon be only an island. It is the other way about from France: the provinces are carrying revolution to the capital. The sea sweeps down on the land, Viking strategy. Perhaps we shall become the spearhead, against our own wish, of the slaves' revolt against Britain and American capitalism. Liebknecht[6] as war-lord in the decisive battle and the Navy in the van.

Friday, 8 November 1918   *Magdeburg*

At five o'clock yesterday afternoon Ebert and Scheidemann, on behalf of the Social Democratic Party leadership, handed the Chancellor[7] a declaration

Contemporary Cartoon of Friedrich Ebert (Thomas Theodore Heine)

which included the demand that the Emperor's abdication and the Crown Prince's renunciation of his rights be effected by noon today. The Chancellor has gone to see the Emperor at General Headquarters.

At half past eight this morning Schloessmann arrived with the information that rail traffic to Berlin is interrupted. I decided to take Pilsudski by car. Next came the news of demonstrations in the streets, with officers having their epaulettes torn off and their swords snatched from them. I requested the Command Transport Officer to let me have a military vehicle immediately. Because it was uncertain whether the Elbe bridges had already been seized or not, I arranged for it to be brought out of town and to wait for us on the far bank of the river while I fetched Pilsudski. Schloessmann and the Transport Officer changed into mufti to avoid molestation; I went at least so far as to borrow a civilian hat and coat. In this gear we made our way through side-streets to the citadel.[8] Everything was quiet there as yet. Some two dozen men from the Convalescent Company lounged around the gate. In the guard-room the Duty NCO was asking for orders.

We wasted no time and hurried across the courtyard to the building where Pilsudski and Colonel Sosnkowski had been confined. They were pacing the garden together, Pilsudski in Polish uniform, Sosnkowski in mufti. I expressed my pleasure at being able to tell them that they were free. My instructions, I added, were to convey them to Berlin so as to enable them to depart for Warsaw this very evening.

Plaue and Brandenburg proved to be perfectly peaceful. Unrest did not show itself again until Wustermark. The village was all agog, with the railway embankment as the focal point of interest. A militia picket, drawn up just behind it, stopped us. An officer of hussars, in the middle of the militiamen, disclaimed all acquaintance with or responsibility for them. Two tightly packed trainloads of sailors, 'deputations', as the picket NCO explained, were passing through in the direction of Berlin. Nobody thought of stopping them.

Saturday, 9 November 1918   *Berlin*

The Emperor has abdicated. Revolution has won the day in Berlin.

This morning, as I left home, I saw a soldier haranguing a crowd. That was in the forecourt of the Potsdam Station, alongside a machine-gun company drawn up ready for action. But between Friedrichstrasse and Unter den Linden everything was at this time (half past ten to eleven) quiet. I could go in uniform, unmolested, to the bank opposite the State Library.

Dinner, with Hugo Simon and his wife, in the Cassirers'[9] dining-room although they were not at home. Schickele brought up the idea of using sailors to carry revolution to Alsace, proclaiming it a Red republic, and thereby saving it for the German nation. While he was talking we could hear and see, through the windows of the room at the back, the shooting that was going on in the neighbourhood of the Palace. Slow infantry fire, with individual shots lighting up the sky as they did during a quiet night at the Front. The Palace, we were told, was already in the hands of the revolutionaries, whereas the Imperial Stables was in part still held by officers and the Youth Defence Force.

At ten o'clock with Kestenberg and Schickele to the Reichstag for discussion of the Alsace idea. In front of the main entrance, and in an arc of illumination provided by the headlights of several army vehicles, stood a crowd waiting for news. People pushed up the steps and through the doors.

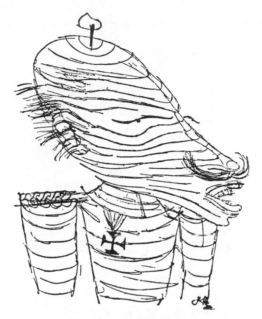

'The Angry Kaiser' (Klee)

Soldiers with slung rifles and red badges checked everyone's business. Kestenberg, using Haase's[10] name, had no trouble in gaining us admission. The scene inside was animated, with a continual movement up and down the stairs of sailors, armed civilians, women, and soldiers. The sailors looked healthy, fresh, neat and, most noticeable of all, very young; the soldiers old and war-worn, in faded uniforms and down-at-heel footwear, unshaven and unkempt, remnants of an army, a tragic picture of defeat. First we were directed to a party committee room where three young sailors, seated at a conference table and entrusted with the issue of arms permits, examined, approved, or rejected applications with all the seriousness and self-importance of schoolboys.

We started looking for Haase. Groups of soldiers and sailors stood and lay about on the enormous red carpet and among the pillars of the lobby. Rifles had been stacked. Here and there some individual was stretched full length and asleep on a bench. It was like a film of the Russian Revolution, a scene from the Tauride Palace in Kerensky's day. The door of the Council

Chamber flew open. Whereas the lobby was comparatively dark, the light inside was glaring. My first reaction was what an ugly place it is. Never has it seemed to me less dignified and more like a gin-palace, this ridiculous neo-Gothic crate, bad imitation of an Augsburg chest. A multitude swarmed among the seats, a sort of popular assembly, soldiers without badges, sailors with slung rifles, women, all of them with red arm-bands, and a number of Reichstag members, Dittmann, Oskar Cohn, Vogtherr, Däumig, each surrounded by a small group. Haase stood bent over the Council table, hammering home a point to a young civilian who is said to be one of the principal Bolsheviks. We pushed forward and Schickele introduced me. The proposal for a sailors' invasion of Alsace evidently came as no surprise to Haase. He discussed it briefly and suggested a conference for tomorrow. Then others demanded his attention.

We forced our way out of the Council Chamber again and climbed two or three floors to a committee room where a woman, apparently the wife of a Reichstag member, was issuing identification papers. I received, on Kesternberg's recommendation, a card according to which, as 'bearer of this credential', I am authorized 'to maintain order and security in the streets of the city'. Signed Oskar Cohn, Vogtherr, Dittmann. I have become, so to speak, a policeman in the Red Guard. I was also given an identity card certifying on the part of the Workers' and Soldiers' Council that I am 'trustworthy and free to pass'. Both identification papers carry the Reichstag stamp.

Kestenberg and Schickele went home. On the strength of my new papers, I passed the barrier on the Potsdamer Platz and walked in the direction of the Palace, from which the sound of isolated shots still came. Leipziger Strasse was deserted, Friedrichstrasse[11] fairly full of its usual *habitués*, Unter den Linden opposite the Opera in darkness. The Schinkel[12] Guard Room was brilliantly lit, with clouds of smoke and lots of soldiers. The white stone figures of naked warriors and victory goddesses had the Schlossbrücke to themselves. Lights burned brightly but desultorily in one or another part of the Palace; everything was quiet. Patrols all around; they challenged and let me through. In front of the Imperial Stables a good deal of splintered masonry. A sentry told me that 'young rascals' are still hidden in the Palace and the Stables. There are secret passages through which they disappear and re-appear. A couple of officers and a few loyalist soldiers were still firing from a house in the Enckestrasse. Some cars with armed men rushed over the Schlossbrücke, were stopped, turned around, and sent off to Enckestrasse 4. Beyond the Schlossbrücke again a barrier. At both corners of Königstrasse a skulking rabble in small packs which reassembled as often as the pickets broke them up. A sergeant said they were waiting for the chance to pillage; they must be cleared out. Slowly I made my way home.

In the Leipzigerstrasse I encountered a fleeing crowd. Various people shouted that loyalist troops had arrived from Potsdam and shooting would start at any moment. I turned away into the Wilhelmstrasse but heard nothing. A few shots are supposed to have been fired in Potsdamer Platz about this time. It was close on one o'clock when I got home. So closes this first day of revolution which has witnessed in a few hours the downfall of the Hohenzollerns, the dissolution of the German Army, and the end of the old order of society in Germany. One of the most memorable and dreadful days in German history.

Sunday, 10 November 1918 *Berlin*

At the Cassirers. Discussion of the situation with Schickele and others. Most of them took a pessimistic view. The crucial point is whether the Liebknecht lot, and with them the Red terror, gains the day or whether the more moderate sector of the Social Democrats. Schickele thinks the Bolsheviks have already won and that Haase is taking an equivocal line. All efforts should therefore concentrate on keeping Haase and the right-wing Independents away from Bolshevism and engaging their sympathies for the Constituent National Assembly.[13] While we talked, shooting was going on in the neighbourhood of the Reichstag. Apparently machine-gun fire. Later we heard that it occurred during a public meeting in front of the Bismarck Memorial.

Dinner with the Schickeles at the Excelsior. Also at our table were his friend Dr Licktrig and Theodor Däubler. Unless they exercise their option, Schickele will become a Frenchman and Däubler an Italian. That alone, as applied to these two German writers, illustrates the complete nonsense and brittleness of the proposed peace terms. Schickele declared his firm intention of moving to Berlin, regardless of the fact that he does not like North Germany. None of them has anything but contempt for the Emperor who has done nothing except disfigure, and so ruin, the character of Prussia. There seems to be no question but that Germany will become a republic. The King of Saxony was deposed today. The Grand Duke of Hesse, Schickele said, is in protective custody. The composition of the new Government has considerably reassured Schickele and everyone else to whom I have spoken.

The head of the Red Guard responsible for security in the Excelsior, a comrade belonging to Sailor Regiment No. 1, outlined his programme to me. It comprises obedience to the new Government, maintenance of peace and order, and opposition to any kind of violence, including pillage. He is a young man of twenty-three or -four and has taken part in the revolution since Kiel, a straightforward fellow who echoes the outlook of the vast majority of our revolutionaries. By and large the attitude of the people, despite the shootings, has during the first two days of the revolution been admirable: disciplined, calm, orderly, trying to be fair, and in practically every instance scrupulously well behaved. A counterpart to the readiness for self-sacrifice in August 1914. So great and tragic an experience, endured so bravely and with such purity of mind, must spiritually weld the nation into a metal of indestructible temper. If only its political instinct, something every Italian chestnut-seller has, were not so rare a phenomenon!

The end of the evening provided a comic interlude. Däubler had promised his sister, on account of danger in the streets, to stay the night in the hotel. When however he registered as 'Austrian', the manager vigorously declined to have him as a guest because as a 'foreigner' he has no identification papers. There was a scene until I, as a delegate of the Soldiers' and Workers' Council who on the score of my credentials am responsible for maintaining law and order, intervened and commanded the manager to keep Däubler. The manager bowed in the good old Prussian way to discipline, even though of revolutionary origin, and allotted him a room. No more of sound and fury, servility alone remains.

Monday, 11 November 1918   *Berlin*

Today the dreadful armistice terms have been signed. Langwerth says that anything else was out of the question: our Front has cracked completely. The Emperor has fled to Holland.

Tuesday, 12 November 1918   *Berlin*

Spent the afternoon at the Reichstag in the quarters of the 'New Fatherland League'. I agreed, at Kestenberg's invitation, to join its executive. Clubs like the 'New Fatherland League', the 'Activists' (the group around Kurt Hiller), and so on, formed to discuss and decide important political questions beforehand, just as in the French Revolution, have taken over Reichstag committee-rooms and hold their sessions alongside the Soldiers' and Workers' Councils. Although entry to the Reichstag is now under strict control (it is impossible to get in without the Soldiers' Council red pass), its appearance inside has not altered since the first night of the revolution except for the even greater accumulation of filth. Cigarette butts everywhere; waste paper, dust, and dirt from the streets litter the carpets. The corridors and lobby teem with armed civilians, soldiers and sailors. In the lobby rifles are piled on the carpet and sailors lounge in the easy chairs. The disorder is vast, but quiet reigns. The old attendants, in their parliamentary livery, flit about, helplessly and shyly, last relics of the former regime. The members of the bourgeois[14] parties have completely disappeared.

In the city everything is peaceful today and the factories are working again. Nothing has been heard of shootings. Noteworthy is that during the days of revolution the trams, irrespective of street-fighting, ran regularly.

Nor did the electricity, water, or telephone services break down for a moment. The revolution never created more than an eddy in the ordinary life of the city which flowed calmly along on its customary course. Moreover, though there was so much shooting, there were remarkably few dead or wounded. The colossal, world-shaking upheaval has scurried across Berlin's day-to-day life much like an incident in a crime film.

Wednesday, 13 November 1918   *Berlin*

At one o'clock I went to see Haase in the Chancellery. A large number of petitioners, in soft felt hats, waited in the lovely Empire vestibule. There never used to be such a throng. A little boy, acting as messenger, told me to go to the first floor. Several tail-coated attendants from former days continue to perform their duties there. I was last here a week ago, when Prince Max was still in charge, at the outset of the débâcle. Neglect of the place has made rapid strides since then. The riff-raff has moved in. The Congress Hall was empty except for a 'man of letters' with a red ribbon in his button-hole.

Haase entered from one of the drawing-rooms to the left and led me in there. A small, insignificant-looking man with a friendly manner, he reminded me of Chlodwig Hohenlohe,[15] in a Semitic version. He was sitting at Bismarck's writing-desk, recognizable by its copper top. The topic of our conversation was the establishment of contacts with France, in particular about doing so right away with the French Socialists. Haase said that he would have best liked to go to Switzerland himself for this purpose, but at the moment it is not possible. The French know however that he was against hostilities even before August 1914 and conformed simply so as not to split Party unity. Schickele is to be in charge and I am to collaborate with him. The cultural contacts moreover, which lie in my hands, are extremely important. I told him that I shall of course gladly continue to place myself at his disposal, though prepared to withdraw at once if he or the new Government prefer someone else. Haase replied that he is very glad to have me and I am to visit him again before my departure.

At five to Paul Cassirer and found Schickele there. They are leaving tonight for Switzerland via Munich. Cassirer dreads the danger of a reaction. The whole middle class, in his view, is already fed up with the revolution. The Potsdam regiments, who have elected their officers to the Soldiers' Council, can easily turn everything upside down again. Both Schickele and Cassirer gave the impression of being peevish, reticent, and flustered.

Thursday, 14 November 1918   *Berlin*

This morning Hatzfeldt asked me to come for a discussion and, in the course of it, inquired whether I would accept the appointment of Minister at

Warsaw. The Polish Government demands the recall of Lerchenfeld and Oettingen[16] and the immediate nomination of a Minister. My main task would initially be to see that our troops are evacuated from Poland and the Ukraine. An extremely arduous and responsible task. I accepted.

Immediately afterwards I ran into Erzberger. He drew me into his office and gave it as his opinion that I ought to remain here. This is the time when energetic personalities are needed, otherwise a peace treaty is out of the question. The Entente is not going to conclude any such thing with the present Government unless middle-class elements are included. He regretted his absence during the revolution, else no purely Socialist government would have been constituted. He again underestimates, as at the time of the abdication question, the leftward trend that the war has developed among us. His journey to French headquarters has left a very bad impression on him. The treatment was vile, with Foch icy and ineffably superior.

Tea with Countess Bernstorff. Her husband, the Ambassador, and her daughter-in-law were there too. He is getting ready to go to The Hague for the peace negotiations.

At one o'clock as I was walking down Unter den Linden, the Palace guard approached from the Brandenburger Tor, tramping to the strains of the Hohenfriedberg March, just as they used to do, but carrying revolutionary flags, the men without badges, the non-commissioned officers or file-markers with black-red-yellow[17] Greater German armbands. The standard of marching was somewhat more sluggish than that of the Guards before the war, but tidy and entirely soldierly. A large crowd wearing red ribbons and armbands accompanied the detachment. On reaching the Passage, so badly damaged through the shooting during the days of the Revolution, the band played the song *Es liegt eine Krone im grünen Rhein*. It sounded like a funeral march and cut me to the quick. I thought of lost Alsace and the French left bank of the Rhine. How are our feelings about that ever to be salved? However fine the League of Nations may prove to be, this is a wound it can but perpetuate.

Many soldiers are now wearing the black-white-red badge again above the red revolutionary one which has taken the place of the Prussian colours.

Friday, 15 November 1918   *Berlin*

At nine to Erzberger in the Budapester Strasse. I warned him against gravely shaking the position of the Government by forcing in representatives of the middle class. For the moment the main thing is to hold the front against the Spartacus[18] group and, alongside that, preparation of the elections for the National Assembly. Erzberger heaped abuse on the cowardice of the middle classes and especially the officers, who did not offer the slightest resistance to the revolution. The Life Guards colonel who forbade the soldiers to open fire ought himself to be shot. Now at least it is not necessary to retreat before the Spartacus lot without a fight. As regards the peace preliminaries, he laid down the following principles: he wants to come to terms as fast as possible, perhaps within a week, in order to save the left bank of the Rhine from occupation. The right of occupation is valid only for the period of the armistice. To complete the peace preliminaries quickly, he is prepared to surrender Alsace-Lorraine. There is no other way of doing it and Alsace-Lorraine is lost to us anyhow. The question of Poland he intends to postpone for the major peace negotiations. The peace preliminaries should not go beyond conceding in principle a neutral Poland and discussing preparatory work on ethnographic and other studies. No Polish frontiers to be established in the peace preliminaries. Under no circumstances must we lose Upper Silesia. Economically it is essential to us, it is not indisputably Polish territory, it never belonged to Poland, and the Poles merely immigrated. Upper Silesia is a *central issue*. Danzig can become a free port or we can concede to the Poles as a free zone a different branch of the Vistula estuary and a piece of the lagoon. That is a matter of money.

On the Potsdamer Platz I saw for the first time since the revolution an officer with epaulettes.

The Foreign Ministry of the Republic – a week ago, when the monarchic concept was a matter of course, the notion would have seemed preposterous. And yet I fancy that people's real outlook is only *now* coming to the fore. The monarchic idea was long before slowly done to death by the Emperor's utter personal failure, especially during the war, as well as by his flashy and disquieting incompetence.

Sunday, 17 November 1918   *Berlin*

The first post-revolution Sunday. During the late afternoon there were large crowds of Sunday strollers going via Unter den Linden to the Imperial Stables in order to see the traces of fighting on the buildings. All very pacific and characterized by vulgar curiosity. The very marked damage to the Imperial Stables was especially gaped at. The only difference between this and former Sundays was the absence of policemen and the presence, though in no great numbers, of armed sailors, guards and patrols.

In the morning I went to the Foreign Ministry and called on various people in connection with my Polish mission. First Nadolny, to collect information about the Ukraine. Our Soldiers' Councils, he told me, are adopting a neutral and reserved attitude towards all the political tangles and fighting which is going on there; this is in agreement with our Government. The arrival of Entente forces in the Ukraine is imminent. After that, the presence of our troops will no longer serve any purpose as they are simply acting as a barrier against the Bolsheviks. They should therefore remain until the time of the Entente's entry,[19] but then be withdrawn straightaway. I am to work at high pressure in Warsaw to see that their transit through Poland is guaranteed. It renders imperative close understanding with High Command East.

Next I saw Bernstorff. He, like Erzberger, wants discussion of Polish affairs postponed until the big peace conference. I am to say at every opportunity, public and private, that we would in any case have been prepared to deal with the Polish Question on the lines of Wilson's Point Thirteen[20] and so they (the Poles) should refrain from committing any follies now.

From Bernstorff to Solf, who had nothing to add but warned me urgently against establishing any links with Zionist or other Jewish political trends because this would rouse Pilsudski's suspicions.[21] I am to get on the best possible terms with Pilsudski.

Tuesday, 19 November 1918   *Berlin*

Today I received my appointment as Minister, signed by Solf and confirmed by the Executive Council of the Soldiers' and Workers' Council.

In the afternoon farewell visits and staff problems.

At ten o'clock at night left from Friedrichstrasse Station in the special train put at my disposal for the duration of my mission. It consists of a Pullman, a sleeper, and a dining-car, exuding a slightly American millionaire atmosphere. Apart from taking along Niemozecki (the Polish chargé d'affaires) and his wife, I was accompanied by Rawicki, Dr Meyer, Gülpen, von Strahl, Otto Fürstner,[22] a courier, and lower echelon personnel (cipher clerks, office manager, shorthand-typists, and so on). About twenty people in all. Chatted with Niemozecki and others until midnight, then to bed and slept well. Shortly before seven in the morning, at Alexandrovo, the head of the German Soldiers' Council (a youngster with a very smart military carriage) and an officer of the Polish Legion reported to me. Everything is quiet in these parts. The railway lines, which had been torn up, have been repaired. We can travel straight through to Warsaw. The shuttle-service of refugees from Poland and Germany has continued undisturbed for some days. But the Soldiers' Council formally complained to me that the Poles have failed to render available three hundred coaches. The punctuality and love of order among my compatriots has not suffered through the revolution. The Council has moreover enlisted the services of an officer, a lieutenant, though many of his brother-officers are, as I was told, 'gone'.

Wednesday, 20 November 1918   *Warsaw*

At breakfast a discussion with Niemozecki. He emphasized his wish for a close and amicable relationship between Poland and Germany. I agreed and said that this will only be possible if both Poland and Germany make sacrifices and relinquish dangerous aspirations. We have accepted Wilson's Fourteen Points and this involves the abandonment of certain territories, but we cannot cede Danzig. Niemozecki confirmed that this is 'Impossible!' The best way to lay the groundwork for mutual lasting friendship between Poland and Germany will be, I continued, for us to negotiate directly and to lay before the Peace Conference an agreed programme. That, though, depends on there existing a strong Government both in Poland and Germany. If Pilsudski can establish himself, then a direct understanding may be feasible. The Entente, Niemozecki commented, is playing a two-faced game whose object is permanently to estrange Poland and Germany. It has made large promises to the Poles, but now seems to be backing down from them.

He went on to tell me that he wants to resign from his diplomatic career and to settle in Warsaw, in which case he hopes to be able to supply me with sound information and render me other services. I have a notion that he is trying to trap me.

Had luncheon served in the Pullman for Niemozecki, Rawicki, Meyer, Gülpen, and myself. We travelled through the areas which were the scene of the major hostilities in 1914 and 1915. There are still some ruins to be seen. At Warsaw I was welcomed at the station by a representative of the Polish Ministry for Foreign Affairs, a representative of the War Ministry, an officer of Pilsudski's personal staff, and another half dozen Polish Legion officers. A Polish military car (probably one 'requisitioned' from us and painted with the red Polish eagle) drove us to our hotel, the Bristol.

On my arrival I was at once visited by Major Ritter, liaison officer for Supreme High Command in Warsaw. He evidently wanted to be ahead of the representatives of the Soldiers' Council. He was discreet, but his account clearly revealed the deplorable behaviour on the part of the Governor-General who, ten days ago, tamely allowed himself to be removed by the mutinous German soldiery and the Legionaries. Without a blow falling, the Poles 'took over' munitions, raw materials depots, horses, and furnishings worth millions. A rump German Soldiers' Council, with no foundation of authority, came forward to act as a 'liquidation commission' and awarded itself large allowances and other perquisites. Ritter demanded that I should remove it.

His visit was shortly followed by the representatives of the Soldiers' Council. I took the line that, in accordance with our promises to the Polish Government, there is no longer any room for German military personnel in Warsaw. Consequently the military members of the Soldiers' Council must at once stop the liquidation process and leave. I shall attend to the orderly settlement of matters. They submitted.

Next came a parson who pleaded with me to make the half million German civilians in Poland my concern. This is a genuine and major problem seeing that they are now exposed to hate and ruin as a result of our Occupation officials' conduct.

After I had seen a Herr Sarnow (my predecessor's secretary, whose description of events more or less confirmed Ritter's), I received a Herr Korff, chairman of the German Aid Association. He had taken into his care the Legation funds and wants to hand them over to me. An important manufacturer, he has lived fifteen years in Warsaw. He says that he is ashamed to meet his Polish friends and only goes out at night, so badly did our armed forces and officials, from the top downwards, behave. The damage done to German reputation is immeasurable and irreparable. The blame, he conceded, lies mainly with the officers. They no longer bothered about their men and in part were venal, like the officials. A case of utter loss of moral authority.

Our talk was abruptly terminated by the arrival of an officer from Pilsudski's personal staff. Pilsudski asked to be excused for cavalierly claiming my attention before even the official formalities were discharged between us, but something very serious had happened. Allegedly as a reprisal for having to give up their arms, German troops stationed at Brest-Litovsk had set fire to houses in two villages and made prisoners whom they abducted and threatened to shoot straightaway. Would I please intervene so that sentence should be duly passed on them? Highly unfavourable repercussions might otherwise occur. I promised to telegraph High Command East. This done, I sent a verbal note to the Ministry of Foreign Affairs confirming dispatch of the message, but simultaneously drawing attention to the imprisonment without trial of fifteen German subjects, one of whom is alleged to have been executed by the Poles. I would appreciate reciprocal regard for our good relations.

Undoubtedly the conduct of German officers and officials in Poland on 11 November was disgraceful, but it was not much better in Berlin on 9 November. My feeling is that everywhere it was a *system* that failed, not individuals, a system which finally relied entirely on brute force and broke down helplessly the moment this slipped out of its grasp.

Thursday, 21 November 1918   *Warsaw*

At eleven o'clock I made my initial call on Wassiliewski, the Minister for Foreign Affairs. He received me in the company of Filippovicz, his Deputy Secretary of State. Handing over my credentials, I said a few friendly words and the Minister, reading from a manuscript, reciprocated. How much was sincere, how much was insincere, it was impossible to glean from this first meeting. The only positive point that emerged was in respect of the imprisoned Germans. Filippovicz (who, apart from Polish, speaks only English) promised to let me have news about them by five o'clock this afternoon and to effect their release shortly.

At five I was received in official audience by Pilsudski. I handed him the original of my credentials and made a short speech. He replied in his capacity as Head of State. Notable was that he spoke of 'our' (his and my) task in the development of relations between Poland and Germany. I seized on the phrase and expressed pleasure at his having mentioned a 'joint task which you and I have been allotted'. He complemented this with 'the joint task to guide our two peoples out of their old enmity into new amity'.

Death Mask of Jozef Pilsudski

He looks very ill, his features pale and sunken. But he still has his old air of vigour and benevolence and his manner is cheerful. He wants to put his country on a constitutional basis as soon as possible, he said, and to divest himself of the irregular power which has devolved on him. The claims of socialism must be propitiated with words a long way; the times demand it. Whether deeds will keep pace with words is a different matter. Conditions in the river Bug lines of communication area cause him considerable worry. Our troops there are setting fire to villages and abducting their inhabitants. That presents a grave peril to the friendship we are both trying to achieve. He wants to secure a clear state of affairs, via negotiation, as soon as possible.

I told him that I have already requested High Command East to attach a liaison officer to my Legation. This was obviously a source of relief to him. I then mentioned the imprisoned Germans. He correctly interpreted my very carefully formulated hope that he will be able to maintain his position as a question. He sees a threat, he replied, only in the presence of Russian and Ukrainian Bolsheviks and supporting gangs in the south-east of the country as well as the very unruly circumstances prevailing in the south-west, in the Dombrova area, where the revolutionary spark may dart over from Germany to Poland. For the rest he just goes ahead and leaves the shouting to others. The opposition at Posen is no danger because it will always stay within constitutional bounds. We then chatted about private affairs and revived old memories, which always makes Pilsudski happy. It is quite obvious that his most enjoyable days, his real youth, were those he spent fighting with his Legionaries.

Friday, 22 November 1918   *Warsaw*

At half past eight Major Ritter came to report about the negotiations with the Poles, due to start today, on the evacuation of troops from the Ukraine. At half past eleven I called on Nieniewski, the Deputy Chief of Staff. In the old days we served at the same staff headquarters.

I was barely back in the hotel when Pilsudski arrived, without prior notice, and accompanied only by an aide-de-camp. A decree, signed by him yesterday, has made him dictator of Poland. That rendered his visit the more surprising. Heads of State do not normally return calls personally. In the course of our conversation he reverted to yesterday's aphorism about it being our joint task to guide our two peoples out of their old enmity into new amity, adding that conditions in the Bug lines of communication area do imperil the success of this task, all the more as the fall of Lemberg[23] will focus public interest on the problem. He could not confirm that Lemberg has already fallen, but its capture is absolutely imminent. He alluded proudly to the fact that he had brigaded his old First Legion units and sent them there, mentioning incidentally that currently the Polish Army has a strength of thirty thousand, an establishment which within a fortnight will be adequately trained. He stayed about half an hour, chatting and telling me his domestic plans. He wants to move into a small palace. He also said that at the moment he barely has a second shirt to his name, but showed me with pride the sword of honour presented to him by his Legions after two years of war.

In the afternoon, between a stream of visitors, I dictated my first report on the situation here. At half past seven Hutten came. He had spent the morning waiting vainly in my bathroom because, after Pilsudski, I had had Wassiliewski with me. He grumbled about High Command East and the Bug lines of communication area where our soldiers are living like savages, killing people, committing arson, and so on. He was insistent that I should complete my day by calling on Count Sczeptycki, Chief of the General Staff. He was gone barely ten minutes when I received a message from Sczeptycki that he must see me this evening still on a most urgent matter. I replied that I would receive him at half past ten.

He arrived punctual to the minute, alone, and transmitted to me verbally the demand that we evacuate immediately the lines of communication area left of the Bug. If we do not, Poland will appeal for help to the Entente. He emphasized twice that he was speaking in his capacity as Chief of the General Staff; tomorrow I shall be presented officially with the same demand by the Government. This means that I am faced, at a moment when I am completely cut off from my Government, with a barely disguised ultimatum. Sczeptycki based the demand on the atrocities alleged to have been committed by our soldiers. When I reminded him of the misdeeds committed by the Austrian Army, to which he belonged only a year ago, he admitted that in the current state of gang warfare such incidents can hardly be avoided. All the same, public opinion has become excited by them to such a degree that neither this nor any other Polish Government can or could resist it. In fact, of course, it is our weakness and the contempt for the behaviour of our officials and many of our officers that has encouraged the Polish Government to put forward this unceremonious demand.

Saturday, 23 November 1918   *Warsaw*

In the morning visited Archbishop Cardinal Kakowski. He resides in a palace which is large but furnished in middle-class style and smells of chlorine. His private chaplain led us into an old-fashioned drawing-room and the Cardinal, a youngish man with a rather common face and pale blue eyes, soon appeared. He and the chaplain evinced great interest in our revolution, asking whether all our dynasties really have fallen, whether things have settled down now, and whether the Bolsheviks can still prove dangerous. The German revolution is a far greater hazard to Poland than the Russian, they maintained, because everything in the West finds favour here. I purposely brought the talk round to Pilsudski. The Cardinal pulled an irritated face, an expression verging on contempt, and made it obvious that he is no admirer of his. Pilsudski is very popular; *le peuple a besoin d'un héros* (our conversation was in French); it was his arrest which turned him into a martyr and national hero. I suspect that the Cardinal holds this particularly against us. We have established a competitor to himself and his saints. Pilsudski is no soldier, he continued, and understands little of military affairs, never having served as a regular officer. He left me with an impression of hurt vanity and aristocratic disdain for a popular hero.

At half past twelve a Polish officer brought back from the radio tower my telegram about Sczeptycki's ultimatum, which had been handed in by Gülpen at six. It was not transmitted because it needs my personal signature. I took it back and wrote Sczeptycki a pretty curt letter 'requesting' him to issue instructions that will ensure his agreements with me being implemented. Meanwhile I would not be in a position to convey to Berlin the contents of yesterday's talk between us. Within an hour Sczeptycki's personal assistant, a little Count Josef Michatowski, appeared to proffer apologies; matters are not yet properly organized, there is considerable disorder in the execution of business, nothing of the sort will occur again, and from now on all my telegrams will be dispatched without the slightest ado.

Up to the present, half past three, Sczeptycki's presaged ultimatum on the Polish Government's part has not as yet arrived.

During the afternoon I called on the Lutheran bishop, Bursche, and visited the hospital where the last of our troops are lying. The bottomless misery of war is to be seen there, including the consumptive cases who caught their disease in Russian prisons. And the poor devil who has lost his leg and said, with tears in his eyes, that his occupation has gone with it too.

In the evening, towards ten, I was having my meal in the dining-room with Meyer when we heard a buzz of voices and the noise of a large crowd in the hall. We went to see what was the matter. A waiter rushed up and whispered, 'Take to your heels, here, through the back door.' I caught the crowd yelling, 'Down with Kessler.' They were preparing to storm my room. 'Kessler, out, out.' One or two of the pack's wild men ran up the stairs. Another, standing on a table gesticulating, made a speech that I did not understand. The manager approached and said that we must leave the hotel tomorrow before ten, or he would be shot. I discussed the situation with Meyer, went upstairs, and fetched Gülpen, in front of whose door the scared Legation staff was congregated. The three of us went to 6 Sachsenplatz to talk to Pilsudski. He was not there, but the guard gave us a guide to a fairly remote street where he was said to be. He led us to a rather old-fashioned apartment with semi-elegant but threadbare furnishings. First we were met by the aide-de-camp Winiawa, then Sosnkowski, who has become a general and corps commander of the Warsaw district. I told the latter that I was here in a private capacity, not as Minister, to inform him of the Bristol's invasion by some one to two hundred people who threatened the manager on my account. The manager is therefore putting us on the street at ten in the morning. As I prefer not to leave in this way, I would ask him to calm down the manager and place the hotel under military protection. Sosnkowski agreed and asked me to wait for Pilsudski, who must arrive in a few moments. We settled down to a pleasant chat, although Sosnkowski was clearly embarrassed when I recalled that the mob threatened to return at ten, but for all that he referred to a report from the Bug lines of communication area about forty people being shot in a heap by our troops. As the clock soon turned one, I went without awaiting Pilsudski's arrival.

Sunday, 24 November 1918   *Warsaw*

This morning no sign yet of Sosnkowski's protective measures. At nine Gülpen brought three men from the Sachsenplatz who planted themselves with fixed bayonets in the corridor in front of my room. At half past eleven a platoon arrived to act as Legation Guard. Around noon a lieutenant reported to me as being charged with finding a Legation residence for us; he hopes to do so by tomorrow. At a quarter to one a crowd, several hundred strong, assembled outside the hotel.

In the afternoon visited Korff. Received a report from Gülpen that the crowd stretches from the hotel to the other side of the street and the Legation Guard is jammed against the hotel door. I prepared a message for Berlin which I shall try and transmit in cipher. This morning Wassiliewski told Meyer that the Ministry of Foreign Affairs assumes every guarantee for our personal safety. Later, speaking to Strahl, he narrowed this down by saying that, although the Ministry cannot assume guarantees, it will do everything within its power for us.

At seven Meyer reported that the crowd had swept aside the Guard, forcibly entered the hotel, and searched my room as well as those of all other Legation members. The manager had earlier had our luggage taken to the fifth floor. There was also a message to send somebody to the Ministry forthwith. Meyer went himself and was informed that we must move this evening. At nine o'clock the Ministry would indicate a residence to us and place it at our disposal. Meyer insisted on seeing Wassiliewski and protested against our treatment as a breach of international law because the Polish Government, despite its guarantee, has failed to protect us from search of the extra-territorial quarters used by the Legation. I prepared with Meyer messages for Berlin which tomorrow I shall send with one of our cipher clerks by rail, since all telegraphic communications have been interrupted.

At the Ministry Meyer was advised that seven rooms in two different dwellings stand at our disposal, but that they are unheated and in part unlit. I went with Fürstner to view the space offered us by Theusner, until now the German director of the Polish Loans Society.

Monday, 25 November 1918   *Warsaw*

At half past eleven to Wassiliewski. I said that, regardless of yesterday's occurrences, I still desire to pave the way for friendly relations between Germany and Poland, but I must tell him that the situation does not lack a certain gravity. At half past three I shall send to inquire from him about offices and at six about an appropriate residence capable of being militarily well protected. He wrote down the two times on a slip of paper and promised that everything will be punctually completed. I have seldom seen anyone so embarrassed and helpless. He assured me that the demonstrations were directed against the Government rather than my own person. Not even a mention of the Bug lines of communications area atrocities.

It was six o'clock before we were notified of a tiny lower-middle-class apartment to be used as offices. A Legation Guard of ten will have to be accommodated in the kitchen, so little room is there. I swallowed this piece of incivility under protest to the Ministry official who was sent to conduct us there. We are still without a residence. The public attitude towards us seems today less hostile. The paper which published the first mischief-making article writes this evening that a German Legation in Warsaw, with numerous staff, is undoubtedly necessary, but that I have made the mistake of daily receiving hundreds (!) of people. The writer does not reveal how I am supposed to have performed this feat.

The negotiations have begun about evacuation of the Ukraine and use of the Polish railways for this purpose. They got off to a good start partly on account of the presence of a medical staff officer and a lance-corporal from High Command East. These arrived this morning and first declared themselves entitled to negotiate with the Polish Government on the strength of credentials issued by Hoffmann. I had them told by Gülpen that the right to negotiate with the Polish Government is confined to myself. Should they nonetheless attempt any dealings, I shall not recognize the upshot. On the other hand I am ready to admit them to my commission as experts and advisers. This they accepted. They say that speed is essential. The High Command East troops want to go home and it is barely possible to exercise restraint over them. If the Polish Government makes difficulties, the whole six hundred thousand of them will force their way through Poland. This statement appears to have impressed Sczeptycki.

Tuesday, 26 November 1918   *Warsaw*

This morning moved into the office premises. A machine-gun and six men are posted in the parlour with a field of fire across the entrance.

Interview with Filippovicz. I asked again when the German officials taken into 'protective custody' by the Polish Government will be released. It is not very well possible to release all at once, he replied, but he proposes to let them go 'in batches' of three or four, the first this week already.

I met Niemozecki. He foresees a more radical state of affairs and line of policy by the Government, probably also public disturbances, at the latest within a few weeks. The Polish news agency (WAT) is distributing an article by Korfanty in a Posen paper about my always having been a left-wing democrat and indeed internationalist. It was Korfanty who, on the day of the hostile demonstrations, held a glowing pro-Entente speech from my window to the crowd below.

At one o'clock our Guard suddenly departed on the plea that it had received orders to return to its headquarters immediately. Sent Meyer to see what was up and to demand fresh protection.

Dinner with the Swiss Consul, Wettler. Also there the Norwegian Consul and a married couple, he German, she Polish. They told us the story of a cabaret sketch they saw last night. A Jew cannot obtain his telephone connection. He implores, he abuses the operator, he threatens, until finally he yells into the machine, 'If I don't get my connection at once, I'll go to Beseler. Oh yes, of course, Beseler isn't here any more. But, Miss, if you don't make my connection right away, I'll go to Kessler, who has replaced Beseler.' And he gets his connection at once. Propaganda, quite skilful too.

Wednesday, 27 November 1918   *Warsaw*

The Guard is back, nine men strong with a German-speaking sergeant in charge. During the morning a call from Morawski to introduce his deputy, a Count Raczynski; no mention of the Note. Also a call by Studnicki, who has had rough treatment by the Press because the mob found his visiting-card in my room at the Bristol. He would like to see the 'eastern provinces', meaning a large slice of Russia, returned to Poland. The Poles are developing an appetite like a freshly hatched sparrow. Studnicki is a small, somewhat untidy man with attractive, kindly eyes who speaks German badly but is said to love Germany. A theoretician and idealist, it seemed to me, rather than a realist.

Thursday, 28 November 1918   *Warsaw*

Still no instructions from Berlin and no answer whatever to my telegram about the Bug lines of communications area.

Dinner at the Angielski with Theusner and Otto Fürstner. Band playing and the place full to overflowing. Many pretty, quite smart women. Through the window of a house opposite could be seen girls and Legionaries dancing together. A demonstration passed down the street, bawling 'Down with the Government!' As I was leaving, the head waiter quickly bundled me through a side-door. Later Fürstner, who went down the main staircase with Theusner, told me that four or five young people, including an officer, had been waiting for me outside and shouted my name as they emerged, obviously meaning to provoke an incident. They want to chalk up some good marks for themselves, quickly, before the Entente arrives. Not very brave, but prudent.

Friday, 29 November 1918   *Warsaw*

This morning a rash of posters headed 'To Arms!' and calling for war with Germany. Unsigned. Evidently the work of the National Democrats subsidized by the Entente. At midday little groups could be seen everywhere, studying the text but not saying anything. Studnicki, who called during the course of the morning, begged me to attach no importance to the matter.

Saturday, 30 November 1918   *Warsaw*

My Polish valet, on waking me, reported that last night 'thousands of people' demonstrated until five o'clock in the morning in front of the house where the Legation offices are situated. They fetched out the porter and demanded to know where I live. The porter says that they threatened to shoot him if he did not tell them. The demonstrators included many women. They pushed right up to our offices.

Yesterday evening, according to the papers, the mob stormed the Prime Minister's offices, hoping to haul out the Ministers. It was presumably the same lot who landed at the Legation at one and it proves how closely the mischief-making against us and the Government is linked.

At half past ten I was informed that the Legation Guard had received orders to leave. Hereupon I sent the staff home, closed the offices, and instructed Meyer to see Filippovicz. The latter will again proffer excuses but no protection. In these circumstances an orderly process of work is impossible.

I had a visit from Zeligowski, the new Posen Police President. He said that clearly I am being watched; he had seen some very suspicious characters hanging around my door. As he is meeting Korfanty and Scyda today, I told him that he can tell them from me that the National Democrats are behaving very foolishly and contrary to Polish interests in seeking to drive me out and to rupture relations with Germany. My task is to try and effect with the Polish Government an orderly evacuation of the Ukraine. It will be impossible, once these negotiations fail, to hold back half a million men well equipped with guns and ammunition. They will break out on the day that I take my departure and my Government must disclaim all responsibility for whatever happens then. I am the sole bulwark between Poland and this seething flood. Zeligowski appeared impressed and proposed a discussion this afternoon between Korfanty and myself in some neutral spot.

Meyer returned from Filippovicz who, he said, outdid himself in apologies. Meyer, on my instructions, demanded the requisition of an empty villa, the provision of adequate military protection in charge of a German-speaking officer, and an audience for myself with Pilsudski.

At six to Pilsudski, who has moved to the Belvedere Palace. He received Meyer and myself in a large, old-fashioned and fairly sparsely furnished drawing-room on the first floor. His manner and attitude, for all his simplicity, is quite that of the Head of State. An odd metamorphosis since our encounter at Magdeburg. He looks ill, pale and thin, and complained about his health. His face is furrowed, but the fire in his eyes, with their mystical and now deeply melancholy expression, still burns. I said that, the mob last night having broken for the third time into my Legation, I must put forward certain requests: a mansion for which, although it is to be militarily requisitioned, I shall pay the full price and a strong guard under a reliable and German-speaking officer.

Pilsudski promised, under the proviso of consultation with the Government, to fulfil these demands. He apologized for what had happened, adding that the demonstrations are directed as much against himself as against me.[24] Hitherto he has tried to manage with indulgence. Now he has decided to suppress disorder by force. He has issued orders which may lead to bloodshed. (As he spoke, his face grew still more pale and ashen. His lineaments reflected a dreadful inner struggle and grief.) Tonight already certain arrests will be made. That is what the National Democrats have asked for. He deplores the need, but his mind is made up. He will put as firm a stop to Bolshevism on the right as on the left. At the same time he must tell me that popular excitement against the Legation is not groundless. The reports of atrocities by our soldiers in the Bug area, the exclusion of Polish officials from the Suwalki region which is indubitable Polish territory, the fear of Russian Bolsheviks following on the heels of our retreating forces in Lithuania and White Russia, these things are splendid stuff for agitation. If matters continue along these lines, he may himself be bound to make certain dispositions. (In other words, a third ultimatum.)

I replied that those who are promoting a breach in German–Polish relations and the recall of our Legation strike me as strangely stupid. As soon as this happens and our soldiers in the Ukraine learn of it, they will take the bit between their teeth and beat a homeward path. Poland will be trampled underfoot before the Entente can offer help. He fully agreed.

I once more gained the impression that Pilsudski really does want a settlement with us. He will also not be deterred from pursuing his own path resolutely and deliberately. The question is what power he actually has or can acquire in time. Clarity of vision and goodwill are not enough against Entente intervention and Bolshevism. He admitted that the National Democrats are trying by every means, including agitation against myself, to provoke an incident whose consequences will be Entente intervention. And he did not seem any too sure that they may not succeed in their purpose.

After my interview I sent a telegram to Berlin, again drawing attention to the dangers of the Bug lines of communication area problem and again urgently asking for instructions. Since my arrival in Warsaw, regardless of the critical situation and of the ultimatum, I have not had a single political directive or other telegram from Berlin. The Ministry of Foreign Affairs gives no answer whatever. Meyer thinks that perhaps everything is in a state of dissolution and nobody dares to take a decision. Unconfirmed reports state that Eisner has demanded the resignation of Solf and Erzberger. Meyer says that the whole Ministry would stick to Solf and resign with him.

Meyer and I dined alone at a small tavern. And thus ends this historic month of November 1918 which will always, together with August 1914, have a memorable ring about it.

Sunday, 1 December 1918   *Warsaw*

Still no courier or instructions. It is just as though Berlin had forgotten our existence.

Our offices are now under the protection of an infantry platoon and two machine-guns. A guard stands in the street in front of the door. So Pilsudski has kept his word.

Various gatherings of a National Democratic character have been announced for today. The one at ten in the evening in the Sachsenplatz is sure to lead to scenes.

I moved yesterday into private quarters. Today my landlady came to me, very politely but very frightened, and made it clear that she will be thankful if I take myself off again. The city mob is after me and there is no telling what may happen. Finally she returned my papers because she is not going to take the risk of registering me with the police.

This evening farewell dinner for Fortress Hospital III which tomorrow leaves for Germany with all the sick and wounded. It is the last of our fully established units in Poland and with its departure there ends the occupation of this country into which we marched in such fine fettle and with such high hopes in 1914.[25] Now I have to be glad that these poor fellows, who were no longer safe here, can escape unshorn. The Commanding Officer, a senior medical staff officer from Stettin, disclosed himself as incurably Pan-German. In the melancholy circumstances of this dinner his phrase-mongering was both innocuous and irritating. When I left, after eleven, a large crowd was moving towards the Belvedere, solemnly and rhythmically chanting 'Down! Down! Down!' This dark, savage horde made one's flesh creep. Towards one o'clock I checked how things were at the Legation offices. The Guard reported that the mob had passed without trouble.

Monday, 2 December 1918   *Warsaw*

At last a courier has brought instructions from Berlin. Supreme Army Command agrees to evacuation of the Bug lines of communication area west of the Bug, apart from one bridge-head near Brest-Litovsk. Polish forces will be allowed, prior to our evacuation, to take over a part of the area eastward in order to prevent its occupation by the Bolsheviks. The decision appears to have cost a struggle, for the SAC agreement to these terms is dated 27 November while a message of the previous day from High Command East (which has arrived at the same time) describes evacuation of the Bug lines of communication area as impossible. Wrote to Pilsudski tonight, telling him of the Government's agreement to evacuation of a part of the Bug area, and suggesting immediate negotiations on the manner of implementation. This secures for the Polish Government a success which will doubtless stabilize its position. Yesterday's gatherings proved a fiasco for the National Democrats.

In the evening a visit from old Count Milewski. Only four weeks ago, he complained, he applied for a passport to his old friend Beseler. When he returned, he found '*ce bolchévique de Pilsudski*' reigning at the Belvedere. In all countries we must stick together, we nobles, against the raging rabble.

Wednesday, 4 December 1918   *Warsaw*

At five o'clock this afternoon the opening conference with the Chief of Staff Count Sczeptycki, in the Bristol, on the Bug area evacuation. Present, in addition to Sczeptycki, were Filippovicz, his aide Jodko, Winiawa on behalf of Pilsudski, and Captain Górka. I had with me Meyer, Rawicki, Major Ritter, Major Schmidt and Captain Rabien, the last two representing the Chief Railway Transport Officer and High Command East respectively.

Jodko conducted proceedings on the Polish side. He began at once with the question by what date we propose to evacuate the area as far as the Bug. The Polish Government will find it difficult to extend the deadline beyond midday, 23 December. In our view, I replied, the deadline must depend on the time necessary to remove our stores and equipment. This requires expert opinion and I have today requested the officer commanding the lines of communication to visit me. I cannot discuss a deadline until I have heard what he has to say. Jodko then demanded the organization of, and a distribution of arms to, the Polish population of Lithuania in order to enable them to resist the Bolsheviks. I shall try and persuade our Government, I answered, to advise the Polish Government of its evacuation in such good time as to enable defence to be prepared. At this stage Jodko permitted himself to put forward wishes respecting Posen[26] affairs. I sharply reminded him that for the present Posen belongs to Germany and that I therefore reject any ventilation with the Polish Government of conditions there. He became very red in the face but kept quiet.

The conference took place in Sczeptycki's bedroom, because he is ill. A strange lot, these negotiators. Sczeptycki is a shrewd Pole who pretends to be a hothead and guileless fighting man. Jodko is an old social democrat, with the head of a Socrates and a sharp schoolmasterly voice, who is not in fact as strong as he likes to make himself out to be. Winiawa, Pilsudski's military assistant, is, as he maintains, the complete soldier, but there is an agreeable whiff of the Paris Latin Quarter about him. Filippovicz has brought back from exile the manner of an American professor as well as his broken English. The team tried to lend an air of determination and passionate conviction to their demands, but they are really spurred on by their feeling of weakness.

Friday, 6 December 1918   *Warsaw*

A number of French prisoners of war, mostly wearing tricolour insignia, loitered about the streets today. The public took little notice. On the other hand, Rabien, going to the theatre in the evening, was cheered. There was a performance of *La Belle Hélène*. Four French officers sat in the proscenium box. The actor playing Agamemnon stepped forward and, in Polish, greeted glorious France as a sister-nation. The *Marseillaise* followed. A French captain in the box expressed thanks. The *Marseillaise* was played again, to the accompaniment of thunderous applause. A scene for Daumier or Flaubert.

In the afternoon there arrived from Biala the representative of Bug lines of communications area headquarters, Major Wolpmann, and the chairman of the area Soldiers' Council, Lance-Corporal Müller. Discussion at the Legation and then I took them to dinner, with Korff, Rawicki, and Fürstner, to the Europejski. Even I thought the spruce General Staff major and the Lance-Corporal in his sheepskin jacket (an Essen decorator, by trade), a slightly odd combination for a smart meal in one of the Europejski's private rooms. As I entered with the pair, Korff paled visibly. However, the superiority of the simple soldier over the staff officer became manifest so quickly that prejudices disappeared. Clear-headed and circumspect, he became in no time and quite naturally the focal point of the conversation. The major sat beside him like a courtier, politely agreeing, while Müller with unconscious dignity dominated the company.

Saturday, 7 December 1918   *Warsaw*

A lieutenant arrived this morning on orders from the Ministry of War at Berlin. He brought us the news that elections to the National Assembly have been proclaimed for 16 February[27] and that probably German Austria will participate. We are so cut off that we knew absolutely nothing about this. He also told us that the troops returning from the Western Front are anything but Red and are marching back with their officers at the head of their columns. The Independents and the Spartacus people are consequently suffering a set-back and are already very nervous about it.

In the morning a discussion with Wolpmann and Müller on deadlines for the Bug area evacuation. They propose a phased withdrawal, the first to last until 23 December and the second to 1 February.

In the afternoon conference at General Staff Headquarters with Sczeptycki and a crowd of individuals from all sorts of Ministries. Jodko again did most of the talking. He negotiates as though he is addressing a public meeting and repeatedly diverged from the main topic to dilate on Lithuania, a tactic supported by Winiawa blethering away excitedly.

Sczeptycki had no objection to the passage of armed columns, but Jodko declared that his authority did not extend to such concessions and he must advise me in writing on the matter. That means we are going to have to barter yet another valuable right for evacuation of the Bug area.[28] This was the afternoon's climax, with the proceedings assuming the character of the Polish Diet. Everyone chattered at the same time. Only Sczeptycki sat there indifferently, allowed the talk to pass him by, and behaved as though he no more than half belonged to the company, which quite likely is what he really felt. This insight into the Polish way of conducting public affairs evidently gave Müller food for thought. He, with his red arm-band, made the sole sensible contribution, and to watch a German lance-corporal, as representative of the revolution, negotiating on equal terms with the Chief of General Staff of a foreign country was a remarkable sight.

Dined again with Wolpmann and Müller. The latter maintained that a German victory would have proved a misfortune because it would have exacerbated and perpetuated class differences. As a result of defeat and revolution, the whole nation will be brought closer together and join in working at political and economic problems. If peace and orderly economic conditions can be upheld, Germany will emerge from defeat stronger and happier than before. But if the Entente reduces us to wage slaves, that will mean a fresh war.

Sunday, 8 December 1918   *Warsaw*

Today a courier has at last arrived, though without newspapers. The telegrams include one from High Command East to the Ministry of Foreign Affairs. HCE has the impertinence to claim that they tried to enlighten me about the actual state of affairs there so that I 'should champion not merely Polish, but also German interests at Warsaw'. The light has not yet dawned on generals of Hoffmann's type. The puzzle is whether narrow-mindedness or impudence has the upper hand among these braggarts and intriguers. Fortunately their teeth sit too loosely in their jaws to be much good for biting. These people, whose manoeuvres have landed Germany in its present dreadful disaster, have the face to want to lay down rules of diplomatic procedure. The courier mentioned that, when he left Berlin on Friday afternoon, a shooting-match was in progress between Spartacists and Government troops. Some twenty dead.

Monday, 9 December 1918   *Warsaw*

Complete peace and quiet. A Cracow paper published an article on what a bad impression my appointment as Minister to Warsaw has made on the Entente and how it signifies that Poland is out of step with the Allies. None of the Warsaw papers carries anything on these lines; it is Cracow which would appear to be out of step.

Tuesday, 10 December 1918   *Warsaw*

This morning a minor Foreign Affairs Ministry official brought me a note from Wassiliewski. It bears yesterday's date and advises me that, with effect from 9 December, I am deprived of the right to send telegrams in cipher.

At a quarter past four visited Wassiliewski. He did his best to be cool and unfriendly. It has been noted that we dispatch and receive a great many cipher telegrams; this procedure is unpopular. The situation is very difficult and the measure imposed cannot for the present be rescinded. Unfortunately, I replied, the negotiations about the Bug lines of communications area and about Lithuania will be the main sufferers. If I have to depend on the courier, rapid progress will be impossible. The negotiations are not producing any result anyway, Wassiliewski retorted; we are exactly where we were three weeks ago.

My impression is that the Government, apart from fear of public opinion, is acting partly under Entente pressure and partly out of irritation at the length of the proposed evacuation deadlines. Perhaps it has managed to persuade the Entente to order us to evacuate. What our forces in the Ukraine will do in that case, whether they will keep quiet or break out, is an open question. If they break out, France can use it as a pretext to denounce the armistice. Consequently the risk that a breach of relations here involves for us is enormous. I have decided to visit High Command East, on the one hand to confer with Hoffmann and obtain concessions about the Bug area and Lithuania, on the other to talk undisturbed to the Government in Berlin.

Wednesday, 11 December 1918   *Warsaw*

Sent Meyer in place of myself to High Command East because I realized that it would be better for me not to leave Warsaw at this critical juncture.

Gave Meyer a report for transmission to Berlin and precise written instructions for his negotiations with Hoffmann. Strahl, visiting the Ministry of Foreign Affairs, had an icy reception from Morawski and Raczynski. A policy line has evidently been issued. Bluff or fear of the Entente? Probably both. I shall try at any rate to prevent or delay the breach because the dangers it would bring are enormous but will diminish with every day that peace comes closer. I would moreover rather see Pilsudski at the Peace Conference than Dmowski, who is on such intimate terms with the French.

Thursday, 12 December 1918   *Warsaw*

Spent the evening with Korff and B., formerly a fairly senior Russian Ministry of Foreign Affairs official who was born in Warsaw and has good connections here. He told us about a meeting at which Grabski demanded my immediate withdrawal from Warsaw. The step was to be effected by a Polish ultimatum to Germany to evacuate instantly Upper Silesia and the provinces of Posen and West Prussia including Danzig. My passport would be handed to me on receipt of my negative answer. Pilsudski rejected this proposal on the grounds that the Polish army lacks boots, munitions, and training, and that this state of affairs rendered the conduct of a war impossible. The hostile Press campaign is, according to B., what remains of Grabski's efforts and has been organized by him, although it is financed by two American correspondents, Daniel W. Strickland of the *Saturday Evening Post* and Charles B. Sherman. (This seems a pretty unlikely tale to me.) Even my attempted assassination is possible, he added, because a breach with Germany is being sought at any price. As recently as a fortnight ago a conspiracy against Pilsudski on the part of officers belonging to the Musnicki Corps was discovered only just in time: he was to be arrested and shot.

Grabski's main argument, B. said, is that Poland must become in the eyes of American and British capitalists the only safe country among a ring of Socialist-infected states – Germany, the Ukraine, and Russia. It must be achieved by throwing out its own Socialist government and myself, passing over power to the National Democrats, and signing an alliance with the Entente. The latter will then entrust to Poland the territories east of the Elbe, eastern Galicia with its oil wells, and Danzig and place limitless capital at its disposal. That way, and that way only, can Poland become a Great Power.

B. gave a very curious account of Rasputin, whom he had known. Rasputin was a perfectly honest son of the soil who, at the age of twelve, was engaged at Court to tend the lamps burning in front of the icons. In that capacity he occasionally entered at night the room of the young grand duchesses, having to light the lamps there, but nothing noteworthy ever arose out of that. It was the ladies of the Court who, when they observed the influence he had, positively sidled up to him and were responsible for his turning into a rake and a glutton. The Empress never had intimate relations with him. She merely showed herself in his company to prove that she was a good Orthodox Russian, but that was how the gossip started. The Tsar looked on him as 'the voice of the black earth' and saw no need for the Duma as long as Rasputin could echo to him directly the thought of his people. Gradually Rasputin acquired enormous influence and earned a corresponding amount of jealousy and enmity. During the war he was always against the continuation of hostilities, increasing the antipathy of Britain and the party of the grand dukes still more. Britain spent immense sums on efforts to eliminate his influence. In the last analysis, though, he always remained a simple peasant and lamplighter. Everything else is romantic trimmings.

Friday, 13 December 1918   *Warsaw*

A day of tragicomedy. I had been notified to expect at midday two representatives from the Bug headquarters who would negotiate with Sczeptycki accompanied by a representative on my side. At six there appeared a General Staff officer, Captain Knackfuss, and the splendid Lance-Corporal Müller who came the other day. Headquarters, they said, are prepared to evacuate the whole of the country west of the Bug, except the bridgehead at Brest, by 28 December. Indeed, Knackfuss added, they will *have* to evacuate it even if the Poles do not demand it because the troops are needed for protection of the railway line; the militia men posted there have become restless and unreliable.

At eight o'clock a visit from Dr Bader, head of the Political Department in the Ministry of Foreign Affairs. He came, he announced, to hand me a not very pleasing communication whose contents I may however have anticipated. Hereupon he passed me a communication whereby the Polish Government broke off diplomatic relations with Germany and requested me, with the entire Legation, to leave the country '*immédiatement*', but expressed the hope that relations would be resumed on the return of normal conditions. The reasons given for the breach were the dilatory progress of the negotiations about the Bug lines of communications area and about Lithuania (autonomous protective measures), the German Government's uncertain tenure of power, and the attitude of High Command East which rendered the prospect of a satisfactory solution of the difficulties hopeless. In this respect special reference was made to the last conference and the prolonged time limit proposed for evacuation, amounting to rejection of the proposed Polish deadline (23 December). The signature appended to the document was that of Deputy Minister Filippovicz.

Bader added that he had instructions to inform me, orally and confidentially, that the reasons stated in the document were not the real ones, but that the Government must ask the Legation to leave because my person is no longer safe and the Government is not in a position to shield me. There are two conspiracies against me, one on the part of individuals who have already made their way into the Legation once, the other on the part of elements whom the Government cannot restrain (presumably NDs). It wants, at whatever price, to spare me Mirbach's[29] fate. I told Bader that it is a pity for the breach to have occurred just an hour after High Command East and Bug headquarters have made me concessions which would have ensured a favourable conclusion to the negotiations. But I regard the breach as an unalterable fact and I request that tomorrow a special train be placed at my disposal. The tone of this interview, in contrast to its subject-matter, was friendly and almost cordial.

I called the staff together and informed them of the breach, sent a message to the Swiss Consul asking him to assume the protection of German interests, advised Ritter, Müller and Knackfuss, Korff, and so on, of the situation, and dispatched Strahl, as arranged, to the Ministry of Foreign Affairs to discuss departure details. He returned after an hour, very excited. He had again told Bader, 'purely privately', how ill-timed the breach was on account of the major concessions from High Command East. Hereupon Bader asked him to leave the room for a moment because he wanted to telephone to the Minister. After half an hour, when he was called in again, Bader informed him that he (Bader) must see me once more this evening and, until he called, I was to treat all today's events confidentially and not to make any further moves.

Bader came at eleven, declined to take off his coat because his stay would be very brief, and asked me to return him the document. Having been signed by Filippovicz instead of the Minister, Wassiliewski, it is formally incorrect. How, I asked, am I to regard this step? Does it mean that the document no longer exists? 'Yes,' replied Bader, *'nul et non avenu.'* Wassiliewski requests that I visit him tomorrow. I said that I shall call at eleven. So, after being broken off for three hours, relations have been provisionally resumed. Bader did not say whether the conspiracies against me will also be withdrawn. Seldom can any Government have displayed such an example of vacillation and fear of its own courage. The excuse of the invalid signature is sheer musical comedy.

Saturday, 14 December 1918   *Warsaw*

Filippovicz has resigned on account of yesterday's incident. Wassiliewski tendered his apologies and stated that there had been an 'abuse' for which the 'official concerned' (Filippovicz) 'has been immediately relieved of his appointment'. I should regard the transmitted document as invalid. He pointed to Filippovicz's signature, declaring that he had no right to sign such a paper. Wassiliewski, in notable contrast to the last occasion on which we met, was distinctly affable. I told him that I now possess an extensive mandate and asked that we should negotiate as quickly as possible, expressing the hope that we might reach agreement and be able to initial the treaty about the Bug area and Lithuania today. He was evidently pleased. The crisis seems over for the moment, with the Ministry at last settling firmly for a definite policy, that of neutrality.

At half past four a conference session at General Headquarters. I was accompanied by Meyer, Ritter, Rabien, Lance-Corporal Müller, and Captain Knackfuss. The Poles were headed by Sczeptycki and Jodko. I brought with me draft agreements. Broad unanimity about the Bug area and Lithuania was quickly achieved and details were left to a commission to work out. Thus the fate of large, populous territories and of thousands of individuals was decided in a matter of hours. Normally it would have taken a major war to come to the same conclusions. Or, more properly speaking, it is the upshot of the war that has been laid down for these territories. Jodko was at pains to behave with ostentatious amiability towards me. It is at his initiative that another session is being held today and that at the end of this it may prove possible to initial the draft agreements. There are three of these, on the Bug area, Lithuania, and the railroads, as well as a supplementary agreement which lays down instructions for implementation.

The evening papers give the impression that Filippovicz's fall has produced a united front between the Pilsudski Government and ourselves. We now have a party behind us because the Government stands or falls with me.

Ate in a tavern with Müller, Schoeller, Meyer, Rabien and the courier, Lieutenant Schuster. Polish officers at a neighbouring table adopted a threatening and arrogant attitude.

Sunday, 15 December 1918   *Warsaw*

Today the breach of relations is final. Bader and Morawski called at ten in the morning and handed me a document, this time signed by Wassiliewski. On the basis of numerous more or less idle excuses it breaks off relations and requests me to depart '*immédiatement*' with the Legation. Bader said that news 'from the West' (presumably meaning Posen) and the lack of result at yesterday's talks were responsible for the decision.

I protested vigorously against the second reason because complete agreement was reached and Jodko, asking for postponement of signature, did not raise a single point of factual objection. He merely stated that he would like to examine again the wording of the agreements. Bader knew no answer to this. What has really happened, of course, is that the Entente has exercised strong pressure, not being prepared to put up with Filippovicz's removal and demanding that of the Legation in atonement.

At the same time as I was notified of the breach of relations, I was handed two documents protesting in a most provocative and arrogant tone against alleged atrocities by our forces in the Bug area. They are evidently meant, clumsy fabrications though they are, for a White Book. We are not responsible for this breach of relations. In Warsaw we have put up with unheard of things without ever losing patience and always trying to smooth matters out, while I have for my part always exercised utmost pressure on High Command East and the Government to meet the Poles half-way. Clearly Pilsudski and his Government did not want the breach either. It is the National Democrats, relying on France, who have brought it about. Here too France has shown itself to be insatiable in its desire for vengeance. Its demonic hatred has not by any means been pacified by our defeat, it seems. The French will continue to hate us and fight against us until they or we are exterminated.

During the afternoon special editions of the newspapers announced the breach, or 'suspension', of relations with Germany. People bought copies with considerable interest. I had sent Gülpen to Pilsudski about release of our police inspectors. Pilsudski was very friendly, Gülpen reported, but said that only now could he breathe freely again, so desperately has he been pressed by right and left alike. We had visits all day from German subjects fetching passports to enable them to leave with the Legation. At five o'clock came the Swiss Consul. He accepted responsibility for the protection of German interests, but only provisionally because, he said, he must in the altered circumstances request permission from his Government before finally assuming the task.

At ten o'clock a young Polish lieutenant reported to me; he will act as convoy officer as far as the frontier; then another officer, and finally a transport officer with a car and a truck. The railway station had been taken over by the military. Gülpen was warned earlier that 'we are afraid of an assault by some lunatic'. The convoy officer pushed us quickly through the crowd of onlookers, nosey but peaceful. The special train, made up of my Pullman, an ordinary carriage, and a luggage van, was waiting. In the end only some sixty extra people accompanied us; the majority of Germans have chosen to stay in Warsaw. At half past eleven a representative of the Ministry of Foreign Affairs arrived and handed me a farewell letter from the Minister.

The station hubbub of civilians, military, and luggage-loading lasted about an hour. A large part of the files had simply been bundled because no packing-cases were available. Whole batches of them were slung into the luggage van. In all other respects the arrangements made by the Poles were exemplary. At midnight we left the station. I invited the two Polish lieutenants into my Pullman. Nothing could have been friendlier than the talk we had with them. The possibility that tomorrow we might be enemies made not the slightest difference. About half past one the train halted. Then we were told that we were returning to Warsaw: the route via Alexandrowo is not free and we must proceed by Mlawa and East Prussia. At two o'clock we were back in the suburban station and moved slowly around the periphery of the city to reach the other track.

Monday, 16 December 1918   *Mlawa*

Shortly past noon a Prussian officer (wearing epaulettes) reported to me. It was gone half past twelve when we left Mlawa. The Polish officers stood on the platform, saluting. At seven minutes past one we crossed the frontier at Illowo.

Tuesday, 17 December 1918   *Berlin*

Arrived at eight in the morning. Staff and luggage detrained at Friedrich-strasse Station. Brandenburger Tor, Pariser and Potsdamer Platz decked with flags and garlands for the returning troops. Noticeable that not a red flag to be seen; nothing but black-white-red, black-white, and here and there black-red-gold. The majority of soldiers and officers are wearing badges and epaulettes again. The contrast with mid-November is considerable.

At half past nine a reporter from the *BZ* came for an interview. At eleven I gave Ludwig Stein an interview on political affairs for *Voss*.[30] He told me that certain people have me in mind as State Secretary in succession to Solf. Then I went to report to the latter at the Ministry. I found him deeply despondent, grey in the face and utterly despairing of the feasibility of carrying out the duties of a State Secretary under the present Government. As regards what I had done at Warsaw, he declared himself fully satisfied. Asked what I thought about registering a protest on account of the Polish Government's proclamation of elections on German territory. Relations between the two countries had, after all, simply been interrupted, not broken off. Said that I thought a protest in order.

From Solf to Haase at the Chancellery. He received me in a very friendly manner and approved my handling of affairs at Warsaw. 'Nobody could have done more.' I had been the victim of *force majeure*. More than anything, Haase gives an impression of great suppleness combined with basic stubbornness, iron hand in rubber glove. A small, dogged, somewhat Jesuitical Jew with a clear, hard look.

Wednesday, 18 December 1918   *Berlin*

As I left the Ministry just before two, a home-coming division was marching down Unter den Linden. All the men wore steel helmets. Numbers of them had bunches of flowers attached to their tunics, their rifles, or their helmets.

The limbers and guns were garlanded and innumerable black-white-red, Prussian and Greater German colours of all sizes, but not a single red flag, could be seen. The officers, wreathed with flowers too, rode at the head of their formations. Both sides of the street were lined with an enormous crowd. There was some faint cheering and from houses decked with banners people waved. But to me it was a heartrending spectacle. I felt grief, shame and love for this courageous host, returning crowned with glory though crushed by misfortune. Here, in Unter den Linden, the pathos of the immense tragedy found expression in this festooned melancholy.

Thursday, 19 December 1918   *Berlin*

The Congress of Workers' and Soldiers' Councils in the Reichstag continues to squabble, and unauthorized deputations from time to time ride roughshod over its wishes. Liebknecht's agitation is achieving a general state of unrest.

Karl Liebknecht (Kursell)

The Government is afraid of intervening vigorously, but, if it does not do this now before the troops back from the Front have been demobilized, the Spartacus people, who are armed and being paid thirty marks a day, will later have the upper hand. The Fifty-Third Sailors' Committee, in occupation of the Imperial Stables and other buildings, has already gone over to Liebknecht. Since then the sailors, as a result of Liebknecht's proddings and financial resources, have become much more radical.

Friday, 20 December 1918   Berlin

In the afternoon a conference with Lewald about arrangements for an inquiry into the abuses which took place in Poland. Kries, the former Chief of Administration, and a senior civil servant in the Ministry of the Interior, was also there. Lewald's object was to exculpate the civil administration which had been subordinate to him. Kries admitted the corruption at lower levels. At the start, he said, everyone was incorruptible. By 1916, however, venality at lower and medium levels had become marked. In 1917 the big swing towards corruption in general and fairly far up the hierarchy set in. It was the Jews who made the overtures and were responsible for the dishonesty. For the Poles this German corruption had been more grievous, oppressive and aggravating than the Russian because with the Russians the most senior officials could be bribed, and the bribery therefore served its purpose, whereas with the Germans it was sometimes the case that the lower echelon, after being paid, was unsuccessful with the higher and the investor lost his money without return.

Saturday, 21 December 1918   Berlin

At noon the burial of victims of the 6 December putsch. Liebknecht seized the opportunity for a demonstration. The funeral train started from the Victory Column, where the coffins were lying in state and Liebknecht made a speech. I encountered the cortège on Potsdamer Platz. The coffins, in pairs on ordinary drays, were buried beneath wreaths of red flowers with red ribbons attached. The draymen wore their working clothes, round hats on their thick skulls. Behind them followed a contingent of Red sailors, then several thousand men and women walking in tidy ranks and carrying large numbers of red flags and banners which swayed on poles above the immense black and grey procession like poppies on long stalks. In the December sunshine the overall impression was neither very awe-inspiring nor very solemn, but astringently picturesque.

A visit from Oscar Fried. He is back from conducting concerts in the Ukraine and talked about the disintegration of our forces there. The Ukrainian civil war, which is going in Petlura's favour, is a danger to them. The Entente is doing nothing and will probably take good care to keep away from those parts. Fried met Petlura at his headquarters and then ran into all sorts of skirmishes and shootings on the way back to Germany.

When I returned to the Ministry, Meyer told me that our fears have now been realized: our forces in the Ukraine have broken loose and will probably march back on their own through Poland. The reason: Petlura's people, contrary to what was agreed, blocked the rail section Golocz-Kowel to them.

Hereupon they went berserk and set off independently. Various wireless messages, including one to the Polish Government, are being dispatched tonight. The danger is that the armistice may be denounced on this score. The Poles, at any rate, will regard the breakaway of the troops as a put-up job and and a retaliation for my expulsion.

Sunday, 22 December 1918   *Berlin*

Visited Paul Cassirer. He is back from Switzerland where he and Schickele are in touch with the French Socialists. He claims that Grumbach is now wholly on our side for fear of French imperialism and is working on *Humanité* in harmony with our ideas. The N–K Agency is now at his and Schickele's disposal and through it they can have news of items published in the Northcliffe Press. Here he has had talks with Bolsheviks (Spartacus adherents). Their programme, far from envisaging any sort of peace with the Entente Imperialists, wants war to the knife with them, and let the German bourgeoisie starve in the process. They want to force the Entente to stay mobilized, hoping that this will spark off revolution. Cassirer describes the German revolution so far as sheer political jobbery. Nothing essential has been altered; only a bit more nepotism here and there. Spartacus is a danger for the days to come. The majority Socialists will enjoy preponderance in the National Assembly, but conditions favour the Spartacists and will frustrate the majority's steady labours.

As I left the Ministry at one, another home-coming division, steel-helmeted and flower-bedecked like that the other day, was marching down Unter den Linden. But at the corner of Wilhelmstrasse it was awaited by a crowd of war-wounded, shaking their crutches in the air or carrying placards: 'Not Charity, but Justice' and 'Throw out the Guilty who have reduced us to Misery and Poverty.' The procession, obviously mounted by Liebknecht, moved forward in the path of the division, jostled the troops, got in their way, broke in among their ranks. It was a distressing incident which visibly affected the soldiers. Their faces were taut and the atmosphere was tense. The onlookers were just as upset, but remained quiet.

Lunched in the Adlon with Rudi Schröder, whom I had not seen since the outbreak of war. Afterwards he recited to me three poems that he had dedicated to Hofmannsthal. The revolution has made hay of his plans.

Monday, 23 December 1918   *Berlin*

Meeting of our committee for foreign affairs: Prittwitz, Roediger, and others. I raised the question what foreign policy we could now have and how we can implement it. With the passing of the old system of power politics, the methods appropriate to it have also become obsolete. About five I left with Roediger to go across to the Ministry. We saw, as we entered, some argument being carried on between armed sailors and people inside who wanted to leave, but we paid no attention.

In the evening, towards ten, there was a rumour of shooting having broken out again and there being twenty dead. Some said that it had occurred at Potsdamer Station, others said at Alexanderplatz. I drove to the latter to see what had happened and was given the (correct) information that the shooting had taken place in the neighbourhood of the Palace. A group of sailors stood outside the Imperial Stables and told the tale of how their comrades, having gone to the Commandant's office to demand pay, suddenly came under fire from the direction of the University. Two of them were killed. Hereupon they had put the City Commandant, Wels, under arrest and removed him to the Imperial Stables. That happened around eight.

As I passed down Unter den Linden, I met a unit in steel helmets. Big, handsome fellows, it was some moments before I recognized the Third Battalion of Uhlan Guards, my own regiment. Some young officers explained that Ebert had just now sent for them. While we were speaking, other soldiers in half-tattered uniforms and civilians surged round the troops and pestered them. Our men ignored the newcomers. After a few minutes an order was issued and the contingent disappeared inside the University. I had not seen my regiment since August 1914, during the assault on Namur. A sorry re-encounter, this, in a night of revolution fraught with the danger of civil war and social dissolution.

This shooting business, the blood spilt, and the arrival of the Potsdam troops have brought things to a head. If the Government possesses any vigour of mind, it will take advantage of the situation to evacuate, by force if need be, the marine division which has gone completely extremist. The majority of soldiers and civilians is hostile to the sailors, regarding them as mischief-makers. On the other hand the sailors only turned radical after discovering the trick which Metternich[31] had played with them. That made them very ready to listen to Spartacus propaganda. Every day something fresh occurs in Berlin's streets, at the price of Germany going to the devil.

Tuesday, 24 December 1918   *Berlin*

This morning Christmas Eve began with an artillery action. Government troops tried to bombard the sailors out of the Palace and the Imperial Stables.

At eleven I went to the Ministry and found Meyer exultant. The Government, he said, is at last taking a stern line. Let them put a few sailors up against the wall! He was mildly reproachful at my not sharing this counter-revolutionary mood.

Towards noon I walked up Unter den Linden. The Republican Security

Guard had thrown a barrier across the street from Friedrichstrasse, but it was possible to circumvent this. There was a fairly large crowd in front of the University. Otherwise all was quiet. But large, pallid patches on the Palace walls, traces of the artillery bombardment, were visible at this distance already. An immense crowd swarmed unimpeded in the Lustgarten. Shell-fire had very badly damaged the main Palace portal facing the Lustgarten. One of the pillars lay shattered on the ground and both wings of the iron doorway, riddled with holes, hung crooked on their hinges. The balcony over it, from which the Emperor made his speech on 4 August 1914, was smashed to pieces and remnants dangled down. The windows of the façade were no more than dark cavities, no panes, the sills splintered. The most grievous damage had been sustained by the balcony's beautiful caryatids, where a Michelangelo-like arm was shot away and their expressive heads were bowed still more movingly than before. Sailors were on guard in front of the portal.

Things looked the same on the Palace square. Sailors with machine-guns stood at the windows, which were battered to pieces. The square was black with people. They were waiting for something, though without knowing what – whether a battle, a mass meeting, perhaps Liebknecht's appearance – just waiting and unafraid because for thousands curiosity outvied fear. At the same time these bystanders formed the best bulwark of defence for the mutinous sailors. Until these spectators were dispersed or pushed back, the Government troops would be unable to renew their attack. Suddenly a Government troop of light artillery emerged from the Breite Strasse and was at once surrounded by a seething mob yelling insults, which revealed that many here were on Liebknecht's side. A sergeant, wearing a red-black-gold armband, climbed on a limber and made a speech audible right across the square. A parley is going on, he announced, and brothers should not shoot and kill each other. It worked, mainly, probably, because of the calm way he spoke. The troop was let through and drove off.

Spartacus agitators started small meetings all over the square. People argued with them, but they listened too. A tall, fanatical-looking fellow, with flickering eyes and a malevolent look shouted down a decently dressed man who was trying to convince him. Action, he snarled, is what is wanted, not simply words all the time. The Government has talked enough. Let it take socialism seriously or it will find its shilly-shallying cut short. Elsewhere a tatterdemalion old man, collarless, preached reason: Always let reason take its course, a little reason on both sides and mutual understanding will prevail. Every speaker had his audience. These small assemblies, with their some-times frantic, sometimes balanced manner of discussion reminded me of Hyde Park on a Sunday evening.

The Christmas Fair carried on throughout the blood-letting. Hurdy-gurdies played in the Friedrichstrasse while street-vendors sold indoor fire-works, gingerbread, and silver tinsel. Jewellers' shops in Unter den Linden remained unconcernedly open, their windows brightly lit and glittering. In the Leipziger Strasse the usual Christmas crowds thronged the big stores. In thousands of homes the Christmas tree was lit and the children played around it with their presents from Daddy, Mummy and Auntie dear. In the Imperial Stables lay the dead, and the wounds freshly inflicted on the Palace and on Germany gaped into the Christmas night.

Wednesday, 25 December 1918   *Berlin*

All the newspapers, even *Vorwärts*,[32] confirm this morning that the Government has capitulated. It would have been better never to have started shooting.

During the afternoon there was another major Spartacus demonstration, proceeding from the Siegesallee to the Palace and there fraternizing with the victorious sailors. Then the crowd marched to *Vorwärts*, occupied the building, and ran off leaflets headed '*The Red Vorwärts*', with the following announcement: 'Today, 25 December 1918, *Vorwärts* has passed into our, the revolutionary workers' possession, in accordance with the new justice born with the revolution of 9 November. . . . Long live the revolutionary sailors' division, the revolutionary proletariat, the international socialist world revolution! All power to the Workers and Soldiers! Down with the Ebert-Scheidemann Government! Arms for the workers! Disarm the bourgeoisie and their accomplices! Signed: the shop-stewards and representatives of the Greater Berlin Works.' The whole thing printed on red paper.

Some other leaflets, on white paper, have a similar content. Two members of the security section of Police Headquarters brought me specimens to a bar where there was dancing and I was surprised to meet Theodor Däubler. These old soldiers told me how they had put *Vorwärts* back in the hands of its lawful staff. The younger of them did not however seem so very immune to Spartacus attractions and was proud of having spoken to Liebknecht. The other gave it as his opinion that if things go on like this, we shall soon see the Tommies in Berlin.

Thursday, 26 December 1918   *Berlin*

At nine a meeting of our political association. Rietzler's information was that at today's Spartacus meetings Ledebour and Liebnecht were elected People's Plenipotentiaries and that the second of these is to be proclaimed Head of Government tonight or tomorrow. The existing Government has all in all perhaps a hundred reliable troops at its disposal.

At ten o'clock Rietzler, two others and myself walked to the Palace to hear the Liebknecht proclamation. The square was the quietest and most deserted place I have long experienced. No more than one small popular gathering being addressed by a young, well-dressed Spartacus adherent with a pleasant manner. Obviously an intellectual, he explained to his audience how the German nation is not yet ripe to rule itself and must first go through a lengthy, laborious preparation. That is why there must be Workers' and Soldiers' Councils instead of a National Assembly. Rietzler tried to enter into discussion with him, could not hold his own, became frightened, wanted to get away, and was only able to do so with the crowd's jeers ringing in his ears. And Rietzler is the man who is supposed to instil Ebert with courage tomorrow! The core of the political problem is whether there are anywhere any serviceable and reliable troops available. Or, if not, whether the sailors can be bought and bribed to leave. Sheer Byzantine conditions! The sailors are venal all right, but what are they to be bought with? Seldom can a Government have been so disgracefully weak.

Friday, 27 December 1918   *Berlin*

The crisis continues undiminished. Hatzfeldt attended today's Cabinet meeting and says only the Independents – Haase, Dittmann, Barth – participated. Landsberg looked in for a moment; Ebert and Scheidemann stayed away. A point of discussion was a Polish proposal for an agreement on a common defence of Vilna against the Russian Bolsheviks; the Poles, in exchange, would guarantee the evacuation of our troops from the Ukraine. The Cabinet, influenced by Cohen-Nordhausen, declined the offer. No falling out with the Bolsheviks, ran the argument; on the contrary, there ought to be a treaty and commercial agreements with Bolshevik Russia.

Dinner with Hiller. Other guests were Paul Cassirer, Kestenberg, Hilferding, and the Independent Ministers Breitscheid and Hugo Simon. The last two made no secret of the fact that their ministerial status may continue for only a few hours. Everything depends on the Central Council. If it decides against the Independents remaining in the Reich Administration, then they will resign their Prussian Ministerial posts as well. Simon, who played the leading part in the financial arguments with the sailors, says that his main object was to get them out of the Palace on account of their pilfering. Although they had handed over the keys to the wine cellars, they retained those of the plate-room. The looting had been dreadful in one wing of the Palace which he inspected. The sailors did finally agree to relinquish the keys, but not to the City Commandant, whom they loathed. The Commandant, however, made it a point of honour that he should be the recipient. From that the whole unhappy tangle had arisen. Now the German Government, and possibly Germany itself, is menaced with collapse because of this idiotic point of protocol.

Breitscheid has strong reservations about Rantzau, especially his homo-sexuality. It is a matter of indifference as such, but it could prove a handicap to the freedom of manoeuvre he can permit himself. And then, there is the question of the profiteers with whom he associated at Copenhagen.

Saturday, 28 December 1918   *Berlin*

The problem of whether I want to accept the Berne Legation as a stepping-stone to the promotion of relations with France has become pressing. Yesterday Schickele cabled me about it and Breitscheid, Hilferding, and Kestenberg all sounded me out. This morning Kestenberg again raised the subject. A luncheon-party was arranged at Cassirer's home to give the four of us further opportunity to discuss the subject. After declining several times, I finally declared myself prepared in principle to accept the appoint-ment provided that I am relieved of attending to local affairs and of purging the Legation, whose staff has to be reduced to less than a tenth of its strength. My only real task, one of international importance, should be the establishment of relations with Britain and France.

I told Breitscheid and Hilferding that I see our position in the following terms. A dictated peace is inevitable. To obtain its abrogation, we must either wage a new war, choose Bolshevism, or, as certain political parties in the Entente countries oppose a dictated peace, give these our support so that they may come to power and rescind the settlement. To my mind, a new war is out of the question during the foreseeable future; Bolshevism is too costly a policy as long as any other hope exists; and therefore I favour the third course.

Before the lunch I went over the Palace. The damage done by the shelling is surprisingly small. A grenade landed in the Hall of Pillars and, tearing to shreds a Skarbina painting, pierced the rear wall. The private apartments of the Emperor and the Empress, especially the dressing-rooms, have been pretty badly looted. With a single exception, the Empress's wardrobes have been emptied and deep inroads made into those belonging to the Emperor. The handles of his walking-sticks have been screwed off, the staffs smashed and thrown away. Photographs, powder-boxes, and mementoes have been scattered around. The Empress's writing-desk has been broken open. Rumour says that the contents, including correspondence between the Emperor and old Queen Victoria, are being hawked around the town. The Emperor's trinket stands, their glass shattered, have been cleaned out. It seems difficult to say how far the sailors have been responsible for the pillage. But these private apartments, the furniture, the articles of everyday use, and what remains of the Emperor's and Empress's mementoes and *objets d'art* are so insipid and tasteless, so philistine, that it is difficult to feel much indignation against the pilferers. Only astonishment that the wretched, timid, unimaginative creatures who liked this trash, and frittered away their life in this precious palatial haven, amidst lackeys and sycophants, could ever make any impact on history. Out of this atmosphere was born the World War, or as much of the guilt for it as falls on the Emperor. In this rubbishy, trivial, unreal microcosm, furnished with nothing but false values which deceived him and others, he made his judgements, plans, and decisions. Morbid taste and a pathologically excitable character in charge of an all too well-oiled machine of state. Now the symbols of his futile animating spirit lie strewn around here in the shape of doltish odds and ends. I feel no sympathy, only aversion and complicity when I reflect that this world was not done away with long ago, but on the contrary still continues to exist, in somewhat different forms, elsewhere.

It was a shock to be confronted with the dead sailors, some in coffins, others on stretchers, laid out in a ground-floor doorway that I often used when attending Court functions. Some relatives, small folk, were having the lids lifted for identification. A stale smell of corpses hung in the cold air. The prosiness of the relatives' almost business-like behaviour befitted the senselessness of these deaths. Nobody could really say why these youngsters were sacrificed or to what purpose they themselves threw their lives away.

Sunday, 29 December 1918   *Berlin*

The funeral of the sailors was magnificent beyond all expectation. I watched from the Lustgarten. The seven coffins stood in front of the bombarded Palace portal. An immense crowd as far as the eye could reach. The whole vast space from the Palace to the Opera, irregularly framed by austere and splendid buildings which comprise what is perhaps the world's most sober and beautiful site,[33] attained homogeneity through the presence of this enormous proletarian assembly. Somebody made a speech from the Palace dais. Then the cortège moved forward, headed by the seven black and silver coffins, each decorated with wreaths of red and white flowers and mounted on seven Imperial hearses driven by coachmen from the Imperial stables. In their wake followed delegations carrying wreaths and flowers, red or red mixed with white, in such numbers as I never before saw. Especially lovely were wreaths of red roses stacked on biers almost as high as the coffins. They formed hanging gardens, a blaze of colour which wound its way through the sombre mass of onlookers.

I did not wait for the procession to pass the spot where I stood, but walked to the Brandenburger Tor. I arrived just in time to see the Democrat Party's demonstration, singing *The Watch on the Rhine* and holding black-red-gold banners aloft, set out down Unter den Linden. Predictably, it met the cortège at the corner of Wilhelmstrasse. The throng being so great, to make way was impossible. 'Discretion is the better part of valour,' said the

Democrat file-leader and about turned in the direction of Brandenburger Tor. That broke up their ranks. Spartacus adherents got among them, everything was thrown into utter disorder, and there were yells of 'Up with Liebknecht!' and 'Down with Liebknecht!', though not, oddly enough, 'Up' anybody of the Democrat Party. Suddenly a sergeant, carrying a black-red-gold banner, bawled, 'After me! The street belongs to everyone! We won't put up with being stopped! We'll make a breakthrough!' and attempted to launch a charge down Unter den Linden. People began to fight. It looked as though a major collision was about to occur. But then a man in a felt hat was lifted above the shoulders of the crowd and started making a speech on the lines that the Democrat Party is the party of good order, consequently it must not itself disturb good order, and therefore it ought to turn back. The whole business degenerated into a farce of respectability which lacked only one facet, a night-watchman to lead the demonstration away.

This evening there was news of three Majority Socialists, Noske, Loebe-Breslau and Wissell, having joined the Government as fresh people's plenipotentiaries. Noske[34] is said to be energetic and intelligent.

Monday, 30 December 1918   *Berlin*

Dinner-party at Privy Councillor Berger's home. Other guests were Becker of the *Deutsche Tageszeitung*, Frau Taegert (the friend of the Crown Princess) the Westernhagens, Georg Bernhard and his wife. A Nationalist, reactionary circle, monarchist but not pro-William II. Frau Taegert of course supported the Crown Prince. There was, however, more than anything else antipathy to the present Government and fear of anarchy. Becker vehemently opposed my suggestion that the Ebert Government ought to be supported. On the contrary, everything must be done to encompass its downfall, he argued, while omitting to say what should follow. An unfruitful policy.

When I described the impression that the Palace made on me, Frau Taegert confirmed how out of touch the Emperor and Empress were with their own day and age. Even during the war, 'the good Empress' had no idea what a Social Democrat is and it proved difficult to convince her that Socialists 'don't gobble children'.

I found Becker's sharp condemnation of Ludendorff surprising, although he was adamant that the story of a 'nervous breakdown' was false. Six weeks before those last fateful September days Ludendorff had already requested the Imperial Government to make peace as quickly as possible. When over and over again nothing happened, he finally lost patience and, consistent with his character, was perhaps a trifle too rough in what he said on the telephone. It gave rise in Berlin to the notion of a nervous breakdown, but that was a mistake. He had to be extremely emphatic because every single army commander had told him that their units were incapable of continuing the struggle.

Tuesday, 31 December 1918   *Berlin*

The last day of this dreadful year. 1918 is likely to remain the most frightful date in German history.

Saw Hermann Keyserling. Tomorrow he goes to the Bismarcks at Friederichsruh for several months. He thinks that, from a foreign policy point of view, we cannot be far enough to the left (barring Spartacus) because only socialist policies, contrasting with reactionary conditions among the Western Powers, can again put us in the leading international position. We must become the paragon of a socialist country and then, with our seventy million inhabitants, we are bound to have the leadership of Europe. The crucial point, I replied, is how we are to combine broad social measures without reducing production. If we can solve this problem, we really shall be ahead of the rest of the world. Keyserling has considerable misgivings about Rantzau, whom, he says, he knew intimately.

1919

Wednesday, 1 January 1919   *Berlin*

Waiters are on strike in various parts of the city. This evening I was about to sit down and order a meal when a deputation of them entered the restaurant, stopped all activity, and presented the manager with an ultimatum. Either he subscribed within ten minutes to the strikers' demands or his business would be closed down. Five minutes later an employee announced his capitulation. The strikers, with red tabs stuck in their hats and carrying a red flag, left. Blackmail completed, we could return to the matter of food. Many places have already been shut, others attacked and wrecked. This afternoon a party of Roman Catholics together with some Protestants stormed the Religious Affairs Ministry in order to haul out the Minister. We are returning to the days of strong-arm law. The Executive is wholly powerless.

Thursday, 2 January 1919   *Berlin*

Yesterday the art dealer Lippmann absconded to Holland with valuables belonging to the Empress and accompanied by certain sailors with whom he is on intimate terms. A little satyr play, seeing that L. was only able to render the Empress this service thanks to his relations with sailor members of the Executive Council whom he sheltered in his home during the revolution.

Saturday, 4 January 1919   *Berlin*

Justi, Curator of the Berlin Museums and formerly a protégé of the Emperor, is now right up-to-date and loyal to the revolution, telling stories about the Emperor which show the latter in a poor light. It is remarkable how frequently and with what lack of affection tales of this sort have been told by those who were close to him, including the Crown Prince and his other sons. This is no new phenomenon, but happened already before his downfall and in the days before the war. He was both shy and intemperate, screaming his head off to hide his embarrassment. His brutality and his cheap posturing were means of self-protection and self-deception, a purely personal matter for which all of us are now paying the price by way of political destruction and economic ruin. This rabbit roaring like a lion would be history's most ridiculous monster if his performance had not resulted in such suffering and rivers of blood. The mendacity of his behaviour undermined policy and the state, substituted sham and show for sound Prussian tradition, and distorted the perspective of almost the entire nation.

Sunday, 5 January 1919   *Berlin*

At five o'clock this afternoon I drove to the Alexanderplatz. At that hour, at any rate, Police Headquarters was in the hands of the Spartacists.[1] Liebknecht was addressing a large crowd. He speaks with unctuous solemnity, like a parson, intoning his words slowly and expressively. He was hidden from sight because, although he stood on the balcony, the room behind him was in darkness. Only a part of his words were intelligible, but his sing-song inflexion carried over the heads of the silent and attentive crowd right across the square. When he ended there was a roar of approval, red flags were flourished, and thousands of hands and hats rose in the air. He was like an invisible priest of the revolution, a mysterious but sonorous symbol to which these people raised their eyes. The demonstration seemed half-way between a Roman mass and a Puritan prayer-meeting. The wave of Bolshevism surging in from the East resembles somewhat the invasion by Islam in the seventh century. Fanaticism and power in the service of a nebulous fresh hope are faced, far and wide, by nothing more than the fragments of old ideologies. The banner of the prophet waves at the head of Lenin's armies too.

Monday, 6 January 1919   *Berlin*

Eleven o'clock, corner of Siegesallee and Viktoriastrasse. Two processions meet, the one is going in the direction of Siegesallee, the other in that of Wilhelmstrasse. They are made up of the same sort of people, artisans and factory girls, dressed in the same sort of clothes, waving the same red flags, and moving in the same sort of shambling step. But they carry slogans, jeer at each other as they pass, and perhaps will be shooting one another down before the day is out. At this hour the Sparticists are still fairly thin on the ground in Siegesallee. Ten minutes later, when I reach Brandenburger Tor, vast masses of them are coming down Unter den Linden from the east. At Wilhelmstrasse they encounter just as immense a throng of Social Democrats. For the moment everything is peaceful.

Suddenly, shortly after one, a tremendous uproar: 'Liebknecht, Liebknecht! Liebknecht is here!' I see a slender, fair-haired youth running away from a mob. They catch up with him, strike at him. He keeps on running. I can see the fair-haired head, with the breathless, flushed boy's face, amidst the fists and brandished sticks. From all sides there are shouts of 'The young Liebknecht! Liebknecht's son!' He stumbles, disappears under the seething mob. I feel sure that they will beat him to death. But suddenly he is visible again, his face mangled and blood-stained, exhausted but supported by Spartacists who have rushed in and now drag him away.

Meanwhile a hansom cab is surrounded by the mob, which tries to drag out the occupants. One of them is supposed to be Liebknecht himself, but I can see pretty clearly that he is just an elderly man with spectacles and a soft hat. The crowd nevertheless rocks the cab from side to side. The old nag staggers from one side to the other as though drunk. But rescue arrives here too in the shape of Spartacists who punch their way through the throng and run off in triumph with the wearily trotting chestnut bay and its rickety cab.

Now Spartacus approaches in serried ranks. Towards half past one I find myself behind their lines. Here and there a cry of 'Home, the women and children!' But nothing happens as yet. Going back through Leipziger Strasse, I meet a crowd of armed civilians lined up in front of a department-store. Impossible to tell whether they are on the Government or Spartacus side. A strong detachment of Government troops moves across Potsdamer Platz at the double. There is shouting all the time. Berlin has become a witches' cauldron wherein opposing forces and ideas are being brewed together. Today history is in the making and the issue is not only whether Germany shall continue to exist in the shape of the Reich or the democratic republic, but whether East or West, war or peace, an exhilarating vision of Utopia or the humdrum everyday world shall have the upper hand. Not since the great days of the French Revolution has humanity depended so much on the outcome of street-fighting in a single city.

Shortly after four (it was still reasonably light) I looked for a moment into the Ministry of Foreign Affairs. Empty. No clerks, no attendants, let alone senior officials; just soldiers at the windows. As I left, some shots were fired. Nobody knew why. My pass enabled me to get through the barricade at the Wilhelmplatz, which meant that this area, including the Chancellery, was still in Government hands.

I went to the Kaiserhof and, to anticipate all eventualities, took a room. Service was normal, though guests were few and far between. At five I went to my room. Quarter of an hour later there was a sound of shooting. I heard soldiers in the street below shouting to each other, then saw them running across the wet, glistening pavement and taking cover. Silence followed.

At half past five violent shooting, the rat-tat-tat of machine-guns, the pounding of artillery or trench mortars, the blast of grenades, the roar of battle. An interval, but ten minutes later the same again. I went downstairs. Soldiers were in the hotel, waiting for Spartacus to launch an attack. Government troops, they said, still held the key central points.

I decided to go home. Shooting began again the moment that I stepped into the street. At the first opportunity I began making my way towards the

Wilhelmplatz underground station. All around me was now a battle area, bleak, dark and lonely as a no-man's-land. The Wilhelmplatz station was closed, so I went back to that at Friedrichstrasse, found it open, and got into a train for Potsdamer Platz. Still an enormous crowd there. In Potsdamer Strasse once more shooting, so I had to take cover.

Tuesday, 7 January 1919   *Berlin*

At ten this morning a chatter of machine-guns outside the house. Passers-by as well as occupants sought shelter in the entrance. The fighting was only fifty yards away, with Government troops making an attack across the canal towards the Railway Administration Headquarters held by Spartacists.

At eleven o'clock I watched a big Spartacus parade in the Siegesallee. Shots were being fired in the Königgrätzer Strasse. On the Brandenburger Tor were Government troops with a machine-gun. The Wilhelmstrasse was again choked with people, Government sympathizers. The windows of all Ministries and palaces were crowded with soldiers.

At four in the afternoon I was passing the Brandenburger Tor when there was an outburst of rifle-fire and tossing of hand-grenades. Panic. Hundreds of people rushed in the direction of Tiergarten. I remained where I was and could see that Spartacus was trying to push forward from Unter den Linden to Wilhelmstrasse. Someone said that a group of Spartacists had climbed Brandenburger Tor and captured the section of Government troops. At any rate the machine-gun up there was not firing any more at the Spartacists passing below.

The Independents are negotiating with the Government over a compromise. But Spartacus has declined to participate and so far the negotiations have come to nothing.

About half past five the Pariser Platz and Wilhelmstrasse were in the hands of Government troops. The leader of a patrol confirmed to me that Spartacus was in possession of the Brandenburger Tor as well as the War Ministry and the Leipziger Strasse end of the Wilhelmstrasse. The situation is extremely unclear. The Government has not merely failed to achieve anything, but has been forced on the defensive and finds itself hard pushed.

At nine o'clock, at home, I could hear machine-gun fire in front of the door. Towards one in the morning a hot exchange of shots in the street. At two, more rifle-fire.

Wednesday, 8 January 1919   *Berlin*

The Wilhelmstrasse is impassable. A gun has been mounted in front of the Chancellery. At intervals a machine-gun fires from the balcony of the

Ministry of the Interior to prevent Spartacists from bringing a machine-gun into position on the roof of a house at the corner of the Neue Wilhelmstrasse. I made my way to the upper part of Unter den Linden. To the rat-tat-tat of distant machine-guns life proceeded almost normally. A fair amount of traffic, some shops and cafés open, street-vendors peddling their wares, and barrel-organs grinding away as usual.

On my way back I found Pariser Platz barricaded, but I was allowed through. Beyond Brandenburger Tor a vast crowd could be seen in the Tiergarten area. I was crossing the square when shooting broke out. The machine-gun on top of Brandenburger Tor was firing into the Tiergarten crowd, which dispersed amidst agonized screams. Then silence. It was a quarter to one. When the shooting began again, I was proceeding towards the Reichstag. That was also Spartacus's line of fire. Bullets whizzed past my ear.

At four o'clock I was in the Friedrichstrasse. There was a good deal of traffic and a lot of people stood discussing matters in small groups when suddenly there was a sound of shooting from the Unter den Linden end. Yet the Leipziger Strasse, except for its closed shops, looked perfectly normal and the big cafés on Potsdamer Platz were open, brightly lit and doing business as usual.

According to an evening paper, Haase and Breitscheid are making a last effort at negotiations. If it fails, a catastrophe will probably follow. Today's fighting gives the impression of being merely a prologue to the real tragedy. At half past seven I had a meal in the Fürstenhof. The iron gates were just being shut because a Spartacus attack was expected on the Potsdamer Railway Station opposite. Single shots were dropping all the time. As I left, about nine, street vendors with cigarettes, malt goodies, and soap were still crying their wares. I looked for a moment into the boldly lit Café Vaterland. Despite the fact that at any moment bullets might whistle through the windows, the band was playing, the tables were full, and the lady in the cigarette-booth smiled as winsomely at her customers as in the sunniest days of peace.

Thursday, 9 January 1919   *Berlin*

The negotiations have broken down. The Greater Berlin Citizens' Council has published a proclamation, beginning 'To Arms!' The Government has again declared its determination to recover mastery of the situation.

The streets gave a quieter impression than they have done recently because Government troops are dispersing street-meetings. Unter den Linden and Wilhelmstrasse were impassable. Towards one, as I crossed Potsdamer Platz, some shots fell. There was a panicky rush for the sidestreets. The weather has been lovely, a premature spring day.

During the night there was half an hour's shooting in the Karlstrasse, then only a few desultory pistol-shots, shortly afterwards again machine-guns and grenade bursts. These sounds have become as familiar as they were at the Front. During the shooting there could be heard the clip-clop of cab-horses and the steps of pedestrians calmly making their way home.

Friday, 10 January 1919   *Berlin*

During the night a proper skirmish developed for possession of the Mosse publishing-house and printing-works. So far it has been in the hands of the Spartacists.

Saturday, 11 January 1919   *Berlin*

The impression made by the shelled Leipziger Strasse was eerie. The lightless façades of the houses towered even more hugely in the darkness. At street-corners people could be seen taking cover because uncertain what to do. At every crossing a small, murky, shapeless throng dithered before the empty but fire-raked side-streets as on the edge of a chasm. Trams still ran, without lights, but throwing off electric sparks which crackled like fireworks and were briefly reflected in the wet, glistening roadway. Patrols encouraged the frightened groups to use the trams as being comparatively the safest means of conveyance. Many however were not prepared to take the risk and stayed stuck in doorways. This dumb panic in a tangle of streets turned into a battlefield was one of the most weird scenes these revolutionary days have presented.

Monday, 13 January 1919   *Berlin*

In the afternoon, in the neighbourhood of the *Vorwärts* building and the Belle-Alliance-Platz, a hail of shots. Apparently from the roof-tops. The area was cordoned off but pedestrians showed anxiety, presumably the main purpose of the Spartacist snipers. In general, though, the rising in Berlin is at an end.

At twenty to eleven at night there was an outbreak of violent fighting, with rifle-fire and the pounding and chatter of heavy and light machine-guns. Right outside my door, it seemed. Sometimes it sounded as though the door was being stove in by rifle-butts. The uproar lasted twenty minutes, followed by sudden complete quiet. The Spartacists, their major effort having failed, are conducting a guerrilla war, by day from the roof-tops,[2] by night from out-of-the-way streets. Liebknecht has disappeared.

Tuesday, 14 January 1919   *Berlin*

Sad to say, our revolution has not been the triumph of a growing body of political opinion, but simply the consequence of the old political structure crumbling away because it was rather too sham and rotten to withstand outside pressure. Had it not been for the war, it would have continued in its jog-trot way a long time yet. Nevertheless it will be a terrible thing if, for lack of any desire to bring it about, all this destruction and suffering does not prove to be the birth-pangs of a new era and it turns out that nothing better than a patchwork job can be done. The feeling that this is what could happen, the fear of such an outcome, has been the spur pricking the best among the Spartacists. Social Democracy of the old sort wants purely material changes, more equitable and better distribution and organization, but nothing new of an idealist nature. On the other hand it is this vision which inspires enthusiasts farther to the left, and it is true that only that could compensate for the war's awful blood-letting.

The problem is whether sentiments and ideas of sufficient power and profundity are on hand as to be capable, if allowed free rein, of transforming prevailing conditions; or whether, having failed to win the war and make a material profit on it, we are buoying ourselves up with mirages of paradise. On the answer to this depends whether Spartacus was right or wrong.

Today the band of the Republican Defence Force stood playing *Lohengrin* among the splintered glass in the courtyard behind the badly battered main gate of Police Headquarters. A large crowd collected in the street, partly to see the damage and partly to hear *Lohengrin*. Nonetheless shooting continues. No spot in the whole city is safe from Spartacus roof-top snipers. This afternoon several shots whistled past me when I was on the Hallische Ufer.

Wednesday, 15 January 1919   *Berlin*

Rantzau has given a Press interview which will startle all those who know him. '*What we care about is democracy's ultimate victory in the world. . . .* This victory will not be attained by intrigues and lobby gossip. Just as little . . . as by spreading confusion in the ranks of our enemies. . . . The most vital requisite for membership of the League of Nations is *moral conviction*!' Rantzau's 'moral conviction' about democracy – with brother and aunt Lord Chamberlain and Mistress of the Robes! The 'moral conviction' of Rantzau against intrigue and lobby gossip, when he is the most unscrupulous intriguer in the whole of the Ministry of Foreign Affairs. If there is one thing that can rob us and him of every vestige of credit in the world, then it is Tartuffism on such a shameless scale. Worse than Kühlmann's. Who is supposed to be taken in by this? Who is supposed to give credence to it? Wilson, perhaps? Rantzau gives the impression of an old *cocotte* trying to persuade herself and others of her dewy virginity.

On the basis of Marx, the old kind of social democracy evolved a new material outlook and men capable of putting it into practice. But in the ideological sector matters have not proceeded beyond an embryonic and fragmentary state. Nothing comparable to Marxist fertility of imagination in the field of practical and human affairs has sprung from the seed of Schopenhauer and Nietzsche. That is the trouble, now that we stand on the threshold of overt action. Only the materialist front is ready for the opportunity.

Berlin is, so to speak, occupied by Government troops. At every street-crossing stand soldiers with steel helmets, fixed bayonets, and a load of hand-grenades. Open-air meetings are forbidden. The Government's convictions may be a little shaky, but at least it has a respectable number of bayonets to stiffen them. It relies, like every other Government, on the military force at its disposal.

Thursday, 16 January 1919   *Berlin*

Liebknecht and Rosa Luxemburg have met with a dreadful and fantastic end.[3] The midday edition of *BZ* has published the story. Last night Liebknecht was shot from behind while being taken in a truck through the Tiergarten and, so it is said, trying to escape. Rosa Luxemburg, having been interrogated by officers of the Guards Cavalry Division in the Eden Hotel, was first beaten unconscious by a crowd there and then, on the canal bridge between Kurfürstendamm and Hitzigstrasse, was dragged out of the car in which she was being removed. Allegedly she was killed. Her body has at any rate disappeared. But, according to what is known so far, she could have been rescued and brought to safety by party comrades. Through the civil war, which she and Liebknecht plotted, they had so many lives on their conscience that their violent end has, as it were, a certain inherent logic. The manner of their deaths, not the deaths themselves, is what causes consternation.

Friday, 17 January 1919   *Berlin*

Today they started taking down from the Brandenburger Tor the decorations, the laurel wreaths, the red streamers and banners, and the mottoes 'Peace and Freedom' which were put up for the entry of the troops into the city from the Front. The whole Spartacus rising, centred on the area between Brandenburger Tor and Wilhelmstrasse, was enacted within this

'Memorial to Karl Liebknecht and Rosa Luxemburg' (Grosz)

festooned setting. Now there stands at the corner of Unter den Linden and Wilhelmstrasse a 105 mm gun, its crew wearing steel helmets.

Doubtless a healthy and well-mannered young officer or *Junker* makes for pleasanter company than the average proletarian. Just as much as Liebknecht and Rosa Luxemburg, with their deep and genuine love for the poor and downtrodden and their spirit of self-sacrifice, are personalities preferable to careerists and trade union officials. The crucial point, though, is that it is probably more important to raise the general level of a nation than to breed outstanding physical or ethical specimens. Which shall apply, the aristocratic or the eugenic ideal? Not that it alters the fact that the Guards subaltern is, as Liebknecht and Rosa Luxemburg were, individually a finer type, as well as standing higher in the human scale, than the proletarians and little men who are on top today.

In the evening I went to a cabaret in the Bellevuestrasse. The sound of a shot cracked through the performance of a fiery Spanish dancer. Nobody took any notice. It underlined the slight impression that the revolution has made on metropolitan life. I only began to appreciate the Babylonian, un-fathomably deep, primordial and titanic quality of Berlin when I saw how this historic, colossal event has caused no more than local ripples on the even more colossally eddying movement of Berlin existence. An elephant stabbed with a penknife shakes itself and strides on as if nothing has happened.

Saturday, 18 January 1919   *Berlin*

In the afternoon a visit from Wieland Herzfelde. He frankly admitted to being a Communist and supporter of the Spartacus League. Not, he insisted, like Liebknecht for sentimental and ethical reasons, but because Communism is a more economic method of production than what we have at present and in the state of Europe's pauperization is essential. He also regards terror as necessary because human nature is not naturally good and therefore sanctions are ineluctable. On the other hand terror need not be of the bloody sort. He had in mind a form of boycott. The Spartacus rising, he maintained, was a spontaneous flare-up organized on amateur lines. Reports about Russian planning and Russian money were nonsense. The rising broke out against the wishes and expectation of the League's leaders.

I discussed with Herzfelde the publication of a new periodical of a literary, artistic, and political character, brought out at irregular intervals, cheap (not more than fifty pfennigs per number), newspaper-style make-up but in accordance with his own typographical ideas, and directed in the first instance towards street sales. In answer to my question as to which of the younger writers and artists are imbued with the Spartacus–Bolshevist outlook, Herzfelde named Däubler, Grosz, himself, the whole of the Malik publishing-house and everybody connected with it, as well as many others. These would support the periodical with contributions.

Sunday, 19 January 1919   *Berlin*

Election day. In the morning registered my vote in a bar in the Linkestrasse. A procession of men and women voters. Everything quiet and humdrum, neither excitement nor enthusiasm. Representatives of the various parties stand around the queue and silently thrust ballot forms into the voters' hands. Cooks, nurses, old ladies, whole families with father, mother, maid, and even small children troop in and take their place in the line. As undramatic as any natural occurrence, like a rainy day in the country.

Wednesday, 22 January 1919   *Berlin*

I met Kautsky and his wife. He was in a quandary about how to get to the Socialist Congress because of Swiss entry permit rules. I drafted a telegram for him to Herbert von Hindenburg at Berne, so that matters shall be settled directly with the police there.

Until half past eight this evening Berlin sat in darkness. No trams, no telephone, and at five o'clock closed shops because the power stations had gone on strike. The overall dislocation outdid anything caused by the revolution and the Spartacus rising. This time life really came to a standstill, throughout the city, not just here and there. Shooting is the workers' least effective weapon, amateurish and out-of-date, revolution in a romantic wrapper. I saw for myself in the Wilhelmstrasse how big the dislocation was. At half past five the Chancellery, the Ministry for Foreign Affairs, and the Ministry of the Interior stood, immobilized and deserted, in complete darkness. Fourteen hundred workers at the electricity plants brought the machine of national administration to a halt to a degree never achieved by the Spartacists' armoured cars, machine-guns, and marauding methods.

Perhaps this gives a hint as to how wars, through the growth of more effective forms of pressure, will come to be eliminated from the international scene. One day mass slaughter and artillery barrages will seem just as simple-minded and old-fashioned in conflicts between nations as machine-guns do in class warfare. Economics, not military superiority, decided the World War. It can be objected that economic agencies must within certain limits bow to military sanction when the latter is capable of being forced on them. The blockade, for instance, was a military means of coercion in the defeat of Germany. Nonetheless, it remains an open question whether in modern conditions military coercion would achieve its object for long in the face of united opposition inside a plant or inside a country. In other words, whether enslavement is, in modern circumstances, feasible in the long run. The Bolsheviks, just as much as a violently anti-Socialist or imperialist government, may have to undertake the experiment and to admit their impotence.

Saturday, 25 January 1919   *Berlin*

Funeral of Liebknecht and the victims of the Spartacus rising. The Spartacists gave notice that the procession would assemble at and start from the Siegesallee at noon. Some hours earlier the Government issued orders for the entire central part of the city and Tiergarten to be cordoned off. Very large forces of soldiers, artillery and machine-guns were deployed at Siegesallee, the Reichstag, Brandenburger Tor, and Potsdamer Platz. Passes were needed to get through the barricades. As a result the Siegesallee was completely empty when the funeral procession began to wind its way towards east Berlin. It was headed by drays carrying four each of the thirty-three coffins. The one with Liebknecht's remains, distinguishable by a blazing-red ribbon, lay with three others on the foremost dray and was driven by a coachman in faded field-grey uniform. A real proletarian burial for the people's tribune. Very different from the ceremonial obsequies accorded the seven sailors borne on conveyances taken from the Imperial Stables. The contrast between this proletarian mass burial in dreary east Berlin and the numbers of military men and the amount of material employed to ensure the procession being kept at a distance from the better quarters of the city was very indicative too of the state of the revolution. Its impetus has disintegrated into two parts. The troops guarding the city centre are also Socialist sympathizers and probably no wholly middle-class Government could have depended on them. What gives Ebert his power, which on this occasion he has converted into the shape of troops, is the eleven million votes behind him.

Monday, 27 January 1919   *Berlin*

Emperor's birthday. The revolution began just about a year ago today.[4]

Tuesday, 28 January 1919   *Berlin*

Wieland Herzfelde came to lunch and showed me proofs of his periodical. They included a cartoon by George Grosz,[5] *Every Man His Own Football*. I advised him to use this caption, because it is both funny and striking, as the periodical's provisional title. He wants to ram home the first number with the public by adopting fair-ground methods and he plans to distribute through street-vendors and soldiers, students in hansom-cabs, and copies handed from cars. The contents are to be half caricature, half serious. Grosz will be the main contributor and proposes to write a series called 'The Handsome German Male'. The principal aim will be, in Herzfelde's own words, 'to sling mud at everything that Germans have so far held dear', meaning moribund 'ideals', and thereby to let in a little fresh air and smooth the way for fresh ideas. As he knows too little about foreign affairs, he asked me for some guidance. I gave him a rough outline of my views. He commented that they 'much appeal' to him. The whole undertaking has an Aristophanic quality which may be successful in keeping lively spirits on their toes and runs contrary to every element of conventionality, outworn tradition, 'Great Man' sacrosanctity, and the stupidity as well as fustiness to be found among radicals. His leading article 'No, Karl Marx!' is only a beginning. A good deal is childish, but a fresh breeze blows through it.

Friday, 31 January 1919   *Berlin*

Talked over luncheon with Alfred Nostitz[6] about Austria and Spartacus. He rates the political capacities of the German-Austrians higher than I do. In his view, the Austrian Empire could still have been saved ten years ago, not under German-Austrian hegemony but with the German-Austrians as one of its components. As for Spartacus, he says quite rightly that its trouble has been to ignore economic facts and necessities. That put it into diametrical opposition to Karl Marx. Odd, that this point should have been misconstrued by so well trained and intelligent a Marxist as Rosa Luxemburg.[7]

Sunday, 2 February 1919   *Berlin*

The guard of honour sent in advance to Weimar for the National Assembly's protection has been disarmed there. This morning *Vossische Zeitung* carried a story about 'New Communist Insurrection Plans'. Yesterday and today other papers have published similar reports.

The Georg Bernhards and the two Bergers (the Privy Councillor and his brother) came to dinner. The Privy Councillor, with a smirk, told anecdotes meant to show how cosy life can be under a Socialist Government. For instance, Ernst, the Police President and a Social Democratic, is as caustic with his men as Blücher was. As for Reinhard, in charge of the well-known Volunteer Regiment and former commander of the Fourth Guards Regiment, he is altogether *ancien régime* and cannot be allowed to speak in public because of his heartfelt turn of phrase, 'His most gracious Majesty'. I said that it was precisely on account of this sort of thing that I give the present state of affairs short shrift. It is all too flimsy and untenable. The paradox whereby a Social Democratic Government allows itself and the capitalist cash-boxes to be defended by royalist officers and unemployed on the dole is altogether too crazy.

Monday, 3 February 1919   *Berlin*

Today the Government has gone to Weimar. The probability of its return seems to me dubious. Something very like a state of war has broken out between Bremen and the Government troops sent there to deal with the Bremen Spartacist municipal government.

Wednesday, 5 February 1919   *Berlin*

The Government forces have taken Bremen. The Spartacists have been defeated.

George Grosz: self-portrait

In the morning I visited George Grosz in his studio in Wilmersdorf. He showed me a huge political painting, *Germany*, *A Winter's Tale*, in which he derides the former ruling classes as the pillars of the gormandizing, slothful middle class. He wants to become the German Hogarth, deliberately realistic and didactic; to preach, improve and reform. Art for art's sake does not interest him at all. He conceived this picture as one to be hung in schools. I made the reservation that, in accordance with the principle of conservation of forces, it is uneconomic to use art for purposes which may be achieved just as well, if not better, without artistic propaganda. For instance, warnings against venereal disease; here an anatomical exhibition is more to the point. On the other hand there are complex events of an ethical character which perhaps art alone is capable of conveying. In so far as this is the case, a didactic use of art is justified.

Grosz argued that art as such is unnatural, a disease, and the artist a man possessed. Mankind can do without art.

He is really a Bolshevist in the guise of a painter. He loathes painting and the pointlessness of painting as practised so far, yet by means of it wants to achieve something quite new or, more accurately, something that it used to achieve (through Hogarth or religious art), but which got lost in the nineteenth century. He is reactionary and revolutionary in one, a symbol of the times. Intellectually his thought processes are in part rudimentary and easily demolished.

Thursday, 6 February 1919   *Berlin*

Opening of the National Assembly at Weimar. Ebert made a good and dignified speech, notable for the fact that he envisages in certain circumstances a rupture of the negotiations with the Entente.

Victor Naumann has been appointed, with the rank of Minister, head of the Press Department in the Ministry of Foreign Affairs. A Clerical and a man close to the Habsburgs (Emperor Charles), Czernin, and the Bavarian royal house, of whom nobody has been able to tell whether he was in the employ of the Austrian or the Bavarian court. Either Erzberger or Rantzau has made a very queer choice, and certainly not one on Social Democratic lines, for Germany's official spokesman.

Friday, 7 February 1919 *Berlin*

A visit from Wieland Herzfelde. I told him briefly how I see the state of the world. There are three main ideas and power structures which make for real international division and are in conflict with one another: clericalism, capitalism (including its offspring Militarism and Imperialism), and communism. The three protagonists of our day are the Pope, Wilson, and Lenin, each of them with enormous, elemental power and human potential behind him. The immensity of this historic drama, the simplicity of its lines, the tragic quality which lies in the inevitability of the destiny it unfolds, all this is almost unexampled. Asia, uninvolved, represents a nebulously menacing quantity. Germany is being stealthily entrapped into clericalism while Bolshevism tears at it, from within and without, and capitalism, through the mediation of Wilson, offers it a Cinderella role at its own table. Consequently the fight for Germany is on. For its soul, the inherent strength of its people, and its advantage as an area of manoeuvre. All parties sense that in this global catastrophe the decisive battle must occur here. Possibly Germany, by allying itself with Asia, could escape from the tragedy. But how? What are the practical possibilities? Or does the way to freedom lie in gradual and democratic socialization? Will fate, the colossal tragedy in which it is involved, allow Germany time for that?

Afterwards I went with Herzfelde to George Grosz. He is doing a caricature against neo-clericalism in Germany for the first number of Herzfelde's periodical. I bought a picture from him which, although unfinished as yet, impressed me very deeply by its magnificent use of colour. This is my second purchase from him. It recalls the colour symphonies of Odilon Redon whose work, Grosz told me, he knows only from reproductions. He has attained this luminosity of colour, the outcome of years of effort, through his practice with water-colours. He envisaged something of the kind much earlier, but lacked the skill.

All education is violence of a sort, just as every state is. Education, society, and the state simply exist to sublimate the cruder forms of force into more refined ones. That amounts to a difference in manner and degree, not of principle. The creature educated is no less violated, forced out of his orbit, denatured (this is indeed the real object of culture) than if coerced by means of less lofty purpose. Nor can it be maintained that he in any case suffers less thereby. It is just that the onlooker is spared the revolting sight of physical violation, blood, pain-distorted features, screams of agony, and death. The process of social incorporation is no less cruel than war, but the onlooker's sensitive nerves find it more bearable. That is the essential difference. Besides, a return to physical violence would be a backward step, upsetting to the concord of coercion by culture and state, and in this respect a shrill, ugly spectacle. Looked at objectively, sublimation of violence can be economy of force. For instance, to enslave a man rather than to kill him is 'preservation for the good of society'. It has nothing whatever to do with humaneness. It is purely a matter of practical consideration which can be rescinded if higher expedience should require it.

Saturday, 8 February 1919   *Berlin*

Hilferding, Theodor Däubler, and Hugo Simon (the former Independent Minister of Finance) lunched with me at home. We discussed the possibility of founding a club without political ties but for people of an independent frame of mind. Hilferding, contrary to Simon and myself, rejects the notion of breaking off negotiations with the Entente if it tries to impose excessively harsh conditions. Däubler described the wretched rates of pay on which intellectuals depend and thinks it is at least one reason why so many of the younger ones are going over to Communism.

Sunday, 9 February 1919   *Berlin*

A visit from Simon Guttmann, who seems to have become a complete Spartacist. According to him, the young intellectuals are almost without exception against the Government. It is impossible to exaggerate their bitterness. They say that this Government is worse than the Imperial one, which at least tried to get something done. The present one does nothing and ducks every responsibility unless it is a matter of shooting people. The revolution has not changed things one iota. Everything continues on the old pattern. Probably the nation's entire structure will have to be recast. There is a German émigré opposition which is at least as strong as that against the old Government. Many of these people say that Germany needs to be defeated a second time before any good will come of it. They are deliberately working to create difficulties for Germany with the Entente. Dr Meyer, who has assumed leadership of the Spartacus movement, is abler and more prudent that Liebknecht, Guttmann added.

Had luncheon with Romberg.[8] He says that he has had enough of the Foreign Service and now wants to look around at home to see what the prospects are. None of the political parties satisfy him, but the Social Democrats seem to him relatively the most capable. I suspect that he will settle for a species of Christian Socialism with membership drawn from decent families. Very laudable, but not viable.

He has certain reservations about my Berne project. In the present situation it is easier and more appropriate for us to seek an understanding with Britain than with France. It is no longer in our interest to try and exercise a moderating influence on France. Quite to the contrary. The more idiotically France behaves, the better for us. He thinks it more important that I should stay here and give my attention to Polish affairs. Quite right, I answered, but then I must be invited to participate in such matters. To sit here and do nothing is not in my nature.

Afterwards had a conversation with Langwerth at the Ministry of Foreign Affairs. Told him my anxiety about Spartacus and that I feel in my bones a second revolution to be near. It upset him considerably and he repeatedly implored me to talk to Rantzau as the only man capable of doing anything. It is astounding how little he knows about Spartacus. The Ministry lives in a little world of its own and calls the policy it evolves international affairs.

In the evening friends abducted me to a bar where the dancing goes on until morning. There are hundreds of such places now.

Monday, 10 February 1919   *Berlin*

Wieland Herzfelde called early. I am much impressed by the energetic, hard-working, and witty personality of this young man.

Kestenberg came to lunch. We talked not only about the idea of a club such as Simon, Hilferding and Däubler proposed, but also the formation of a 'Fabian Society'. The latter's business would be to restore confidence in the political, economic and moral condition of things, by way of debate and objective analyses, among people of intellectual standing who have lost their bearings through the course of events. To my mind, rules would need to include a veto on public activity and initially the society would have to have a strictly behind-the-scenes character.

In the evening went to a lecture on Bolshevism which was followed by a disgracefully trivial discussion. The overwhelming fact of Bolshevism, for all that Berlin had a week of Spartacus, has left very little mark on the middle classes.

Tuesday, 11 February 1919   *Berlin*

The Provisional Constitution was approved at Weimar yesterday. That officially ends the revolution. But in fact it is merely a phase that has come to a close.

Today the National Assembly elected Ebert as President of the Republic. A master-saddler has been raised to the throne. He is respectable, likeable, and efficient, but how much he will contribute to the invigoration of political life is at least questionable. He will not cut any capers, and to that degree is an improvement on William II, but he is no Cromwell either, I fear.

Wednesday, 12 February 1919   *Berlin*

Luncheon with Romberg and Nadolny.[9] I asked Nadolny what Rantzau's ideas are if at some point we have to decide to reject certain Entente conditions and not to renew the armistice. He replied that, for all Rantzau's and Ebert's threats, there is no intention of breaking off negotiations. Time, it is thought, is on our side. Every fresh extension of the armistice effects a further estrangement between France and its allies on account of the exorbitance of its demands. Therefore our policy is to wait and to protest, but not to cause any open breach. It all depends on whose nerves prove stronger. They who have time can afford to wait, I commented, but if a real mess occurs at home before the Entente yields, we shall willy-nilly have to side with the Russian Bolsheviks, whereas now we still have free choice in the matter.

Thursday, 13 February 1919   *Berlin*

Early this morning the Berlin police arrested Radek.[10]

Friday, 14 February 1919   *Berlin*

Lunch with Hugo Simon, Breitscheid, Hilferding, and others. Hilferding vehemently criticized the threats by Ebert and Rantzau to break off the armistice negotiations. Either it is idle talk or Germany faces famine and Bolshevism. We should, he thinks, work out a precise and constructive programme of how we believe Wilson's Fourteen Points can be applied (to Poland, reconstruction, and so on) and not confine ourselves to having conditions imposed on us and protesting.

Sunday, 16 February 1919   *Berlin*

Today's newspapers publish the Entente's League of Nations plan. A bundle of barren legal paragraphs animated by the old spirit and barely disguising the imperialist intention of a number of states to enslave and pauperize their defeated enemies. That is the first impression it gives: a contract to be imposed on poor relations. What should our reaction be? Rejection would only be possible on the basis of a better plan which dealt with the whole question from a broader and more profound aspect, from a human and not merely juridical angle, and provided a convincing solution. A mistake that leaps to the eye is that the plan has originated with states, political entities which are by nature rivals, rather than with those major economic and humanitarian interests and associations which inherently incline to internationalism. Those are the bodies (international labour organizations, international trading and raw materials federations, major religious communities, the Zionists, international banking consortiums, and so on) which should be furnished with power and sanctions *against* these political entities and become invested with ever more legal independence of any individual states. A framework and set of rules for that purpose is what is needed, and not one which will, just the other way round, provide the ridiculous old élite of Great Powers with even more ascendancy than before.

A League of Nations, on the lines I visualize, would be the natural agency for the liquidation of war debts, reconstruction, and international administration of colonies (raw materials production areas). A preliminary question: are we in any position to oppose Wilson? And are the advantages of my solution so obvious as to render opposition worth while?

Monday, 17 February 1919   *Berlin*

Lunched with Hilferding. He completely rejected my League of Nations ideas. In his view, the matter will quite simply have to be left to the Powers because they will not agree to anything else. What is necessary is to try and improve on Wilson's plan by individual amendments. (All this is precisely the opposite to my proposal.)

Yesterday the armistice was again extended; the conditions are shattering. Rantzau let it be known that he was thinking of resignation, but then remained after all.

Tuesday, 18 February 1919   *Berlin*

Lunched with Romberg. Told him my League of Nations ideas. He was very interested and urged me to take action on them. He regards Max Weber as very capable and a good speaker, but also as academic and without much talent for practical affairs. Prince Max, too, is more distinguished for the integrity of his personality and his understanding of other nations' outlook than for his speed of political decision.

Somebody who came to our table told Romberg that he and Kühlmann[11] last night stayed at a party until five in the morning. Romberg merely commented, 'Bad taste.' A mild reproof for Kühlmann who, to a far-reaching degree, shares responsibility for Germany's misfortunes. Berlin dances and Kühlmann, who caused the smash, dances too. Ludendorff will at least spare us that sight. But Kühlmann continues in character. He was and remains, behind all the trappings of intellectual capacity and cynical indifference, a thick-skinned voluptuary.

Wednesday, 19 February 1919   *Berlin*

A visit from Herzfelde. He complains that the bourgeois women newspaper-vendors are boycotting his periodical because they suspect it of being sympathetic to Spartacus. I have had a letter from Anselm Ruest asking indirectly for financial assistance for his magazine. Publications, some interesting in part, are shooting out of the ground like mushrooms. But there is a lack of money, paper, and intellect.

Thursday, 20 February 1919   *Berlin*

Called on Walther Rathenau[12] at his mother's mansion opposite the Italian Embassy. Handsome staircase and well-appointed rooms in Renaissance and Empire style. I had not met him since the revolution, but wanted to discuss with him the political situation and especially the League of Nations problem.

For some time now, he told me, he has been receiving visits from dozens of British and Americans who want to see him personally but are unanimous in their attitude of condolence that he should belong to a nation which they regard with a mixture of loathing and contempt unique in history. Their behaviour is the same as Christians adopt towards outstanding Jews whom they accept but pity because of their awful Jewish connections. As a Jew, he is perfectly familiar with such politely disdainful turns of phrase and the accompanying looks. What seems harsh to him is that, having had to put up with this all his life, he is called on to endure it a second time as a German. One should however stick to one's own people, whatever convenient way out there may be, and not use them as a stepping-stone to one's advantage.

He made no bones about his strong attraction to Bolshevism. He thinks it is a splendid system and that a century hence Bolshevism will rule the globe. The current Russian version is like a magnificent play performed as melodrama by third-rate actors. Germany, if Communism should come in, will give just as appallingly crude a performance. We lack the men to handle such an extremely complicated system. It requires more delicate and sophisticated talent than we possess. We have nobody of the requisite stature, though the British and Americans may. German organizational capacity is confined to parade-ground style; Bolshevism demands the staff college touch.

He is against the notion of opposing Wilson's League of Nations with one founded on international organizations. The contempt and hatred felt for Germany in the world today are so strong that they will affect every international body, whether freemasonry or the Church or the Socialist International, of which Entente countries are members. Therefore nothing should ever be based on any international body wherein the Entente nations participate; we shall always be at a disadvantage. But all existent international associations and links are tied up with the Entente.

His plan is a different one. We ought really to reject any entry into Wilson's League. But public opinion here, especially the Social Democrats', will not stand for that. So, assuming the worst, we shall join. Other countries, like Russia, for example, will probably stay outside. With these we should seek totally unpolitical contacts, forming a sort of *Salon des Refusés* via inter-parliamentary conferences, scientific congresses, and similar events, and drawing the bonds between us ever tighter. When the inevitable intrigues and divisions inside the League of Nations begin, then the moment will have come to disrupt it, with the support of the black-balled, and to compel the creation of a better organization.

All this sounded to me like yet another gambit in the familiar game of diplomatic chess. My confidence in it therefore corresponded to the success of our previous moves! Rathenau enunciated it as if he were imparting a piece of esoteric wisdom. He is however only concerned with the more distant future, he added, because there is nothing to be done about the present state of affairs. A bolt can be adjusted here, a nut there; that is all. At the outbreak of war he organized the raw materials supply, but with a bad conscience, for he asked himself whether it would not be better to let things take their course, providing for a painful but speedy end and 'giving a push to what was on the downward path'. Such assistance excepted, he is devoting himself entirely to the future.

This is the age of little men. They all look alike – Scheidemann, Naumann, Kühlmann – 'scrub', the lot of them, and completely interchangeable without anybody noticing. In Germany only taproom politicians make their way. 'Popularity' and trundling through saloon bars is essential to success. Not an exercise for intellectuals. The only really big man in Germany, as far as he knows, is Hugo Stinnes who, having made three to four hundred million marks during the war and being interested only in his own and his family firm's fortunes, is not available to rule the country. The same crowd of faces is to be met in Parliament and Government today as yesterday. The revolution has thrown up just one new man, Noske, who appears to have talent. The rest of them, the officers, the civil servants, the policemen in the streets, the middle-class froth-blowers, are the same as before. How is it feasible in those circumstances to face the world and to proclaim that the German people had undergone regeneration? That is why Eisner[13] is guilty of misrepresentation. His publications and self-accusations would serve some purpose if they voiced the feelings of fifty million Germans. As barely a few thousand Germans share his feelings, these manifestoes amount to deception. No revolution has taken place among us. Nothing has happened at all. Just a little military strike.

Rathenau spouted all this with a self-assured loquacity which often puts matters in a false light even when he is right. He is an adept at striking false attitudes and displaying himself in a freakish posture, as Communist ensconced in a damask-covered chair, as patronizing patriot, as ultra-modernist strumming an old lyre. He is a political virtuoso, but unfortunately also the 'great man' concerned for the figure he will cut with posterity and permitting the thought of it to weigh down his mind, which fifteen years ago was richer and nimbler. Now his conversation, for all its stateliness and apart from a few shrewd observations, is sterile. His manner is a mixture of bitterness and conceit. No doubt his impenetrable attitude towards women plays a part in all this. There is something of a masculine old maid about him, his way of thinking and his arrogance.

Today when I met Willy, my submarine sailor friend, he was utterly depressed. I asked him why. Eventually he shyly admitted that he cannot get over the surrender of the Fleet. He no longer sees any fun in life. Everything was fine at sea, with real comradeship and good and bad times shared together, and his shipmates' motto always was 'Be brave even after disaster.' He still has a photograph of his ship and that, at any rate, cannot be taken from him. Does he believe in the possibility of a similar comradeship with all our fellow-Germans and indeed the world at large? He can see what I am driving at, he replied, and the notion is a splendid one, 'but there are too many wicked people in the world.'

'Be brave after disaster.' This simple rule of life on the part of a simple sailor is one of the most admirable and courageous that I know. The almost unconscious despair of this poor, plucky boy is also a part of our national tragedy. How much more estimable and human than Rathenau's hollow condescension.

Friday, 21 February 1919   *Weimar*

In the morning travelled to Weimar in the National Assembly train.

Early today Eisner was assassinated in Munich by a young Count Arco. This afternoon, Nadolny, who has been staying with me for the past two days, brought the news that the Spartacists have avenged Eisner by waylaying the Bavarian Ministers Rosshaupter and Auer, killing the former and severely wounding the latter. Nadolny was asked by Landsberg whether he thinks that the Government armed forces here and at Berlin are reliable. If yes, then it is a matter of setting one's teeth and seeing matters through. If not, then there may be a breakdown all round.

I outlined to Nadolny my League of Nations idea. His enthusiasm kindled slowly, but, the clearer its concept became to him, the keener he grew. He regards the notion of labour holding the key to peace (and being able perfectly simply to enforce this on a rebellious state through a strike decreed by the Executive Authority) as far superior to that of a league of sovereign states. To that degree it is well suited to rival successfully Wilson's more old-fashioned concept. He wants me to work out details so that it will be possible to envisage, and to promote, the plan in a practical way.

Met Stresemann[14] in the Government Pullman car. Obedient to Nadolny's suggestion, I invited him for Monday evening. My plunge into the spider's web of Weimar intrigues!

After talking to Nadolny, my impression is that the National Assembly is likely to prove a hybrid between taproom and papal conclave politics. That is to say, major policy matters will be handled in taproom style and minor ones in the more lofty and refined one of the College of Cardinals. A queer change of scene for me, whose background here has hitherto been entirely conditioned by people like van de Velde, Hofmannsthal, Gordon Craig, Maillol, Rodin, Bodenhausen, Ludwig von Hofmann, and Nietzsche. Like a chimney-stack in the countryside.

Saturday, 22 February 1919   *Weimar*

This afternoon a talk with Rantzau[15] shortly before he left for Berlin. His valet is away, attending to family affairs, and so Rantzau had to pack his own things; he was somewhat exhausted. I outlined to him my League of Nations idea, for which Nadolny had prepared him. He seized on my hint that this could prove a way of accommodation with Russia and the Bolsheviks. Without a doubt, he said, the really grand design of policy would be for Germany to ally itself with Russia against the Entente. He has such a line of action in mind. Indeed it is the one that he would most like to pursue. I must have noted during the course of his speech the bow he made in the direction of the Bolsheviks. His only fear is that, by striking out along this path, we shall initially experience a very nasty, dangerous passage, and this is why he has so far shrunk back from it. But if the Entente drives us to desperation and we do have Bolshevism at home, then this is the road that he will take and squeeze every possible advantage out of the move. He has already warned a British journalist at Copenhagen that, should the Entente's measures deliver us up to Bolshevism, then he will see to it that Bolshevism does not stop at *our* borders.

My League of Nations idea was obviously attractive to him mainly as a stepping-stone towards Russia. Or that, at least, was the prospect on which he dwelt longest. His only criticism was that national enmities have already invaded such organizations as the Workers' International, the Church, and so on. He asked me to let him have a written exposé. I brought this to him at the station in the evening and offered, should he be interested, to draw up a League of Nations constitution, my only proviso being that he should put at my disposal a member of the Legal Department to help with the formulation of clauses. He agreed, but thought it would be difficult to send someone to Weimar; I would need to come to Berlin for the purpose.

Concise definition of my concept: supreme power (military enforcement, boycott, et cetera) respecting war, peace, and international law shall not lie with a league of sovereign states but with *an organization of those organizations which in any case support peace and are international.*

Sunday, 23 February 1919   *Weimar*

This afternoon visited Frau Foerster-Nietzsche[16] and found Pachnicke, the Reichstag deputy and bigwig of the Democrats, sitting with her. He is a trifle patriarchal, a trifle precious, and he smacks of being 'too good for his world'. What lies behind it is unfathomable. I suspect him of quoting Horace but having parish-pump politics in mind.

The confrontation with Frau Foerster-Nietzsche and Pachnicke had a distinct touch of comedy about it. Even in her seventh decade, she remains a flapper at heart and enthuses over this or that person like a seventeen-year-old. (It is, incidentally, the best quality she displays in her relationship to her brother.) So in spite of her name, she is the female counterpart to Pachnicke and the embodiment of precisely what her brother fought against. The comic touch is enhanced by the fact that Pachnicke, as a student, wrote to Nietzsche and begged him to become his spiritual 'father'.

The denizens of the cultural quagmire bustled around with unsuspecting pleasure until the whole swampy world broke down in the catastrophe of World War and revolution. What our university products have always lacked is harsh contact with reality. For the nation to recover, every boy should be left for at least two years to see how, cut off from all assistance, he can best get on. Having learned a handicraft at thirteen or fourteen, he should pitilessly be thrust into the world between eighteen and twenty. Let that serve as a substitute for military service. Everything else, all the drivel about standardized primary schools, closer touch with the people, democracy, is balderdash. The capable proletarian's superiority of character is founded on this training through action. Everything sound about every form of education derives, directly or indirectly, from this. Perhaps such exposure to reality for all will only be feasible in a totally newly ordered society.

Attended the session of the National Assembly. Preuss[17] spoke in an infin-itely tedious, colourless, spiritless, ponderous, and dragging manner on behalf of his draft Constitution. Not a touch of the greatness appropriate to this historic moment. After an hour I fell into a doze and then left.

PROF. HUGO PREUSS
Staatssekretär d. Innern.
Berlin.

Hugo Preuss (Kursell)

The sight of the house, decorated in pale green silk and white, with the public in the boxes and circle seats and illuminated by the auditorium light-ing, is not very impressive, though quite cosily provincial and respectable. This environment will stimulate neither intellectual flights nor historic decisions of any revolutionary or desperate variety. Danton or Bismarck would seem monstrous apparitions in these dainty surroundings. The grandeur lent to the spectacle of the revolutionary days in Berlin by the mass of the populace and the background is altogether missing. Much blood would need to be shed on this stage to consecrate the scene. So far the atmosphere is that of a Sunday matinée in a petty court theatre. The petit bourgeois character of the revolution becomes plainly visible; the representatives of all parties, with but few exceptions, belong to the lower middle class. Dr Allos' cabaret, which is performing here for the entertainment of the Assembly's members, very aptly meets the intellectual demands which the appearance of the Assembly suggests.

Although Stresemann possesses a robust determination which could prove a powerful factor, he wholly lacks the fine moral sensibility which is now coming into fashion and which will be essential in future to perform productive action on Germany's behalf. Consequently he is one of those problematic personalities who, like all problematic personalities, feels with some subjective justification that the world is an unjust place.

Tuesday, 25 February 1919   *Weimar*

In the afternoon visited Ernst Hardt with Georg Bernhard. Apropos of van de Velde's recall to Weimar, Hardt expressed the view that post-war Germany must keep in mind its own interests on the strictest national basis or perish. The rich and mighty Germany of pre-war days could allow itself to dilly-dally internationally in cultural affairs. For the time being that is done with.

I referred to the radicalism and internationalism of our young intellectuals. He thinks (and Bernhard agrees) that these are simply temporary manifestations and that a vehement reaction will follow when the Entente's chatter about fraternization and a League of Nations is seen to be trumpery. For my part I believe that youth tends simultaneously in both directions and towards two extremes, radicalism and reaction, internationalism and chauvinism, and that in the coming years the battle between these will be unprecedently fierce.

Afterwards I went with Bernhard to a party at the house where Hirsch, the Prussian Prime Minister, has been quartered. The company was playing skat[18] and drinking champagne. The Minister of Police, Ernst, was there too. A stocky, stubborn petit bourgeois, satiated, respectable, and without any imagination to worry him: he embodies quite well the character of the present regime. He told me that he has a 'purely Party library' of two thousand volumes. I asked him, in his capacity as Police President of Berlin, how he expects Spartacus to behave. There is probably a major uprising still to come, he replied. At the moment the bonfires are sporadic and spread all over the country; but one day there will be a proper conflagration and then nothing less than large-scale blood-letting will suffice to quench it. Everything depends on effecting demobilization as quickly as possible because the old troops have all been corrupted. Those who have been freshly enlisted are, in his opinion, wholly reliable. He talks like a conservative old artisan.

Wednesday, 26 February 1919   *Weimar*

During the morning finished dictation of my draft League of Nations constitution and gave it to the Cranach Press[19] to set up in type.

Invited Wolfgang Heine to dinner. Our conversation was odd in so far as he was continually at pains to try and convince me of his conservative and national outlook, whereas I tried to convey to him in all sincerity my adherence to socialism. That is characteristic of the whole current state of affairs and why, out of sheer mutual courtesy, nothing happens. Just like two Germans trying to pass through a door and bringing everything to a standstill. He was positively staggered by my League of Nations concept, saying that it dispels the darkness like a flash of lightning. He wants to study my draft constitution.

Thursday, 27 February 1919   *Weimar*

In the morning went to the National Assembly. A clash between Cohen and Noske, who levelled at him the accusation of taking Russian money. Cohen tried to vindicate himself, but only brought down a still more vehement attack on his head. Noske also attacked the Independents for always pleading for peace and order but in fact supplying the trouble-makers with ammunition. When the Government tries to forge weapons for the protection of public order, he said, the Independents do their best either to blunt or break them. Cohen was twice called to order; a Centre member once drew Noske's attention to the inadmissibility of a turn of phrase. The Assembly became very excited and there were loud cries of 'Oh, oh!', but it remained commonplace for all its huffing and puffing.

Lunched with Stresemann. He offered to let Rantzau have material which would show Erzberger[20] as having agitated even after 19 July 1917 for the annexation of Longwy and Briey. I explained my League of Nations idea and he seemed to approve of it, commenting that in Britain the trade unions will not be able to resist the power it offers them. He is going to let me have information about the big international shipping and raw materials associations.

Saturday, 1 March 1919   *Weimar*

In the afternoon Becher[21] came over from Jena. He looks surprisingly well and completely changed, slightly coarser, embarrassed and blushing when he mentions the past. He brought with him his second play, *Hans im Glück*, scenes from *Ikaros*, and a major poem, *Zion*, which he read to me. He left the play with me, but declared that he does not want to publish either this second effort or his first. Before he does that, he insists that his dramatic technique shall be as individual and original as the verse technique and lyrical style of his poems. He also told me that the anarchist Mühsam wrote and asked him to come to Munich right away so as to help with the revolution, just as in January he was invited to go to Berlin and fight as a Spartacist. But he does not feel that he has sufficient political and economic knowledge and experience to participate. The notion of dabbling in politics as an amateur and possibly causing harm is repugnant to him.

Later in the day went with Minister of Justice Heine through my draft League of Nations constitution. We sat in the 'Gothic Chamber' which is at the disposal of Government members as a conference-room and is meant to call to mind the Commons at Westminster. Located behind the Assembly President's chair on the stage, it consists of parts of the *Lohengrin* sets and easy-chairs. Here the regal proletarian Scheidemann, inflated like a peacock in his brief glory, wandered round arm in arm with Preuss and Erzberger, deliberating affairs of state. As they passed up and down, the Gothic trappings quivered slightly in the breeze. I joined them. Erzberger, with his baggy cheeks and sly, sensual lips, received me smilingly. He always looks like someone who has fed well and is in the process of giving a tip. What with Scheidemann being pompous in his concertina trousers and Preuss a sheer monstrosity, the three of them constituted the quintessence of German humdrumness.

At supper Heine discoursed on art and literature quite in the authoritative manner appropriate to our princes. What little change, apart from that of one or two personalities, there has been in Germany!

Sunday, 2 March 1919   *Weimar*

In the morning a visit from Becher. He compared his former condition, under the influence of morphia and cocaine, with things as they are now. His sensibility, as a result of the stimulants, used to be extremely fine and nimble, while emotionally he was dulled and shrivelled up. Now his sensibility is slighter and more sluggish, and his sensuous associations take their course more slowly, but his emotional sensitivity has become more profound.

I told him of Rathenau's view that Bolshevism is a splendid system, but that we do not yet have the right individuals to handle so superior an organization in the way it requires. This applies to every form of education, he commented. The problem is always whether first to train a person theoretically and then thrust him out into the real world or whether to let him experience reality at once, so that he will either learn from it or go under.

Shortly after two o'clock we arrived in Berlin. A general strike has been proclaimed for tomorrow. Today already a number of newspapers apparently did not appear. The Government's inactivity is said to have turned the mood of the workers against it.

Monday, 3 March 1919   *Berlin*

On waking I could hear the trams and knew that there was no general strike. This evening the *8-Uhr-Blatt* announces that the Workers' Councils of Greater Berlin[22] have decided on a general strike immediately. The paper itself is in a limited edition because the staff is already on strike. None of the Ullstein, Scherl, or Mosse publications have come out at all. After seven o'clock no more trams. The Government is showing fright by placarding walls with posters proclaiming that socialism 'is here'. Too late, like the Emperor's abdication in November. A large part of the Majority Socialist workers are rumoured to be against the Government. This could be the start of the second revolution.

Tuesday, 4 March 1919   *Berlin*

A state of siege has been proclaimed. I recall Berger telling me at Weimar that Scheidemann said that he will only feel happy when a state of siege exists again. I doubt, though, whether he feels especially happy at the moment.

At seven o'clock saw Rantzau. Gave him my opinion of the situation and the part he should play. I laid particular stress on the fact that he is the only Minister in Berlin just now and that therefore it will be no act of disloyalty for him to negotiate with the Independents[23] on Governmental reconstruction. It is absolutely essential, and this is the last minute to do it, that the Government should be reconstructed. The masses wholly distrust Scheidemann, Erzberger, and certain other Ministers. No measures initiated by these discredited politicians can prove effective. Apart from that it is necessary for Germany's economic reconstruction to be based on the system of workers' councils. These must have both the right and the duty to raise production, look after the unemployed, and maintain peace and order. Responsibility, and therefore sufficient power, must be transferred to them. But the present Government, especially Scheidemann, is after its preceding pronouncements not in a position to implement the workers' council system to this extent. Consequently Scheidemann, Erzberger, and the Centre Party as a whole must be forced to drop out and be replaced by the Independents, the stipulation being of course that the Independents guarantee work and quiet.

Rantzau warmly agreed with my views, telling me that others have also proposed that he should take matters in hand and call on the Independents.

At ten I discussed the position with Hilferding and Breitscheid. Finally we agreed that they should talk tomorrow morning with Haase and one or two other leading Independents. Then Hilferding will formulate the conditions upon which the Independents are prepared to join the Government and assume responsibility for work and order. I am to see the two of them tomorrow at half past twelve again.

I went to Rantzau and told him that tomorrow the Independents will probably ask me to approach him and inquire whether he will undertake the Government reconstruction, meaning, properly speaking, the *coup d'état*.

Rantzau was fully aware of the momentous significance of the decision. It may result in a complete upheaval, at home and abroad. The point of uncertainty in his own mind seemed to be whether it will be of greater advantage to him to line up with the Independents now or to wait for a month or six weeks and join the Spartacists and Russians. If he goes ahead with the Independents and the Spartacists come to power, he brooded, he will have no cards left. There are no certain winners in politics, I answered; it is a game of hazard. Yes, he agreed, and that is precisely their attraction! The thought of the stakes involved darted through my mind.

He understands that Scheidemann must go and Haase become Minister President, and he does not appear to be prepared to do much in defence of Noske. On the other hand he has strong misgivings about the Centre being thrown overboard completely. It will endanger the *Anschluss* of German-Austria and promote the creation of an independent Rhine Republic.[24] He also regards the establishment of diplomatic relations with Russia at this moment as extremely risky because there is no subject on which the Entente views us with greater suspicion than Bolshevism. To release Radek at this juncture is out of the question. All this is a matter of negotiation, I replied. My intention is simply to see that practical discussions are started as soon as possible between the Independents and himself. Rantzau thanked me effusively and said that he will be at my disposal at any time tomorrow. From this I could see how much the prospect attracts him.

Wednesday, 5 March 1919   *Berlin*

In the afternoon I reported to Rantzau about my negotiations with the Independents. He was rather upset because he had just received news that his cousin Klüver had been thrown into the Saale by the mob at Halle and had not been seen since. Klüver was a regimental comrade of mine and, as a General Staff officer, conducted the operations of Government forces against Halle. Rantzau has spoken to Simons about my League of Nations idea and we are to work at it together.

Afterwards Wieland Herzfelde visited me, bringing the second issue of his periodical, now called *Die Pleite*.[25] Grosz's caricatures are brilliant. That of Ebert as a monarch in an easy-chair is a masterpiece. On the other hand the literary contents are terribly pedestrian, the precise opposite of what I expected, a collection of manifestoes, yelps, and solemn pronouncements instead of wit and colourfulness. Herzfelde said that that is the way his friends and collaborators (Spartacists) want it. They objected strongly to the first number's flippancy. For all their internationalist pose, they remain German in their bad characteristics: *de lourds Allemands*. They believe neither in the power nor in the seriousness of wit. As far as they are concerned, wielding a club alone can kill. Logically enough, force is the only means their organization knows.

In the evening I attended a meeting where a staff member of the *Berliner Tageblatt* made an undignified, ridiculously naïve speech. If allowed to do so, he suggested, we should without the slightest criticism, as repentant sinners and deeply grateful, join the Paris League of Nations. I fiercely contradicted him, exposing the true character of this so-called League of Nations as an imperialistic alliance between certain Great Powers.

Thursday, 6 March 1919   *Berlin*

In the morning I was told of severe skirmishes, with mortars, on the Molkenmarkt and Alexanderplatz and of a number of houses being demolished in the Neue Friedrichstrasse. Since yesterday barricades and wire entanglements have been erected all over the city, partly by Spartacists, partly by Government troops. There were no papers this morning, so I went to see for myself the state of things. At the corner of Unter den Linden and Friedrichstrasse a fire-brigade car, with someone dead or wounded on a stretcher, drove by at full speed. At the Palace everything is at present, shortly before one, quiet. The Rathaus is in the hands of armed patrols of the Republican Security Guard. The latter and a People's Naval Division are attacking the Police Headquarters, where Reinhardt Government troops[26] are lodged. At the corner of Königstrasse and Neue Friedrichstrasse a fairly phlegmatic crowd stands behind a barrier erected by the Republican Security Guard and listens to the shooting; there is nothing to be seen. Bullets are whizzing across the Alexanderplatz and from time to time the dull thud of a mortar can be heard. Both parties are in possession of artillery and mortars. That makes these the most serious scrimmages since the beginning of the revolution. The crowds do not seem very enthusiastic. Hilferding tells me that a speaker for the People's Naval Division and, later, the Divisional Commander who went to Police Headquarters for negotiations were shot dead by Reinhardt troops as they were leaving.

At twenty past one a force of Republican Military Guard marched, with its band, down Unter den Linden. At the corner of the Linden and Friedrichstrasse stood other troops, apparently belonging to Reinhardt's Free Corps, the officers with shoulder-straps. In their midst was an armoured car with mounted machine-guns. The Republicans passed the enemy unchallenged.

At a quarter to five I ran into Victor Naumann in the Wilhelmstrasse. He was going home and told me that Bergen had instructed all Ministry of Foreign Affairs staff to do the same. The walls of the city are placarded, today of all days, with posters, asking 'Who has the Prettiest Legs in Berlin? Caviar-Mousey-Ball. Evening 6 March.' Suddenly, at half past six, the lights went out. This signifies that the strike now includes the power stations.

Siege conditions have extended as far as the Potsdamer Station and Tiergarten. The Margarethenstrasse has been cut off by Reinhardt troops. The officer in charge states that Spartacus forces want to seize Potsdamer Platz. The affair gives the impression of having a much more serious civil war character than the Spartacus uprising. A major operation instead of a guerrilla action. Not that this will prove decisive; the latent discontent will remain and grow. A victory by Government forces will merely postpone, for a few weeks at most, the main explosion. Reinhardt and Scheidemann are now acting just as Westarp wanted to do in January 1918. They are making the same mistake in believing that machine-guns and trench mortars can solve psychological problems. The same arguments I employed against Westarp at that time now impel me to seek a reconstitution of the Government, by a *coup d'état*.

Friday, 7 March 1919   *Berlin*

Leaving the Foreign Affairs Ministry towards six, it struck me that most of the large stores were already closed and had let down their steel shutters. This morning only a few shots were fired in the centre of the city and none were to be heard this afternoon. So this nervousness is surprising. The electricity has been on since this morning and is still burning at this moment, a quarter past seven. The underground is operating. On the walls are Social Democratic Party posters calling on 'the working population of Berlin' not to support the strike. The overthrow of the sailors' uprising by Reinhardt troops, although factually unconnected with the strike, is psychologically important. This morning, surveying the steel-helmeted Reinhardt pickets, I saw for the first time since the revolution a glimmer of the old Prussian spirit[27] again. Perhaps one day traditional Prussian discipline and the new socialist one will coalesce to form a proletarian ruling caste which will assume the role of a Rome propagating new brands of civilization at the point of the sword. Bolshevism or any other label will do. The penurious Prussian *Junker* officer has always been a sort of prole. Let faith in Liebknecht, or whatever the name may be, take firm root in these German masses, trained to discipline as they are, and woe betide their enemies. If not today then in the generation to come!

Saturday, 8 March 1919   *Berlin*

This morning we had newspapers once more. The last two days have seen more bloodshed in Berlin than any since the start of the revolution. According to the *Lokal-Anzeiger* there have been five to six hundred dead. Ernst has had his 'blood-letting'. For the moment the strike has been suspended.

The workers have put forward fresh conditions: removal of the volunteer regiments from Berlin and repeal of the state of siege.

Kestenberg says that at the Chancellery they are drunk with victory. As far as the Majority Socialists are concerned, every angel in heaven is busy twanging his harp. They imagine that all difficulties have been overcome because, with Reinhardt's assistance, they have mown down the uprising in Berlin. So Kestenberg thinks it unlikely that they will be prepared to enter into any compromise with the Independents or allot them any ministerial posts. In the northern parts of the city, seething hatred of the 'West' is said to be the preponderant mood. Reinhardt soldiers who go through the streets alone there are torn to pieces by the mob. Soon, it is thought, no one wearing a stiff collar will be safe in those quarters.

About a quarter to five I was passing down the Wilhelmstrasse when a lorry stationed in the courtyard of the Chancellery was being loaded with prisoners, both civilians and soldiers. The guards outside the building hustled passers-by along. I produced my identity papers, stopped and watched what was happening. Suddenly a soldier with a whip jumped on the lorry and several times struck one of the prisoners just before the lorry drove out into the street. The prisoners, mainly soldiers, stood with their arms raised and hands crossed behind their heads. Shameful, to see men wearing German uniform in that position.

I went inside the Chancellery and asked for the Commanding Officer. In his absence I saw the Adjutant. (These were Reinhardt troops.) I reported to him the incident of the prisoner being struck, demanded an inquiry, and had my testimony recorded. The lieutenant expressed his regret at the incident, but explained in exculpation that the prisoner was found to have on him the papers of three officers who have disappeared. There was, he added, a completely reliable escort on the lorry. Otherwise there would be grave danger of the prisoner not reaching Moabit alive at all. The bitterness of the Reinhardt troops is boundless. Last night a sergeant was stopped in the street by Spartacists and shot out of hand. Two soldiers have been thrown into the canal by Spartacists and others have had their throats cut.

All the abominations of a merciless civil war are being perpetrated on both sides. The hatred and bitterness being sown now will bear harvest. The innocent will expiate these horrors. It is the beginning of Bolshevism.

The electricity is on again. Business as usual in the cabarets, bars, theatre, and dance halls.

For some weeks, dating approximately from Liebknecht's murder, a new factor has crept into the German revolution and during the last two days has grown uncannily, the blood-feud element which in all great revolutions becomes ultimately the driving force and, when all others are extinguished or have been appeased, is the last ember to remain burning.

Sunday, 9 March 1919   *Berlin*

Yesterday Government troops seized the Bötzow Brewery, the Spartacists' 'Fort Eichhorn'.[28] Today the struggle is for the Frankfurter Allee. This is being kept under machine-gun fire by the Spartacists and 15.5 centimetre howitzer shelling by the Government. Flyers are participating in the struggle. It is a proper battle.

Simon Guttmann telephoned this morning that Wieland Herzfelde has been arrested for publishing in *Jedermann* the condemnation of the White Terror by the Bavarian Soldiers' Councils.

In the afternoon took a walk through the centre of the city to inspect the damage caused by the most recent fighting. Generally speaking, it is less than the newpapers suggested, but certain buildings are pretty badly affected, there is a lot of glass lying about in the streets and in some parts it is covered with a thick layer of pulverized brick. Police Headquarters has some fresh scars to add to its old ones. Every single window of Tietz is smashed. On the pavement in front of the store is a pool of blood. The house opposite, at the corner of Prenzlauer Strasse, is wrecked from the roof to two floors down, either through aerial bombing or shelling. In the Prenzlauer Allee, in the neighbourhood of Bötzow, the cemetery wall together with a tree and a lamp-post has been flattened, evidently from a mortar hit. By far the worst sight is the Kleine Schützenstrasse where two houses, facing each other, have been nearly completely destroyed by mortar fire. On the other hand the Volksbühne, reputedly badly damaged, is untouched. Barbed wire and barricades manned by Government forces everywhere. A good deal of shooting still, though not quite clear by whom or what for.

At six I went to Haase's home. He views the situation as being extremely serious. He does not believe that it is any longer possible for the Independents to enter a coalition with the Majority Socialists nor that it would serve any useful purpose. The Independents would simply share the obloquy attaching to the Socialists. I did my very best to make him change his mind. If there is no Government reshuffle, I argued, the catastrophe of a bloody Bolshevism is inevitable: the workers have lost all faith in the present set of ruling politicians, consequently attach no value to their promises, and so are tending towards despair. If Haase refuses to act, I see no prospect of deliverance.

Monday, 10 March 1919   *Berlin*

Yesterday Noske proclaimed martial law in Berlin: 'The cruelty and bestiality of the Spartacists fighting against us compel me to issue the following order: Every individual caught in the act of armed conflict against the Government forces is to be shot immediately. Noske.' That is the answer to the Lichten-berg murders. A reply will not be lacking. We are quickly dragging one another down into a chasm of blood.

I had a visit from Simon Guttmann. The bitterness on both sides, he says, is boundless. The 'West' (Friedenau, Wilmersdorf, and so on) talks of nothing but slaughtering all Spartacists. In the 'East' the popular demand is for every Government soldier caught to be executed right away. Spartacist escorts are unable to protect such captives. Mediation between the parties no longer appears possible. One must tremble for every prisoner who falls into the hands of either party.

Guttmann takes the hoisting of the Imperial standard over the Palace seriously. The building was so closely guarded that no Spartacist could have stolen in. He claims it as a fact that a part of the Government forces wanted to proclaim August Wilhelm emperor.

The *Berliner Tageblatt* howls against the Spartacists and Independents like a dervish foaming at the mouth, an exhibition of bloodthirstiness deliberately calculated to appeal to the taste of its middle-class readers in the 'West'. At the same time working-class wives are allegedly treading wounded soldiers under foot on pavements in the 'East'. And this evening the Government announces that executions have begun. A batch of thirty, for a start.

Noske is ensconced in the Ministry of War behind barbed wire. With seven officers, twelve non-commissioned officers, and fifty rankers as his personal guard, just like Nicholas II or the tyrant Dionysus.

Tuesday, 11 March 1919   *Berlin*

The fighting against the Spartacists around Lichtenberg and the executions continue. Apart from a glimpse of numerous steel-helmeted patrols and a few barbed-wire entanglements, none of this leaves any mark on the 'West'. But the brutalities and the shootings defile the moral atmosphere.

In the afternoon a conference at the Ministry of Foreign Affairs with Simons, one of the senior officials, about my League of Nations plan. Rantzau, he maintains, told him that we should not be too virulent in our criticism of the Paris project because we might after all have to join in. Simons thinks that Rantzau firmly intends to wreck the Paris League from inside by fomenting within a short time such misunderstandings between all the Great Powers that they will be thoroughly at odds with each other.

Simons believes that my idea has a distinctly promising future. At this stage, he suggests, a representative assembly on my lines could play the part of an upper house to the international parliament composed of national delegations. He wants me to publish the project under my own name. In view of my diplomatic status of Minister, it will be realized that I have not made this move without Government support. On the other hand it will not be as binding on the Government as if it were to undertake publication officially. The point is to be discussed at a conference with Rantzau.

Wednesday, 12 March 1919 *Berlin*

A warm spring day. The memory of those who have been shot during the past few days and who can no longer experience this warmth impinges itself, reluctantly, on the mind.

The Commanding Officer at the Chancellery has written me in reply to my denunciation of the thrashing administered to a prisoner four days ago: 'Sergeant-Major Kluge states that he indicated a prisoner with his whip. He did not hit him.' That is a lie. I saw exactly how he struck a prisoner three or four times.

Dinner with Bernstorff (the ambassador). He is in charge of the peace negotiations. He made no bones about our having to reject the conditions. Rantzau is going to Paris and will say no. I pointed out that in that case everything will depend on *who*, as head of the Government, will be prepared to accept responsibility for such a rejection.

Thursday, 13 March 1919 *Berlin*

Today, with Däubler, saw a lawyer on Wieland Herzfelde's behalf. Däubler tells me that soldiers went to arrest George Grosz in his studio. He managed to escape on the strength of some false papers he had on him and is now a fugitive, sleeping in a different place each night.

The White Terror proceeds without restraint. The execution of twenty-four sailors by Government troops in the courtyard of a house in Französische Strasse appears to have been sheer gruesome murder: the sailors simply came to collect money from the paymaster's office.

Young, who was at Lichtenberg, says that there were only about a couple of hundred Spartacists there and the Government troops could have marched in straightaway, if they wanted. Why did they choose to let matters take their course? At Halle, where he also went, everything was perfectly peaceful until the Noske forces arrived. He is convinced that the spirit animating Noske and his regiments is the old militarism raising its head again. In so far as he identifies militarism with brutality and arrogance, Young is probably right.

At Weimar today Noske made a speech, boorish and utterly deplorable in tone, predicting victory over the enemy at home. Repulsive! Every decent-minded person must spurn a Government which so frivolously and shame-lessly plays with the lives of its fellow-citizens. During the past week,

'The White General' 1918 (Grosz). The cartoon refers to the cruel suppression of the
German Revolution by the Army

thanks to its wanton lies and bloodshed, it has caused a breach in the nation
which decades will not suffice to mend. Tonight the popular mood towards
it fluctuates between loathing and contempt. The feeling about Napoleon III
after his *coup d'état* may well have been like that prevailing now against
Noske and Scheidemann.

Friday, 14 March 1919   *Berlin*

I cannot get out of my head the memory of the execution of the twenty-four
sailors in Französische Strasse, where during all these days there was no
trouble. It is one of the most abominable civil war crimes I have ever
heard. This evening I tried, but failed, to find distraction in Reinhardt's[29]

production of *As You Like It*. I am haunted by these murders and shootings which are the order of the day in Berlin.

I have had a letter from George Grosz in which he writes, 'As at the moment I find myself in embarrassing straits, I shall be grateful to hear from you whether I can anticipate some advance for the picture reserved on your behalf.' No more than that. He gives his studio as his address, so seems to be back. I have written that I shall call on Sunday between twelve and one to settle matters.

Saturday, 15 March 1919   *Berlin*

The executions continue. The city again bristles with machine-guns as though a major operation were under way. Heavy machine-gun sections are stationed at two points in the Charlottenstrasse. Steel-helmeted patrols, armed with hand-grenades, stop cars, exude a very martial air, and create a distinctly tense atmosphere. Yesterday, in his capacity as Minister of Justice, Wolfgang Heine made a speech in the Prussian National Assembly against the Independents, branding them as pimps of the Spartacists. That scarcely seems like coalition. But then Heine has always, in my view, been a reactionary at heart.

Sunday, 16 March 1919   *Berlin*

In the morning to George Grosz's studio. He asked me to wait for a moment while a friend, who had spent the night there, disappeared. A fugitive Communist, presumably.

Grosz says that numerous artists and intellectuals (Einstein,[30] for instance) are making their escape from one abode to another. The Government intends to deprive the Communists ruthlessly of their intellectual leaders. He himself feels safe again and is even preparing a second issue of *Pleite* with still more caustic caricatures. He told me something of what he has seen during the past few days of the fighting qualities of Spartacists, even the gaol-birds among them, whose fervour and reckless bravery have been incredible. They have converted him to a totally fresh outlook on the proletariat: the artist and the intellectual must take duly modest place. Still more shattering was something he saw in the vicinity of the Hotel Eden. A lieutenant shot a soldier out of hand who did not have his identity papers on him and gave an impertinent answer. The man's comrades, whether from grief or fury, wept. Grosz now professes himself to be a Spartacist. Force, he argued, is essential to implement its idea because there is no other way to overcome middle-class inertia. I contradicted him on the ground that any idea is debased by alliance with force.

Bernhard seems to hope that the congress of Soldiers' and Workers' Councils (on 8 April) will remove Scheidemann and his fellows through an internal party resolution. That would certainly be the only constitutional

Café scene (Grosz)

method of shedding them. Otherwise there is nothing left but a *coup d'état* or third revolution. He regards it as impossible that this discredited, blood-spattered Government can maintain its position much longer. The Communists have no one, though, of statesman-like qualities. In the entire party Rosa Luxemburg was the only statesman who might have been capable of ruling Germany.

Wednesday, 19 March 1919   *Berlin*

At one o'clock met Ludwig Stein. He claims to have spoken at Berne to Haguenin and Poncet, as well as the British military attaché, the French Embassy counsellor Clinchant, the Italian Minister Farinolla, and other Entente personalities. What the Entente fears most is Bolshevism, but the French Government asserts that the alleged danger of Germany succumbing to this is 'camouflage'. Nevertheless Haguenin, Poncet, and Clinchant take it seriously and Haguenin has been sent to Berlin to study the matter, Stein would like to make his apartment available as 'neutral ground' where meetings can take place. Our task, he emphasized, will be to convince Haguenin of the Bolshevist danger and to supply him with evidence.[31]

Friday, 21 March 1919   *Berlin*

This morning a visit from Wieland Herzfelde shortly after a telephone call notifying me of his release. He spent about a week in Moabit and Plötzensee prisons. His descriptions of them are so dreadful that I felt sick with nausea and indignation. They exceed Dostoevsky's *House of the Dead*. The ill-treatment of prisoners, from being spat in the face to standing against the wall and being beaten to death, is so general and their torture in the presence of officers such a matter of course that Wieland's belief in trained lynching, with set instruction hours, almost seems to make sense. He says that the prisoners' bitterness is so great that to plead for the life of a single bourgeois is downright dangerous. Should their side come to power, they want to exterminate the middle class, one and all. The picture Wieland paints is of a totally dehumanized military generating an equally dehumanized blood-thirstiness. In the prevailing situation, and after what he has seen, he feels it impossible to strike a lighthearted note in his periodical. Only a struggle waged with the most extreme means matters any longer.

Saturday, 22 March 1919   *Berlin*

A Soldiers' and Workers' Council republic has been proclaimed in Hungary,[32] thanks to the Entente's surrender of almost the whole of the country to the Rumanians and Czechs. Michael Karolyi[33] has resigned and called on the proletariat of the world for help against the Entente. The new government is reported to have entered into alliance with Soviet Russia.

At three o'clock a meeting with Prittwitz, Neven-Dumont, Pabst-Weisse, Kraus and Dr Scheurer to listen to Herzfelde's experiences. We agreed that something must be done at once to improve the prisoners' lot and then to call to account officers who incite or tolerate atrocities. Kraus and Scheurer suggested that we were robbing the Government of its sole weapon to maintain internal order, but the rest supported my view that to shrink back from the issue would be worse and as cowardly as the acceptance during the war of all evils through similar reasoning.

In the evening I talked to Kempner. He promised that on Tuesday the Democratic Party will put a question in the Assembly at Weimar. He and Nuschke have a great deal of material about the murder of the sailors in the Französische Strasse. I urged the rigorous punishment of officers who are in the least implicated.

Sunday, 23 March 1919   *Berlin*

A visit from Hellmuth Herzfelde. In connection with his periodical, he expressed his utter repugnance to the publication of poems by Däubler or Becher or indeed anything that is just art. He and his friends, he explained, are becoming more and more hostile to art. Wieland's and George Grosz's achievements are, it is true, artistic, but only so to speak as a by-product. The main thing is to echo the heart-beat of our days. He went on to reject past artistic achievement too, even if in its own time it did possess precisely this quality of contemporaneity. He and his friends do not want either to document their actions or to create any kind of durable record and thus to impede posterity.

Tea with the Stresemanns. I gave him Herzfelde's account of prison conditions and mobilized him for action against the atrocities. He also had a totally wrong picture of the murder of the sailors, believing them to have been captured while fighting. When I told him what really happened, he was horrified. He promised to intervene personally at Weimar and to see the Minister of Justice tomorrow.

Monday, 24 March 1919   *Berlin*

In the afternoon, at the Kaiserhof, I was introduced to Markovski, the Soviet Government representative who has remained here in secret. Gropius[34] was there too. Markovski described conditions in Russia to me.

Thursday, 27 March 1919   *Berlin*

Haguenin and Hilferding to lunch. Haguenin has been suddenly recalled to Paris. He says that the situation has become critical, but did not appear to know why he should have been recalled so suddenly and hopes to return in about a week. He ascribes the difficulty of the situation to France being put in a very awkward position by America's notice of credit withdrawal. The Poles and Czechs have also led France by the nose.

Monday, 31 March 1919   *Berlin*

Däumig has been arrested. A fresh piece of folly which will sooner or later probably result in his becoming head of the Government, provided that he is not murdered in prison. This morning *Vorwärts* manifested its good taste by waxing indignant over the news, and printing it as a headline in heavy type, that 'The Assassin of Jaurès is Acquitted.' Tonight its leading article returned to the theme of this 'unatoned murder'. The paper would do better to concern itself with the fouling of its own Social Democratic nest here.

A delegation from the Executive Committee of the Soldiers' and Workers' Council notified the Public Prosecutor that, unless Däumig was released, the workers would proclaim a general strike. The authorities let him go immediately. This Government is weak-kneed as well as sanguinary.

Deutsch, of AEG, indulged in gloomy prophecies. Our economy will not be restored until the workers are back at their benches for ten to twelve hours a day! The workers' councils will be the ruin of everything. Frau Deutsch foresees the moment when she will have to move into a four-roomed apartment and declares that she would sooner die. These pre-war society women, mummies stringing pearls around their sallow old necks, are a horrid anachronism amidst the torrid passions and spilling of blood among the masses.

Thursday, 3 April 1919   *Berlin*

In the evening at Cassirer's, where there were a lot of foreign journalists. Talking to Ward Price,[35] I heard more about how factories and Government offices in rural districts of Russia manage to obtain an autonomous supply of victuals, which Markovski mentioned to me. In many parts of Russia factory workers are also still peasants who twice a year go back to the land to sow and to reap the harvest. That makes it perfectly natural for them to bring their provisions from home to their places of work. Price added that, were it not for this form of self-supply, the towns would have starved and the Soviet regime would have collapsed.

Saturday, 5 April 1919   *Berlin*

The *BZ* publishes the Munich resolution to proclaim a Soldiers' and Workers' Council Republic in Bavaria. The first piece of Germany to go over to Bolshevism. If the Communists can maintain their position there, it will be a German and European event of outstanding importance.

Monday, 7 April 1919   *Berlin*

Tonight the Soldiers' and Workers' Council Republic has been proclaimed at Munich.

In the afternoon saw Farinolla. Told him my view of the situation, which is pessimistic. He regards global Bolshevism as inevitable. In Italy, the downfall of the monarchy is certain, though whether it will be succeeded by Communism is uncertain. In France, the soldiers returning from the trenches do not hate the Germans but are determined to clean up affairs at home, and he foresees a bloody revolution. He brushed aside my objection that the peasants and small investors will stick to what they have. Their hatred of those previously in power who unleashed the war is stronger than their greed, he asserted. In Britain, Lloyd George is managing temporarily by making it a principle to grant the workers their demands until the peace negotiations are ended. But there too the workers are now self-confident. Recently a labour leader, returning home from Berne via Paris, telephoned the British ambassador, Lord Derby. Given a message by a secretary that the ambassador was not available at the moment, he replied that the ambassador was to come to the telephone *immediately*! And Derby actually came. That is symptomatic of how things stand.

Farinolla uttered a cautious warning against Haguenin and spoke about France with considerable irritation. He asked me to let him have proof that France has already entered into commercial relations with us. The French, he grumbled, want everything for themselves and grudge Italy even the sale of oranges and grapes to Germany. Italy is powerless against them because it lacks even ten days' stocks of coal.

Tuesday, 8 April 1919   *Berlin*

The Wilhelmstrasse is jammed with artillery and machine-guns. On the Wilhelmplatz two machine-guns are mounted on lorries to dominate the street right and left. Noske guards everywhere, steel-helmeted and loaded with hand-grenades.

Wednesday, 9 April 1919   *Berlin*

Have arranged with *Sozialistische Monatshefte* for publication of my League of Nations pamphlet.

Attended the Soldiers' and Workers' Council Congress. Violent attack on Noske and the Government by Brass and an emotional reply from Wissell. Germany's desperate situation, he protested, renders far-reaching socialization currently impossible. As I see it, socialization either increases production, in which case this is the time to implement it, or diminishes it (as Wissell clearly assumes) and should therefore never be undertaken. The objection can be raised that Germany is not economically ruined, but that the workers, as a result of the war, do not want to work any longer. But why should they work less in socialized enterprises than they do now? This seems to me an extremely weak line of defence, especially coming from a Social Democrat.

In the evening Committee dinner of the 'Democratic Club'. Sheer waste of time. With but few exceptions, the most appalling collection of philistines. A mixture of corpulence and moneybags that can only arouse disgust. What is supposed to be democratic about them, other than their middle-class manners, is inconceivable. In France the same species at least keeps little girls; in Britain, Bible classes. Here this fauna, thanks to the revolution, crawls out of its cocoon as republican.

O Brutus! O Robespierre! O Lassalle! These are the creatures now being preserved at the cost of bloodshed.

Thursday, 10 April 1919   *Berlin*

Listened to a lecture by somebody from the Saar. The French, he said, are behaving correctly and doing their best to look after the population. No intent to annex, at least not politically; but economic exploitation.

Saturday, 12 April 1919   *Berlin*

In the afternoon Wieland Herzfelde brought me the third issue of *Pleite*. Street-vendors, he reported, are afraid to handle it; they might be killed. But he is having four to five thousand copies distributed in factories. He is even having a second edition of his pamphlet *Protective Custody* printed. I showed him my League of Nations draft. He examined it from his Communist viewpoint and commented that it goes farther than Bolshevism in so far as it assumes it to have been put into effect. He undertook to spread the concept among his people. He has an idea of his own which complements it: individuals should not be organized in states but in freely chosen legal communities (on the pattern of religious communities). Everyone should be allowed to elect the law according to which he wants to live.

Things are happening! A colossal fermentation of ideas is in process or paving the way for a new – peaceful or bloody, but genuine – revolution.

A contrast with the totally uninspired one of 9 November. Revolution is just beginning.

Sunday, 13 April 1919   *Berlin*

In the afternoon saw the Kippenbergs, who are here only for today. They knew nothing about the murder of the sailors, the conditions in Berlin prisons, and so on. Nothing has been heard of all this at Leipzig.

Yesterday the Dresden mob dragged Neuring, the Saxon War Minister, out of his office, threw him in the Elbe, and killed him with rifle-shots.

Monday, 14 April 1919   *Berlin*

Lunched with Hugo Simon and Hilferding. Simon says that he regards a German financial catastrophe as inevitable. Schiffer, who resigned yesterday, frittered away valuable time and allowed assets to disappear abroad. Funds are seeping into innumerable rills where it will no longer be possible to lay hold of them.

The bank employees' strike continues and is very inconvenient. For me too, as it is impossible to get any cash.

Tuesday, 15 April 1919   *Berlin*

Lunched with Hutten-Czapski in the new Wilhelmstrasse bar, a small, very smart place, opened on Sunday by a former orderly of the Warsaw Governor-General. We ate cutlets and paid 150 marks per head. The clientele consisted of gilded youth and its ladies. Also Richard Kühlmann, with not a grey hair on his head and looking thirty-five. He came to our table. When he was gone, old Hutten remarked, 'One of the biggest criminals in German history.'[36] But Kühlmann does not care, is well off, and has fun. He was accompanied by some pretty cousin or other. Society, all the little guardee Hohenlohes and industrial Horstmanns, is not aware of the revolution yet. They are simply delighted to be back, from Mesopotamia, Courland, France, Georgia, with no bones broken. Kühlmann joins the club as a somewhat elderly member.

Maundy Thursday, 17 April 1919   *Berlin*

A visit from Simon Guttmann. Talk about Spartacism. I asked whether the Spartacists have any leaders capable of taking over the Government. Not at the moment, he replied, but the cadres are growing and in six months they will be ready. The existing Government can carry on until then. He is contemptuous of the Independents, alleging that there is no real difference between them (Breitscheid, Haase, and the rest) and Scheidemann. He repudiates the Marxist principle of expropriation of the means of production because it sees matters in terms of machines, not human beings. What needs to be confiscated is what a man does not need, dead property, whether it happens to be a means of production or not. I gave him my League of Nations draft.

Went to Cassirer's. He returned from Munich yesterday and told us about the Soldiers' and Workers' Council revolution. His descriptions suggest a carnival, but a bloody one. I had a long discussion with him and Breitscheid about this Council system. My vindication of it was based on the argument that it gives representation to a working unit as an effective community, which a constituency is not. Only an effective community can discern who is fitted for leadership and therefore undertake valid elections. Constituency elections are scraps-of-paper elections because the electors lack data to judge the candidate. Breitscheid agreed, Cassirer denied that modern factory conditions create effective communities. On the contrary, machines are atomizing mankind, he insisted.

Good Friday, 18 April 1919   *Berlin*

Schücking lunched with me at the Adlon and said that at yesterday's Cabinet meeting I enjoyed 'a great triumph'. Simons had expounded my League of Nations concept and hereupon Schücking was instructed to work out a draft based on the idea. This would then be tabled as the official German alternative to Wilson's plan. The Cabinet thinks that perhaps it will not be possible to have it implemented right away, but its presentation will restore the initiative to Germany and gain sympathy in wide circles. And finally, because it is sound, the proposal will probably succeed. Schücking added that work on the new draft is proceeding at a feverish pace. Assuming Cabinet approval, it will be published on Monday or Tuesday. That would be ahead of my own publication. I am however to be expressly acknowledged as the originator of the concept.

I am really surprised how vigorously this idea, since I first ventilated it, is making progress: the notion of the state restrained by the universal forces of humanity. Born of despair, it can perhaps shape humanity's future and guide it to a fresh flowering. Good Friday magic. In the evening, listening to a folk song, only the contrast of the deep humiliation of our nation impinged painfully on me. Suddenly my nerves gave way almost completely.

Saturday, 19 April 1919   *Berlin*

In the evening *Voss* editorial meeting to discuss the publicity treatment for my League of Nations plan. It was decided to devote the whole of the front page to the subject, introducing it as 'The German League of Nations Plan'. The Government, Bernhard urged, should not be allowed to anticipate my presentation; that would make a mess of things.

Easter Sunday, 20 April 1919   *Berlin*

Saw Romberg in the Ministry of Foreign Affairs and asked him to see that premature Government publication does not frustrate my own efforts. He was very upset. Yesterday's arrival of the Entente's impertinent summons[37] and our contemptuous answer have created so critical a situation that the Government must make some positive counter-proposals immediately. Only two trumps are available for the purpose, my League of Nations concept and a far-reaching international social programme. Nevertheless I begged Romberg to intervene on my behalf as it is difficult for me to talk to Rantzau about this matter without appearing touchily conceited.

At nine at night Romberg telephoned that Rantzau allows me precedence. Only for a few days, though. The Government cannot afford to wait long. They are evidently in very deep waters, with nothing to offer the nation if the peace conditions have to be rejected. So they are clutching at my idea as at a straw, not caring whether it goes under with them or not.

Tuesday, 22 April 1919   *Berlin*

Today the *12-Uhr-Mittagsblatt* announces that the Government will publish on Wednesday evening (that is, simultaneously with my address in the Upper House) a 'German League of Nations Plan' and that Erzberger is one of its progenitors! They mean the Schücking draft based on my ideas, but Erzberger claims its paternity. Apparently he finds his fat person not yet famous enough.

I went to the Ministry and spoke to Romberg and Roediger. The latter telephoned Simons who said that nothing will be issued *before* my address. Erzberger gave the story to the paper. This rascal wants to create the impression beforehand that his great intellect has once more saved Germany. Not that anybody knowing his botched League of Nations scheme will be deceived.

Simon Guttmann, visiting me in the morning, praised especially my surrender of democracy for the sake of human personality. In my project the individual plays a vital part instead of functioning as a mere digit, which is the case with democracy's version of universal suffrage. He called my concept a good basis for future developments, a step forward with which he, as a Communist, can declare himself in agreement. Formal democracy is, in his sight, a means to eliminate human personality.

Wednesday, 23 April 1919   *Berlin*

The scrap over publication of the Government's League of Nations plan and publicity for my ideas continues.

This evening I gave my address in the Council Chamber of the Upper House. The floor and the galleries were full, I spoke for about an hour, I was followed by Bülow, Schücking, and Pabst-Weisse (all supporting my proposal), Steinthal (doubtful about it), and Gleichen (who opposed me in a strangely confused, wishy-washy speech). The audience listened to Steinthal in icy silence and hissed Gleichen. Schücking struck a light, pleasing note, more an intelligent chat than a speech. A storm of applause from the whole gathering greeted my final words when I vigorously rejected formal democracy but affirmed my faith in it, in a purged form, as the shape of things to come. This clearly hit the target.

Thursday, 24 April 1919   *Berlin*

Voss devoted five columns of its front and second pages to my address. In the evening I was interviewed by the Vienna *Tagblatt* and Stockholm *Aftontidningen*.

The simultaneous publication of the Government's draft and my concept has obviously caused immense confusion. The New York *Sun* correspondent telephoned me to say that American journalists have got them mixed up and that undoubtedly this jumble will be reflected in their Press versions. The same confusion appears to reign in Vienna. Palpably this muddle is precisely what Erzberger wanted when he insisted on the Government's publication of its plan at the same moment as my address in the Upper House. A crafty pettifogging rascal. It is almost funny.

Friday, 25 April 1919   *Berlin*

Haguenin's guest at lunch in the Adlon. Also present were Georg Bernhard, who this morning published a very friendly leading article about my League of Nations project, Redlich, and a French professor Hesnard. I had a long, confidential talk with Haguenin. He complained that the Ministry of Foreign Affairs does not make proper use of him. His Paris connections, particularly with Poincaré and Clemenceau, would have been of considerable service to us if we had cared to avail ourselves of him. My own memorandum about Poland, for instance, made a great impression and the Conference's decisions were substantially influenced by it. Had Paderewski[38] not turned up, the results would have been still better. Danzig was on the point of being relinquished completely when Paderewski managed to have this settlement

reversed. (From this it emerges that Danzig is to come under Polish administration.)

At this point I interrupted him to state that the Danzig problem is one
which can prevent the conclusion of peace. To cede Danzig to Poland is
impossible for us.

He could have told Rantzau quite a number of things in confidence,
Haguenin continued, but Rantzau has not received him since his return from
Paris. He would also like to supply appropriate members of our peace
delegation with introductions to establish private connections at Paris. But
to do that he must know who is going; so far he has not been told. There
are people who distinctly favour Franco–German collaboration in financial
affairs, although this is a matter fraught with considerable difficulties.
Distrust of Germany, particularly German businessmen, prevails in the
French business world. This reflects the distrust and fear of Germany's
strength which is the hall-mark of public opinion in France. This viewpoint
is shared by Foch, who regards it as a '*malheur irréparable*' that he did not
have the chance to impose a Sedan on Germany. There is general belief in
a recrudescence of German militarism, of which the Noske forces are taken
as being symptomatic, and that is why public opinion is today far less
favourable to Germany than a few weeks ago.

I asked how the French Government's prospects are. Clemenceau,
Haguenin answered, has aged much since the attempt on his life and is now
influenced to a positively senile extent by those around him (Mandel, and
so on). He will resign as soon as peace is signed. Then individuals like
Thomas, Briand, Renaudel will come to the fore. Clemenceau is on very
bad terms with the Socialists; Thomas, in particular, he really hates because
he fears him, while on occasion having to ask for his help. I again counselled
direct discussions, dealing with specific points, on financial and social
problems between Germans and French. He is afraid, Haguenin said, that
the Ministry of Foreign Affairs thinks the object of his being here is to soothe
Germany '*pendant qu'on l'opère*'. Probably the Ministry is not altogether
wrong about that.

Saturday, 26 April 1919   *Berlin*

A luncheon-party at Berger's which included the Prussian Prime Minister
Hirsch, the former Minister of the Interior Loebell, and Captain Taegert
(Navy). Loebell expressed regret that the Government did not use my
League of Nations draft rather than its own which will prove diplomatically
worthless. After the meal Taegert, who is a Nationalist, explained to me in
front of the Social Democrat Prime Minister that our sole salvation lies in
a 'Monarchist Social Democratic Bolshevism'. He indulged in this utterly
idiotic notion with great seriousness and many supporting arguments.

Monday, 28 April 1919   *Berlin*

This afternoon Rantzau and the Peace Delegation left for Versailles.

Tuesday, 29 April 1919   *Berlin*

Went to a performance of Strindberg's *Father*. Maria Orska played the woman like a leopard, a slinking feline beast of prey; Hartau, as the father, was a lion on the rampage. It was like sitting in front of a cage in the zoo. A translation of Samson and Delilah into modern and animal idiom. Splendidly done, including the performance of the two main parts, but a spectacle which I observed without being touched in the slightest.

Thursday, 1 May 1919   *Berlin*

National holiday. Everything closed, even the restaurants. The impression is of a national day of mourning for the failed revolution.

Saturday, 3 May 1919   *Berlin*

A visit from Wieland Herzfelde. He described Communist meetings which he has attended. On every occasion he found Russians there, much better trained than the Germans, unemotional, coolly calculating, like staff officers. They always speak to the point and despise the German worker for his political naïvety and backwardness. Herzfelde thinks that even before the revolution there must have been a large number of Russian Communist agitators active in Germany. The German Communist Party's main worry is lack of money. Conditions are downright lamentable. Apart from that, many of the Communist workers are obviously hysterical. It is evident from the debates, where the Russians treat arguments with cold superiority while the Germans become excited to the point of senselessness. Herzfelde is now distributing some ten to twelve thousand copies of his *Pleite*.

Thursday, 12 June 1919   *Berlin*

Since 7 May, the day when the peace conditions were handed to us, I have been so depressed that I was in no mood to write anything. Now the prospects are *slightly* better. The Entente is apparently no longer quite so obdurate and is preparing modified conditions. I shall try and put things down again.

There has been talk recently, particularly in the foreign Press, of my succeeding Rantzau. I have denied, in an interview with the *New York Times*, that I have the slightest intention of supplanting him.

Friday, 13 June 1919   *Berlin*

Today the Entente's answer to our counter-proposals was supposed to be handed over, but this has again been postponed. Rosa Luxemburg's funeral. Everything passed off quietly.

Sunday, 15 June 1919   *Berlin*

Pacifist lunch. A Herr Meyer-Bremen tables a resolution which pledges those who sign it to perform no war service or give any kind of assistance to war by acts or abstentions of their own. That would of course be the only root-and-branch method, were it to be generally adopted.

In the evening attended a lecture about school reform. Many children present, half of them wearing glasses, which is a sad sight for a youth movement.

Monday, 16 June 1919   *Berlin*

Lunched with Hilferding. He foresees catastrophe as inevitable. Thinks that Erzberger will sign. But either way there will be an explosion within a few weeks. He still believes that we should sign[39] without fuss though under protest. Regards my proposal as too complicated for the mass of people. Proscription lists of those who are to be arrested in case of non-signature have already been prepared, he maintains. His name is among them and he fancies that he would have difficulty in obtaining his release, once he was caught, because of the execration in which his *Freiheit* is held. This, he mentioned incidentally, has passed the two hundred thousand copies per edition figure.

Tuesday, 17 June 1919   *Berlin*

Yesterday the Entente handed over its reply. This morning again no newspapers except for *Vorwärts* and a few hole-and-corner publications. Therefore no details available. *Vorwärts* only quotes the contents from French papers. *Berliner Mittagszeitung* publishes a Reuter report with the text of the covering note accompanying the Entente reply. Ostensibly its key-point, stated in uncivil terms, is Germany's war-guilt, 'the greatest crime against humanity ever committed'. Rantzau and the Delegation left Versailles last night. Delegation members are said to have had stones thrown at them on the way to the station, some being hurt. This all looks like a fresh war.

The *Neue Berliner* (*12-Uhr-Mittags*) appears (in spite of its being 'independent') with an enormous headline, 'Attempted Murder of the German Peace Delegation'. It was like 1914. And just as stiflingly sultry and sunny as it was then at the end of July.

Sunday, 22 June 1919   *Berlin*

Scheidemann and Rantzau have resigned. The new Bauer Cabinet proposes to sign the peace treaty under protest and with reservations. These relate to acknowledgment of Germany's sole war-guilt and extradition of the Emperor as well as other so-called criminals.

The German Navy, interned at Scapa Flow, has scuttled its ships.

This evening I have been indescribably depressed, as though the entire sap of life has dried up inside me.

Monday, 23 June 1919   *Berlin*

This morning students and soldiers removed the French flags we are supposed to surrender from the Arsenal and burned them in front of the statue of Frederick the Great.

This afternoon, since the Entente has declined to accept our signature *under reservation*, the military leaders have announced their resistance to the Government, the Centre Party has withdrawn its agreement to signature, and the Government has decided to resign. This evening the ultimatum expires. The tension is terrific. Very oppressive weather. Counter-revolution, war, insurrection threaten us like a nearing thunderstorm.

In the morning a letter from Dietrich Bethmann, who according to his own account is one of those principally responsible for the war. He makes mysterious allusion to my 'ambition' (which I do not possess) and implores me to do everything to prevent any extradition.

August Müller, who is a *mauvaise langue*, says that on the day before the Entente delivered the peace treaty (5 May) Ebert gave an enormous drinking-party for Ministers and former Ministers. At one in the morning Trimborn, of the Centre Party and a former State Secretary in the Ministry of the Interior, made a carnival speech in Cologne dialect. The party broke up towards three, with everyone heavily laden. The consequence was that when the peace treaty terms arrived during the next night, not a single Minister could be got out of bed. He (Müller) received the terms at the delegation headquarters alone except for *one* other member (whose name I do not recall), and vainly tried to get hold of any one of the Ministers. They were exhausted from the preceding night. Erzberger moreover declared that next day was time enough to take cognizance of the terms! And that without knowing how short the respite for decision might be.

Bitterness against Erzberger[40] is supposed to have been enormous amongst all of them. Müller said that, if somebody did not get rid of him, he would club him to death himself. No German jury would condemn him for such action. I am very much afraid that Erzberger will share Liebknecht's fate. Not undeservedly, like Liebknecht, but self-incurred on account of his pernicious activity.

Tuesday, 24 June 1919   *Berlin*

Today Noske negotiated with the rebellious military leaders. Apparently he achieved some sort of agreement in spite of the peace treaty's 'odium paragraphs'. The generals have temporarily submitted. Looting in the north of Berlin continues.

In the evening a meeting at Gerlach's to listen to a disquisition by Montgelas on the war-guilt question. Present were Quidde, Nuschke, Wehberg, and Dr Gumbel. Eduard Bernstein was invited but did not come. Montgelas proved that the initial war mobilization acts were on the Entente side. On 24 July there was the partial mobilization of the British Navy and on 28 and 29 July the Russian general mobilization, two days *before* Austria. The point that Montgelas diplomatically described as requiring clarification is why the Serb answer, known in Vienna on 25 July, was not cabled or telephoned. Sent by courier, it did not arrive in Berlin until 27 July. The delay strongly influenced the Berlin Government during these critical hours to adopt an intransigent attitude. Immediately the Serb answer became available, moderating pressure was put on Vienna by Berlin. Meanwhile, however, matters in Russia and elsewhere had taken their course.

This, it is clear to me, is the core of the war-guilt question as far as we are concerned. It also throws a fresh light for me on what Dietrich Bethmann[41] told me. At Vienna he and Hoyos, on his own admission, made the most of every opportunity to bring about war. I surmise that he was partly guilty of the singularly slow transmission of the Serb answer. He may have been afraid that his cousin Theobald would 'give in', should he learn of its contents in time.

The conviction in Vienna that Russia would *not* attack was incredibly rash. In point of fact Russia was already mobilizing. Montgelas demonstrated the frivolity prevailing at Vienna not merely by the semi-official Press statements, but also by the neglect to begin mobilization until two days after Russia began its mobilization. For two days the frontiers lay open to the partially mobilized Russian forces! That has to be taken into account, along with the intrigues of Bethmann and Hoyos, in order to understand the calamitous state of mind at Vienna which may have determined the outbreak of war.

Only now do I appreciate that Bethmann's self-accusations and pangs of conscience were not merely a pose, but unfortunately meant in bitter earnest. As this is hardly likely to be known for some time to come, people are going to run their heads against a wall about the war-guilt question by looking for the answer in Berlin, whereas the key to it lies in Vienna, at the German Embassy there and with Hoyos at the Ballhausplatz. The eerie association between Hoyos, wooden-faced, drily calculating, crazily clever, and Bethmann, the romantic with an instinct for entangling every situation, who fomented tragedy with his hazy fantasies and hot-headedness and was conceitedly gratified at playing a part in important affairs, provided the impetus towards the outbreak of war.

Only today I had a letter from Bethmann in which he warns me oddly enough against 'personal ambition'. He says that he defends me in Switzerland against all those who attack me on this score! To what should I aspire? As things are, I have more influence than if I were Minister of Foreign Affairs, the position to which the newspapers keep promoting me. Why should I, without serving myself or my country in the slightest, push myself forward to be Rantzau's successor? Bethmann will 'defend' me until everybody believes the newspapers are right. He is, to a pathological degree, what the French call a *brouillon*. And at a decisive moment of history the fate of humanity, on account of Tschirschky's and Theobald Bethmann's weakness, lay in this man's hands!

Gerlach passionately advocated the theory that the German Government was *wholly and entirely* responsible for the outbreak of war. At that moment, he insisted, the rest were 'pure innocents'. Montgelas, Quidde, Nuschke, and I were against him. While recognizing the role of Dietrich Bethmann and Hoyos, it was only the coincidence of the same game being played in St Petersburg and Paris (Poincaré), and with relative lethargy in London, that ultimately brought about the outbreak. Had Dietrich and Hoyos possessed no cronies on the other side, they would have played their game in vain.

On our side the basic facts in the situation were: in Berlin a weak central government in the person of Theobald Bethmann, a 'leading' statesman whose soul was a pawn for which London and Vienna were rivals. In Vienna Tschirschky was driven forward, and partly imposed on, by Dietrich Bethmann just as Berchtold was impelled in the same direction and with even cooler calculation by Hoyos. Kühlmann, who was on holiday in the country, remained impenitently nonchalant in spite of the danger while in London Lichnowsky, with his illusions about Grey and supported only by Schubert, struggled against Vienna. Berlin was no more than the point where these influences, active and passive, clashed. Real will-power of any sort never materialized at Berlin. It remained a mere telephone exchange.

Montgelas told a story which confirms this view of mine. Falkenhayn was *against*, Moltke *for* declaration of war. Finally Falkenhayn succeeded in persuading Moltke to *recall* the declaration of war on France which had already been issued. Instructions were given, but the telegram was on its way. Too late! (The source of Montgelas's information was Haeften.) Not even the military displayed a firm, clearly considered determination.

Saturday, 28 June 1919   *Berlin*

Our plenipotentiary, Bell, and the new Foreign Minister, Hermann Müller, have signed the peace treaty at Versailles.

Sunday, 29 June 1919   *Berlin*

Lunched with Romberg, who has resigned on account of the treaty being signed. He probed me about Rantzau and a dictatorship. His idea is that a triumvirate consisting of Rantzau, a Social Democrat, and an Independent (perhaps Hilferding, in charge of socialization), should assume power. He asked me to sound out the Independents about Rantzau.

Wednesday, 9 July 1919   *Weimar*

Ratification of the peace treaty in the National Assembly. A dignified session except for the note struck by Fehrenbach when the public applauded after the speech made by Traub, the Nationalist. The harsh, pedantic tone in which Fehrenbach spoke was inappropriate to the tragic magnitude of this frightful moment.

Wednesday, 23 July 1919   *Weimar*

Van de Velde, who has recently returned, and Victor Naumann had dinner with me. Naumann, who has proposed that I become ambassador at Brussels, says that Haniel and Rosenberg are much in favour of my appointment. Van de Velde was enchanted by the idea. He promised all sorts of support and recommendations, including one to Lefebvre, the King's secretary.

Thursday, 24 July 1919   *Weimar*

Spent the evening with Naumann, Nadolny, and Schücking. I am generally regarded, Nadolny stated, as an 'Independent'. I drew his attention to the fact that I am a registered member of the Democrats and prefer to avoid the class struggle. I would therefore have some difficulty in describing myself as an Independent. Van de Valde tells me that he was informed in Switzerland of my conversion to the Spartacists.

Friday, 25 July 1919   *Weimar*

Today there at last occurred the expected major political collision. Beginning with two speeches during the morning, the tension erupted in the afternoon in one of the most dramatic sessions that any Parliament can ever have experienced.

The Nationalist Graefe, slender, finely built, somewhat Spanish, with his highly-strung manner, and refined, pale face ending in a pointed, slightly silvery beard, attacked Erzberger and the revolution, making them responsible for the catastrophe. Particularly Erzberger, as the originator of the indiscretion about Czernin's[42] direct report to the Emperor William in April 1917. Graefe's speech was a most effective piece of oratory. His expression remained serious throughout. In a beautiful, cultivated timbre he levelled the grave charge that in 1917 the conclusion of peace was balked by Erzberger's action. Finally a quotation from a speech by Bismarck was used to suggest that possibly Erzberger was bribed by Austria or France.

Erzberger, who until now had been grinning all over his plump face, went white, then red, and screamed, 'Impudence! What do you mean by that?' Graefe remained imperturbable. He repeated the quotation. From this moment forward the feeling of a life-and-death struggle, with two gigantic opposing forces having each other by the throat, prevailed.

As Graefe sat down, it seemed that no oratorical effort could screw the situation to a higher pitch. Indeed Erzberger, with his commonplace appearance, his boorish dialect and his grammatical errors, presented a sad contrast, although his opening phrase was dexterous and dramatic: 'Is that all?'

I had a full view of his badly made, flat-soled boots, his comic trousers rising via corkscrew crinkles to his full-moon bottom, his broad and thick-set peasant shoulders, of the whole fat, sweaty, unattractive, utterly plebeian creature. I could see every clumsy move of his clumsy body, every change of colour in his chubby cheeks, every drop of sweat on his greasy forehead. But gradually this comic, uncouth figure grew into a personality enunciating the most frightful of indictments. The badly framed incoherent sentences piled fact on fact, formed themselves into ranks and battalions of accusation, and fell like flails on the members of the right, sitting white, cowering, and ever more isolated in their corner. When he quoted the Pacelli[43] telegram, horror held us all in its grip. Old Nuschke, standing close to me, looked as though he had seen a ghost. Into the silence a Centre member, in a strangled voice like a sigh, spoke the words, 'And my boy was killed after that!'

Then a noise, like a murmur rising to a roar of breakers, broke the stillness. The entire left, three-quarters of the House, was on its feet and facing the small, pallid group of the right, trembling with rage. Yells of 'Murderers, murderers!' It looked as though the whole massed block of the left would fall on the right and throttle it where it sat. There was a smell of blood in the air. A number of voices cried, 'Impeach them!' 'That will come, all right,' Erzberger answered. The words were barely out of his mouth before the right sprang up, with Hugenberg, Semler, Roesicke, Graefe, clamouring to speak. Semler, the colour drained from his cheeks and looking like a cartoon of Saint-Just, leapt in front of Erzberger, who had left the rostrum, and wanted to go for him with his fists, but was dragged away by his fellow members.

The dreadful tragedy of the situation – a nation faced with the truth for the first time – towered over the execrations. Had it been a little less awe-inspiring, I truly believe that blood would have flown. My own overall impression is that Erzberger and his opponents are just about worthy of each other.

Saturday, 26 July 1919   *Weimar*

Dernberg came to dinner. He was sceptical about Erzberger's revelations and 'imagines' that the unpublished British 'peace offer' was in fact nothing more than the British answer to the papal Note, containing nothing more than intimation of the already familiar Entente conditions. He has, he added, become cautious of accepting what Erzberger says; he knows many yarns spun by that source. Erzberger appears to have admitted today to Richthofen that the British Note was quite short and had nothing new in it. If that is so, it would mean that he has trifled with the National Assembly and the nation's gravest affairs in an incredibly shameless and impudent way.

Wednesday, 6 August 1919   *Berlin*

Today five years ago! The evening at the Habsburger Hof, with Varnbüler coming in with news of Bethmann's speech and the invasion of Belgium. Only five years ago, and yet a whole epoch lies between then and now! I recall that we were shy of emerging into the street in uniform because of the public ovations we would receive, which we found ridiculous.

This afternoon Naumann telephoned that there is a wild attack on me by Léon Daudet in the *Action Française*. My advice was to do nothing.

Daudet is a notorious pornographer who is not taken seriously even in France. The matter leaves me cold, but evidently it is a prelude to the cacophony which will break out if I am appointed to Brussels. Proof enough that the prospect frightens the French, or at least Léon Daudet's kind who want a permanent state of war with Germany.

Thursday, 7 August 1919   *Berlin*

A visit from Wieland Herzfelde. He was depressed and thinks that the revolution is probably over. The downfall of the Soldiers' and Workers' Council Government in Hungary (yesterday the Archduke Joseph was appointed Regent) and the bad news he has had from Moscow make him very pessimistic. As long as three weeks ago he told me that in his view the revolution has been postponed for fifty years.

Friday, 8 August 1919   *Weimar*

A year ago today began the war's decisive battle. I was negotiating with the Bolsheviks.

In the afternoon to Berka. On the return train journey an elderly, prosperous-looking man said that he would like to slaughter Erzberger. Someone ought to place a couple of hand-grenades in his car. He spoke quite loudly, with the compartment packed to overflowing. Nobody expressed the slightest objection.

Wednesday, 20 August 1919   *Weimar*

Discussed with Rubakin the translation of my book[44] into Russian and its distribution in Russia. He says that he is familiar with my principles and is in agreement with them. He will take up the project (and of course wants to make money out of it).

Thursday, 21 August 1919   *Weimar*

At five o'clock this afternoon Ebert's swearing-in at the National Assembly. The stage was festively decorated with the new German colours and plants, gladioli and chrysanthemums placed on a floor covering which in its day has obviously been the mossy turf of *A Midsummer Night's Dream*. The organ played and everyone in their black jackets crowded between the plants like guests at a better-class wedding. The House was crowded except for the seats belonging to the Nationalists and Independents, which remained ostentatiously empty. A number of secretaries and shorthand-writers spread across the Nationalists' seats.

After an organ prelude, Ebert appeared on the stage in a frock-coat, small, broad-shouldered, with gold-rimmed spectacles. He was followed by Bauer, the hobbling Chancellor, and the whole Government, all of them in solemn black too. Ullstein's *Berliner Illustrierte* saw fit to publish today a photograph of Ebert and Noske in bathing trunks. The memory of the picture haunted the ceremony.

FRIEDRICH EBERT
Mitglied des Rats der Volksbeauftragten.
Berlin.

Friedrich Ebert (Kursell)

When Ebert was supposed to take the oath, the text was found to be missing. A search was instituted and, the organ having stopped playing, a fidgety interval ensued. Finally someone pushed their way through the frock-coats to the front with the piece of paper. Ebert spoke the words of the oath in quite a pleasing, clear voice. Fehrenbach pronounced the official welcome. Ebert made a speech. All very decorous but lacking go, like a confirmation in a decent middle-class home. The Republic should avoid ceremonies; they are not suited to this type of government. It is like a governess dancing a ballet. All the same, the whole occasion had something touching and, above all, tragic about it. This petty drama as conclusion to the tremendous events of the war and the revolution! Pondering the deeper significance of it can bring tears very close.

Friday, 22 August 1919   *Weimar*

Met Rubakin. He wants to institute people's libraries, each with a thousand volumes in Russian, and to have them run by the cooperatives there in order to promote a pro–German frame of mind.

Tuesday, 2 September 1919   *Berlin*

A visit from Wieland Herzfelde. Politically very depressed. He does not think that any revolutionary events are in prospect at all, and according to his information the Berlin workers are determined not to let themselves be provoked into any. It is my impression too that the revolution is provisionally over. Counter-revolution is on the march, with the monarchy clearly in the background. The revolution has come to a dead end through the incapacity of the Social Democratic Government team, the far greater experience and cunning of conservative civil servants (like Berger, Nadolny, and the rest), the difficulty of creating socialism in a ruined country, and the physical exhaustion of the famished proletariat. Nothing can stand permanently still, so we shall now have the retrogressive movement, counter-revolution. That will be Germany's real defeat.

Thursday, 4 September 1919   *Berlin*

Becher does not think much of the workers' revolutionary energy. In Thuringia, where he is in the confidence of the Communist Party hierarchy, there is no thought of an uprising. Indeed, if someone tried it, the Party would do its best to thwart them. The Communist Party is lacking in leaders, in experience, in everything that is essential to a successful revolution. Moreover it is riddled with informers. The workers regard the whole revolution simply as a means of acquiring cars and silk stockings. The German worker is a revolutionary only when he is hungry. A Communist revolution would be possible in Germany only, if a link with Russia were established, with Russian leaders and Russian Red Guards.

He told me of a play that he now wants to write on the island of Rügen, where he is going: *Workers, Peasants and Soldiers. The Awakening of a People*. The dramatis personae consists first of a single individual spreading his revolutionary ideas, finally of a whole people. At the end the drama is even to include the audience and the action will reach into the stalls.

In the afternoon two staff members of *Vorwärts* and the Vienna correspondent of the *Frankfurter Zeitung* came and asked me to assume the leadership in Germany of the World Youth Movement. I proposed several other names, but ultimately behaved like Caesar with the laurel wreath. I insisted only that my acceptance is conditional on my obtaining the effective direction, not merely the name, and that it shall be the *workers'* youth the Movement principally seeks to attract.

They gave as reason for wanting me my 'Searchlight' article. The editor of *Marxist*, in which it appeared, is supposed to have said that no contribution has shown such sympathy for the worker's soul during the paper's existence.

Friday, 12 September 1919   *Berlin*

Stiflingly hot day, like the preceding ones. Wieland Herzfelde lunched with me. We talked about the Munich hostage murder trial, news of which has filled the papers for days. Thanks to brilliant counter-revolutionary wirepulling, it is creating enormous propaganda against the Communists. Although I can see through the purpose, I said, it nevertheless makes a strong impression on me because it reveals the Communist state of mind, that is, the outlook prevalent among at least some Communists, which is exactly the same as that of the vilest reactionaries and military butchers. He admitted the justice of this and says that the point is appreciated in many Party circles. It has caused a split between those who place priority on reformation of the Party outlook and others who want to snatch power as quickly as possible. He belongs of course to the first group.

Meeting of the World Youth League committee. I have accepted the chairmanship. We agreed that the League, though politically neutral, should principally seek to instil a new frame of mind on a socialist basis.

In the evening to the New Fatherland League. A businessman, Ebert by name, who has returned from Soviet employment in the distribution of foodstuffs in the Chernigov district, aired his experiences and views. He said that he was a Communist, but what he saw in Russia convinced him of the impossibility of putting Communism into practice. He was however unable to answer my question what *facts* had driven him to this conclusion and simply kept on muttering 'The war is the reason. The war, the war.' When I pointed out that the war had not been caused by Communism, just as little as the raw-materials scarcity was, he lapsed into an embarrassed silence.

Individual facts mentioned by him did no more than confirm what we have already long known. For instance, anything can be obtained in the black market, though at a very high price; bread costs forty-five roubles a pound. Or, again, intellectuals have to sell newspapers and workers receive high wages. He, as an official, was initially paid 650, later 1,000 roubles per month. When he was asked, on the basis of prices he had quoted, how he managed to live on this amount, his reply was that he existed on bribes, not his salary. His paymasters were the 'speculators' (profiteers). According to Ebert, everyone in Russia today is a profiteer, even if he has only half a pound of flour to offer. The state of corruptibility is greater than it was under the Tsars, just as Red Army discipline is better than it was in the

Tsarist forces. The workers' living conditions are not much worse than at the time of the Imperial régime. The peasants have their fill of everything except machines. Production has decreased enormously since the revolution, not only for lack of raw materials, but because people have become lazier. On the whole he failed to convince me that Communism had failed on account of its impracticability. Rather, I would say, due to external circumstances.

Saturday, 13 September 1919   *Berlin*

A visit from Rubakin. The finance for his Russian library plan, he said, is now assured and the project will come to fruition in the next few months. Steps are also to be taken now to establish his big institute, Intellectus et Labor. He asked me to share the German representation with Albert Einstein and Professor Nicolai. France will be represented by Romain Rolland, Belgium by van der Velde, Switzerland by Ferrière and Baudouin. De Kay, the American, will supply the funds. Rubakin brought with him de Kay's book, *Women and the New Social State*. Later, dipping into this, I saw that on certain fundamental points about the League of Nations (especially that it must be a league of workers, and not governments or states) de Kay and I are unanimous. A remarkable fact, seeing that hitherto neither of us has known about the other's ideas.

Sunday, 21 September 1919   *Berlin*

A telegram that Mama is seriously ill.

Monday, 22 September 1919   *Berlin*

A fresh talk with Richthofen to tell him that Hermann Müller, if he is not up to his job, must go and not be allowed to retain the Ministry of Foreign Affairs as a sinecure. We have not thrown out the Hohenzollerns in order to replace them at vital points with Social Democrat princelings, in the shape of trade union secretaries, whom we are then unable to get rid of. Richthofen granted Müller's incompetence, but does not believe it possible to enforce his dismissal at this stage. The most that can be done is to put a State Secretary at his side. If he (Richthofen) is appointed, the arrangement will not last for more than a week before one or other of them resigns, and he has confidence in his power to ensure that it is Müller, not he, who goes. But that is the only way he sees of dealing with the matter.

News of poor, dear Mama's death on Friday last week. Hers was a great, but unhappy personality. She was gifted with beauty, passion, imagination and wit far beyond the average, but she lacked worldly wisdom. I lose in her more than a mother: a background which maintained its powerful spell upon me, regardless of all distance. We had not seen each other for five and a half years, but were soon at last to meet again in Switzerland. That is truly tragic for her too.

Wednesday, 24 September 1919   *Berlin*

Papa's birthday. I still do not know whether and when Mama's funeral took place. Very depressed.

Friday, 10 October 1919   *Berlin*

Lunch with Albert Einstein, Nicolai, Rubakin, Sytin (the Russian publisher), and Hugo Simon to discuss Rubakin's people's library project. Several million volumes are to be injected into Russia. Simon, brought in for the financial aspect, thinks that the printing and publishing side will have to raise about a million marks before there is a chance of obtaining any banking credit. Some three million will be required in all. Profit is calculated at forty million, a part of which will have to be secured for Rubakin's institute.

In the evening saw an exhibition of Slevogt's etchings. Slevogt was there, having just arrived from the Saar. His account of the petty-minded persecution inflicted on the inhabitants by the French is a gloomy one. The popular fury is intense, but he fears that the territory is lost to Germany because the French policy of paltry daily chicanery is wearing people down.

Tuesday, 14 October 1919   *Berlin*

Met Helphand[45] (for the first time) in the Kaiserhof. Victor Naumann and Pernot were also there. Haguenin joined us later. Helphand is an enormously fat Socrates whose face seems as big as his body. For over an hour he lectured us, in fluent, precise, but badly spoken French, on Russia and Bolshevism. He is entirely against the latter, but thinks that nothing could be more mistaken than the Entente's effort to crush it through force and blockade. That gives Lenin and Trotsky the chance to appear as patriots. The proper way to deal with the matter would be to improve production and organization and to deliver raw materials, foodstuffs, machines, and so on. Social Democratic efforts at organization must put an end to anarchy in Russia just as in western Europe. Lenin and Trotsky would not oppose such a turn of affairs, although Bukharin is too narrow-minded to have any truck with it.

Thursday, 4 December 1919   *Berlin*

Trial of the murderers of the sailors. Marloh's own evidence stamps him as a murderous marionette stuffed with parade-ground rules and lacking either heart or intelligence. A monster who is not even wicked, but a ghastly caricature of Prussian militarism, which reduces its entire orientation to the absurd, from the beginnings under Frederick William I to this conclusion. The fellow knows nothing else but slogans and the sergeant-major's cane. So he murders thirty youngsters 'out of patriotism'! – Reichardt, on the other hand, is a smooth, evil rascal, the other embodiment of Prussian militarism.

Ultimately the shooting of Katte and that of the thirty-two sailors is motivated by that spirit of unnatural inhumanity which can only inspire the most extreme abhorrence.

Saturday, 6 December 1919   *Berlin*

Berlin's official state of siege, begun on 3 March, has been raised.

Sunday, 21 December 1919   *Berlin*

At Cassirer's the Lasker-Schüler woman pestered Däubler to introduce me to her. For four years I have tried to avoid this beastly person. Däubler behaved in such an elephantine way that I could not avoid the introduction. I said how-do-you-do and took my leave.

1920

Today the Peace Treaty was ratified at Paris; the War is over. A terrible era begins for Europe, like the gathering of clouds before a storm, and it will end in an explosion probably still more terrible than that of the World War. In Germany there are all the signs of a continuing growth of nationalism.

Cartoon by Grosz

The morning paper reports that yesterday there were more than thirty dead and four hundred wounded in front of the Reichstag. Left in the afternoon for Basle.

Thursday, 15 January 1920   *Basle-Zurich*

Visited Basle Minster in the morning. Climbed the tower. German landscape all around, so thoroughly German and yet politically not in union with us. Beyond, lost Alsace. Between them the Rhine, the living, untamed, headstrong soul of Germany, *one spiritual continent*, composed of a hundred provinces and principalities. *Les Allemagnes*. That is why outsiders have never recognized our unity. Nevertheless, as profoundly *one* as an oak with countless boughs and branches. The false concept of the centralized state, evolved by Rome and France, is not suited to this variety. The problem of how we are to maintain ourselves against the outside world has not been solved, is barely understood. Adoption of the Latin concept of the centralized state is at all events wrong for us. The prime fact is – we exist. And are perhaps all the more dangerous and indestructible for being as incomprehensible and diverse as Proteus.

Friday, 16 January 1920   *Zurich*

After nearly six years of war and revolution met Wilma at the Hotel Royal. This meeting, the prospect of which slightly frightened me, passed off as though we had parted yesterday.

Tuesday, 20 January 1920   *Zurich*

In the evening visited Busoni[1] with Wilma and Annette Kolb. He was in a disagreeably sarcastic mood. Would like to return to Berlin, but puts on airs at every practical suggestion and adopts temperamental Beethoven poses.

Saturday, 13 March 1920   *Caux*

This afternoon I was with Jacques[2] at Faist's bookshop in Montreux when an old German lady came in and excitedly announced that counter-revolution had broken out at Berlin; Hindenburg was to be President. The news was in the *Messager de Montreux* office. We went there. She was perfectly right. Behind the pane lay displayed a typewritten Wolff telegram reporting the *coup d'état* plus a second message quoting a proclamation on the part of the new Government. Kapp,[3] founder of the 'Fatherland Party', an anonymous pamphleteer and unstable adventurer, has put himself at the head of it as 'Chancellor'. General Lüttwitz has treasonably gone over to him with the troops under his command and been rewarded with the appointment of

'Defence Minister'. Subsequent messages amplified the picture of this Government of gamblers: Parson Traub as 'Minister for Religious Affairs', Colonel Bauer as Chief of the General Staff, Jagow as Police President.

It all smacks more of farce than history. Berlin has evidently been taken over by the counter-revolutionary forces and the old Government has disappeared. Where to, nobody knows. The Social Democrats have proclaimed a general strike. That, it is to be hoped, will wring this gang's neck. Else the position would become extremely grave. If these people were able to stay in the saddle, civil war, foreign intervention, and chaos would be almost inevitable. How deluded men like Jagow or Colonel Bauer must be if, in view of the overall situation, they lend themselves to such an utterly hopeless stunt. Their end will be like that of the Soviet republics at Budapest, Munich, Bremen, and the rest of them.

In the late evening a telephone call from Zurich that Erzberger, Schiffer and Rauscher have been caught and imprisoned by the counter-revolution, but that the general strike is in operation. Munich (including the Reichswehr garrison) and Cassel have declared themselves for the old Government. The latter proposes to summon a session of the National Assembly in the provinces. The worst of it is that Ludendorff[4] seems likely to be behind Colonel Bauer. We can but hope that Lüttwitz will turn out to be no more than the German Revolution's Kornilov and that his exploit will give fresh impulse to the revolutionary movement.

Tuesday, 16 March 1920   *Berne*

This morning visited Nasse, who left Berlin on Tuesday. The Kapp people, he said, meant their *coup* to take place in May, but had to strike prematurely because the Government got wind of their plot. The British were in sympathy with them because they hoped to make use of a reactionary Government in Germany against Russia. Nasse's answer to my question whether, when speaking of the British, he meant General Malcolm, head of the British Element in the Allied Commission, was in the affirmative. He more or less took sides against Kapp, but did not appear to condemn the affair entirely. He did however unreservedly agree with me that Kapp and his associates are not people who can be tolerated at the head of German affairs under present conditions.

Thursday, 18 March 1920   *Lugano*

In the morning to the Italian Consul and fetched my visa. Met there Richard Kühlmann, who was also dancing attendance among the crowd of petitioners but finally departed in disgust.

Dinner at the Palace Hotel with Wilma and Jacques as guests of the Kühlmanns, who are on their honeymoon. Kühlmann was sleepy and passive until after the meal I turned the talk to politics. Hereupon his conversation became shrewd and absorbing. He apportions the main blame for the war to Berlin, and then to Russia. He is not so certain about Poincaré's responsibility. But he has never been able to unravel exactly *who* at Berlin wanted war. In answer to my remark that the Emperor, Bethmann and Jagow were all three vacillating characters who would certainly not have taken the decision, he observed that three vacillating characters in such position were just sufficient in number to bring about a catastrophe.

He allowed that there was a tussle between our Vienna and London Embassies as to whether it should be war or peace, but thought that Tschirschky had possessed neither the support nor the standing to exercise a decisive influence. And still less of course, Dietrich Bethmann. (Here I differ somewhat, knowing the influence of Dietrich on his cousin, the Chancellor.) Nonetheless there are details, Kühlmann said, which are wholly inexplicable, such as why the Serb answer to the ultimatum was not sent at once *directly* by our Minister at Belgrade to Berlin; instead Berlin relied on its transmission by the Embassy at *Vienna* and calmly waited until the people there passed it on with forty-eight hours' delay. It is impossible to believe that this was an accident.

I suggested that it was very regrettable, indeed disastrous, that he, Kühlmann, was absent from London during the critical days. Once the ultimatum had been dispatched, he replied, his presence could have altered nothing. He has confirmed this point with British politicians. Moreover, to avoid giving offence, he did not want to return to London until Lichnowsky recalled him. Lichnowsky liked to do things himself. And eventually Lichnowsky sent him a telegram, in not very urgent terms, that it might be quite useful if he returned. He left at once and on 29 July was back in London.

His first knowledge of Austria's intention to force a war came from his brother Charles who told him, *before* dispatch of the ultimatum, that the Dresdner Bank felt certain of an impending conflict and was clearing up its affairs accordingly. The Government in Berlin should have known how matters stood as soon as the Dresdner Bank did. That renders its alleged ignorance exceedingly suspect. He summed up his own career by saying that he constantly had to carry out measures and political directives, such as the Baghdad Railway project and the Brest-Litovsk negotiations, of which he disapproved. Presumably that is the secret of his impassivity and the catastrophic effect he ultimately had on the fate of Germany.

Naturally he disapproves of the Kapp Affair, but in his opinion the general softness and sloppiness of our internal politics will ensure that not a hair of these traitors' heads is touched. He told me to mark his words: not one hair! Personally he would put them up against a wall without another thought.

Once again I was impressed by his immense cleverness and farsighted political intelligence. But he utterly lacks warmth of feeling or fervour of conviction. In his inmost heart he cares nothing for the fate of Germany, whose destinies were entrusted to him at the crucial moment. Any passing love affair takes precedence.

Friday, 19 March 1920   *Lugano*

The Kapp farce is over. Kapp and Ludendorff are reported to have fled from Berlin. The Government has issued warrants of arrest for Kapp, Bauer, Jagow and their accomplices. But there is still fierce fighting between workers and Reichswehr at Berlin, Leipzig, Nürnberg, Chemnitz, Dresden and in the Ruhr. The Government is drifting leftwards again.

Saturday, 20 March 1920   *Lugano*

Yesterday Noske resigned, today he *stays*. The papers paint a picture of a growing revolt by the workers. What I said to Kühlmann the day before yesterday, that only now are we faced by real revolution, may yet prove correct. At various points in Berlin the mob has captured officers of the retreating Kapp forces and murdered them. The bitterness of the working classes against the military seems to be unlimited, and the successful general strike has greatly increased their consciousness of their own power. Opposed to them stand a disrupted, half-treacherous Reichswehr and a feeble, irresolute Government. So, at least, it looks from here. Nobody knows what is happening in the east of the country except that Silesia and East Prussia are apparently still loyal to Kapp.

The Italian Consul, who on Thursday gave me a visa without the slightest hesitation, today stopped me on the promenade and asked me to postpone my trip for a few days '*parce qu'il y avait une petite difficulté*'. There had been a telephone call from Berne. '*Vous êtes un diplomate ; alors ce n'est pas si simple.*' But the Consul-General, Count Caccia, was going to Berne on Monday and proposed to discuss the matter with the Minister. I would perhaps be able to start on Wednesday.

Friday, 26 March 1920   *Lugano*

Today, for the first time since the putsch, Berlin newspapers, *Voss* and *Tageblatt*, are again available. Unfortunately there seems to be no doubt about Ludendorff's participation. How shattering that from 1916 to 1918, the most frightful moment in German history, a man with such atrocious lack of political judgement should have been in dictatorial control of our destiny. Ludendorff and Bauer played the decisive roles then and it becomes appallingly clear that what caused them to plunge Germany into the abyss was the same state of narrow-minded delusion as has animated their preposterous *coup* now. We have been the victims of political imbeciles and adventurers, not of great though unfortunate soldiers. This stunt of theirs stains our history retroactively. Ludendorff sinks to the level of an idiotic professional genius who was also a ruthless gambler. He becomes the military equivalent of the 'German professor' who abandons every ethical standard and loses every shred of common sense where his field is concerned. A tragicomic figure as the principal in a drama which was a matter of life and death. A worthy counterpart to the Emperor, in whom the grotesque was simply more obvious. Not that in the sequel Wilson, Clémenceau and Lloyd George proved more deserving of respect. A form of society which culminates in such specimens and takes its inspiration from them stands self-condemned. '*Le ridicule tue.*' So does misproportion in an organism when it becomes too palpable and noxious.

Sunday, 28 March 1920   *Lugano*

Something funny for a change. Friday's evening edition of *Berliner Tageblatt* has a tribute by Alfred Kerr[5] to Hoelderlin on the hundred and fiftieth anniversary of his birth. Its jewelled phrases include '(He was) *a melody in trousers*.' A melody that sometimes sounds like Brahms's song '*O wüsst ich doch den Weg zarück.*' Stuff like that is concocted and printed in Berlin in the middle of a revolution.

Wednesday, 7 April 1920   *Brissago*

The French have occupied Frankfurt.[6] They pretend, with revolting hypocrisy, to be the defenders of the German workers against Prussian militarism. On the other hand the German Government has behaved with unparalleled clumsiness in this whole Ruhr business. It has done everything all round to provide pretexts for suspicion.

Monday, 12 April 1920   *Brissago*

With André Germain and two other friends to the island residence of the Baroness St Leger who in her own lifetime has locally become something of a legendary figure. She is supposed to enjoy magical powers, to have had seven husbands who visit her on Christmas Eve, and so on, and so on.

Living alone on her island, apart from an old gardener, an aura of super-stition envelops her. It was the gardener who received us at the landing-stage and accepted our visiting-cards, which he carried inside to the Baroness. After a while he returned with permission to show us the garden. This, although giving an impression of neglect and of being in process of be-coming a wilderness, has a powerful and highly individual atmosphere. Within a few moments of strolling among its masses of evergreens and clusters of palms, with only the monotonous lapping sound of the lake's waves and the sight of the grandiose mountain setting, it impressed us as the reflection of a great, untamed, entirely subjective personality striving for expression.

Apart from Sanssouci, I know of no garden whose spirit so catches that of a single individual. The Circe who has created and inhabits it, the old recluse and Baroness, crossed our path, by accident it would seem, in the neighbourhood of the house. As the gardener made a move to lead us towards her, she waved us away with brief, emphatic gestures. But then, as though attracted by her very distrust of us, she took a few paces nearer. I seized the opportunity to address her and pleaded to be shown the dolls which she makes. She looked at me and my companions with an undisguised antipathy which clearly showed, without the slightest pretence at politeness, in her sharply contoured, somewhat Semitic features framed by ringlets and a downy, black goatee beard. Gradually she became more conciliatory, let herself be talked over, tripped away into the house, and suddenly stood in front of us again with a deceptively life-like boy in her arms. She treated the doll just like a child, spoke to it, made it display its graces to us, and, when we expressed our admiration, took us inside the house to a room where a whole row of just as life-like little boys and girls, in fanciful cos-tumes and with glittering dolls' eyes, sat on a sofa. It was really just like a children's party. She took each little creature into her arms, introduced it to us, and exercised it in a series of movements and bows. Evidently this was the world for which she lived.

The old woman, standing before us with these somewhat cloyingly smiling dolls in her arms, really seemed like a sorceress. Dynamic and ugly, authori-tative and still distrustful, she reminded me now of Disraeli in old age. And yet there hung behind her the portrait of a young and very beautiful woman with black, wavy hair, which probably was the way she looked forty years ago.

For thirty years she has lived here on these islands. Their beauty is her creation. When she came here, she told us, there had been nothing but rocks and incredibly bold snakes which had furiously darted up their heads and spat at her as an intruder. First she had had to extirpate the snakes, then transport basketsful of earth from the mainland. Every shrub and every tree had been individually planted and fostered. It had taken thirty years for this paradise to grow. Now people trooped in, brought their cameras, and behaved as though it was common property. We must understand that sometimes she defended herself like a wildcat, 'So, so, so!' Curving her fingers like claws, she lunged them at us and spat as the snakes must have spat when she first intruded upon them.

She confirmed that in ancient days there had been a temple of Venus here, then a cloister which had been in ruins since the sixteenth century, and she showed us reproductions of inscriptions. What deeply upset her, though, was that her garden appears in the photographs too and is even used to lend attraction to the scene. We parted from this strange woman with a not easily definable sensation. In the evening I heard that she is supposed to have been a pupil of Liszt.

Tuesday, 4 May 1920   *Berlin*

Mrs Warren's Profession at the Lessingtheater. I was deeply impressed by the big scene in Act Two between mother and daughter. A really magnificent piece of theatre.

Sunday, 9 May 1920   *Berlin*

Frau ohne Schatten at the Staatsoper. Loveliest of fairy-tale operas, just enough symbolism to lend significance to the plot, and wrapped in a pearly robe of glittering, rainbow-coloured music.

Thursday, 13 May 1920   *Weimar*

In the evening visit to Frau Foerster-Nietzsche. She insists that she is a 'nationalist'. Whereas her brother did not even want to be a German, but a Pole! She has had her head turned by all these Countesses and Excellencies.

Sunday, 16 May 1920   *Duisburg-Düsseldorf*

At eleven o'clock delivered a lecture on the League of Nations in the big hall of the Stock Exchange. The audience was attentive, but clearly regarded my entire concept as new and rather bewildering. Consequently only one question.

In the afternoon to Düsseldorf. I was accompanied by a teacher who was to see about the details of my lecture there. He told me about the outbreaks of violence. Three of his pupils were shot as Red Guards. Some of the youngsters, put up against the wall by the Reichswehr (about two thousand are supposed to have died in all), met their death heroically, with cheers for better days to come. But he was not prepared to be categoric on whether a strong belief in the future is general among the younger proletariat. The population, homeless individuals jumbled together from many various regions, is too chaotic for that.

Monday, 17 May 1920   *Düsseldorf-Ruhrort*

In the evening addressed metal workers in the large room of Ruhrort Station Hotel. Smoky suburban hall, tightly packed with people sitting at tables and drinking beer. Speaker's desk on a stage. I talked for an hour and a quarter on the theme of 'Workers and the League of Nations'. Loud applause at the end and no protests, but also no questions or debate. The subject seems to be too new, too unfamiliar to the workers for them to know what to ask or to challenge.

Tuesday, 18 May 1920   *Düsseldorf*

Spoke at Hagen. Lower-middle-class and workers' audience. Ringing applause. The idea obviously caught on. I spent the afternoon at the Folkwang-Museum. Fuhrmann led me round and later I visited Rohlfs who, regardless of his age and fragility, seems to be still astonishingly productive. I bought four water-colours; they averaged a thousand marks. Also talked to the sculptor Hermann, who looked me up while I was with Rohlfs. Küster, secretary of the Peace Society, says that everything was perfectly quiet and orderly at Hagen during the Reds' rule, although this was their headquarters.

Thursday, 20 May 1920   *Düsseldorf*

To Cologne during lunch-time. Visited the Cathedral and East Asian Collection. Freely accessible despite British occupation. Many British soldiers and cars in the streets, but otherwise the picture of the city is unaltered. No impression of the Occupation lying very heavily on it.

Tuesday, 25 May 1920   *Hamburg*

News that during Whitsun the pacifist Paasche was murdered on his estate by Reichswehr soldiers. Of course 'while attempting to escape' (just as under

Diaz in Mexico or under Noske in Berlin) and of course the case will again be 'examined' by the 'appropriate military court', just as the cases of Marloh and Hiller. At present those in Germany who make themselves politically unpopular stand in greater danger of their lives than they would in the most disreputable South American republic or at Rome under the Borgias. But neither that nor the state of economic misery stops life looking superficially

Cartoon by Grosz

glossy, as exemplified by the continued growth of a crowd of war-profiteers as well as respectably rich individuals for whom nothing is too expensive and no pleasure too extravagant.[7] Rot is attacking the roots of this splendidly flourishing tree, though there are no signs of it among the foliage. But probably it will one day suddenly crash. Already there is talk of a new right-wing putsch. That could hasten the downfall.

Saturday, 29 May 1920   *Berlin*

Frau von Gerlach asks me to tea for tomorrow: 'As my husband may shortly have to leave Berlin, we would be highly delighted to be able still to talk to you about this and that.'

Schwann-Schneider, who came to see me about my lecture at Tegel tomorrow, said that Gerlach had to cancel his meeting on Friday here in

Berlin because of a threat to murder him. Similarly, when he proposed to
speak at Hamburg, he received a warning from there that it would 'be the
end of him'. F. G., whom I met in the evening, volunteered that a Reichswehr
non-commissioned officer in close touch with the *Femebund*[8] told him that
Gerlach 'is now the next after Paasche'.

Sunday, 30 May 1920   *Berlin*

Lunch with Georg Bernhard. As he rightly says, the danger is not that my
ideas will not be put into practice, but that they will be taken up by others,
particularly the political parties, and put into practice badly.

Afterwards at Gerlach's. I warned him, in accordance with F. G.'s
information, against Captain Schneider, whose accomplices are planning his
murder. He has had warnings from others too. The whole family was in a
considerable state of excitement, and this atmosphere was heightened by
the presence of the murdered Paasche's housekeeper, all in black. But there
was also an Italian diplomat, and Frau von Gerlach veered between tension
and tea-table manners. She asked me, in case of emergency, to assume the
care of her fourteen-year-old boy; I promised to do so.

Sunday, 6 June 1920   *Berlin*

A crucial date for Germany. The German Republic's first Reichstag
elections. Fears of a putsch have proved unfounded. Indeed the streets are
quieter and emptier than on ordinary Sundays, perhaps because it rains
now and again. At eleven in the morning I was the sole voter at my polling-
centre, whereas on the occasion of the National Assembly elections eighteen
months ago I had to queue.

Wednesday, 9 June 1920   *Berlin*

Meeting of the Wednesday Society. Jordan-Mallinckrodt spoke about the
German economic structure. Those present included the former Chancellor
Michaelis (long, erect, flat-topped head set on a small body, a medium-
grade bureaucrat personality totally out of proportion to the global scale
of events on which he exercised a baneful influence), the Vice-Chancellor
Koch, August Müller, and at a later stage Stresemann, hailed as the victor
of the day. I sat next to his personal assistant and party organizer Rheinbaben,
who accepted congratulations, half-jokingly, half-seriously, as the future
Minister for Foreign Affairs. He admitted pretty frankly to me that for
Stresemann and his Party everything now depends on Britain's attitude.
If Britain grants them facilities in respect of raw materials, foodstuffs,
payment conditions, and so on, matters will come right.

Wednesday, 16 June 1920   *Berlin*

In the evening addressed the Wednesday Society on the subject 'Should Germany join the League of Nations?'

Thursday, 17 June 1920   *Berlin*

In the evening spoke at the University on the invitation of the Socialist Students Union. The speech, judging by the applause, was a great success. Afterwards, it is true, a Communist denounced me as a bourgeois counter-revolutionary because I do not want to 'smash' the League of Nations and let loose the 'world revolution'. There is no helping these gentry; they want force. They don't worry their heads about 'What happens *then*?' and 'What is the *objective* which force is meant to serve?' Else they would see that the answer cannot differ substantially from mine. The blinkers of the revolution-ary catchword narrow down vision no less than do those cramping the counter-revolutionary one. The result is parrot-like recitation of party slogans.

My last words, condemning this breed of revolutionaries and quoting Lassalle[9] on my behalf, were again greeted with the plaudits of stamping feet, but some of those who had participated in the debate raised a good deal of noisy objection and shuffled their feet. The Nationalist students present remained silent.

Friday, 18 June 1920   *Leipzig*

To Leipzig. In the evening a lecture on Poland to Upper Silesians. On the train I met Noske and had a long talk with him. He was very bitter, not merely about Lüttwitz, but Seeckt[10] and Oven too. Seeckt spent the crucial night rocking to and fro on the heels of his highly-polished boots, but could not be persuaded to agree to any measures against the rebels. Noske clearly regards him as no more reliable than Lüttwitz.

About the situation now, Noske said that he saw Ebert yesterday and implored him not to surrender the reins of power in any direction. If he let in a right-wing Government and handed over the armed forces to it, these would be built into an instrument to which reactionary elements could look for firm support. Officers still wavering in their allegiance would then be drawn over to that side. In answer to my question why he had not dismissed Lüttwitz sooner, he replied that Lüttwitz had been represented to him as a deeply religious man who, having sworn an oath of loyalty, would keep it. His dismissal would moreover have upset the officer corps. The Inde-pendents, Noske continued, were impossible because they would break up the armed forces, just as Loeffler, having suggested reduction of the Reichswehr to fifty thousand men, was impossible as Minister of Defence.

Noske is manifestly a perfectly sincere and dyed-in-the-wool militarist whom the officer corps, with the help of his prejudices and their catchwords, has led by the nose. He has indeed something of a bear with a nose-ring about him. Though 'unemployed', he looks prosperous enough, travels

GUSTAV NOSKE
Kommandant von Berlin
Mitglied d. Kabinetts d. Mehrheitssozialisten

Gustav Noske (Kursell)

first class, wears brand new yellow boots, and consumed during the journey large quantities of ham rolls and beer. Were there not so much innocent blood on his hands, he would be a slightly comic, almost likeable figure. Where, in that immense frame of his, he keeps his social conscience and his Social Democratic red heart is another matter and his own secret.

Friday, 25 June 1920   *Berlin*

Stresemann, Berger and Rheinbaben lunched with me at Hiller's. (A nice little bill, by the way. Thousand marks for four, just a simple lunch.) Stresemann, with a party meeting timed for two, stayed until a quarter to three, regardless of Rheinbaben's vehement entreaties. Far better, he declared, to let the members blow off steam first and then, fifteen minutes before the Reichstag session and election of the Reichstag President, put in an appearance and take matters in hand. A sovereign display of contempt for his Party vassals.

Berger and Stresemann outlined their ideas on foreign policy. Both count heavily on the British, and Stresemann confirmed that Lüttwitz and Malcolm had been in negotiation for weeks before the Kapp Affair. Berger described how, in his capacity as State Commissioner, he had been in constant touch with Brussilov,[11] who at that date already predicted the Polish attack on Russia. Brussilov told Berger's agents that he is no Bolshevik, nor a Tsarist either, but a supporter of bourgeois democracy inside Russia and an advocate of cooperation with Germany abroad. He predicted not only the Polish attack, but the collapse of Poland, Russian entry into Warsaw, and a Fourth Partition of Poland. Berger (who was at pains to emphasize that he acted without knowledge of the Ministry of Foreign Affairs) thinks that the Russians need to re-establish a common frontier with Germany and that this is why Poland's annihilation is of vital importance to them. Once Brussilov is installed at Warsaw, Germany will become indispensable to the Entente as a bulwark against Bolshevism. The British will re-equip our forces and we shall have to mass troops on our eastern frontier, though secretly assuring Brussilov that we shall not attack him. On the contrary. As soon as we are re-armed, we shall, with Russian support, demand revision of the Versailles Treaty, and it may then be possible to achieve this without bloodshed. France will no longer be able to oppose such a step or it will find itself having to fight Germany alone, without Britain.

Saturday, 26 June 1920 *Berlin*

Harden[12] to lunch. Oddly enough, he was enthusiastic about Stinnes and maintained that the latter is too intelligent ever to practise a policy of force against the workers. He attacked Bernhard's views on European affairs in so far as these are hostile to Britain. (Stresemann too is pro-British now.) The present Government he regards at any rate as better than the last, which was beneath contempt. He questioned me closely about my adherence to the Democrats, who are 'done for'. Bourgeois democracy has proved itself impossible for Germany. He had upbraided the Democrats, in *Zukunft*, for not nominating me as a Reichstag candidate, but now he is glad that its failure to do so has kept me out of all the party hustle and bustle.

He recalled the days of 1905–6 when we struggled against the disastrous Morocco policy, the start of Germany's downfall, and he reminded me of a letter I wrote to him then but had since completely forgotten. He printed it in *Zukunft* as an anonymous contribution, whereupon Holstein[13] came running to him and wanted to know, on account of its excellence, who the author was. Henceforward Holstein (whom I never met) always 'sang your praises'.

It is strange, but Harden was unaware of my *political* activity in Berne, my links with the French, and was highly surprised (or pretended to be so) when I mentioned them.[14] He remained until half past four, having evidently greatly enjoyed his visit. So did I. His conversation is very witty, knowledgeable, sensible and not in the least extreme. Quite different from what he publishes.

He had heard of my League of Nations projects that I harbour 'most interesting, but ultra-Bolshevist ideas' for the League. I have sent him for his enlightenment my 'directives'.

Friday, 9 July 1920   *Berlin*

First meeting of the executive committee of the 'New Fatherland League' whose purpose is propagation of my League of Nations concept. Under discussion were approaches to the AFA, trade unions, shop stewards, and political parties. At the end Lindhagen pleaded for stronger emphasis on the ethical and Christian aspects, saying that the League of Nations must see its principal task in the creation of the New Man. I objected that this was the business of the Sermon on the Mount, not that of my brochure or any new organization. The Christian Church has been employed on the problem for two thousand years. The best we can hope for is that a world organization will clear away certain impediments to the evolution of the New Man.

Sunday, 11 July 1920   *Berlin*

Dietrich Bethmann lunched with me. He is completely ruined, is trying to sell his art treasures, and proposes to become an art dealer. We talked about 'war-guilt'. He admitted that, apart from certain contributory Russian factors, Germany was to blame for the outbreak of the war. The ultimatum had been so framed as inevitably to provoke hostilities. We had nonetheless been right, for in October Russia's 'practice mobilization', at a cost of 250 million roubles, would have lain in store for us, and that would have been synonmous with a declaration of war. Germany had to precipitate war in August, according to Dietrich, because otherwise the Entente would have provoked it under some excuse or other which would have left Austria with an outlet into neutrality. Then we would have been on our own. He certainly did all in his power to frustrate a peaceful settlement. And said today that, faced once more with taking the decision, he would act in precisely the same way.

He also believes that, in alliance with Russia, we shall inside a year be at war with France again.

Monday, 12 July 1920   *Berlin*

As my barber was shaving me this morning, he whispered that in three months' time the Bolsheviks would be in Warsaw and then we would turn, hand in hand with them, on France. He would join up a second time for that. I only mention this because it is precisely among ordinary people that feeling against France and in favour of a new war has recently spread more and more. The most improbable individuals come out with it.

Thursday, 26 August 1920   *Geneva*

In the morning saw, by appointment, Albert Thomas at the International Labour Office. They have hired a big, monastery-like building (La Châtelaine), standing in a fine park of its own, fairly far outside the city. Everything appears to be still in the stage of moving in and settling down. Carpenters, painters, charwomen run about between the officials. The rooms are as yet cheerlessly bare and drab. It all smacks strongly of still being at the rudimentary stage. The remainder of the League, domiciled at the Hotel National, will not be much more advanced. Thomas received me very courteously and readily answered my questions. Despite his brown, bushy, crinkled full beard, he has a young face with an intelligent, benevolent expression. I concentrated my inquiry on the Office's practical activity (so far), on its relations with the independent international workers' organizations (especially the international trade union movement), and Thomas's personal views on the intervention of these organizations in national policy.

When I mentioned the British workers' resounding undertaking against the war (their 'Council of Action') and tried to probe Thomas's reaction, he winced. Clearly the question was very embarrassing to him. The timidity of the civil servant, dependent on the goodwill of governments, revealed itself. To me this was very interesting as a symptom of the attitude of League of Nations officials in general. He did however wriggle through to a sort of recognition and approval of the Council of Action by saying that the British workers had only been able to achieve so immense an effect because the overwhelming majority of public opinion was behind them, whereas French workers' impotence derives from public opinion against them.

Saturday, 2 October 1920   *Brunswick*

Pacifist Congress (since 30 September). Hiller's resolution on conscientious objection had created chaos. The Peace Society was nearly blown apart. Meetings were held in a fierce state of excitement. Which was worrying, because of my own speech and resolution. When today it was my turn, around eleven, I had to contend with a distinctly unfavourable atmosphere. But my success was enormous, far beyond what could be expected. The Congress was almost unanimous in voting to interrupt its debate so as to pass my resolution. Schücking, who was in the chair, said that for years he had not heard such a speech in the Reichstag. Afterwards I was besieged from all sides with requests for lectures. Within half an hour I had assumed engagements to speak all over Germany.

Monday, 22 November 1920   *Königsberg*

Spoke in the hall of the stock exchange. Unheated, icy. Discussion. Two Communists declared themselves satisfied with my *goal*, but rejected my *road* to it (via the League of Nations). A Social Democrat rebuked me for not (on the score of 'class conceit') joining the SPD.

Wednesday, 24 November 1920   *Königsberg*

All Königsberg papers have published detailed reports of my speech, even the reactionary *Ostpreussische*. This last closes with the remark that my views are 'dangerous'. The rest more or less agree with my ideas and in part go into raptures about my oratorical gifts.

Friday, 26 November 1920   *Tilsit*

Have here addressed the Hyperboreans. I am lodged at an antediluvian hotel ('The Royal Court') which smells and is tumbling down. The waiters, porter, and so on, are ancient and have been a lifetime on the staff. A portrait of the Emperor, smarmy and gorged, hangs almost pertly over my old, soiled, and crippled couch. The meeting, in the 'Civic House', also passed off in a comically provincial atmosphere. I had just begun to speak when the glee club began to rehearse in the room next door. I broke off, saying that, out of consideration for my audience, I could not continue. The chairman sent his secretary to look for another place. Finally we moved upstairs, the audience carrying their chairs, to the first floor. Apart from that, a tumultuous success.

In the afternoon I crossed the Niemen into what is now 'Memel Territory'. The division of Germany is encountered right outside Tilsit. The quiet, broad, rapid river forms the boundary. Once before, at an historic moment, East and West, in the persons of Napoleon and Alexander, met here. The landscape is vast and melancholy, steppe-like, with low hills on the horizon and broken up by the gleam of lonely tributaries. Heavy clouds hung over the scene today as I watched the flight of birds of passage over the waters. It had the sadness of folk songs, all in a minor key. The sight compensated me for my hotel and meeting.

Tuesday, 30 November 1920   *Danzig*

Danzig is a little Babylon. Unbelievably international and cosmopolitan in the midst of its Gothic German gables. Profiteers, whores, and sailors. Americans, Poles, and Jews shading off into Germans. Many of the Poles with a veneer of Americanism. At night, drunk as swine, they demonstrate in the dance-halls a charming combination of American and Polish facets of intoxication. Eastern Europe under the influence of Wilson. Money flies; gold delirium. Such a circus hasn't been seen for years.

Thursday, 2 December 1920   *Berlin*

Yesterday the wife of the British Ambassador, in response to my 'Children's Aid' article, visited the eastern parts of Berlin and said, on her return, things are not as bad as I made out! But this evening Henckel telephoned, putting me in touch with Colonel Stuart Roddie who accompanied the Ambassadress yesterday and went out there again today. Obviously, he said, she was taken to see quite the wrong parts. What he saw today exceeded his worst expectations. He has at once made a written report to the Ambassadress and will tell her in the morning what terrible things he witnessed.

This morning the chairman of the Association of Berlin Street Vendors said that my article is having terrific sales. He therefore proposed that I should have it distributed at two marks a copy by women who are out of work, with one mark for the publisher, forty pfennigs for the children, and sixty pfennigs for the women who sell the pamphlet. He is convinced that he can dispose of it in thousands.

1921

Tuesday, 11 January 1921   *Geneva*

I have had an excellent Press, even from the anti-German *Suisse Tribune*. In the evening I gave a lecture (in English) to the International Women's League. Many members of the two League of Nations secretariats were present. A very interesting discussion followed. Lloyd spoke up in favour of a Continental (European) policy. In answer to a question from me, he said that he counts Britain as part of Europe and regards it as being of greater importance to Britain than the Empire.

Friday, 4 February 1921   *Berlin*

First night of *Josephslegende* under Strauss. Enormous, almost unprecedented success. The audience was really '*Tout Berlin*' – the Chancellor, Simons, Seeckt, numerous Ministers, the outstanding figures in society, art, and literature, Albert Einstein, and so on, and so on. The applause would not stop. We had to appear on the stage again and again. Durieux[1] beyond praise. Afterwards at Felix Deutsch's.

Wednesday, 9 February 1921   *Berlin*

Ate with Colonel Roddie (British Embassy) at the Adlon. Apart from myself, nothing but Englishmen from the Embassy or Military Mission. Roddie, according to Schubert, is in Lloyd George's confidence. The Paris decisions, he told me, will not be dictated to us for *signature*, but only be *communicated* to us as a unilateral Allied statement. He had this from d'Abernon.

Thursday, 10 February 1921   *Berlin*

Lehmann-Rüssbuldt asked me this morning whether I would go to Amsterdam with Albert Einstein on behalf of a pacifist group. The object would be to get in touch with the International Trades Union Congress about the Paris decisions. The group includes Eduard Bernstein, Gerlach, Walther Rathenau, Heinrich Ströbel, Hugo Simon, and so on. In other words, the 'New Fatherland League'. I agreed, but only on condition that Simons consents and favours the idea.

Monday, 14 February 1921   *Amsterdam*

Early at Bentheim. Passport and customs formalities. Einstein, apparently using a sleeping-car for the first time, seemed fascinated by everything.

During the journey I asked him whether the inferences of his theory of relativity can be applied equally to the more or less astronomically constructed atom. Einstein said no: size (the minuteness of the atom) comes into it here. So size, measurement, greatness and smallness, must be an *absolute*, indeed almost the sole absolute that remains, I said. Einstein confirmed that size is the ultimate factor, the absolute that cannot be got away from. He was surprised that I should have hit on this idea, for it is the deepest mystery of physics, this inexplicability and absoluteness of size. Every atom of iron has precisely the same magnitude as any other atom of iron, no matter where in the universe it may be. Nature knows only atoms, whether of iron or of hydrogen, of equal size, though human intelligence can *imagine* atoms of varying magnitude.

In that case, I said jokingly, man is more intelligent than God, God is stupid, and in fact stupidity, the lack of human intelligence, is the one thing which we can say about God with certainty. Man with his inexhaustible complexity of imagination reposes in God like a pearl in an oyster. God is so old that He has no further use for intelligence. On the contrary, replied Einstein, the farther one penetrates into nature, the greater becomes one's respect for God. (Which, after all, does not contravene my joke, for what would be the good of intelligence to 'God'?)

Sunday, 20 February 1921   *Berlin*

Lunched at General Malcolm's with Lord and Lady d'Abernon. After the meal Malcolm took d'Abernon and myself into the smoking-room and left us alone.

I told d'Abernon my view that we are nearly as much interested as France in the reconstruction of northern France, whereas for Britain the recovery of Germany's purchasing power, and that of eastern Europe, is just as important, if not more so. The reparations problem can only be solved in this context. As long as Germany remains so wretched and impoverished, it can pay little or nothing. How much it may be capable of paying at all depends entirely on the extent to which its purchasing power and economy are restored. The two questions, reparation and economic rehabilitation, are in my view inseparably linked. We can name the figure we are capable of paying, any figure whatever, only when we know if and to what extent our economy is going to be assisted. The one is the indispensable and unshakable prerequisite to the other.

D'Abernon replied that this argument is substantially different from what has hitherto been heard from German sources. Herein lies a possible basis for the London negotiations.

Monday, 21 February 1921 *Berlin*

Lunched with Simons (just back from southern Germany) and told him about my talk yesterday with d'Abernon. This link between German reparations and Allied aid for the German economy is nothing new, he commented. It was with this in mind that the Brussels conference was convened. Paris sabotaged the Brussels meeting, but that is the point of departure to which d'Abernon is clearly trying to return. He is evidently going about the matter with great vigour. He has requested an appointment for this afternoon, probably to repeat what he told me yesterday. But he, Simons, feels that it is not altogether in our interest to come to an agreement with the British too quickly. We should at least wait until the Americans enter the game. The French will make a frightful fuss if we make our payment dependent on reciprocal aid. Roughly, though, that is how he also envisages the London discussions.

Saturday, 26 February 1921 *Geneva*

At six o'clock visited Albert Thomas at his home. I explained how I see things and I told him that my opinion is shared by Gerlach, Breitscheid, and the German left-wing parties as a whole. It is in Germany's economic interest to recognize frankly its obligation to pay because it needs French economic rehabilitation on its own behalf. But the Paris decisions are no good because they completely overlook how France is to get its money. They have shifted political and military considerations to the fore instead of concentrating-attention on the technical and economic measures. That is why he, as Director of the International Labour Office, is entitled and has an obligation to intervene before it is too late. In a fortnight Foch may be in the Ruhr. The situation is as dangerous and formidable as it was in July 1914. Everyone must do their duty.

Thomas, clearly somewhat embarrassed, began by saying that 'in great part' he shares my standpoint. Nonetheless Simons, through his speeches in southern Germany, has '*coupé les bras*' of those who would still like to do something. He does not see how an intervention is to be managed at this moment. Briand's downfall, if he makes the slightest concession at London, is certain. Poincaré is '*d'une activité trépidante*'; all he is waiting for is a sign of yielding on Briand's part.

Obviously Poincaré thoroughly scares Briand and people like Thomas. Even if Germany were to sign the agreement in London, I replied, it would still be built on the very shaky foundation of assuming that the current military and political situation, including the preponderance of Foch, will last forty-two years. That is ridiculous. Our *common* aim must be to place reparations to France on a firm footing, meaning an agreement freely accepted by France, Germany, and the whole world, including organized labour, as being sensible and advantageous.

Thomas now palpably felt on safer ground and became more approving. These, he maintained, are the lines on which he has been working for the past week. He is just back from Paris, where he talked to Briand. Then, I remarked, he must see that this subject is one for the League of Nations (in accordance with Articles 3 and 11) and that he, as Director of the Labour Office, must demand a hearing for international organized labour.

Thomas's main trends of thought can be identified as (1) awareness of the (comparative) impotence of the League of Nations and organized labour, (2) fear of Briand's downfall and Poincaré's seizure of power; (3) recognition of the unreliable foundations of the Paris decisions and the conditions that may be imposed in London (allowing for the mutability of military and political circumstances); (4) distrust of public opinion in Germany, reinforced by Simons' speech campaign. (Simons, he said to me, will arrive at London '*dans des bien mauvaises conditions*', his 'inflammatory' addresses having exhausted what was his best asset, his personal credit. I tried of course to pacify him and to explain matters.) (5) dawning realization of the need for his own and organized Labour's intervention. Considerable fright at the prospect of this intervention and a search for backing; (6) fear of the chaos consequent upon a military move by Foch.

A good thing that I am having a letter written simultaneously to Branting so that perhaps Sweden, as a member state of the League, can be brought into action in accordance with Articles 3 and 11. Possibly a grouping can yet be effected which will sufficiently invigorate and strengthen Lloyd George, Briand, and Thomas to demonstrate courage in dealing with their own wild men. What is lacking today among our opponents is not recognition of the facts (d'Abernon is a case in point), but courage, meaning readiness to proceed at risk to their own positions, just as it was with our 'statesmen' of the William II, Bülow and Bethmann calibre. Three-quarters of all catastrophes, major and minor, derive from cowardice. Cowardice is the subtlest and most tragic of human qualities. It holds society together at all points and is at the same time its most blasting force. Man is man through cowardice, and *only* man through cowardice too.

Friday, 10 June 1921   *Rome*

At an early hour to the Vatican. I had an introduction to Monsignor Giuseppe Migone, private secretary and confidant of the Pope, from young Bartolomeo

Migone at Florence. He knew my 'line' because Bartolomeo Migone had already forwarded it to him in Italian. He is putting me down for an audience with the Pope and suggested that I visit Monsignor Cerretti who deals with external affairs in the Secretariat of State[2] and is going shortly to Paris as nuncio. He will make an appointment for me. Migone concurs with my ideas, especially with the stress I lay on the need to create a counterweight to the ebullient nationalism which threatens civilization with destruction. He agreed that the Papacy and the Catholic Church should participate in this task as an influence for compromise.

Saturday, 11 June 1921   *Rome*

At eleven with Migone to Monsignor Cerretti. I got the impression of a clear-headed, matter-of-fact Italian, a brisk and practical realist with but a very thin layer of ecclesiastical unction. We plunged without further preliminaries into the middle of things by dealing with the League of Nations. I underlined its particular importance to Germany.

Cerretti's comments on the League were frankly sceptical. An ironical smile played around the corners of his mouth at my first mention of it and, after I finished, he proceeded to hold a close-knit disquisition on the Vatican's policy towards the League. When Wilson first raised the subject, the Vatican gave the idea a warm welcome. But when it was seen how affairs developed, the defeated Central Powers not being allowed to become members, the 'League of Nations' disclosing itself as an alliance of the victorious countries which accordingly took decisions on various occasions of a purely political and dubiously equitable character, and finally America declining to join, then the Vatican too gradually lost interest in *this* League of Nations, which stood revealed as a hollow dummy, and any desire to adhere to it had progressively faded.

Thursday, 23 June 1921   *Rome*

During the morning I went for a walk on the Esquiline Hill. At the foot of it is San Pietro in Vincoli with Michelangelo's *Moses*, which should always be visualized as having the slaves and giants in the Academy at Florence for its supporters and intellectual complement. They represent insensate, self-ignorant, therefore unfree and ill-fated power, whereas *Moses* is power illumined by mind and feeling, clear-sighted, purposeful, and thereby free.

The problem of power, struggling with itself on its own behalf and for its own justification and redemption, seems to me central to Michelangelo's thought. This struggle is to him the pivotal question of history. What is power for? To what purpose shall all the colossal diversity of power be applied? Tolstoy, who rejects every form of force and wants power to be renounced because he does not know to what purposes it should be applied and because he sees in it no path to saintliness or wisdom, gives a lagging, weary answer to Michelangelo's question, an answer which Michelangelo must have known but rejected. *Moses* is Michelangelo's converse, still more exalted rejoinder, comprising not the answer of the Renaissance but of a more profound, Christian and modern spirit: power is good because there is a way from it to saintliness and wisdom whose embodiment is man, though a higher and profounder type of man. This is also one of the pivots of Nietzsche's thought.

Prittwitz and Lucidi lunched with me. Afterwards the latter accompanied me to the Cardinal Secretary of State, Gasparri, in the Vatican. His appearance and manners are those of a small, fat, rather vulgar businessman. Nothing of a prince of the Church about him, for all his scarlet stockings, scarlet skullcap, and the damask hangings dyed in the scarlet blood of the martyrs. He could, just as he is, be standing behind a shop-counter. Not a trace of ecclesiasticism.

For the League of Nations he has nothing but undisguised scorn. He quoted to us the salaries of bourgeois and other officials at Geneva (bourgeois, six hundred thousand francs; the Italian representative, three hundred thousand; and so on) and suggested that these gentlemen now regard the League of Nations as the finest invention of all times and don't want to see it altered one jot. For the Vatican the question of membership has been settled by Article 10, which it can never accept because in no circumstances can it declare war upon any nation '*à moins qu'un peuple ne fasse une guerre de religion*'. The victorious Powers have simply founded an alliance for the preservation of the fruits of victory. The Argentine has already taken its departure. Peru is on the point of leaving. The Peruvian representative told him that in his report to his Government he described the money spent on the League as 'gone down the drain'.

To say all this caused Gasparri unconcealed malicious delight. He grinned all over his fat, oily face and slapped his knees. At the outset, he added, there was talk of papal membership of the League of Nations. France however objected that '*la Sainte Siège n'était pas une nation*', to which someone replied, '*qu'en effet, ce n'était pas une nation, mais une puissance*'. It is obvious that this sceptical, negative attitude of the Vatican towards Geneva contains a lot of *dépit*, irritation, 'our-toes-have-been-trodden-on', and possibly a helping of Church venom against the invention of the Devil in the shape of that Calvinist pastor and professor Wilson.

When I told Gasparri my ideas, 'which proceed from similar criticisms' to his, he retorted that at any rate such a reform of the League will have to wait a very long time, '*que le Vatican ne pouvait pas se lancer dans la lutte*', but that of course he accords my efforts his 'sympathy'. This was uttered without the slightest unction, indeed rather brusquely, and he obviously regards me as an idealist who wastes the time of cardinals and other men of a mundane, realistic turn of mind.

To be fair, it must be remembered that the Church fundamentally looks on neutral man as wicked. What I dislike, though, is the *ton canaille* which its political representatives flatter themselves is appropriate in dealing with the concept of the League of Nations. It is open to them to proclaim, 'the *Church* is the League of Nations' and to point their fingers at the detestable secular abortion. But this acidulous, coarse mockery without positive content is disreputable.

Saturday, 25 June 1921   *Rome*

At half past twelve a private audience with the Pope. There were just the two of us and so I had the chance briefly to ventilate the questions which interest me. In these circumstances an even sharper edge was given to his deliberate diversion from the subject of the League, evading it with the words, *'Ce n'est pas ici'* (meaning the Vatican) *'que nous pouvons traiter cette question.'* The main thing, he emphasized, is *'qu'il fallait mettre fin à la guerre'*. He asked me, perhaps out of politeness, whether and what I had written on the subject of the League and, at the end, accorded me his Apostolic blessing on behalf of my efforts.

Sunday, 26 June 1921   *Rome*

The links here between the Vatican and the extreme left are evidently numerous and fairly close. An Italian Socialist said to me that behind these two groupings stands the real nation (with divided attitudes but common material interests). That is my conclusion too.

Sunday, 24 July 1921   *Sorrento*

Decent hotel and room. Very crowded here. Saw Caruso, the tenor, with an enormously tall and stout American woman. He looks like Napoleon on St Helena. Always gloomy and preoccupied. Stocky, muscular Neapolitan type.

25 July–8 August 1921   *Sorrento*

Worked steadily. In the afternoon have usually gone bathing at the Capo di Sorrento. Poor Caruso died at Naples on 2 August. It has caused an overwhelming sensation here. He was the 'representative' of Naples, the adored folk-song singer, the incarnation of Neapolitan man. With his voice he took the skies of Naples around the world. The whole of Naples followed him to his grave with more than royal honours. The newspapers allege that he has left over two hundred million lire.

Sunday, 11 December 1921   *Paris*

Arrived early in Paris, which I left on 28 July 1914, the Tuesday before the war. Strange, how seven so terrible years can be completely wiped out in a moment of unreflecting thought. I felt as though I was returning to the old familiar scene after but a brief absence. Only, unless my first impression is wrong, people have become somewhat morose, less friendly.[3] Otherwise everything has remained astonishingly the same. The changes in Berlin are incomparably greater.

In the evening Marc Sangnier gave a big banquet as the conclusion to his congress. There were several hundred guests from twenty-one nations. I sat on Sangnier's right and followed him as speaker. We Germans were treated with the utmost politeness and friendliness, not cold-shouldered at all. My speech was repeatedly interrupted by downright frantic applause.

Monday, 12 December 1921   *Paris*

A soirée given by Mme Ménard-Dorian. Some fifty to sixty left-wing politicians and people of similar sort, mainly from the Ligue des Droits de l'Homme. Ferdinand Buisson, Senator d'Estournelles de Constant, the deputies Marc Sangnier and Moutet (Caillaux's[4] defence counsel), old Professor Aulard, General Sarrail, Henri Lichtenberger, Victor Basch, Grumbach, etc.

Matters proceeded rather along the lines of a collective interview or debate, with Buisson in the chair. D'Estournelles de Constant extended formal greeting to us (that is, the Austrian and German delegations consisting of Redlich, Tiedge, the student Meskau from Berlin, and myself) and then invited me to speak. I addressed the company for about ten minutes. Apparently to its satisfaction, for there were continual murmurs of '*très bien*', '*ah, c'est bien, ça*', and other tokens of approbation.

Redlich followed on behalf of Austria, and failed to make much impression, so I thought. He entered into too much detail and he went on too long.

The rest of the evening I spent under a meticulous cross-examination, mainly on the part of Aulard, Victor Basch and Grumbach. Aulard asked me about German adhesion to the League of Nations. I gave my usual answer: not *against* the wishes of France, but if France agrees, immediately.

My statements, especially my attitude on League of Nations affairs and my rejection of Lefèvre, Barthou, and people like that, met with approval.

Finally Grumbach made a highly charged and somewhat equivocal speech, partly for, partly against, but in the ultimate analysis more for than against Germany. I was allowed the last word. Afterwards they all bore down on me with congratulations.

Tuesday, 13 December 1921   Paris

Lunch at Marc Sangnier's. Very elegant apartment, a number of footmen, magnificent floral table decoration: ambassadorial style.

After lunch I had a fairly long talk with old Buisson (eighty), President of the Ligue des Droits de l'Homme. He displayed the most lively interest in what I told him about my lecture tour in Germany and the reception I was accorded by the working classes. Up to that point rather apathetic in a senile way, he became downright rejuvenated as he listened to me, his eyes flashed, and he kept on repeating, '*Mais, c'est très important, ce que vous dites là, mais il faudrait qu'on sache ça en France.*'

Wednesday, 14 December 1921   Paris

In the afternoon visited Mayer, whom I had not hitherto met. A big, stout manufacturer, of Catholic and southern German stamp, with polite but slightly provincial gestures. He conceded that feelings about Germany have never been so favourable here since the cessation of hostilities. But he looks on Marc Sangnier as a lone albatross and warned against any too optimistic assessments (wherein he is undoubtedly right). He defended Briand and maintained that Poincaré is neither as strong nor as important as he appears. Only Barthou is a highly dangerous personality whom it may prove necessary to weather. Mayer, without being outstanding, seems to have quite a well-trained judgement on internal affairs.

Afterwards I saw Hoech, purest pre-war Foreign Ministry specimen. Apparently got his posting here simply because of his well-lined pockets. Manufacturer's son, gold-plated (the generation *after* Mayer). Probably quite assiduous insofar as all sorts of pleasurable diversions don't impede him. Kühlmann's *maître de plaisirs* at Bucharest. He reminded me that in 1914, when he was attaché in London, he had conducted negotiations with Nijinsky[5] on my behalf. Unsuccessfully, come to that.

Thursday, 22 December 1921   Paris

In the afternoon visited Jean Cocteau. He was very friendly and emphasized the need to forge afresh the intellectual bonds between France and Germany.

Jean Cocteau: self-portrait

The task is easier to fulfil, he added, *'entre gens bien élevés'* than between those of Bohemian breed.

Friday, 23 December 1921   *Paris*

During the morning went again to Cocteau in order to meet Zimmer, responsible for the *Revue Rhénane* at Mainz. Zimmer makes no secret of the fact that he is subsidized by the Quai d'Orsay. I told him at once that I neither could nor would have anything to do with efforts, such as those of Maurice Barrès or even Dorten and Smuts, to promote the secession of the Rhineland. He denied any such intention on his own part. His publication aims purely at intellectual, not political, goals and *'servir de trait d'union'* at that level. Cocteau used the simile of *'deux trottoirs roulants qui marchent à des vitesses différentes'*. Only one can be used at a time. Political and intellectual matters must not be mixed. As long as it is a question of *intellectual exchanges*, I said, exclusive of all political objectives and allowing for equal treatment of German authors by way of translations, and so on, I am prepared to help him obtain a hearing among German authors and the public at large. He asked me for a contribution to his publication. I agreed rather vaguely.

Poncet had asked me for lunch in a private room (*Le Cabinet Lafontaine*) at Lapérouse with Colrat (Assistant State Secretary in the Ministry of the Interior) and Robert Pinaud (Comité des Forges). Colrat is a sort of French August Müller, blustering and reactionary (the 'heavy father' type) without any perceptible intelligence, but very ambitious and can probably, because he always talks big, not be ignored. Pinaud is much more experienced, intelligent, polite, and diplomatic, but just as reactionary. All three of them anti-progressive.

My conclusions are that Briand, Loucheur, and those in touch with the major industrial personalities agree on three points: (1) an understanding with Germany is necessary; (2) there is no sentimental objection to such an understanding; (3) they do feel that they cannot move towards the achievement of such an understanding until Germany has of its own accord (a) punctually fulfilled for a while its reparations obligations and (b) put an end to the lack of confidence caused by its political affairs (weakness of the republican parties and Government, strength of reactionary movements) and financial management (concealment of its true export figures, capital transfers, disorderly state finances, inadequate tax collection). They are evidently really afraid of what the future may otherwise hold for them, as politicians and industrial magnates, and for the country as a whole.

Later paid a brief visit to a Russian by the name of Bryantschaninov who has worked out a plan for a new League of Nations, is President of the 'Russian Association for the League of Nations', and wrote me a letter. A mystic, whose target is a world government manned by the sages of all nations. I was received by a Princess Gortchakov. He outlined to me his concept of an '*Internationale blanche, ni rouge, ni dorée*'. His notions seem at some points to touch on those of Keyserling, whom he mentioned.

1922

Sunday, 22 January 1922   *Rome*

At six o'clock this morning the Pope[1] died. He was not an outstanding
personality, but one excellently suited to his office; the exactly right cog in
the powerful machinery of the Church and the still more powerful one of
the world. Cold as ice, clever but with the requisite narrow-mindedness,
he was moderately high-spirited and even benevolent beneath the glacial
exterior of sophisticate and diplomat.

Monday, 23 January 1922   *Rome*

Papal lying in state at St Peter's. In front of the altar of a side-chapel the
body lay, at a slope and between candles, on a scaffolding some six feet high
and draped with purple. The head was strikingly fine and handsome, a
slight puffing of the features lending them an appearance of almost cherubic
innocence and smoothness. The effect midst the surrounding pomp was
impressively exalted. All the coarser and more disgraceful was the contrast
presented by the staring crowd which pushed past, utterly indifferent,
laughing and cracking jokes.

Saturday, 4 February 1922   *Rome*

The square of St Peter's. Forenoon. Sunshine. A large crowd awaits
announcement of the election of the new Pope. All eyes gaze tensely towards
the slender, elongated stove-pipe meandering laboriously up from the gable
of the Sistine Chapel. The miracle of papal designation by the Holy Ghost
is in process. We are a long way from *Parsifal*, Act Three. The dove of the
Holy Grail and the stove-pipe: reality and imagination.
    A race-meeting atmosphere predominates among the crowd. Newspaper
and postcard vendors move between Englishwomen who have brought camp-
stools, prolific families including infants, numerous priests, monks, and
nuns, and, drawn up around the church and the colonnade, soldiers in field
grey. There are also horse-cabs, super-cars, and taxis. On the roof of the
colonnade is congregated the Roman aristocracy and the Diplomatic Corps.
The spirit of *Parsifal* comes closer to that of the stove-pipe than the crowd
does.

Sunday, 5 February 1922   Rome

Again in St Peter's Square. Today the crowd is immense. At a quarter past eleven a woman, standing on the base of the corner pillar on the right of the church, begins to bless the crowd with wide-stretched, grotesque gestures. She also utters incomprehensible phrases, looking fixedly up at the sky with an ecstatic expression. The crowd laughs, cheers, and shouts. Is the woman serious or playing a joke? A female Antichrist? No one knows.

By a quarter to twelve the square is packed. If the crowd were to be swayed by any strength of emotion or even Christian love, it would be irresistible. But it only gazes towards the stove-pipe. Just a mass of specks. If it were to be seized by panic or aroused by an idea, what then?

Monday, 6 February 1922   Rome

Today the Pope was at last elected: Cardinal Ratti, now Pius XI. It rained. Consequently the crowd was smaller than yesterday, reaching only as far as the obelisk, and armed with umbrellas. Fifteen minutes before noon a wisp of smoke could indistinctly be seen rising from the stove-pipe, becoming thicker, then stopping altogether. '*È nero!*' '*È bianco! È bianco! È fatto il Papa! È fatto il Papa!*' Immediately there was a highly dangerous folding of umbrellas and a rush for the church doors. But they proved to have been suddenly closed and a file of soldiers was drawn up in front of them. As the pushing from behind continued, the crush amidst the re-opened umbrellas became almost intolerable. Excitement was at a peak. Everybody tried to keep an eye, between the spread umbrellas, on the loggia high up the façade of St Peter's from where the name of the elected Pontiff would be announced.

Almost three-quarters of an hour passed before there resounded abruptly cries of '*Ombrelli, ombrelli!*' and, in a breathless tension, umbrellas (several thousand umbrellas) were snapped to. The glass door of the loggia was opened, attendants stepped forward and laid over the parapet a large velvet carpet embroidered with armorial bearings. Then there could be caught sight of a big golden crucifix and above the edge of the parapet the head and gesticulating hands of a cardinal. Deathly silence. The cardinal proclaimed: His Eminence – he paused – the Most Venerable Archbishop of Milan, Cardinal Ratti, had been elected Pope and had adopted the name Pius XI. An immense jubilation broke out, hats and handkerchiefs were flourished, and shouts of *È viva!* re-echoed.

The cardinal and the *monsignori* made signs to the crowd to wait. There was still something to come. And after about ten minutes the big surprise occurred. For the first time since 1870 the Pope showed himself to the people of Rome assembled in the open square. Above the parapet of the loggia could be discerned a white arm moving in a gesture of blessing and rather full, not specially remarkable, scholar's features while at the same time there could be heard a deep, melodious, slightly unctuous voice very clearly pronouncing blessing upon the crowd. The latter, whenever the voice halted, answered with a resonant 'Amen'.

The Italian soldiery drawn up in front of St Peter's saluted. On the balcony of Bernini's colonnade the members of the *Guarda Nobile* showed themselves in their scarlet gala uniform and unfurled the papal standard. The moment, for all the martial trimmings not entirely appropriate to the Pope's words, was one of greatness produced by the gesture of a truly Supreme Pontiff or, perhaps, by the resumption of an illustrious tradition. A faint fragrance of the Gospel, a muted echo of the Christmas tidings, was wafted down.

And then there impinged on my mind the memory of a similarly unctuous deep voice, on a sombre wintry night, I had heard speaking from a high balcony in Berlin to a large crowd – that of Karl Liebknecht, in January 1919. Wholly invisible in the darkness, a voice and no more, he addressed the crowd on the Alexanderplatz. Who was the more genuine, more effective friend of peace? Liebknecht or today the Pope?

Funnily enough, at the very moment that Cardinal Bisleti was proclaiming the new Pope from the loggia, a troop of newspaper vendors forced itself among the crowd with special editions of *Messagero* announcing, in a sensational make-up and with a large picture of him, the election of Cardinal Tacci as Pope. The copies sold, for their curiosity value, like hot cakes.

Monday, 13 February 1922   *Rome*

The Pope's coronation. Although the invitation card said half past eight, I made my way to St Peter's at half past six and found it already three-quarters full. The crush, in consequence of the unending stream of fresh arrivals, became a peril to life and limb.

Towards half past nine the festive procession passed. The Pope, borne high over the heads of the assembly in the *sedia gestatoria*, looked like an apparition in white and gold. He bestowed his blessing constantly but abstractedly. His face, round, lined, pale-grey complexioned, was quite expressionless. The crowd, waving handkerchiefs and hats, made such an uproar that the sound of the silvery trumpet notes could only be heard as though coming through a bank of clouds.

The appearance of the Pope was picturesque and historically stately. The occasion as a whole, with the Swiss Guards, the chamberlains either in evening dress or Cinquecento costume, the priests and the cardinals in their ornate purple, was a queer mixture of late classical magnificence, medieval militarism, Renaissance etiquette, and pageant without room for a moment's true reverence or composure. The only feeling it inspired was of a very old, venerable, and splendid, but inwardly utterly dead, spectacle. A mass in a village church is spiritually a thousand times finer.

Saturday, 11 March 1922   *Brenner-Innsbruck*

The Customs examination at the Brenner Pass showed my suitcase to be missing. Rather than leave it to the hazards of two frontier crossings on its own, I made my way through slushy snow to the beastly inn mentioned by Goethe. It was full of noisy Italians, railway officials who drank more than was good for them. The upshot was a scuffle with the landlord, whom they knocked down with chairs, followed by a general outcry and arrival of the carabinieri. The landlord was picked up from the floor with blood pouring down his face. I asked him afterwards what the trouble had been. 'They're Italians and we're Germans. That's all. It happens every second or third day.' But the waitress maintained that this was the first time.

In the evening reached Innsbruck. The hotel guests (they seemed to be nothing but Americans and British) were superficially a smart lot, with the men in dinner-jackets and the women half-naked. After dinner there was dancing, shimmy and fox-trot. A 'winter sport' public, just as at Caux.

Monday, 20 March 1922   *Berlin*

At one o'clock to Rathenau[2] in the Ministry of Foreign Affairs. Our conversation began with a detailed catalogue of complaints on his part about the onerousness of his duties and the difficulties with which he has to contend. Nobody, in his view, can cope with this appointment for more than six months. It is a cranking up the Ministry's entire machinery, and that is superhuman labour. For eight years German foreign policy has lain fallow. Now it has to be reactivated, every day a fresh iron has to be put into the fire, a helping hand has to be given to every part of the Ministry. To enable him to do that, he should see everything. If he omits anything, then that sector slips out of his grasp. He cannot in fact see everything, and so he will perhaps have to divide things up in such a way as more or less to delegate certain sectors to department heads while he himself exercises active control over these minor fields only every few weeks. Even then the burden will remain almost insuperable.

On top of this come the affronts which he must constantly pass over in silence, the answers to the Entente communications, the visits he has to receive and make, the Cabinet meetings and the Reichstag sessions, and the paradox which requires that German foreign policy shall now not merely be sensible but accord with the popular mood. All that is an impossible strain to carry indefinitely. Worst of all, though, is his own countrymen's vindictive hostility. In addition to threatening letters he receives every day, there are police reports which cannot be ignored. As he said this, he drew a Browning from his pocket. His most cordial relations are with the British, followed by the French, Italians, Japanese, and so on; his worst, with the Germans.

We discussed my trip to Paris. He is of the opinion that the phrase '*désarmement morale*' presents at this stage the greatest possible danger to us, now that physical disarmament has been effectively implemented, because it can serve the French with an excuse for maintaining their military control.

Finally the talk turned to Genoa. I said that I propose to go there and that I am informing him of this because I do not want to act without his knowledge or against his wishes. He replied that he is very willing for me to go, but it should remain a private matter between us. I am to tell no one that he has encouraged the idea, else far too many others will seek his blessing also. I am going, I commented, because I believe I shall be able to make myself useful to him and our common objectives and interests. He agreed that my innumerable connections in France, Britain and Italy may render my presence valuable and, if occasion arises, he will be pleased to avail himself of my services. He is very glad that I am going.

My own impression is that he is not as gratified as all that. Perhaps he fears that I shall produce too pacifist an effect and thereby inconvenience the efforts of his own people. The military undoubtedly exercise some influence on his trains of thought. Before I left, he added that we *cannot* promise the French '*désarmement morale*' when our entire youth is moving in precisely the opposite direction towards the worst, most obdurately reactionary, outlook. Were we to offer the prospect of such a disarmament, then they would be justified in subsequently accusing us of dishonesty.

Dined with the Einsteins. A quiet, attractive apartment in Berlin West (Haberlandstrasse). Rather too much food in a grand style to which this really lovable, almost still childlike couple lent an air of naïvety. Guests included the immensely rich Koppel, the Mendelssohns, Warburg, Bernhard Dernburg (as shabbily dressed as ever), and so on. An emanation of goodness and simplicity on the part of host and hostess saved even such a typical Berlin dinner-party from being conventional and transfigured it with an almost patriarchal and fairy-tale quality.

I had not seen Einstein and his wife since their major excursion abroad. They admitted quite unaffectedly that their reception in the United States and Britain were veritable triumphs. Einstein gave a slightly ironic, sceptical twist to their description by claiming that he cannot make out why people are so interested in his theories. His wife told me how he kept on saying to her that he felt like a cheat, a confidence trickster who was failing to give them whatever they hoped for.

Albert Einstein (Strink)

He wanted to know precisely, and made me repeat several times, what message Painlevé gave me for him and what he said about his Paris trip. He is starting on this in the next few days and will stay there a week. He expects university circles here to take it amiss, but they are a terrible lot and he feels quite sick when he thinks of them. In Paris he hopes to be able to do something towards resumption of relations between German and French scholars. He brushed aside his differences with Painlevé as a detail, appearing to attach no importance to them. In autumn he intends to comply with invitations to visit China and Japan, giving lectures at Peking and Tokyo. He must see the Far East, he has confided to his wife, while the big drum is still being banged on his account; that much he insists on obtaining from the hullabaloo.

He and his wife kept me back when the other guests left. We sat in a corner and chatted. When I confessed to sensing the significance of his theories more than I can properly grasp them, Einstein smiled. They are really quite easy, he retorted, and he would explain them to me in a few words which would immediately render them intelligible. I must imagine a glass ball with a light at its summit resting on a table. Flat (two-dimensional) rings or 'beetles' move about the surface of the ball. So far a perfectly straightforward notion. The surface of the ball, regarded two-dimensionally, is a *limitless but finite* surface. Consequently the beetles move (two-dimensionally) over a limitless but finite surface. Now I must consider the *shadows* thrown by the beetles on the table, due to the light in the ball. The surface covered by these shadows on the table and its extension in all directions is also, like the surface of the ball, limitless but finite. That is, the number of conic shadows or conic sections caused by the theoretically extended table never exceeds the number of beetles on the ball; and, since this number is finite, so the number of shadows is necessarily finite. Here we have the concept of limitless but finite *surface*.

Now I must substitute three-dimensional concentric glass balls for the two-dimensional beetle shadows. By going through the same imaginative process as before, I shall attain the image of limitless yet finite space (a three-dimensional quality). But, he added, the significance of his theory lies by no means in these thought processes and concepts. That is derived from the *connection between matter, space, and time,* proving that none of these exists by itself, but that each is always conditioned by the other two.

It is the inextricable connection between matter, space, and time that is new in the theory of relativity. What he does not understand is why people have become so excited about it. When Copernicus dethroned the earth from its position as the focal point of creation, the excitement was understandable because a revolution in all man's ideas really did occur. But what change does his own theory produce in humanity's view of things? It is a theory which harmonizes with every reasonable outlook or philosophy and does not interfere with anybody being an idealist or materialist, pragmatist or whatever else he likes.

Saturday, 25 March 1922   *Berlin*

Stresemann to lunch. He stayed till four, talking about all sorts of things. For instance, shortly before Briand's downfall Poincaré sent out feelers to him and Stinnes through Sir Thomas Barclay. Indeed matters got as far as arranging a meeting between Stresemann, Stinnes, and two other German businessmen on the one hand and Poincaré and three Frenchmen on the other when Briand's defeat balked the encounter.

He passed over to conditions in Bavaria. Although he has advised Prince Rupprecht (Wittelsbach) in the most urgent terms against taking any action, and every week someone travels down to exhort him on similar lines, there is no holding the Prince any longer. Three alternative plans have been prepared. Either a *coup d'état* (proclaiming him King), or a plebiscite throughout Bavaria (with the monarchists hoping to squeeze through an election to the throne), or (what would be the shrewdest and most dangerous move) the installation of a President, who will of course be Rupprecht. In that eventuality, Stresemann thinks, northern Bavaria (Franconia, Nürnberg) will secede from southern Bavaria. So probably will Augsburg; Count Fugger says that neither he nor Augsburg will join in. The monarchists for their part have rosy ideas about incorporating Tyrol and Styria. They are moreover, including Rupprecht, rabidly anti-French. Stresemann does not seem to anticipate a spread of the monarchist movement to northern Germany. He dismisses the notion of a restoration in these parts within any foreseeable time.

Tuesday, 28 March 1922   *Berlin*

In the evening went to a reactionary Russian cabaret on the Kurfürstendamm. Extravagantly modern décor and production: a lamentation for Old Russia's downfall sublimated in a cabaret-like presentation and set over against an invincible faith in Russia's future. The charm and easy touch transform all the nationalist streaks into humanly understandable factors.

Into the middle of the performance burst the shocking news of the murder of Milzalov and Vladimir Nabokov during the course of a lecture given by the former at the Philharmonie. The rumour swept the best part of the audience, almost exclusively Russian, out of the cabaret like a tidal wave.

After a few moments we were practically alone in what had been an auditorium full to overflowing. Only three elegant young Russians (there is a grand duke in the chorus) sat on at the table next to us. When I asked one of them how much truth there was in the report, he replied, 'Well, yes, Milzalov has been assassinated. Pity that the scamp was not done away with sooner. A shame about Nabokov. But Milzalov, the traitor who with Kerensky and others betrayed the Tsar, ought to have been knocked on the head sooner. Infamous, that fifteen thousand Russian officers should have let themselves be slaughtered by the Revolution without raising a hand in self-defence! Why didn't they act like the Germans, who killed Rosa Luxemburg in such a way that not a smell of her had remained?' All this was uttered so complacently as to suggest that he would be quite incapable of murder himself. In his case the shocking news merely mixed with the music of the cabaret and his personal rancour to become a poisonous brew he would not mind seeing others drink. Fine motivations!

Wednesday, 5 April 1922   *Berlin*

Lunched at d'Abernon's. Long private talk with him. In his opinion the German Government is wholly and completely to blame for the inflation on account of the use it had made of the Mint's printing press. On the day that this stops operating, the mark will be stabilized. Exports and imports have only very little bearing on the situation. The major pressure towards a downward trend derives solely from the printing press. Admittedly Germany's economic position is today worse than a year ago and the country will still experience a severe crisis even when the mark is stabilized. Politically, though, Germany's situation is far more favourable than it was twelve months back. That is what we should watch.

He does not seem to expect much from Genoa, and he nearly lost his temper when I referred to Boulogne and Lloyd George's knuckling under.[3] That is the gossip *here*, he retorted, but it is totally mistaken and unjust to accuse Britain of constantly yielding. All the same, it upset his equanimity sufficiently for him to become quite red in the face. My shaft manifestly went home. The soundest prospect for Genoa, he continued, lies in Chicherin's proposal for Red Army disarmament. That makes discussion of the entire disarmament question inevitable, whether the French like it or not.

A pretty farcical situation, when the British Ambassador looks on a gesture from the Bolsheviks as a trump card, and not very convincing evidence of Lloyd George's freedom of action or courage. Now I know why my reference to Boulogne irritated him so much.

Returning to Germany's economic situation, he dwelt on the new sort of middle class he now always sees among the theatre audiences. Neither profiteers nor preponderantly Jewish, but clearly 'respectable' people, large numbers of whom can afford as much as 150 marks for an orchestra stall. Where do these people come from? That is the question he constantly reiterates to himself and finds it an interesting sociological problem.

Thursday, 6 April 1922   *Berlin*

Lunched with Robert T. Dell and Garrison Villard (publisher of the New York *Nation*) at the Adlon. Villard said that opinion in America is veering sharply against France, but the effects of the infernal war propaganda have still not worn off. We have no idea here, Villard emphasized, of the intensity and subtlety of this propaganda, which he repeatedly termed 'diabolic'. (I have recently heard this from someone else too.) Consequently opinion over there still remains strongly anti-German.

What, I asked, would happen if the French occupied the Ruhr? Opinion against France would be deeply exacerbated, Villard replied, but not so deeply as to lead to American action. His explanation for, and in some degree vindication of, the anti-German war propaganda was that when Wilson declared war, the majority of Americans were against it and a popular vote would have shown as many as seventy per cent opposed to hostilities. The Government consequently had no choice but to set on foot a wild anti-German propaganda campaign and justify retrospectively its belligerent course.

Monday, 10 April 1922   *Genoa*

Early this morning saw Prittwitz and Lieutenant-Colonel Simon who, one after another, asked me to be instrumental in arranging a meeting between Rathenau and Seydoux. Went straight over to the Savoy, where the French are staying, and spoke to Hesnard, Poncet, and Philippe Milliet. Put out feelers with Hesnard on a Rathenau–Seydoux meeting. He will give me an answer tomorrow or the day after. Milliet wanted an interview with Rathenau *aussitôt que possible*. Rathenau has treated him coolly in Berlin and he feels resentful about it. Told Simon the replies I had from the French and what their wishes are. So far the Entente organization is working rottenly.

Afterwards I talked to Neurath and Maltzan. Lunched with Kreuter (Wirth's[4] 'right-hand man') and Georg Bernhard. With the latter to the Conference opening in the Palazzo San Giorgio. The area was impressively cordoned off; military pickets, mounted patrols. Near the Palace white-gloved, red-cockaded Royal Guards lined the route to the old banker's mansion, which is decked out with potted plants and red carpets in proper palatial style. Flags on all the houses round about the harbour and gaping crowds at all the windows. Together with the sight of the masts and funnels of the ships in the port, it forms an appropriate background for the first attempt at practical negotiations with the Communists.

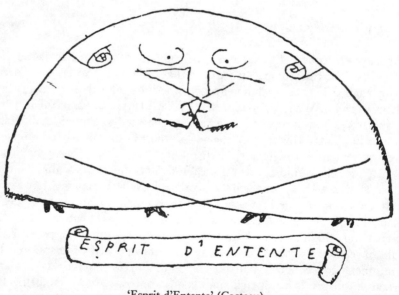

'Esprit d'Entente' (Cocteau)

The main sessions of the Conference are taking place in an ornate, rather stiff Renaissance apartment whose recesses are filled with large, conventional statues: forgotten celebrities, like figures on tombstones. The living celebrities sit at the double horseshoe-shaped table beneath a chandelier burning in broad daylight in order to brighten the somewhat crypt-like gloom of the apartment. All around them is a subdued throng of diplomats, experts, Genoese worthies. A cardinal has a seat close behind Chicherin. A number of sailors act as attendants.

The opening speeches (by Facta, Lloyd George, Wirth, and Barthou, although I happened not to hear the last, being out of the room) were read out and copies passed round simultaneously. They make a pretty tame impression, with Wirth's as the tamest of the lot. His text is a thin brew (sterilized and lacking sting) of what I said a couple of years ago in *Wiedergutmachung und Arbeiterschaft* (Reparation and the Working Class). Wirth receives embarrassingly resounding applause; his appearance here is the minor, anticipated sensation. But up to this point the meeting has been like that of some academic body or the proceedings at a scientists' annual reunion.

The scene does not come alive until Chicherin rises to his feet. Then there is a general stir of expectation. This is to be the big moment. All the same, the first impression is one of disappointment. He reads his speech in French, but his pronunciation is so exotic that at first I think he is speaking Russian. Gradually single words and later whole sentences become intelligible. He announces Russian readiness to collaborate in reconstruction; in other words, to allow capitalist and Communist economic structures to exist side by side and compete with each other. He expresses the hope that Genoa may prove to be only the first of a series of European economic conferences and that these will be the forerunners of a congress in which all the nations of the world, not merely those of Europe, will participate to undertake global rehabilitation. Finally he proclaims that Russia is prepared to undertake disarmament, provided other countries do the same. (Here is the *coup de théâtre* predicted to me last Wednesday by d'Abernon, on which he founded his hopes for this conference.)

Chicherin makes his remarks about disarmament with specially formal emphasis and seems to be trying to speak with particular clarity. When he has finished in French, without receiving any applause because apparently hardly anybody realizes he has come to the end, he himself reads, still more unintelligibly, the English translation. He sits down to a sprinkling of plaudits.

Barthou barely waits for Chicherin to be back in his seat before he leaps up and enters an impassioned plea of protest which would probably have been effective with a French audience but here sounds merely provocative and out of place. He whips himself into an ever greater state of excitement and, with hollow-sounding categorical affirmations and rhetorical flourishes, rejects discussion of the disarmament question at Genoa in his own name, that of his delegation, and that of France. This peroration sounds like a piece of senile bickering. A few of the listeners clap, but the majority sits in icy silence.

Chicherin replies very skilfully and does not disdain the use of malice. It was Lloyd George, he recalls, who said that Genoa should merely be the first of a series of conferences. He (Chicherin) merely wished to quote him. True, disarmament is not on the agenda as agreed at Cannes. But Monsieur Poincaré himself described this agenda as muddled and incomplete. Many other problems which will have to be ventilated at Genoa, such as rates of exchange, were not listed at Cannes. The Russian Government has moreover been especially impelled to put forward its disarmament proposal by Monsieur Briand's speech at Washington wherein he accused the Russian Red Army of being one of the principal impediments to French disarmament. That is why the Russian Government hoped that it would render France and the world a service if it did away with this impediment by giving a binding declaration here at Genoa. But the Russian delegation will of course abide by the decision of the Conference if the latter desires to exclude discussion of disarmament. His listeners smile. In this battle of wits Chicherin has emerged as victor over Barthou.

David Lloyd George

Now it is Lloyd George's turn. He makes the speech which is the star attraction of this spectacle. Although he certainly encouraged the Russians to put forward their disarmament proposal (see d'Abernon's forecast), he quietly drops them after they have rendered him the service of exasperating Barthou and inciting France to display itself to the world as the new Prussia. Genially and jokingly he pours oil on the troubled waters, scouts the notion of a universal congress whose end, if such were to be summoned, an old man like him would not live to see, and then emphasizes that this Conference will prove a failure if it does not lead to disarmament. Nontheless the prerequisite to any general disarmament is decontamination of the international atmosphere, the restoration of confidence between nations, and economic agreement. Precisely this is the purpose of the present Conference. The League of Nations is moreover dealing with the disarmament problem and he is convinced that it is not M. Barthou's intent to place any obstacles in its way. He therefore appeals to M. Chicherin to leave for the present the disarmament problem on one side so as not to wreck the already heavily laden vessel of this Conference. If the ship sinks, M. Chicherin may be among the drowned. But if the ship reaches harbour safely, it is to be hoped that, after a successfully completed voyage, it will put out to sea again. Having learned what sort of a passenger M. Chicherin is, it will be a pleasure to take him along again and perhaps even allow him to steer the vessel.

So here we had, as a matter of form, a disposal of the Russians (all the more marked for its ironic delivery) and, as a matter of fact, a not easily definable attack on the French. The effect produced by this very momentous political performance, executed in a light conversational tone, was outstanding. The whole conference, including onlookers and journalists, applauded wildly for minutes on end. Lloyd George had once more evinced his magical touch and bewitched everyone.

The applause has barely subsided when Chicherin makes a move to speak again. Facta asks him however to desist because this will launch a debate which cannot be concluded here and serves no purpose. Barthou springs to his feet, furious. There are just a few words he wants to say. He must declare. . . . Facta, scarlet in the face, rises and stops him short. What he, as chairman of the Conference, has laid down applies to all, to one party as much as to another. He must request M. Barthou, like M. Chicherin, to desist. But Barthou does not sit down, goes on talking, and demands, in a tone of utmost irritability, to know whether all the Conference participants recognize the agreements reached at Cannes or not, for otherwise the French delegation must draw its own conclusions.

This time the very meagre attempts at clapping are smothered in discreet hissing. Barthou's débâcle and the awkward situation into which France has been pushed by Chicherin's thrust is all too palpable. Facta drily comments that the answer to Barthou's question was given at the beginning of the Conference when he (Facta) read out the conditions laid down at Cannes and none of the participants objected. The subject is thereby closed.

The enduring impressions of this initial session are of Barthou's provincial clumsiness, Chicherin's propagandistic craftiness, Lloyd George's superiority in sophisticated diplomacy and debating technique, and the unworldly donnishness of the German delegation. This opening session of the Genoa Conference has furnished one of the greatest scenes in political comedy in the manner of Aristophanes or some even more superlative writer.

We have watched two small-town actors, Barthou and Wirth, and two superb players, Lloyd George and Chicherin, with the former doubling as the secret producer of the whole affair. The opening performance has alone been worth the fare. To have been able to share in the feelings of the great producer, Lloyd George, would have been beyond price. Throughout Barthou's second and third speeches (his own achievement) he sat with his face resting between his hands. Inwardly he must have been hugging himself with satisfaction.

Tuesday, 11 April 1922   *Genoa*

This morning Rathenau disagreed with me that the Russians brought forward the disarmament problem with the cognizance of the British. Sir Robert Horne asked him earlier whether he knew what the Russians were going to do. From this Rathenau concluded that the British were not aware of Russian intentions. In the afternoon Neurath told me that he heard in Rome on Friday that the Russians proposed to bring forward the disarmament problem with the cognizance of the British.

Wednesday, 12 April 1922   *Genoa–Nervi*

The proposal of the British experts for Russian financial rehabilitation has caused a major sensation. Our side (Maltzan) regards it as an attempt to reduce Russia to the status of the Porte and as unacceptable for the Russians. Chicherin yesterday requested two days' time for reflection; tomorrow he will seek another respite. What attitude we shall adopt is as yet uncertain. Hilferding tells me that he, Bernhard, Maltzan, and 'every decent member' of our political delegation want us to say that we cannot support the British stipulations because they are morally inadmissible and incompatible with the Russian people's right to self-determination and sovereignty. Rathenau, on the other hand, is afraid that the upshot of that would be our exclusion from the reconstruction consortium and he wants to barter our agreement for economic concessions from the Entente. Hilferding and Bernhard are livid about Rathenau and accuse him of a tremendous vanity which finds it intolerable that Stinnes should not take him at his own valuation. According to them, he thinks of nothing all day except what the People's Party is going to say. Here at Genoa he is the big stumbling-block to Germany adopting any European and morally effective attitude.

In the evening dined in Genoa with Ludwig Bauer (of the Basle *National Zeitung*), the Terwins, and Emil Ludwig.[5] The latter made an unpleasing impression on me. Extremely affected, he always moves on tiptoe so as to seem taller and is never for a moment relaxed or natural. A typical scribbler, bowed down by envy and the consciousness of his own lack of talent. Later we were joined by Hilferding, Georg Bernhard, and Kreuter (Wirth's right-hand man). Returned with them to Nervi.

What appears to me to be a crucial point for the future, amounting to a genuinely far-reaching change in the European situation, is the fact that Germany and Russia have been allotted places on equal terms with the five Entente countries in the Conference committees. All the other countries together have been allowed no more than four states (different ones in different committees) to represent their interests. A new Areopagus with a membership of seven, while still lacking the essential American representation, has been constituted to supersede the previous five-member Entente Areopagus and *de facto* Supreme Council. By that token alone the Conference has already borne very important fruit, all the more so for this gain having been won in the face of rabid French opposition but with the acquiescence of all the neutrals and even the Little Entente (including Poland!). Picard's desperate onslaught in the Finance Committee yesterday against this move (he was so excited that, thanks to his gesticulations, he and his false cuffs parted company!) has only confirmed the position the more strikingly and irrevocably.

Maundy Thursday, 13 April 1922   *Genoa*

Ate with Rathenau and Wirth. Also present State Secretary Hemmer and an economic expert. Wirth, whom I met for the first time, disappointed me deeply. Typical Boche in appearance. Fair, fat, apoplectic complexion, soft mass of meat without inner firmness. Moody, over-familiar, a drinker. Yes, son of an innkeeper[6] and obviously a soaker. The fumes of wine and self-admiration seem to have convinced him of his Olympian qualities. Rathenau mothers him like an old chamberlain does a Serene Highness and was very worried whether he may not have imbibed more at the meal than is good for him. I was reminded of *Schluck und Jau*.[7] At any rate, my first impression is of a very low-grade personality, both blurred and shallow in his ideas, though this does not exclude flashes of commonsense. But it will not be possible to uphold his balloon-like greatness for long and it is time to look around for a replacement against the day when he is deflated, which cannot be far ahead. Only now do I understand why Rheinbaben said that Wirth's policy admits of argument but he himself is 'impossible', and why the Foreign Ministry would not let him draft his own speech for the Conference. To sum up: a doorman as Chancellor.

Hilferding, who is acting as go-between with the Russians,[8] was in Rapallo again today and has explained the situation to me. The Russians (on our advice, as Hilferding emphasized) will state that they are prepared to accept the British memorandum as a basis for negotiations, but they must reject every infringement of Russian sovereignty, in particular the proposed consular jurisdiction. This also applies to actual *payment* of debts or interest cost, since they are utterly incapable of discharging even the interest on their debts. The assumption of an obligation to pay would obstruct every prospect of obtaining credits and therefore of reconstruction. That would be far more damaging, not merely for Russia but the whole of Europe, and especially Britain and America, than non-payment on the interest, which in essence concerns only a number of French investors. They will be prepared if necessary, to recognize their debts *pro forma*, but they demand either remission or time to pay (as would be granted to any over extended undertaking) without, of course, institution of a *dette publique* administration since there is nothing to administer.

During today's committee session Hilferding told Rathenau that his ideas are 'brilliant and alluring, but . . .'. Rathenau flashed back that he has suffered this reproach for thirty years, 'but I have built up my career on it'. Repeating the details of the squabble, Hilferding said that he wanted to ask whether Rathenau meant his career with AEG or as German Foreign Minister.

Saturday, 15 April 1922   *Genoa*

The lie of the land is as follows: the main issue is and remains Franco–German relations, which is in turn dominated by the reparations question. So the Conference, including the Russian business, amounts to no more than a secondary relief measure doomed to failure unless a satisfactory solution to the reparations question is reached simultaneously and hand in hand with it. The subject cannot be discussed inside the Conference because (formally) it is a matter between the Entente and Germany only. But it can and must, be discussed outside and parallel to the Conference proceedings. Their success depends on the success of these unofficial reparations discussions.

The Wirth puzzle: In the financial analysis all my objections to him merge in the single one that he utterly lacks sensitivity. That is a personal failing; it has nothing to do with ancestry or social status. Compare Wirth with Lincoln, for example. 'He's a *cad*,' the British would say. And he has learned nothing on the way up (no 'breeding'). The result is that his innate crudeness lies naked to the eye. He is, in the deeper sense of the word, 'vulgar'.

Easter Monday, 17 April 1922   *Genoa*

Just after four o'clock called on Rathenau to congratulate him on the conclusion of the treaty with the Russians, which had just become known. He seemed to be a little worried about the effect it might have on the Conference and the Entente. Had I heard yet, he asked nervously, how the news has been received? There is no doubt but that the treaty comes at a very inopportune moment for the Entente, bursting into the middle of their own negotiations with the Russians. It faces them with the alternative of either reaching an agreement with the Russians as well or leaving us a free hand in Russia. Their position has been substantially weakened, that of the Russians much strengthened.

In the evening I learned of the very considerable excitement that this German–Russian treaty, signed quite unexpectedly yesterday at Rapallo between Rathenau and Chicherin, has caused among the delegations and journalists attending the Conference. The terms include a settlement of war debt accounts (equivalent to abrogation of Article 216 of the Versailles Treaty), most-favoured-nation treatment, and restoration of diplomatic relations. The treaty was actually drafted when the Russians passed through Berlin on their way here. For all Maltzan's promptings, Rathenau was not however prepared to sign it. He only did so yesterday because he was afraid of otherwise falling perhaps between two stools if the Russians came to an agreement with the Entente. For the past two days the latter, without bringing in the Germans, had been at work on them in Lloyd George's villa. This played into Maltzan's hands. The upshot was that Rathenau decided yesterday morning to go to Rapallo ('Sunday outing') and sign.

Met Dr Zifferer, of the Austrian delegation, who described the uncontrollable anger of the French and Lloyd George, raging about German disloyalty. This evening Lloyd George, in a light grey suit, appeared to everyone's surprise at Albert Thomas's dinner for trade unionists at the Hôtel de Gênes and bitterly reproached State Secretary Hirsch for what has happened. Bernhard, who was with me, maintained that this was sheer play-acting on Lloyd George's part because he had known, step by step, of our negotiations with the Russians. True, he was not informed in advance of yesterday's decision to sign, but Rathenau made up his mind to do so on the spur of the moment.

Zifferer thought the Entente would either declare the treaty null and void as not being in conformity with the Treaty of Versailles, or break up the Conference, or demand that we revoke our signature. Poincaré's position would be impossible if the treaty was allowed to stand. Bernhard said the French are behaving as though they mean to leave; trunks are being packed. The French communiqué, which Zifferer showed us, is however comparatively moderate in tone and has even, in the interest of moderation, undergone correction. (He showed us the revised version, pointing out the alterations.) The British one is much fiercer.

The essential point, as far as we were concerned, was that we could not wait any longer without risking that the Entente, without taking the slightest notice of us and *without consultation* (exemplified by the negotiations at the

Villa de Albertis), might conclude an agreement with the Russians. And that the Russians demanded that we should sign *now*. (Naturally, since this treaty provides them with a trump in their Villa de Albertis negotiations.) All the same, it would have been better if the treaty had already been signed at Berlin (thereby avoiding an appearance of bad faith).

Tomorrow should prove the most exciting day of the Conference.

Tuesday, 18 April 1922   *Genoa*

All today's committee sessions have been cancelled. The Entente is conferring on what action to take. My impression is that they would like to find an easy way out, but cannot discover one at the moment. The German–Russian treaty has put a totally different complexion on the Russian problem.

Dined with Ludwig Bauer. He was very much against the 'blunder' we have made. In his eyes it destroys the spirit of mutual confidence which is more essential than anything else. To my mind, the way we handled the matter was undoubtedly faulty. If we are going to quote the Villa de Albertis negotiations in our own support, we should at any rate have *previously protested* against them.

In the evening arrival of a Note from the Political Subcommittee to the German Delegation, stating that Germany is excluded from attendance when Russian affairs are under discussion. It remains to be seen whether Germany will hereupon withdraw from the Conference. Good sense dictates that we should not. We shall have to swallow this slight, just like the Entente our treaty. Neither action is particularly dignified, and certainly not conducive to the restoration of mutual confidence.

To me the vital question is whether the danger existed of the Entente concluding a treaty with the Russians behind our backs or taking their negotiations so far as virtually to have faced us with an accomplished fact. Or did this danger *not* exist? If the danger did exist, in either form, then Rathenau's proceeding was justified. If it did not, it was unjustified. This brings up the question *what* it was that Giannini[9] said and how far it was admissible for Rathenau to rely on *him alone* without obtaining more information or first making a protest.

Meanwhile the capitalist Press, including the Italians, is roaring its head off about Germany's deceitfulness and unreliability. The only exception is *Avanti*. It has come out in our favour with a highly approving leading article which Maltzan took great pleasure in showing me. What we are experiencing is a revival of war-time propaganda.

Wednesday, 19 April 1922   *Genoa*

The uncertainty and excitement continues. Last night's banquet by the

Italians for the foreign delegations is said to have taken place in a very stiff atmosphere.

Prittwitz has confirmed to me that Rathenau tried three times to see Lloyd George during the days preceding his signature, but was rebuffed. This strengthened his suspicion that the Entente was planning to confront us with a *fait accompli*. The tragedy is that Lloyd George asked Rathenau to come and see him when he had already left for Rapallo. Maltzan, he adds, maintains that he tried to telephone the British before the departure for Rapallo, but could get no connection.

Sacchi (*Corriere della Serra*) asked me to lunch. He has calmed down considerably since yesterday and now anticipates that matters will mend.

Wirth and Rathenau spent two hours today with Lloyd George. He spoke very plainly and demanded annulment of the Russo–German treaty. The discussion got nowhere. Our delegation is still debating the matter. A compromise is almost certain. But Maltzan is reported as saying that we shall leave.

At this stage my impression is that the two men principally responsible for and the originators of the treaty, Maltzan and Hilferding, perpetrated a tactical error, though for different reasons. Both of them had their eyes glued to the idea and paid no attention to the manner of its achievement. Maltzan wanted to see it consummated, under any circumstances, out of political fanaticism and possibly ambition. Hilferding looked at it from a purely theoretical angle, irrespective of circumstances, and on that score lost sight of reality and timing. Maltzan was on this occasion (according to Prittwitz's formulation) a monomaniac and Hilferding too donnish. Rathenau's perspective was that of the easily depressed Jew (nervous type). Wirth wanted to 'do something' and 'show them for once', and had an eye on domestic politics. Lloyd George, on the other hand, felt himself to be once again 'boss' of the Supreme Council and, as such, succumbed to blandishments of Barthou and Poincaré, who wanted the negotiations to take place *without Germany*. (This is Raumer's account.) Between them, these half dozen individuals have dropped the precious and painfully restored vase of European mutual confidence and smashed it again. The Russians, for their part, have stoked the fires on both sides and acted as *agents provocateurs*.

The moral of the tale is that a new Europe cannot be created by sticking to old methods and habits (new wine in old bottles), all the more so if their employment is botched and clumsy in the highest degree. They cannot be applied any longer. The art is lost and cannot be revived, even if we had need of it.

Thursday, 20 April 1922   *Genoa*

Another very critical day.

Early in the morning I told Rathenau, at Hilferding's and Raumer's request, my interpretation of the connection between Barthou's representations to

Lloyd George and our exclusion from the Political Subcommittee. They also want it to be published in the Italian Press, in the form of an interview with me. They seem to anticipate some advantage from such a step.

Hilferding gave me a situation report. Wirth and Rathenau spent two hours yesterday with Lloyd George. He gave them the choice between annulling the treaty or renouncing participation in the discussion with Russia in the Subcommittee. A Cabinet council, continuing into the early hours, considered the matter last night. The Delegation appears to have split into two parties. The one, the Ministry of Foreign Affairs in the persons of Maltzan and Simson, is for defiance and discounts the Allied threats as bluff. The other, consisting of Hermes and Schmidt, is looking for a way out. Hilferding thinks our answer will amount to a declaration that we are ready to allow our treaty to be incorporated as part of an overall European treaty with Russia and that it should be regarded simply as a preliminary to, and pattern for, such a treaty. We cannot rescind our signature, nor would the Russians agree to such a step. Chicherin, who ate with Wirth and Rathenau yesterday, made it perfectly clear that he will in no circumstances accede to a rescission. Visconti Venosta visited Rathenau yesterday and hinted that the Italians are very much afraid lest we pack our bags and go, thus breaking up the Conference. All this according to Hilferding.

Just by the Eden Hotel I met Hesnard. He was in a very pessimistic frame of mind, insisting that the Conference will fall apart unless we rescind the treaty promptly and definitely. The French are in no position to control their Press and public opinion. From what he knows of Barthou's plans, refusal on our part to rescind the treaty will mean the end of the Conference.

Wirth's Press chief, Ludwig Stein, and myself had arranged a luncheon for foreign journalists. There were about forty-five people present. At the last moment Hesnard, Poncet, Massigli, and those journalists who are also members of the French Delegation cancelled their acceptance. Barthou is said to have vetoed their presence.

The *Matin* correspondent was very sensible. Lloyd George, he admitted, made a gross error in exclusively conducting negotiations at the Villa de Albertis. He ascribed it to a residue of the *esprit de guerre*. McClure, the British Press chief, who sat on the other side of me, announced that Lloyd George wanted to see all journalists at four o'clock in the Palazzo San Giorgio. The Italians thought this a bad sign. A depressed atmosphere, because we were all agreed that the Conference's failure would be most unfortunate.

I went over to the Palazzo San Giorgio at half past three. The Press conference was held in the same big apartment where the Conference was opened. Lloyd George arrived shortly before four. He sat down in the chairman's place at the foot of an imposing statue of some doge or other, with the Italian Prime Minister and Foreign Minister near him, and rose almost immediately. He spoke fairly briefly and then asked for questions. The tension, when he began, was enormous. The fate of the Conference lay palpably in his hands.

When he stated that in his view the incident caused by the Russo–German treaty is closed, the Germans having consented to suspend their participation in the Political Subcommittee, in so far as it deals with Russian affairs, the relief was profound. It means that he has dropped his demand for rescission of the treaty and (although we have not as yet delivered our reply Note) it ensures escape from the impossible situation. He did not forbear from repeating several times that we behaved disloyally, but he emphasized just as strongly and repeated just as often that our special agreement was *not* intended to torpedo the Conference. He even went so far as to say that perhaps the incident may eventually contribute in bringing the Conference to an auspicious end. His final words were another affirmation of his confidence in the Conference's success.

The good humour and grace with which he said all this worked once more like the spell exercised by a great actor, despite one's awareness of the fact that his words and display of feeling were for the most part put on. He is quite simply of totally different and incomparably greater calibre than any other Conference figure. Satisfaction at having rounded this dangerous corner is general, especially among the Germans – Bernhard, Hilferding, Kreuter, and so on – who came over from the apartment in the Palazzo where they had been in session with the Finance Committee.

Later in the afternoon Hilferding showed me the draft of our reply Note, which he has revised and to which Rathenau is giving the final shape tonight.

The first part, defending our conduct, struck me as thin and not very convincing. The second part, agreeing to our absence from the Subcommittee in so far as Russian affairs are discussed and expressing the hope that our treaty may become part of an overall European piece of treaty-making, corresponds to the attitude I have recommended from the start. Its wording is dignified and conciliatory. In this way we have probably safeguarded our material interests and minimized the moral damage sustained by ourselves and by a truly European outlook.

Dined with Georg Bernhard, Hilferding and Raumer. We were all very relieved at the outcome of the conflict. Bernhard treated us to a bottle of muscat. Afterwards he told me what transpired at the meeting about our reply Note. Wirth was 'splendid', dignified and resolute; Rathenau, 'extremely good'.

Saturday, 22 April 1922   *Genoa*

The Russians have today presented a very conciliatory reply Note in which they promise compensation for losses caused by socialization and recognize under certain conditions the pre-war debts. They attended, with other delegates, the luncheon given by the King!

Hesnard exemplified to me how upset the French are by saying that even Albert Thomas has been infected by their state of mind. He has inveighed against Rathenau in the most passionate way. Hesnard confirmed my guess that Poncet is deliberately keeping away from us.

These *Bloc National* Frenchmen are really of too idiotic, troglodytic an outlook. They deserve nothing better than that their policy should bring about their own destruction. And that applies still more strongly to such sympathizers as Poncet. On account of their cowardice, which is even worse than the narrow-mindedness of the others.

Monday, 24 April 1922   *Genoa*

Lunched with Dell, Steffens, and Hamilton of the *Daily Chronicle*. The last of these is very much of a Bohemian, linen off-white, ravaged looks. Seeing that he acts here for Lloyd George's unofficial paper, he should know what the master wants. Surprisingly, he defined Lloyd George's aim as using this Conference primarily as a means to disengage Britain from the alliance with France. He wants to isolate France here morally and then throw her overboard. France's isolation at Washington had strongly appealed to his imagination and 'he wanted to repeat the performance in Genoa.' France was to be lured into displaying a cloven hoof among a company of angels, but now we and Russia had spoiled his design by not behaving immaculately either. The plan to dissolve the tie with France ceremonially, 'to slow music', is much endangered thereby and may prove impossible.

Dined with Dell and the Communist Rappoport. A real personality; coarse, Bohemian, and repulsively ugly, but exuding vitality, and full of character, energy, and wit. A French-naturalized Lithuanian Jew, he conspired at Vilna with Pilsudski and Lenin's brother against Alexander III. As a result Lenin's brother was hanged, Pilsudski exiled to Siberia, and Rappoport left untouched. He closed the tale with the amusingly cynical comment, '*Moi j'ai fait mon devoir; mais la police n'a pas fait le sien*', which is why he is still alive. In his rabble-rousing speeches he is in the habit of saying about nationalists, '*Ils aiment les peuples comme les beefsteaks: saignants.*'

On my way back I ran into Joffe. He introduced me to Chicherin, and then Krassin, who in turn introduced me to Litvinov. Krassin and Litvinov doubted whether they would reach an agreement with the Entente. There have been considerable difficulties in the Committee today. Chicherin speaks German without the slightest accent, looks like a German professor, and might well be a Berlin headmaster.

Zifferer, who joined us, says that Poincaré's speech at Bar le Duc was 'terrible'. He has given notice of his determination to adopt military measures against Germany, with or without the Allies, if Germany does not fulfil its obligations. If his speech was as Zifferer reports, the situation will undoubtedly once again be aggravated. It will be interesting to observe Lloyd George's reaction.

Tuesday, 25 April 1922   *Genoa*

The morning papers carry Poincaré's speech. *Lavoro* (Genoa) and *Stampa* (Turin) in their leading articles vigorously repudiate its tenor and menacingly recall Lloyd George's words that, if he must choose between the Entente and the peace of Europe, he will have to reconsider his attitude to the Entente. They also quote yesterday's speech by the Chancellor, Lord Birkenhead, made here in Genoa, when he emphasized what Lloyd George had said. The difference of policy between Britain and France becomes ever more marked. A breach between them is now openly regarded as a possibility by both sides. Hesnard, whom I met as a matter of daily routine at eleven o'clock, is trying to allay excitement. Poincaré is mouthing phrases, he maintained, and is in no position to carry out his threats: he cannot afford the breach with Britain on account of French public opinion.

Wednesday, 26 April 1922   *Genoa-Nervi*

Stayed at Nervi during the morning. After lunch to Genoa. Met Hesnard at the Casa della Stampa and went for a walk with him. Most of the French journalists here, he says, are against Poincaré's policy because they can see how France is isolated. But almost incredible letters, written by normally sensible people, are arriving from France. He has seen, for instance, one from a university professor of rather pacifist leanings who writes that Rathenau ought to have been arrested immediately after the signing of the Russo–German treaty! And so on, just like a lunatic.

   In the evening there was a rumour in the Casa della Stampa that Lloyd George has summoned the Allied Supreme Council to Genoa for the purpose of examining Poincaré's speech 'point by point'. In other words, disciplinary action against Poincaré! Ludwig Bauer, with whom I dined, says that at about half past six a Havas Agency telegram and a Reuter one, with identical contents, were being passed simultaneously from hand to hand in the 'Casa' and had caused enormous excitement. Lasswitz, whom I met in the train on my way back, had also heard the rumour (in its most extreme form) that Lloyd George wants the Supreme Council to investigate whether all other Allies are not obliged to take active steps against any Ally who invades Germany except by agreement. It does seem to be a fact that France, after the Frankfurt incident, undertook by its agreement with Britain not to proceed independently and that Poincaré's speech, at any rate in its ideas, constitutes a breach of that agreement. Lloyd George is fighting for his political life and the Conference's collapse would mean the end of him. He has never hesitated on such occasions (as witness his behaviour to Asquith in 1916) to proceed with ruthless brutality.

The issue of *Le Temps* which has arrived today has three successive leading articles preparing the French public for a new war!

Friday, 28 April 1922   *Genoa*

The French Government has rejected Lloyd George's suggestion that the Signatory Powers to the Versailles Treaty should meet in Genoa to discuss sanctions.[10] Barthou is going to Paris *ad audiendum verbum!*

Monday, 1 May 1922   *Genoa*

Lunch with Villard. He told me, in confidence, that Child, the American Ambassador, admitted to him today that America (Hughes) 'is beginning to move', meaning that it is beginning to exercise pressure on France to come to its senses. Child hopes that the Conference will soon end 'before it has done more mischief'. Neurath, with whom I went back to Nervi, confirmed from his conversation with Child the increasing pressure on France by America.

During the afternoon I went to the Excelsior to return Marc Sangnier's visit. When the Russo–German treaty became known in Paris, he said, young men got ready to march to the Front. What hysteria! He does not think Poincaré will march into the Ruhr. I unfolded to him Bergmann's loan plan. He thought it sensible and a good way out. The mass of Frenchmen wants money, not laurels. He is seeing the Chancellor tomorrow again.

Tuesday, 2 May 1922   *Genoa*

Spent the evening with Hilferding, Kreuter and Dell at *Aida*. Quite a good performance in the beautiful Empire style Carlo Felice opera-house. After-wards great excitement on account of the latest French *coup de théâtre*. Barthou having left, the Acting Head of Delegation, on instructions from Paris, refused to sign the proposal to the Russians worked out together by the Allies. After a highly emotional scene between Lloyd George and the Frenchman, the former accepted a French amendment to the paragraph about private property, though not without pointing out that this amendment could lead to 'very serious difficulties'. Thereupon the French, under the proviso of their Government's subsequent confirmation, signed the proposal. It was transmitted to the Russians without delay.

The *Observer* carries an unprecedentedly severe attack on Poincaré and French policy, with cross-heads like 'M. Poincaré as Wrecker', 'The Kaiser of the Peace' (meaning Poincaré), 'France versus Europe', and 'Failure at Genoa Means War'. Garvin is a confidant of Lloyd George and in constant touch with him here.

Thursday, 4 May 1922   *Genoa*

This morning Wirth and Rathenau spent two hours with Lloyd George. During their talk, Rathenau tells me, they touched on all current problems but came to no definite agreement on any particular matter. Lloyd George justified this by reference, among other things, to Barthou's absence. The talk is to be resumed. In any case, contact has been established and the unfavourable atmosphere between the German and British Delegations after signature of the Russo–German treaty has cleared.

The Chancellor gave a luncheon party at which Theodor Wolff, Moissi[11] (he arrived yesterday), Johanna Terwin, and Simson were also present. I sat between Economics Minister Schmidt and State Secretary Hemmer. Schmidt, who had Frau Wolff on the other side of him, paid grave attention to his food and rose from table after having spoken but a single word, uttered in a menacingly imperative tone to the waiter: '*Formaggio!*' Not that there was much more to be heard from the Chancellor.

Sunday, 7 May 1922   *Nervi*

Hilferding says that Lloyd George has had his thanks conveyed to Wirth for the mediation of the German Delegation between Russia and the Entente.

With Hilferding and Dell to Rapallo in an overcrowded train, sitting in the same compartment as Chicherin. We waited an hour in Nervi Station, packed like sardines, while a repair was completed. Chicherin, in a winter overcoat in the boiling heat, bleated sarcastic remarks through his red goatee. He is very funny, slightly satanic in appearance and very cosmopolitan, hardly Russian at all. Speaks German like a German academic.

Monday, 8 May 1922   *Genoa*

In the morning Maltzan told me that Lloyd George yesterday talked to Wirth and asked him to impress on the Russians that they should consult with him (Lloyd George) before giving an answer. So Maltzan set off late last night for Santa Margherita and invited the Russians (Chicherin) to call on Wirth and Rathenau at ten this morning, following this up with a visit to Lloyd George. What the Russians want more than anything else, says Maltzan, is money. If that is forthcoming, they will be cooperative about the private property problem. They are demanding fifty million pounds, but will be satisfied with thirty. In reply to my question as to what form their conciliatoriness would take, Maltzan replied that they would stick to Article 5 of the Villa Memorandum; Article 7 of the new Memorandum they would never accept.

While Maltzan was telling me this, Chicherin arrived with Litvinov. Rathenau and Wirth went down to meet them in the garden. After the discussion Maltzan repeated to me that all that interests the Russians is money, money, money. A consortium is to be set up to allocate financial assistance for specific and verifiable purposes (productivity credits).

·Chicherin and Litvinov have now (eleven o'clock) departed for Lloyd George's villa (where he sits like an uncrowned king, receiving one and all without himself going anywhere).

Visited Krassin at the Excelsior. Long talk with him about their negotiations with the Entente. He started off on a fairly emotional note: 'We *cannot* return empty-handed!' Private loans would not suffice because a number of rehabilitation projects are involved which no private company would be prepared to entertain. He gave as an example a stretch of railway line where at one point there may be a couple of bridges destroyed, farther on a section of an embankment, elsewhere a station, the whole stretch passing through a region whose inhabitants have neither shoes nor food. What private banking-house would be ready to advance money for the entirely unremunerative capital outlays that these projects, large and small, comprise? That is why governmental credits, repayable of course, are imperative, making the country suitable again for the profitable investment of private capital.

Walking in the garden with State Secretary Hirsch, he disclosed to me his fear of outsize unemployment in the autumn, as soon as the mark stops dropping. He is preparing measures to keep a grip on this unemployment, but it is the most serious problem facing us in the time ahead.

I asked whether French occupation of the Ruhr would prove of any advantage to them by way of reparations. Yes, he replied, because the first thing that would happen would be a further steep fall of the mark. The French would not however sell us Ruhr coal for marks, though perhaps for schillings. At the rate of five hundred marks to the dollar, they would extract some seven to eight hundred million gold marks for their reparations alone on the exchange rate profit.

Dell, with whom I travelled back to Nervi, told me about Lloyd George's completely unexpected meeting with British journalists at six o'clock this evening. He replied to questions and made a fierce attack on *The Times*, denying the contents of the interview published there. Dell says that the British journalists as a whole think that Lloyd George wants to dissolve the Entente. Nine-tenths of British public opinion would warmly welcome the breach with France.

Whether he is right or wrong, it certainly looks as though an entirely new grouping of Powers, directed against France, is taking shape here at Genoa. Not at all what was expected from this conference and very much like preparation for a new Continental war. The Treaty of Rapallo is already totally forgotten. Relations between Lloyd George and the German Delegation proceed on a basis of mutual confidence.

Wednesday, 10 May 1922   *Genoa*

I gave a luncheon party in the private room of the Carlo Felice. Present were Krassin, Maltzan, Hilferding, Professor Ernst Cassel, Georg Bernhard, and Heinz Simon. The table was laid out with gold plate and decorated with various sorts of fruit, just as in my *Josephslegende*. Chicherin and Litvinov should have come, but were still engaged on working out the answer to the memorandum.

Conversation touched on points relating to political and economic organization in Soviet Russia. The benefit of the Revolution to the peasants, Krassin said, is that they are rid for ever of the landlord and can now, apart from a delivery of some twenty per cent, do whatever they like with the products of their soil and their labour. They are the broad groundwork on which the dictatorship of the proletariat is based. Wherein, I asked, does this 'dictatorship of the proletariat' consist? In the participation of the trade unions, in the central administration, both political and economic, Krassin replied. This includes, for instance, individual production lines, though the control by workers in single factories has, 'thank goodness', been abolished.

One has to keep reminding oneself that what is at issue during these outwardly petty negotiations, contacts, and conversations is the future of Europe – the life or death of European civilization. Should all these efforts at bridge-building fail, two worlds will stand opposed to each other and go down together in history's greatest struggle. It is difficult constantly to bear in mind the gravity of the decisions being made here in Genoa.

Thursday, 11 May 1922   *Genoa*

Hilferding, Georg Bernhard, Hesnard and I lunched with Philippe Milliet in the little San Giorgio restaurant by the harbour. Milliet started off straightaway with an attack on the Conference as a useless instrument for getting anything done, the reason being the unbearable ascendancy gained by a single personality, Lloyd George. The Conference is being suffocated by him and his autocratic methods. His position here is like that of Napoleon at the height of his power. That is more than France can tolerate. I asked, do the French therefore propose to leave the Conference? Yes, he replied, no useful purpose can be served any more. That probably also means the break-up of the Entente, I commented. Yes, he agreed again, the Entente partners will take their own ways. It is in any case inevitable now. But only for a time. France and Britain will come together again. Lloyd George wants to turn the Entente into an instrument to satisfy the wishes and interests of Britain. Here, at Genoa, France cannot stop him. So it will be better to part company for a while. A sensible line of policy will only become possible *'quand l'Europe aura vomi Lloyd George'*. Franco–German talks are impossible under the circumstances prevailing here *'parce que Lloyd George y fourrerait son nez'*. Germany and France must meet after 31 May elsewhere and come to terms. Direct Franco–German understanding is all the more urgent an objective now that the Entente is breaking up, but, for the reasons stated, cannot be attained in Genoa. What about occupation of the Ruhr? He did not believe that Poincaré would pursue so nonsensical a policy. I repeated my question, whether he firmly believes that the French delegation will leave. Yes, he said, he regards it as certain.

Milliet seemed to me to be inspired by a mixture of grim amusement, exasperation, anxiety about the future, and an effort to assume a mask of fearlessness or indifference. Altogether very much like the German mood in 1913–14. His attitude was that he does not believe in a new war because the masses everywhere are too war-weary. Let the politicians talk and intrigue, but for the next ten to fifteen years they will not succeed in persuading the masses to go to war again. Not unless, of course, there is a real danger, and so on, and so on. The qualification throws the doors wide open to propaganda and a fresh outbreak of hostilities.

Shortly before lunch the Russian answer, sixteen typed pages (!), arrived at our delegation. The original was handed to Facta at noon. We did not see the contents beforehand. The main point is that they want definite pledges of financial assistance and request the appointment of an expert commission which shall investigate individual points under dispute.

Looking at matters completely realistically (omitting sentiment and politics), only two major financial operations or sums of money are necessary to bring peace to the world and put it on its feet again: four million gold marks, or two hundred million pounds, for reparations; and five hundred million to a milliard gold roubles, or fifty to a hundred million pounds, to rehabilitate Russia. All in all, some two hundred and fifty to three hundred million pounds. This money is abundantly available; the people who dispose of it are the large and small, anonymous and intangible 'investors' in Britain, Germany, America, France, and the neutral countries. The total is smaller than is spent in any year on military outlays. But there is (apparently) no means of luring it out of the larger or smaller capitalists' pockets. What colossal, impregnable power money possesses!

Friday, 12 May 1922   *Genoa*

Discussed the Conference with Moissi. As we talked, I became conscious of the growing depression which the atmosphere of this Conference, an atmosphere of sheer amateurism, has exercised over me for the past five weeks. Amateurism and petty, particularist political egotism are the two reefs on which the Conference has foundered. On our side we congratulate ourselves because 'we are returning home with a gain *for us*'. That is considered good enough! '*We* have done well!' True to the traditional outlook, it does not even dawn on people like Wirth or Rathenau or Hirsch that thereby nothing whatever is gained for the rehabilitation or reconstruction of Europe. Inhibited nationalism, hardly less fatal than the open sort.

Sunday, 14 May 1922   *Genoa*

Practices familiar from life at court under Louis XIV or Napoleon are beginning to evolve here around Lloyd George. Typical of this is the way Beneš has fallen into disgrace. Lloyd George, feeling himself circumvented by Beneš, gave a dinner and had it reported in the Press that the representatives of all the Little Entente states had been invited, but '*non era invitato il signor Benesch*'. With those six words Beneš is done for. The confirmation arrived yesterday in the shape of news from Prague that he intends to resign from the premiership of Ministry of Foreign Affairs.

Monday, 15 May 1922   *Genoa*

Luncheon party at the Chancellor's. Sixteen people. I sat next to Rathenau. The gist of his remarks was that at the moment the ruling force in international politics is the French Army. The advantages which France derives from the fact are almost boundless. Consequently all efforts towards disarmament agreement are doomed because it is out of the question for France voluntarily to relinquish these advantages. Democracy has lost face all over the world.

Maltzan told a very indicative and amusing story about Monsignor Pizzardo, sent here by the Pope to negotiate with the Bolsheviks. After several days of consultations with Chicherin, during which he repeatedly expressed satisfaction at the progress made as well as the intelligent, conciliatory attitude of Chicherin, he asked Maltzan, purely as an incidental point, whether Chicherin had not personally shot down the Tsar. Not that it worried the reverend gentleman. He only wanted to know as a matter of historical interest. A Renaissance type!

The Conference is in its death throes. The Allies have agreed, with France deliberately trying to make everything as difficult as possible, to the establishment of a committee to study the Russian question. The committee, which is to assemble in June in The Hague, will consist of two halves, one manned by the Russians and the other by representatives of all states taking part here except Germany. The two halves will meet as occasion requires. In other words, the Russians are only to be 'heard'; and France tried to prevent even that. Whether the Russians will accept this proposal is unknown as yet.

All that is left of the 'pact' which Lloyd George wanted as the crowning symbol of the Conference's labours is the mutual promise by Russia and the fringe states not to attack each other for the period of The Hague negotiations!

The predominant feeling is that the Conference has been a failure. (Sacchi, of the *Corriere della Serra*, remarked bitterly to me today that it simply remains to ensure a decent burial.) Only Germany has gained practical advantage. France has sustained severe moral and political damage. Lloyd George has suffered a very deplorable rebuff. Russia continues outside the community of civilized nations. Europe has not been rehabilitated, though it has at least been reconstituted. Europe exists again, despite France's frantic refusal to recognize the fact. This Europe, the way it has appeared at Genoa, is not a pretty sight. But let it be ugly and scarred: the principal fact is that it exists again. And the second fact of importance is that this Europe has formed itself into an association against the Treaty of Versailles and its consequences. That is why France's attitude is logical. Today France is the enemy of Europe because Europe is the enemy of Versailles.

Wednesday, 17 May 1922   *Genoa*

Lunched at the Eden with Maltzan. Other guests were Dr Dillon and his wife, Simson and Dufour. Dillon thinks that Lloyd George, on account of his set-back here, will either resign or appeal to the country. His position is far less favourable than if the French had manifestly caused the break-up of the Conference. Now it looks as though the Russians are responsible, and that gives him no election slogan. But he will probably rely on the catchword 'Reconstruction of Europe'. The general assumption was that the Conference has been a failure.

We went to the Chancellor for coffee. Rathenau was there too and expressed worry about the political situation at home. At Munich demonstrators hauled down the national colours from the station roof and burned them! Ebert has therefore cancelled his visit to the trade show there and wants to induce Wirth not to stop in Munich on his return journey.

My *last* meeting with Rathenau.[12] Not until after his murder did I see his features again.

The Conference ends in failure. It was a small step forward instead of the stride which Lloyd George anticipated. But it was progress all the same.

On the one hand, a pettifogger at the head of a *Grande Armée*; on the other, the exhausted nations of Europe who are beginning to recognize their common interests and their common enemy and to organize themselves against him. That is the situation after Genoa.

Wednesday, 24 May 1922   *Rome*

With Hilferding visited Modigliani in Parliament. He talked for an hour and a half, very interestingly, about the Socialist Party's situation. Having missed the chance two years ago to seize power and carry out a political revolution, he regards its position, at any rate for the time being, as practically hopeless. He described how the Fascists are systematically ruining the peasant co-operatives and how, thanks to the passivity of the sixty thousand carabinieri, they enjoy Government immunity for their acts of violence. At the very time Modigliani was telling us this, Fascist gangs were trying to enter the Parliament building. We heard yelling and military orders. Soldiers occupied the exits. Modigliani commented that Italy was experiencing *counter*-revolution before revolution.

Sunday, 11 June 1922   *Berlin*

At half past ten this morning a meeting with the French in the Reichstag, which Löbe placed at our disposal. Gerlach presided with Einstein, Buisson, Basch and myself. Basch, Einstein and I were applauded after our speeches for minutes on end. For my part, I emphasized that we look on the rehabilitation of northern France and acceptance of a share in responsibility for the French financial emergency caused by the war as a part of European reconstruction and requisite to European solidarity. Consequently they are for us matters not merely of legal but also *moral* obligation. However, precisely because we regard them as a moral duty, our good will has limits and we must insist on seeing that our payments and services really are devoted to the moral purposes recognized and desired by us, European reconstruction and solidarity, and neither directly nor indirectly contribute to French militarism.

It is just as well that the French, because I outdo even them with my assertion of a *moral* obligation to render reparations, agree to this new basis. That gives us the complete diplomatic initiative.

Monday, 12 June 1922   *Berlin*

Having Chicherin for my neighbour at a luncheon given by Riezler, I discussed with him the subject of his address to the Wednesday Society. He has chosen the theme 'Soviet Russia and Pacifism'. He wants to talk about this because the next step is for the Soviet Government to launch a pacifist policy on a grand scale. He has ventilated the subject with d'Annunzio and the latter now also wants to pursue a working-class pacifist policy on the pattern of Germany and Russia.

These remarks by Chicherin, enunciating an entirely new foreign policy on the part of the Soviet Government, are of course of the greatest interest. I outlined to him my League of Nations ideas and afterwards sent him, at his request, a copy of my 'directives' as well as other material.

We met again tonight at Hilferding's, where the other dinner guests were Raumer, Kreuter, Hugo Simon, and State Secretary Hirsch. Unfortunately Hugo Simon and Raumer deafened the company with an argument about agricultural problems. Chicherin just sat there silent, tired and bored, his pointed nose burrowed into his pointed red beard.

Tuesday, 20 June 1922   *Berlin*

During the morning a discussion with Chicherin at the Esplanade. I wanted to fathom more exactly his attitude towards pacifism and the League of Nations. He began by saying that the Russian Government has no firm programme on these problems. It will determine its attitude as a matter of practical politics according to the circumstances in which they arise. It will not join the League of Nations unless that body previously undergoes reformation.

How, I asked, does he react to my proposal that internationally organized economic bodies should have their own representation in the League to counterbalance the locally limited interests of nations? Chicherin rejected the idea. It is, he argued, not only too complicated but affords additional power to internationally organized capitalism (the Golden International). Nor could he acquiesce in my proposal to include intellectual and religious organizations, such as the Roman Catholic Church. It would strengthen the power of religion, and that is undesirable. The power of the Church, I retorted, is a fact as much as is the power of the bankers. Here, as elsewhere, I take the point of view that facts must be recognized: to include such bastions of power in the structure of the League will diminish rather than increase the dangers which they represent.

My impression was that Chicherin is far from well acquainted with all these problems and not very interested in seeing the capitalist world really effectively organized.

Saturday, 24 June 1922 _Berlin_

At half past eleven Guseck came into my study and said that Ossietzky had just telephoned: Rathenau has been murdered. I was thunderstruck. As soon as I could think coherently, it flashed across my mind that now the Reichstag will have to be dissolved and accounts will at last be settled with these murderers, Helfferich and his consorts on the right. For Helfferich is the real murderer, the man truly responsible for this event.

At three o'clock to the Reichstag. The Chamber, when I reached the gallery, was in a state of confusion and uproar. Members of the left had swamped the places of those on the right. A tangle of members gesticulated and screamed at one another. Only after twenty minutes, and repeated calls to order from Löbe, was a degree of very unquiet peace restored. Löbe paid his tribute to Rathenau. Then Wirth rose from his place on the Government Bench, next to Rathenau's empty seat which was veiled in crepe and had a bouquet of white roses on the table in front of it.

Wirth's speech, vigorous but restrained, and proclaiming severe measures against the gangs of murderers and their accomplices, was repeatedly interrupted by tumultuous applause from the left-wing parties, the Democrats, and the Centre. Applause from the galleries too. At one point half the Chamber roared three times in succession 'Long live the Republic!' The right, like the rest of the Chamber, stood while Wirth was speaking. Even Heim, who at first remained seated, finally got to his feet. The applause at Wirth's peroration was, again including the galleries, tremendous. Hermann Müller moved that Wirth's speech be printed and publicly displayed throughout Germany at official expense.

Another session, for 'notice of a declaration by the Government', was announced for seven o'clock. It only began towards eight. Wirth did no more than drily read out the ordinances issued by the President. There was no excitement and the proceedings were entirely business-like.

The feeling is generally that Rathenau's assassination will have a deeper effect and more ominous consequences than was the case with Erzberger. Rathenau was a cleaner, more likeable personality and possessed of a deeper, more irreplaceable intellectual power. The desire for vengeance has been aroused as strongly, or even more strongly, than after the assassination of the Archduke Francis Ferdinand. A new chapter of German history begins or at least should begin, as a result of this murderous act.

Sunday, 25 June 1922 _Berlin_

In the morning a mass demonstration in the Lustgarten. More than two hundred thousand people, a sea of faces, over whose heads waved countless red and black-red-gold flags. I was supposed to speak but, as I am still hoarse, declined. Speeches were made from various points: the Palace balcony, the Emperor William Memorial, and that to Frederick William III. A little boy, with a black-red-gold flag, perched on the head of Frederick William. The bitterness against Rathenau's assassins is profound and genuine. So is firm adherence to the Republic, a far more deeply rooted emotion than pre-war monarchical 'patriotism' was.

With Kreuter to the Reichstag for the noon session. I went in with Wirth (we exchanged a few words) and stood at the back of the Government Bench. Subject of debate was yesterday's emergency ordinances. Wels made a very stinging speech against the right. Marx, the Centre leader, demanded a clear avowal of loyalty for or against the Republic. Hergt (Nationalist) floundered. Crispien (Independent) tried his hand, in front of an almost empty Chamber, at pretty light-weight thunder.

Then Wirth got up. Only to make a brief remark, apparently. His first words were that, although the Chamber was empty, it seemed to him the moment to repair an omission by saying something which yesterday he had been unable to express appropriately. Hereupon, while the Chamber filled, he paid a warm tribute to Rathenau's memory and spoke words of grief at his death. Then he broadened his theme into a speech that was all the more effective for its air of spontaneity and extemporaneousness. By the end he had brought three fifths of the tightly packed Chamber to their feet, staring in the direction of the right who sat there pale and silent like accused in a dock. I was reminded of Erzberger's great denunciatory speech at Weimar. But Wirth is more convincing and genuine in feeling, less sly and demagogic. It can be sensed that what he says really comes from the depths of his convictions. I judged this man wrongly. He is someone, after all.

At four I went with Kreuter out to the Grunewald to take my farewell of poor Rathenau. He lay in an open coffin in the study where I so often sat with him. His head was leant slightly back to the right, a very peaceful expression in the deeply lined face over whose shattered lower portion a fine linen cloth was laid; with nothing except the grey, closely cropped, dishevelled moustache protruding. A few flowers were spread over his breast and hands. Kreuter and I added red and white roses. We were quite alone in the room. Complete silence reigned. From the dead, furrowed, wounded face emanated immeasurable tragedy. I felt it as I did at Nietzsche's bier.

A progress has been abruptly interrupted which was leading to an unforeseeable point and now will never be consummated. Rathenau, like most great Jews, had something Messianic about him. Not that he was a Messiah. He was more like a John the Baptist awaiting a Messiah, or a Moses who caught sight of the Promised Land but was not allowed to enter it. His death is like that stroke of fate. As a statesman, the legacy which he bequeathes is not a completed achievement but a pointer into the future, a hope whose realization depends on others.

When we left, a servant stood in front of the door. A girl with a large bunch of wild flowers was seeking admission. 'I wanted him to have these flowers,' she said pleadingly. As Rathenau's mother was supposed to arrive at five, we curtailed our visit and drove away together. I went to the Nostitz home. Pastor Siegmund-Schultze was performing a small memorial service for Rathenau among a circle of children who had come together for a summer party. The words he spoke were very simple, but they moved me deeply. I left as soon as he finished.

Tuesday, 27 June 1922   *Berlin*

Rathenau's funeral. From noon on all work stopped as a token of mourning and protest against political murder.

The funeral ceremony was held in the Chamber of the Reichstag. The coffin lay in state, mounted behind the speaker's rostrum and under a large black canopy suspended from the ceiling. The Chamber was hung with black and transformed into a sea of flowers and plants. Enormous palms flanked the coffin at its four corners. The speaker's rostrum was shrouded in black and buried, as was the Government Bench, beneath magnificent wreaths with ribbons in the Republican colours, black-red-gold. The galleries, draped with crepe, were decorated with banks of blue and pink hydrangeas. Long crepe veils hung from the ceiling's arc-lights, which were turned on. The galleries, like the Chamber itself, were packed. There was not one empty seat, not even among the Nationalists. The focal point was the coffin, draped with a huge flag in the national colours. At its foot there lay two immense wreaths, of red and white flowers, to right and left of the colours.

At noon the Chancellor led Rathenau's mother into the Imperial box. She sat down in the seat whose back was still embellished with a crowned W. The old lady was evidently in full control of herself, but her complexion was as pale as wax and the face behind the veil might have been carved from stone. These features, all colour drained from them through grief, touched me most. She stared motionlessly at the coffin. Kreuter, who visited her yesterday, says that she is the embodiment of retribution. Her sole desire is to take time to write to Helfferich,[13] condemning him as the murderer of her son, and then die.

Wirth, having escorted her to her place, left the box. A moment later he was to be seen below in the procession led by Ebert. The orchestra, out of sight in the vestibule behind the coffin, played the *Egmont* overture. Ebert stepped in front of the coffin and spoke, very softly, almost inaudible from emotion, but well. After him came Bell, representing the Reichstag, his tone clearly articulated, his words moving. Lastly, and mediocre, a Pastor Korell, on behalf of the Democrats. Then the musicians played the Siegfried Funeral

March from *Gotterdämmerung*. This undoubtedly brought the ceremony inside the Chamber to its highest pitch of emotion. In the circumstances the effect was overwhelming. Many of those around me wept. The historic significance of this death echoed from the music in the hearts of those present.

The coffin was carried through the lobby to the entrance stairway. At the foot of the steps stood a Reichswehr company, in field-grey uniform, steel-helmeted. The drums rolled and the resonant tones of a funeral march rose muffled into the air, strangely like distant thunder. The coffin, wrapped in the national colours, was laid on the hearse which was swathed in red roses. Slowly, to the accompaniment of drum-beats, the cortège set off. In spite of the rain, or perhaps because of this grey gossamer appropriate to the muffled roll of the drums, the impression made upon the spectators was almost even more intense than it had been in the Chamber. Lassalle's dream of passing through the Brandenburger Tor as President of a Republic of Germany was today fulfilled by the Jew Rathenau because of his martyrdom in the service of the German people.

Wednesday, 28 June 1922   *Berlin*

The meeting tonight of the Wednesday Society was devoted to the memory of Rathenau. Stresemann made the commemorative speech. He expressed himself with great warmth of feeling, while not shirking clearly defined criticism on individual points. Impressive was the way he underlined the duty of everyone to render service to the state as it is (i.e., the Republic) and not to persist in a 'convenient opposition'.

Friday, 30 June 1922   *Berlin*

Wrote a letter to Nernst, advising him on behalf of the Peace Cartel of our 'grievous astonishment' that he should have vetoed the memorial service for Rathenau inside the University, requesting disciplinary measures against those students who threatened to break up the meeting, and suggesting that the University should 'after this occurrence observe the obligation of elementary decency' and institute on its own initiative a memorial service for Rathenau.

Sunday, 2 July 1922   *Berlin*

Since yesterday no newspapers, thanks to a printers' strike. Nobody quite knows what is happening. It seems that more than eighty people have been arrested as participants in or accessories to Rathenau's assassination. The conspiratorial net spread over the whole of Germany. Its members nearly all belonged to the 'Organization E'[14] (Erhardt), and certain of them were undoubtedly in personal touch with Ludendorff, Helfferich, and so on.

An early telephone call from Nernst, asking to see me. I fixed an appointment for half past two tomorrow. He will show me all the documents relating to the veto and hopes to convince me that he could not act otherwise. 'A grave breach of faith,' he said, was committed by the organizers of the meeting.

Tuesday, 4 July 1922   *Berlin*

Last night an attempt on Harden's life. He is severely wounded.

Thursday, 6 July 1922   *Berlin*

There is a rumour that Gerlach has been assassinated. I was telephoned by *Volkszeitung* and the Peace Society. Gerlach left Berlin last night and nothing can be discovered. Probably the rumour is no more than outcome of the extreme nervousness which prevails. The atmosphere of murder, uncanny and intangible, is as oppressive as today's sultry weather has been.

I lunched at Hesnard's with Haguenin, Hilferding, and Georg Bernhard. The catastrophic fall of the mark since Rathenau's assassination (from three hundred to four hundred and fifty today) is also causing great anxiety to the French. They realize that a further drop will render reparations payments impossible and that French policy is partly responsible for the plunge. Poincaré seems no longer quite so sure that his chosen path is the correct one. It has not however stopped him from protesting once more against Germany's election to the League of Nations!

In the evening saw Toller's[15] play *Maschinenstürmer* at the Grosse Schauspielhaus. Untalented rubbish which can only compromise the views he presents just as the untalented, trashy Munich Soviet Republic compromised republican ideas in Bavaria.

Friday, 7 July 1922   *Berlin*

Spent the afternoon with the painter and draughtsman George Grosz. The devotion of his art exclusively to depiction of the repulsiveness of bourgeois philistinism is, so to speak, merely the counterpart to some sort of secret ideal of beauty that he conceals as though it were a badge of shame. In his drawings he harasses with fanatical hatred the antithesis to this ideal, which he protects from public gaze like something sacred. His whole art is a campaign of extermination against what is irreconcilable with his secret 'lady love'. Instead of singing her praises like a troubadour, he does battle against her opponents with unsparing fury like a dedicated knight. Only in his colours does he ever let his secret ideal show through. His is an excessively sensitive nature which turns outrageously brutal by reason of its sensibility, and he has the talent for delineating this brutality creatively.

Drawing by Grosz

Becher and Dr Gumbel dined with me. I warned the latter. I have sound reasons for believing him to be on the list of those due for assassination.

Wednesday, 12 July 1922   *Berlin*

Visited Harden in hospital. He was all wrapped up in bandages. Told me about the incredible savagery of his would-be murderer, who continued to beat down on him with an iron bar as he lay on the ground. 'Can I live in this country any longer?'

Tuesday, 18 July 1922   *Berlin*

Last night the Rathenau murderers, on being surrounded, shot themselves in Castle Saaleck near Kösen.

Thursday, 20 July 1922   *Weimar*

In the afternoon visited Frau Foerster-Nietzsche. A most unedifying conversation. She led up to it by saying that she fears for my life because of the
Bolsheviks 'who had Rathenau murdered'. This ridiculous rubbish, started
a few days ago by Ludendorff in his interview with the *Daily Express*, is
incontrovertible truth to her because 'assassination is not something that
Germans do'.

So this contemptible lie is now being spread among old Nationalist ladies
to exculpate the Party! I told her what I thought. A pretty vehement squabble
ensued without in the slightest shaking her belief in the purity of the
Nationalist soul and Communist responsibility for the Rathenau murder.

My argument included the following points. First, the five hundred
murders of left-wing politicians committed since the revolution by right-
wing radicals. Were these all Communist or Bolshevik inspired? Second,
not a single Bolshevist agitator has been accused, let alone found guilty, of
murdering right-wing opponents. Third, if what she maintains is true, then
the weapon-stores of the 'German Defensive and Offensive League', the
'Organization E', and the rest, must have been accumulated at the instigation
of the Bolshevists, seeing that their possession suggests intent to assault and
murder.

It is degrading to have to refute such absurdities. The good old lady
simply refers to the right-wing radicals as 'We'! However, she did, though
pretty lukewarmly and after an effort, ask me to remember her to Harden.

Wednesday, 26 July 1922   *Berlin*

A reception by Chicherin at the Russian Embassy on Unter den Linden to
celebrate its re-establishment. The apartments furnished by Tsar Nicholas I
radiated their full glory for the benefit of the Bolshevik social occasion. In
accordance with Russian tradition, Chicherin received his guests at the
entrance to the first room and exchanged a few words with each. To me he
talked about pacifism, which in the light of our meeting at the Wednesday
Society and after was not lacking in a certain irony.

A young Communist attaché, flawlessly fitted out in tails and with the
Soviet star in his buttonhole, attended to guests in the best diplomatic
manner. The company was almost exclusively male and displayed a variety
of dress. Our Foreign Ministry, in the persons of Haniel, Maltzan, Schubert,
Ahrens, and so on, was resplendent in white tie and tails. The majority of
guests was rather less festively garbed, their attire ranging from dinner
jackets to lounge suits. On the whole the impression was less that of a
diplomatic social event than of the meeting of a political club with slightly
conspiratorial overtones.

This somewhat odd effect was reinforced by the presence of the Esplanade page-boys, in their green liveries, whom Chicherin had borrowed for the evening. Rantzau, whose appointment as ambassador to Moscow has now been published, was to be met at every hand's turn. His aristocratically blasé features, crumpled like a used handkerchief, were at one moment to be seen spookishly hovering about groups of people and at another buried in deeply intimate talk with individuals. Löbe, in morning coat and white evening tie, typified the jolly working man dolled up in his Sunday best and stood out as the complete contrast to Rantzau. Also in a morning coat, but with the black tie appropriate to a professor, was Hoetzsch, the representative of enlightened nationalism, smiling as always, indeed beaming like a ripe, rosy-cheeked apple in the sun. Breitscheid, the sauntering beanstalk, declined all offers of food and drink with the sarcastic refrain, 'Do bear in mind that there's famine in Russia.' Wirth only put in a momentary appearance.

Saturday, 29 July 1922   *Berlin*

In the afternoon visited Harden, the second time since the attack on him. He is much better. Though still in bed, he is now very lively, all his wits about him. He described how he got to know Frau Foerster-Nietzsche when he visited her in the temperance hostel in the Behrenstrasse. He gave an amusing imitation of the way that, with an air of Christian ardour amidst this company of pious nuns and pastors' daughters, she had utterly annihilated the notion of Christ. He then unfolded an astonishing range of knowledge in the field of Parisian theatrical lore, telling tales about Hortense Schneider (my first love, when I was six or seven), Jeanne Granier, Réjane, Sarah Bernhardt, and so on. From there we jumped to a long talk about conditions at the universities. He also mentioned Rathenau, making an obvious effort when, tight-lipped, he used the phrase 'Let us say our *friend* Rathenau.'

Sunday, 30 July 1922   *Berlin*

At noon a 'Never Again War' demonstration in the Lustgarten. About a hundred thousand people, with red and red-black-gold flags. Many youth movement adherents. Thirty speakers. I spoke from the Palace staircase near the bridge.

Wednesday, 2 August 1922   *Berlin*

First night of the Moscow Experimental Theatre at the Apollotheater. Went with Max Goertz and Guseck. Dramatized Dickens. Marvellously spirited and realistic acting, for all that it is strictly stylized. They are entirely free of that artificiality which is so distracting about our Expressionists. The impression is of pure naturalism. The masks are an astonishing achievement, their faces real works of art where the painting and modelling is concerned, yet without interfering with the play of the features. The actor Chechov is unforgettable.

Monday, 7 August 1922   *Paris*

Considering the absolutely middle-class and reactionary character of the majority of the French, including their national economy, it seems impossible that any socially or internationally progressive spirit could ever reign here. Yet a similar state of affairs has always prevailed in French art and literature. Throughout the nineteenth century, the Academy and the preponderant majority of the 'cultured' public was completely middle-class and reactionary, rejecting and deriding any innovation and every innovator, from Ingres, Delacroix, and Baudelaire to Verlaine, Manet, and Rodin. Nevertheless, France during that period was the country always ahead of others where art was concerned and today a visit to the Louvre shows those old Academicians banished from its walls, their places taken by those revolutionaries who in their own day were recognized by only a tiny minority. Perhaps from this something can be deduced about the process of political and economic evolution in France, the country where a talented and determined minority can most easily succeed. *Perhaps!* The French Revolution, for example. But the argument holds equally good for a reactionary minority, such as the people around Léon Daudet, provided they are endowed with the necessary qualities.

In the evening I went to a revue in the Cigale in Montmartre. There was a really first-class young dancer, obviously Russian trained, who might well do for *Josephslegende*. Also the inevitable Chicherin caricature; he is all the rage here. Last night, in the revue at the Marigny, there was a Chicherin too, excellent as regards the likeness, performing Russian dances and turning somersaults.

Friday, 11 August 1922   *Paris*

The greatest contrast between Paris and Berlin, between France and northern Germany, is the harmony which prevails in France, by a long tradition of mutual cooperation, between social functions. It is not a harmony between individuals, but between the functions they represent. The small investor, the *cocotte*, the notary, the civil servant, the workman, and so on, work so easily together as *social functions* and have become such accepted types that the whole social organization looks like a product of nature; it is 'naturalized'.

With us every form of function is still in a state of evolution. Artificial organization has to be called in to help. Most of the operative social structure seems haphazard, arbitrary, unstable.

This is especially true of Berlin, which looks like a swarm of separate entities when compared with Paris. This 'naturalized' interaction of French society can be sensed in Molière already, so that types (reflecting constantly recurrent functions in it) convey an almost perfect picture of it. In France everyone, whether *cocotte* or banker, finds their niche. With us everyone must first establish his stance in the world for himself. Here everyone just slips into the long-made bed and the long-settled posture of his social function.

Sunday, 13 August 1922   *Paris*

In the morning with Wilma to Marly and visited Maillol. I had not seen him since 1914. He greeted me with outstretched arms and tears in his eyes. I too was much moved to see him. He is considerably aged, grey and shrunken, and has produced little during the eight intervening years, but there are two consummately beautiful achievements – the torso of a young woman striding forward and the model for a war memorial, a naked wounded warrior with steel helmet. Apart from these, he has done only three war memorials for small towns in his native region, giving them as presents and using female figures previously created, such as my own *Crouching Woman* and *Pomona*, which merely needed to be draped. He complained that he has not had a single commission since my last. The Government has not ordered a single war memorial from him.

Thursday, 17 August 1922   *Munich*

Early in the morning with Max to the Glyptothek and the Neue Pinakothek. There is brutality and an almost insane loathing of nature in every brushstroke by Van Gogh. Yet the overall effect is always delicate, fresh, and attractive. The brutality of the brush-stroke dissolves into a luminous, gentle harmony. That is nature, and Van Gogh is perhaps the only painter whose canvases show it like that.

Tuesday, 22 August 1922   *Lugano*

Arrived in the afternoon for the congress of the 'World Women's League'; I am to give a lecture on the League of Nations. Was introduced to a German-American woman who was not only tactless (Why do you travel about so much? What do you do politically?) but excelled herself by ventilating to me, against the fundamentally pacifist background of this congress, her view that Ludendorff ought to be murdered. Notwithstanding my vigorous repudiation of any such idea, she persisted. A pretty start to a congress of 'pacifist' women and painful evidence of how shallow and stupid people can be where their own ideas are concerned. This woman, who wants to have Ludendorff assassinated for the sake of peace, is a worthy counterpart to Bernstorff who, to unleash war, wants to join the League of Nations.

I am sorry that I came.

Thursday, 21 September 1922   *Rapallo*

Arrived here early to visit Gordon Craig whom I had not seen since 1914. He seemed hardly aged at all as he came with his son, almost grown up now,

Edward Gordon Craig: self-portrait

down the country road to meet me. We went back to his little house, steep above the sea, from which it is separated only by the road and the olive trees. Very simple, but a bower of flowers. The entrance is up a small external staircase, also smothered in flowers. He has hung the interior with grey sail-cloth and the walls are covered with bookshelves of polished pine. They contain almost exclusively works on the theatre, puppetry, and ballet, and must be a unique specialist library, all that remains of his Theatre School at Florence. Light and spare, dedicated with almost religious fervour to a single purpose in life, the rooms are like monastic cells. I cannot help feeling that this single-mindedness is, in our age, somewhat childish. It was like paying a visit to a nursery, particularly when Mrs Craig and the son Teddy suddenly came out with some bloodthirsty Fascist opinions.

However that may be, Craig, his wife, and their two children have been living here for the past five years, since the Theatre School failed, with all their thoughts and hopes fixed on a non-existent theatre, their project for an ideal theatre enterprise for which they only need to find a patron. I said that, if I had to live and work here, I would feel that the instrument I was playing had some strings missing. Craig laughed and retaliated that, on the contrary, this is an experiment in playing on two or three strings 'with the rest of the piano left out'.

He expressed regret that he and Reinhardt never collaborated:[16] Reinhardt, precisely because the differences between them are so great that they complement each other, is the only producer with whom he could have worked. Stanislavsky, the Russians as a whole, and the Americans as well, are impossible. 'I don't want to have anything to do with Russians or Americans. I cannot abide them.' Reinhardt, he went on, has the hard-headed commonsense which he himself lacks. He is still confident that in time he will be given the management of a theatre. Until that happens, he has to live marooned here where, as he puts it, he can exist with his wife and children on his income of £250 a year while in London the same amount would not last six weeks. Last year they were able to make a trip, all four of them, to no less than seven Italian cities, but the problem had been how to scrape together the necessary eight thousand lire without running into difficulties here. The children are growing up wild, without schooling.

We then discussed the edition of *Hamlet* which I want to bring out under the Cranach Press imprint. Walker has still to prepare the type-face, but we agreed provisionally that next autumn Craig should come to Weimar (all expenses paid) to supervise the printing of his wood-cut engravings.

In the evening I invited the family to the New Casino Hotel. He talked about his working methods. When his imagination is set alight, he cannot stop until suddenly the flames are extinguished, and then he cannot go on at all any more. That is why he is always nervous of undertaking anything, hesitates and makes difficulties for himself and others, because he can never foretell how long the fire of his imagination will keep burning.

It is close on tragic to see this undoubted genius, whose vision and ideas have for the past twenty years inspired the theatre the world over, from Russia via Germany and France to America, not exercising his gifts but living like an island exile while festival playhouses, international drama exhibitions, and revolutions in theatrical production still draw on his capital. Before we parted, he said that in art he has no faith whatever in the countries of northern Europe. If there is going to be progress at all, then it will take place here in Italy. The people still have the essential stuff of drama in them: actors with naïve talent for straightforward impact and audiences with a similar capacity for enjoyment. In northern countries artificiality and criticism reign supreme. Even the Russians are nothing but 'clever monkeys' when they are let loose on the stage. There is nothing genuine behind their optical tricks. The Italians, for all their lack of taste, have the touch of the genuine, the life-blood of great art, in them.

Sunday, 29 October 1922   *Berlin*

In Italy the Fascists have attained power through a *coup d'état*. If they retain it, then this is a historic event which can have unforeseeable consequences, not only for Italy but the whole of Europe. It may be the first step in the successful advance of the counter-revolution. Until now, as in France for example, counter-revolutionary governments have still at least behaved as though they were democratic and peace-loving. Here a frankly anti-democratic and imperialist form of rule gains the upper hand again. In a certain sense Mussolini's *coup d'état* is comparable (in the opposite direction, of course) to Lenin's in October 1917. Perhaps he will usher in a period of fresh European disorders and wars. What place, for instance, has Mussolini's Italy in the League of Nations whose principles (right of self-determination, peace, etc.) he spurns?

Monday, 30 October 1922   *Berlin*

Mussolini has been appointed Prime Minister by the King of Italy. This may turn out to be a black day for Italy and Europe.

Saturday, 4 November 1922   *Berlin*

Lunched at Haguenin's with Barthou and Manchère, Karl Melchier, Hoetzsch, Felix Deutsch, Schacht, Andrić. With Barthou I launched straight into a conversation about Rimbaud, helping to bridge the gulf between us. Clearly he was pleasantly surprised and invited me to visit him in Paris at the end of the month to show him my copy of *Sagesse*, marked with notes for me in Verlaine's own hand. During the meal Barthou was palpably at pains to make himself agreeable to one and all. At intervals he made short addresses to the company at large by speaking loudly and on a high note, attracting everyone's attention. During one of these minor oratorical performances he praised the *'parfaite loyauté et bonne volonté indiscutable'* of Wirth and Hermes, but added that the Reparations Commission is slightly worried because it looks as though the German Government has not as yet thought out any firm proposals.

Tuesday, 7 November 1922   *Berlin*

Nine thousand marks to the dollar. The daily rate of exchange shows the progress of our decline like the temperature chart of a very sick patient.

Tonight I gave a small dinner at the Esplanade to set up a new association between leading representatives of the republican parties. I invited Köster, Hugo Preuss, Georg Bernhard, Hilferding, Breitscheid, Hugo Simon and Gerlach. The last of these was away; the rest came. We decided on a weekly meeting between ten or twelve people who should act, to use Preuss's expression, as a sort of republican *camarilla*, influencing the responsible leaders of German politics.

The main question discussed this evening was that of the Chancellorship, whether Wirth is still feasible or not, and who could perhaps succeed him right away. We were unanimous that Wirth's performance has recently been totally inadequate. Candidates considered for the post were Adenauer,[17] Hermes, and Oeser, but none of them came up to the mark. Hilferding and Bernhard advocated the retention of Wirth, in spite of everything, but with a completely reconstituted Cabinet limited to men of real ability. Hilferding opposed the idea of a Social Democratic Chancellor on grounds of foreign policy.

Tuesday, 14 November 1922   *Berlin*

Had our *camarilla* dinner at Hiller's. Newcomers were Löbe and Gerlach. Hilferding and Breitscheid arrived from their party meeting with the news that the Social Democrats have voted by one hundred and fifty to twenty against the 'big coalition', Wirth having yesterday made his continuation in office dependent on a 'big coalition' coming into being. This means his downfall. And in fact Köster, who came late, confirmed that the Cabinet has resigned.

Adenauer and Hermes are the prime candidates for succession. The Social Democrats are very loath to fill the Chancellorship because of the difficulties ahead during the winter and for reasons of foreign policy. However, if there is no other solution, they will acquiesce, Hilferding said, and in that case Otto Braun will be their first suggestion.

I raised the question of the Foreign Minister. Everyone seems to be accepting the prospect of Cuno, although he is thought incompetent, as an inevitable stroke of fate. Bernhard quoted Rathenau's remark at Genoa: Cuno is a fat cigar which will have to be smoked some day for the sake of its lovely band. Köster condemned Cuno as wholly unfit, but Hilferding was less downright. I do not know Cuno, but took the line that this is not the moment for experiments. *Vestigia terrent*. Zimmermann and Rosen cost us enough.

Wednesday, 15 November 1922   *Berlin*

Hauptmann celebration at the University.[18] The New Hall, with an ugly mural by Arthur Kampf, is vaguely reminiscent of Michelangelo. Hauptmann sat between Ebert and Löbe in front of the podium. Some Professor of Literature (I think his name was Petersen) made a colourless and boring speech followed by further professional effusions. The only distinction gained, and that for tactlessness, was on the part of Roethe, chairman of the Goethe Society. Instead of speaking from the podium he stepped in front of Hauptmann and thrust his address under his nose, forcing him to stand during the whole of it.

The only two speakers who had anything to say were a student and Löbe. The student spoke so glowingly and with such youthful enthusiasm that he swept his audience along with him. The only exception to this was a professor, with gold-rimmed spectacles and all the other appurtenances of a Boche, next to me. Barely able to control his rage throughout the ceremony, he did not fail at this point to proclaim his disapproval by audible mutterings. Hauptmann read a short and not very profound speech, but I was glad to hear him firmly declare himself on the side of humaneness and reconciliation.

The most memorable point about the celebration was the grotesquely narrow-minded behaviour of the students and professors. The students' union solemnly resolved (by a majority, I believe, of four to two) not to participate in the event as Gerhart Hauptmann, having admitted to republican sympathies, has evinced himself as being no longer a staunch German! And from Sam Fischer[19] I hear that this Petersen, who made the formal address, visited him two days ago to ask him to cancel the invitation to Ebert because it would be disagreeable for the University to have the republican head of state appear within its walls. When Fischer refused, Petersen said that he should then at least cancel Löbe's invitation, seeing that to put up with two Social Democrats simultaneously was a bit much!

At the end of the celebration d'Albert gave a magnificent rendering of the *Appassionata*. Whereupon another of the professors in my row distinguished himself by growling bad-temperedly to his neighbour, 'That was of course a composition by the pianist himself, wasn't it?' Beethoven seems to be as little familiar to the University of Berlin as Ebert is.

In the evening a gala performance of *Florian Geyer* in the Grosse Schauspielhaus. Hauptmann sat in a box next to the stage, with a spotlight on him and looking like Goethe's double, or the Goethe protagonist in any Goethe film. At the end of each act Kloepfer (in the part of Florian Geyer) hauled him over the sill of the box on to the stage. The audience roared, with enthusiasm of course, which was slightly different from the original first night when, during the frightful to-do, I nearly fell out with Seebach and Bodenhausen.

Afterwards a festive supper-party for Hauptmann in the Deutsche Gesellschaft. I stayed with him, his wife, Ivo and 'Scheelchen' until half past two. I congratulated him on his earnest support, in his speech today, for reconciliation between the nations. He now qualified this by saying that there are cases, such as when someone spits in your face the third or fourth time, where retaliation must be made. Later, contradicting my assertion that he is the first genuinely popular poet in modern German literature, he contended that Goethe was also a popular poet because he derived his themes and his inspiration from the people, and not from complicated intellectual processes as Schiller did. *Faust, Werther, Gotz,* and Goethe's most beautiful poems originated with and were written for common folk just as much as his own *Weber* or *Biberpelz.* I thought the comparison, coming out of his own mouth and in conjunction with his outward resemblance to Goethe, distinctly striking.

Tuesday, 21 November 1922   *Berlin*

The Cabinet under Cuno has been formed without any Social Democrats. The welcome given it by the Press is almost compassionate in tone.

Wednesday, 22 November 1922   *Berlin*

Meeting of the Peace Society in Löbe's official residence as Reichstag President. He led us through the apartments. Atrocious Wilhelminian taste, oppressively florid and vulgar. The style was intimation of the catastrophe to come.

Friday, 24 November 1922   *Berlin*

This evening Hauptmann reading of *Kaiser Max Brautfahrt* and a selection of his poems in the Philharmonie. The Great Hall was packed with people and overflowed with enthusiasm. Festive mood. Schoolgirls presenting roses. All a trifle reminiscent of the hip–hip–hurray atmosphere on which William II thrived.

Afterwards a soirée at d'Abernon's. Very smart. Mainly Diplomatic Corps, foreign and German. Recital by Bellincioni, whom I thought dead; her voice is old but wonderfully controlled. Baby Kühlmann, in emerald green, with bobbed hair and a white Spanish shawl which once belonged to the Empress Eugénie, whispered to me that she was not dancing 'because I'm in my sixth month'. Renata Schubert (very beautiful, with marvellous earrings and pearls) introduced me to the slightly plump Mrs Houghton, wife of the American Ambassador. With d'Abernon, very assiduous in his attention to the ladies, I was only able to have a few words.

Monday, 27 November 1922   *Berlin*

Stresemann asked me whether I would go as Minister to Brussels; there are several major tasks to be performed. I have not the slightest ambition to be given another ministerial appointment, I replied. I am completely independent, I am thoroughly happy with the activities I already pursue, and I know from experience the intrigues which sour life for everyone in the Foreign Service. It would therefore mean a very great sacrifice for me to re-enter the Foreign Service and I would only be prepared to make it if I was convinced that I could thereby really render the country a service. Such a conviction would depend on whether the German Government, instead of confining itself to vague declarations of goodwill, at last came forward with firm proposals on the reparations question.

Tuesday, 28 November 1922   *Berlin*

Dinner with the Bergers (former head of the Security Police and Minister at Dresden). Sumptuous apartments in the Roonstrasse, princely furnishings. Lots of antiques, in part extremely fine and valuable. Millionaires' meal: young Thyssen, Otto Wolff, Vera Guttmann ('the richest woman in Germany'). Also remnants of former Court society: Count Platen, Frau von Loebell, Stohrer.

The gem of the evening was Frau von Wassilko, the Ukrainian Minister's wife. Small and thin, she seemed to consist entirely of brilliantly dyed red hair and diamonds, with quantities of paint and enamel where the face usually is. She is supposed to have been a Viennese night-club singer, later the mistress of the Shah, and is now Madam Minister at Berlin and Berne. The diamonds on her fingers were the size of pigeon's eggs and of the finest water. Rows upon rows of them, intermingled with strands of large pearls, were wound around her neck and hung down to her lap. My first notion was that, representing a Soviet Republic, she was wearing the entire Ukrainian aristocracy's confiscated jewelry. Then I was told that her husband is here on behalf of Petljura, not the Soviets. Weismann, Stresemann, and former Minister Heine were the representatives of the new Germany in this remarkable and ponderously rich company. A setting for Balzac.

Sunday, 10 December 1922   *The Hague*

Congress of the International Trade Unions Federation. Its purpose is to draft constructive plans for the prevention of war through cooperation between trade unions, pacifists, and intellectuals. The opening ceremony took place in the main hall of the Zoo Administration. Fine working men's choirs, singing of the *Internationale*, etc. The hall was cram-full. Chairman is the Englishman J. H. Thomas, with Leiphart, Jouhaux, Mertens, Oudegaast, and Fimmen as Vice-Chairmen.

Thomas said in his opening speech that there were more than six hundred delegates from twenty-four nations present, representing forty million people. The Congress was unique and there had never been anything approaching it in character. It must have *practical* results. Thomas speaks slowly and clearly, with a trenchant turn of phrase, but he 'drops his hs', the hall-mark of the cockney, and that gives him a touch of the semi-literate. Thomas's speech was the only real business. The rest was just addresses of welcome alternating with choirs.

In the evening there was a reception for Gerhart Hauptmann (the Dutch are now doing honour to him) under the aegis of the German–Dutch Society. I went with van de Velde. Tonight the Trade Union Congress is also being celebrated on a large scale by the socialist youth of The Hague. I tried to persuade Hauptmann to accompany me there quite briefly and to speak a few words. First he accepted, then he had second thoughts. It might be a political affair, he is a bad extempore speaker, it was all rather sudden, he couldn't quite see what he was involving himself in, and so on. In short, he begged me to excuse him if he preferred not to go. Then he was borne away in an easy chair by gentlemen in tails in order, I believe, to be read poems or excerpts from his plays.

I escaped with van de Velde to the young proletarians. We found them in the Zoo hall, grouped around a large red flag on the stage, all very fresh-complexioned and fair. They made an attractive picture, listening to a young German worker whose ringing, high-spirited speech ended with the words, 'But if soldiers for peace are wanted, then here they are!', pointing to his youthful audience. There was thunderous applause, followed by a closing speech in French by another youngster. I was told that earlier the boys and girls gave a very nice display of dancing. What a pity that the author

'Cathedral of Socialism' 1919 (Lyonel Feininger)

of *Die Weber* and *Hannele* would not be moved to make a sudden appearance among these lively youngsters. It confirms my estimate of Hauptmann as a non-revolutionary. This quality has now however attained almost ultra-conservative proportions. Strange, what an indecisive mouth and pinched lips he has.

Wednesday, 13 December 1922   *The Hague*

Third day of business sessions. Rotstein, the Bolshevik, proposed fourteen points whose acceptance would, he claimed, ensure peace for the internationally organized working people of the world. The skittish parallel to Wilson's Fourteen Points, advanced for the identical purpose of maintaining permanent peace, was in itself irritating and robbed the proposal of belief in its seriousness. Its insincerity, irony, playing to the gallery, could be sensed.

There was another situation blending irony and tragedy. While Helene Stöcker was proclaiming the undoubted right of every human being to life, and so justifying conscientious objection to military service, Friedrich Adler, the murderer of Stürghk,[20] was prowling about the hall like a sick beast of prey. Large, heavily built, bowed, with the velvety eyes of a predatory beast behind gold-rimmed, flashing spectacles, he is one of the Congress's prize figures. Yet in the eyes of God Techow[21] acted no differently from Adler.

Apart from the Bolshevik Rotstein, the main speakers today were the Menshevik Abramovicz, a pale, tragic figure, drawn with suffering; Grumbach, full of rhetoric and bellowing like a bull, an Alsatian Danton; the Spanish socialist Caballero, a toreador; Ben Tillett, the historic British Red, with the appearance of a middle-aged gentleman; Wels, friend of Noske and an apostle of peace, with a hackneyed refrain of indignation about the misdeeds of the Entente; and finally Friedrich Adler, quite sagacious, a sprinkling of scepticism. In the afternoon I talked about general strikes and the League of Nations, demanding its extension in accord with the Brunswick Resolution.

Friday, 15 December 1922   *The Hague*

Last Congress session. All resolutions were passed, the Russians opposing of course. For good measure Radek made a mischievous speech, assuming the mask of youthful ardour. From behind it, and his flashing spectacles, there suddenly crept into his face an expression somewhere half-way between that of Facta and a wolf and at the same time having something of the look of a street urchin after a particularly successful prank. A truly impertinent, amusing, and frightening Mephistophelian face.

Sunday, 17 December 1922   *London*

Arrived early at Harwich. Reached London at ten, after more than eight years' absence.

I left with Rodin on a Friday morning, a week before the war began. I remember our Channel crossing and how Rodin, when we sailed from Folkestone and I asked him whether he wanted anything to eat, replied, '*Non, je n'ai pas faim. Je regarde la nature. La nature me nourrit.*' Then the arrival at Boulogne, with the ultimatum in the papers and my instant firm conviction that war was inevitable and Austria *wanted* it. Thereafter the parting with Rodin at the Gare du Nord in Paris and the arrangement (unreal, to my mind) to meet for tea next Wednesday at Countess Greffule's. By Wednesday I was sitting in Cologne, waiting for war to be declared.

I recalled it all as the train carried me through the sooty, mean London suburbs.

In the late afternoon I walked along the Embankment towards West-minster. The sun shone on wet streets and heavy clouds scudded low across the sky. The whole city was bathed in a violet and golden light that turned the Thames to glowing copper.

Monday, 18 December 1922   *London*

In the morning shopping. Not much change in the shops. They are as good class and elegant as they used to be. But there is no longer the astounding amount of bustle and luxury as in 1914 and which is still to be met in Paris. It can be sensed that the country has become poorer and the shoppers rarer.

In the afternoon Wilma arrived. In the evening we went to a theatre, Daly's, and saw a musical comedy by Jean Gilbert (*The Lady of the Rose*). To my astonishment, at least half the men in the stalls were in lounge suits, the rest in dinner jackets, and only five or six in tails. A real revolution or, more accurately, the symptom of such.

Thursday, 21 December 1922   *London*

During the morning at the Embassy to see Sthamer. He gives the impression of being an intelligent, matter-of-fact business man, lacking in polish and without much intellect, but with quite a fund of commonsense. All the same a bit old-fashioned and not very clear on the point that there is a new world, different somehow from what it was before 1914.

Friday, 22 December 1922   *London*

This morning Wilma went back to Paris. I visited Arthur Henderson in the Labour Party offices (Eccleston Square). My purpose was to appeal to him to put his weight behind the establishment of the League of Nations committee agreed at The Hague. He promised to write a letter along these lines to the IBG at Amsterdam and to speak to Thomas. His ideas on reformation of the League of Nations accord with mine. He wants it to evolve from organizations representing producers, consumers, and 'citizens'. He does not think, though, that the existing League of Nations can be reconstructed on this basis.

1923

Today the Allied Reparations Conference (Bonar Law, Poincaré, Theunis, Torretta) assembles here.

In the afternoon to the Embassy. Mayer believes that the French will above all require '*des gages*'; Hoesch fancies that '*des gages*' is what they want even more than payments. Our offer, Mayer thinks, is sure to be rejected, but he hopes that tomorrow Bergmann will at least be heard.

He is still very upset about Millerand's remarks yesterday at the New Year's Day reception for the Diplomatic Corps. The Nuncio Cerreti, dilating on the ideas in the Pope's peace encyclical, said that first feelings must become assuaged and then all other problems will be reduced to technicalities which bankers and economists can settle. Millerand, who knew beforehand the line that Cerreti was going to adopt, retorted with passionate emphasis that far too many people everywhere forget Germany's responsibility for the war and it will only be possible to found a firm peace on the basis of truth and justice. (In other words, by punishing Germany.) For a moment Mayer was undecided whether to leave the room on account of this affront, but dismissed the idea in order not to stir up a conflict on the eve of the Conference. All the same, the manner in which Millerand spoke is scandalous.

In the evening saw *Michel Auclair* by Vildrac at the Théâtre du Vieux Colombier. In front of us sat a Faubourg St Germain party: elegant women, with low-cut dresses and long pearl necklaces, and a number of youngsters. They were discussing the situation. One of them, about twenty-eight, in a dinner jacket and with the Légion d'honneur, commented, '*Que voulez-vous, c'est stupide, mais on ira dans la Ruhr. Nous sommes engagés. Plus moyen de reculer, avec cette Chambre terrible!*'

In the evening with Wilma to a Satie[1] and Poulenc[2] concert in van de Velde's theatre.

In the entrance I ran into Misia Edwards[3] (now married to Sert), Sert and Diaghilev. Our first encounter since the war. We were all deeply moved. Misia could hardly speak. To someone who greeted her, she replied, *'Excusez-moi, en ce moment je suis si troublée!'* And to me, when I remarked how odd it was that we should meet again precisely here in this theatre where we had shared so many experiences, *'Cela devait arriver comme cela, j'en étais sûre.'*

Erik Satie (Cocteau)

Satie's *Belle Excentrique* makes very amusing use of the shimmy, cake-walk, and other rhythms in a bizarre kaleidoscope. *Socrate* is dignified Louis Seize, Gluck in modern dress. A lot of good taste and poise, but a trifle thin in invention. Plenty of applause (Satie came on the stage) and some hissing.

Friday, 5 January 1923 *Paris*

Yesterday the Conference broke up under the motto 'maintenance of the Entente'!

In the morning visited Poncet. I expressed regret that Bergmann should not have been received and called it a mistake on Poincaré's part. Poncet replied, *'Que voulez-vous? L'idée de monsieur Poincaré depuis quelque temps déjà est qu'il ne faut pas causer avec les grands industriels allemands avant de leur donné "une leçon".'* First humiliation, then negotiation. I imagine that fear of German recovery and a fresh threat to France lies behind it. So Samson is to be put in chains before his strength is harnessed.

Saturday, 6 January 1923   *Paris*

In the afternoon went to see Sert and his wife (Misia). She said again how she was moved nearly to tears when we unexpectedly re-met the other day. *'Pendant la guerre, vous étiez pour nous l'image qui représentait l'autre côté. Nous pensions à vous, quand on disait: l'Allemagne.'* It was a strange conversation. I had to tell her about the last days in London. *'Nous vous en avons un peu voulu de ne nous avoir pas avertis.'* I explained to her that I had not known anything myself. She looks on the present situation as extremely dangerous, almost desperate.

Monday, 8 January 1923   *Paris*

Lunched with Jean Cocteau at 'Boeuf sur le Toit', a sort of artists' tavern on the most modern lines, in the Rue Boissy d'Anglais. English furniture, Picassos on the walls. Also at our table was his friend Radiguet, whom he introduced as a kind of new Rimbaud. Rather coarse, peasant-like features, with a vague resemblance to Rimbaud, but dull and not radiantly handsome as Rimbaud was. Cocteau described a long illness he recently had. He has talked to Misia. She said the same to him about our re-encounter as she did to me, but added that she was not merely moved but also *'gênée'*. Cocteau dwelt on the fact that someone who is not even French should feel that way. The qualification gave an edge to his remark. I sensed something similar in Sert himself.

There was of course a good deal of discussion about the Ruhr occupation. Cocteau could not do much else, with myself present, than deplore it. He would like to see his ballet *Les Mariés de la Tour Eiffel* produced by Reinhardt in Berlin; Radiguet would like to find a German publisher for his two novels which are appearing shortly. I invited them both to luncheon on Friday.

In the afternoon visited Jouve. He appears to be living apart from his wife. We had a long talk about politics and literature. Certain Frenchmen, he says, take the line that France can now win the political and economic hegemony of Europe and retain it for perhaps fifty years, when indeed collapse will set in. But to them this notion of short-lived glory is acceptable and *'après nous le déluge'*. France's tragedy is to be a second-class nation which by every means *'veut se pousser au premier rang'*. Intellectually it is still in the first rank, but it clings to tradition to a startling degree. Valéry, currently acclaimed as the greatest poet, is a *'versificateur'* trying to mould Malherbe and Mallarmé into a traditional pattern. The sixteenth century is now the ideal admired in poetry and in fiction the seventeenth century. The Vieux Colombier is creating a tradition for itself compounded of Craig, Reinhardt, and the Russians. Everyone feels the urge to wear stays instead of trying to breathe freely. (My conversations with Cocteau, who is attempting to modernize du Bellay, and Satie, who preens himself on a return to eighteenth-century music, confirm this.) In short, reaction in art and literature is trumps here too. I invited him to join me on Friday with Cocteau, whom he has not met. He asked time to consider whether indeed he wants to meet him. Jouve is by far the more human of the two.

Saturday, 3 March 1923   *London*

The French have suddenly occupied Mannheim, Darmstadt and Karlsruhe, or at least taken possession of the railheads in those towns. During the morning called on Lord and Lady Parmoor. She is a Quaker, he an important barrister. I mentioned the subject of accommodation for Ruhr children in Britain. Parmoor replied that Sthamer talked to him about this two days ago and he has since made inquiries. Unfortunately it is out of the question. The state of public opinion will not yet allow such a step. The risk of demonstrations, Press attacks, and indeed physical assault on the children would be involved. Anti-German feelings are undoubtedly dying down more and more, but a part of the nation, though a dwindling one, still remains in a wholly belligerent frame of mind.

Rodin came to lunch. It is painful to see him looking as thin as parchment, weak and old. He is the only friend I have left from my childhood days.

Dinner with General Thomson at the United Services Club. His other guest was Massingham, of *The Nation*, just back from the Riviera. He did not meet a single Frenchman, he said, who is in his right mind. 'They are all lunatics.' There is absolutely no talking to them. I tried to drum into him that many of them genuinely want reparations and real security (not imperialist expansion), and that this fact is the only one which provides the basis for any hope. But he would not be persuaded.

Thomson was again very vivacious and amusing. He is a ladies' man and, with his slim, spruce figure and handsome, well-bred, youthful features, makes a distinctly aristocratic impression, but for all that he stood as a Labour candidate at the last election. He told us how things were in the Imperial General Staff during the weeks preceding August 1914. He held an appointment in the Operations Department under Sir Henry Wilson, the later Field-Marshal. Cliquish comradeship was the rule, with all officers on Christian name terms and intolerant of newcomers not recruited from 'Society'.

Once, shortly before the war, Wilson called a meeting of his staff (seventeen strong) and asked what they would do if instructed to proceed against the officers stationed in Ireland and in rebellion against the Government's policy there. This insinuation that they should refuse to obey orders was met by silence until Wilson called on Thomson, of whom he was not quite sure, to reply first. He requested that the matter should be put in writing, when he would give a written answer too. For the moment he could only express the feeling that they were 'coming perilously near to a conspiracy'.[4] He was seconded by certain officers on whose support Wilson had counted and so the latter, much annoyed, abandoned his project.

French's resignation occurred in the same context of events. The specific cause, as he told Thomson the same day, was a remark made by the King. He received French in audience, discussed the position *vis-à-vis* the rebellious officers, and gave it as his view that it was 'a matter between officers'. In other words, they were entitled to refuse obedience to the Government. French immediately tendered his resignation; it was accepted. His step was all the more to his credit because he was 'broke' and had no idea that anyone could exist on less than five thousand pounds a year. Massingham, to whom the story was new, criticized the King's attitude vehemently. (He muttered beneath his breath, but I believe I caught the words, 'To think of it, that puppy!')

This rebelliousness on the part of the King against his own constitutional Government was indeed worthy of Emperor William II. I would never have thought it of George V. It vividly reminded me of lunch at the Asquiths' on that Wednesday, ten days before the outbreak of war, when the Irish Guards hissed Asquith on his way from Buckingham Palace to Downing Street and made him late for the meal. (Afterwards old Jules Roche, a fellow-guest, whispered to me in a corner, *'C'est triste d'assister à l'écroulement d'un grand empire.'*) Such was the atmosphere in which Grey negotiated about the Austrian ultimatum and the question of war or peace in Europe.

Monday, 5 March 1923   *London*

Ate at the Dufours'. The guests included Wheeler, counsellor of the American Embassy, and his wife. I took her in to table and she told me that the United States will certainly intervene as soon as Congress meets (in November). Harding is only waiting for the opportunity. We must hold out until then. But her way of telling me was not wholly convincing and she seemed ill-informed about things which everybody knows. Detmold said that his 'Society' relations, who so far cut him, have taken to inviting him since the Ambassador lunched with the King. They explicitly notified him that after the foregoing event they can have him in their homes again.

Wednesday, 7 March 1923   *London*

Early to the Embassy. Bernstorff[5] is as disappointed as I am about Cuno's[6] speech. It looks to me as though Cuno must grab his chance if he is not to stake his policy purely on a gamble. He will incur heavy responsibility if he declines Simon's offer and matters subsequently go wrong in the Ruhr.

Thursday, 8 March 1923   *London*

At nine to Rheinbaben, in his pretty modest Russell Square hotel, and found him still in his shirt. I urged him to write to Stresemann. The latter should go to Cuno and press him to advise Bonar Law of the Government's proposals, as suggested by us. Rheinbaben agreed. Then I told Dufour at the Embassy about my talk with Simon[7] and drafted with him a telegram to Berlin, very emphatically recommending a letter by Cuno to Bonar Law. The short time available is a great difficulty because presumably there will first have to be a Cabinet meeting to decide on this fresh and decisive turn in German policy. The letter can only be brought by special courier. Wrote to Schubert and vigorously advocated the move through Simon.

Lunched with the Ambassador. He said that he will write on the same lines as myself and hopes that our operation will be crowned with success. He too is of the opinion that British public opinion must be offered something positive. At any rate he is now with us, body and soul.

Saturday, 10 March 1923   *London*

In the morning to the Embassy. Telegram from Berlin that a letter from Cuno, containing what we wanted, is on its way and will arrive Monday. But the Ambassador is first to ask Curzon whether the step is agreeable and prepare him for it. Curzon is in the country. Sthamer is going down to him at Kedleston this morning still.

Sunday, 11 March 1923   *London*

This morning the Ambassador asked me to come and see him. With much show of sympathy and regret, he disclosed that Berlin, while in agreement with the basic idea of my move, can nevertheless not make up its mind to send Bonar Law such a letter. Apparently this is the point which wrecked the scheme. He is extremely sorry about it, having thought my suggestion a sound one, and he sticks to his view that it is not possible simply to remain inactive. I sensed that he was holding back something. My answer was that I also deeply regret Berlin's attitude. The consequences will be twofold. Those here who would like to help us will gradually become tired and apathetic if they see that we have no idea how to help ourselves; and in Germany such lack of imagination will not help to hold the Government's defences for long. The *form* of my proposed move is irrelevant, but somehow or other Cuno must emerge from his passivity. Otherwise there will be a repetition of what happened during the war when we missed every chance of peace because we were never ready to make some small sacrifice.

Dufour has instructions from the Ambassador not to tell me anything which has not already been said. A pretty tomfool piece of mystery-mongering. We debated what to do to save what can be saved. We agreed that I should inform Simon tomorrow that it is too difficult and problematical for the German Government to put forward its proposals without outside encouragement. Such will be given by his putting a question in the Commons as to whether it is known if the German Government will be prepared to submit the whole reparations issue to an impartial tribunal.

From Bernstorff I learnt what really transpired. Sthamer went to see Sir Eyre Crowe yesterday and asked *whether* a letter from Cuno along the lines suggested would be agreeable to Bonar Law (instead of simply stating that such a letter *will* arrive tomorrow). Crowe replied that such a letter would not be welcome to the British Government and that we should either approach France directly with proposals or go to the Allies collectively.

Incidentally the mystery-mongering, suddenly set on foot against me by the Embassy, seems suspicious. It looks as though somebody at Berlin is brewing mischief and the Embassy has received some sort of warning. Possibly Helfferich, Rosenberg's intimate friend, is at the back of it. The Ambassador's manner today was that of laying a wreath on my grave. All the same, it must be admitted that the blame for the outcome of this move lies principally with the British Government (in particular, Sir Eyre Crowe) rather than the German. By scaring off the latter from formulating its proposals, it has in my view been incredibly blind to British interests. But perhaps Bonar Law is in fact physically not robust enough to carry great responsibilities, a manikin in the seat of a man.

Monday, 12 March 1923   *London*

At the Embassy Dufour showed me two telegrams from Berlin. One is the text of a memorandum for the British Government incorporating my proposals. The other is an instruction to be careful, in order to avoid any impression of double-dealing or intrigue, about involving the Opposition in the course of events. So at the last moment, when already committed to folly, reason has prevailed in Berlin. Dufour cannot imagine what has caused the change of mind. At any rate Sthamer will after all see Curzon today and hand him the German Government's memorandum.

Dufour and I agreed that only *after* the Ambassador's visit shall I acquaint Simon, strictly confidentially and for his personal information alone, with the German Government's step. We feel that it would be rather risky for the Opposition to come into action tomorrow already. As Parliament does not go into recess until the twenty-ninth, there may be time to postpone the matter a few days.

Saw Dufour again at half past nine this evening. The courier had just arrived with the letter for Bonar Law from Cuno. Or, rather, two letters. A shorter one in more general terms and a longer one quoting my proposals almost word for word. Dufour and I were unanimous that it is the longer one which should be presented. Unfortunately the Ambassador has not yet been able to talk to Curzon, who did not return from the country until five. Sthamer (having already requested to see Curzon) prefers to wait until he sends for him. Another difficulty is the levee tomorrow morning. Both the Ambassador and Curzon will have to attend. Dufour will try and arrange for the interview to take place *before* then, but that is very uncertain.

At ten to the Commons. Simon was just speaking. I had a ticket for the Distinguished Strangers' Gallery from him and stayed to the end of the debate, a distinctly lively affair. Then I talked to Simon in his private room, saying that unfortunately I am not yet in a position to disclose to him all that I would like.

Nonetheless, in strict confidence and 'as between you and me', I can tell him that the German Government has decided to make an approach to the British on the lines discussed between us. Nothing has happened so far because of Curzon's absence until this afternoon. I can therefore give him no details about the contents of the message because we want these, as a matter of good faith, to reach the British Government first. The Ambassador will do everything possible to make the approach before tomorrow's session of the House. But it depends of course on Curzon.

Simon hardly hid his disappointment. Naturally we do not want to cause the British Government any disappointment, I continued. We are anxious, above all and at any price, to avoid the appearance of having intrigued against or laid a trap for it. Perhaps he can so frame his question as to include a query about the French and Belgian Governments' intentions too. That will diminish the impression of its being a pre-arranged affair. Simon agreed that it will be better that way and added that, if conformable to the contents of our message, he will advise Bonar Law beforehand of his intention to put his question. Then Bonar Law will perhaps send for him and tell him what is in the message. Asquith also intends to speak. That will be very important to our cause on account of the great standing he enjoys in the country. The point is to force the Government to do something. Success nevertheless depends to a major degree on the contents and timely delivery of our message. Tomorrow is the last chance before Easter to lend weight to our cause by having it debated in the Commons. I asked whether it will be quite impossible to bring the matter up later but still before Easter. Yes, utterly, he replied, for in that case Bonar Law, if he thinks it expedient, can keep the message to himself.

I promised to ring him up as soon as the Ambassador has seen Curzon and at the same time to let him have details about the form and content of our proposals. He said he would remain at home the whole morning and await my call.

Left the House at midnight and walked home in pouring rain.

Bernstorff fretted to me about Sthamer's inadequacy to the present situation. Can anyone imagine the German Ambassador, in charge of what is the most important post during the Ruhr occupation, sitting tight and doing nothing, seeing nobody and suggesting nothing? He is not even active on the social side although the moment has arrived when it is once more possible to gain ground even in Conservative circles. I had a feeling that Bernstorff wanted to sound me out, though to what purpose was not apparent.

Tuesday, 13 March 1923   *London*

Two Frenchmen were shot at Buer. On the strength of that the French have shot seven Germans in the course of various incidents there. In Paris the excitement seems to be frantic and out of all proportion to the two murders. Clearly the French Government is out to give rein to popular fury against Germany.

At half past nine I told Dufour of my talk with Simon and was insistent that Sthamer should see Curzon before the levee. Then I saw Sthamer himself. Not only was it out of the question for him to see Curzon so soon, he said, but it was indeed 'against my instructions' to treat the matter with such urgency. While deploring that Berlin did not take immediate action, dithering to and fro instead, he had for his part done all he could to support the project. Would it not be possible, I asked, to have a word with Curzon at the levee, requesting an immediate interview? That he promised to do, provided he could catch him. Otherwise it might be four or five in the afternoon, too late for today's debate, before he had a chance.

No doubt about it that Sthamer lacks drive. Stirring his senatorial[8] phlegm is uphill work. His nerves are steeped in a triple layer of protective fat.

At one o'clock, when the levee was over, I was with him again. In the interval he had not spoken to Curzon, but to Sir Eyre Crowe who told him that Curzon will be unable to receive him today, only tomorrow, because he first wants to consult Bonar Law. Sthamer concluded that 'this puts paid to the matter' and expressed regret. It puts paid only to a procedural detail, I retorted. The main point, that we have induced the German Government to formulate and hand over proposals, stands. What has to be done now is to acquire positive benefit from the fact by some other means.

In the circumstances there is really nothing more to be done today. But I cannot rid myself of the feeling that Sthamer, by displaying a little more vigour and less fear of acting 'against my instructions', could have got the Note conveyed to Bonar Law in time for something to happen. I telephoned Simon that the matter has to be dropped for today. I believe that I caught a note of irritation as well as disappointment in his tone.

Wednesday, 14 March 1923   *London*

To everybody's surprise the Government majority dropped to forty-eight (from 109) in the vote on Simon's motion. Had we presented our proposals promptly, the result would probably have proved even more sensational.

Sir John Simon rang me up at a quarter to eleven and asked whether I had anything to tell him (meaning the contents of our proposals) because he wants to put a question to the Government as soon as possible. Otherwise someone on the Labour back benches can get in first, 'which will not make the same impression' as if it comes from the Opposition front bench. I congratulated him on his success last night and expressed my regret that we could not make use of all the material available. Yes, he said, that was a great pity, for 'we would have changed the face of Europe' if he had been able yesterday to put the question he intended.

Went to Dufour and obtained his agreement, as Sthamer is definitely seeing Curzon today, to inform Simon of our proposals.

I drove to Simon's office in the Temple and acquainted him confidentially with Cuno's proposals in his letter to Bonar Law. He seemed highly delighted. Have I any objection to his talking to Asquith and passing on this information? I said no, if he regards that as useful. He at once telephoned Asquith's secretary and arranged for us to meet him at half past five in the House. No doubt, he continued, the Francophiles will now claim that the French were perfectly right to march into the Ruhr, since it has proved the only way to induce us to make such proposals, and he and his friends will be accused of having seen matters in a false light; but that is quite unimportant from the overall point of view of European, British, and German interests. He went on to ask, 'as a matter of historical interest', whether his discussion with me in the Reform Club did really exercise any influence on the German Government's decision. I confirmed, to his evident pleasure, that this was indeed the source of the change in German policy.

We went on to consider what should be done now. I said that if the British Government advises the French Government of the proposals (which has to be anticipated), then the French will leak their knowledge straight away and begin a violently hostile Press campaign. That will thwart any positive effect from the start. Consequently it is of utmost importance that the proposals shall become known in Britain at least concurrently and before this Press campaign is launched. Simon was at one with me. This was precisely why he wants me to meet Asquith, so that the latter shall give his opinion and lend his support to the tactics to be adopted. Probably it will be best for Asquith himself to put a question to Bonar Law in the House, perhaps after reaching an understanding with the Prime Minister. But we must first hear how Asquith feels about that. He, Simon, is merely Asquith's 'lieutenant'.

The marvellous view from Simon's windows to the green sweep of the Temple's lawns provided our talk with a Shakespearian setting. The contrast between its aristocratic radiance and spaciousness and the gloomy holes where Simon's secretaries have to ruin their eyes by artificial light is typically British.

The afternoon's discussion took place in Asquith's private room in the Commons. An immense ostentatious Gothic apartment with an open fire of medieval proportions burning away in the hearth, it reduced the room in which Simon received me the other night to a mere antechamber. Asquith now gives the impression of being an elder statesman, an ancient medicine-man with slightly red nose and a mane of white hair. He deports himself monosyllabically and with an air of distant wisdom as though a bank of clouds separates him from the common run of humanity, not excepting Simon, and as if he were used to speaking through a megaphone. Oracularly, with a faint aroma of banquets and brandy. And, of course, during eight years this man did rule an empire of global dimensions.

We plunged straight into the middle of things. I began by explaining my position to Asquith. I am here entirely unofficially, but I act in close personal contact with the Ambassador who knows, and acquiesces in, what I am doing. Then I informed him that the German Government has decided to make a diplomatic *démarche*, that Sthamer was at this moment with Curzon, that the German *démarche* probably takes the form of a personal letter from Cuno to Bonar Law which Sthamer was delivering, and that the Cuno proposals are such and such.

Asquith commented that people may well ask why the German Government is making this approach to the British, and not the French Government. It can only yield results if the British tell the French about the Cuno proposals. Consequently it really amounts to a request for British mediation.

I replied that the German Government has avoided any sort of request for mediation, deliberately leaving the British Government absolute freedom of decision. Direct communication with the French has not recommended itself to us for various reasons. In the first place we feel that we cannot negotiate directly with the French Government because, in our view, it has broken its treaty obligations towards us. Another factor is that in recent instances it has refused even to receive proposals (such as Bergmann's) from us and we must therefore assume that it is just as little prepared to listen to us now. We do not however want to let the whole world suffer on account of this behaviour by the French Government, but to play our part in ending the current situation, injurious as it is to everyone, without unnecessary delay. These are our grounds for having decided at least to acquaint the British Government of the sacrifices we are ready to make in order to put an end to the illegal and disastrous invasion by France of German territory. The British Government can use this information in whatever way seems appropriate and useful to it. My personal opinion is that any success deriving from our readiness to make such sacrifices depends on our proposals becoming known quickly and before a French Press campaign can render them worthless in the eyes of the world.

Asquith agreed the validity of my reasoning, laying special emphasis on the fact that the refusal of the French Government even to listen to such proposals as we have recently made provides a very strong justification for the course now adopted by us. Nevertheless, it is hopeless to expect France to evacuate the Ruhr solely on the strength of these proposals. It will maintain that it is being required to sacrifice a tangible pawn for mere promises. Nor will it acquiesce in the substitution of a British, American, or neutral occupation for a French one.

Simon agreed. He suggested that in order to render our proposals acceptable to sensible Frenchmen and convincing to British public opinion, France must be conceded the right to remain in the Ruhr at the ready until the bank consortium has reached a decision on the amount and guarantees necessary for the loan. A short limit, perhaps two months, must of course be set on the time allowed to reach the decision and it must be stipulated that the French leave the Ruhr immediately afterwards. The collaterals held by them there will have to be secured by other measures in accordance with the finding of the banking committee or the court of arbitration. I replied that I could not comment; I did not know whether the German Government would regard such a proposal as a basis for discussion. But for my part I took note of it.

Asquith supported Simon's suggestion, saying that only along this road can there prove to be decisive progress with the problem of actually getting the French out of the Ruhr in the shortest possible time. Does he believe, I asked, that the French will entertain such a mode of procedure? 'Yes,' he answered, after a pause for Olympian reflection. As for his own course of action, he must first know how Curzon received Sthamer's communication and what he had said. He will want, if he is going to put a question in the House, to inform Bonar Law beforehand and to be able to deduce from Curzon's behaviour what Bonar Law's answer will be.

Simon and he then discussed how to proceed, with Simon quite obviously trying to urge Asquith to take the matter in hand, though always in the highly respectful and discreet manner appropriate to coaxing an old demigod or centaur to take a leap. But things remained open because Asquith persisted that he must first know how Curzon has received the communication. So I promised to pass tomorrow morning news of this to Simon, with whom I left.

Simon told me that he thinks Asquith will take the matter up. He will have another word with him this evening. But the rider that the French should be allowed to stay in the Ruhr for the brief period before expiry of the time-limit on the financial decision is also necessary for the sake of British public opinion. This will otherwise be cajoled into believing that again it is only a question of an empty promise, a German 'trick'.

Thursday, 15 March 1923   London

In the morning saw the Ambassador. Yesterday's meeting with Curzon, he said, took a strange turn. At Curzon's request he handed over simply a memorandum, not Cuno's letter to Bonar Law. Yet our approach is apparently not unwelcome to the British Government. In fact the situation has been reversed. Now the British Government is putting out feelers which go beyond our own memorandum. He, Sthamer, has been in telegraphic communication with Berlin since yesterday evening. We must wait for the upshot of this exchange of ideas. He can see just a tiny chance of the British Government intervening for us. In any case these highly delicate threads must not be jolted in their embryo stage of development by any lumbering outside intervention on our part. That is why a question today or tomorrow in the House is undesirable. I calmed him down with the assurance that Asquith and Simon have promised to do nothing without our approval. Then, he replied, I should ask them 'to lie low' until the beginning of next week.

Friday, 16 March 1923   London

All the newspapers are full of stories about German feelers, British mediation, and so on. The most tangible is the report from Berlin in the *Daily Chronicle*. Developments are moving so fast that, contrary to my original intention, I thought a fresh talk with Simon necessary at once.

We made an appointment for noon at the Commons. He seemed upset (at Berlin's indiscretion) and worried because, as he said, there is no doubt that the Government will be faced with a barrage of questions. A member of his own party (and without Simon's foreknowledge) put such a question yesterday already and received an evasive answer. There is moreover the danger of a French Press campaign. I quoted Sthamer's view that matters are not yet ripe for our agreed move. Possibly the German proposals, so far as I feel able to judge, have not yet been definitely formulated. That was why I would like to ask him to wait, in the hope that this delay need not be protracted beyond Wednesday. I would advise him immediately the Ambassador regards the matter to be so far advanced as to render it suitable for ventilation in Parliament. He agreed to wait, but did not disguise his keen impatience, concern, and even, so it seemed, a trace of suspicion.

Saturday, 17 March 1923   *London*

Dufour told me this morning that Sthamer's discussion with Bonar Law and Curzon yesterday was very unsatisfactory. They called the proposals in our memorandum wholly inadequate and the guarantee of 'security for France' an essential prerequisite to solution of the crisis. The security they envisage is an international control system and demilitarization of a German border strip (Robert Cecil's idea). I said to Dufour that, to my mind, this is the juncture at which we should raise the question of Germany's security. Only *reciprocal* control and demilitarization, meaning control and demilitarization to the same depth on both sides of the border, can be acceptable to us and fair. As for the discussion with Bonar Law and Curzon, we never expected our step to achieve a British intervention at once, but simply to be preparatory to a move in the Commons and trying the effect of sensible German proposals on British public opinion. I advised the dispatch of a fresh telegram to Berlin urging that we should expand our proposals as recommended by Asquith and Simon and thereafter no longer delay our move in the Commons. Dufour agreed to cable Berlin today on these lines.

Monday, 19 March 1923   *London*

With Dufour in the morning. Still no telegram from Berlin.

In the afternoon to the League of Nations Union. The speaker was Lord Robert Cecil, who sails for America the day after tomorrow. In a speech at Paris a few days ago he propounded internationalization and control of the Rhineland by the League of Nations. I said that I had come today to tell him that, as a German supporter of the League, this speech alarmed me because his proposal to subject the western border of Germany unilaterally to League control will seem to the vast majority of all Germans inadmissible and offensive.

Cecil asked where I read his speech. Its reproduction in the Press was faulty. Our Government will do well not to be too intransigent. He would regard it as a considerable benefit for us to see the Allied occupation replaced by a League police force. He wants to see all the political and economic control measures done away with, the Rhineland Commission too, and only to place the railways and the Rhineland's demilitarization under control, and a League control at that.

Bernstorff told me that my lecture has been a great success. Everyone is talking about it. Formerly he was always asked, 'Do you know the Kaiser?', then 'Do you know Stinnes?', whereas now everyone's question is, 'Do you know Count Kessler?' Fine company one gets into!

Tuesday, 20 March 1923   *London*

In the morning saw Dufour. No telegram yet from Berlin. Visited the Tower. Saw the cells, Tower Green where so much royal blood was spilt, and the Crown Jewels. They epitomize why this blood flowed and in a sense constitute a shining isle rising out of this sanguinary sea. The large ruby given by Peter the Cruel of Castile to the Black Prince, and set like a drop of blood over the sovereign's forehead in the royal crown, seems symbolic of British world dominion which sprang from such frightful murder and bloodshed.

In the afternoon to the Ambassador. He is reluctant to ask Berlin once again about expansion of our memorandum on the Asquith and Simon lines. Among other things there is the technical complication of its already having been delivered in Washington. He conceded that relinquishment by the French of their Ruhr pawn prior to the banking consortium having devised other guarantees would be illogical and is not to be expected. With the argument that Asquith's amendment is a detail which really flows naturally from our offer, I persuaded him to allow me to tell Simon that we agree to a question being put in the House and to say that in our view the withdrawal of French troops from the Ruhr only after the establishment of fresh guarantees is a matter of course. He only asked me to wait until tomorrow morning because a telegram from Berlin may after all arrive by then.

Wednesday, 21 March 1923   *London*

No telegram from Berlin. I telephoned Sir John Simon (after talking to Dufour) and made an appointment with him at his chambers.

Simon was clearly irritated by the numerous postponements and delays. For the first time he lacked zest. Previously I had to hold him back. Today it was he who was full of doubts. The situation, he insisted, is very different from what it has been during our previous talks, especially since the French Government's announcement that it will regard every form of interference as an unfriendly act. That always happens, he grumbled, when time is frittered away and all sorts of impediments and 'cross-moves' make an operation more difficult. He will discuss the subject with Asquith today, but Asquith will not ask the question without first having notified Bonar Law. If Bonar Law says such a proceeding is undesirable, he will probably drop the project.

Thursday, 22 March 1923   *London*

No news from Simon. Presumably Asquith is conferring with Bonar Law today.

Saw Sir John Simon at the House of Lords during the luncheon interval of a legal action in which he is appearing as counsel. Asquith, he informed me, regards the matter as still resting where it was when we met him. That is because it has not yet been clarified whether the German Government makes evacuation of the Ruhr a prerequisite to agreement to a conference and acceptance of a loan or whether its memorandum can be interpreted as conforming to Asquith's proposals. Incidentally, why don't we publish the memorandum in the British Press? Because, I retorted, we think his (Simon's) advice to let the matter become known through Parliament a tactfully sound move and have so far taken it as our guiding principle. The response in the Press would be strong too, he commented. And, by the way, he would like to draw my attention to the fact (it is in this morning's papers) that on Tuesday or Wednesday there will again be a major Commons debate on the Ruhr, inspired by Lloyd George and likely to prove of little comfort to us because General Spears will propose internationalization of the Rhineland. But at the moment he (Simon) had no time to enlarge on this, having already foregone his lunch on my account. It is quite true that he invited me to eat with him, and when I declined because I had a guest of my own at the Cecil, he simply ordered a sandwich.

As I see it, we must abandon the tactics we have hitherto followed and adopt in fact Simon's proposal to publish the memorandum, or its contents, in the British Press. Probably it will be best for the Ambassador to write a letter to *The Times* for publication on Wednesday morning before the Commons debate. That way he can drop in Asquith's amendments. The letter will then undoubtedly become a focal point in the debate and receive appropriate recognition before screams reverberate from Paris. On Tuesday I shall warn Fisher and Macdonald of what is happening. They can then trim their speeches accordingly.

In the afternoon talked over this plan with Dufour. He agreed and (provided Sthamer assents) he will wire to Berlin today still. Let us hope that by this means we shall achieve the same effect as would have obtained ten days ago if Sthamer had not back-pedalled so.

In the morning Dufour told me that Sthamer had rejected my proposal. He does not want to write to *The Times* nor to pass suggestions in this sense to Berlin. The telegram drafted by Dufour has not been sent.

Dufour recommended me to talk to Sthamer myself. I went upstairs and explained the situation and my reasoning in detail. His first objection was his feeling that the German Government is itself not too sure of what it wants and whether indeed it desires publication of the policy laid down in the memorandum. I answered that the whole move has been aimed at publication by Bonar Law in Parliament. If the Government does not know what it wants, it is all the more appropriate for us to help it make up its mind.

Sthamer's next objection: publication in the British Press will make it too much of a British affair; Bonar Law told him that Germany should turn to France or the Allies as a whole. (Sthamer is evidently afraid of impairing his own position here if he disregards this advice.) My reply was that all I care about is to see the German policy, plus Asquith's qualification, stated in the British Press on Wednesday morning. The form, and whether the British Press is alone in printing the news, is immaterial to me. The facts can be revealed to the Press at large in Berlin, for instance in the form of an interview accorded by Cuno or Rosenberg. The one essential point (in order to prevent a French harassing operation between announcement and the Commons debate) is that they shall appear neither earlier nor later than Wednesday morning in the British Press.

This, Sthamer said, is a totally different proposition from the one I made last night and he can acquiesce in it. (Not, be it noted, that he thought it worth while to think out this modification himself; he simply wanted to shelve the issue.) He will compose a telegram to Berlin along these lines. In order to encourage the Government, he will affirm, basing himself on information received from me, that such a publication will be of substantial value to the Asquith group during the Commons debate on Wednesday and that such a move can be anticipated as also meeting with the approbation and support of the Labour Party. In other words, he is putting the whole of the responsibility for this fresh step on my shoulders, a responsibility which I shall gladly shoulder. I would have wired to Berlin myself if Sthamer had definitely refused. His timid and bureaucratic aversion to taking action is a handicap in the long run.

Tuesday, 27 March 1923   *London*

Just after nine o'clock to the Embassy and found a half-decoded telegram from Rosenberg. He will make a statement according to our ideas to the Reichstag Foreign Affairs Committee today and see that it is published in the morning Press here tomorrow.

Telephoned Simon and Fisher, fixing appointments with them for 'an important communication'.

At ten visited d'Abernon at his home, 8 Portland Place. I discussed our memorandum with him. He seemed ill-informed on its contents. 'Lord Curzon did not think much of it. There was nothing in it.' To which I retorted that it contains precisely the notions which Bonar Law at Paris declared (p. 78 of the Blue Book) as essential to a solution of the reparations question. Curzon had not thought much of it, he rejoined, because the French Government will refuse to entertain such proposals. The French Government is 'hopeless', I replied; there is nothing to which it will agree. But if its attitude is accepted as final, then there is nothing one can do except twiddle one's thumbs and wait.

D'Abernon agreed that there is nothing which will satisfy the French Government. Only the pressure of public opinion in Britain and elsewhere, I went on, can alter the situation; therein lies the value of our proposals. But in their present form, d'Abernon demurred, they are not reaching public opinion. It is in fact 'very important that Germany should put itself right with public opinion'. To offer a firm amount, though, will be nonsense. The most that the world market can raise as a loan will be two milliard gold marks. Anything in excess of that is unreal.

Afterwards to Sir John Simon. I announced to him Rosenberg's speech and that it will contain the memorandum's contents, but not, for technical and diplomatic reasons, Asquith's rider. The best thing, it seems to me, is for Asquith to interpret his amendment as being implicit in Rosenberg's speech, in which case the German Government will probably not repudiate the idea.

Simon was obviously delighted with my information and straightaway, under my supervision, wrote a long note for Asquith, who intends to speak tomorrow. He added that he will also confer with Asquith and Grey on the subject immediately after lunch. He was extremely friendly when we parted, escorted me to my car, and expressed the hope that we shall see each other again shortly.

In the afternoon told Fisher (for transmission to Lloyd George), and Ramsay Macdonald much the same as Simon. The former called the contents of our proposals highly satisfactory. I mentioned specifically the misgivings which Spears's proposals for unilateral control of a strip of German territory inspired in me. The Versailles Treaty (Articles 42 to 44) has already permanently demilitarized the Rhineland and placed it under League of Nations control (Article 213). If the present talk about demilitar- ization means anything, those responsible for the concept must be aiming at something more than the demilitarization foreseen by the Versailles Treaty. Probably this 'something more' envisages control of the railways and an international police force. If an area under such control is established on both sides of the border, I shall not mind. But if it is to be confined to German territory, then I must say that it will constitute a measure intolerable to the German nation because it will brand it as the only one among all nations which needs to be placed under police supervision. It will reduce it to a nation only able to act on a 'ticket of leave'. Hence such a measure can never prove lasting and never create durable security because the German nation will do away with it at the first opportunity, by force if necessary. It will moreover bring Germany into irreparable opposition to the League of Nations, which will be degraded to the status of Germany's jailer.

Fisher heard me out and agreed that 'reciprocity' would be appropriate, but was of opinion that France will never accept that. French nerves are in a bad state and a sedative is required.

Our discussion took place on the terrace of the Houses of Parliament, sitting in the unusually warm spring air and looking at the wonderful picture of the Thames, with its lights and bridges and a faintly bluish fog hanging over it.

Later in the afternoon I spoke to Macdonald in his room in the Commons, telling him the same things I told Fisher. He appeared deeply interested, listened most attentively, and did not dismiss my suggestion that he should intervene in tomorrow's debate. He then told me that the Labour Party delegates who visited the Ruhr have today rendered a partial report. The workers there are now getting *higher* wages (even when judged as *real* wages) than before the occupation: fourteen thousand marks instead of five thousand. Some Party members have questioned how this is possible since there is less production than before. Where does the money come from? From the Ruhr Funds, I suppose, was my reply. Our workers' and civil servants' organizations in the unoccupied territory impose regular deductions from their own salaries for this purpose.

Wednesday, 28 March 1923   *London*

The morning's papers carried as good as nothing about Rosenberg's statement yesterday. In *The Times* a downright misleading report. I was very disappointed, telephoned Dufour at eight, and met him at the Embassy at nine. He had a copy of the Reuter wire brought to him. It showed that Rosenberg's statement was very fully and well quoted, but the newspapers printed versions which were so short and badly cut as to be unintelligible. I therefore wrote private letters to Asquith, Fisher, and Macdonald, enclosing copies of the uncut Reuter message. Also copies to Trevelyan, Charles Buscher, Snowden, Morel and Brailsford.

Afterwards to the House, where I was in time to hear the second half of Asquith's speech. He had in front of him the notes drafted by Simon under my supervision and brought out all the points I had made to Sir John. Baldwin's speech was good and statesman-like. The front-bench speaker, McNeill, was superficial and weak in his defence of the Government's passivity. He was downright untruthful when he maintained that Rosenberg's statement renders acceptance of his proposals conditional on a previous evacuation of the Ruhr, which was precisely what Rosenberg did not say, and that he had simply suggested the creation of a bankers' consortium. In fact Rosenberg announced the far more important concession that the German Government will submit to the decision of both this bankers' consortium and the 'international tribunal' (which McNeill never mentioned) and give whatever security is required by either of them.

Sthamer and St Aulaire (the French Ambassador) sat in front of me and d'Abernon was in the Peers' Gallery. Sthamer left before McNeill's speech, shaking hands with St Aulaire. Unfortunately all the Opposition speakers were absent during McNeill's speech, which he made during dinner-time, and so no one corrected him. The question of the Rhineland's international-ization was only raised by General Spears. His speech was extremely feeble and barely audible.

We have gained two big advantages. First, thanks to my intervention with Fisher and Dufour's with Grigg, internationalization played no part in today's debate. Second, Asquith and Macdonald have welcomed Rosenberg's proposals as a suitable basis for discussion. Thereby the German Govern-ment has won the support of both Opposition parties, a very important factor if the Ruhr occupation continues for long.

Thursday, 29 March 1923   *London*

A visit from the *Frankfurter Zeitung* correspondent. He severely attacked Sthamer for being too lethargic. I agreed up to a point, but I defended him on account of his thoroughly loyal support for my efforts. Few ambassadors would have suffered so much usurpation of their privileges and at the same time have given their help without the slightest resentment.

Saturday, 31 March 1923   *London*

In the morning I said goodbye to Sthamer and Dufour. The Ambassador was, as always, very courteous and thanked me for what I had done here. This, he said, was alone responsible for the move in Parliament and, even more importantly, bringing about the change of attitude in Berlin. I told him that I am probably returning the week after next. I did not sense any special delight on his part. Is there, I asked, anything in particular that he would like me to mention or stress at the Ministry of Foreign Affairs? He requested me to emphasize his own feeling of an increasingly pro-French sympathy recently in the Foreign Office. He is uncertain to what this should be ascribed, but perhaps the British and French Governments have already reached some sort of working agreement. On the other hand the unpopularity of the French among the British public at large is undoubtedly growing. A contributory factor is the business losses incurred through the occupation of the Ruhr. A similar trend can be observed in Holland, Scandinavia,

Switzerland, and even Belgium. In this respect it looks as though matters are coming to some sort of a head against France. We then parted on very amiable terms. Thus ends my stay in London which on this occasion really has been of political importance.

Tuesday, 3 April 1923   *The Hague*

Went to Lucius at ten and stayed until half past one. The first hour I had to listen to shallow chatter about art, on the lines that he is an Epicurean and cannot bear the sight of 'anything ugly'. It does not prevent his place being an example of how cluttering up a small amount of good stuff with a very large quantity of medium good plus trash produces dreary triteness. Finally we got round to politics.

He had plenty more to say (especially how suitable he would be as Ambassador at Paris, but he doesn't feel like accepting the posting, and so on), though he talks so fast, jumbles together so much, and goes into such endless detail that it is difficult to keep up with his ideas (which, incidentally, are never very profound or new). He visualizes himself in a thousand different situations displaying countless facets and sparkling details of his personality. This constantly interrupts and distorts the flow of his matter. Women, club cronies, Rodin, Stumm, Halberg, Bismarck, and others, in visions relating to himself and his nearest and dearest, perform a wild fling and tear flickeringly and confusingly, like figures by torchlight, through the topics of the day.

As regards the quality of his 'sparkle' (his own term) and his artistic sense, he is rather like a pocket edition of William II, for whom he does not care. He recalls, among other things, the latter's stylish remark on the occasion of his last visit to Doorn (Lucius maintains that he is not going there again) about Rathenau, 'Serve him jolly well right!' (being murdered). And about Ballin, 'He never knew that he was a Jew.'

He took delight in pointing out to me comments about this blue-blooded specimen which he had underlined in Waldersee's memoirs. Yet that is the epoch to which Lucius himself belongs. A mixture of pleasure-seeking, false culture, political meddling, self-assurance and, last but not least, bad manners is the hallmark of William II's time. Typically, Lucius even tells the story of how he successfully corrected Rodin, who remarked, '*Je ne savais pas, cher ami, que vous étiez sculpteur.*'

The most deeply rooted characteristic of the Wilhelminian period (and the source of catastrophe) was the absence of a sense of proportion and modesty (awareness of one's own limitations), no religion, and no sense of the individual's relative status in the universe. The world has relieved itself of this sort of creature simply as a consequence of this sort of creature's utter inability to adjust itself to the world. In a symbolic and profound sense,

William II really was Antichrist, although in his own person a very insignificant, shallow, and contemptible example. Perhaps profundity, and, even more, personal wickedness, is not a specific ingredient in the figure of Antichrist, but simply this shallow, guileless superficiality. Perhaps a truly wicked and ambitious man, like Caesar Borgia or Napoleon, never can be the diametrical opposite to the quintessence of spirituality because the gravity of his wickedness attracts him to a place in the world which makes it impossible for him ever to be in complete antithesis to it.

Wednesday, 4 April 1923   *Berlin*

Arrived early. At noon to Schubert, who received me with great to-do on account of my success in London. He was describing the effect of my reports and proposals (they do appear to have played a considerable part) when we were interrupted by the return of Rosenberg from Copenhagen.

At half past five I went with Schubert to Rosenberg. He welcomed me with open arms. 'Well, here comes Kessler the Conqueror who shakes the position of British Prime Ministers and initiates in the Commons one Ruhr debate after another!' He thanked me profusely. In the light of the modest practical upshot of my efforts, it seemed somewhat too much and I found it rather embarrassing. He was at pains to make clear to me how meticulously Berlin had followed my suggestions. Three times, for instance, a session of the Foreign Affairs Committee was postponed for my sake and, when it finally took place, Stresemann was induced to dispense with a break so that Rosenberg should be able to make his speech precisely at four o'clock. They are also in other directions doing all they can to improve relations with Britain.

Friday, 6 April 1923   *Berlin*

In the afternoon visited Hilferding. He returned yesterday from the Socialist International meeting at Brussels and outlined to me the proposals, still secret, which have been worked out there on reparations. The main point is a payment of *thirty* milliards, in gold. Not forty, which Maltzan suggested as likely, and less than my thirty-five.

Saturday, 7 April 1923   *Berlin*

In the morning a telephone call from Schubert that he must see me today on a matter of utmost importance and urgency. I sent a message that I would come to his office at six.

Then a visit from Lehmann-Russbüldt. He brought a memorandum from the Thuringian Chief of Police which alleges that, on the basis of careful calculations, the overall fighting strength of the counter-revolutionary associations in Germany is seventy-one thousand men. Add the Bavarian police, numbering nine thousand and in league with the Oberland Association, and the total comes to eighty thousand. That portion of the Reichswehr stationed in southern Germany can probably be thrown in for good measure. This makes the figure a hundred and ten thousand. As against that, the Republic has only some forty-five thousand men in its reliable Prussian, Saxon, Thuringian, Baden and Hamburg police forces. No reliance can be placed on the Reichswehr. So Lehmann and others want to establish workers' units 'in defence'.

I expressed grave misgivings. Once admit that Hitler's[9] militancy renders necessary counter-militancy on the part of the Republic and it has to be admitted that French militancy renders necessary German 'defensive' counter-militancy. That is however the old principle of procedure which we finally want to be rid of.

In the afternoon visited Hilferding. He dined last night with Rosenberg who was very hostile to the new proposal. He and Bergmann tried in vain to impress on him the need for a further move. Schubert was present, but never said a word.

While we were talking, Hermes telephoned and asked to see Hilferding immediately; he was sending his car. I accompanied him and waited in the ante-room. As we left, Hilferding told me that Hermes is entirely for the new proposal, naming a definite figure, and will push the matter vigorously in Cabinet.

Hilferding made an appointment to see Ebert at six and I went to Schubert. The 'very urgent matter' was yesterday's dinner with Rosenberg. He began telling me about it, but with all sorts of reservations, until I said that Hilferding had already informed me exactly of what transpired. The German nation, he continued, stands on the brink of events more fateful and dangerous than those of 1918. Since the day before yesterday he has become convinced that we are approaching a financial catastrophe. What is to happen if in a few weeks the dollar rate of exchange races up to a hundred thousand marks or more? We shall then have to accept whatever conditions are dictated to us. There is moreover the danger, initiated by Loucheur's trip, that France will ally itself with Britain *against* us if we do not anticipate the move with sensible proposals.

1924

I talked for quite a while to Albert Einstein at a banker's jubilee banquet where we both felt rather out of place. In reply to my question what problems he was working on now, he said that he was engaged in thinking. Giving thought to any scientific proposition almost invariably brought progress with it. For, without exception, every scientific proposition was wrong. That was due to human inadequacy of thought and inability to comprehend nature, so that every abstract formulation about it was always inconsistent somewhere. Therefore every time he checked a scientific proposition his previous acceptance of it broke down and led to a new, more precise formulation. This was again inconsistent in some respects and consequently resulted in fresh formulations, and so on indefinitely.

The ironical (*narquois*) trait in Einstein's expression, the *Pierrot Lunaire* quality, the smiling and pain-ridden scepticism that plays about his eyes becomes ever more noticeable. Here and there, watching him as he speaks, his face recalls the poet Lichtenstein, a Lichtenstein who smiles not only at the superficial manifestations of human arrogance but at the causes of it too.

In the evening saw Sternheim's play *1913*. Sternheim exposes with highly dramatic and comic vigour the decisive factors in the German national structure shortly before the war. The character Krai is Stresemann in adolescence, the 'Teuton youth' with political ambitions who is 'corrupted' by the rich manufacturer's daughter, not a *cocotte*, as traditionally happens. A strong and profound play.

In the afternoon saw Abegg in the Ministry of the Interior. He lectured me for an hour about the state of the police problem. The Reichswehr had behaved thoroughly stupidly on points relating to military supervision. The call-up of short-term volunteers and the business of the Black Reichswehr had now gone well beyond the bounds of reason. The concealment

Street-scene by Grosz

of weapons was handled in the most careless way. The Reichswehr Ministry's political adviser had fooled Ebert completely. Gessler too had been led astray. The Entente was as well informed as our senior circles, if not better, about this Treaty contravention by the Reichswehr, which is moreover reactionary even though Seeckt has so far always acted loyally.

Contrary to the Reichswehr, the Police was reliably Republican. Former Imperial officers who were members of the Force had also gradually had a Republican, constitutional outlook instilled into them. Last year, during the Küstrin putsch,[1] it had only been thanks to the Force that the Republic had been saved from utmost danger. The Küstrin putsch had been intended simply as the start of a general uprising against the Republic. Fort Hahneberg at Spandau had already been in the hands of the rebels and remained so for five days until every hope of the putsch's success disappeared. It was perfectly clear that parts of the Reichswehr had been hand in glove with the rebels, else these could not have taken over the Spandau fort. Only the firm intervention of the police had preserved the Republic. And now the Entente wanted, as a gesture of thanks, to dissolve the Force! Neither he (Abegg) nor Severing could implement that idea. If matters got so far (and this was Severing's view too), then a right-wing government would come into power.

1925

Dinner with Wilma. The Sautreaus and Georges Duvernois (he now holds a senior local government appointment) were there too. We discussed the disgracefully indiscreet and spiteful book about Anatole France, just published and causing so much excitement, by his former secretary Brousson. Duvernois told the story of how, when he visited him in June after his first serious illness, France said to him, '*Maintenant j'ai été là-bas*' (i.e., in the land of the dead) '*et je sais ce que c'est : eh bien, mon ami, il n'y a rien !*'

Mme Sautreau went on to tell a number of anecdotes about France and his long–established friend Mme de Caillavet (a Frankfurt Jewess by birth). She was barely twenty when the latter invited her (Mme Sautreau), because she was Björnson's daughter, to a big dinner-party where France was also present. He asked her, across the table decoration of a thousand francs' worth of roses, '*N'est-ce pas, vous êtes Socialiste, Madame?*' To which she maintains that she replied, with a gesture towards the roses, '*Oui, tout comme vous, Monsieur.*'

The Caillavet household, regardless of its grand style, was indescribably untidy and dirty. The seats of the chairs on which guests sat at table rubbed off to such a degree that all the ladies afterwards showed large red marks on their light evening dresses. After dinner Mme de Caillavet said to France, quite audibly and in front of all the guests, '*Tout le monde sait que vous êtes amoureux de Mme Björnson : allez vous asseoir à côté d'elle.*' Thereupon France led the young Miss Björnson into an adjoining drawing-room and began to tell her some incredibly filthy stories to which she, as the true daughter of her father, listened unflinchingly while she gazed at him icily out of her large blue eyes.

Of insignificant appearance, France was very dirty about his person. On one occasion Mme de Caillavet loudly remarked, '*Je sais qu'il va voir une maîtresse aujourd'hui, car il s'est lavé les pieds ce matin*'. France paid a visit to Björnson when he lay dying in the Hotel Wagram at Paris. The room was big, well-lit, and painted white. Mrs Björnson, of regal appearance and always dressed in white, sat beside the bed. Three Norwegian nurses, also in white, stood next to it. France was totally overwhelmed by this intensity of light and this majestic cleanliness. Björnson and he exchanged only a few words, but, on leaving, France said to her (Miss Björnson), '*Je sais maintenant que j'ai été malheureux toute ma vie.*' Eventually, after Mme de Caillavet's death, he married her lady's maid. In answer to my question as to why he should have done this, Duvernois replied that France had become unable to go out alone any longer. '*Ça a fini par créer une situation impossible; on ne savait jamais où la placer à table. Alors, pour simplifier, France l'a épousée.*'

Very funny was Mme Sautreau's account of the reception given last summer by Fritz von Unruh's French translator at his mother's home in Paris. A number of ladies prominent in society, Mme Sautreau, Mme Dubost, Mme Paul Clemenceau, and so on, were among those invited to meet the author. When Mme Sautreau arrived, she was told that Unruh was talking to journalists in an adjoining room; the ladies must wait. He poked his nose around the door for no more than a moment and then, having inspected the females present, disappeared again without a word. After a time Mme Sautreau decided to forego the pleasure of this meeting and departed. On the stairs she met a stream of arrivals who, when she told them how things were, also turned on their heels. This preference for the company of journalists to that of ladies (very unlike Unruh) has left a bitter taste in the mouth of the Parisian feminine world.

Monday, 5 January 1925   *Banyuls*

Arrived early at Port-Vendres. In the harbour I saw Maillol's War Memorial, recognizing it from afar by the way it has been sited on the high wall of the piazza, between town and harbour, as a silhouette against the sea and the hills. The figure is simply a variant of his Cézanne memorial. The inscription on the base, typographically hideous, is distracting. My summary impression was that it is cold and conventional. The figure might, at a pinch, be by one of Maillol's better pupils. I was disappointed. But, on looking at it longer, I did find in it traces of Maillol's outstanding qualities, such as the noble rhythm and carefully studied flow of line. All the same it is not one of his best works.

On by car to Banyuls and reached Maillol's house at two. He was sitting on his garden-terrace and was very surprised to see me so soon, having thought that I would come by train. I mentioned the Port-Vendres memorial. He said at once how dissatisfied he is with it. '*Ça ne fait pas bien, on ne voit pas les "morceaux" cue j'ai mis; car j'y ai mis des morceaux, le dos, par example, qu'on ne voit pas. Je pense peut-être à le retourner, pour qu'on voit au moins le dos.*'

We went to his upper studio and worked at the Virgil. He made some changes, also promising to produce two new woodcuts to fill the gaps in Eclogues III and VII.

His son Lucien joined us and altered something in one of his large footballer pictures. I had not seen him since 1914. Thanks to the war (he was a flyer), he has developed quite differently from his father. He is much less gentle, more of a townsman, less refined, less cultivated, and has, on the surface at least, something pushing and vulgar about him. But his pictures prove his considerable talent.

In the late afternoon strolled with Maillol through the softly grey-tinted countryside in all of whose colours there appears to be an admixture of silver. The cemetery next to the old Romanesque church, an avenue of graves with sepulchral chapels and cypresses, vividly recalls Pompeii. In the fields beyond, Maillol showed me what he regards as the most beautiful grave in the district, a low tomb surrounded by a small grove of olive trees and cypresses, right in the middle of a meadow. He modelled his Virgilian woodcut on this tomb, he told me, just as the spring with its nymph in Eclogue IX had its origin in a small spring where we picnicked years ago.

On the way back we visited his mother, who is ninety-four. The old lady still moves about quite nimbly. Her small face, lined but fresh-complexioned and with a pair of very vivacious eyes, was framed by one of those black veils which all the local women wear. Her conversation was lively and completely clear-headed.

In the evening ate with the Maillols. He complained of great tiredness and too much work. In his lower studio he is engaged on a glorious youthful female nude, a sort of Venus or goddess of youth, which will turn out to be one of his most perfect achievements. He has a young Spaniard to help him, but said that the need to be constantly working at this creation left him no peace.

Tuesday, 6 January 1925   *Banyuls*

Before ten to Maillol to fetch him for our trip to Céret. We went down to his studio and he played about with a spatula on his clay models. '*C'est une variante de la vôtre à Berlin,*' he said of a small, crouching female figure. '*Mais celle-ci, je voudrais la faire pour être vue d'un seul côté, tandis que la vôtre, elle a quatre côtés. Celle-ci, je voudrais la faire comme un bas-relief. Mais il y a toujours une jambe qui gêne; il y a toujours une qui ne rentre pas. Je cherche; avec de la patience, j'arriverai!*'

He proceeded to deal with the subject of women who were slender and those who were short and sturdy. '*Hier, à la gare, j'ai vu une jeune fille avec des jambes épatantes. Du reste, ici, on n'a qu'à regarder, toutes les jeunes filles ont des jambes admirables. Il y a des gens, quand ils arrivent ici, qui les trouvent trop courtes; ils veulent des jambes longues. Mais ils n'entendent rien à la sculpture. En sculpture, il ne s'agit pas d'aimer les jambes courtes ou les jambes longues, mais il s'agit de trouver l'harmonie. D'Annunzio, quand il est venu à Marly avec vous – vous rappelez-vous? – a dit que ma sculpture était très bien, mais que mes femmes avaient les jambes trop courtes; ça prouvait qu'il n'entendait rien à la sculpture! On peut faire les jambes longues ou les jambes courtes; mais il faut que ça s'emmanche, il faut trouver l'harmonie. J'ai épousé une femme courte, j'ai toujours eu les jambes courtes devant les yeux ; c'est pour ça que j'ai cherché l'harmonie des jambes courtes. Si j'avais épousé une Parisienne aux jambes longues, j'aurais peut-être cherché l'harmonie des jambes longues. Avant d'être marié, j'avais des Americaines du Sud qui me posaient, des femmes minces et longues, et j'ai fait une peintre avec des harmonies de femmes longues.'*

I took a long look at the beautiful nude of a slender young girl (no feet yet and the head only sketched in clay) which in fact proves that he is masterly at portraying finely built young creatures. The arms are also still in the experimental stage, in clay, and, stretched out behind, signify a garment being flung away by a bather striding into the water. Maillol said that he might change the arms to come forward and be pressed against the breasts because at present the space between torso and arms is too ample. *'C'est une figure que je n'ai pas faite d'après une idée, mais pour laquelle je me suis servi d'un torse que j'avais fait d'après une jeune fille.'* However that may be, it is one of his most beautiful figures. We discussed making a copy for me in light red ceramic.

Our first stop was Elne. We made our way from the station into the town to see his War Memorial in the cathedral square. He has simply draped his *Pomona* and put a scroll with an inscription in her hands. He is very pleased with this figure; I find it heavy, unattractive, and puny, in the context of its site, in front of the apse of the huge Romanesque cathedral and facing the sea, the plain, and the mountains.

From Elne we went on to Céret to visit Manolo. He lives in a small peasant house on the road leading into the town. But first we lunched with Lucien Maillol in the hotel and then inspected Maillol's War Memorial here. This is a really great and touching work. An ordinary woman of the people who sits mourning, her head on her hand. The figure itself is powerful and expressive, the stone, a light grey, fits into the surroundings; and the position of the sculpture, in a broad and shady square under massive plantain trees in front of a row of simple old grey houses over which can be seen towering an immense mountain ridge, is completely successful. It is the only one of Maillol's three war memorials which attain its purpose. He himself today repeatedly called the one at Port-Vendres a failure (*raté*) and I find the one at Elne trivial and unprepossessing. But here at Céret he has achieved one of the few wholly satisfying monuments of our time. Admittedly the surroundings help a lot.

Manolo is a small, tubby, clean-shaven Spaniard of about fifty who looks like a retired toreador. Nobody would suspect his former career in crime from his appearance. His wife, much younger and a former Parisian *cocotte*, is of a lean ugliness full of character and gives the impression of a strong personality with a male streak in it. His work has a noteworthy force of expression and he has an exceptional gift for reducing the essence of what he sees and wants to delineate to a simple formula and presenting it convincingly. Sometimes, it is true, the process is rather arbitrary, as he himself pointed out and is trying to correct.

Maillol and Manolo. I studied their features. The elongated, finely drawn, sensitive, somewhat tired traits of Maillol, with the grey peaked beard and light blue eyes, the face of a Greek shepherd poet. And next to him Manolo's bullet-head with its rotund, firm but slightly plump Sancho Panza aspect of the Southern materialist who enjoys life but fears the Devil. It may be that these two types are the basic ones of Mediterranean civilization, that of Greece, Rome, Spain, and France.

Wednesday, 7 January 1925   *Paris*

Back in Paris at eleven. In the evening dined at the home of Mme Sautreau with Wilma, Mme Paul Clemenceau, and Painlevé.

After the meal a long talk with Painlevé about disarmament. He (like all French politicians) regards the question of Germany's *material* disarmament as secondary because Germany, whatever the arrangements, would be in a position to rearm in a very short space of time. Demilitarization of the police, he added, is a '*mesure enfantine*' insofar as it is meant to prevent their enrolment in the army, a step which it could delay by twenty-four hours at the most. The real issue is disarmament of a frame of mind. It is unfortunate, but the zenith of desire for peace in one country invariably coincides with its nadir in another: *il n'y a jamais concordance* and so no progress occurs. He does not take the bluster of our Nationalists and People's Party ranters very seriously, recalling that after 1870 vengeance-lyrics of the Deroulède sort were acclaimed with huge enthusiasm at popular meetings all over France without either the nation as a whole or those who were exhilarated by them really wanting revenge.

Painlevé looks on the present French Government as '*solide*'. Even the nationalists know that they cannot bring it down. A *coup d'état* need not be feared; the overwhelming majority of the Army would not participate.

Later Mme Sautreau told some fairly malicious stories about other society ladies. Quite amusing, and she certainly brought them to life. I told her that she treated her friends like cooks do gherkins, '*elle les conserve dans le vinaigre*'.

Saturday, 10 January 1925   *Paris*

At seven o'clock to Painlevé at the Palais de la Présidence. An eighteenth-century dwelling, it owed its construction to that lover of the Duchess de Bourbon who built for her the mansion bearing her name. There was a passage connecting the two houses. Today the President of the Chamber, by using this to reach the scene of his authority, follows in the footsteps of the lover who formerly availed himself of this route to the Duchess's bed. The Palace is big and has finely proportioned rooms. All the same, apart from some handsome tapestries, it is shabbily furnished in the taste of the July Monarchy and Second Empire. The banisters would disgrace a suburban tenement.

Monday, 19 January 1925   *Cardiff*

Midday left for Cardiff. In the evening gave a lecture at the University College on Germany's home and foreign policy. About three hundred students attended. Afterwards answered questions. Certain students, I was told, had planned a hostile demonstration, but everything passed off extremely well. At the end they honoured me with their 'war-cry', a fearsome hullabaloo, their highest form of compliment.

Despite the darkness I could distinguish the massive outlines of Cardiff Castle in the centre of the city. One of the most imposing medieval fortresses I know, it is the property and residence of the Marquis of Bute.

Tuesday, 20 January 1925   *Cardiff–Abergavenny*

In the morning to Llandaff and visited the cathedral. An immense, partly Romanesque (Norman), partly Late Gothic building, picturesquely sited on a hilly slope covered with graves, cypresses between them. This situation is the finest thing about it; the cathedral itself has undergone a lot of restoration.

At ten o'clock made a tour of Cardiff Castle under the guidance of a Bute man-servant wearing green livery and a top-hat. The huge square site was originally a Roman camp. On its foundation-walls the Normans built their fortifications without altering the original layout in any way. The Roman walls, sixteen feet thick and consisting of boulders embedded in mortar, remained as the base and inner components of the medieval walls. For the past twenty years the Marquis has been laying them bare beneath the Norman superstructure. This must be one of the best preserved of all Roman forts. Its date, my guide said, has been established through inscriptions. It is supposed to have been constructed in AD 250 and underwent extension during succeeding decades, the time when the Roman Empire was threatening to fall apart through civil war. That shows how little the palace revolutions and struggles affected the enormous Imperial structure and its strong administrative organization initially. Very likely the importance of the encounters in the second half of the third century between emperors and pretenders (with Ferrero as the most grotesque figure among these) is much exaggerated.

'Rosary Crucifix' (Gill)

Midday left for Abergavenny to visit Gill[1] and discuss with him the *Georgics* commission. His address had been given me as Capelyffin (pronounced Chapel-y-fin, signifying *capella ad finem*) near Llanvihangel. At Abergavenny nobody had ever heard of it. I therefore took a car and drove first to Llanvihangel on the assumption that Gill's home must be quite nearby because he answered my wire from there. My driver had never heard of Capelyffin either. At Llanvihagel we were told it was another twelve miles away, high up in the Black Mountains. The driver grumbled that he could not guarantee our getting there because the roads are so bad and narrow. He himself had never been beyond the monastery of Anthóny at the foot of the mountains.

We drove between meadows and hedges along a narrow road through a beautiful lonely valley which did indeed appear to lead into the wilds. I was reminded of my journey a year ago up the Rio Grande. Past the ruins of Anthóny, a medieval monastery, the road became ever narrower and my driver more despairing. We arrived at a steep slope. A local told us that Gill lived in another monastery higher up, founded by Father Ignatius.

Proceeding between more hedges and meadows and finally climbing a steep path, I reached a dilapidated monastic building, passed along a cloister passage under repair, marched through an ante-room to where I could hear voices, and suddenly stood in a medium-sized room where a number of women and girls and two very dignified-looking monks were sitting in front of a large log-fire.

One of the women stepped forward. I recognized her as Mrs Gill. Had I not met her husband on the road? He left a couple of hours ago to meet me, but we must have missed each other. Then she introduced the two monks. One of them, a handsome middle-aged man of grave though friendly appearance, is the prior of an island monastery and was about to return to his sea-girt home because of some celebration there tomorrow.

I sent my car back to look for Gill. He arrived about an hour later, a Tolstoy-like figure in a smock and cloak, half monk, half peasant. He was accompanied by his son-in-law, a young sculptor and draughtsman.

There was nothing dramatic about this re-encounter after the war years, but we were both moved. Later Gill said that for him and his friends, and evidently for me too, art has now taken second place to achieving a regeneration of life. Pre-war life was too superficial. That is why they are here, 'trying hard to be good', though it is not always easy. Yet he must go on working, even if only in order not to starve. In fact he is very busy. He showed me some fine small box-wood carvings and reliefs made by himself and his son-in-law, numerous woodcuts and copper-engravings, depictions of saints and the Crucifixion, portraits, and so on. They are all of a high standard.

He and his wife as well as the children (which is more surprising) profess themselves well in this monkish seclusion. Ditchling had been too petit bourgeois, leaving them only a choice between London and the wilds. They decided to give first preference to the wilds and up to now the experiment has proved successful. They have no sort of help, do everything themselves, cook over an open fire, (like we did when we bivouacked during the war), lead a squatter existence four hours from London, and are happy and completely content.

I showed Gill Maillol's woodcuts and we went through my copy of the *Georgics*. He agreed to carve the initials. I set out again in the dark of night and was back by eight o'clock in The Angel, not at all a bad country hotel, at Abergavenny.

Monday, 26 January 1925   *Berlin*

Winterfeldt telephoned and asked me to come and see him about a 'not very pleasant business'. I went to his office and he told me that a large number of the old gentlemen are demanding my resignation because neither my conduct in foreign affairs nor my pacifist outlook is compatible with the principles and traditions of the Canitz Society.

I replied that I am of course very ready to resign since I have no desire to remain a member of a society which regards my outlook and conduct as incompatible with its own. I would however like to establish the fact that my conduct in foreign affairs has always been based on closest liaison with the Ministry of Foreign Affairs and has repeatedly earned me the unqualified approval of those responsible for the direction of our foreign policy. As for my pacifist outlook, I see as a politician no means other than peaceful negotiations to improve our position abroad and to alleviate the rigours of the Versailles Treaty.

This incident shows how, after leaving me alone for six years, the reactionaries and war-mongers are getting puffed up again. They think their time has come and are no longer afraid of a set-back when they might need my good offices. Winterfeldt clearly did not relish his task and tried to keep his own views out as best he could.

Thursday, 29 January 1925   *Berlin*

In the evening saw Pirandello's *Six Persons in Search of an Author* at Reinhardt's theatre. A piece of virtuosity which occasionally passes the bounds of staggeringly good craftsmanship and becomes real art. The problem of twirling together two or three plots simultaneously, and each time carrying the audience across the gaps without a break in the mood, has been solved by Pirandello with consummate nerve and confidence.

Friday, 30 January 1925   *Berlin*

The Peace Cartel had issued invitations to a meeting to discuss the evacuation of Cologne and the disarmament question. Representatives of the Democratic and the Social Democratic Parties as well as of the Reichsbanner were to be on the platform and it was hoped that at any rate a common front and some agreed step would be achieved. The idea originated with Küster (of Hagen) and the Cartel's Westphalian groups. Ebert,[2] a son of the President, was the delegate for the Reichsbanner's Berlin area command. Unfortunately he proved vulgar, tactless, and indiscreet. These factors turned his speech on the views of the Berlin Reichsbanner into the sensation of the day.

For a couple of hours the discussion rippled along, with all sorts of proposals being made as to how the Government should be tackled about the short-term volunteers (Black Reichswehr). Then up got Ebert, a sturdy, somewhat squat young man with a dark, bullet-shaped cranium. He did not really know, he said, why he was invited. He thought the subject was going to be how to speed up the evacuation of Cologne. So far there had only been talk about the Black Reichswehr. (He was incorrect, seeing that I had spoken at length about security and the security pact.) The Reichsbanner is better informed about the Black Reichswehr than anybody else, having worked for months collecting the material in as much detail as possible. He himself has been out for weeks, systematically visiting every village in the borderland. What has been learned so far about the Black Reichswehr is downright hair-raising. There will be more to come and soon enough. Within three months they hope to have on record every man jack who belongs to the Black Reichswehr. But they would regard it as monstrous to publish the material now and thereby attack the German Government from behind. (This is one point on which I entirely agree.) The way that they (the Berlin area command) see matters is that if the German Government thinks it necessary to have a Black Reichswehr, then it must be constituted from the Reichsbanner, not reactionary associations.

Saturday, 31 January 1925   *Berlin*

Lunched with the *Matin* correspondent Lauret. Others present were young de Margerie (son of the French Ambassador), another couple of Frenchmen, and Alfred Kerr.

De Margerie described the clash in Paris between Carl Sternheim and Madame de Noailles at André Germain's. Madame de Noailles talked about Goethe, Nietzsche and other great Germans; Sternheim rejected the lot as being insignificant. Mention of Unruh's name put him into a positive fit. In his eyes, he himself and possibly Georg Kaiser were the only German writers he would allow, though Kaiser of course copied him.

Kerr spoke in quite good French dully about California.

Tuesday, 3 February 1925   *Berlin*

Dinner with the Bergens at the Adlon. Other guests were Bernhard Bülow, Count and Countess Klinckowström (he formerly in the Life Guards, she *née* Kanitz), and Frau von Oheimb.

Countess Klinckowström, an attractive and cultivated, though not beautiful, young woman (best type of well-bred Prussian stock) complained about the unimaginative reactionary outlook of the younger generation. At seventeen she herself was half a Communist, but their young private tutor, a theological student, is never stirred by a quiver of doubt about any and every old-established tradition. And what he has to tell about the spirit animating his fellow-students is too dreary for words. Odd, to hear such words from her. And she is staunchly nationalist too.

Klinckowström told the story of how he received an official letter from Eulenburg-Prassen, the most respected aristocrat in his province, saying that Major-General X had asked him to inform Klinckowström that there were allegations of French being spoken at a party in his house. What had in fact happened was that one of his guests exchanged a few words of French with a Swiss governess who had been part of the family household for thirty years.

The evening came to rather an abrupt close for me because Frau von Bergen announced her intention of accompanying the Klinckowströms to the Palais Mascotte and asked me whether I would go along too. In front of the Adlon Bergen, Bülow, and Frau von Oheimb on various pleas departed. When we arrived at the Mascotte, it turned out that we were either the guests of, or supposed to sit with, Prince August Wilhelm.[3] This would have been most embarrassing for me, so I quickly said goodbye to Klinckowström after the Prince, coming forward to greet us, had kissed the ladies' hands. I asked him to make my excuse to Frau von Bergen. As the wife of an ambassador, she might well have told me what was going to transpire. Astounding, the free and easy way with which the monarchists are picking up threads and taking over again.

Monday, 16 February 1925   *Berlin*

Big dinner party at Felix Deutsch's home. I saw and met Frau Ebert for the first time. She makes an almost aristocratic impression and could be a countess from east of the Elbe, rather heavily built and ruddy complexioned, but not lacking in graceful movement. She showed good taste in appearing in this highly fashionable company in a perfectly simple low-cut dress and without a single piece of jewellery except for a tiny golden cross which any working-woman might wear. She clearly has tact and dignity.

Regina Deutsch[4] told me that immediately after Rathenau's assassination his mother destroyed all his letters from herself. That put paid to what, she maintains, was their plan at some date to publish their correspondence. I asked why old Frau Rathenau had behaved that way. 'Jealousy! The jealousy of an old woman of eighty.'

Friday, 20 February 1925   *Berlin*

To tea with Albert Einstein, who is off to the Argentine in a few days. Also there was a French colonel, head of the chemical division of the Inter-

Allied Military Inspection Commission. Everything is all right with the German chemical industry, he said. There can be no question of it manufacturing poison gas or being in any way not completely back on a peace-time footing. Morgan's[5] article contains a lot of nonsense. He has obviously written it only to have his name bandied about.

Einstein, when I mentioned his successes, replied that he has merely been luckier than others. He knows a large number of scholars who are intellectually as well fitted as he to make major discoveries, but they have just been less fortunate. I commented that he seems nevertheless to have some special sort of feelers to tell him where the solution to a problem lies. He and the French colonel talked about scientific problems.

Tuesday, 24 February 1925   *Oxford*

To Oxford, where in the evening I spoke at Balliol on behalf of the League of Nations Union. Stayed with the Master of Balliol (Lindsay). In the train met Gilbert Murray.

Lindsay has a house inside Balliol. I have been given a handsome room with a large, though unfortunately very cold, bathroom adjoining. Before dinner I sat with Lindsay and his wife in his study. Students came in a number of times to talk to him or ask for appointments. The contact between students and teachers is much closer here than with us. Unmarried dons live in college and in the evenings a circle of young people gathers in their rooms. All very Socratic.

We ate in hall, where afterwards the meeting took place too. I sat with Lindsay and three or four dons (all in gowns) at the high table, the students in their black gowns at long, narrow tables below us. My impression was of a gently murmuring company of monks. The students finished their meal within a very few minutes (fifteen at the most) in order to get away again. Striking, how noiselessly everything proceeded. Utterly different from what it would be in America or France or at home.

After dinner we went to the Common Room while the tables were cleared. Then I made my speech, to an audience composed mainly of students and dons, on Germany's attitude to the League of Nations and security matters. A discussion followed. Questions usually showed sympathy for Germany. At the end Murray seconded a vote of thanks to me proposed by a student.

Wednesday, 25 February 1925   *Birmingham*

At midday I left Oxford for Birmingham to be the guest of Mrs George Cadbury (widow of the cocoa king) at Northfield Manor, her magnificent country-seat. The Cadburys, like all British cocoa kings, are Quakers. In the darkness I caught no more than a glimpse of the large park in which the house lies. My meeting took place at Woodbroke Settlement, a sort of Quaker educational institute for budding missionaries and 'international workers'. At seven o'clock we had a meal with the students. It was somewhat frugal – an egg, tomato salad, and a pudding washed down with lemonade. All of the students are nice, decent individuals.

I spoke in the chapel, a very simple wooden building. The cocoa million-airess was in the chair. Besides the British members of the community, the students included Germans, French, Americans, and a Zulu. Eleven nationalities in all, they told me. After the meeting we sang a hymn in the hall of the main building. The place has an appealing atmosphere. There is no question about that. But there is no room for the resolution of more profound problems. Such difficulties are just papered over or indeed just sugared over. Such a coating may be enough to inspire a few exceptional characters to lead an exceptional life and to perform exceptional achieve-ments, but it provides no foothold for the ordinary run of humanity. It bears, like Pre-Raphaelite art, the stigma of superficiality.

Thursday, 26 February 1925   *Birmingham–Wolverhampton*

Visited Bournville under the guidance of Mrs Cadbury's very pretty eighteen-year-old daughter. An enormous plant, ten thousand workers, men and women, all neatly dressed in white. The odour of cocoa, though, is so pervasive that I was nearly sick. The Cadburys have built a model town round the plant, with delightful cottages, park-like gardens, baths, dining-halls, an ideally planned school, and a charming old English manor house which was brought here stone by stone and re-erected. The employees are happy. They have their own council which operates on the newest lines. The enterprise is the most complete extension to the working classes of middle-class capitalist civilization with all its blessings and amenities. Neither money nor effort can take this method of management any farther. Above all else there is, with the Cadburys, a genuine ideal behind it, the very best and most charitable of Christian goodwill.

Yet a big question mark hangs over it all. Regardless of the owners' liberality, does there not ultimately remain an element of workers' exploita-tion in so far as they receive less than their share from the proceeds? Can the system as a whole, based as it is on the profit motive and not real need, become any better thereby, any more rational or moral? Does this method take matters any farther or does it only lead them still more deeply into the morass of an irrational and immoral economic process? Are we not simply faced here with a sort of inbreeding on the part of highly developed capital-ism, the outcome of which will be decay rather than evolution into fresh productional procedures?

Little fair-haired Miss Cadbury is rather too frail to bear the burden of being this enormous production machine's crowning achievement and justification. The same applies to Mrs Cadbury's splendid international philanthropy, which in the last analysis derives from nothing more than the benevolent temper of the Lady of the Manor.

In the afternoon I left for Wolverhampton. Spoke to a meeting, under the auspices of the Labour Party, of mainly working-class people.

Friday, 27 February 1925   *Manchester*

The morning papers report that Ebert, after an operation for appendicitis, is in serious danger. At ten o'clock set out for Manchester and was received at the station there by Mr A. C. Wilson. At one o'clock a meeting at the Students' Union. In the evening another at the Quaker meeting-house. Great success. I have seldom felt better and more sure of myself.

Saturday, 28 February 1925   *Manchester–Bradford*

During the morning Wilson accompanied me to the John Rylands Library. The curator showed us some magnificent medieval manuscripts, principally from the Crawford Collection.

At two o'clock with Wilson to Huddersfield. The city's MP, Hudson, and the Mayor were waiting at the station and we drove straight from there in the Mayor's car to the meeting. A hundred and fifty people, trade union delegates and representatives from other associations, were present. There was growing applause as I spoke, for an hour and a half, about Germany's attitude to the League of Nations, the 'protocol', and security pacts. The Mayor, wearing his golden chain of office, was in the chair. During the closing speeches I was embarrassed to hear myself referred to as 'the great international figure' who had addressed the audience. Hudson, who arranged the occasion, was obviously delighted with its outcome.

On the journey from Manchester to Huddersfield the cold, harsh, treeless landscape made a deep impression on me. It resembles a sharply etched, pitiless face. Here is the birthplace of the Industrial Revolution, world-wide industrial capitalism, and English radicalism. It has an archaic grandeur, grey and sombre, a soul compounded of coal dust, and yet with a hard, untamable energy such as can be sensed in the Roman Campagna. This is the real England, without the mask it wears everywhere else. Rarely has a landscape impressed me so deeply in so short a space of time. It is like lifting the veil from a secret long suspected, but never clearly defined.

At seven we were back in Manchester. I bought an evening paper immediately because I was anxious about Ebert's condition. Walking out into the street, I read the news of his death!

First Rathenau – now Ebert.

Monday, 2 March 1925   *Bradford–Leeds*

In the evening a meeting in the big but only half full hall of Leeds University. Having now spoken in a number of large cities, my strongest impression is of the indifference to the League of Nations, the 'protocol', international security, and the rest, which prevails among the vast mass of the public in this country. The problem of peace is of as little interest to it as in France or Germany. I, and those like me, remain preachers in the wilderness for all the touchingly zealous efforts of pioneers like Hudson. Seen in this light, though, these small, otherwise so dismal and intellectually wretched pacifist associations (leagues for human rights, peace societies, and so on) acquire a different aspect and significance.

Tuesday, 3 March 1925   *Newcastle*

On arrival at Newcastle I received a wire from Paul that my little Lulu has died. A small world of staunchly faithful emotions in which I figured as the focal point has been obliterated for ever. Through the long years of war-time partings she stayed loyal to me until there came the hours of convulsive joy when I did return. We humans are too intricate in our feelings for such affection. I recall her long, lovely and thoroughbred paws, her sprightliness, her comical passion for sugar, and all those little quirks of character which made a personality of her. The ties with which she bound me to a long distant past were many.

Mama (who normally could not stand dogs) used to stroke her. Heymel often played with her. She was poor Fip's unswerving friend. I recall our journey from Paris when she was six months old and looked so funny as she frolicked on the bed of the sleeper. To the end, even on my last visit to Weimar, she put her entire individuality into the storm of barking with which she always greeted my arrival. The news spoiled Newcastle for me.

Wednesday, 4 March 1925   *York*

In the morning visited the Cathedral. I was once again overwhelmed by its boldness of concept, grace, and greatness. The thirteenth century was perhaps Europe's most integrated and richest age. It gave us everywhere our most outstanding buildings, our most splendid paintings, a wealth of un-surpassed poetry, saints like Francis of Assisi and Dominic, rulers like Frederick Hohenstaufen, St Louis, Innocent III, and, the crowning grace, Dante. This was the century in which Europe was really born and the white race raised above all others.

In the afternoon to the Commons to listen to what was expected to be a major debate on foreign affairs prior to Chamberlain's journey tomorrow to Paris (meeting with Herriot) and Geneva. Hudson had procured for me a seat 'under the gangway',[6] meaning that I actually sat in the Chamber itself directly behind Members.

Herbert Fisher rose to question the Government about its policy. He spoke in place of Lloyd George, who is ill, and made two particular points. The Liberal Party will not permit the continued occupation of Cologne[7] to be mixed up with the subject of security. Furthermore it will have no truck with a security pact between Britain and France which leaves out Germany. What Fisher said was good, but he is a poor speaker.

Chamberlain, with his shiny topper on his head and his legs stretched out full length, had so far presented the perfect figure of a clubman on the Government bench. He stood up immediately after Fisher's speech, placed the immaculately ironed hat on the table of the Clerk of the House, and began his answer. In addition to that indefinably youthful appearance which characterizes an English boy past school-leaving age, he has a clean-shaven sharply contoured, lean face. It carries little trace of intellect, but resembles that of a boiling chicken or a bad reproduction of features on a fine old medal executed in relief.

His delivery was abominable. He stuttered, continually corrected himself, from time to time got stuck, and was evidently undecided as to how much he should or should not say. The contents of his speech were pretty hollow and unsatisfactory. He admitted that he does not yet possess any policy because, as he put it, he has not as yet come to any conclusions about what policy he should follow(!). He wants to make use of his journey to obtain the information. This pitiable confession was received by the House in silence. He went on to refer to Grey's speech of yesterday, appearing to adopt its arguments as his own (a point on which Grigg later nailed him down).

His two most important statements, and the only ones that he expounded more or less clearly, were that the problem of security has nothing to do with prolongation of the Cologne occupation and must not be linked to it and, secondly, that the German Government has in fact offered to guarantee the existing Franco–German boundary and the British Government regards this offer as very important. Indeed he went so far as to express the hope, formulated with some warmth and even uttered with some solemnity, that this offer by the German Government may prove to be the bridge across which Europe will proceed out of its present melancholy condition towards a better future.

Chamberlain had been speaking for a while without having said much, though he did push forward as far as the German offer, when Kirkwood, the

Labour member, sang out, 'Well, now there's something terribly important!'
He repeated this comparatively harmless interruption two or three times
until the Chairman (the House was sitting in committee) called him to order.
He did not obey, whereupon the Chairman required him to leave the
Chamber. Chamberlain sat down in the middle of his speech. Kirkwood
remained in his seat. The Chairman then named him, suspended the
session and, with great ceremony, sent for the Speaker, who came in his
array and upheld Kirkwood's exclusion.

Now Ramsay Macdonald intervened, but without success. This was
followed by the exodus of the whole Labour Party from the Chamber
amidst jeers from the Conservatives. The Liberal Opposition stayed seated.
With the House now reduced to a third of its number, Chamberlain resumed.
The scandalous incident had however clearly put him off his stroke. His
remarks became still more uncertain and confused than before and, when
Grigg got up to reply, he was obliged to apologize for having forgotten a
very important passage which he meant to insert earlier.

Never in my life have I experienced so lamentable a performance on the
part of a Foreign Minister in a Parliament. Even our Rosenberg, who can
only read from a manuscript and does that badly, is better. How such a
helpless, awkward, indecisive, vague man is expected to discuss the world's
most serious problems with some degree of good sense is incomprehensible.
I would not let him act for me even in eviction proceedings.

The Labour Party was very indignant about the mischievous procedure
of the Committee Chairman (a Conservative) against Kirkwood. Macdonald
will put a question about it. For the moment the Labour Party, which is the
official Opposition, has withdrawn from participation in the business of the
House.

Wednesday, 11 March 1925   *London*

In the morning a discussion with Ramsay Macdonald in his room in the
Commons. He now has the one in which I talked to Asquith two years ago.
A large fire was blazing in the hearth to combat the cold, clear weather
outside. During most of our talk he stood leaning against the mantelpiece
(a British habit), with his hands folded behind his back and stretched out
towards the fire.

He is distinctly opposed to our proposal for a guarantee pact.[8] He accuses
our diplomacy of having been in recent years nearly always 'clumsy' and that
this is once more the case. Our proposal raises questions for whose solution
Europe is not yet ripe: that of our eastern border and of what guarantees
Germany can offer France. We are still in the middle of hostilities. France
hates and is suspicious of us. Many in Britain hate and are suspicious of us.
Nothing positive can be expected from a conference on security matters

as long as this frame of mind lasts. Conferences must only be held when it can be anticipated with almost complete certainty that good results will ensue. He had summoned the London Conference only when he felt sure that it would lead to a successful conclusion. But were Britain, France, Germany, and Belgium to sit down together now in order to discuss our pact proposal, France would at once throw up the question of our eastern border and the military guarantees to be offered by us. We would either have to submit or let the conference collapse on account of our obduracy, in which case the whole of Europe would once more throw up its hands in horror at Germany's wickedness.

Arthur Henderson came in towards the end of our talk. He was even more emphatic in his opposition to our proposal than Macdonald. My own feeling is that, over and above objective reasons, tactical and party political grounds influence this attitude which the Labour Party chooses to adopt. They want to use the question of the 'protocol' and peace as their principal battering-ram against the Government so as to win votes and catch a fresh breeze behind the Party sails.

Friday, 13 March 1925   *London*

Visit from Eric Gill. We lunched together with Will Rothenstein. Gill and I discussed his commissions for me, the Virgil and the Caslon type-face initials. Later he showed me at the Goupil Gallery his beautifully sculptured head of Christ Sleeping, which he has just finished. In reply to a question about woodcuts, he said that he would very much like to do some for a Latin edition of the *Song of Solomon* to be printed at my press. He also suggested that we undertake the production of an Indian work, *Ananga-Ranga*, a treatise on love, which he is extremely keen to illustrate. I asked about the contents. 'Well, in reality, thirty-four ways of doing it.'

Gill is a completely innocent mixture of religion and eroticism. He defines his religion as being 'fully in love with Christ', dresses in a sort of monk's habit, and, barring the fact that he is married, in Wales leads the life of a monastic anchorite.

He looks like a mendicant friar, with a shaggy beard and unkempt, fairly long hair. His gaze, out of bloodshot eyes, is guileless yet strong-willed and has on occasion an almost fanatical gleam. His grey-brown woollen gown reaches practically to his feet, while his black felt hat is so old as to have become nearly grey too. He finds it 'such a comfort', he told me, to have all his clothes made at home. One of his daughters is learning to weave and he hopes that in time all the family's clothes will be homespun.

He has misgivings about my intention of having galvanoplastic copies made of his initials because the galvanoplastic process is a child of modern industry, or capitalism, which is bringing ruin on the world. In answer to my objections, he retorted that he is not fighting capitalism, but is content if he personally does not participate in the capitalist process but does 'what is right'.

It is not his concern how others behave. He is however convinced that the whole of modern civilization will break down within a few years, whether we like it or not, so strong is the revolt against it which is growing on all sides.

He really is a quite extraordinary and noteworthy personality, with his great artistic talent, utter repudiation of modern commercialism, and eccentric piety translated into an all-embracing sensuousness. He rejects morality in the usual sense, but his sensuous austerity (a true combination of sensuousness and austerity) recalls the outlook of certain Church Fathers in the desert. Van Gogh probably provides the nearest analogy.

Thursday, 19 March 1925   *London*

Saw Noel Coward's *Vortex* at the Comedy Theatre. He also plays the lead, a young drug addict. A very powerful piece. Coward's performance is superb. With shattering realism yet masterly restraint, and no cheap tricks, he acts the tragedy of the son of a vain, pleasure-seeking, thoroughly depraved and heartless beautiful woman. The ending, though, is inconclusive because there is in fact no way out of the situation.

Friday, 20 March 1925   *London*

During the morning called on Mrs Snowden at the Victoria Hotel, their present abode. He, Snowden, was attending a temperance congress in the provinces. She is just back from a lecture tour in America and had much the same experience as myself of nearly being killed with kindness. One of her lectures was attended by two thousand people, every one of whom wanted to shake hands with her. She had spent the previous seventeen nights on trains. When the thousandth or twelve-hundredth person approached, she fainted. After being carried out and sprinkled with eau de cologne or water, she came to, was led back into the hall, and forced, regardless of her protests, to shake hands with the remaining eight hundred.

Mrs Snowden ascribes Macdonald's obstinate support of the 'protocol' to personal vanity.

Monday, 23 March 1925   *London*

Rothenstein took me to lunch (very bad Italian place) with Sir Sidney Lee, who wanted to meet me. I told the biographer of Edward VII politely what

I think of his hero's complete empty-headedness. He not only agreed that the enormous mass of the royal correspondence contains scarcely a single political or other idea, while a mental decline after 1880 is obvious from it, but also quoted without contradiction a *New York Times* judgement that Edward VII and the Emperor William II were two of a kind. A remarkable feature of his letters to women is the business-like way, without a trace of gallantry or amorous chatter, he arranges his rendezvous with them. These 'love letters' lack charm, wit, or imagination; like the rest, they are just utterly dull. As King, he meddled in politics more than was compatible with the British constitution. Happening to be at Copenhagen when the Entente Cordiale was signed between Britain and France, he proposed on the same day to Isvolski (Minister there at the time) an entente with Russia. Isvolski asked for permission to put down their conversation in writing and this record was initialled, in duplicate, by the pair of them. Lee had seen the King's copy. I promised to send him the German edition of Isvolski's reports, with which he is unfamiliar. Evidently a fairly cautious court historian, his intellectual gifts make no dazzling impression and he looks pretty senile.

Tuesday, 24 March 1925   *London*

Attended the Commons debate on the Protocol and our pact proposal. The calibre of speeches was generally high. Henderson's plea on behalf of the Protocol, quite skilful though badly delivered, echoed towards the end my suggestions and softened the rejection of our proposal. Chamberlain, in contrast with the abortive mumble he produced before his trip to Geneva, spoke clearly and thoroughly held his hearers' attention. But the event of the day was Lloyd George's philippic against the Protocol and against Poland, which he accused of already having five contested territories, currently seeking surreptitiously to obtain a sixth (Danzig), and personifying the real danger of war on the Continent.

The speech caused a sensation. That, in order to draw attention to himself, was probably what its author intended. It totally lacked his usual wit and fascination. Although he did produce a few quite funny remarks, the impression was of a burnt-out volcano belching nothing better than a few puffs of smoke. The vital spark was lacking. An actor too old for his heroics. There was something gruesomely grotesque about this effort to regain the limelight by a demagogic attack on his own creation, Versailles. The convict as public prosecutor. The old lady of easy virtue as the champion of public morality.

Chamberlain interrupted him, emphatically rebutted his allegations, and left the Chamber in protest. Macdonald, in his mellowest tenor and with skilfully simulated indulgence, described Lloyd George as a bull in a china shop who can perhaps be tolerated in home affairs but who becomes a European problem when he intervenes in matters of foreign policy. Otherwise Macdonald's speech was comparatively weak. He rejected and was disdainful of our proposal, yet more indulgent than I expected, saying that if it brings peace closer it has his blessing.

The debate's most sparkling oratory came from young Duff Cooper (Conservative), the husband of Diana Manners and clearly a first-class talent and coming man. Herbert Fisher did his best to mend the damage done by Lloyd George, but also declared himself against the Protocol. Baldwin's was the last speech, a distinctly witty one in which he warmly supported the German move. So far the Labour Party's opposition has only had the effect of confirming the Government in its support for us.

Sunday, 29 March 1925   *Paris*

In the morning saw Hoesch and told him how things are across the Channel. The British Government is catching at our proposal as a last straw in the absence of any other saving notion of its own. That, he commented, is Herriot's position too. So, despite the boorish attitude of the Press here, the French Government will eventually take up our proposal in one form or another, he thinks.

Monday, 30 March 1925   *Paris*

Wilma's dinner-party consisted of Hoesch, Henri Lichtenberger, François Crucy, Lady Barlow, and a Mme Malaterre. At table the talk about Coudenhove showed everyone to be well disposed towards him, but, as Lichtenberger observed, no French politician of any standing will join his Pan-European Union as long as he proposes to exclude Britain. Herriot, Crucy told me, is really very much in favour of our pact proposal. There is considerable anxiety, though, regarding the possible outcome of our presidential election.

Later the conversation turned to Anatole France. Crucy, who had been a close friend of his, recalled Einstein's visit to him at the Adlon in Berlin when Professor Nicolai was also there. France clearly found nothing much to say to Einstein and at once engaged in a very lively conversation with Nicolai. Einstein, on the other hand, was much impressed by their encounter. What baffled Crucy was the reason for France's strange lack of contact with Einstein. The occasion, I suggested, may very well have been as if Jehovah had suddenly met with Voltaire. Einstein is a deeply religious man, convinced of the existence of God, whereas France was a sceptic. Jehovah's appeal to Voltaire would be small, but Voltaire and his scepticism might strike

Jehovah as yet another emanation of His own divinity, a fresh facet of the Godhead, and as such a source of some gratification. Crucy laughed and said that I was probably right. He went on to complain how Brousson, le Goff, and other writers like them, are now muddying France's reputation. They can sling all the dirt they like, I replied, but they have no more than glimpsed the grandeur of France's intellectual status. It is like a Rembrandt portrait which radiates an even more mysterious light for all that it has been painted with dirt.

Wednesday, 1 April 1925   *Banyuls*

I found Maillol suffering from a bad cold and feeling sorry for himself. He suffers, or complains, more about small personal ailments than other people do. He has been unable to sleep for a fortnight because of headaches, he says, and that is why he has made no progress with the initials for the Virgil edition. Bowed and sunk down into himself, he walked around the house in a light blue ulster, a knitted yellow waistcoat, a thick pale blue shirt, and a hat on his head. His clear, light blue eyes twinkled from under bushy grey eyebrows and out of his lined, but noble and ruddily complexioned, face. As colourful a figure as a beautiful old bird of Paradise.

Roundel made for Kessler's Cranach Press (1925). The figure is by Maillol, the lettering by Gill

What do I want the initials for at all? They are costing him endless time, a whole day each, and anyway he doesn't know how, before his departure for Paris, he is to finish the work he wants to do. But, if I insist, he supposes he must get on with the job. All this, with a vain effort to conjure up a thoroughly hurt look, tumbled out with an artful, benevolent smirk, half that of a guilty schoolboy and half that of an old sage. He proceeded to take sample proofs of the two initials for the First Eclogue. When they proved too heavy and in need of correction, he accepted the fact without demur, thus succeeding in making me feel almost intolerably beastly. He asked me to return tomorrow at ten, uttered the hope that he would be better by then, '*et alors nous travaillerons*'.

Horrible, setting a genius a task the way a schoolboy is set a lesson. But that is how it always has been between us. Without gentle pressure and ruthlessness in face of his continual complaints neither his great *Crouching Woman* nor his great relief nor the figure of Colin would ever have been finished.

Thursday, 2 April 1925   *Banyuls*

Maillol still has a cold, but with the sun shining he went to work and completed two of the Virgil initials by adding ornamentation to the letters carved by Gill. First he painted the ornament on the wood-block with a fine Japanese brush and then he cut it out with a knife. In the case of both letters he achieved with these very simple means astonishingly rich effects.

When I expressed my admiration, he replied that only a century ago potters in Spanish villages attained even more astonishing results by even simpler means. I urged him to make a third letter with an ornamentation similar to one of the other two, but he would have none of that. Each letter must have an individual embellishment and he must think of something: '*il faut inventer chaque ornement, sans cela ce serait embêtant.*'

While he was busy, I read him the French translation of my essay about him. He put me right on certain biographical details. He did not, for instance, come to take up sculpture via Gauguin and his decorative studies, but as a very young man took lessons at Perpignan and later, at twenty or twenty-two, worked with Bourdelle.

Friday, 3 April 1925   *Banyuls*

Violent downpour with thunder and lightning in the morning. I sat with Maillol while he worked; he stops as soon as I am not there. I had brought him the stalks of two irises with buds as a model. He put them down in front of him, but remarked, '*Ça ne donne rien pour ce que je cherche. Il ne s'agit pas de trouver un motif, il s'agit de trouver de la couleur, de trouver l'effet*', meaning the background to the letters.

In the afternoon he carved the small leaping buck for the Second Eclogue.

The crudeness of his tools – no tracing-paper, just ordinary paper which he holds against the window, and the tracing is done with the point of scissors left lying around by his wife.

In the evening I ate with the family. Maillol mentioned that he has sold one or two bronzes to Japan and often receives visits from Japanese artists. This turned the conversation to East Asian art. Will Rothenstein, I said, during a lecture in London showed slides of old Indian carvings which vividly reminded me of Maillol figures. The explanation for that is easy, he replied, because at one time he made a very close study of Indian sculpture. It cannot be copied, though, as Gauguin tried to do. Only general lessons can be drawn.

Saturday, 4 April 1925   Banyuls

Spent the morning with Maillol, who felt better for the sunshine and blue skies. He took the sprig of blossoms for the Third Eclogue and completed the woodcut by the addition of a twig which he drew and carved. I discussed with him the price of the four new woodcuts, offering eight thousand francs. He thought it too much, but I stuck to the figure.

Lunched at the hotel. By two I was back with Maillol and asked him to ornament some of the three-lines-high capital letters alphabet which Gill had carved for me. For a start I only talked about four or five letters. With his fine small Japanese brush he painted the ornamentation in white on the block. Then gradually I got him to decorate the whole alphabet. At four o'clock, after only two hours, all of the twenty-six letters were done (including a very beautiful four-line J) except for the G which was botched and spoiled in cutting yesterday. He invented a different embellishment for each letter. Once, when I made some remark, he complained, '*Vous m'avez coupé l'inspiration. Je ne retrouve plus ce que je voulais faire.*' All the same he required less than five minutes for invention and execution. It was an almost unbelievable performance, but now I understand how the monks worked who decorated medieval manuscripts with opulently ornamented initials.

Each letter with its rich blue-white embellishments against the black background looked afterwards like a tiny majolica tile. He impressed on me that Gill, when doing the carving (he refuses to cut this alphabet himself because his eyes are not good enough for such precision work), should on no account try to imitate the irregularities of the brush-stroke, but cut as far as possible identical and regular lines. '*Plus ça sera régulier, plus ça paraîtra riche.*' He seems to draw almost effortlessly on an inexhaustibly copious stock of imagination.

When I think that Johnston simply does not trust himself to design an alphabet of ornamental capitals and would in any case take years to do it, while even Gill would be occupied for months on such a project, whereas

Maillol has never seriously concerned himself with the decoration of literals but shakes them so to speak out of his sleeve, the profusion of forms alive in him appears miraculous.

Sunday, 5 April 1925   *Paris*

Unruh's book about Paris has, thanks to the vulgar tone he adopts towards Mme de Noailles and others who gave him a friendly reception, produced the effect of a public scandal. Annette Kolb calls it, in her quaint way, 'worse than a battle lost'. Unruh, she says, is thought tactless, miserably ill-bred, and far too big for his boots. Rilke on the other hand is the drawing-room pet, 'exactly as the French imagine a German poet to be'. Apparently he has fallen right into Mme Klossowska's clutches.

Saturday, 18 April 1925   *Berlin*

At twelve to Schubert. Told him my impressions about Britain and France. Hindenburg's election as President, I said, would be a 'foreign policy disaster'. Schubert confirmed that this is his view too. Stresemann had struggled to the last moment against Hindenburg's candidature. It is Stresemann's duty as Foreign Minister, I retorted, to stand up publicly against it. The same line of thought, Schubert replied, had crossed his (Schubert's) mind, but the time for such action is not yet; it will be more effective during the last few days preceding the election. The danger, though, is that Stresemann's initiative may result in just the opposite of what is wanted. He has gradually become so unpopular that many will say, 'If Stresemann is against it, then that's precisely why we'll vote for Hindenburg.'

Sunday, 19 April 1925   *Berlin*

Lunch with Stresemann at his home. His wife looks much younger with bobbed hair. Afterwards I talked alone with him for an hour. He is frankly and honestly in despair at Hindenburg's candidature. His features assumed their gloomiest expression when I turned the discussion towards the subject and outlined the catastrophic consequences which Hindenburg's election would have on foreign policy. He fought this move to the last, he said, but for the sake of Ebert, who was still alive, he did not join the Loebell Committee on its formation. That proved a serious mistake because the Committee *voted* on candidates, a wholly improper procedure. Small parties, 'with seventeen registered electors', were allowed one vote each and the People's Party with three million electors only three. That was how it became possible for it to be outvoted. If he had been sitting on the Committee, he would not have put up with that. Hindenburg himself was in fact against running in the election and a statement to this effect had already been drafted. Then Tirpitz made a secret trip to Hanover and talked Hindenburg into changing his mind. (Tirpitz, in other words, bamboozled Stresemann.) Hindenburg will not however be elected; that is his consolation.

Cartoon by Karl Arnold showing Gustav Stresemann as the guardian angel of the young Republic

At the end he became very mournful, all the same, saying that two years of his life's work will go to wrack and ruin if it does happen. Expounding foreign policy to Hindenburg, as President, is something at which his imagination so far boggles. He ought to initiate the public into the dangers this candidature represents, I told him. The consequence could quite easily be negative, he countered, because people who reject foreign interference in our home affairs may vote for Hindenburg precisely on that score. The whole business, he continued, amounts to an intrigue directed against himself, its purpose being to avoid election of a President with whom he is on good terms. The objection to Jarres was that he is 'a friend of Stresemann'.

The longer we talked, the gloomier he became. But he lacks the courage to stand up openly against Hindenburg. 'People have been told the truth from the Ministry for Foreign Affairs point of view. A public declaration against Hindenburg on the part of the Minister for Foreign Affairs is a different matter.'

Monday, 20 April 1925   *Weimar*

In the afternoon visited Frau Foerster-Nietzsche. As always, she was extremely friendly. She waxed indignant against Fritz Unruh's very silly and tactless Paris book, especially the way that he abuses her 'dear Countess Noailles'. We discussed business. Admirable, the resignation and courage with which this old woman of eighty mentioned the complete loss through inflation of the accumulated funds (eight hundred thousand gold marks, in round figures) of the Nietzsche Endowment. 'Everything gone, down to the last penny.' She added, almost cheerfully, 'Now we live on royalties. It is nearly a miracle, but it is so.' Munich well-wishers moreover gave twelve hundred marks (!) at Christmas as the basis for a new fund. This courage of hers, which in situations of this sort comes out so strongly, borders on the heroic and compels esteem for Nietzsche's sister. Afterwards she spoke very nicely about Wilma.

Sunday, 26 April 1925   *Berlin*

Arrived at seven and went to the voting-booth in the Linkstrasse at ten. Rainy, cold morning. The drizzle kept the streets empty. On the Potsdamer Platz just a few swastika-carrying youths, with heavy cudgels, blonde and stupid as young bulls. There were few flags in this district, and those few were fairly evenly divided between black-white-red and black-red-gold.

A worrying day. My calculation is that Marx and Hindenburg will each obtain some fifteen to sixteen million votes and that Marx's majority can with luck be five hundred thousand to a million.

It poured incessantly. The people in the streets seemed indifferent. The lorries with black-white-red and black-red-gold supporters drove noisily between the crowds taking their Sunday walk under umbrellas. Nobody, looking at the streets, would guess that a decision vital to Germany and Europe was in the course of being made.

I have at any rate done my duty, which Stresemann has not. He soothes his conscience with the notion that Hindenburg 'won't be elected after all'. That, as German Foreign Minister, is a risk that he has no right to take. It is too big and the consequences that would follow on Hindenburg's election can prove too disastrous for the German nation. Left in the lurch by those in authority and the man at the helm, as in 1914, it will rush un-suspectingly upon its fate. That is why I *had* to say at least what I did at Bielefeld.

In the evening I waited for the election result at Democratic Party head-quarters. Shortly after one the outcome was definite: Hindenburg has been elected. The sequel is likely to prove one of the darkest chapters in German history.

Tuesday, 28 April 1925 *Berlin*

At the theatre saw Krupp von Bohlen and his wife, sitting like modest petit bourgeois in the stalls. Talked to them during the interval. He takes the view that Hindenburg will inevitably disappoint those who expect him to work a miracle and will therefore lose his nimbus. In foreign policy too he will have to make unavoidable concessions. Bohlen, oddly enough, does not reject the idea of permanent League of Nations military commissions in the Rhineland. The Allied military occupation is already now not very oppressive. 'Isn't that right, Bertha?' His wife duly approved. But he sees difficult times ahead. We are, he thinks, at the start of a very severe economic crisis. So far we have only had a foretaste of it.

Tuesday, 12 May 1925 *Berlin*

Arrived in Berlin last night. Today attended Hindenburg's swearing-in at the Reichstag. Enormous police contingents in the Budapester Strasse and at the Brandenburger Tor. By eleven o'clock the galleries inside the Reichstag were full to overflowing. Luckily I had a numbered seat with a good view. The hall was pretty skimpily decorated. Just the black-red-gold presidential standard affixed to a wall-covering behind the Reichstag President's chair and a black-red-gold banner, flanked by blue hydrangeas, draped over the presidential table. As Lewald said to me, 'Suitable to the inauguration of a new mayor in the back of beyond!'

Precisely at twelve Hindenburg and Löbe, both of them in frockcoats, entered through one of the small doors behind the Reichstag President's chair. They almost went unnoticed, but suddenly there were cheers on the extreme left, the Communists shouted 'Long live the Soviet Union', and marched out of the hall in goosestep. Then Hindenburg, standing on the spot where Rathenau's coffin had stood, swore the oath of office, hedged in right and left by black-red-gold, and read a declaration from a piece of paper inscribed with such huge letters that it would have been possible, with the aid of an opera-glass, to read them from the gallery. The old gentleman nevertheless had some trouble in deciphering them. He read hesitantly, with pauses, and at the outset addressed Löbe as *Herr Reichspräsident*.[9]

The impression was of a somewhat self-conscious old general enunciating unaccustomed and incomprehensible material. The emphasis laid on the declaration on the constitution's *republican* and *democratic* character and on *popular sovereignty* was however stronger than expected. That was indicative of the tactics which the intelligent monarchists and right-wing politicians behind Hindenburg (men like Luther and Loebell) are going to adopt in the first instance, tactics directed towards winning over or at least lulling the republicans, but which cannot fail also to strengthen the Republic.

A young diplomat with the Legation at Riga said to me, as we were leaving, 'We have now witnessed the *birth* of the German Republic.' With Hindenburg it becomes respectable and so do its black-red-gold colours, which will now appear everywhere with him as his personal banner. Something of the veneration in which he is held will rub off on them and make it more difficult for the swastika-wavers to drag them down in the mud again. Today already they are much more prominent as part of the street decorations in the centre of the city than has been the case so far. The Wilhelmstrasse, normally venturing only upon a very modest and essential black-red-gold splash, is today steeped in these hues. If the republicans do not abandon their vigilance and unity, Hindenburg's election may yet turn out even quite useful for the Republic and for peace.

Friday, 15 May 1925   *Weimar*

Visited Frau Foerster-Nietzsche. During tea General Hasse paid a first call. He and his staff have been transferred here from Cassel yesterday. Frau Foerster-Nietzsche almost fell on his neck. She has retained the girlish heart that cannot resist the sight of a soldier's tunic. More irritating is that, as she herself told me, she should have allowed her little great-nephew Oehler to sit, steel-helmeted and girded with a drum, on the coachman's seat of her carriage during the entry of the troops which took place yesterday amidst great popular participation. In other words, she supports the idiotic nursery game of soldiers.

All the philistines are delighted about Hindenburg. He is the god of all those who long for a return to philistinism and the glorious time when it was only necessary to make money and accompany a decent digestion with a pious upward glance. They are waiting for Hindenburg to 'consolidate' conditions, meaning adjustment to Philistine standards. Farewell progress, farewell vision of a new world which was to be humanity's conscience money for the criminal war. At long last, until the day the butcher arrives and demands his toll, it is going to be possible once more to live cosily as a stuffed sheep or gorged goose. I am still sickened by my experience this afternoon of intimacy between Frau Foerster-Nietzsche's trashily sentimental militarism and the narrow-minded General Staff outlook.

Tuesday, 26 May 1925   *Berlin*

Fancy dress ball at the d'Abernons'. I went in a red tail-coat and white breeches, the dress we used to wear at the Imperial Hunt banquets in Grunewald before the war. The costume attracted some attention. D'Abernon and others complimented me on its striking combination of elegance and simplicity.

Took Frau Stresemann in to supper. She wore Baden peasant costume, as also did her two sons. She complained bitterly about the attacks on her husband, 'such a dear, good man'. They will be glad when the day comes for them to return to the Tauentzienstrasse and be left in peace. Besides, with her husband's wretched salary, official entertainment costs them a mint of money. I spoke to her about the bad state of the pact negotiations and asked her on my behalf to warn Stresemann again to beware of Briand, who is a saboteur and a criminal. At this point d'Abernon joined us.

There were noticeably few Germans present. From official circles only Frau Stresemann and a few young Ministry of Foreign Affairs attachés. The Diplomatic Corps was there in full strength. The Italians danced a tarantella (a pretty sight), and the British, Americans, and Dutch an English country dance in which Frau von Gevers, in Dutch peasant dress, also took part. Lady d'Abernon, with whom I sat out one dance, looked unbelievably young and charming as a Gainsborough farmer's daughter in a light, flowered material and cap. The whole scene was very colourful and gay. The only difficulty is to see why, at this moment when the international situation is so tense and grave, diplomatists (of all people) should have to disport themselves as peasant lads and lasses.

Wednesday, 16 December 1925   *Berlin*

Dinner at the Stresemanns'. Grand affair, with the guests including Bosdari (the Turkish Minister), Kühlmann, the Rüfenachts, Schachts, Zechs, and so on.

As I crossed the Potsdamer Platz on my way there, the postal edition of the *Vossische Zeitung*, with news of a projected attempt on Stresemann's life, was being distributed. Stresemann, whom I congratulated on the failure of the plot, had just heard of it from Police Headquarters. He complained bitterly about the inadequate protection afforded by the courts and the fact that nothing should happen to a man like Pudor who is openly preaching his death. Berger, who arrived later, said that the judiciary used to operate with a bias towards the executive, later acted on a par with it, and now it is against it. Whoever undertakes proceedings against the executive is sure of winning. He quoted the indemnities for the former sovereigns as an example. So far as these are concerned, I put in, they should receive no more than the revaluation ratio. Stresemann thoroughly agreed with me.

Tuesday, 22 December 1925   *Berlin*

Opening night of a series of guest performances by Diaghilev and his ballet company at the Deutsche Künstler-Theater. They danced *Biches*, *Tricorne*, and *Sailors*. Storms of applause. I went behind the footlights and congratulated him.

Diaghilev (Cocteau)

Monday, 28 December 1925   *Berlin*

In the evening with Max to the Russian Ballet. Afterwards supper with Diaghilev, Lifar, Nouvel, Boris Kochno and Max at Förster's. Diaghilev told us a gruesome story. *Just once*, in 1915, he discovered a new Nijinsky, a young Spaniard called Garcia. When he visited him at Barcelona, the old landlady spoke of *el loco* (the madman), but he took no notice and brought him to London. One day Garcia went out and, seeing a red lantern burning in front of St Martin-in-the-Fields, asked a beggar woman who sat in the porch whether the building was a brothel. Then he gave her all his money and said,

'What a joke. In London even God lives in a whorehouse.' Next he tried to force his way into this 'brothel', eventually breaking in the door. As he did not turn up for the evening performance, Diaghilev, after looking for him, informed the police. Late at night they found Garcia inside the church: naked, suspended in front of the altar, and quite mad. He is believed to have died meanwhile in the lunatic asylum to which he was taken.

1926

Friday, 1 January 1926   *Paris*

The year of Locarno has ended.[1] Let us hope that, after eleven years of war, the first year of peace begins.

Saturday, 2 January 1926   *Paris*

Lunched with Misia Edwards-Sert, Poulenc, Jean and Valentine Victor-Hugo, Pierre Bertin of the Comédie Française, and the pianist Marcelle Meyer. We ate in the hotel-room downstairs and then sat in Misia's small silver brocade cage on the sixth floor. Poulenc, whom I met for the first time, is a big, broad-shouldered farmer's son, rather taciturn and difficult of approach but likeable.

Talk turned largely on mutual acquaintances: Diaghilev, Cocteau, Radiguet. When I spoke about the Russian Ballet's miraculous salvation and rejuvenation through war and revolution, Misia told us how badly off Diaghilev had been during the war. In Spain he nearly starved. It took months before the French Government granted him an entry permit, but at last Sert was able to fetch him from Barcelona. On the way to the frontier he asked Diaghilev whether he had anything compromising on him. No, nothing at all, he never carried anything compromising on him. Well, at any rate look whether you haven't anything in your pockets, Sert urged him. Only a few old letters. Yes, but what letters? Finally Diaghilev brought out a fat wad of papers, including two letters from Mata Hari. The French had just arrested her for espionage. There was barely time to destroy the correspondence before they reached the frontier.

Valentine Victor-Hugo and Misia tore to shreds Cocteau's poem about Radiguet. It is quite untrue, Misia said, that poor little Radiguet died with his eyes riveted on Cocteau. On the contrary a horrible thought, he died quite alone in hospital. *On a fait le vide autour de lui* because he had typhoid and, partly from fear of infection and partly under doctors' orders, practically nobody visited him. Cocteau put in only a very rare appearance. Valentine Hugo recalled how Radiguet was already in a bad way during his last summer. He had been a terrible drinker and loved doing everything to excess. Pierre Bertin commented, '*Il allait toujours jusqu'au bord de l'abîme pour voir.*' For example, he once swallowed an entire set of heavy sleeping pills in order to experience the effect of an almost lethal dose. They all agreed that he had been one of the truly great who revived the tradition of French story-telling practised by Mme de Lafayette, Voltaire, Balzac and Stendhal. Misia said Cocteau has undergone *une crise religieuse*. A missionary, Father Maritain, converted him. Cocteau has told her that, at the sight of the old priest, he felt '*qu'il étais un saligaud*'. Now he is '*un ange. Claudel, lui, l'a toujours été un ange paysan, avec les pieds bien plantés sur la terre. Cocteau, lui, c'est différent. Mais sa conversation l'a rendu délicieux. Plus de nervosité un calme, une sérénité qui vous fait du bien.*' Valentine Hugo declared *Orphée* to be a masterpiece.

Wednesday, 6 January 1926   *London*

Telegram from Max: Paul Cassirer has shot himself, but they hope to save him.

Thursday, 7 January 1926   *Berlin*

Memorial service for Paul Cassirer. The whole of Berlin's art world was present. Max Liebermann spoke first, I followed. Although Ernst Cassirer telephoned me at half past eleven last night, still trying to persuade me *not* to mention Tilla Durieux[2] (hostility of the family and friends), I did so of course. She was there, deeply veiled. (They tried to prevent that too.) I went up to her afterwards. Cassirer's death has deeply upset me.

Wednesday, 13 January 1926   *Berlin*

Visited Tilla Durieux. She was embittered. Not one of the family had come near her at the service. After twenty years she and Cassirer parted over an utterly petty incident, but she might have returned to him after a couple of months. Evidently indignation against the family dams up for the moment greater anguish, and she is by nature cool and unbending.

Tuesday, 19 January 1926   *Berlin*

With Max to the first night of Richard Strauss's *Elektra*. The orchestra, under Bruno Walter, played with splendid, headlong, tempestuous verve. Clytemnestra was superb, but Wildbrunn made rather a plump Elektra.

In a box behind us were Richard Strauss, Pauline, and a family called Strauss with whom they are staying. Pauline invited us to supper after the performance. The house is far out on the Heerstrasse, near the Stadium where until recently there was nothing but pine-woods. Apparently, though, this part is being transformed into a smart western suburb for those who have cars.

Richard Strauss

At table Pauline showed herself at her best and her worst. Motherly concern that all her guests should have enough to eat, especially Max who sat next to her and whose plate she kept on cramming with eggs, cold meat, and salad. But *Woyzeck*[3] (Büchner's play, not the opera) she spurns because she really cannot preoccupy herself with the troubled soul of a squalid non-commissioned officer. What affair is it of hers (the implication being, 'me, the daughter of a general')? *Carmen* is also the story of a non-commissioned officer, I observe. Yes, but romantic, Spanish, and a Merimée creation, protests Pauline. A German non-commissioned officer seems to me worth as much attention as a Spanish one, I retort, adding that I rate Gretchen above Mary, Queen of Scots. People do say, and Pauline bends forward to whisper it stealthily, that Count Kessler has become quite a Red. Oh no, I answer, I am just a simple democrat. Pauline: A democrat, you, who are a Count? In that case you are fouling your own nest. I: You will forgive me, but whether I am fouling my own nest or not is a matter upon which I must reserve judgement to myself.

Strauss was becoming more and more uncomfortable. Now he intervened and, by declaring that his wife knows nothing about politics and I should take no notice of her remarks, tried to put a stop to the talk. Later Pauline, aware that she had gone too far and obviously somewhat taken aback by my rap over the knuckles, led me into the study to explain to me her political outlook. She is a general's daughter and aristocrat (all this in broadest Bavarian): in southern Germany they hate the north Germans, the Prussians: they want a south German state, Bavaria and Austria together: Catholics and Protestants in one state won't do.

She seemed to anticipate that the brilliance of these concepts (which, she assured me, enjoy the full blessing of the Bavarian Royal Family) would propitiate me.

I am a north German, I replied. All the same I do not want the south Germans to starve and therefore I cannot subscribe unconditionally to her ideas. Before such sentimental amalgamations are discussed, the United States of Europe must be brought into existence. She acquiesced delightedly in European unity.

Wednesday, 20 January 1926   *Berlin*

Dinner-party at home for General Wauchope, his ADC Burton, the British Military Attaché Hume, Sir Andrew McFadyean, and the Nostitzs.

After the meal Wauchope took me aside and said, 'You know right-wing circles better than I do. So you will also hear what I am so frequently told there – that people are ashamed of their country becoming so compromised through the wife of the German Foreign Minister.' 'How?' 'Well, they say that she often dances all night with twenty-year-old boys. Can you imagine Lady Chamberlain doing that? The wife of a British Foreign Minister might perhaps have an affair, but she would not be allowed to embarrass her husband and her country publicly.'

In other words, our nationalist friends go running to a British general and do their best, by undermining respect for the German Foreign Minister through filthy imputations about his wife, to diminish as far as possible international respect for Germany and its scope for action. There's the true face of these nationalist *Junkers*' 'patriotism'! A truly edifying sight, the way these heroes sacrifice themselves *pro patria* by rendering themselves contemptible to a British general as dirty talebearers. Hats off to so much loyalty! Wauchope was not prepared to give me the names of these patriots.

29 January – 2 February 1926   *Berlin*

Discussed the present situation with Koch, Erkelenz and Breitscheid at the Reichstag. Told Koch formally that I would like appointment as a fully-fledged member of the German Delegation to the League of Nations (not in the Secretariat) and asked him to talk to Stresemann about it.

Lunch at the Nostitzs' included Hilferding, Georg Bernhard, Ernst Toller, and Annette Kolb. I said that in Paris one moves from *salon* to *salon*, whereas in Berlin I always feel as though I am going from one public meeting to another. In fact this luncheon was just like a public meeting, with everyone haranguing everyone else and claiming to be right, and lacking either elegance or wit. Not a single well-turned phrase, not one well-aimed shaft, just loud-mouthed opinions. Toller, in conversation, is hyper-excitable and touchy to a degree, speaks softly and stares at his interlocutor with glowing eyes.

Saw Werfel's *Maximilian and Juarez*. Reinhardt's production is excellent. The play is a workmanlike adaptation of the old Sardou historical melodrama to what today's public wants, done in good taste but devoid of any poetic significance.

Friday, 5 February 1926   *Berlin*

Dinner at Schubert's. The Nuncio Pacelli, the Dutch Ambassador, Princess Hatzfeldt (whom I took in to table), the Bergens, Zechs, Countess Sierstorpff and so on.

Talked to Countess Zech about Pacelli (who looked like a portrait by Bronzino come to life) and Catholicism. The latter and Pacelli are embodiments of the old universality of the Roman Empire and the Church. On the other hand Protestantism, in the person of Calvin, has created the new universality of capitalism, a monster perhaps, but nonetheless the begetter of the modern universal European world. Yet what sort of a figure does the representative of this Protestant and capitalist world, a typical banker, a Morgan, say, cut when measured against a Pacelli? We belong to this Protestant and capitalist world and must put up with it. All the same, this antithesis between Catholicism and capitalism is fundamental to the dialectic of our historical epoch.

Princess Hatzfeldt discussed home and foreign affairs with me on the basis of a moderately conservative policy at home and adherence to Locarno abroad. Looking at this gathering of the variegated Stumm-Bethmann clan, my feeling was that power lies in the hands of precisely the same set as before and during the war, the enlightened liberals, tepid monarchists, and anti-Wilhelminian Bethmann family group, consisting of the Bethmanns, Stumms, Harrachs and their cognates (Kühlmann, the Hatzfeldts, Schubert, Mutius and the rest).

Frau von Bergen told me that her father (Dirksen) wanted to invite the Crown Princess and Stresemann to a party, but the Crown Princess declined to be seen in his company. Which is downright ungrateful, seeing that he enabled her husband to return to Germany.

Sunday, 7 February 1926   *Berlin*

In the morning to a performance of Mozart's *Requiem* by the Berlin Phil-
harmonic. Bruno Walter conducted.

Dinner at Hilferding's. The guests included Annette Kolb, Vollmoeller,
a young writer called Friedenthal, and a Hungarian painter whose name I
can't recall.

The main subject of talk was Mussolini's idiotic anti-German speech
provoked by the damn stupid utterances of Held, the Bavarian Prime
Minister. Mussolini is on the look-out for an opportunity to win some
laurels cheaply and wants to pick a fight, never mind where, with a weaker
opponent. Now Held and his fellows have drawn Mussolini's attention to
Germany as a promising outlet for his pugnaciousness.

Vollmoeller, was, as always, extremely amusing, quirkish and barbed. He
described d'Annunzio's feelings about Mussolini. The former is convinced
that the latter tried to have him murdered and that the woman who threw
him out of the window was Mussolini's emissary for the specific purpose of
getting rid of him in this way.

Monday, 8 February 1926   *Berlin*

Dinner-party at home for the d'Abernons, the Lichnowskys, the Andreaes,
Frau von Schwabach, Baby Goldschmidt-Rothschild, Kolbe and Musch
Richter. After the meal came Vollmoeller, Hume, Max and Guseck. Lady
d'Abernon again looked young and charming; she really is almost incredibly
youthful and attractive. Mechtilde, so slender, was beautiful too. And then
Baby, glowingly voluptuous and alluring. Three notably lovely women.

D'Abernon displayed enormous interest in, and a surprisingly expert
knowledge of, Maillol and my large Seurat.[4] His verdict on Maillol's
Crouching Woman was that it is the finest piece of modern sculpture he
knows. He kept on going back to it and inspecting it from all sides.

The library, dining-room, and study once more seemed to make a deep
impression on everyone. With these exquisite women moving through them,
they really did look festive and artistic.

Tuesday, 9 February 1926   *Berlin*

A soirée at Frau von Friedländer-Fuld's apartment on Pariser Platz. Baby
Goldschmidt-Rothschild and Francesco Mendelssohn acted Hofmannsthal's
Gestern, followed by a parody called *Heute* with Baby and Curt Bois taking
Mendelssohn's place.

Interesting was how the younger members of the party, Goertz, Meiern, even Simolin and Helene, condemned the Hofmannsthal play. They thought it 'dated'. The truth is that the war has dealt cruelly with this piece, written for an audience that no longer exists and perhaps never did exist. Hofmannsthal wrote for 'society' without any inner urge and much as though slipping on a gay Venetian fancy-dress. Now the colours have faded, the disguise is transparent, and there is little body inside it.

Thursday, 11 February 1926   *Weimar*

In the afternoon visited Frau Foerster-Nietzsche. She was bursting with the news of her Mussolini friendship and demanded to know whether I had heard of it. Yes, indeed, I said, I had both heard and regretted it, for Mussolini compromises her brother's reputation. He is a danger to Europe, that Europe which her brother longed for, the Europe of all good Europeans. The poor old lady became rather 'agitated', but she changed the subject and the rest of our conversation passed off peacefully. She will be eighty soon and it is beginning to show.

Saturday, 13 February 1926   *Berlin*

Dinner-party at home for Mme Mayrisch and her daughter, Hugo Lerchenfeld with wife, the Willy Radowitzs, Horstmanns, Lancken, Simolin, and Hannah Wangenheim.

At one o'clock, just as my guests were gone, a telephone call from Max Reinhardt. He was at Vollmoeller's[5] and they wanted me to come over because Josephine Baker was there and the fun was starting. So I drove to Vollmoeller's harem on the Pariser Platz. Reinhardt and Huldschinsky were surrounded by half a dozen naked girls, Miss Baker was also naked except for a pink muslin apron, and the little Landshoff girl (a niece of Sammy Fischer) was dressed up as a boy in a dinner-jacket. Miss Baker was dancing a solo with brilliant artistic mimicry and purity of style, like an ancient Egyptian or other archaic figure performing an intricate series of movements without ever losing the basic pattern. This is how their dancers must have danced for Solomon and Tutankhamen. Apparently she does this for hours on end, without tiring and continually inventing new figures like a child, a happy child, at play. She never even gets hot, her skin remains fresh, cool, dry. A bewitching creature, but almost quite unerotic. Watching her inspires as little sexual excitement as does the sight of a beautiful beast of prey. The naked girls lay or skipped about among the four or five men in dinner-jackets. The Landshoff girl, really looking like a dazzlingly handsome boy, jazzed with Miss Baker to gramophone tunes.

Vollmoeller had in mind a ballet for her, a story about a *cocotte*, and was proposing to finish it this very night and put it in Reinhardt's hands. By this time Miss Baker and the Landshoff girl were lying in each other's arms, like a rosy pair of lovers, between us males who stood around. I said I would write a dumb show for them on the theme of the *Song of Solomon*, with Miss Baker as the Shulamite and the Landshoff girl as Solomon or the Shulamite's

Josephine Baker (Serge)

young lover. Miss Baker would be dressed (or not dressed) on the lines of Oriental Antiquity while Solomon would be in a dinner-jacket, the whole thing an entirely arbitrary fantasy of ancient and modern set to music, half jazz and half Oriental, to be composed perhaps by Richard Strauss.

Reinhardt was enchanted with the idea, as was Vollmoeller. We fixed on the twenty-fourth of this month for dinner at my apartment to discuss the matter, the two of them and the Landshoff girl, Miss Baker coming later. Vollmoeller asked me to invite Harden too. It was past four when I left.

Sunday, 14 February 1926   *Berlin*

Saw Zuckmayer's *Fröhliche Weinberg*, ribald farce with political highlights and lots of sturdy sex stuff. The whole thing no more than an entertaining brawl, not to be compared with Hauptmann's *Biberpelz*.

Monday, 15 February 1926   *Berlin*

Dinner-party at home for the Einsteins, Roland de Margeries, Countess Sierstorpff (maiden name, Stumm), Theodor Wolff, Helene, and Jean Schlumberger (of the *Nouvelle Revue Française*). Later there came Mme Mayrisch and daughter, Goertz, Guseck, Alfred.

Einstein sublimely dignified, despite his excessive modesty and wearing laced boots with a dinner-jacket. He has become a little stouter, but his eyes still sparkle with almost childlike radiance and twinkling mischief.

His wife told me that recently, after numerous admonitions, he at last went to the Foreign Ministry and fetched the two gold medals awarded him by the Royal Society and Royal Astronomical Society. She met him afterwards to go to the cinema. When she asked what the medals looked like, he did not know because he had not yet undone the package. He has no interest in such trifles. She gave me one or two other examples. This year the American Barnard Medal, awarded only every four years to outstanding scientists, has gone to Niels Bohr. The newspapers recalled that last time Einstein was the recipient. He showed her the paper and asked, Is that true? He had completely forgotten. He cannot be induced to wear his *Pour le Mérite*.[6] At an Academy session not long ago Nernst drew his attention to the fact that it was missing: 'I suppose your wife forgot to lay it out for you. Improperly dressed.' To which Einstein retorted, 'She didn't forget. No, she didn't forget; I didn't want to put it on.'

A discussion ensued at table about the Sirius moon. Einstein explained the sensational discovery of its gravity and the significance of this for the deflection of red in the solar spectrum. Turning to Hertz (a nephew of the great physicist), he said, 'Your uncle wrote a great book. Everything in it was wrong, but it was nonetheless a great book.'

My Maillol figure once again attracted general admiration, on the part of Einstein too. Countess Sierstorpff told me that she is a 'pacifist'. An incident last summer was responsible for her conversion. My guests were a very animated company and remained until two in the morning, the last to go being Schlumberger, Goertz and Guseck. The Mayrisch girl, now that her mother has taken her in hand and forbidden her to wear her ugly horn-rimmed spectacles, looks very pretty. She and the de Margerie daughter added a delightful note of young feminine charm.

Wednesday, 17 February 1926   *Berlin*

Lunch at McFadyean's with Sir Eric Drummond. He is here to discuss with Stresemann the details of Germany's entry into the League of Nations. I said that I had been sorry not to witness our entry in 1924, when I was in

Geneva, but in fact it is an advantage for it to happen under Hindenburg. Drummond answered that there are other respects in which it is perhaps quite good for the delay to have occurred; France now leans decidedly more to the left and is in a much more pacific mood.

Evidently the interior furnishing of the new Council Chamber, to be built at Geneva, is causing him a good deal of a headache. A specific problem is whether the delegates are to have desks or not (as is the case in the House of Commons). Stresemann advised against desks because delegates, if provided with them, will write letters rather than listen to speeches. Drummond inclines to the same view, but thinks he will not be able to avoid their provision.

In the evening I went again to the negro revue starring Josephine Baker. All these shows are a mixture of jungle and skyscraper elements. The same holds good for the tone and rhythm of their music, jazz. Ultramodern and ultraprimitive. The extremes they bridge render their style compulsive, just as it does with the Russians. In comparison, our own products hang like a limp bow string, lacking inner tension and therefore style, with far too much of a 'cosy parlour' origin about them.

Monday, 22 February 1926   *Berlin*

At tea in the Adlon I was introduced to Elsa Brändström.[7] Strikingly pretty, slim and fair-haired, she was providence in person to our prisoners of war in Russia and Siberia, a Nordic Joan of Arc who for years on end was the one truly human being whom hundreds of thousands encountered. She exemplifies what a simple person with good will, courage and tact can achieve. A real heroine, she made the same deep impression on me as Nansen did. With fine, slenderly moulded features, but a nose firm enough to indicate determination, and blue eyes which are beautiful as well as very clear in expression, she has an unaffected way of speaking that implies her story to be nothing out of the ordinary. In fact she spent five years in Siberia, during two of them cut off completely from contact with her family, suffered a terrible bout of spotted typhus, and twice was condemned to death as a spy. Yet she remains as natural and full of goodness as on the first day, apart from looking as lovely as a débutante. People like this, whose inborn strength becomes beneficence without loss of vigour, are genuine paragons. What is so profoundly moving about her is not that she saved thousands of lives, but the faith of these thousands in humanity.

She told me how once she received news of her father being dangerously ill. She could have gone home. She stayed because she knew that her father would receive every possible help, whereas thousands would lose their last hope if she left them. Miraculously, so it seemed, her father recovered. Years later, when they met again, he said that he would have despised her if she had returned. Today the former German prisoners of war in Siberia are still like a family to her. Through the Russians they have acquired the best of all qualities – respect for the enemy, deep and warm-hearted humanity, comradeship without regard for rank. The Bolsheviks were better than the Tsarist officials. Her stories about the casualness of the Imperial regime were hair-raising. In 1915 they put a trainload of Turkish prisoners into a Moscow siding, leaving the inmates of the sealed coaches to freeze to death. When the carriages were eventually opened, ice-picks had to be used to remove the corpses. The same thing happened at Pensa and other places. Not out of wickedness, simply out of casualness; Nitschevo! And she narrated many other things too, all in the same straightforward and matter-of-fact way while drinking tea or dividing up a piece of cake with a fork or playing with a pearl necklace. In Saxony she supports a home for the children of prisoners of war whom she promised on their death-beds to look after their offspring. I had the distinct feeling that I was in the presence of a simple but very great individual, a secular saint to whom one wants to go down on one's knees.

Wednesday, 24 February 1926 *Berlin*

Invited for dinner Harden, Max Reinhardt, Oscar Fried, Vollmoeller, Frl. Landshoff, Goertz and Guseck. Stag-party, including Frl. Landshoff in dinner-jacket, very attractive, her boyish appearance enhanced by horn-rimmed spectacles and a cosmetic intimation of black down. Harden, who looks every day more like a cross between Voltaire and an old actress, was entertaining and witty. He keeps quiet a long time, then suddenly looses a stinging shaft, his tone almost timidly gentle and his manner faintly recalling the *ancien régime*. An amusing war of words, mainly about Jews and Soviet Russia, was waged between him and Fried, who is less subtle and much clumsier in repartee.

Around midnight the Landshoff girl and Guseck went to fetch Josephine Baker. I had cleared the library, so that she should have room to dance. But at first she was not in the mood and sat for a long time in a corner, evidently embarrassed at exposing her nudity in front of Helene and Luli Meiern, who had also meanwhile arrived, because 'they are ladies'.

She did not recover from her shyness until I began to describe to Reinhardt and Vollmoeller the first scene of the ballet I plan for her. My plot is how Solomon, handsome, young, and royal (I have Serge Lifar in mind), buys a dancer (the Shulamite, Miss Baker), has her brought before him, naked, and showers his robes, his jewels, his entire riches upon her. But the more gifts he lavishes, the more she eludes him. From day to day he grows more naked and the Dancer less perceptible to him. Finally, when it is the King who is altogether bare, the Dancer utterly vanishes from his sight in a tulip-shaped cloud, first golden in colour and composed of all the jewels and stuffs of which he had stripped himself to adorn her, then turning black. At the end of the scene, in the semi-gloom, there enters the young Lover, wearing a dinner-jacket, and . . . . For the present, I told them, I would keep the continuation to myself.

Reinhardt and Vollmoeller argued that this scene should really be the end. It has such dramatic and choreographic tension that they cannot imagine it rising to a higher climax.

Josephine Baker was as though transformed. *When*, she implored, will the part be ready for her to dance? She began to go into some movements, vigorous and vividly grotesque, in front of my Maillol figure, became preoccupied with it, stared at it, copied the pose, rested against it in bizarre postures, and talked to it, clearly excited by its massive rigour and elemental force. Then she danced around it with extravagantly grandiose gestures, the picture of a priestess frolicking like a child and making fun of herself and her goddess. Maillol's creation was obviously much more interesting and real to her than we humans standing about her. Genius (for she is a genius in the matter of grotesque movement) was addressing genius. Suddenly she stopped and switched to her negro dances, spicing them with every sort of extravagance. The climax was reached when Fried tried to join in the clowning and she caricatured, ever more preposterously, ever more dizzily, any and every movement he made. Where Fried was just ungainly, with her it became a wonderfully stylish grotesquerie which struck a balance between what is depicted in an ancient Egyptian relief frieze and the antics of one of George Grosz's mechanical dolls. Now and again Luli Meiern also improvised a few movements, very delightful and harmonious; but one twist of the arm by Josephine Baker and their graces were extinguished, dissolved into thin air like mountain mist.

Reinhardt thinks that the people around Unruh, especially 'pernicious' Heinz Simon, are turning him into a megalomaniac. He will shortly produce Unruh's *Napoleon*, but says that from the start he has felt suspicious about the dialogue, lifeless, crumbly, and so unrevolutionary on the part of an author who claims to be a great revolutionary.

Sunday, 28 February 1926   *Berlin*

Looked up Richard Strauss after hearing him conduct *Frau ohne Schatten* at the Opera. The audience could be heard clapping frantically long after the curtain finally dropped. He invited me home to supper, but, having promised to go to Vollmoeller, I had to decline. He seems very tired and worn out from all this conducting and money-making.

I reached Vollmoeller's apartment past midnight. Once more the company was a weird collection, with nobody knowing anyone else. The only fixed star in this firmament is the Landshoff girl, his very attractive mistress and again in men's clothes. It is a *déclassé* atmosphere that Vollmoeller creates around him as being appropriate to the *déclassé* poet that he is or feels himself to be. The names of the women, in every stage of undress, were unintelligible and it was impossible to tell whether they were lovers, tarts, or ladies. The young Jews could be ballet-masters or publishers. The actresses had been 'just discovered'. Sprinkled among this lot were Pallenberg, Luli Meiern, Goertz, Meiern-Hohenberg, and Charell. The gramophone ground out popular hits all the time, but Josephine Baker sat on a couch and ate 'hot dogs' instead of dancing. Mechtilde Lichnowsky, Reinhardt, and Harden were supposed to come, but never appeared. So it continued until three, when I took my leave.

A cheerless, almost tragic atmosphere for a man like Vollmoeller, who really has talent, to steep himself in. I read today his *Achtes Wunder der Jungfrau Maria* (Eighth Miracle of the Virgin Mary). He has a lapidary style, of almost Doric austerity, which no one else now in Germany possesses. But the material is shallow and it is difficult to see why he chose it. Beneath its classical surface it is evilly lascivious and there is some confusion of thought, an effort to combine disparate elements.

Monday, 1 March 1926   *Berlin*

Goodbye to my Seurat, *Les Poseuses*, which I have (alas!) sold to Scotland for a hundred thousand marks. For nearly thirty years I have enjoyed the serene charm of the picture's delicate tints and masses, so natural in effect. I part from it as I would from an individual dear to me. I should not have agreed to sell.

In the evening Max and I went to Toller's play *Der entfesselte Wotan* (Wotan Unbound) at the Tribüne. Ralph Roberts, as the hairdresser on the rampage, was farcically funny, but the piece is sham Sternheim without Sternheim's caustic sense of reality. Toller fumbles about on the surface where Sternheim strikes the target good and hard. On leaving the second Toller piece (a Renaissance love affair and sham Hofmannsthal) after its first, utterly trivial scene, we ran straight into the author's arms. He had just arrived and seemed somewhat disappointed to see us go. I invented some reason and he spoke about his trip to Russia, on which he starts tomorrow.

Wednesday, 3 March 1926   *Berlin*

At lunch met Heinz Simon. I told him that the effect of Unruh's book in Paris is most unfortunate. Simon tried to defend it by saying that it is only a small group of writers which has taken offence. Quite right, I replied, but it happens to be the group which has been at greatest pains to effect a reconciliation with Germany and treated especially Unruh with marked friendliness. Simon hinted that Unruh strongly resents my attitude to the book.

Dinner at Schwabach's.[8] Other guests were the Schuberts, Dirksens (junior) Hannah Wangenheim, Lancken, Countess Lehndorff. I sat between Renata Schubert and Frau von Dirksen.

Renata remains, outwardly and inwardly, the beautiful, smart, presumptuous aristocrat for whom Stresemann, Luther, and parliamentarians as a whole are still just a grotesque ragtag and bob-tail middle-class 'crowd' which, contrary to good order, has seized power. She is indeed, with her superbly shaped shoulders and her gestures, her old and slightly old-fashioned family jewelry, her always rather weary expression and biting, cynical comments, the Republic's only real *grande dame*. Beside her Frau Stresemann (let alone Frau Löbe) looks like a typist tricked out in her Sunday finery.

From the Schwabachs I went to the ball of the Democratic Students Association at the Esplanade. Bourgeois elegance of the type that Renata regards as so comic. Young men in dinner-jackets and lots of perspiring young girls.

Saturday, 6 March 1926   *Helmbrechts (Franconian Forest)*

Left Berlin early to speak on behalf of the Reichsbanner at Helmbrechts in the Franconian Forest. Train as far as Hof. From there started at seven o'clock for Helmbrechts, about twelve miles away, in an open car belonging to a Herr Winzheimer. It got stuck in snow-drifts a number of times before finally breaking down short of a village called Volkmannsgrün. Guseck and I made our way to an inn and drank grog while Winzheimer tried to find some horses. The innkeeper, two old peasants and two youngsters were at first highly suspicious of us, unable to make out what we could be. They questioned us cautiously, asking where we were from and where we wanted to go.

Eventually Winzheimer re-appeared to tell us that no horses were available. I decided to do the rest of the way on foot. It had meanwhile turned half past nine. The snow had stopped and, under a starry sky, Guseck and I tramped along the frozen highway. After about three-quarters of an hour we heard singing in the distance. It was a column of the Reichsbanner from Helmbrechts, who had been advised by telephone of our approach and was marching out to meet us. So we ultimately arrived in the pretty little town, with its medieval lanes and everything under a mantle of snow. The meeting-hall was full to overflowing. Our reception was most enthusiastic, for all that these good people had been waiting two and a half hours and it was half past ten by now.

I spoke for about an hour on the subject of Locarno and the imminent important event at Geneva.[9] A great success. Winzheimer had in the interval been able to have his car repaired and we left at midnight, back to Hof across the hills, just in time to catch the fast train at one fifty-one back to Berlin.

Thursday, 18 March 1926   *Weimar*

Had the registrar of the Nietzsche Archive to lunch. A cousin of Frau Foerster, stockily built, he is quite pleasing in manner, cultured, and has seen the world. Discussed Archive matters: honorarium for Frau Foerster, extension of the copyright period, creation of a Society of Friends of the Nietzsche Archive. I agreed to the latter, but believe the most sensible thing would be, after Frau Foerster's death, to merge the Archive with the Schiller–Goethe Archive.

Monday, 22 March 1926   *Berlin*

In the evening went for the first time to the new Society for Politics, Science and Art. Found there Becher, Heinrich Vogeler, George Grosz, Piscator, Samuel Sänger and others.

Vogeler has taken up residence in Moscow completely and is employed in the Soviet art propaganda department. According to him, there already exists a school of young, highly individual Russian painters. A couple of years ago they were still devoted to the abstract trend, but they are past that stage now and practise a sort of synthetic realism. Vogeler thinks they show great promise. He has, incidentally, aged so much that I scarcely recognized him. Has been given pretty poor quarters in Moscow, but travels all over the country. Has just been up in the Murmansk coastal area and, when he gets back, is supposed to go to Turkestan.

George Grosz says that he has recently returned to painting; the last few years he has done practically nothing but drawings. He hopes gradually to acquire greater facility and then to do, as he puts it, 'modern historical paintings', such as *Parliament*. Something on the lines of Hogarth's political satires.

Sänger talked to me a long time about Geneva. Will I, if we are invited, go as German representative? He has mentioned me as a possibility to Stresemann, who gave an evasive but not negative answer. I replied that I won't stir a finger to land there. The *force des choses*, Sänger retorted, are nonetheless preparing the way for me.

Drawing by Grosz. A comment on post-war decadence

On the whole the Society made a fairly lively, stimulating impression on me. A semi-Bohemian atmosphere which is quite amusing. Beer and hot sausages served at a buffet beneath a picture of an old whore by Dix (who was there too).[10]

Tuesday, 23 March 1926   *Berlin*

Dinner-party at Carl Fürstenberg's[11] in the Behrenstrasse. The Chancellor, the Stresemanns, Schachts, McFadyean, old Monts, the Rüfenachts, Kanitz, Lancken, the Roland de Margeries, Frau Deutsch, Frau von Schwabach, and so on. It looks as though Lancken, Kanitz and I are becoming a sort of standing bachelor reserve for dinner-parties (even though Lancken is married).

I took Luther[12] aside and told him how pleased I was to hear that he proposes to have his portrait painted by Dix. Yes, he said, the tale is going the rounds, but the matter is by no means certain yet. If only Dr Luther were involved, he would have no hesitation in sitting for Dix. The question is, and he doubts whether the answer is in the affirmative, whether Dix would succeed in also presenting the German Chancellor. Slevogt has just done a thoroughly good portrait of him, so that he does not feel particularly enthusiastic about going through the process again right away. I agreed that posing is a tiresome business. Well, he admitted, he derives quite an amount of pleasure from watching how a painter brings out his personal traits. In fact he finds it positively uncanny.

I studied him while he was speaking. He has a heavy, bullet-shaped head, nothing much out of the ordinary, but a finely formed mouth and a young, lively and thoroughly good-natured expression. His features may be undistinguished, but they do not lack character. They reveal vitality, determination, some intellect, and above all flexibility. I told him my analysis. No cartoonist has yet done him justice, he commented. There is a certain ingenuousness in the way he reveals his pleasure at his own success. He is a good example of the type of German who has a tough exterior, but inside is kindly with a sensitively agile mind. I remarked that it was new and surprising to encounter a German Chancellor interested in advanced modern art. This, I could see, was music to his ears. He is evidently out to attain a reputation as a patron of the arts, an ambition inculcated by the activity of Osthaus and the excellent Essen Museum during the time he was Lord Mayor of that city.

Friday, 26 March 1926   *Berlin*

In the evening an 'informal gathering' at the American Embassy. An enormous crowd of people mainly unknown to each other. As soon as I arrived, the Ambassador wheeled me in the direction of a gentleman whom he introduced as Mr Stetson, American Minister in Warsaw. This Stetson (a member of the Stetson hats family), a small, pale, sickly-looking person with reddish eyebrows and moustache, at once attacked me about ill-treatment of the Polish minority in Germany. The Poles, he alleged, have always dealt with the Germans in Poland 'with the greatest moderation' and 'there have never been any complaints'. How long, I asked, has he been Minister? Since August. In that case, I suggest, he should refer to his Legation's files. They doubtless contain the two judgements of The Hague Court of Arbitration, dating from before his days as Minister, wherein the Court condemned the Polish Government's attempted expropriation of German farmers in Poland as a breach of treaty obligations and declared the measure null and void. He knows nothing about that, said Stetson. Precisely, I retorted, that is why he holds the views he does.

At this moment Schubert entered the room. I made a sign to him to join us and introduced Stetson. I added that Mr Stetson had just explained to me the examplary treatment extended by the Polish Government to the German minority there. Schubert turned scarlet and proceeded to describe with considerable vehemence the true state of affairs. Stetson listened impenitently and without budging an inch. Finally, as we went in to eat, Schubert planted him next to Luther. While the latter also apparently did his vigorous best with him, I recommended to Köpke that a telegram should go to Maltzan at Washington, ensuring that Stetson's incorrect reports should at an opportune moment be rectified. As a last resort I spurred Gerlach on to try and enlighten him. The hatter in the soup[13] was the liveliest item in an otherwise pretty dreary evening.

Tuesday, 13 April 1926   *Lugano*

Arrived midday at Basle and travelled straight on to Lugano. This place is packed because the entire flow of Germans which would normally flood Italy has become congested in the Ticino. Huguenin, the café owner, who has just spent a month at Nervi, says that all the hotels there are completely empty 'on account of the Mussolini speech'. Here there is not a room to be had. Although we booked at the hotel a fortnight ago, we have been found accommodation privately. A few hundred million lire is what Mussolini's speech will have cost his country. The price of having a funny man at the head of their Government is proving a little high for his compatriots. *Un polichinelle un peu cher!*

Max says that Locarno is wholly under the spell of Stresemann. There are photos of him everywhere. He is immensely popular, behaves with utmost friendliness to everyone, and goes four times a day to Frau Scheurer's *pâtisserie;* she raves about him. But there is always a posse of detectives in his wake.

Friday, 16 April 1926   *At sea*

Sailed at noon in the South America-bound *Principessa Mafalda,*[14] ten thousand tons. She belongs to the Navigazione Generale Italiana and is a pretty, friendly, even luxurious ship (for all that the luxury is a little past its prime). Furnishings are in fairly unelaborate Louis Seize style, the cabins are large, airy, painted white and have beds, and the meals are excellent. Only a few first-class passengers. They include the Genevese conductor Ansermet, his wife and daughter. All their luggage was lost at the Italian border, so they are travelling to South America without any! During the afternoon the view of the Ligurian coast, with the snow-covered Alps glistening in the distance, was lovely. After nightfall rather heavy seas in the Gulf of Lions.

Saturday, 17 April 1926   *Barcelona*

The Spanish coast in sight since early morning. One small clean white town after another strung along the sea-shore like pearls on a rope, with low, gently rounded hills rising behind them and overtopped from afar by the Pyrenees. At noon landed at Barcelona. Its modernity surprised me. Nothing drowsily southern or operatic about it, but crowds of busy people hustling along spacious modern streets and avenues shaded by plane-trees. Half Paris, half Buenos Aires. An atmosphere totally different from Italy, much more up-to-date and genuine. In Italy whatever is modern is simply a superficial polish deliberately imposed. Here it seems to spring out of the soil and to emanate from the hardworking population.

In the evening down to the Parallelo to see Spanish dancing. Unfortunately the cinema has done much to spoil this. The working classes no longer want to watch folk dancing at its most consummate; they prefer the semi-nude society women and *cocottes* the film world has accustomed them to. So third-rate provincial 'Parisian' dancers instead of the thoroughbred, unique Spanish dancing that the Parallelo used to offer.

Sunday, 18 April 1926   *Barcelona*

Bull-fight. Loathsome memory, despite the colourful, savagely lively, grandiose spectacle. The slaughter of the helpless old horses, whose bowels are torn out of their bodies, is shocking and disgusting. The bull too, entering the arena as a young, splendid creature and half an hour later leaving it as a bleeding carcase, arouses nothing but anger and pity in me. The most colourful, glittering display is no compensation for animals who don't stand a chance being killed to provide Sunday afternoon sport for coarse-grained crowds. By the end I felt as though I had been bludgeoned, mentally apathetic and physically fit to vomit.

Saturday, 24 April 1926   *Palma*

Rain. Have been reading *Don Quixote* with growing admiration. Every word of it is like ripe fruit from which succulence can be squeezed. The perfection of prose narrative. Raymond Lull[15] is buried here in the Church of San Francisco.

Monday, 26 April 1926   *Palma*

By car to Sollér via Valldemosa and Miramar. Glorious drive through the mountains and along the mountainous north-west coast on excellent roads.

At the Carthusian monastery in Valldemosa, twelve hundred feet above the sea, visitors are shown the rooms where in 1838 George Sand and Chopin spent the winter; an ideal spot, lovely, rugged, and remote, for a romantic pair to stay.

On the right of the road, soon after leaving Valldemosa, there lies a farmhouse, formerly the property of the late Archduke Ludwig Salvator whose estates began at this point. Pretty and well-built, it now belongs to some heir or other of the Archduke, a Greek doctor. The interior does not evince much taste, but two modest photographs of the Empress Elisabeth as a very young woman are deeply moving. Her features, of a radiant and austere beauty alike, were so exquisite as to merit adoration even in these mediocre reproductions.

We continued along the steep, rocky coast. The scenery is more magnificent than that of the Riviera or Capri. The Archduke's own country-house is a very unassuming building. This accords with the striking fact that the whole of his enormous property was turned to useful agronomic purpose without any attempt at empty luxury in the way of mansions, parks, and so on.

The last Habsburgs had a fine sense of how to die in truly splendid surroundings – Maximilian of Mexico, the Empress Elisabeth, Archduke Rudolf, here Archduke Ludwig Salvator, and even the site of the modest grave of the last of the Emperors in the little village church on Madeira are all places which command aesthetic respect. How different from the last of the Hohenzollerns. The Habsburgs departed like gentlemen, the Hohenzollerns like draymen.

Thursday, 29 April 1926   *Palma*

Last day here. Overcast. Once more to the Cathedral. Though bare and gloomy, the interior makes an overwhelming impression on account of its proportions.

In the evening embarked on the 'luxury ship' *Jaime I*. Quite a pretty little three- to four-thousand tonner. A drawback, though, that the wooden cabin partitions are as thin as paper and therefore whatever happens on board is completely audible. As the sea was rough, the night was frightful. Not merely a sea-sick family next door, but half a dozen sea-sick young and not so young Englishwomen along the corridor. They vomited, groaned, rang for the steward, vomited again, groaned again, and rang for the steward again. In between the children, if they were not also vomiting, howled; their mother spewed fit to sever body and soul; their father cursed in the intervals of his regurgitations in a bass key. Never again Majorca: *es la ultima vez! Jamás, jamás!* At dawn a cargo of sea-sick dogs and chickens, crowing and cackling away, added to the harmony. The small ship rolled and tossed untiringly. That I was not sea-sick too was truly an achievement.

Saturday, 1 May 1926   *Barcelona*

Pahissa came to lunch. Eventually he talked about Primo[16] and conditions in Catalonia. Objectively, it seemed to me. Spain, he says, has been saved by the 'Directory' from the Communism which threatened to overwhelm it.

He returned in the evening and took me to see *Sardañas*, a most astonishing, improbable spectacle. In the heart of this modern metropolis, on a pavement somewhere in front of a café, artisans and middle-class people, children, soldiers, sailors join in a dance of unbelievable buoyancy and grace. The orchestra consists of four brass instruments, four wood-winds, a double-bass, and a *flaviol*, a flageolet with a very strange, shrill tone. The triteness of everyday life is transformed into a scene animated by charm, rhythm and beauty. The dances date from time immemorial, but (according to Pahissa) they have become fashionable again only during the past twenty years as an affirmation and symbol of Catalan nationality. Politics, the protest against Spain, is the impetus behind this movement. As I told Pahissa, it is the sole form of imaginative nationalism that I have run across so far.

Sunday, 2 May 1926   *Barcelona*

In the afternoon watched a bull-fight again. A young, very skilful matador, an absolute master of his profession, was worth seeing. Nevertheless the cowardly, brutal way the horses are surrendered to the mercy of the bull remains revolting. What is so astonishing is that the people who enjoy the sight of this nauseating cruelty to animals should be identical with the delicate, light-footed dancers of the *Sardañas*. Brutality and charm, ferocity and a sense of beauty exist in them, side by side, as it did with the Greeks.

Altogether the Spanish spirit seems to me to be compounded of elements closer to the ancient Greeks than is the case with any other European nation, possibly because it has been moulded by similar geographic and historical factors. During the centuries decisive in the shaping of their national character the Greeks and Spaniards were *frontier* peoples, fighting for their existence against the threat from the Orient of far more advanced civilizations. An almost fanatical self-assertion of their own more primitive cultures demanded of its prerequisite ruthless cruelty. To this must be added a religiosity streaked with mystic and tragic traits and steeped in notions of gore and sensuality. A third, contrasting, ingredient was natural gaiety and charm, the desire to sublimate their sensuality and to transmute it into a delicate, attractive, sportive quality. What they never did was to make a clean cut between the serene achievements due to success in this respect and the mystic, tragic, blood-soaked mythology from which it sprang. Instead the Greeks and Spaniards became peoples whose spirit harboured differing strains of character and the reflexes of the rest always brightened or sullied whatever aspect might rule supreme at any moment of their swift fluctuation.

Tuesday, 4 May 1926   *Valencia*

Arrived early at Valencia. My first impressions were of a profusion of flowers, mellowness of light, streets so entirely lacking in character that they might just as well belong to a poor Brussels or Paris suburb, and a great deal of dust, dirt and disorder quite different from Barcelona. Here is the Spain I knew.

The only real object of interest is the old silk exchange, the *Lonja de la Seda*, an enormous Gothic hall dating from the days of Ferdinand and Isabella (around 1490), a proud structure redolent of wealth and austerity, an embodiment of that Spain which became a world empire, discovered America, and drove the last Moors out of the country. The hall is divided into three aisles separated from each other by imposing, slender, spiralling columns which merge with the Gothic roof like the trunks of palms. The walls, apart from the very beautiful tracery of the windows and the richly decorated door-posts, are plain. The alternation between austere simplicity and sumptuous ornamentation underlines both the rigour and opulence. This *Lonja* is one of the most grandiose and attractive of Gothic secular buildings, architecturally a far more successful and homogeneous achievement than Or San Michele at Florence or the Loggia dei Lanzi. It is the only reward a trip to Valencia has to offer.

Sunday, 16 May 1926   *Paris*

With Henry van de Velde, Thylla van de Velde, and Max by car to Chartres. Van de Velde was utterly overwhelmed. As we entered the Cathedral, he murmured, '*Ça m'étouffe, je ne peux plus respirer.*' He constantly drew our attention to the beauty and rhythm attained by the masses, quoting it as proof of the fact that embellishment is of no importance whatever.

Yesterday he showed me his magnificent designs for the Schelde embankment at Antwerp. They also rely exclusively on the rhythm produced by enormously massed structures (skyscrapers).

Tuesday, 18 May 1926   *Berlin*

Arrived at eight and spent the morning at the PEN Club meeting. Jules Romains was in the chair. The speakers included Fulda, Galsworthy, Piérard, Martin du Gard. In the evening PEN Club banquet at the Kaiserhof.

Fulda in the chair. Galsworthy spoke well and in German. A moving speech was made by the Swede Björnsberg, whose fine features and manner of expression intimate a hard-fought spiritual struggle. Fulda was trivial, coming up to expectations. Jules Romains was amusing, but void of either intellectual depth or warmth of feeling. I sat between Martin du Gard and a Monsieur Berge. The numerous speeches and the long session at table (until half past eleven) was tiring. But a good and harmonious atmosphere prevailed.

Wednesday, 19 May 1926   *Berlin*

Lunched at the Esplanade with the von der Heydts. Others present were the young Dirksens, Frau Weissmann, Kümmel (the Far Eastern art expert), Voretsch (Minister at Lisbon), the art dealer Flechtheim, and Cohn of the Ethnological Museum. Really an 'Asiatic' lunch, as von der Heydt said, purely for Far Eastern art enthusiasts. Frau Weissmann told me that her husband yesterday had a skirmish with Stresemann because he has licensed, in his capacity as State Secretary in the Prussian Ministry of the Interior, the film *Battleship Potemkin* for public performance. In her view it is the most artistic film ever made and to ban it would be out of the question. After the meal the whole party went to Gutmann (the art dealer in the Bellevuestrasse) to take a look at an Indian bronze bought by von der Heydt.

Piérard (the Belgian author of the *Vie tragique de Vincent van Gogh*) came to tea with Helene to see my van Gogh. The fall of the Belgian Government he told me, has again rendered doubtful, or at least postponed for a long while, fulfilment of the project to build a special institute for van der Velde. In the evening saw *Potemkin*. Magnificent photography and highly effective dramatic construction. Best kind of popular art. I can understand that the right-wing parties and militarists loathe it.

Friday, 21 May 1926   *Weimar*

Dinner with the Bassianos. They are here, with a whole crowd of relatives and friends from Rome, for the first night of his opera *Hypatia*. Roffredo himself was not present, being detained at rehearsal, but there were his brother Gelasio (former Italian Ambassador at Washington), Count and Countess Lovatelli, Countess Piccolomini, Roland de Margerie and his wife, a Professor Luciani who spoke an unknown language alleged to be French, Hofmannsthal,[17] and Helene Nostitz (who had first declined the invitation, but then towards the end came after all), so that the company numbered thirteen. I sat between Princess Bassiano and Luciani, with Gelasio opposite. A lot of talk about d'Annunzio. The re-encounter with Hofmannsthal, for the first time in nine years, was entirely harmonious. He called this afternoon, but I was not at home.

Sunday, 23 May 1926   *Weimar*

Hofmannsthal lunched with me alone, as he asked that we should. We discussed the outlook for the German novel. He is pessimistic because, he maintains, the world of the novel must have for its basis a 'society', like

Hugo von Hofmannsthal (Colin Spencer)

Paris or London has, and a real capital, such as Paris or London. I mentioned Russian post-war storytellers and the current younger generation: Ivanov, Lebedinski, Babel, and the rest. Hofmannsthal is unfamiliar with them and asked how, now that neither money nor in a certain sense love are any longer available as plot factors, they manage about the tensions and antitheses indispensable to lending impetus to the action of any large-scale tale. He is probably right that *he*, at any rate, is incapable of concocting any novel out of things as they are. We both rank Max Weber very highly, but he thinks better of Rohan than I do. He is very sceptical about a political union between Austria and Germany, arguing that the only people in Austria who seriously want it are those belonging to circles corresponding to Stahlhelm and Werwolf in Germany. (These, it so happens, today held a pretty pathetic parade in the rain here at Weimar.) He would prefer to see closer economic links with the Successor States[18] so that Vienna, which is at present totally redundant and dying, can once more resume its function as the luxury metropolis of eastern Europe.

Thursday, 27 May 1926   *Paris*

Russian Ballet. *Romeo and Juliet*. Lifar and Nikitina as the young lovers very beautiful in their movements. The music, by a British composer,[19] weak. In the interval Misia Sert introduced me to Picasso and his wife.

Friday, 28 May 1926   *Paris*

In the afternoon visited Maillol at Marly and found him in a bad mood. He has not touched a piece of sculpture for six months, he said, and feels paralysed. He has no idea what is the matter. '*Je n'ai même pas pu mettre les bras à ma statue*', referring to an extremely fine statuette of a female figure. Since his return to Paris he had not been to his studio, not even to unlock it, and he did not want to see it.

I persuaded him to go there. He grumbled all the way and accused his stone-mason of spoiling the figure for his Cézanne Memorial: '*il a fait le nez de deux centimètres trop court; comment voulez-vous arranger ça?*' I calmed him down and expressed admiration of the figure all the same, which seemed to please him. Finally, though with considerable reluctance, he unlocked the door. Finished and half-finished objects stood about in great disorder and under a blanket of dust. He pointed to a heap of hollow moulds, lying on the floor, '*C'est ça qui m'a tué*,' he declared. The moulds were models for a bust of Daniel de Monfred (Gauguin's friend) which Monfred had nagged him into making and he could not refuse because once upon a time, when he was going through a bad patch, Monfred had for a few months saved him from starvation. But the head did not interest him, it was '*tout en bosse, il m'embêtait et je m'obstinais dessus. Si encore ç'avait été le buste d'une jolie femme!*' This bust had been his downfall because it had gone against the grain to work at it. He had not been able to do a sculpture since, though he had made many drawings.

In the afternoon visited Baby Goldschmidt-Rothschild. She received me in bed, between pink damask sheets and in blue pyjamas, the Chinese bed upholstered in yellow satin. A setting appropriate to the bedroom scene in a play about adultery. Curt Bois, the actor, arrived at the same time as myself.

Francis Poulenc (Cocteau)

Afterwards went to a house-concert at Mme Dubost where the Pro Arte group performed excellently. An interesting piece (especially the third movement) was a quartet by Darius Milhaud. Many young French musicians were present: Auric, Milhaud, Poulenc, and so on. Also the Weissmanns from Berlin.

In the evening the Russian Ballet. *Pastorale* by Auric. Helene caused annoyance by forcing herself on a supper-party given by Misia Sert on a boat moored in the Seine. Her excuse for coming with me was that Nabokov[20] had invited her; Misia was polite but distant. The occasion was the inauguration of the launch as a dance-bar, an idea started by some young Polish painters and under the patronage of Misia Sert, Baroness Rothschild, and others. The band, furnished impromptu by the painters, played brilliantly and deafeningly.

Nothing specially Bohemian about the affair, though it was Polish enough, with the electricity not working, so that we ate and danced by the light of candles stuck in bottle-necks. Food and drink was bad and fantastically expensive hundred and fifty francs for a bottle of champagne. The final blow came when the cloakroom clothes-rack collapsed and everybody had to search for their things among the appalling muddle of hats and coats. A swarm of Polish counts (Rzewuski, Hutton-Czapski, *et al.*) and Russian dancers. In the mysterious shimmer of a few candles everyone took a turn with everyone else; Helene with Goertz, Lifar with Misia Sert. Diaghilev came to our table and tried to tell Goertz, in the teeth of the frightful din of the jazz which itself faced competition from the wind and the rain lashing against the boards of the barge, details of his story about the dancer Garcia. All that was needed, to carry the dramatic character of this Polish entertainment to its logical conclusion, was for the hulk to spring a leak. But let it be said on behalf of the Poles that, in spite of the casualness of the whole business, the bounds of propriety were never exceeded. All the rules of polite society were respected even when, at the end, everyone was scrabbling round on the floor in the darkness and looking for hats and evening cloaks among the wreckage. Helene discovered the Slav strain in her blood and thought it all delightful.

Thursday, 3 June 1926   *Paris*

Lunch with Claude Anet in the Rue du Bac. Just he, his wife and a woman lawyer, French but with a Polish name, whose husband is in partnership with Paul Boncour. Pretty, tastefully furnished ground-floor apartment with fine Persian faiences and pictures by Vuillard and Bonnard. A simple meal. Macaroni, leg of mutton, strawberries. About his success in Germany, which financially comes in very useful to him, Anet said, '*Je vis de l'étranger.*' He insisted on hearing my Pilsudski experiences.

With Helene and the Brions to the musical soirée given by Painlevé for Seipel, who lectured at the Sorbonne earlier in the day. The reception took place in the Hotel Claridge, not in the Ministry of War, because, so the gossip goes, Painlevé was expecting the fall of the Cabinet at the time he was issuing his invitations and so preferred to be careful about the location. A small, elegant, well selected company consisting of French intellectuals and generals, Austrian and German diplomats, and a sprinkling of French parliamentarians. Mme Clemenceau was entirely at home in the role of hostess. Marya Freund sang in German and French. A lot of German was spoken, spontaneously and regardless of the French generals in their dress uniform; nobody seemed to take much notice.

Seipel,[21] to whom Zifferer introduced me, referred to my activities at Geneva in 1924. He appeared well informed on the subject and commented that I had been expected to become the German delegate to the League. Severe, sharply contoured features, the voice that of a countryman, but surprisingly low in pitch and gentle. Then Madame de Noailles summoned me and we renewed our acquaintanceship. With all the excitable, rapturous exclamatoriness that is innate to her, the little dark woman was wearing black gloves with her evening dress and gesticulated so livelily as to make me feel that black vipers were leaping into my face. She revived recollections of our meetings in Weimar, with Frau Foerster-Nietzsche, and so on. Then she suddenly swooped down on Rakowski and forced him into a corner. Something very vehement about Bolshevism was squirted in his face. At the same moment Ravel, completely white-haired now and looking like an Aryan edition of Oscar Fried, seized my hand. '*Cher ami*, so long since we have seen each other,' etc. It was in fact a matter of reunion all round, with a spirit of European good will predominating despite glossy French uniforms, not at all the mood associated with a Minister of War's reception, a major European social event. In this respect it is perhaps permissible to suggest *que cette soirée marque une date*.

Saturday, 5 June 1926   *Paris*

Dinner at Martin du Gard's, with Helene, Paul Valéry, and Edmond Jaloux. Immaculately spruce, utterly modern furnishings as though straight from an arts and crafts show, frigid and lacking the slightest touch of intimacy. Valéry is a short, meagre man with artistically disarrayed strands of grey hair, fine, deeply-set eyes, and a quiet, musical intonation. At table he was caustically malicious about Cocteau and the fashionable 'Thomist School' – the followers of Thomas Aquinas, Jacques Maritain, and the rest. He said that he is writing the preface to the volume on France in Wasmuth's *Orbis Terrarum* series and proposes to enlarge on the theme that, with the exception of the Russians, there is no European nation ethnographically more hybrid than the French, a quality reflected in its language which is so highly furbished, '*polie comme un caillou*', precisely for this reason.

I had to leave immediately the meal was over because I had invited Mlle de Koranyi (daughter of the Hungarian Minister) and Jacques to be my guests at the Russian Ballet. She is a pretty, intelligent girl who told us how many of the Russians in Paris are now being reduced to poverty. Recently she hailed a taxi and was startled to recognize in the driver a Russian prince with whom she had frequently danced during the previous winter. For a moment she hesitated, then shook hands, and got in. During the journey she wondered

whether she should give him a tip or not. Finally she did so, but said at the
same time, '*Vous viendrez prendre le thé un de ces jours, quand vous serez libre,
n'est-ce pas?*' A truly tactful and ingenious solution.

Sunday, 6 June 1926   *Paris*

Drove Helene to Meudon to Jacques Maritain, who was so insistent on
meeting her. On the way she asked me what the word *pédéraste*, which she
so frequently hears applied here, means. I advised her to ask her husband.

I then went home and fetched Wilma to go to Madame Clemenceau's
Sunday reception, where we met the Sautreaus and others. Painlevé had
also said that we should have a talk there, but I could not wait for him
because I had promised to pay Nabokov a visit. I found him in a wretched
pension behind the Panthéon, 3 Rue de l'Estrapade. A dirty, evil-smelling
staircase leads to a tiny room containing nothing but a piano, a rumpled
couch which evidently serves him as a bed, a chair, and a few photographs
on the walls. The impression of ghastly poverty is one that his appearance
in public, his well-groomed exterior and his air of *grand seigneur*, never so
much as hints at. Nor did he now show the slightest embarrassment,
receiving me as though I were a guest in his mansion and proceeding to play
a cantata which he has composed on some verses by Lomonosov. I was dis-
tressed by the contrast between inspiration and miserable surroundings, just
as I witnessed it in the case of Munch in Berlin.

He reiterated his contempt for French music as a whole and added a
vigorous condemnation of every Oriental, national, folk-song strain
(*l'exotisme*), not excepting jazz, wherever it may occur in music. '*Si vous me
demandez pourquoi je déteste l'exotisme en musique, je vous répondrai: parce
que j'aime Bach.*' His loathing extends to Russian music in so far as it displays
national characteristics of the kind found in Rimsky-Korsakov and others.
He only exempts Borodin as having managed to rise a little above Orientalism
into the sphere of pure music. His gods are Bach and Mozart: the peak of
achievement is when music '*entre le temple*', attaining to religion.

He said that I simply must meet Maritain, at present the most interesting
personality France has to offer. He is evidently much impressed by the
Thomists and quoted zestfully a pretty stupid remark by Stravinsky: '*D'un
côté il y a Luther, le Protestantisme, Kant et cette vieille vache de Sand,*'
(pronouncing her name like 'sand') '*de l'autre, le Catholicisme et le bon vin.*'
But, in spite of this rather callow, excessively Catholic radicalism, Nabokov
really does give the impression of being an inspired young giant.

Friday, 11 June 1926   *Paris*

In the afternoon called on the Duchesse de Clermont-Tonnerre, then Mme

Ménard-Dorian, and later Baby Goldschmidt. In the evening Hoesch, the Anets and Serts dined with me at the Ambassadeurs to the accompaniment of the Florence Mills negro revue. Parisian society at its most elegant, the genuine '*Tout Paris*', ate here crushed together at small tables. I met Boni de Castellane, the first time since the war, and thought his appearance much the worse for wear. Next to us sat the Italian Ambassador with a large company, the actress Maud Loty, and so on. The first time for fifteen years, since the first night of the Russian Ballet, that I saw '*Tout Paris*' together again in its full glory. Hoesch was delighted, beside himself with pleasure at the smartness and glitter of the spectacle. The same applied to Claude Anet.

Sunday, 13 June 1926   *Paris*

Lunched with Maillol at Marly. During the meal Daniel de Monfred, Gauguin's friend and white-haired now, came in. When I spoke about the Ambassadeurs, Maillol said, '*C'est aux "Ambassadeurs" que j'ai fait ma première décoration en arrivant à Paris, oui, j'ai décoré les "Ambassadeurs"!*' He had been '*sans le sou*' at the time and was taken along by friends to help with his decoration and earn a few pence. Eventually he was the only one who saw the colour of money because, sacked as being no good, he was paid off. Those who continued got nothing because the management meanwhile went bankrupt. Recalling the story, Maillol grinned all over his face. He added that he also did a major decoration for the Moulin Rouge, consisting of two pierrots and freely copied from Willette, a work that perished in the fire of a few years ago. The decoration enjoyed a triumphal unveiling. Maillol turned up for it in fancy-dress, wearing green tights with black sleeves and gloves, in the character of a *fusain* (charcoal crayon). The performers carried him round the building, shoulder-high, amidst ovations. Then they stripped him to the skin, except for his tights. Maillol, much enlivened by these reminiscences, seemed greatly improved all round and said that he can, thank goodness, work again.

Tuesday, 15 June 1926   *Paris*

Lunched with Misia Sert. The other guests were Hoesch, Mme de Jouvenel, and Sert's extremely pretty niece, to whom Hoesch paid assiduous attention. Sert maintains that the greatest living French writer is Léger (St John Perse), whose spare time occupation is to act as *chef de cabinet* to Briand. He also told me how radiantly handsome, *la figure couleur d'acajou*, Radiguet looked as he lay on his death-bed. Cocteau had refused either to visit him or to bother in any way. They (the Serts) paid for the funeral. He went on to talk about Sitges, a village near Barcelona, which shows a strong streak of paganism in its daily life. It will happen, for instance, that a boy of twelve or fourteen goes to sea, returns after ten years, falls in love with his half-forgotten sister, has children by her, and, though of course they are not wed in the eyes of the Church, continue to live with her as his wife, respected by one and all, to the end of his days.

First night of Cocteau's *Orphée*, under Pitoeff's direction, at the Théâtre des Arts. Tickets cost a hundred francs each (the same as for the Russian Ballet) and the audience was the usual smart and international set, including many Americans, British, and even Japanese. The play, which the Serts have long praised as a masterpiece, disappointed me. I thought it fumbling, neither true tragedy nor true comedy. Its focal point is an impossible, unintentionally funny figure of an angel (calculated appeal to the fashionably Catholic trend of taste). The part is played by a revoltingly mawkish, effeminate young man who appears to have escaped from some dreadful hairdresser's. This sugary youth completely spoiled my taste for a production which was not improved by the fact of Mme Pitoeff being once again far gone in pregnancy, a detail lending the part of Eurydice a touch of the grotesque. I was so ruffled that I quickly took myself off after the performance, greeting neither Cocteau nor the Serts.

Wednesday, 16 June 1926   *Paris*

Dinner-party given by Hoesch at the Embassy on the occasion of the composers' and dramatists' congress currently in session here. Fulda, Arnolt Bronnen and Wegener from Germany; Auernheimer and Zifferer from Austria; and, naturally, lots of Frenchmen – Tristan Bernard, Lugné-Poe, Yvette Guilbert (whom I reminded of our lunch in Bernard Shaw's apartment shortly before the war, when Rodin and Mme Greffulhe were also there), Jules Romains, Claude Anet, Gémier, and so on. The plethora of red and white roses decorating the beautiful Empire drawing-room of Queen Hortense lent a very brilliant touch to the affair. The atmosphere between French and Germans was quite unforced and full of good fellowship.

Bronnen,[22] whom I met for the first time, made a very odd impression. Brusque, uncertain of himself, bumptious, with bad breath, and in lounge suit (the rest of course in tails) but with a monocle stuck in his eye, he haphazardly spouted nonsense whenever he opened his mouth. With me, for instance, he eulogized recent Russian drama as being far closer to us than any French works. When I replied that, although I know the output of young Russian poets and novelists, I am unfamiliar with any playwrights, his answer, delivered with utmost naïvety, was that he does not know any either! He is obviously a second-rate, weak, highly-strung character who would like to simulate superiority, playing in literature the counterpart to the junior officer of the reserve who attends summer camp and puts a rasp into his voice because he cannot keep up the role in other respects. A contorted philistine, shallow, no guiding light, morbidly vain. In brief, *un grand homme de province* without much to him. He spoke to nobody or, if he did, merely returned an uncivil, loutish rejoinder to a polite approach. (To Wegener he retorted, 'You know, Herr Wegener, I don't like you and you don't like me either.') Taciturn and restless, he strutted through the brightly lit, beautiful rooms like a night-bird flown in by mistake. Soon nobody took any notice of him.

Hoesch moved nimbly and gracefully between all these writers and actors. He does undoubtedly exercise a certain charm on the Parisians. Jules Romains and Claude Anet went very thoroughly with me into their prospects of being performed in Berlin. I happened to mention Büchner and his *Woyzeck*, which was unknown to Romains. He said that he would like to translate him; I promised to let him have a copy.

Coudenhove arrived late. We stood for a long time by the table between the two windows in the main apartment. Although he talked very intensively to me, only his thin lips and the slight, almost childish pucker in the cheek of his Mongolian features moved; every other part of his face remained quite freakishly still. Close to us sat Yvette Guilbert, in one of Queen Hortense's beautifully carved chairs, fanning herself, a rather well-developed, red-haired lady now who in no way calls to mind the spindly grisette, with the long arms and long black gloves, immortalized by Toulouse-Lautrec. Coudenhove claims that his pan-European ideas have met with greater understanding in Britain than on the Continent.

Monday, 21 June 1926   *Paris*

The referendum,[23] as could be foreseen, failed by about fifteen million votes. I am still ill. A sort of meningitis. The coughing has somewhat subsided.

MY ILLNESS

(recorded at Capri according to my nurses' notes)

On *Thursday, 24 June* I left Paris for London on the midday train, arrived at a quarter to seven, drove to the Hotel Cecil, and was conducted to my room. A window was open, I was cold, caught a fit of the shivers, could not pull the window down, had to call a manservant. I went to dinner, had no appetite, and got into bed.

Friday, 25 June I lay in bed all day. From that point on my recollections become gradually blurred. It was on *Monday, 28 June*, I think, that I had Mr Noel, the hotel doctor, fetched. He at once diagnosed pneumonia.

On *Tuesday, 29 June* there came Miss Wrigley, henceforward my day nurse, and faithful Miss Bostock, who remained with me until Capri, for night duties. Noel called in Dr MacDonagh, whom he described as 'outstanding' and who probably did save my life. A man of great parts, conscientious, tactful, and pleasant, he treated and healed me in a manner entirely unsparing of himself.

On *Thursday, 1 July* there occurred an intestinal haemorrhage.

On *Friday, 2 July* Wilma arrived by air from Paris. Next to MacDonagh's skill, I owe my life to her love and care. For two months she remained day and night outside my door, hardly eating or sleeping, worn out by constant fear and anxiety, suffering more deeply than I did.

Monday, 5 July was the critical day as regarded the pneumonia. My temperature suddenly dropped by several degrees, I was reduced to utmost weakness, my heart gave out. Nurse Wrigley caught hold of me and put me on my back, forced brandy between my lips, and summoned the doctors. I was given an oxygen injection, a process repeated several times during the next few days in addition to receiving oxygen respiration.

On *Thursday, 8 July* Max and Fritz arrived in the evening by air from Berlin and Christian and Jacques came from Paris. This led to a tragicomic incident. At eleven o'clock at night, when I had already had my oxygen injection as well as a sleeping tablet and was beginning to dose, the door opened, all the lights in the room were suddenly turned on full blaze, and at my bed-side there appeared, accompanied by Dr Noel, four sombrely dressed men which it took me some seconds to recognize as respectively Christian, Jacques, Max and Fritz. I had not been told that they were coming to London. This was now the classic death-bed scene, faultlessly produced, and I interpreted it as such right away, greeting them as well as my feebleness allowed and whispering to the nurse, bent over me, 'Tell them that I am not dying yet.'

As the haemorrhage continued, I became daily weaker. On this *Thursday, 8 July* I had the first blood transfusion. A splendid London arrangement enables such transfusions to be made without delay. The Boy Scouts, under the aegis of the Red Cross, have created an organization whereby, day and night, young people are available for immediate blood donation. One of these youngsters was brought along on my behalf.

Next day, *Friday, 9 July*, as my weakness increased, a second blood transfusion was undertaken. This had an unhappy effect. My temperature at once rose to 103 Fahrenheit. Noel told Wilma that if it went up one more degree he could answer for nothing and she should be prepared for the worst. The crisis passed, but my weakness became worse from day to day.

On *Tuesday, 13 July* I was as good as dead. MacDonagh explained to Wilma that only one thing could still save me, a third blood transfusion, but it was also possible that it would kill me on the spot. The danger was equal either way. I could be dead in an hour. He could not take the decision. It was for her to determine whether the blood transfusion experiment should be risked. Wilma, after consulting Guseck, resolved on this last effort. I was given the third blood transfusion and it saved my life. I recovered consciousness and during the next few days was kept alive by oxygen injections and artificial respiration. But the haemorrhage continued and on *Wednesday, 14 July*, to staunch it, I received for the first time coagulin.

On *Thursday, 15 July* when the worst was already past, Leschke, director of the Charité,[24] called in by Wilma on MacDonagh's advice, arrived from Berlin, stayed three and a half days, and charged three hundred and fifty pounds. In reply to Guseck's expostulation, he stated that normally he only attends kings and prime ministers, this is the amount they pay, and he could make no exception. He sat a good deal beside my bed and said that in Berlin he would talk about me to Stresemann; I must accompany the German delegation in September to Geneva, and so on. For the rest he merely encouraged MacDonagh to continue with his treatment and on the eighteenth, without having contributed much, departed with his fee.

As I was very restless at night and sleeplessness increased my weakness still more, I had on *Tuesday, 20 July* my first shot of morphia. From now until September, at Broadstairs, I was constantly and increasingly under its influence. The effects gradually grew into a condition of complete temporary hallucinations and semi-madness. I imagined events which had never occurred, broke into convulsive sobbing when my stories about them met with incredulity, was nervous and touchy to a degree, and yet could not do without morphia at night. More especially because, if I was not given heroin, the most dreadful muscular pains in the thighs turned the nocturnal hours into a hell for me. All other sedatives, tried on Leschke's advice, were utterly useless and simply made me still more nervous. But the intestinal haemorrhage, under the influence of coagulin, did begin to subside and on *Saturday, 24 July* a fresh intestinal treatment was started.

The succeeding weeks were a time of slow improvement, but I was now plagued by violent fits of coughing. They frequently lasted hours on end. This was in addition to the muscular pains in my legs. On *Wednesday, 18 August* the experiment of trying to heal my lung via injection of my own viruses was undertaken. By *Monday, 23 August* I was sufficiently advanced to be able to be transported by ambulance to a sanatorium at Broadstairs.

The weather was exceptionally fine and from the first day on I was able to spend some hours daily in the sun. After a few days too I made my first efforts at walking. Nobody who has not been forced by illness to stay in bed for a long time can have any idea what great strength it needs to take a few steps.

On *Tuesday, 14 September* Wilma returned to France. I stayed until *Friday, 1 October* at Broadstairs under the care of a young, excellent, delightful and highly conscientious Dr Raven. The injections were continued. On *Friday, 17 September* Raven gave me a stronger injection. The result was that from midnight until five in the morning I had the worst fit of coughing of my whole illness. I coughed four to five hours without a break. I spat blood and particles of tissue. My chest felt as though it was being torn apart from the torture and strain. I was sat up in a chair and given morphia. Nothing helped. I thought I must die. Finally, towards five, I slipped into sleep from exhaustion. When I woke, the cough was gone. I never coughed again. When Raven visited me, he admitted that the injection dose had been excessive, but evidently the violent outbreak of coughing had disposed of the remains of pneumonia because the affected part, at the bottom left of the lung, was barely discernible any longer. My real convalescence began on this day.

So on *Friday, 1 October* I returned, much stronger already, with Guseck and Miss Bostock to London and the Hotel Cecil. I took an attractive suite of rooms overlooking the Thames.

On *Tuesday, 5 October* the three of us travelled down to Southampton to embark on the *Homeric* for France.

On *Wednesday, 6 October* Wilma and Jacques met me at Cherbourg. We slept there and drove next day in Wilma's car to Jacques' villa at Deauville.

I stayed until *Tuesday, 12 October*, when I drove with Wilma and Miss Bostock to Rouen. Our journey continued via Paris and Switzerland (where Wilma left us and Goertz met us with his car) to Genoa. We embarked in the *Colombo* for Naples, remained there five days, and on *Saturday, 6 November* crossed to Capri. Guseck arrived and Goertz and the faithful Miss Bostock left, for Berlin and London respectively. I looked for a villa to rent and found a fine, roomy house perched on a height and with a lovely view of the bay of Naples, Vesuvius, Sorrento, and the Calabrian coast as far as Paestum and beyond. The Ca' del Sole belongs to a Captain Borselli, Fascist and confidant of Mussolini who sends him to America for propaganda purposes. I rented it from his wife, an Australian, for three and a half thousand lire per month.

On *Monday, 13 December* I visited, at the wish of Dr Pemberton, my British medical adviser on Capri, the German oculist Praun in Naples. I had suffered from vision defect in the left eye ever since the start of my illness. I talked to Leschke about it in London. With my left eye I would see standing behind Leschke, when he was to the left of my bed, figures in duplicate and triplicate which, as I told him, I knew not to be there but which were hallucinations that I could not eliminate. Neither Leschke nor MacDonagh nor Noel took any notice. Finally I got Pemberton to make an examination. It turned out that a portion of the left eye's field of vision was obscured and the sight of the lower half gone. Praun diagnosed scotoma, forbade me to read and write, and prescribed strychnine injections in the left temple. He ascribed my condition to the severe losses of blood consequent on the intestinal haemorrhage.

1927

On *Sunday, 9 January* another visit to Praun. He disclosed some very dismal possibilities, not excluding a disorder of the nervous system and urgently advised me to undergo a thorough examination, even though this cannot be managed in Italy. I was very depressed.

On *Monday, 10 January* Pemberton suggested, in view of Praun's alarming diagnosis, that I visit Professor von Wyss at Zurich.

On *Wednesday, 26 January* Dr Walter von Wyss told me that he could undertake a lumbar puncture only in a nursing home.

At noon on *Thursday, 27 January* the puncture and a blood test were made The results were completely negative, as Wyss informed me two days later, but the consequences of the puncture were highly unpleasant. I developed violent headaches, dizziness, and nausea. My temperature sank continually until on *Monday, 31 January* it was down to 35.8 degrees Centigrade and my pulse measured only sixty-two. On that day I felt seriously ill, but it proved to be the nadir of my condition. On *Tuesday, 1 February* I was able to go out and went to Professor Vogt, the oculist. He examined me, although he had a broken leg, and then handed me over to his assistant. My head was X-rayed by Professor Schry.

Wednesday, 2 February 1927   *Zurich*

Today Professor Vogt told me that my eye is incurable and that therefore any treatment is superfluous.

Tuesday, 8 February 1927   *Paris*

During the morning went to the Louvre and looked at the *Mona Lisa*, this sturdy and mysterious peasant woman, and the head of Amenophis, perhaps the most profound portrayal of a highly-strung intellectual that art has ever produced. Even the *Mona Lisa* seems shallow in comparison.

Wednesday, 9 February 1927   *Milan*

Met Max at Arth-Goldau and in the late afternoon arrived here. As I did not fancy the prospect of *Rheingold* at the Scala, we went to a cinema. *Faust*, a German film, poor.

Friday, 11 February 1927   *Rome*

Arrived early with Max. To Ostia to see the freshly discovered Roman apartment houses. They really do look like modern stores and tenements. The big, smart department store (*orca*) of Epagatos, several storeys high and with salesrooms leading off broad corridors built around a central courtyard, is the precise counterpart to a Tietz or Wertheim. The same applies to the apartments in the tenement buildings and provides a complete contrast with Pompeii. A modern family could move straight into one of the ground-floor apartments, with large windows facing the garden, and not even notice that they are living in an ancient house.

Tuesday, 15 February 1927   *Rome*

This morning called on Prittwitz at the Embassy. He told me that, although Mussolini's position is entirely secure, he hardly ever now meets a *convinced* Fascist. The fact of a Fascist, corporative state is accepted without argument, but there is great disappointment and disillusionment. The republican trend inside Fascism is gaining ground again. The King has been divested of his last function by Mussolini's assumption of supreme command over the Army and he is in eclipse. All the same, for the present Mussolini is unlikely to make any move towards his official elimination. Corruption among Fascist civil servants is rife right to the top. Our arbitration treaty has in the first instance given us all that we need and we should not, Prittwitz thinks, enter into any further dealings with Mussolini because, if we do, he will only use it as an occasion to betray us to France.

Saturday, 26 March 1927   *Rome*

Lunched with Prittwitz alone. I said that I had somewhat revised my notions about Mussolini and Fascism. There are elements in the Fascist state, like its corporative structure, which cannot be condemned out of hand. Mussolini moreover does now represent Italy and anyone who wants to be on terms with Italy must come to terms with Mussolini, just as Bismarck, much against the inclinations of his conservative Prussian party friends, resigned himself to Napoleon and Bonapartism.

Prittwitz agreed with me on both points, adding that people in Germany have been too quick to condemn Fascism out of hand as an entirely reactionary movement. That is not at all the case. On the contrary, it is in many respects an interesting attempt to effect an evolution in the contemporary structure of the state. There is no question of Mussolini being a charlatan;

he is genuinely a statesman who, having seriously grappled with the problem of politics and formed his own conclusion, seeks to put it into practice. It is the methods adopted to achieve this objective, the acts of violence and the total absence of any provisions for control of the all-powerful officialdom, which are open to criticism. Control exists solely in Mussolini's personal talent for organization. Let him be replaced by someone less gifted or less honest, then there will be no control whatever because any sort of supervision from below, on the part of those who are ruled, is lacking. Moreover, nothing has been undertaken to regulate the succession to Mussolini, should he die. There are stories about his having written a political testament which foresees, in the event of his sudden disappearance, a form of directory consisting of civil and military members, and he is supposed to have included a list of those to be appointed. But will this really work in the case of his sudden death? Violence, absence of control, and lack of a properly regulated succession are the major items on the debit side of the regime's ledger.

Italy's complete intellectual stagnation under Fascism, I said, seems to me a very distinct symptom of profound flaws in its intellectual structure. Prittwitz agreed that, as things stand, serious discussion of any political or social problem is utterly out of the question and that this is responsible for the stagnation I mentioned. 'The peace of the graveyard,' I commented. 'Yes. If you photograph a beggar in the street and publish the picture, proceedings *must* be taken against you. You have disparaged Italy in the eyes of the world and a prison sentence is inevitable. That of course makes criticism in public of social shortcomings impossible.' Is Fascism really doing anything to improve conditions in Italy? Prittwitz has no doubts whatever about that. Road building, afforestation, and land reclamation are cases in point. Projects are put into execution and do not, as in the past, just remain ideas. Archaeology is also benefiting greatly. Mussolini is an enthusiast about anything that concerns history and the former greatness of Rome. This explains the relatively large amounts spent on excavations. He is not a cultured person or possessed of any deeper traits of refinement, but he is mentally receptive, rendering it pleasant and easy to negotiate with him because he is open to conviction. If he can be proved to have been in the wrong or to have based himself on false information, he will frankly admit his mistake.

My impression is that Prittwitz views Fascism as a problem about which no conclusions can as yet be drawn, but whose permutations he watches with interest and without bias. That is my attitude too.

Sunday, 27 March 1927   *Rome*

Hutten called before lunch. As always, he was amusing and full of anecdotes. Bülow is staying for the winter, as usual, at the Villa Malta. Recently Hutten spent two and a half hours with him, swapping reminiscences about Hohenlohe, Holstein, Eulenburg,[1] and others.

That brought up the subject of Phili Eulenburg and his quarrel with Holstein, the reason for which will now probably never be cleared up as all those in the know are dead. Hutten also pleads ignorance except that when he told Holstein on some matter to write to 'your friend' Phili, Holstein rapped out 'For the past fortnight Eulenburg has ceased to be my friend and we shall never be friends again.' But he would not say why, although in the end he suggested casually, 'Ask Hohenlohe. Tell him that I give him permission to divulge to you the reason for my quarrel with Eulenburg.' In the evening, at table, when Hutten broached the subject with Hohenlohe, the latter seemed ready to explain, but then, looking at his wife and daughter, decided, 'It is better that you should not know,' and Hutten never learned any more. We chatted about Eulenburg. 'There was no holding him back,' Hutten observed. He had, on the Chancellor's instructions, instituted investigations and the Berlin police reported that Eulenburg had passed the night in a hotel with a boy he had picked up in the street. 'When was that?' I asked. 'When he was no longer ambassador,' Hutten replied. That had clinched the Eulenburg Affair.

Wednesday, 30 March 1927   *Rome*

Towards evening I visited the small Protestant cemetery close by the Cestius Pyramid where Keats and Shelley lie buried, each with his best friend beside him. Trelawney next to Shelley, Severn next to Keats. The inscription over Keats's anonymous grave is heart-breaking, a shattering expression of unquenchable grief carved in stone for eternity. And, what is more, grief based on false premises! As gripping and crushing a situation as in any Shakespearian tragedy. Like Castor and Pollux, the two pairs of friends lie united for ever as monument to a community of feeling far beyond the usual empty epitaphs and false bonds of conventional family and marriage ties.

Monday, 11 April 1927   *Capri*

Today Pasqualino, who is thirteen and helps in our kitchen, has been arrested and thrown into prison for allegedly molesting a girl in public. He pines in a cell because, so it seems, spring got the better of his thirteen years. But the regime is 'moral' and therefore a thirteen-year-old child is locked up with habitual criminals. Moral hygiene! The Capri chief of police is said to be a place-hunter who wants to make a career and displays zeal in order to be able to report to Rome the number of morally tainted individuals he has expelled from the island.

Monday, 9 May 1927   *Capri*

Check of the inventory with Mme Borselli. Two pictures have vanished without trace, a lot of linen has been stolen, a good deal of crockery, two silver spoons, and so on, are missing. Mme Borselli is terribly punctilious about it all. I leave the Ca' del Sole with very mixed feelings.

Thursday, 12 May 1927   *Pompeii*

During the morning the usual tour of Pompeii, but in the afternoon, starting at half past four, we saw the first performance that has taken place for two thousand years in the ancient theatre: Euripides' *Alcestis*, in Italian. A very fine and in parts (especially the first half) very harrowing production. The strangely obscure personality of Admetus perhaps defies (like that of Hamlet) the range of any actor. The play's stupendous boldness of imagination and genius nevertheless remains as fresh as ever. There is a romantic, Shakespearian quality too in the structure of the work, with its compound of tragic and comic elements. And finally, as is the case with Shakespeare, the spectator is left with the feeling that the human soul is a riddle to which events, situations, and catastrophes occasionally supply clues without revealing its ultimate springs of inspiration.

Sunday, 15 May 1927   *Rome*

By car from Naples to Rome. Glorious scenery, magnificent and endearing alike. The view from Monte Cassino[2] is of an exalted beauty, but the monastery disappointed me. A rather indifferent, showy baroque building, trying to be impressive but without a vestige of genuine feeling and not to be compared with Montserrat even as regards dramatic effect. On Montserrat the church affords a sense of being the scene of an intangible mystery; here it is an ostentatious state apartment whose sole purpose appears to be to demonstrate God's wealth.

The frescoes by Pater Desiderius are, in glaring contradiction, really serious in character and very vivid, an almost miraculous achievement in these surroundings. But the monk who led us round made it impossible to appreciate them. He jabbered the whole time at breakneck speed. Whenever I tried not to listen to him and to contemplate the frescoes, he seized my arm and shook it in order to arrest my attention.

Monday, 23 May 1927   *Zurich*

My birthday. A year ago I celebrated it in Weimar and two days later left Germany.

Today I paid two visits to Professor Vogt. My eye, he says, is possibly a little better, at any rate no worse than in February. The vision on one side is somewhat improved, but he thinks further progress unlikely.

Tuesday, 24 May 1927   *Zurich*

Exactly a year ago today, in the evening, I left Berlin for Paris. It was meant to be quite a brief stay. Instead, through illness and convalescence, I have been kept away a whole year from Germany, where I return tomorrow. Almost I did not return at all!

Wednesday, 25 May 1927   *Zurich–Frankfurt*

Today, after exactly a year, I have come back to Germany. At two o'clock I left Zurich and passed the frontier at Basle. Both Max and I were struck at Freiburg by the ugliness of the people crowding into the train. A nasty, grey, cold day too. Not a pleasant return home. A chilly feeling, both literally and metaphorically.

Thursday, 26 May 1927   *Leipzig*

During the morning inspected the preparations for the Book Exhibition.[3] The central spot in the hall of honour has been allocated to me, which is distinctly flattering. But the showcase is still a very poor sight and I was not able today to obtain the display trestles.

Friday, 27 May 1927   *Leipzig*

Worked all day at completion of my showcase. At intervals looked at the rest of the exhibition. No doubt whatever that the Russian exhibit is the most interesting, novel, and artistically valuable. Next, from a typographic standpoint, comes the Dutch. The British have been clumsy. Of their first-class presses only Vale Press (Ricketts) is represented; Doves Press, Hornby, and so on, are missing. The Belgian exhibit, particularly as regards illus-trators, is interesting and the Czechoslovak one quite good. The Exhibition's absolute nadir is reached by the French book bindings; they are a positive horror. The Italians show nothing deserving second thought. The German section is something of a disappointment. Second-class book producers like Mathéy, Gruner, Steiner-Prag have thrust themselves into the limelight by having large individual stalls and thereby grossly exaggerating their significance in the German book world. Nobody would guess the part that *Pan*, *Insel*, *Blätter für die Kunst* or people like Peter Behrens, Rudi Schroeder, Poeschel, and I have played in the evolution of a decent German book typography. Kippenberg is right to be angry.

Sunday, 29 May 1927 *Leipzig*

Sammy Fischer and his wife asked me to lunch with Gerhart Hauptmann. The latter was enthusiastic about my Virgil edition and suggested that I should print a *de luxe* edition of his forthcoming *Till Eulenspiegel*. He invited me to visit him at Bad Liebenstein, where he is now staying, so that he can read the work to me.

Earlier in the day I discussed with Kippenberg the project for a Cranach Press edition of Rilke's letters to Rodin and a volume of early Rilke prose.

Dinner with the Kippenbergs. Van de Velde also there. I mentioned the idea of publishing an edition of Petronius with woodcuts by Marcus Behmer. Kippenberg was enthusiastic and would also like me to print an edition of *Vathek* illustrated by Behmer. He told me repeatedly that my exhibit here has been the best. Van de Velde said the same.

Monday, 30 May 1927 *Weimar*

After a year's absence, back to Weimar. The house has been rebuilt and fresh additions have been made to the garden. It was a great pleasure to see the place again. In the evening van de Velde and Guseck had dinner with me and afterwards we sat on the terrace.

Tuesday, 31 May 1927 *Weimar*

Worked the whole day with van de Velde at plans for the further reconstruction of Cranachstrasse 15. After dinner a long talk on all sorts of topics. About the Russians, whose exhibit I praised, he said, '*La Russie liquide une situation; elle ne construit pas une nouvelle situation.*' The fresh impetus in the world, of which there are clear signs, will probably come from others. He spoke about the *Cours de l'Histoire de l'Architecture* which he is holding in Ghent. The more deeply he studies the history of architecture, the more definitely he recognizes that there has always existed only *one* sort of architecture which, beneath the wrapper of various successive styles, has always had the same objective in mind. He is especially full of admiration for Gothic.

In the morning van de Velde left for Brussels and in the afternoon I went over to the Hauptmanns. Immediately after my arrival he and I went for a walk, first to the villa of the oculist Count Wiser and then in the park.

A part of our conversation was devoted to the contribution made to German culture by the eighteenth-century principalities. I suggested that it was of dubious value. The sag in German literature around 1780, leading away from the realist and social attitude of Lessing, *Die Räuber*, and *Clavigo*[4] in the direction of Schiller's 'historical' plays and Goethe's 'classical' epoch, was caused to a considerable degree by inevitable deference to the feelings and outlook of the Weimar court. As a result we have been cheated of the realistic and political writings that, after such beginnings, we were entitled to expect. Schiller's histories and *Wilhelm Meister* are not compensation enough. This line of thought seemed new to Hauptmann. He agreed with me and added that this is the reason why we have no outstanding German novels.

Later Frau Hauptmann joined us and we continued our walk and conversation until eight. For dinner Hauptmann ordered a cold punch, partaking lavishly of this as well as two bottles of champagne after the meal.

He told me how pleased he is that in the autumn his revised version of *Hamlet*[5] will be produced by Wiecke at Dresden. He has already arranged for the copyright of his adaptation. In his view copyists were responsible for utterly distorting the fourth and fifth acts of the play as originally conceived by Shakespeare. He proceeded to describe to me the alterations he has undertaken. I asked whether he would let me have these amendments and additions for my edition of *Hamlet* which will carry the Craig woodcut illustrations. I would insert them in red type in the text or as footnotes. He readily agreed.

At ten o'clock Hauptmann looked me up in my room and invited me to come over to his apartment so that we could 'plunge into work', meaning the reading of *Till Eulenspiegel*.[6] He has a very big, attractive drawing-room where he has set up a small library and has everything he needs for his work. He took the manuscript and began to read to me, softly, in order to spare his voice, but with masterly clarity and intonation.

He had explained to me earlier that he has taken the hexameter for his basis, and has also adhered to its scansion, but that the versification is something new and individual. His reading confirmed the claim. Goethe's rigid hexameter pattern has gone completely. The way that he read and articulated the verses, especially the Prologue which he has only recently composed, sounded like rhythmic prose and in places recalled the inflexions of Hölderlin's *Hyperion*. The effect is sumptuous and full of variety. I fear, though, that for the eye of the reader the scrupulously observed hexameter form will prove a little misleading. Great verbal artist that he is, his achievement is to have distilled from German speech its own peculiar rhythms and blended them into something akin to the hexameter. He maintained however that his choice of the hexameter was neither fortuitous nor irrelevant, but had been essential to his purpose and was alone instrumental in suggesting certain things to him. Apparently he did not quite relish the emphasis I laid on the singularity of his versification and my remark that it sounds like rhythmic prose; I fancied that I caught a shade of displeasure in his reaction.

He repeatedly interrupted himself during the course of the first two Adventures and grumbled that this or that is 'much too long'. He also jumped certain passages, explaining that at the outset he was so preoccupied by the matter of the poem as not to have attended sufficiently to its form. That is what he must do this summer, clean up these older parts and cast them in the right mould. He will do it on the proof-sheets, as he has with all his previous writings. My own impression of the work, which may become Hauptmann's *Faust*, was distinctly favourable. I would say that it is, next to *Quint*, his most outstanding and profound performance.

In the afternoon a consultation with Count Wiser about my eye. He thinks that things are not so bad and that, if I wear his glasses, he will be able within a reasonable space of time to put me right. Towards half past six I was going back with Frau Hauptmann to the hotel when we were met by Hauptmann himself, slightly pale and *défait*. This afternoon, he told us, he thought that he must die. Stomach-ache and flatulence suddenly attacked him so violently that he felt as though he was going to burst. He used laxatives, suppositories, and so on, but nothing helped. For an hour and a half he had the most dreadful spasms, but now he felt better.

Meanwhile Sigmund Feldmann, who is their guest, joined us from inside the hotel. He, Hauptmann, and I remained in the garden by ourselves. A chit of seventeen, fair-haired and slender, floated past us; Hauptmann's mortal terror vanished in thin air. 'Shall I fall in love again? I am almost inclined to. It is what goes with it that is so painful. Leaving a person who through the years has almost become a part of you in order to follow a young, unknown one. . . . No, better not.' Nevertheless his eyes pursued the girl with a slightly woebegone expression until the unsuspecting Frau Hauptmann approached from the hotel and the four of us strolled through the village to the edge of the forest beyond.

I brought the conversation around to Hauptmann's *Hamlet* adaptation. The key-point, he said, is that he makes Hamlet, not Laertes, responsible for the uprising against Claudius. It is Hamlet, not Laertes, who speaks the words, 'Oh thou vile king, give to me my father.' Hamlet has struck up an alliance with Fortinbras and returns with him to Denmark to avenge his parent and reconquer his inheritance. This is the only way to render the last two acts intelligible and it frees Hamlet from the appearance of being no more than a spineless procrastinator and argumentative dabbler. Goethe came close to appreciating the switch which occurred in the roles of Laertes and Hamlet, but he did not take the point to its logical conclusion. I was much impressed by Hauptmann's arguments and I believe that he may well be right.

I suggested to him that, setting up *Till* in type, we should print it as prose, only inserting a sign at the end of every verse-line to indicate the hexameter. This was what we did with the Schroeder rendering of Virgil. Hauptmann seemed to regard the proposal worth consideration. He will give the matter thought.

Saturday, 4 June 1927   *Bad Liebenstein*

At ten o'clock with Hauptmann again. He continued his reading, beginning with the night scene where the young soldier who has shot the angler comes to Till's camp fire. I was deeply moved.

In the afternoon a visit by Tesdorp, who is the original of Till. He is a big, slender man, in his mid thirties, not handsome but with dazzling white teeth and a pleasing almost constant smile. He and Hauptmann are on intimate terms and Frau Hauptmann calls him 'my fifth son'. During the war he was a lieutenant in the Air Force. Now he is the representative of a large British firm. His ambition, as soon as he has money enough, is to buy a two-masted schooner and, with his wife and a one-man crew, to make it his permanent home, spending winter in some Mediterranean harbour and the fine seasons of the year roaming the seas.

Whit Sunday, 5 June 1927   *Bad Liebenstein*

During the morning Hauptmann continued his reading of *Till* and again from half past four to a quarter past seven, which was pretty exhausting for both of us. But he insists that the experience has been very useful to him. He can now see exactly what has still to be done, tidied up and polished.

Whit Monday, 6 June 1927   *Bad Liebenstein*

During the morning Hauptmann finished his reading. I told him that I miss, at the close of the poem, Eulenspiegel's laughter, his laughter at death and ultimate things. Eulenspiegel should literally die of laughter. That, he agreed, is quite correct and conforms to his original plan, though he had dropped it for the moment. He proceeded to search his notes and read to me the draft passage.

Thursday, 9 June 1927   *Weimar*

Kippenberg, who is here for the Goethe Convention, came to lunch. Discussed printing of the Rilke letters and prose volume, *Till Eulenspiegel*, *Hamlet*, and other publishing business.

Saturday, 11 June 1927   *Weimar*

Listened to Wundt at the Goethe Convention talking about the influence of Goethe's personality. His superficial address succeeded in multiplying my doubts about the value of 'German *Weltanschauung*' and 'German philosophy'. Their exaggerated individualism, notion of history, nationalism and overestimation of inherent as opposed to rational factors did, in the final analysis, result in the World War and all the misery and barbarity of our age. Wundt basked of course in the undimmed glory of this attitude towards life!

Tuesday, 14 June 1927   *Berlin*

Dinner at Sammy Fischer's with the Gerhart Hauptmanns, Hugo Simons, Einsteins, Kerrs, and so on. Hauptmann said that he is grateful for my suggestion about Eulenspiegel dying of laughter. He is definitely going to add the scene, but is not yet certain how; he has various possibilities in mind.

I do not recall how the talk veered to astrology, but Hauptmann assumed the role of its defender against Einstein, or, more accurately, asked Einstein what he thought of it, obviously anticipating that Einstein would allow it some significance or other. Einstein however rejected it utterly and in as gruff a manner as, given his conciliatory character, he is capable of. The Copernican system, he declared, conclusively made a clean sweep of the anthropocentric view which thought of the entire firmament as revolving around the earth and humanity. That was probably the severest shock man's interpretation of cosmos ever received. It reduced the world to a mere province, so to speak, instead of its being the capital and centre. And it put the Passion in a totally fresh light.

Hauptmann held out stoutly on astrology's behalf. Einstein would very shortly see a book by Johannes Schlaf which proves the whole of the Copernican system to be wrong. (Hauptmann himself slightly smiled at this.)

Well, even though regarded objectively that may be nonsense, it must be granted that imagination does play a part in the formation of our philosophy of life and that this subjective factor cannot be altogether eliminated. The same applies to speech, for the formulation of any ideology in words lends backbone to it.

That is evident, parried Einstein, from Lévy-Bruhl's book about primitive ideas which he is just reading and where he meets demons on every page. Faith in the influence of demons is probably at the root of our concepts of causality. (Clearly what he meant was that man's notions have evolved from faith in demons to faith in astrology, i.e., in the influence of the stars; and from there, via Copernican astronomy, to the causal doctrine of a purely mechanistic interpretation of nature.)

Kerr, who sat listening with his vulgar little wife, constantly interrupted with facetious remarks which he thought witty but which were not even funny. The subject of God was a special butt for his derision. I tried to silence him and said that, since Einstein is very religious, he should not needlessly hurt his feelings. 'What?' exclaimed Kerr. 'It isn't possible! I must ask him right away. Professor! I hear that you are supposed to be deeply religious?' Calmly and with great dignity, Einstein replied, 'Yes, you can call it that. Try and penetrate with our limited means the secrets of nature and you will find that, behind all the discernible concatenations, there remains something subtle, intangible and inexplicable. Veneration for this force beyond anything that we can comprehend is my religion. To that extent I am, in point of fact, religious.' Before that he brushed aside categorically, indeed slightly irritably, my remark that his discoveries have had as revolutionary an effect on our view of the world as those of Tycho Brahe and Copernicus. 'There is *nothing* so revolutionary about my observations.'

At dinner, when I made a passing comment on his resemblance to Goethe, Hauptmann flashed across the table, 'Yes, but then I am a son of Goethe.' Slightly baffled, I asked, 'How am I to understand that?' He modified the statement to the degree that he is of the same stock. He is also related, he maintains, to Alexander von Humboldt.[8] His son Benvenuto, being taken at the age of four past Berlin University, pointed at the figure of Humboldt: 'That's Daddy!' This close consanguinity with Goethe and Humboldt seems to have become a sort of mystic article of faith with Hauptmann.

Sunday, 3 July 1927   *Baden-Baden*

Early departure from Frankfurt for Baden-Baden via Mainz, Worms, and Speyer. At the last of these cities we stopped for lunch in the Wittelsbacher Hof, eating in the dining-room where in 1924 three Separatist leaders, Heinz-Orbis and two henchmen, were murdered. One of the bullets which prostrated them is still stuck in the panelling. The head waiter who served us was present at the time and described the scene, reminiscent of the more gruesome during the French Revolution. The three Separatists had been sitting at a table, drinking hard. Suddenly some young men entered. 'Hands up! This concerns only Heinz-Orbis and his fellows. Others have nothing to fear.' The words were hardly spoken before the salvoes rang out, the Separatists lay dead on the floor, and one of the assassins, turning out the light, shouted 'Everyone of you stays here quarter of an hour; whoever moves will be shot.' The murderers disappeared into the night without leaving a single trace.

Tuesday, 5 July 1927   *Zurich*

By car from Basle to Zurich. Today a year ago occurred the crisis in my illness.

I visited Wyss. Then I went to the Kokoschka Exhibition. His talent lies in catching the delicacy and subtlety of human expression, especially in the eyes, mouth and hands. He disguises and yet emphasizes this by means of a completely extraneous coarseness and brutality.

Thursday, 7 July 1927   *Sils Maria*

To the Nietzsche house and Nietzsche memorial. Both are exactly as one would wish them to be. The small, modest house was open, but nobody to be seen. The memorial was rendered even more impressive by the sight and sound of the sublime, magnificently rugged *Zarathustra* landscape, the rustle in the tree-tops and of the waves on the shore of the lake.

I wrote Frau Foerster and sent her edelweiss from the *Zarathustra* mountains.

Friday, 15 July 1927   *Coire*

In the cathedral I chanced upon the grave or better, the tombstone of Jürg Jenatsch. The inscription runs GEORGIUS JENACIUS, with a coat of arms. It impelled me to go into a bookshop and buy Conrad Ferdinand Meyer's[9] novel of the same name.

To my surprise I found it to be an outstandingly great work.

Perhaps only our age, we who have experienced the war and the revolution, can fully appreciate its profundity and truth. Every nationalist and political assassin should be forced to read it so that he can see the reflection of his visage. With glowing passion and startling veracity, Meyer has here etched the features of the 'nothing but nationalist'.

Jürg Jenatsch is a monster, but a monster far ahead of his day and one whose descendants were to dominate the world in the nineteenth and twentieth centuries. The contrast between Jenatsch (fanatical nationalist) and Rohan (man of honour and peace) is the one which also shapes the contemporary scene. The author's depiction of Jenatsch, with his colossal unscrupulousness, his criminal good conscience, and his frenzied determination to attain power, anticipates the type that the war has produced.

Thursday, 21 July 1927   *San Bernardino*

I spent the evening with Pellegrini, the painter, Dürr, the writer, and Oeri, the editor of the *Basler Nachrichten*. Dürr advanced, clearly and fascinatingly, the theory that Conrad Ferdinand Meyer, Jacob Burckhardt, Gottfried Keller, Jeremias Gotthelf, Nietzsche, Gobineau, and all the rest of the great intellectuals active in Switzerland around the middle of the nineteenth century (Gobineau was a legation counsellor at Berne) were pushed into aversion of democracy and conversion to an aristocratic philosophy of life by the spectacle presented by the victory of Swiss democracy. 1831 saw the beginning in Switzerland of a cultural levelling process which lasted until about 1875 and produced to a varying degree detestation, fear, hate, and contempt among all these men. The lower middle class, which mistook its semi-education for culture, came to power and pushed the old, highly cultivated patrician families aside. Switzerland thus forestalled developments all over Europe. At the same time there arose in the cantons petty tyrants who pursued a harsh, ruthless rule on the lower-middle-class's behalf. Since then Switzerland has become conservative.

I was very interested by this exposure of where the roots of Nietzsche's 'Superman' concept and his hostile attitude to democracy lie and, secondly, to learn that they did not derive from purely idealistic notions but were the upshot of political experience and factional sympathies aroused by his Swiss environment.

The attitude of Dürr, this very typical Swiss citizen, towards Fascism seemed to me significant. Pellegrini, the artist, supported it. Oeri rejected it because it represses intellectual freedom. Dürr fears that it will corrupt the Italians' best qualities. The experience of many centuries has rendered them a pusillanimous people. Fascism is trying to inject an artificial heroism into them. The experiment will fail, but the Italians' naïvety, charm, urbanity, and sensitivity will be lost in the process.

I had to struggle with Pellegrini against the idiotic myth that Mussolini has introduced order into the Italian rail and postal services. Oeri, who attended the Genoa Conference in 1922, *before* Mussolini's day, confirmed that the trains at that date ran as punctually as they do now and that the Italian post is still as unreliable as it was then.

Sunday, 31 July 1927   *Berlin*

During the last few days I have read several plays of Plautus, whom I did
not know, in the original. I was astonished at the vigour, effectiveness,
terseness of the dialogue as well as its wit, imagination, colourfulness, and
rich variety. The *Arsinaria* surprised me most of all. They combine demonic
depravity with raging mockery of the upper crust, the middle class and the
gentry, which sounds like the rumble of approaching social thunder and is
prophetic of Spartacus. Nowhere else in ancient literature can I recall so
acrid a smell of slaves' sweat and spleen.

Wednesday, 3 August 1927   *Berlin*

A visit by Kippenberg. He overflowed with enthusiasm for the latest pro-
ducts of French literature: Maurois (*Ariel*), Morand (*Buddha vivant*),
Mauriac, Valéry, and so on. They provide, in his view, what today's intel-
lectual readership demands, the 'spiritualization of reality'. The old classics,
Balzac, Dostoevsky, even Goethe, are 'dead'. Nobody buys Goethe any more.
He has practically had to give away his stock of Dostoevsky, except *The
Brothers Karamazov*. Rowohlt has had the same experience with Balzac.
To me the most surprising was the admission by Kippenberg, Goethe
enthusiast though he is, that Goethe is no longer a draw.

Thursday, 11 August 1927   *Berlin*

Constitution Day. Flags on all Government buildings, buses, trams, and
underground; but very few on big business houses, department stores,
hotels and banks. A moderate display among private houses, and on the
whole probably a larger number than in former years.

   In the evening I saw the American film *What Price Glory?*, the best war
film I have so far seen and the only one that has had the courage to show war
as it really is, in the round and from all sides, without concealment. During
various scenes the audience broke into stormy applause.

Sunday, 14 August 1927   *Berlin*

Looking back on Constitution Day, my conclusion is that an increasing
proportion of the nation, right into circles of the People's Party, regards the
republic for the time being as an incontestable fact, whereas the great
majority of the 'captains of industry', the powerful financiers, the civil

service, the Reichswehr, the bench, the large and medium-sized landowners (*Junkers*), and university professors and students are hostile to the republic.

Tuesday, 23 August 1927   *Berlin*

Last night Sacco and Vanzetti were executed.[10] The outburst of indignation in every country is unparalleled, a mass emotion as on an outbreak of war. There is hardly anything to distinguish this crime from thousands of others which society, under the cloak of civilization, perpetrates all the time. Nevertheless it is a good thing that now and again the sluggish mind of the masses, when some scandal assumes sensational proportions, should be pricked by perception of the horrors continually coexistent with, but hidden behind the veil of, modern civilization's brilliance and false glitter.

    Quite accidentally, certain 'cases' penetrate the consciousness and feelings of the general public. What is characteristic of, and historic about, them is that they suddenly stab the normal apathy like a dagger plunged into millions of souls and that the suffering shared awakens these to a sensibility which transforms the 'cases' into turning-points of history. The Dreyfus Affair and the deaths of Giordano Bruno and Socrates are examples. Such a case, to the most intense degree and with unforeseeable consequences, is the slaughter of Sacco and Vanzetti. In the consciousness of mankind it will remain, like Lady Macbeth's 'damned spot', an indelible stain on American civilization.

Thursday, 1 September 1927   *Paris*

During the morning passed in the train through the valley of the Meuse, from Liège to Namur, where in 1914 I experienced such dreadful hours. Once more I had a swiftly passing sight of the bridge by which I rode into Liège, a city in flames; of that other bridge between Seille and Andenne across which I saw the swarms of ashen-faced hostages being led away; of the long highway on the right bank of the Meuse down which we retreated from Namur. I tried to relive the events of 1914. I was taken aback how pallid the memory of them had become. Faint and unreal, they haunted like mere ghosts the firm, indestructible reality of the landscape which has survived while those horrors, and the dead too, have (alas, how quickly) disappeared.

Tuesday, 6 September 1927   *Paris*

At eleven o'clock Maillol came to fetch me. He had asked me to find with him a site in the Tuileries gardens for his Cézanne memorial. He has been offered a spot in the corner of the terrace left of the Seine and the Place de la Concorde, but he has very properly rejected this because the background would be dominated by the Eiffel Tower. *'Voyez-vous ma statue toute petite avec la Tour Eiffel lui sortant du ventre!'* He favours the location above and to the right of the terrace entrance because it is circumscribed and framed by flowers.

Afterwards we lunched at the Café de la Paix. He is learning to drive a car. No mean achievement at sixty-five, he remarked proudly. *'Mais vous verrez, l'année prochaine, si vous venez à Banyuls je vous conduirai.'* He talked about the beginnings of his career in Paris. *'J'étais tout seul; je ne connaissais personne. Sans cela, j'aurais peut-être continué à faire de la peinture. Mais je n'arrivais pas à faire ce que je voulais en peinture, et je n'avais personne pour me donner des conseils.'* He did at that date however paint a number of women's heads which were good, but most of them are lost; he has no idea where they are. I have at Weimar at least one of them, I said, which he himself sold to me, perhaps twenty years ago. He knew nothing more about it and was totally unable to recall what sort of a head it could be.

He told the story of how necessity drove him to paint the scenic decorations for Maurice Bouchor's puppet theatre. They included one of a brothel, for a play by Hroswitha, and another of a Byzantine bath where he did the mosaics in the manner of van Gogh. This so roused the admiration of Puvis de Chavannes that he had Maillol introduced to him. Chavannes and Renan regularly attended Bouchor's shows, but Bouchor continued his habit of giving away all the seats until he finally lost his money. Those were the days when Maillol fulfilled an order for tapestry at a fee of three hundred francs, from which he still had to pay for the wool and a needlewoman. Nevertheless he lived on his remuneration for six months. *'Ça c'est du génie, vivre six mois de trois cent francs!'*

After lunch I drove him to Marly and then visited Paul Valéry to ask him to translate Virgil's *Georgics* for me. Valéry, with his carefully parted silver-grey hair, smart black suit, and the Legion of Honour button in his lapel, looks like an old French marquis.

He declined my request. In the first place he is too busy and in the second he does not care for the *Georgics* because he knows nothing about agriculture. So much so that Mallarmé once had to explain to him what corn was, an occasion on which Mallarmé had coined one of his most beautiful phrases. It was at the end of July or beginning of August 1898, when he was staying with Mallarmé in the country and the corn was growing golden already. As they walked by a field, he inquired what this *herbe* was. *'Mais, mon cher, c'est du blé.'* After a pause, during which he gazed at the golden corn and a thought about the coming Paris concert season, one of his keen interests, crossed his mind, Mallarmé added, *'C'est le premier coup de cymbales de l'automne.'*

Valéry went on to say that he would be very willing to cooperate with

Maillol and myself on publication of some shorter Latin work which appeals to him or possibly some of his own poems. Why not, I asked, a complete edition of his works, *de grand luxe*, at three or four hundred francs per volume? The idea pleased him and I promised to bring him, during the course of my next visit to Paris in December or January, detailed proposals for its implementation.

Speaking of his own work, he remarked that for the past five years he has no longer done what interests him, but has simply fulfilled commissions. Although he has no faith whatever in his critical capacities, the result is that he has gradually composed an entire history of French literature by way of short prefaces. He has more such commissions for years ahead. Until 1917 nobody took any notice of him. Suddenly he became the fashion and since then he has no longer been his own master. To flatter him, I commented, '*C'est la rançon de la gloire.*' '*Voilà ce que tout le monde me dit; mais je me suis promis plusieurs fois d'étrangler celui qui me répétait le mot.*'

My general impression is of an old *grand seigneur*, a fairly harmonious mixture of philosopher and businessman laced with intellect and malice, a gleaming surface of manners and intelligence over an abyss of obscurity which is difficult to define and perhaps deliberately veiled.

Thursday, 15 September 1927   *Paris*

Last night the unfortunate Isadora Duncan was strangled by her own shawl when it was caught in the back wheel of the car in which she was travelling. The shawl which was so much a part of her dancing has caused her death. Her stage property and slave has taken its revenge on her. Seldom has an artist been so intimately beset by tragedy. Her two small children were killed in a car accident; her husband committed suicide. Now her own life has been ended by this object which was so indispensable to her.

On the evening before the death of her children I was in her box at the Russian ballet. She invited me to luncheon at Neuilly the next day, but I had to refuse because I had an engagement with Hermann Keyserling. The children were supposed to dance for me after the meal. I have always had a feeling that fate intervened and, if I had accepted, the children would not have died.

Poor Isadora. In her early days I had a low opinion of her dancing and considered her awkward, amateurish, and uncultured. She knew of this through Crail. Later she once asked me to Neuilly, demonstrated a dance to me, and, when I expressed my genuine admiration, said in her Americanized French (which had a certain affiliation with her Californian interpretation of Greek art), '*Oui, quand vous m'avez vue*' (pronounced *vou*) '*avant j'étais vertueuse*' (pronounced *vörtouöse*), '*je ne savais pas danser: mais maintenant . . . !*'

Isadora Duncan (Cocteau)

One day in Paris she came to the ladies' afternoon of Mme Metschnikov, wife of the famous savant. When she entered, the old lady was surrounded by friends of her own sex and generation. She did not know Isadora and, on hearing her name announced, went up to her with the words, '*Que puis-je faire pour vous, Mademoiselle?*' The reply came like a shot from a gun: '*Je voulais vous demander, Madame, si vous permettriez que Monsieur Metschnikov me fasse un enfant?*' Curtain, with Mme Metschnikov in a faint and the other old ladies doing their best for her. But finally Mme Metschnikov came round and asked, her wits still shaken, '*Mais pourquois, Mademoiselle : connaissez-vous le Professeur Metschnikov?*' '*Oh, non, Madame! Mais je pensais que si le Professeur Metschnikov me faisait un enfant, celui-ci aurait la tête du Professeur et les jambes de moi, et que ce serait très bien.*'[11]

I once met her, at the very beginning of her career, in the house of Luise Begas in Berlin. It was snowing and slushy. I was just leaving as she arrived. I believe it was the first time I saw her. She wore a wide mauve cloak, reaching from her shoulders to the ground, a sort of cowl, and her feet were bare except for goloshes. These she removed in the hall and then, to my surprise, strode bare-footed into the drawing-room.

She became a protégée of Countess Harrach, in those days the most beautiful woman at the Berlin court and a friend of the extremely prudish Empress. The latter summoned one of her ladies to debate the morality of female barefoot pedestrianism. The lady-in-waiting (who told me the story next day) reassured her, and that was how it came about that a sort of Christian Ladies' Association was formed in support of Isadora. Everything went splendidly until it could no longer be ignored that the Vestal Virgin was very shortly to have a child. Hereupon the Association collapsed in a turmoil of thunder and lightning and Isadora had to leave Berlin.

Poor Isadora! She never could rid herself of something philistine and school-marmish, however much she tried by way of free love and selection of her children's fathers to break the bounds of convention and American Puritanism in her art. Yet she was a real artist, and art and tragedy constituted as ineradicable an element of her private life as did her Californian philistinism. Dancing of the calibre which today we hold in high esteem, and even the Russian Ballet, would not have been possible without her. She sowed a seed which has blossomed. The manner of her death could have been the inspiration for one of Holbein's *Dance of Death* illustrations.

Wednesday, 21 September 1927   *London*

In the morning to the British Museum and read Belleforest's *Hamlet* story in his *Cinquième tome des Histoires*, 1582. His ending (Hamlet slays the king and succeeds to his throne) corresponds much more to Gerhart Hauptmann's version than the accepted Shakespeare text does.

Monday, 26 September 1927   *Paris*

At two o'clock Eric Gill came to the hotel to fetch some money. He left London yesterday, to bring his little boy to school in France, without any. We went through everything again and he promised to come in April to Weimar to work on the *Song of Songs*. In the autumn he wants to begin the Boccaccio edition. I suggested that he should drive with me to Maillol at Marly, but he declined because he wants to do life-drawings at some academy or other. But he did ask me to convey his respects to Maillol as a truly great artist.

A comment on his eccentric eroticism: he asked me, in front of his ten-year-old son, where to buy erotic photographs here. He also said that it is high time to create works of art to destroy the morality which is corrupting us all. What, I laughed, would the Abbot of Ash think of that statement? He would disapprove, Gill replied, but all art is a revolt against conventional morals and is composed of two elements, a moral and an anti-moral one, in conflict with each other.

I found Maillol at home with a slight 'flu, but in good spirits. I showed him Gill's book. He thought the etchings '*pas mal, mais trop faciles*'. He is doing a very similar set of etchings for an edition of Ronsard, scenes between lovers, but he does not content himself with such paltry compositions, mere contours, which he can reel off. He does not make things so easy for himself,

Eric Gill: self-portrait 1927

but seeks to give them light and shade, to lend them substance. He showed me a number of sketches for the Ronsard volume. Inevitably, since the number of positions for the consummation of love is not unlimited, there is close

'The Soul and the Bridegroom' 1927 (Eric Gill)

resemblance between the designs and poses chosen by Maillol and Gill. But those by Maillol have a far greater intensity and carnal atmosphere than is the case with Gill's somewhat cold-blooded eroticism. I mentioned Paul

Valéry's wish to have a complete edition of his works printed by me with illustrations by him. To my surprise he did not turn down the project. Instead he requested me to tell Valéry that he will consider the matter because he would not only be delighted to collaborate with him, but it would give him the opportunity of acquiring Valéry's works, which are normally unobtainable.

Tuesday, 27 September 1927   *Paris*

Discussed with Paul Valéry the subject of the collected edition. He reckons that there will be six or seven volumes in all. He was worried that there will be no more than three hundred copies of each.

I found him quite alone, without any domestics to open the door, suffering from an attack of lumbago, and in a very nervous state. He spoke so softly and swiftly that I had difficulty in following him. He has so much to do, he complained, he does not know '*où donner de la tête*', what with trips to be made to Vienna, England, Spain, and heaven knows where, a mass of literary obligations to fulfil, family worries, and all the rest. Obviously he attaches excessive importance to 'recognition' and also has a keen nose for business. He is like a shipwrecked mariner who has just reached land and is immoderately careworn and delighted at the same time.

He will go and see Maillol next week ('*si je trouve le temps*'). As I said that I have never yet succeeded in obtaining copies of his poems, he presented me with *Charmes*, *Album de vers anciens*, and *La jeune Parque*.

Wednesday, 5 October 1927   *Weimar*

Visited Frau Foerster-Nietzsche. She is of course full of the approaching Nietzsche Congress at which Oswald Spengler is to give a lecture. I told her that it is uncertain whether I shall be able to attend as I have a previous engagement with the Hauptmanns at Agnetendorf. She looked somewhat disconcerted, but merely asked me to see whether Hauptmann cannot come over to the Congress. She proceeded to talk about her 'dear friend Mussolini', the comfort of her old age, who has recently sent her greetings. Out of politeness I did not comment. In complete antithesis to this Mussolini infatuation, she then proclaimed her adherence to the 'United States of Europe', which her brother had been the first to advocate.

Wednesday, 12 October 1927   *Weimar*

I made an excuse to Frau Foerster for declining her invitation to a luncheon with Oswald Spengler. However, since she wrote and wished to know which of her guests did not suit me, I answered truthfully that I prefer not to meet Spengler in private because, in view of his political methods and intellectual arrogance, I do not want to make his acquaintance.

Thursday, 13 October 1927   *Weimar*

This afternoon I was with Frau Foerster. She treated the Spengler incident mildly, though emphasizing the friendship that she feels for him. Otherwise she was, as always, charming and kind. It is a pity that her provincialism, so inappropriate to Nietzsche, is so all-pervasive. An example is the reiterated emphasis she lays on being an expatriate German (it is thirty years since she has been out of Germany) and that therefore she cannot be other than a Nationalist. (When she was in Paraguay, there was of course no such thing as a Nationalist Party and the old Conservatives wanted her brother's works pulped, one and all. Indeed the *Kreuzzeitung* even demanded that the police should impound copies in private possession.) Painful to hear such nonsense from Nietzsche's sister in the environments of the Nietzsche Archives.

Saturday, 15 October 1927   *Weimar*

Opening of the Nietzsche Congress with Spengler's lecture on 'Nietzsche and the Twentieth Century'. The hall was full to overflowing. I had a chair carried in for myself, but many had to stand. The lecture proved a débâcle. For an hour a fat parson with a fleshy chin and brutal mouth (it was my first sight of Spengler) spouted the most trite and trivial rubbish. Any young worker in a Workers' Educational Association who tried to inform his fellows about Nietzsche's philosophy would have done better. Not *one* original idea. Not even *false* glitter. Everything uniformly shallow, dull, insipid and tedious.

In short Spengler succeeded in making Nietzsche a bore. Only a few ludicrously wrong assertions enlivened the gloomy hour. In Britain, for instance, philosophers have never pondered politics 'because Britain is no polity'. (Hobbes's *Leviathan* and the rest are non-existent or, more likely, Spengler has never heard of Hobbes and his successors.) Again, interest in the cognition theory in the nineteenth century was as much an anachronism as 'anyone today ordering baroque or Louis XV instead of modern furniture'. (Mach, Wundt, Spencer, the entire field of scientific perception, physiology and psychology are null and void, excommunicated by Spengler.) And again, Kant and the guillotine are parallel manifestations. (This flash of inspiration was repeated several times, for fear, no doubt, that somebody might miss this precious piece of enlightenment.) So the big gun has burst or, more properly speaking, since never a shot was fired, it has simply fallen apart in dust.

The whole assemblage was obviously nonplussed. Frau Kippenberg (beside whom I sat and who, at the start, took almost personal offence at my saying that Spengler's lecture did not interest me and I was attending only out of courtesy to Frau Foerster) said that my verdict, 'speech by an un-talented sixth-former', was far too mild. Riezler, who rang me up, raged that it was 'unheard of', 'a real scandal'. Heinrich Simon, of the *Frankfurter Zeitung*, took the same view.

Saturday, 22 October 1927   *Weimar*

Lunched with Frau Foerster-Nietzsche. What, she asked, did I think of Spengler's lecture? I told her the unvarnished truth, and she listened to me without protest. On the other hand I also told her, what is correct and clearly delighted her, that in other respects the Congress was a sound success. She has, despite her eighty-one years, survived the strain of the event well, though looking frailer and more tired than usual. She recalled many lively memories of her life in Paraguay and of the atrocities performed under the Lopez dictatorship, tales that sounded as if recounted by Hudson or Cunningham Grahame.[12] About the execution of entire companies of soldiers who had buried treasure at the dictator's orders, so that none should live to tell the tale of where the loot was buried. About an English mistress of Lopez who returned subsequently to uncover a treasure, was recognized, and had to flee disguised as a scullion. About a company of British adven-turers who procured permission to explore the jungle for rubber, disappeared without trace, and of whom it was rumoured that they went in search of Lopez's treasure and departed with an iron chest full of gold which they had raised out of a jungle swamp.

She went on to tell me about the reconciliation with the Wagner clan. Last year, during the festival here for Siegfried Wagner and after a preliminary reconnaissance by Countess Gravina, the whole Wagner family called on her. Subsequently she gave a luncheon party for them. On this occasion the reconciliation was formally sealed when they all held hands around the table and she read them her brother's *Sternenfreundschaft*. Siegfried issued an official invitation to her to share the family box at Bayreuth. She cannot be cross with him, she added, for she still sees in him the little boy who announced that he loved her more than anything else in the world.

The world-shaking Wagner–Nietzsche feud has petered out in an atmos-phere of social cosiness and in a manner appropriate to the 'courtly' style so typical of the Bayreuth crowd. The 'Princess of Albania'[13] was present and, duly touched, took cognizance of the reconciliation. The whole business is infinitely commonplace and removed in sentiment by several thousand miles from the closing chords of *Götterdämmerung*, let alone the end of *Zarathustra*. But who is to say whether Richard Wagner might not have effected a reconciliation with Nietzsche over a cup of coffee? Hardly, though, Nietzsche with Wagner.

Sunday, 23 October 1927   *Weimar*

A good joke by Carl Fürstenberg, told me by Hilferding. Louis Hagen conducts Fürstenberg through the apartments of his newly acquired manor. Each is fitted in a different style: Louis XVI, Louis XV, Louis XIV. Finally they reach a room where there is just simple, old-fashioned plush-covered furniture. 'The living-room from my parents' home,' Hagen reports. 'BC, I presume?' asks Fürstenberg.

Sunday, 6 November 1927   *Weimar*

Saw Krenek's *Jonny spielt auf*. A sketch extended to an evening's entertainment, with good, bad, and indifferent all mixed up together. Not very original, musically, but talented. Afterwards the Craigs to supper. Craig was in excellent form and sharply condemnatory of Piscator's[14] and other production novelties. In principle, he argued, novelties on the stage are always bad and the public is right to have no truck with them. We discussed *Merchant of Venice* and Machiavelli's *Mandragola* or Grazzini's *La Spiritata* as subjects for illustration by Craig.

Friday, 11 November 1927   *Weimar*

Wrote the first pages of my Rathenau biography.

Monday, 14 November 1927   *Berlin*

Kurt Weill arrived at half past seven and we talked about the ballet project. He would like to do it, he says, but he has meanwhile accepted a commission from his publisher to compose a big opera and has already received an advance for it. He must therefore ask the publisher whether he will give him leave, so to speak, for two or three months for the ballet. He proposes that this music should be mainly *sung* from behind the scenes, using only a very few instruments – flute, saxophone.

Monday, 21 November 1927   *Berlin*

Talk with Frau Lily Deutsch about Walther Rathenau. What she told me was, on the whole, critical rather than positive and accompanied by an

Kurt Weill (Dolbin)

undercurrent of disappointment. His ruling passion, she said, was the determination to possess power. Everything else was a mere appendage. The same was true of people. They were all 'only episodes', as far as he was concerned, and this applied to herself also. The letters she received from him could just as well have been written to any other woman, although she was the person who stood closest to him.

She went on to describe in great detail their relationship, which never attained to intimacy. She was speaking very frankly, she commented, but it was a fact that, notwithstanding Rathenau's passionate nature, matters did not go beyond a certain stage. Perhaps such a thing, self-possessed restraint despite vehement feeling, was only possible among Jews. And the AEG, Rathenau's fear of a scandal and what it would mean for his position in the firm, played a part in the matter too. He never jumped over that shadow nor were his feelings so vehement as to induce him to take the step.

Rathenau was a man who literally *knew everything*. His intelligence was phenomenal and much greater than he dared to show. His intellect enabled him to see far into the future. In economics he was far ahead of his day. His lasting importance lay only in his economic ideas. These would in time prove fundamental.

It would be quite wrong to suggest any primacy of sentiment in his nature. He was really totally unemotional, merely hankering for this or that feeling. She repeated the point several times: sentiment was a minor matter with him. All that counted was intellect and the determination to have power over others. When he courted people, it was in furtherance of his determination to win power over them. That applied not simply to important individuals like the Emperor or Bülow, but also to quite insignificant ones.

Lotte K., for instance, had been a small, hunch-backed member of the *Vorwärts* editorial staff; Rathenau accepted her devotion because at that date (after the revolution) he wanted to be in someone's good books on the *Vorwärts* staff. A similar case was that of Wilm Schammer, a staff writer on an anti-Semitic hole-and-corner paper in Nikolassee, whom he wanted to get over on his side.

Frau Deutsch thinks that, although he was a radical in the economic field, Rathenau was at heart a monarchist whose ideal it would have been to attain power under the old Imperial regime. During the revolution he once said to her, 'We ought really to be standing on the barricades. But I can't. I can't bear the smell of little people.' And it was perfectly true that certain things appertaining to the five senses, like evil smells, and so on, made him ill.

'With Rathenau,' she continued, '*everything* was spurious except his determination to possess power and his intellectual activity. He had a *very* sensuous nature, but to this day I have no idea what vent he gave to his passions. He knew that such things stand in the way of "success" and therefore he held them in check. He grew up in a world whose sole objects were money, career, and power, a dreadful world. When we met, he told me, "I have never known anyone like you before, who *wants nothing*." ' He was a romantic through and through. His determination to possess power was as much a piece of romanticism as his idolization of blonde and noble Teutons. This romanticism was connected with his Jewishness; sensitive Jews are often romantics. Once when she was very ill, he said to her, 'When you are well again, let us go to Granada and Seville. That is where we belong, where our home is' (meaning among the Moors and Arabs). His pedagogic strain was characteristically Jewish too, originating with the Talmud. It was a very marked quality of his.

Wednesday, 23 November 1927   *Berlin*

After lunch a long talk again with Frau Deutsch about Walther Rathenau. His mother, she said, was a hard, cruel woman. There were constant scenes between her and her husband and with her son as well. Often Rathenau ran away from table because he could not stand the scenes any longer. His parents did not allow him any literary interests. They forbade him to read Shakespeare and punished him when they once caught him reading one of the plays at night. He had to acquire all his intellectual equipment on his own and worked continually at his self-improvement. His concern for externals, democracy, patriotism, republicanism, were pose; his interest was entirely concentrated on himself. But he struck deep roots in German culture and could not detach himself from Germany; that part of him was real.

He had, according to Frau Deutsch, a presentiment of his death. Shortly after his appointment as Foreign Minister, Wirth told him, teeth chattering, the following story: he had a visit from a Catholic priest who, even though breaking the secret of the confessional weighed heavily on his conscience, felt that he must report to Wirth what had been confided to him – Rathenau was the next on the murder list. From Wirth the priest went to Pacelli and obtained from the latter absolution for his breach of the confessional secret.

Rathenau repeated the story to her without much excitement and asked what he should do about the matter. To which she replied, 'Nothing.' To that degree she was also to blame for his murder. Subsequently she did advise him to put himself under police protection. For a while he did so, but then became irritated by it. He could not bear always to have people around him who watched his every step and he countermanded the precautions.[15]

In the later afternoon I saw Edith Andreae, Rathenau's sister. Her manner was even more self-possessed and matter of fact. She was perfectly willing to talk. My first question related to her mother. In contrast to Lily Deutsch, she described her as highly cultivated, sentimental, romantic, extremely musical, and as a young woman strikingly beautiful. Her parents were rich and she grew up with every luxury. Her husband's much poorer circumstances made her unhappy in the early years of her marriage and, as a southern German, she had difficulty in attuning herself to the much more prosy Berlin atmosphere. Walther had been her only comfort and she invariably stood by her son in the arguments between him and his father. He had moreover received his intellectual stimulus entirely from her. His father preferred the second son, Erich.

How, I asked, was a reconciliation effected between Walther and his father? That occurred in 1902, when Erich died. The father was in a state of utter collapse. Walther took things over, worked out his father's speeches, discussed everything with him. Gradually his father became so used to his care that he could no longer do anything without him. That was when the close bond between them came into being.

After Erich's death, the mother withdrew completely into herself and was harsh, suspicious, and jealous of Walther. This jealousy went so far as to include Edith. If brother and sister wanted to talk to one another, they had to hide from their mother. This lasted until Walther's death, when her mother again underwent a transformation. She was literally restored to vitality and recovered her kindliness. It was her own idea to write to the mother of her son's murderer[16] and, when she did so, she did not even show her daughter the letter.

Rathenau was an out-and-out romantic, his sister asserted. His enthusiasm for the blonde Teutons was pure romanticism and she used to tease him about it, saying to him, 'If you had met Siegfried or Arminius, you would have run away from them because you would have thought their hands too dirty.' The same applied to his love for Germany. The war crushed him because 'his beloved' was overthrown. (Lily Deutsch also told me that the war really broke Rathenau.) And the war was responsible for his suffering from his Jewishness again. He had felt slighted when, as a young man, it prevented him from obtaining an Army commission. But it really hurt when, in the war, he longed to help his 'beloved' and his Jewishness hung like a millstone round his neck.

1928

Came over from Weimar to meet André Gide at Viénot's. Big social occasion.
Also there was Madame de Prévaux, granddaughter of Liszt. Gide seemed,
or pretended to be, pleased at our meeting. He read a passage from his
Enfant prodigue, but suddenly interrupted himself with the exclamation, '*Non,
c'est trop belge, c'est trop mauvais. On ne peut lire cela. J'ai fait mieux depuis.*'

Cartoon by Karl Arnold, 1928. A comment on the gulf between the rich and poor.
Some are fat by choice, some are thin by choice, and others are thin of necessity

In the morning went to see Wirth to ask him about Rathenau. How did he
come to pick on him? When he was Minister of Finance, he replied, he
realized at Cabinet meetings that his colleagues just chattered away without
having a proper grasp of affairs. He therefore got into the habit of calling for
Rathenau to discuss with him matters relating to finance and Allied reparations. Rathenau was a physicist, he (Wirth) a mathematician, and both of

them were interested in philosophy, so they had many points in common. Soon a semi-political, semi-intellectual friendship developed between them. That was why he took Rathenau and Dernburg with him to Spa, as his two mainstays. At Spa Stinnes[1] openly demanded the Bolshevization of Germany, but Rathenau in a brilliant speech opposed him and converted Dernburg and Seeckt (!). From that moment (1920) began the policy of fulfilment of the Entente's demands. The Ministry of Foreign Affairs, especially Rosen, was furious about Rathenau having accompanied Wirth to Spa.

In the following year, after the London ultimatum, circumstances rendered it natural for him to bring Rathenau into the Cabinet as Minister for Reconstruction. He had, so to speak, already grown into the part. Towards the end of the year the Democratic Party withdrew Rathenau from the Cabinet; Rathenau was furious about this. Next year, when a Foreign Minister was needed to cope with the Genoa Conference, Stinnes tried to have Rosenberg, his loyal supporter, appointed, but Wirth sent for Rathenau. Stinnes was economically so powerful that nobody except Rathenau dared to oppose him. He (Wirth) and Ebert had done their utmost to bring Rathenau and Stinnes together and to achieve a compromise between them, but their efforts were in vain.

Tuesday, 15 May 1928   *Eilsen*

In the morning went for a two hours' walk with Hauptmann. He told me about his new drama, *Schwarze Fastnacht*, and we talked about Rathenau. Stresemann, he remarked, is not exactly kind to his memory. For instance, speaking to Benvenuto, Hauptmann's son and Rathenau's godchild, he commented that 'Cobbler, stick to your last' is the only proverb appropriate to Rathenau's role as Foreign Minister.

In the afternoon we discussed dates for the *Hamlet* edition. He promised to let me have his manuscript by 15 September, enabling us to effect publication by Christmas. Then, I do not recall how, our conversation turned to Hofmannsthal's *Der Turm*. Hauptmann described it as 'a débâcle'. He fetched his copy, with various passages marked in red, and read extracts. Hofmannsthal, he criticized, was infatuated by individual words and would write whole scenes, totally inorganic and undramatic, just so as to introduce them.

In the evening, at table, he said that Tolstoy's *Power of Darkness* had 'opened the door' for him to his own work as a playwright. Ibsen had influenced him little, if at all. But Tolstoy, that was a different matter! True, the concept of *Bahnwärter Thiel* had already taken fairly firm shape, but *Power of Darkness* rendered the last step possible. Ibsen's characters were all artificial, whereas Tolstoy's were genuine creations. In his own work the drama derives from his characters. That is the way it was with Goethe, in *Clavigo* for example, though not with Schiller.

Incidentally, Hauptmann claimed that Hofmannsthal's *Der Turm*, precisely on account of its errors, has inspired his *Schwarze Fastnacht*.

Sunday, 20 May 1928   *Berlin*

Reichstag election. In the evening ran into Koch in the Democrat head-quarters. He was very depressed about the Party's losses.

Monday, 21 May 1928   *Berlin*

During the morning saw Gaus at the Ministry of Foreign Affairs about publication of Maltzan's reports in my *Rathenau*.[2] He is not worried about revelation of the contents, but he does regard direct quotation from post-war files as something so out of the ordinary that readers will inevitably suspect the fact as having some political motive behind it. Dirksen, whom he called in, suggested that perhaps the Russians should be consulted, but Gaus saw no occasion for that. He reiterated that he has no objections, but that it would be more correct for me to raise the point once more with Schubert. He might do a minute on it.

Wednesday, 23 May 1928   *Berlin*

My sixtieth birthday. Many congratulations and flowers. Newspaper articles, but only one good one.

Tuesday, 29 May 1928   *Berlin*

At eleven o'clock conference in Dirksen's room with Gaus on publication of the Maltzan reports. He repeated that there is no objection to verbatim quotation, but the Ministry requests that such passages should be presented as my personal description of events, not as an extract from the files.

Lunched at the Schuberts'. He said that he hoped his decision would not make things too difficult for me. He was unable to adopt a different line because he had simultaneously had to entertain a request for publication of the Ministry's files for 1914–18 and had to reject this for political reasons. Those files contain, as I would be aware, things which it is impossible to publish today. Recently, skimming through them, he came across a truly mad story. Shortly before the war, in summer 1914, America offered Germany an arbitration treaty on the same pattern as had earlier been concluded with Britain and France, and it even renewed the offer after the outbreak of hostilities, in November 1914. On both occasions the German Government scornfully declined the invitation because it would mean 'a relinquishment of sovereignty'. The Emperor's marginal comment made the same point!

Wednesday, 13 June 1928   *Vienna*

The Hofmannsthals to dinner at the Bristol. Afterwards we went to the Schubert Festival Concert in the Josefsplatz. There were lights in the apartments of the grandiose baroque palaces which frame the square and therefore it was possible, standing in the darkness under the canopy of a clear Italian night-sky, to look through the open windows into the stately *salons*. The whole scene, with not too many people walking about while listening to the music, had an almost purely Italianate quality. I cannot, though, think of any city in Italy which could offer such a sumptuously imperial baroque setting.

Richard Strauss and Hugo von Hofmannsthal (seated at the table)

Thursday, 14 June 1928   *Vienna*

Lunched with Richard Strauss, his son and daughter-in-law, at the Hofmannsthals' in Rodaun. An uneven flow of conversation because everyone wanted to talk about different things. Strauss aired his quaint political views, about the need for a dictatorship, and so on, which nobody takes seriously.

In the evening attended the second performance of *Egyptian Helen*. Very disappointed and bored. Libretto and music alike weak and decadent. I am glad that I did not have to discuss it with either Hofmannsthal or Strauss. The last time that I saw Hofmannsthal!

Sunday, 24 June 1928   *Berlin*

My *Rathenau* book is officially out today. The major newspapers, *Voss*, *Börsen-Curier*, *Frankfurter*, *Kölnische*, and the rest, give whole columns to quotations from it. *Berliner Tageblatt* has an excellent leading article on the subject.

Saturday, 21 July 1928   *Homburg*

Today's issue of *Die Menschheit* publishes a letter from Poincaré to the Separatist Matthes. He defends himself against the accusation in *Rathenau* (never made, though Master Matthes has evidently humbugged him into the belief that I allege it) of wanting at the time of the Genoa Conference to 'annex' the Rhineland. Drafted a reply to Poincaré.

Tuesday, 24 July 1928   *Homburg*

Dewall, of the *Frankfurter Zeitung*, has advised me not to wait for Poincaré's reply, but to have my answer to him printed at once in *Menschheit* and other papers.

Sunday, 12 August 1928   *Frankfurt*

Very impressive Reichsbanner parade in the Ostpark. Some eighty thousand men. Almost even more impressive was the march through the streets, which lasted several hours. The population formed a lane many rows deep on both sides and all windows were packed with cheering spectators. Obviously the Republic is an accepted fact in Frankfurt. Numerous 1848 banners were carried in the procession. In the afternoon returned to Homburg.

Monday, 13 August 1928   *Homburg*

Poincaré's reply to my letter has arrived. He denies, through his secretary, that he encouraged the Separatist movement. The letter is dated 30 July and went by courier bag to Berlin, where it was posted on the eleventh with a completely wrong address.

Wednesday, 15 August 1928   *Coblenz*

In the morning travelled from Homburg to Coblenz in order to collect material for my rejoinder to Poincaré. Poincaré insists *'que le Gouvernment français n'a jamais voulu, en ce qui le concerne, favoriser une mouvement séparatiste; il a d'ailleurs jugé qu'il ne lui appartenait pas d'interdire les manifestations spontanées'* (!!) *'d'une partie des populations'*. I am looking for conclusive data which will prove the encouragement, manifest to everyone, given during the years 1922–4 by the Poincaré Government to the Separatist movement.

First to the Town Hall and saw the deputy of the Mayor (who is away) and then to the Provincial Governor. I gave him Poincaré's reply to read. He laughed at the impudence of it. The fact that the French 'favoured' the Separatist movement and that it was indeed their creation, is notorious throughout the Rhineland. But, he added, it is precisely facts shrieked from the roof-tops which are often difficult to prove. If I wanted to collect material for a publication, that could be put together in no time. What will be practically impossible is to frame a brief letter which will conclusively prove what everybody knows about Separatism and the French. Whatever individual example I quoted, a denial would be immediately made or the case be described as an exception. In short, he was unable to furnish me with anything that I can use.

Tuesday, 21 August 1928   *Homburg*

At Frankfurt showed my revised rejoinder to Heinz Simon, who found it good. We agreed however that publication should be postponed until after signature of the Kellogg Pact[3] and the negotiations at Paris and Geneva. That way I shall not incur the reproof of having spoiled the party for the French.

Friday, 24 August 1928   *Treves–Verdun–Reims*

Drive via Luxemburg and Longwy to Verdun and from there via the Champagne country to Reims. The burned-out villages on the hills near Verdun herald a truly shattering landscape, a landscape that first inspires horror and gradually a feeling of desolate tragedy. Mile after mile of military cemeteries, charred trees still stretching their limbs to the sky, ruined farms, and constantly in the distance the bare, grey and white shimmer of the chalk downs. Horror and anguish alternate at the sight of this picture. The densely packed little white crosses in the graveyards, thousands upon thousands of them, seem in the broad landscape insignificant, for it is the landscape which harbours the souls of the dead crying for vengeance on those responsible for this crime and which constitutes a perpetual admonition to peace.

And then, to crown it all, the damaged, dreadfully maltreated Cathedral of Reims, scoured by fire, its stones as eaten away as if they had lain thousands of years fathoms deep in the sea. Infinitely grand, unnerving, exaltedly terrible, and yet of an unearthly beauty in its devastation. The whole calamitous area between Verdun and Reims should be transformed into a European sanctuary where in condemnation of war and for the consecration of peace, hosts of pilgrims from all corners of the world could annually congregate and pay homage to the great, stricken cathedral. At present the only hosts of pilgrims consist of tourists, principally Americans, carrying cameras and concerned for their tightly stuffed sightseeing programmes. They desecrate the scene like droppings. This landscape, site of Attila's 'Catalaunian Fields', Valmy, and finally the Battle of the Marne,[4] has fulfilled the destiny graven upon its face. Those who come here now should do so in the spirit of the Greeks when they viewed the awe-inspiring mythical figures in their tragedies – to be purged with pity and terror.

Thursday, 27 September 1928   *Berlin*

In the evening saw Brecht's *Dreigroschenoper*,[5] music by Weill. A fascinating production, with rudimentary staging in the Piscator manner and proletarian emphasis (apache style). Weill's music is catchy and expressive and the players (Harald Paulsen, Rosa Valetti, and so on) are excellent. It is the show of the season, always sold out: 'You must see it!'

Sunday, 30 September 1928   *Berlin*

Today's second morning edition of the *Frankfurter Zeitung* publishes my last two letters to Poincaré. Only about a hundred, out of the original five thousand, copies of Rathenau are still on hand. The print-run of the new edition is complete and will be on sale in a few days.

In the evening saw Theodor Dreiser's *Clay in the Potter's Hand* at the Renaissance Theatre. Hartung's production is a Brahm[6] resurrection, just as the play is an early Gerhart Hauptmann resurrection, though weaker, more sentimental, and with a whiff of American morality, especially in the last act. Nevertheless it made an immense effect, mainly in the third act, the court scene, where Frida Richard (the Jewish mother) and Hermann Vallentin (the old Jewish father) gave performances that are among the best I have ever seen. I shall never forget Frida Richard as the mother, utterly broken, but stubbornly and almost speechlessly defending the innocence of her son. Her acting recalls Eleonora Duse, Jaccori, Rossi or Salvini at their most moving.

Friday, 5 October 1928   *London*

Tea at the Dieckhoffs. He says that relations between the Foreign Office and the French Embassy could not be more intimate, whereas the attitude adopted towards the rest of the diplomatic world, including ourselves, is much more distant. Every step taken is previously discussed and agreed between the two Governments. The British are irritated with the Americans; Houghton does not feel happy here.

Dieckhoff told the story of Emil Ludwig's reception by Sthamer. Ludwig sent in his name simply as 'Herr Ludwig'. Sthamer at once received him, without in the least suspecting who he was. 'Do, please, sit down, Herr Ludwig. You are German?' Ludwig, scenting a hint at his Jewish appearance, 'Yes. I am the author of a Bismarck biography.' Sthamer, suddenly realizing what had happened, threw up his hands and exclaimed 'O Lord!' Ludwig assumed this to be a contemptuous assessment of his work; he quickly took his leave. Sthamer, thoroughly embarrassed and annoyed at his own gaucherie, could not bring himself to issue an invitation to Ludwig. Whereupon Ludwig steamed off in a tremendous pique.

Tyrrell tried to comfort Sthamer with the following anecdote. Ludwig complained to Tyrrell once about the modern lack of respect in Germany for great men. 'When Moltke and Bismarck strolled down Unter den Linden, all the passers-by raised their hats. Do you suppose anyone takes off his hat when I walk down Unter den Linden with Feuchtwanger?'[7]

Tuesday, 9 October 1928   *Paris*

Saw Giraudoux's *Siegfried* in the Comédie des Champs-Elysées. The French and German characters are cardboard figures, therefore tedious and exasperating. The main impression is of the false light in which a well-meaning Frenchman sees even the externals of German life, such as the ridiculous 'German' clothes of 1921 appropriate to a farce of the 1860s! The production and acting are wretched and as absurdly out of date as the costumes. Coming from London or Berlin, the drop in standards met in the Parisian theatre is very marked. Like going to the provinces and finding that the fads and fashions of thirty years ago are the latest thing.

Monday, 15 October 1928   *Paris*

During the morning visited André Gide in his new apartment, 1bis Rue Vanneau. He was still in the middle of moving and received me in his half-filled library. I wanted to talk about the *Hamlet* translation. He has done the first act, but has not progressed beyond that. He asked what Hauptmann thinks of the rendering. When I told him, he commented, '*Voyez-vous, c'est ce que j'ai toujours dit, qu'il était profondement corrompu.*' I outlined to him the revision that Hauptmann has undertaken. He fairly definitely rejected my proposal to complete his translation for the Cranach Press. He is so behind-hand with work that he cannot assume any further commitments. For instance, he promised to let the American *Forum* have his new novel for the November issue, but he has been unable to finish it because for four months in the summer he felt paralysed and could not put pen to paper. The *Forum* has however refused to allow him more time and now he must do everything to try and meet the date-line.

As previously arranged, looked up Maillol in the workshop of his caster Rudier. Maillol was preparing the plaster foot of his *Venus* for its casting in bronze. In the courtyard some figures from the fountains at Versailles stood next to Rodin's *Thinker*. The latter looks distinctly puckered and small beside these firmly rounded, clearly contoured forms, designed to be visible at a considerable distance.

Maillol, studying the figures with Rudier and myself, commented that recently, when *The Thinker* lay on the ground, he observed '*des morceaux superbes*', particularly the torso and the back. Now that it is standing, '*on ne voit plus ces morceaux*' because the arms hide the former. Rodin, he went on, was masterly at implementing details but had no idea how to bring them out. The statue's arms, he added, half jokingly, should be hacked off in order to display the splendours of the torso. (Maillol in any case dislikes arms, even in the case of his own figures. He thinks his Venus better without arms.)

The *Burghers of Calais* group was also standing in the yard. This, and *The Thinker*, was ordered by the Japanese millionaire Matsukata for presentation to a Japanese museum. In the interval of the order being fulfilled, he went bankrupt and for the present the figures are stranded here. I asked Rudier whether anyone can still have Rodin's sculptures cast. He replied that fresh casts of all his works are obtainable from the Musée Rodin, which has the monopoly and is maintained from the proceeds.

Monday, 22 October 1928   *London*

This afternoon finally got hold of Craig. First spoke to him on the telephone and then saw him in my hotel. He arrived with his secretary, good-tempered and smiling as usual. Tomorrow is his son Teddy's wedding. We discussed in detail the unsuccessful *Hamlet* prints. He climbed down a peg or two. Also dealt briefly with *The Merchant of Venice*. He has done some costume designs for an American *Macbeth* production, he said, and this has given him fresh zest, so that he hopes to tackle the blocks for *The Merchant* in a better frame of mind, but I must leave him time.

Eric Gill turned up at a later stage of the talk. He is just moving to High Wycombe and looked very tired. I introduced Gill and Craig to one another, and they had tea with me. When Craig was gone, Gill said, 'I expected him to be quite different. Why, he is a charming old boy!' Seeing them side by side, it is much more Gill, extremely grey already and today terribly exhausted, who looks like an 'old boy'. Craig, for all his grey hairs, continues to have something youthful and boyish about him. Again discussed the *Song of Solomon* with Gill.

Saturday, 27 October 1928   *Berlin*

Saw Reinhardt's production of *Romeo and Juliet* at the Berliner Theatre. An incredible muddle. So much intellect and so many bright ideas that the upshot is an inferior provincial performance. A Palladian setting, with Juliet's bedroom in the courtyard between screens and the balcony scene acted backstage so that Romeo's words are totally inaudible and Juliet's nearly so. Dreadful. At one point, during Juliet's duologue with the Nurse, the audience broke into loud laughter. Elisabeth Bergner and the Nurse, greatly upset, rushed offstage between the screens and an interminable pause followed, with the house lights left down, while presumably Juliet was being soothed by some manager or other in the wings. The production had an icy reception, except from an obvious claque. At the end the real members of the public, including those in the more expensive seats, left without applauding. Young Franz Lederer and Elisabeth Bergner make a handsome pair (he bears a striking resemblance to Byron), but that is all the performance has to offer.

Monday, 29 October 1928   *Berlin*

Saw Bruckner's *Verbrecher* at the Deutsche Theatre. A problem play attacking the processes of justice. Its main theme is that 'We are all criminals' or, what amounts to the same thing, there are no criminals, only sets of circumstances, 'social conditions', breeding crime just as swamps breed flora (Rousseau's argument). As a work of art, the play seems to me to be at about the same level as Sudermann's *Ehre* and Brieux's problem plays like *La Robe Rouge*, neither worse nor much better. Only the way that the stage is divided into six locations and the strong emphasis laid on homosexual aspects lends it a shimmer of 'modernity'. The homosexual aspect is thrown into even franker and bolder relief than in Heinrich Mann's *Bibi*. The audience did not take the least offence, not even at one of the very unambiguous concluding scenes in the 'boudoir' (the furnishings permit no other description) of an elegant young man who holds on his lap, caresses, and kisses a pretty fair-haired boy, apparently aged about sixteen. Theatregoers seem to have made up their mind about this entire problem and barely regard it as topical any more. Sexual attraction between women and between men and boys is accepted as natural and a foregone conclusion as much as it was by the Greeks, though as yet only on the stage!

Tuesday, 30 October 1928   *Berlin*

An evening at Piscator's attractive, bright flat, designed by Gropius, without frills but pleasant and providing a good background for people. A fairly large party, forty to fifty people, a number that increased until past midnight. Apparently it was given in honour of Granovsky, the Russian Jewish producer. Many actors and actresses on hand.

Bertolt Brecht

I was introduced to Brecht.[8] Strikingly degenerate look, almost a criminal physiognomy, black hair and eyes, dark-skinned, a peculiarly suspicious expression; very nearly a typical twister. But in conversation he thaws and comes within an ace of being naïve. I told him, apparently to his great delight, stories about d'Annunzio. Superficially, at any rate, he has a head on his shoulders and is not (like Bronnen) unattractive.

Afterwards Herzfelde once again discussed with George Grosz and myself his notion of making a film solely from shots of actual events. Grosz was opposed to the idea or, at best, very critical. 'It can make an interesting document, but reality as such does not interest me. You see, I am what you may call an artistic person and what I aspire to is the fabulous. The camera can achieve all sorts of interesting snippets, but never the magical effects of draughtmanship.'

'Civil War' 1928 (Grosz). A comment on the unsettled political conditions of the period

Grosz seems altogether to be experiencing a strong move away from realism. He complained that our time rationalizes everything and has absolutely no appreciation for man's irrational needs. What left-wing circles, the Social Democrats and the rest, strive for, improvement of living conditions among the broad masses, hygiene, and so forth, are simply matter of course objectives for anyone who has a heart. They are, however, a mere beginning, not a goal, and that is what people do not understand.

Sunday, 11 November 1928   *Berlin*

Read the letters from the Empress Frederick to her mother,[9] edited by Ponsonby. In spite of everything already known about the relations between the Emperor and his mother, they are here revealed as having been much worse than this correspondence could have been expected to show. The Emperor behaved with almost unexampled brutality, malice, baseness and cruelty towards her. It recalls Tacitus' account of Nero and Agrippina. Had the period allowed it, he would hardly have been deterred from murdering her. Every fresh publication renders the portrait of this weakling, coward, ambitious brute and braggart, this nincompoop and swaggerer who plunged Germany into misfortune, yet more repulsive. Not a facet of him is capable of arousing pity or sympathy. He is utterly contemptible.

Wednesday, 28 November 1928   *Berlin*

Talk with Roland de Margerie[10] and Viénot about my correspondence with Poincaré. Roland said that my idea of replying to Poincaré via my secretary caused a great deal of amusement. In answer to my remark that I had been right also in the *substance* of the matter, he commented, 'Poincaré let you have the last word.' Viénot described how he was recently received by Poincaré; our exchange of letters was mentioned. To his surprise, Poincaré was quite mild, '*pas du tout aigri*', though maintaining that he, and not I, had been right in the substance of the matter.

The counsellor of the Belgian Embassy had himself introduced. He told me that during the period in question he was Secretary to the Inter-Allied Commission at Coblenz and he could acquaint me with a lot of relevant material. I was right of course about Matthes and many others, '*des gens tarés*'. There were however also people '*de bonne foi*', such as Jarres, who had been for the 'ditching' of the Rhineland.

Thursday, 27 December 1928   *Paris*

In the evening to a performance of Diaghilev's Ballet at the Opera. Stravinsky's *Rossignol* and *Petruschka*. After the performance I was waiting for Diaghilev in the corridor behind the stage when he approached in the company of a short, haggard youngster wearing a tattered coat. 'Don't you know who he is?' he asked. 'No,' I replied, 'I really can't call him to mind.' 'But it's Nijinsky!' *Nijinsky!* I was thunderstruck. His face, so often radiant as a young god's, for thousands an imperishable memory, was now grey, hung slackly, and void of expression, only fleetingly lit by a vacuous smile, a momentary gleam as of a flickering flame. Not a word crossed his lips. Diaghilev had hold of him under one arm and, to go down the three flights of stairs, asked me to support him under the other because Nijinsky, who formerly seemed able to leap over roof-tops, now feels his way, uncertainly, anxiously, from step to step. I held him fast, pressed his thin fingers, and tried to encourage him with gentle words. The look he gave me from his great eyes was mindless but infinitely touching, like that of a sick animal.

Paris
1912

Diaghilev and Nijinsky (Cocteau)

Slowly, laboriously, we descended the three, seemingly endless flights until we came to his car. He had not spoken a word. Numbly he took his place between two women, apparently in charge of him, and Diaghilev kissed him on the brow. He was driven away. No one knew whether *Petruschka*, once his finest part, had meant anything to him, but Diaghilev said that he was like a child who does not want to leave a theatre. We went to eat in the Restaurant de la Paix and sat until late with Karsavina, Misia Sert, Craig, and Alfred Savoir. But I did not take much part in the talk; I was haunted by this meeting with Nijinsky. A human being who is burned out. Inconceivable, though it is perhaps even less conceivable when a passionate relationship between individuals burns out and only a faint flicker briefly lights the despairing, inert remains.

At lunch talked to Diaghilev, Lifar and others about my ballet. Diaghilev is still against using Weill for the music. '*Il faudra vous trouver un musicien.*' Weill, in his view, simply follows in Donizetti's footsteps, but camouflages the fact by inserting the appropriate number of discords at the right moment. He spoke about Berlin with enormous enthusiasm. When he was there in October, he never knew how he should spend his evening because the theatres had so much to offer. Berlin is the one capital he has been unable to conquer. He has enjoyed triumphs in all other great cities of the world, but '*devant Berlin, je suis comme un collégien qui est amoureux d'une grande dame et qui ne trouve pas le mot pour la conquérir.*' His Berlin efforts had always proved a material disaster, involving deficits of a hundred to a hundred and fifty thousand francs.

1929

Friday, 4 January 1929   *Berlin*

Dinner party at the Ows', including Kühlmann and Mrs Harold Nicolson,[1] whom I met for the first time. Talking about Brest-Litovsk, Kühlmann emphasized with great self-satisfaction that he deliberately crossed swords with Trotsky only dialectically because he set store by defeating Trotsky at that level. For myself, I find this gratification, a triumph of personal vanity over a non-essential, the dialectical game, extraordinary at a moment of history when Germany's fate was hanging in the balance. Even more extraordinary is that Kühlmann should continue to pride himself on it eleven years after the event and its catastrophic consequences.

Tuesday, 22 January 1929   *Berlin*

Mrs Harold Nicolson, Virginia Woolf and her husband, Leonard Woolf, came to tea. Virginia Woolf, no longer young and on the tall side, slightly desiccated and somewhat ravaged in appearance, has the pleasant manners of a well-bred Englishwoman. Leonard Woolf, clever and imaginative, is a bundle of nerves who trembles as he speaks. We discussed Mrs Nicolson's Rilke translation and the possibility of it being printed by the Cranach Press. Virginia Woolf is very typically upper-middle-class of the best kind, don's daughter, while Mrs Nicolson is just as typically aristocratic, the great lady, of slender build and great elegance, with ease of manner and style in every movement, a person who has never experienced a moment's embarrassment or a feeling of social barriers.

Tuesday, 23 April 1929   *Berlin*

In the evening a concert by young Yehudi Menuhin.[2] The boy is truly marvellous. His playing has the afflatus of genius and the purity of a child. His fantastic virtuosity remains a totally secondary factor, as though it were something to be taken for granted. A wonderful feeling for style, without the slightest suggestion of cheap effects or sentimentality. On the contrary, pure and profound sensibility. He played Beethoven's *Romance in F Major* (Opus 50) as I have only heard Joseph Joachim[3] render it.

Virginia Woolf. Woodcut by Vanessa Bell

Friday, 10 May 1929   *Berlin*

The Rumbolds gave a lunch at the British Embassy 'to meet the Maharaja of Kapurthala'. A tanned-looking, elegant man in a cut-away, he was treated with practically royal honours. I told Harold Nicolson the story of his father's fall on the occasion of Lichnowsky's royal dinner-party in London; it was new to him. He is an entertaining personality, but somehow I do not like him, without quite being able to make out why.

Monday, 13 May 1929   *London*

At the Savoy saw *Journey's End*, the play that is here having a success similar to that of *All Quiet on the Western Front* with us. A few strong scenes, but rather too much 'funny' business for my taste. The oddest part was the audience, which laughed with unconstrained heartiness. The terrible tragedy of the whole situation was, as it were, dissipated between the jokes.

Whit Sunday, 19 May 1929 Paris

Pagnol's *Topaze* at the Théâtre des Variétés is a harsh, malevolent, destructive play. Descended from Mirbeau and Becque, it is still more virulent and anti-social. Pagnol spares himself the trouble of explaining how the honest, lamb-like schoolmaster is transformed into the cynical profiteer and shark of the last act.

Wednesday, 22 May 1929 Berlin

First night of the Scala company's guest performance at the State Opera. *Falstaff*, conducted by Toscanini. Glittering audience, glittering performance. *Tout Berlin* present and thrilled. Toscanini conducts dazzlingly, with a verve, delicacy, and sureness that are astounding and enchanting. But, for my part, I found the dazzle greater than the depth; I was not deeply stirred. The Mayor of Milan, a gentleman of very bourgeois appearance with wife and daughter of the same calibre, contributed to the gaiety of the evening by keeping two gigantic lackeys, in scarlet livery with lots of gold trimmings, standing stiffly to attention behind him in his box throughout the performance.

Thursday, 23 May 1929 Berlin

My birthday, unfortunately! In the afternoon tea with Jenny de Margerie to meet Paul Morand and his wife. She turned out to be an old acquaintance to whom I had been introduced before the war. At that time she was unmarried, a Princess Soutzo, and lady-in-waiting to the Queen of Rumania. She at once reminded me of an amusing occasion at Countess Greffulhe's when Edmond Rostand, almost on his knees before the Queen, gushingly assured her that she was the original of his 'Princesse Lointaine'.

She told a very characteristic story of Proust, whom we both met at Larue's. One evening during the war, again at Larue's, Proust demanded music although this was forbidden in cafés for the duration of hostilities. Proust however insisted and finally said that, if no other music was available, he would fetch the Poulet Quartet. He went out to do so and, seeing that by two o'clock he had not come back, the Princess returned to her hotel, the Ritz. Between three and four she was suddenly woken by Proust. He stood outside her door and announced that he had hauled the Poulet Quartet out of bed, M. and Mme Poulet were standing in the hall downstairs but the double bass was ill with pneumonia and asked to be excused, the unfortunate consequence of which was that the Quartet would not now be able to play for her.

Sunday, 9 June 1929   *Berlin*

Saw Max Reinhardt's new production of *Die Fledermaus* at the Deutsche Theater. 'Press and Gala Performance', by invitation only. *Tout Berlin.* In the stalls behind me sat Kühlmann with a pretty young woman whose face I do not know. In the stage-box were two old ladies. One was the widow of Johann Strauss, the other of Hans von Bülow, having been Cosima's successor.[4] A brilliant performance under Reinhardt's stirring direction.

Monday, 15 July 1929   *Berlin*

Read in the *BZ*, midday edition, that Hofmannsthal's elder son, Franz, has shot himself. At half past two cabled Hugo. In the evening went to Stroheim's film *The Wedding March.* A work of genius which, with the savagery of a George Grosz, shows up the hollowness of pre-war Vienna's glamour and its sugary trashiness of sentiment (that of Hollywood as well, incidentally). Here is the precise obverse of what has always enthralled Hofmannsthal and held him spellbound.

Tuesday, 16 July 1929   *Berlin*

Hofmannsthal has died, at the funeral of his son, from shock at the suicide. I am stunned.

Thursday, 18 July 1929   *Vienna*

Arrived here early for the funeral of poor Hugo. The service took place at three o'clock in the parish church of Rodaun. The coffin, altar, and altar rail disappeared under a sea of roses. Every rose garden in Vienna must have been pillaged to produce such splendour. The church was cram-full. I sat beside Johanna Terwin and behind Richard Strauss's son. The absence of Strauss[5] himself and Max Reinhardt was unexpected. A beautiful violin solo, but not very impressive service.

A crowd of onlookers had assembled outside the church. Nosy sightseers from Vienna (the women, including some Americans, in light-coloured summer frocks), and many peasants and small tradespeople from the vicinity. It must have been a concourse of several thousand that joined the procession and escorted the coffin to the cemetery. The throng and the heat gradually marred the atmosphere. I walked next to Rudi Schröder. The extraneous distractions intruded as jarringly on his grief as on mine. A really disgraceful scene occurred on arrival at the cemetery. A wild scramble between mourners and onlookers to pass the police posted at the entrance resulted in a proper scuffle. Eventually Schröder and I were admitted, but by now any vestige of funereal sobriety had been replaced by a feeling of participation, under sweltering conditions, in some sort of *Kermesse* spectacle. For a moment, as I scattered earth over it, I glimpsed the coffin in its vault. With that of the son who shot himself visible immediately below, it struck me how thin and frail it seemed. Then all was over.

A part of my own life is gone with Hugo von Hofmannsthal. Only a week ago he briefly summarized in a letter to Goertz[6] our enduring relationship. The last time I saw Hugo was at that dreary, disagreeable lunch in June a year ago when Richard Strauss talked such nonsense that afterwards Hofmannsthal wrote to apologize.

Friday, 19 July 1929 *Vienna*

In the morning took a drive to Schönbrunn and there, in the park, read Hofmannsthal's *Der Tor und der Tod*. After lunch I went out to Rodaun and found Gerty Hofmannsthal and the family wonderfully composed, almost gay. She believes, and it is a consolation to her, that the death of the son was *not* the cause of the father's death. The doctors, diagnosing advanced hardening of the arteries, gave up Hugo three years ago. After Franz's death he had been quite calm, carried on his normal routine, wrote a lot of letters, and talked long and eloquently to her and Raimund about the death, though he also wept much and bitterly.

On Monday he got up and came to meals as usual. At three o'clock they were about to leave for the funeral. He had just put on his hat when he suddenly exclaimed that he felt dizzy and sat down on a chair. She took off his hat and led him into the study. On the way he could still stoop to pick up a glove that he had dropped. In the study he sat down again. She asked whether she should loosen his collar. His answer was indistinct and, to her horror, she noticed that his face was aslant. She scrutinized him sharply. 'Why are you looking at me like that?' But he did not go to the mirror, as he would formerly have done, to see whether anything was wrong. His speech was already laboured. She helped him to lie down on the sofa and he gradually lost consciousness.

Meanwhile the funeral was taking its course. Raimund said that, even as he hurried to the church, he felt convinced that he would not again see his father alive. Both he and his mother think it fortunate that Hugo was spared an awakening to hopeless, protracted suffering. But Gerty is grieved that he never received the letter from Richard Strauss confirming arrival of the revised version of *Arabella*, Act One,[7] and congratulating him on its success.

With Hofmannsthal a whole chapter of German culture has been carried to the grave. He was the last of the great baroque poets, belonging to that same tree whose finest fruits were Shakespeare and Cervantes. Baroque – the grafting of genuine feeling upon consciously artificial matter. Notable in this connection is Hofmannsthal's ceremonial approach to his themes. He handles them, particularly in his prose writings, much as a priest officiates with the host and he attaches to this ceremoniousness a certain similar sense of the numinous. To take a direct grip on his themes is repugnant, indeed impossible, to him and lacks in his eyes both respect and efficacy. He seeks matter to which he can transfer the expression of his own feelings (as in *Der Tor und der Tod*) and does not find it in reality. So he pursues his search for it in the arts, in literature, and creates his own artificial matter. That is genuinely baroque.

Tuesday, 23 July 1929   *Weimar*

Julien Green and his friend, a M. de St Jean, had a meal with me. They have been here a week and propose to stay longer because they like Weimar so much. Green is a powerfully built man, almost a peasant in looks, somewhere in his late twenties and with a calm, agreeable, well-balanced air. This, I imagine, is what Flaubert was like in his youth. He reads German, but speaks it badly. Notable is the slightly disdainful manner in which he talks about American literature in general and Sherwood Anderson in particular. For three years he studied at the University of Virginia, founded by Jefferson, but he is clearly the complete Frenchman.

Monday, 19 August 1929   *Homburg*

Read in the newspapers about Diaghilev's death. Deeply upset. A part of my world has died with him.

Friday, 30 August 1929   *Berlin*

A visit by Erich Maria Remarque to discuss his contracts. He came at Hutchinson's suggestion and stayed an hour and a half. He has the head of a Saxon peasant boy, an incisively contoured face with furrows, fair-haired with blue eyes beneath fair eyebrows. A firm expression that sometimes slips into lyricism. He told me his story in great detail and almost without a pause for breath. As a boy, from a lower-middle-class home in Osnabrück, he was very unhappy at the lack of any intellectual mentor. At fifteen he swotted his way through the *Critique of Pure Reason*,[8] though without much appreciation.

It always seemed to him extraordinary that he should exist at all. He spent a disconsolate youth interspersed with thoughts of suicide.

During the war he and all his fellows believed that everything would come right once there was peace. In fact they found themselves just as helpless in the face of peace as of war. He had no idea what he wanted to do. For a time he worked with Continental-Rubber at Hanover, writing snippets of advertising verse and copy. Then he became a sports reporter on one of the Scherl newspapers in Berlin. He used to imagine how splendid it would be if the *Berliner Tageblatt* would print a contribution of his in its literary pages.

He began to write *All Quiet on the Western Front*[9] simply as an exercise, took six weeks to complete it, and never had the slightest difficulty with it. Indeed, he finds writing perfectly easy when he has got his material firmly into focus. What he tries to do is to see his characters against the background of the infinite. His sentences may not be as polished as those by a professional writer, but they touch their reader's heart more deeply. Arnold Zweig[10] (author of *Sergeant Grischa*) has accused him of being slapdash, but Zweig's artistry comes between his book and the reader, whereas he (Remarque) is only concerned to get close to the reader.

The success of his novel has depressed rather than gladdened him. Previously he thought that success could bring contentment, but now he has realized that it cannot suffice a man. He was never so near to suicide as in the months following the publication of his book. He was only rescued from his depression by the thought that perhaps it has somehow been of use. Giving help to a cause or person is the one thing that matters.

Dinner at the Hugo Simons'. Arnold Zweig was there and, pretending to present bouquets, was venomous about Remarque. As if someone had attacked the latter, though everyone was singing his praises, he said, 'No, no, it's a good book', the word 'good' being pronounced with condescension. 'Remarque is a "good" amateur and he could even have turned his book into a great novel. His amateurism lies precisely in having failed to see the angle from which he should have tackled his subject. He lit on it, but passed it blindly by. There, where he describes the farmer's lad who can't stand the war any more when he sees the trees in blossom and thereupon runs away. That is where *I* would have started the story and centred everything else around this boy. Then it would have become a great book.' Altogether Zweig was at pains throughout the evening to prove himself maliciously witty. As he has only the malice and not the wit, the upshot was merely excessively tedious literary tittle-tattle.

Thursday, 3 October 1929   *Paris*

I was sitting in the barber's chair when I overheard 'Stresemann is dead'; I was on needles. The *Paris-Midi* carried the official announcement. He died of a stroke at half past five this morning. It is an irreparable loss whose consequences cannot be foreseen. That too is the way that people feel here. Everyone talks about it. Barbers, waiters, drivers, newspaper sellers. *Paris-Midi* carried the headline '*Une événement d'une portée mondiale et un deuil pour la cause de la Paix*'. To the Embassy, where I signed the book. The top signature is that of André Tardieu, Minister of the Interior. The Ambassador is on leave.

This frightful year 1929 continues to garner its harvest. Hofmannsthal, Diaghilev, Stresemann. One landmark after another of the world, as I and my contemporaries knew it, disappears. Truly an '*Année terrible*'.

The sensation produced here by Stresemann's death amounts to consternation, the Embassy Counsellor told me this afternoon. Briand called on him at ten o'clock already to pay his condolences and spoke with very warm commiseration. The feeling generally is not simply one of consternation, but also of anxiety about the future.

What I fear, as a result of Stresemann's death, are very grave political consequences at home, with a move to the right by the People's Party, a break-up of the Coalition, and the facilitation of efforts to establish a dictatorship.

Friday, 4 October 1929   *Paris*

All the Paris morning papers publish the news of Stresemann's death in the most prominent make-up. It is almost as if an outstanding French statesman had died, the grief is so general and sincere. The French feel Stresemann to have been a sort of European Bismarck.

A legend is in the making – by his sudden death Stresemann has become an almost mythical personality. Not a single one of the nineteenth-century's great statesmen, neither Pitt nor Talleyrand, Metternich, Palmerston, Napoleon III, Cavour, Bismarck, Gambetta, or Disraeli attained such world-wide recognition or such an apotheosis. He is the first to be admitted to Valhalla as a genuine European statesman. In its leading article, *The Times* states that 'Stresemann did inestimable service to the German Republic; his work for Europe as a whole was almost as great.'

The death of Byron, whom he admired so much, is the nearest comparison to the general sorrow and world-wide recognition accorded to Stresemann at his death. During the war, when I subscribed to *The Times* at my own expense so as to let him have a European perspective on affairs, neither he nor I foresaw such a close, such European *gloire*, for his career. It is a striking fact how, since the war, almost exclusively Germans have obtained world fame in all spheres of activity – Einstein, Eckener, Köhl, Remarque, Stresemann, and the rest, with only Lindbergh, Lenin, and Proust perhaps achieving similar stature. Much of the distinction which the mass of news-

Gustav Stresemann

paper readers attaches to these individuals is distorted and exaggerated, but the phenomenon is nevertheless noteworthy.

Monday, 7 October 1929   *Berlin*

It becomes ever more obvious to what an intense degree the nation as a whole has participated in the obsequies for Stresemann. Hundreds of thousands paid their last respects to him at his lying-in-state. One newspaper has justly commented that his was a national, not a state, funeral. He leaves behind an immense prestige which renders it all the more certain that an embittered struggle for this heritage will be kindled inside the People's Party, Parliament, and the entire nation. The People's Party's very odd memorial celebration furnishes evidence of that. Every possible means is being tried to falsify the picture of Stresemann into that of an anti-republican and chauvinist so as to salvage for the right the moral capital he has bequeathed.

Tuesday, 29 October 1929   *Berlin*

During the morning to Hilferding. The Cabinet, he said, has discussed and sanctioned the move which I propose to make with Snowden.[11] He, for his part, remains pessimistic about it.

Afterwards saw Curtius, whom I met for the first time. We began by talking about Stresemann. Curtius told me how he spent the last evening with him, staying until nearly ten o'clock. Stresemann had a bronchial catarrh, but did not pay much attention to it and was otherwise strikingly fresh and in good shape. In fact, he had recently been much fresher and healthier than a year ago, when he was patently a very sick man. At The Hague, regardless of the considerable efforts and excitements involved, he became fresher rather than wearier as the Conference proceeded.

On the evening before his death he discussed with Curtius his plans for the future. As soon as he had recovered from the catarrh he wanted to take a short holiday, then attend the second Hague Conference, and, immediately the Young Plan was accepted by the Reichstag, again take a longer holiday. On 30 June 1930 he would conduct the liberation celebrations in the Rhineland and thereupon retire. That would leave him a number of years ahead to enjoy life a little. A few hours later he was dead!

Thursday, 7 November 1929   *London*

In the afternoon I attended a reception given by Mrs Snowden, using this opportunity to arrange for myself an appointment with Snowden. The reception took place at 11 Downing Street, the lovely old official residence of the Chancellor of the Exchequer. Beautiful, white-panelled rooms with fine old pictures, brocade curtains, splendid marble fireplaces. It was slightly odd to see the rather proletarian company in this setting. Mrs Snowden, looking very smart, received me with great warmth and promised to make it her business that I should sit next to her husband and be able to talk to him alone. Henderson arrived soon after me and I chatted with him. Then I sat down next to Snowden, who greeted me very cordially: 'I am really glad to see you again', and so on. I said that I would like to make an appointment with him because here, in the drawing-room where at any moment we might be interrupted, it was simply not possible to tell him what I have to convey to him. He asked what the subject is. I told him and he invited me to come at eleven on Saturday.

Saturday, 9 November 1929   *London*

At eleven to Snowden in his official residence at 11 Downing Street. He sat at his desk by an open fire in a small, attractive room on the ground floor.

I took an armchair opposite him and we plunged into the middle of things. I elucidated the proposals for a new basis of negotiation which I had worked out, proposals which try to do justice to the difficult position in which both Governments find themselves.

Snowden listened very attentively and in a friendly manner to my statement, raised no objections, and at the end was going to make some notes. But I said that, if the proposal interested him, I would like to put it down in writing and let him have it today still. He accepted, commenting that I am aware of his views on this whole problem of the liquidation of alien private property. He made a gesture indicating that the responsibility for the matter is not his.

Dined alone at the Savoy and allowed myself half a bottle of champagne to mark my success of the day.

Wednesday, 13 November 1929   *London*

At six o'clock called on Snowden again. For three quarters of an hour, on the basis of my letter, he discussed with great seriousness and in detail, point by point, the problem of German property.[12] (He was not deterred by the fact of having yesterday sent Sthamer a very brusquely worded letter which rejected all further discussion of the question and demanded, in the form of an ultimatum and with threats, that the German Government should at last sign the agreement proposed by the British.) He neither accepted nor dismissed my proposals, but took shelter behind the excuse that, before he can reach a decision, he must await the report of the commission in Paris where his Treasury people are negotiating with Fuchs and the others. There seemed to be all sort of difficulties, he remarked, before the Young Plan could be implemented. He found especially worrying those connected with the International Bank.

He then produced a copy of the rude letter he had written Sthamer and which Otto Bismarck showed me yesterday.[13] I pretended not to know the contents, read them carefully, and confined myself to the comment that it is also our wish and to our interest that the commission's negotiations should be concluded as quickly as possible, thereby enabling the second Hague Conference to take place and the Young Plan to come into force. I must however tell him once more how valuable would be a gesture on the part of the British Government which would allow us to say that it has displayed generosity in its attitude. The German Government, Snowden retorted, would immediately draw the conclusion that it should demand the entire liquidation surpluses because, in the case of such a gesture, it would interpret the British Government's helpfulness as an admission of being in the wrong.

Nevertheless, he seemed deeply impressed, remained throughout calm, serious and sympathetic, and summarized the discussion in the phrase, 'You have touched my heart, but not my purse.' His final words were that he will listen to my broadcast on Friday and he hopes that I shall call on him again during my next visit to England.

Thursday, 14 November 1929   *London*

To tea with Leonard and Virginia Woolf in Tavistock Square. Woolf expressed himself in very warm terms about my book and added that he has reviewed it for tomorrow's issue of *The Nation*. Virginia Woolf said, 'You know, you have been spoiling my sleep this last week, by my husband insisting on reading to me passages of your book.' We spoke at length about Rathenau and Stresemann.

Afterwards I went to see Bernard Shaw, who has moved from Adelphi Terrace to 4 Whitehall Court. Very luxurious and with a marvellous view over the Thames. His wife was, as always, very pleasant and cheerful. She has put on a little weight, but Shaw, for all that he has gone completely white, remains as slim and nimble as a stripling. He was at his sprightliest, talking of matters past and present. We recalled our joint campaign for good will between Britain and Germany before the war and the luncheon given by Lichnowsky, when Shaw vainly tried to warn him[14] against Grey. Then he told the tale of his meeting last summer with Richard Strauss. 'The astonishing thing was that as long as Strauss and I were alone in Brioni,[15] nobody seemed to take any notice of us; but when Gene Tunney' (the boxer) 'came and joined us, we could not get away from the photographers; they were always around us taking photographs and films and following and watching us.'

We then spoke about Lawrence (Colonel Lawrence, Lawrence of Arabia), who is an intimate friend of the Shaws, and his eccentric shyness of publicity. Once Lawrence complained about every move of his being followed by the Press. 'Well, of course, they notice you,' Shaw replied. 'You always hide just in the middle of the limelight.'

Before I visited the Woolfs, I had a dress rehearsal in the BBC building of tomorrow's broadcast with Garvin. Everything was again discussed in detail and the precise timing fixed.

Friday, 15 November 1929   *London*

In the morning *The Times* carried the semi-official rejection, in a brusque, imperative, and quite unusual tone, of our claims in respect of German property. I felt straightaway that I could not speak on the wireless about Anglo–German relations just on the day when the British Government has given Germany such a slap in the face. Went to the Embassy and discussed the point with Dieckhoff and the Ambassador, also Bernstorff and Otto Bismarck. They unanimously approved my view that in these circumstances I cannot today make my broadcast address.[16]

I telephoned to Sir John Reith, Director-General of the BBC, and said that on account of a bad cold I shall be unable to speak today. If he could come to the hotel, I would like to add something to him in confidence. He arrived within fifteen minutes. I do have a cold, I told him, but the real reason I have decided not to speak *today* is the communiqué in *The Times*. It would be impossible, were I to speak, to pass over the matter in silence. Were I to mention it, I would have to explain what impression it will make in Germany. And that would quite definitely not contribute to the improvement of Anglo–German relations.

Wednesday, 20 November 1929   *Berlin*

Arrived early. Shortly afterwards I was telephoned by Ow. Harold Nicolson,[17] he informed me, has called at the Foreign Ministry to declare, in the name of the British Government, that neither the Treasury nor the Foreign Office had anything to do with the publication five days ago in *The Times* of Snowden's letter. In this connection Nicolson, as part of his official *démarche*, uttered the conjecture that publication derived from a German source and the surmise that I (!!) may have been the originator. Sthamer, Ow continued, has received instructions to make a counter-move, see Henderson, and declare that I have nothing to do with the business.

Friday, 29 November 1929   *Berlin*

In the afternoon saw Harold Nicolson at the British Embassy. He was very friendly and boyish and, with his legs dangling over the arm of his chair, talked like one British undergraduate to another. He described how, in his communication to Curtius, he purposely brought in my name, although he exceeded his instructions by doing so, because in that way he provided me with the opportunity to defend myself.

Friday, 6 December 1929   *Berlin*

A big dinner-party at the Morgans' (Dawes Commission). This morning's newspapers carried the text of a memorandum by Schacht[18] which is hostile to the Government and Hilferding in particular, sounds like a pronunciamento, and has been the sensation of the day. I was therefore not a little astonished to find that the order of seating for the meal provided that Schacht and Hilferding should sit to right and left of Mrs Morgan and opposite me. I told Hilferding that I was prepared for a bull-fight at table. However, the two merely turned their backs on each other and exchanged not a word.

Sunday, 8 December 1929   *Berlin*

Dinner at Baby Goldschmidt-Rothschild's on the Pariser Platz. Eight to ten people, intimate party, extreme luxury. Four priceless masterpieces by Manet, Cézanne, van Gogh, and Monet respectively on the walls. After the meal thirty van Gogh letters, in an excessively ornate, ugly binding, were handed round with cigarettes and coffee. Poor van Gogh! I saw red and would gladly have instituted a *pogrom*. Not out of jealousy, but disgust at the falsification and degradation of intellectual and artistic values to mere baubles, 'luxurious' possessions.

Thursday, 12 December 1929   *Berlin*

In the morning went to see Nicolson at the Embassy to discuss the further handling of the Henderson business. I then told him about pre-war Weimar, the Grand Duke, and so on. This led us to talk about pre-war days in general. In his opinion Germans as a whole overrate Edward VII. Nicolson's father knew him extremely well and always maintained that the King was terribly lazy and without any real knowledge of affairs. He did have one major quality – 'He was somebody you could trot out on occasion' to captivate some victim. In 1908 (?)[19] Isvolsky, who had arrived in London to discuss the Dardanelles, was so thoroughly softsoaped by the King that he utterly forgot ever to mention the Straits. Nicolson ascribes the main blame for the war to Bülow, not the Emperor (which coincides entirely with my own view). The Emperor assessed certain matters perfectly correctly and much more accurately than his entourage. It was only his mania about the Navy (including his faith in Tirpitz) and his hatred of his Uncle Edward that proved catastrophic.

I must add what Nicolson said about the after-effects of the war. For Britain they have been much worse than for Germany or France. Germany can base its reconstruction on the industry and scientific 'spirit of investigation' of its people. Britain has always relied on its tradition, its sense of 'fairness', and its 'team spirit'. These have been deeply shaken by the war, and it is difficult to see what is to replace them. He expressed himself very pessimistically about Britain's future, much as Beatrice Webb did when I was in London.

In the morning I was rung up by Wise, who is here for a day on his way through to Moscow. I asked him to lunch in the Automobile Club. Discussed with him my description of the Genoa Conference. He said that he induced Lloyd George to read it and talked to him about it in detail. How, I asked, did Lloyd George like it? All right, Wise replied, except as regards events relating to signature of the Rapallo Treaty. He wants, with Lloyd George's assistance, to put forward his differing interpretation in an article for a periodical. The Treaty of Rapallo was a catastrophe whose significance Lloyd George summarized in the words, 'If there had been no Rapallo, there would have been no Ruhr.'[20]

1930

The Nostitzes and Vollmoeller were my luncheon guests at Savarin. Vollmoeller told some piquantly colourful yarns about the Marchesa Casati. One of them could well have been spun by Barbey d'Aurevilly. The owner of a beautiful Louis XV mansion with a large garden in the Faubourg St Germain, she once rang up the Cardinal Archbishop of Paris at three o'clock in the morning and implored him to come to her instantly as she must inform him of a matter vitally affecting her spiritual welfare. The Cardinal declined to put himself to this trouble in the middle of the night, but after prolonged parley he instructed a priest of his household to go on his behalf. The priest arrived, sounded the bell, gained admission, and was conducted along one of the avenues towards the house. He was half-way there when the Marchesa, stark naked and a candelabra in each hand, stepped forward and tried to recite a long litany. The priest, shaken to the core, turned and fled as though he had seen the Devil incarnate. Next day the Cardinal filed a complaint with the police, accusing the Marchesa of an *attentat à la pudeur* and blasphemy. The incident ended with her disappearance for six months into a mental nursing home.

A fellow-guest at the Schwabach luncheon in the Esplanade was my old enemy of 1914, Lady Cunard.[1] After six weeks of hostilities, which Margot Asquith, Mechtilde Lichnowsky, and the rest vainly tried to end, because I insisted on a formal apology for her indescribable behaviour at the *Josephslegende* rehearsal, she finally threw her arms round my neck in a dark corridor at the Duke of Westminster's house, tearfully asked for forgiveness, and begged me to accept an invitation to her home. I agreed to a luncheon and she left the choice of guests to me. I selected Margot Asquith and Mrs Astor and they attended the peace celebration a fortnight before outbreak of the war.

    The peace was negotiated by Countess Greffulhe who came from Paris to London and at our first talk about the matter, in the Piccadilly Hotel, declared that I must *absolument* make it up with Lady Cunard. When I failed to react docilely to her exhortations, she demanded, '*Vous la détestez donc bien?*' I began, '*Non, mais enfin ...*' '*Allons, oui,*' she spiritedly interrupted me, '*vous la détestez ; mais quand on déteste tellement une femme on est bien près de l'aimer !*' And now today Lady Cunard was suddenly on the scene again (she is related in some way or other to Frau von Schwabach), completely unchanged except for looking still more malicious than she did formerly. She has acquired a truly vixenish expression, which was sub-cutaneous in the old days, but she was as charming as though nothing had ever happened between us.

Thursday, 13 February 1930   *Berlin*

Dinner at the Theodor Wolffs'. Molnar, Emil Jannings, Flotow, Kardorff, and so on. Molnar is a cheerful-looking old man with white hair and a fresh complexion. Jannings maintained that the live theatre is doomed to extinction; the talking film will kill it. Just a few theatres in the metropolises will, with external financial support, manage to survive. When people can see and hear the world's best actors and singers in the cinema for a few marks, nobody is going to visit some provincial theatre to watch the same show being done by mediocre performers.

Wednesday, 12 March 1930   *Berlin*

Luncheon at the French Embassy. Other guests were the Duchesse de Gramont (*née* Ruspoli), whom I took in, the Thurns and Taxis (she is a daughter of Pauline Metternich,[2] pretty coarse in appearance with few aristocratic traits), the Etienne de Beaumonts, and Chanel, the famous dressmaker. Beaumont told me that last year she paid seventeen and a half million francs in taxes. She started, people say, as the friend of an elderly gentleman who left her his fortune.

Old Hutten-Czapski took her in to table. Afterwards he asked me who his neighbour was. 'A seamstress,' I replied. He nearly fell over with indignation. But when I added, 'A seamstress who last year paid seventeen million francs income tax,' he was immediately mollified and merely muttered, 'Oh, well, in that case . . .' She interested me because, a friend of Diaghilev, she was with him at the time of his death in Venice. He died very peacefully and happily, she said, without realizing his condition. On the contrary, he was busy to the very end with plans which were a source of great contentment to him.

In looks (she is very pretty) and pronunciation, the Duchesse de Gramont reminds me strangely of Karsavina. Perhaps we were placed next to each other because we have both been victims of her step-daughter Clermont-Tonnerre (twenty years her senior) in her scandalous and lying memoirs.

Friday, 14 March 1930 *Leipzig*

Left Weimar at seven in the morning for Leipzig to join the jury responsible for choosing the fifty best printed German books of 1929. Besides myself, the seven-man jury included Poeschl, Klingspor, Fedor von Zobeltitz, the trade unionist Dressler, and Steiner-Prag. The session lasted all day, from nine until seven, with only an interval for lunch. It was not altogether easy to find fifty books which could decently be given a prize. The superiority of the private presses over the commercial publishers was manifest. If we had not basically decided to put the commercial publishers in the foreground as the more important, we would have had to give prizes to a far larger number of private printings.

At the close of the session Poeschl made a little speech, stating that he had been requested to tell me, in the name of the jury, that my *Hamlet* production was the finest German book of the year and that they would make it their business to see that this opinion became known at large. Privately, Poeschl told me that the *Hamlet* caused him a sleepless night, so excited had he been by it. How we achieved the two-coloured printing from a single wood-block is beyond his comprehension. Coming from Poeschl, who is probably the best contemporary German printer, that says a lot. The Cranach Press edition of Goertz's *Zwei Novellen* is also among the fifty books awarded a prize.

Thursday, 27 March 1930 *London*

First night of Cochran's 1930 revue at the London Pavilion. In the stalls I ran into Bernard Shaw and his wife and they introduced me to Lord Berners.[3] He has written the music for Lifar's first ballet, *Luna Park*. Shaw laughed when he saw me, greeting me with the words, 'I was going to write to you. I owe you an apology. I have "taken your name in vain" in my new book in which I am collecting all I said during the war. But I will show it you before I publish it.'

Thursday, 10 April 1930 *Paris*

To tea with the Etienne de Beaumonts. They reside in a truly princely palace in the Faubourg St Germain (2 Rue Duroc). Built by Brogniart, the architect of Versailles, for his own family and afterwards turned into the Spanish Embassy, it has for the past century ('*depuis le retour de l'émigration*') been the home of the Beaumonts. The drawing-room is of positively gigantic proportions, the whole in the most ornate Louis XIV style, all white and gold, and overlooking a Louis XIV garden. The Count and Countess were alone and showed me the entire house. They possess a large number of paintings, pastels and drawings by Picasso which do not accord perfectly with the Louis XIV surroundings but at any rate look better there than modern trash. When I said that I had been quite unable to get into touch

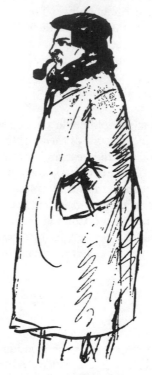

Picasso: self-portrait

with Picasso, they replied that they too have not seen him for a year, although they are his closest friends. Whenever they invite him, he accepts, but ten minutes before they are to sit down for the meal a message arrives that his children have scarlet fever, or his wife is indisposed, or something of the sort. He does not answer letters on principle and telephone callers are informed that he is not at home. All his friends have had the same experience. Nobody knows what he is up to.

Saturday, 12 April 1930   *Paris*

In the afternoon visited André Gide. He is planning a longer stay in Germany and talked a lot about the collected edition of his works in German. He presented me with a copy of the translation of the Samurai love stories, commending them as '*tout à fait étonnantes*'. Afterwards we went together to the Gallimard bookshop. He talked a lot about his pre-war trip to Weimar, when he stayed with me, and the impressions he gained of the small Court there. He wants to write about them, '*peut-être pour une publication posthume*'.

Monday, 14 April 1930   *Banyuls*

Arrived early at Port-Vendres and proceeded by car to Banyuls (Hotel Soler), where I found a note from Maillol that he has a cold but expected me after lunch. When I went to his home, I saw that his cold is really bad, but otherwise he is perfectly cheerful.

I broached carefully the subject of the Horace edition. He said neither yea nor nay, but simply complained about having so much work that he has not a minute to spare. He is supposed to sculpt a Debussy memorial for St Germain, an André Chénier memorial for Carcassonne, and a war memorial for Banyuls. There are moreover the etchings to complete for Vollard's edition of Ronsard. I told him that Vollard is totally incapable of handling this production and what a pity it is that he, Maillol, who knows how a book should be, is a party to such a half-baked affair.

He agreed and asked whether *I* would not print the Ronsard edition for Vollard. I said that I would be glad to cooperate with Vollard, even though I cannot abandon the misgivings which I have on principle about etchings as a form of book illustration. Eventually we arranged that Maillol will write to Vollard and we shall try and persuade him to do the Ronsard with me.

In the evening Maillol told the story of how, as a young man, he published a small periodical, *La Figue*, for which he made drawings in the style of the contemporary fashion designer Cham. Showing us some caricatures (woodcuts) by Cham in a few almanacks of the 1870s, he emphasized how excellent, even in his mature view, they are. Everything that Toulouse-Lautrec has to offer is contained in one or two of Cham's *cocotte* illustrations.

Tuesday, 15 April 1930   *Banyuls*

Went with Maillol to his studio outside the town. He showed me drawings made by his model, a young Parisian whom he used for his last statue and with whom he is obviously head over heels in love. The drawings, which bear clear traces of his influence, are good. '*Elle a du talent, cette jeune fille. Elle écrit, mais elle ne veut pas écrire pour vivre. Je voudrais lui trouver du travail pour qu'elle ne soit plus modèle, pour qu'elle ne pose plus que pour moi. Mais n'en dites rien à ma femme; elle ne peut pas la supporter. Elles étaient amies, et voilà que ma femme ne veut plus la voir. Je m'intéresse beaucoup à cet enfant.*' So the customary domestic drama is back in Maillol's life.

I promised to try and find her some employment and inquired whether, if he taught her the technique, she might not be able to help with the cutting of the wood-blocks for my Horace edition. He seized eagerly on the idea.

I mentioned that Demeter is finishing a bust of me. After the war, said Maillol, was when he would have liked to make a bust of me. '*Quand je vous ai vu après la guerre, vous aviez une tête comme Napoléon. Il aurait fallu vous voir par les grands plans.*' I record the fact with all due modesty.

Wednesday, 16 April 1930   *Banyuls*

Today the storm is raging worse than it did yesterday; the whole house is shaking. In the afternoon I visited Maillol at home because he could not go to his studio on account of the wind. He showed me the new issue of the periodical *Formes*. It contains an article by Jules Romains about him. '*C'est assez bien; mais il ne conclut pas.*' Romains interprets Maillol's contrast with Rodin as being conscious and deliberate; he gently deplores his 'primitive-ness' by exhorting him to be less 'primitive'. Maillol's rejoinder to this is that, at the outset of his career, he did not worry his head about Rodin at all. As for his 'primitiveness' (meaning his archaic style), he is not intentionally primitive but simply tries to execute his forms as perfectly as he can. '*Je ne peux pas construire une figure comme Phidias; si je le pouvais, je le ferais; mais je construis aussi bien que les sculpteurs d'Olympie.*'

He then talked very circumstantially again about his little model, whose name is Lucile Passavant, and laid emphasis on her talent. '*Je lui ai dit que si elle travaille, elle n'aurait pas besoin de montrer son cul à tous les sculpteurs de Paris. D'abord ça a très bien marché avec ma femme, elles étaient amies. Mais maintenant ma femme est jalouse, il n'y a plus rien à faire. Je vous ferai dîner avec la petite à Paris; mais je dois être discret. Tout de même, je devrai la faire venir à Marly pour faire les bras du monument Debussy* (for which she stood as model). Lucien appears to be supporting his mother in hostility to *la petite*.

In the evening dinner with the Maillols. He still has a very bad cold and sat all wrapped up. He asked me about Capri, whether it is beautiful and whether it is possible to find a small house there in some small, quiet place, unexpectedly adding, '*Parce que j'aurais bien envie de me retirer pour un temps quelque part tranquillement, sans ma famille.*'

Thursday, 17 April 1930   *Banyuls*

After lunch said goodbye to Maillol. He complained even more vehemently than yesterday about his wife's jealousy. '*Ma femme me fait plus de mal que mon rhume.*' She no longer leaves him a moment's peace. As soon as they are back at Marly, he wants to go away, somewhere that he will have a rest from her. He cannot stand it any longer. '*Je ne dis pas qu'elle n'a pas raison; mais c'est insupportable.*' I invited him to come to Germany for a few weeks, to Weimar and Berlin. He half accepted.

Monday, 5 May 1930   *London*

I was the luncheon guest of Dame Adelaide Livingstone, the very delightful woman who for some years after the war was the War Graves Commission representative in Berlin. The other two guests were a Mrs Borden, an American, and Colonel Roddie, who during the worst of the post-war years was also a member of the Embassy at Berlin.

Roddie was very nice about my Rathenau book. He recalled how he visited Rathenau's house in Grunewald three or four days before the assassination. As he drove up, he was stopped by two men in civilian clothes. Whom, they asked, did he want to see? He produced his papers and was allowed to pass. Going into the house, he heard music in a room to the right of the entrance, went in, and saw Rathenau seated at the piano, playing by candlelight. Rathenau jumped up and apologized. Roddie told him that he was glad to find that he was taking safety precautions. This excited Rathenau immensely. He hurried to the telephone, rang up some office, and demanded categorically that the police protection be removed, saying that he forbade the molestation of his guests. By the time Roddie left, the police guard had disappeared.

Friday, 9 May 1930   *London*

In the evening Sthamer gave a reception at the Embassy. Big throng. I wandered in the crowd from room to room, each of which is packed for me with historical, ghostly memories. Discussions with Metternich. A lunch at which Richard Strauss, to the horror of Metternich, repeated the Emperor's bellicose utterances. A luncheon by Lichnowsky when Bernard Shaw was there. The appalled reaction of the Russian Ambassador's wife to Princess Lichnowsky's Picassos. Mechtilde Lichnowsky squatting on the floor of her boudoir. The catastrophic Lichnowsky dinner-party attended by the King and Arthur Nicolson. And then the first time after the war that I was back in London, the days of the Ruhr Occupation and my daily conferences with Sthamer, Dufour, and Bernstorff. Finally my negotiations last year with Snowden, and Sthamer's exasperation at the tone adopted by Snowden towards him. All these scenes re-passed before my eyes as I drifted with the crowd. I also recalled my long talk with Stresemann when he offered me the Embassy here, a posting that Schubert evidently thwarted so as to keep it open for himself.

Saturday, 10 May 1930   *London*

During the morning inspected musical volumes with Teddy Craig and Martin Shaw at the British Museum in preparation for the edition of *A Midsummer Night's Dream* with Purcell's music and intermezzi and illustrations by Gordon Craig.

Sunday, 11 May 1930   *London*

To tea with Leonard and Virginia Woolf in Tavistock Square. They are back today from a week's tour by car of Devonshire and Cornwall to try and persuade bookshops to take their Hogarth Press products. Leonard Woolf was extremely angry about the booksellers in small towns who know nothing about books, have no interest in them, and are altogether hopeless. I discussed with him the marketing, number of copies required, prospectuses, and booksellers' rebates for Vita Nicolson's Rilke translation. He thinks that he will be able to dispose of 150 copies.

Went with Woolf to Hampstead to Delisle Burns. There we met Shastri, an Indian who is a friend of Gandhi, fairly light-complexioned, and speaks perfect English. Gandhi's passive resistance movement, he told us, has broken down completely. Gandhi had been under the illusion that the practice of civil disobedience would within a few days force the Indian Government[4] to capitulate and that everything would work according to his wishes and plans if his fellow-nationals would obey just a few 'simple' concepts and maxims. What he wholly overlooked was that these apparently so simple ethical rules are not simple at all. They derive from highly complicated trains of thought which presuppose decades of education and constitute commandments difficult for the ordinary man to follow. The Indian people totally lacks such education. That is why Gandhi's ideas were built on sand and why his movement, breaking down right away, deteriorated into ordinary mob violence.

Burns and Woolf invited Shastri to address the Labour Advisory Board (Woolf is the secretary) next week and to debate his views at this meeting. Shastri forecasts a period of unbroken disturbances in India which may well last for fifteen to twenty years.

Friday, 16 May 1930   *Paris*

In the afternoon visited Maillol at Marly. In the garden were Mme Maillol and Maillol's sister, Mme d'Espie, a woman of over seventy whose former beauty and charm are evident and who today is still attractive. Mme Maillol accompanied me to the studio where, as she phrased it, '*il a modèle*'. Maillol introduced me to his 'model', Lucile Passavant, who was just dressing again. I did not find her very beautiful. She is somewhat plump and rather crudely rouged. But she is intelligent. Maillol showed me some ceramic figures which she has made and they demonstrate an undoubtedly genuine artistic talent.

As his wife stuck to me like a leech, I told Maillol that I would like to inspect the bronze cast in his shed and left the three of them in the studio. He promptly followed and expostulated, '*Voyez-vous comme ma femme est insupportable; elle ne veut pas que je vous parle seul. Je n'en peux plus. Elle me fait des scènes perpétuelles,*' and so on. I had already said to Mme Maillol in the garden that it would do her husband, who is still in poor health, good to have a change of air. She agreed. I now again proposed to him that he should come with me to Weimar. He accepted with visible pleasure and relief, disappointed only to the extent that we shall not be able to leave until next week. He appeared to assume as a matter of course that Mlle Passavant would accompany us and that his wife would not be aware of the fact.

It amounts to a thoroughgoing flight from the married state, and in the case of a sixty-seven-year-old man[5] there is something tragic about that. I have however no scruples about assisting him. For the past thirty years his wife has, with her insane jealousy, stood in his way and prevented him from ever having an acceptable model. He has had to make do with all sorts of random photographs and magazines devoted to nudes.

I invited Maillol to come to lunch tomorrow. If he liked, he could bring along Mlle Passavant and we could *mise au point* the execution of his woodcuts by her. He was delighted. When we returned to the garden, 'Clotilde', as Maillol calls his wife, could not hide her ill-humour at my offering to take Mlle Passavant with me in the car to Paris.

On the way she told me that her mother, a painter, had at the age of nearly forty married a man of twenty. She herself was sixteen at the time. Life at home became intolerable for her. She left and managed somehow to survive until she began to model for Maillol. I find her quite appealing, but she belongs to that type of lower-middle-class, plumpish, made-up Parisiennes whom, as far as their outward appearance goes, I do not care for.

Saturday, 17 May 1930   *Paris*

At noon Maillol and Mlle Passavant arrived for lunch. He was beaming. We discussed details of the trip to Weimar. I told him that it would be pleasanter for me if he and I travelled alone. He can get Mlle Passavant to follow; I could raise no objection to that. But if she came with us, apart from it not being agreeable to me, it might be awkward for him if his wife should insist on seeing him off at the station. He appreciated the point. After the meal we drove to Zay to buy tools and then I dropped the two, radiant as freshly weds, at a cinema where they proposed to watch the film *The Night Is Ours*.

Monday, 19 May 1930   *Brussels*

I spent the morning with van de Velde in his Institute in the Abbaye de la Cambre, an old monastery placed at his disposal by the Government as a school. He guided us around the various departments (sixteen teachers, a printing works, theatre school, and so on). There are many foreign female pupils.

In the evening dinner at van de Velde's new home in Tervuren. It is a very pretty house, shows traces of Le Corbusier's influence, but is permeated with the true de Velde spirit of *sérénité*. After the meal came the married von de Velde children, the twins Tyl and Tylla, with their respective spouses. I found it interesting that everybody here, including the van de Veldes, should say that Paris has become boring and Berlin is now the city where true amusement is to be had. I hear it on all sides.

Saturday, 24 May 1930   *London*

In the evening saw *Othello* at the Savoy Theatre, with Paul Robeson as Othello, Maurice Brown as Iago, Sybil Thorndike as Emilia, and a strikingly pretty and attractive young actress, Peggy Ashcroft, as Desdemona. Apart from her and Robeson, who was a dignified, passionate Othello, it is a moderately successful production. The casting of the smaller parts like Cassio, Rodrigo, Brabantio, and the Duke is comically inadequate and reminiscent of smaller German municipal theatres. The Weimar National Theatre is on the whole a better company and, seeing that it would have done quite well in comparison with this *Othello* performance, I am now less surprised that Brown should have thought of bringing it to London. His own rendering of Iago was presentable but average.

The Savoy Theatre has just been rebuilt and is regarded as the most modern in London. Nevertheless the revolving stage, or some other back-stage machinery, creaked loudly during the most tragic scenes between Othello and Desdemona and Emilia and Desdemona, ruining the tension. The auditorium is modern in the less complimentary sense of the term, constructed in a style which in Germany we have nearly outgrown, all tinsel and meaningless 'modern' ornaments appropriate to a third-rate bar, the way that we built ten years ago. Theatre architecture in London and Paris is half a generation behind Berlin, Hamburg, Frankfurt and Stuttgart.

Friday, 30 May 1930 *Paris*

Aristide Maillol came to lunch. Since our last meeting, he said, *il s'était passé des histoires tragiques chez lui.* His wife, who listens at doors and peeps through keyholes, caught him and Mlle Passavant in his studio amidst tenderness of one sort or another. She rushed in like a fury and '*a déchiré tous mes dessins*', meaning the large nude studies of Mlle Passavant which had hung on the walls and including a large red crayon drawing I had admired. She then became very dark red in the face, '*comme si elle était congestionée*', and fell in a faint. For four hours Maillol and his seventy-year-old sister, Mme d'Espie, had to sprinkle her with water and chafe her hands until she came to. '*Mais ce qu'il y a de plus étonnant, c'est que depuis ce temps, elle est douce comme un agneau. Depuis trente ans elle n'a jamais été aussi douce.*' Maillol seemed enchanted by the fact. I find this sudden meekness rather suspicious. He added *qu'elle n'avait pas à se plaindre.* He continues to love her despite everything. '*Je fais l'amour avec elle comme un jeune homme.*'

We then discussed the details of his 'flight' to Weimar. He is having difficulties about Mlle Passavant's visa because she is not yet twenty-one and neither her mother nor her father 'acknowledges' her. Rudier, Maillol's caster, has friends in the Ministry and is doing his best. They have even, Maillol related, had to concoct '*une pièce fausse*'. We have therefore postponed our departure until Tuesday evening. Mlle Passavant is to travel ahead and join the train at Reims. This '*départ pour Cythère*' is having a somewhat stormy and difficult start and, with a sixty-seven-year-old lover involved, does not lack a certain comicality. Afterwards I took Maillol to the Café de la Paix, where Mlle Passavant was waiting for him. He suggested that we should be a little careful as his wife is in Paris *et pourrait rôder autour du café* to spy on him.

In the afternoon I visited the Gropius exhibition in the Salon des Artistes Décorateurs inside the Grand Palais. It has caused a considerable sensation here. There is no doubt whatever that it is much more interesting than the French arts and crafts exhibition which is set alongside it. My overall impression of the latter was of a certain poverty, of a material, not inspirational, sort. Poor people's art.

Tuesday, 3 June 1930 *Paris*

Jacques brought Maillol and myself to the station, where there was also Lucien Maillol. Departure for Frankfurt at ten. At midnight I heard Mlle Passavant, who had travelled ahead to Reims, enter the sleeper and talk to Maillol.

After lunch I drove with Maillol to the stadium. We sat on the terrace overlooking the swimming pools and watched the bathing and sunbathers. Maillol was in raptures about the unabashed nudity. He continually drew my attention to the splendid bodies of girls, young men and boys. '*Si j'habitais à Frankfurt, je passerais mes journeés ici à dessiner. Il faut absolument que Lucien voie cela.*' I explained to him that this is indicative of only a part of a new vitality, a fresh outlook on life, which since the war has successfully come to the fore. People want really to *live* in the sense of enjoying light, the sun, happiness, and the health of their bodies. It is not restricted to a small and exclusive circle, but is a mass movement which has stirred all of German youth.

Another expression of this new feeling for life is the new architecture and the new domestic way of living. To show him what I meant, I drove with him and Mlle Passavant to the Römerstadt. Maillol was practically speechless with astonishment. '*Jamais je n'ai vu cela. C'est la première fois que je vois de l'architecture moderne qui est parfaite. Oui, c'est parfait, il n'y a pas une tache. Si je savais écrire, j'écrirais un article.*' We went on foot through the Römerstadt and his exclamations of admiration grew ever greater. '*Jusqu'à présent, tout ce que j'ai vu d'architecture moderne était froid; mais ceci n'est pas froid, au contraire.*' I explained to him once more that this architecture is simply an expression of the same new vitality which impels youngsters to practise sport and nudity. It lends warmth in the same way as medieval buildings gained such from the Catholic interpretation of life. This German architecture cannot be understood unless it is visualized as part of an entirely new *Weltanschauung*.

Maillol and Mlle Passavant lunched with me. Maillol brought his drawing for the first book of Horace and Mlle Passavant some drawings of nudes which Maillol highly praised and I thought good.

In the afternoon we drove to Naumburg, Dornburg and Jena. On the road between Weimar and Naumburg we passed truckloads of Red (Communist) athletes with stacks of red flags every few hundred yards. When a couple of dozen had gone by and we continued to meet fresh ones, Maillol remarked, '*Je vois qu'on se remue beaucoup dans ce pays.*' From Naumburg to Dornburg we took the narrow downhill road to Camburg and found it almost entirely obstructed by two truckloads of 'Werewolves'. A little farther on we again encountered a Communist load which, travelling in the opposite direction, was bound to run into the 'Werewolves'.[6] Our chauffeur commented that the collision would result in some cracked skulls. Maillol maintained his previous complete equanimity, merely repeating, '*Oui, on se remue beaucoup ici.*' Uttered by this past master at tranquillity, contemplativeness, and the art of not meeting trouble half-way, the aphorism was not meant as praise.

In Jena we dined at the Black Bear inn. In the dining-room I pointed out to Maillol the picture showing the disputation which in 1522 took place between Martin Luther and Johann Kessler in this very house. My ancestor is portrayed as a fair-haired youth with a small-peaked beard. Surprisingly enough, Maillol thought the picture quite good.

Tuesday, 10 June 1930   *Weimar*

As yesterday the cathedral at Naumburg was closed, we went back there today. A certain coolness seems to have occurred between Maillol and Mlle Passavant. I noticed that she barely spoke to him. She forced herself to smile at me when she was really feeling disgruntled. A pity.

At dinner, in my garden pavilion, I again observed Mlle Passavant's taciturnity while Maillol and I engaged in lively conversation. Finally I said to her that she must excuse us if we two old men chattered so much. Maillol went on to tell us that he never reads newspapers because they waste columns on events that could be dismissed in two lines. '*Les seules choses qui m'intéressent ce sont les crimes.*' In deference to my somewhat bemused look, he added, '*Oui, parce que j'y vois des drames, quelque chose de Shakespearien.*'

Wednesday, 11 June 1930   *Weimar*

Spent the day at the Press. I had arranged to meet Maillol and Mlle Passavant at five o'clock at the Schwanensee bathing pool. They were sitting in the café. It was immediately obvious that yesterday's upset between the two has deepened. She was quite pale, with red-rimmed eyes, and deliberately spoke not a word to him, replying to his questions either monosyllabically or not at all. To me she said that she has a sore throat, but nothing serious and nobody is to worry about her. We sat together for an hour in embarrassing frigidity until I suggested that we go home and send for a doctor. She emphatically declined. '*Ce n'est rien, je vous assure.*'

Maillol appeared at table without her. She had gone to bed, he explained. I commented that she probably does have a cold, but some sort of worry or disappointment seems to me to be a contributory factor. Yes, he answered, she has hinted something of the kind.

In short, we have here the old tragicomedy of the ageing man and a hot-blooded girl, the very stuff of the most ancient comedy. Mme Maillol is avenged! In this instance I am sorrier for Maillol than for Mlle Passavant, who must have known what to expect after having an affair with him for a year. Oddly enough, Goertz told me on Thursday already, straight after seeing her for the first time, that she is a sweet, delightful creature but belongs to the category of women who cannot hold a man for long because they are too sensual and demand too much of him.

Thursday, 12 June 1930   *Weimar*

During the morning Dr Bulcke, whom I requested to see Mlle Passavant, informed me that both of them, Maillol as well, have septic tonsillitis and must remain in bed. He thinks it better to engage a nurse. I visited them at midday. Maillol was in a fairly good state, but she was in very low spirits.

Friday, 13 June 1930   *Weimar*

Maillol is far better, but both of them must remain in bed.

In the afternoon called on Frau Foerster-Nietzsche. She reopened the subject of Mussolini. She recently had Orsini, the new Italian Ambassador, to lunch and gushed to him that Italy now seems to her in the condition that Germany was after 1870, with a hero king for its sovereign and a great statesman, Mussolini, akin to Bismarck. I observed that this resemblance to the German Empire is one that many see. For myself, I only hope that this Italian apotheosis does not end the same way as the German one did!

Monday, 16 June 1930   *Weimar*

Visited Maillol. He is up again. His wife has advised him via her maid at Marly that he should write his letters in ink as pencil is too much of a strain for her eyes. The maid will send him pen and ink by parcel post! She herself has not replied to four of his letters.

Tuesday, 17 June 1930   *Weimar*

Demeter arrived at eight in the morning by car from Berlin and during the morning worked in the Press on my bust. Maillol praised this and that, but then commented, '*Il y a trop de trous. Il faut faire simple et carré. Regardez la tête de Monsieur de Kessler ; il n'y a pas de trous. Il faut voir le modêle de loin, l'impression générale.*'

Maillol, Mlle Passavant, Demeter, Guseck, and John Rothenstein[7] lunched with me. Afterwards we all drove together in Demeter's car to Berka. On the way Maillol fetched a parcel from the Customs. I assured him, when he received the notification, that this would be the pen-holder and ink-stand which his wife wrote that she was sending through the maid. And so it turned out to be. Maillol, laughing but nevertheless irritated, emerged from the Customs building waving the pen-holder in one hand and the bottle full of ink in the other. Mlle Passavant and I told him that he ought to have refused acceptance and had the consignment returned. But his opinion was, '*Puisque ça n'a rien couté, autant valait l'accepter; ça peut toujours servir.*'

Thursday, 19 June 1930   *Weimar*

Supper with Maillol, Mlle Passavant, Demeter and Guseck in the forest near Berka. I had food and drink brought out there, the young people had taken a gramophone and Chinese lanterns, and we spread ourselves in a glade beyond which we could see on the horizon the ridges of the Thuringian Forest. Maillol was delighted by the scenery. When it became dark, the Chinese lanterns were lit, a record put on the gramophone, and the two young men danced with Mlle Passavant. So, later, did Maillol. He had declared that he can only waltz, but he moved quite nimbly on the uneven ground. We stayed until nearly one, with the stars shining brightly and the air warm and scented. An entirely successful evening.

Sunday, 22 June 1930   *Paris*

At eight o'clock left Berlin for Paris. Met a whole crowd of French people returning home from the theatre congress at Hamburg: Tristan Bernard[8] and his wife, Gémier, Florent Schmitt, the publisher Cools, and so on. The entire day our compartment was like a drawing-room, with Mme Bernard playing hostess. Friends from other compartments came and went. There was an endless amount of gossip. Mme Bernard, middle-aged and very charming, received everyone for hour after hour without the slightest sign of weariness, regardless of the heat. Tristan Bernard, collar, coat, and waistcoat discarded and continually wiping his brow, just as indefatigably told one story after another. Good, average, and unintelligible ones whose point became stuck in his beard.

One of the anecdotes, that of General Lyautey's parrot and monkey, was really funny. In Morocco Lyautey was the owner of a monkey and a parrot whom he taught the words '*Charmante Soirée!*' Whenever he had guests or brought some home, his parrot uttered the words '*Charmante Soirée.*' One day Lyautey was away the whole evening. The monkey used the time to tear out all the parrot's feathers. Lyautey, arriving home late, was received by a furious parrot who shrieked, again and again, '*Charmante Soirée, Charmante Soirée!*'

Bernard said of Maillol, '*J'ai pour lui non seulement de l'admiration, mais de la vénération.*'

Monday, 23 June 1930   *Paris*

Once more met in the street that immoderately stout creature, possibly South American or Levantine and looking like a milk pudding, whom I encounter on every occasion and in every place, whether in the street, the theatre, or the restaurants here, whose name I can never discover, and who, always leisurely going his way and apparently content in his obesity, is the only inhabitant of Paris to constitute a steady pole in the evanescent process of things. I call him '*le fantôme blafard*'. To me he is almost as uncanny as the White Lady of the Berlin Palace, a sort of male Countess von Orlamünde. Perhaps he really is an apparition whose destiny is bound up with Paris.

Friday, 27 June 1930   *Weimar*

Worked in the press. In the afternoon to Maillol at Berka. Mlle Passavant has begun to paint with gouache and displays astounding talent. I bought from her one such picture, of a window-sill with flowers, which I thought excellently done.

Monday, 30 June 1930   *Weimar*

At four o'clock Eric Gill arrived, at once drawing attention to himself at the station on account of his extraordinary garb: knee-length stockings, a kind of short black cowl, and a stridently colourful scarf. In Cologne everyone stared at his legs, he reported. Could that be perhaps because his stockings were so thin? He likes to make himself conspicuous as an eccentric.

Tuesday, 1 July 1930   *Weimar*

Rhineland Liberation Day. A good many flags were put out, on the private houses nearly all black-white-red banners. To this day the supporters of those colours have done everything to thwart the Rhineland's premature liberation (which, politically, is a harsh blow to them). Now they put out their flags. The dishonesty of it does not worry them in the least.

With Gill and the Rothensteins visited Maillol at Berka. It had been planned that in the evening Maillol and Mlle Passavant would return with us to Weimar. However, as Maillol manifestly wanted to stay a few days longer, I negotiated with the landlord (who had already let their room) for them to remain another week.

Wednesday, 2 July 1930   *Weimar*

At the press pulled proofs with Gill of his woodcuts for the *Song of Songs*. He began work on my portrait.

Thursday, 3 July 1930   *Weimar*

Gill continued with the portrait. Further *Song of Songs* proofs. In the evening with Gill and the Rothensteins by car to Oberhof and dined at the Golf-Hotel. As all the men were in dinner-jackets and the women in evening dress with low-cut corsages and jewellery, Gill's strange garb attracted even more attention than usual. He was wearing long red stockings beneath the black cowl reaching to his knees.

Tuesday, 8 July 1930   *Weimar*

With Gill to Frau Foerster-Nietzsche, of whom he made a drawing. The picture was simply that of an old lady who might have come out of *Pickwick*. Frau Foerster however, on seeing it, said that she was glad for someone at last to have drawn her as being old. Hitherto artists have all made her far too young.

Monday, 14 July 1930   *Berlin*

Went with Maillol and Mlle Passavant to see the School for Physical Culture in Grunewald. In the magnificent grounds and glorious sunshine the sight of almost naked young people performing athletic exercises was reminiscent of ancient Greece.

In many ways, especially in Germany, we are returning, unconsciously and naturally, to the habits of the Greeks. Nudity, light, fresh air, sunshine, worship of living, bodily perfection, sensuousness without either false shame or prudishness. But it is astonishing how much finer young people's bodies are today than before the war. The whole national physique has improved since people are no longer shy of going naked. Maillol asked me to photograph two youngsters who were '*beaux comme des dieux antiques*'. Unfortunately Mlle Passavant moped the whole time, somewhat spoiling our pleasure.

Afterwards lunch in honour of Maillol at the Simons'. Gropius was there (with his very pretty young wife). Later the whole party drove to the open-air bath at Wannsee. Maillol wanted to make drawings of the bathers. They appealed to him even more than the athletes he had seen in the morning because here they formed less of a pattern. It so happened that not one of us had paper or pencil on him.

Tuesday, 15 July 1930   *Berlin*

A big lunch in honour of Maillol at the Hugo Simons'. The guests included Einstein, Max Liebermann, Renée Sintenis, and the Meier-Graefes. When Einstein entered, I pointed him out to Maillol. '*Oui, une belle tête; c'est un poète?*' I had to explain to him who Einstein was; he had evidently never heard of him. After the meal they were photographed together.

Before lunch Maillol inspected some sculptures by Renée Sintenis to which he took a great liking. '*C'est une grande artiste,*' he told me, '*tout ce qu'elle fait est jeune.*'

Maillol recalled, and Liebermann appeared much interested, that he had known Millet (in Barbizon, at the beginning of the seventies).

Wednesday, 16 July 1930   *Berlin*

In the afternoon said goodbye to Maillol and Mlle Passavant. She returns to Paris tonight; Maillol leaves on Friday.

Monday, 25 August 1930   *Weimar*

Ceremony at Nietzsche's grave. Frau Foerster took my arm and demanded that, being her 'oldest friend', I should escort her.

Monday, 15 September 1930   *Kandersteg*

A black day for Germany. The Nazis have increased the number of their seats almost tenfold, from 12 to 107, and have become the second strongest party in the Reichstag. The impression created abroad must be catastrophic. The repercussion on foreign and financial affairs is likely to be appalling. A hundred and seven Nazis, 41 Hugenberg[9] supporters, and more than 70 Communists total some 220 deputies who are radical opponents of the German state in its present shape and want to do away with it by revolutionary means. We face a national crisis which can only be overcome if all those who accept, or at least tolerate, the Republic stand firmly together and furthermore demonstrate the ability to put straight the economic and financial situation before the next Reichstag dissolution. Provided there is no putsch meanwhile, the next move will presumably be the formation of a 'Big Coalition' between the current Government parties and the Social Democrats. If not, the continuation of government becomes impossible. As a political factor, the German upper middle class seems to be definitely on the point of extinction. Soon it will no longer play any part at all between the rabble-rousers on the one hand and the Social Democratic workers on the other.

It is worth noting that, out of a total of 573 seats, the parties with a distinct *Weltanschauung* (the Centre, the Communists, and the Nazis), have gained 326 seats as against 247 seats won by the 'vested interest' parties. For all the lunacy and infamy of the National Socialist *Weltanschauung*, the result still speaks for the German elector.

National Socialism is a delirium of the German lower middle class. The poison of its disease may however bring down ruin on Germany and Europe for decades ahead.

Monday, 22 September 1930   *La Napoule*

In the evening visited our enormously rich American neighbours, the Clews, and dined in the medieval castle they have had constructed by the sea. The magnificent natural surroundings absorb and endow the movie medievalism with dignity. Henry Clews is a not untalented sculptor. He has ornamented the innumerable pillars of his castle with grotesque human and animal faces to express his loathing of the modern world as manifested by the middle class, democracy, the herd outlook, and so on. His fanatical hatred of everything modern has not however precluded him from taking advantage of all inventions and conveniences the contemporary age has to offer: telephones in every room, splendid plumbing, and so on.

Our reception, when we arrived for the meal, was astounding. Clews was dressed in white trousers and a sort of embroidered, scarlet silk military tunic reaching to his knees. His (very beautiful) wife, in black with golden stars, was the Queen of the Night. Behind them stood three footmen, in white and with their hands tightly pressed against the seams of their trousers. And behind the footmen were two magnificent large white bulldogs looking like Chinese idols. The Gothic hall was candle-lit. We ate at a stone table (good food, excellent champagne) while our host spoke well and sensitively about Nietzsche. He has a profound, polished sensibility even if he does spout a lot of nonsense about Mussolini, democracy, war, pacifism, nationalism, et cetera. I could not rid myself, though, of the feeling that we were being filmed.

Sunday, 28 September 1930   *London*

In the evening Craig came to my hotel and told me about the squabble relating to the correspondence between his mother[10] and Bernard Shaw. He characterized Shaw as a success-seeker and upstart who used to write letters to all the actresses of the day to cajole them into accepting parts in his plays. Now he finds these letters embarrassing.

Thursday, 2 October 1930   *Berlin*

In the evening an official banquet by the Prussian Government[11] in the Palace. Horrible. Formerly the scene was rendered grandly colourful by the handsome, or handsomely apparelled, individuals crowding the apartments. Now a monotone, amorphous grey mass shuffled past the baroque splendours. We have, and it is almost a miracle, in the dozen years since the revolution produced a new sort of beauty, including a younger generation better built and looking than that of pre-war days. But this new world must not be brought into contact with the old baroque one, else an intolerable clash occurs. Never before have I had it so vividly impressed on me that the former epoch is dead and done with.

The baroque world created the background appropriate to itself. We are engaged in doing the same for ourselves. Probably our world, when it has mellowed, will be no less fine than the baroque one was. What cannot be done, without flouting every aesthetic instinct, is to set our world against a baroque background.

Friday, 3 October 1930   *Weimar*

In the evening left for Weimar. In our train, as well as in a second one which stopped at another platform in Weimar, there were crowds of Stahlhelm members travelling to Coblenz for a 'liberation celebration'. In uniform, a field grey hardly distinguishable from the Reichswehr. At Halle they were already bawling 'The Watch on the Rhine' and other 'patriotic' songs. At Weimar they spread over the platform, down the stairs, into the waiting-rooms. Snotty-nosed brats most of them. Drunk too, with their tunics half unbuttoned, in a bickering, brawling mood, abusive to other passengers, utterly undisciplined. Any small unit of real soldiers would scatter such a rabble.

Friday, 10 October 1930   *Berlin*

In the evening saw Reinhardt's production of Hofmannsthal's *Hard To Please* at the Komödie. Helene Thimig in the part of Helene and Gustav

Waldau as Kari Bühl, the man 'hard to please'. Waldau is alleged to have taken, or wanted to take, me as his model. As he is fat and rather ponderous and I am lean and spry, he has superficially not been successful. But Max maintained that he copies my movements, especially gestures, astonishingly accurately. Since I do not know Waldau and, as far as I am aware, have seen him for the very first time tonight, it can only be a case of Max Reinhardt having shown him. Apart from that, I grant that Hofmannsthal has drawn pretty freely on me and (what never crossed my mind until this evening) on my relationship with Helene Nostitz in portraying the figure of Kari and his relations with Helene Altenwyl.[12]

Helene Thimig was magnificent. The delicacy and subtlety of her acting, her play of expression and her radiant purity put her in the class of really great actresses. The play is a little uneven. The third act is weak; but the second act, with its two love scenes and steeped in poetry and human understanding, is a wonderful, immortal achievement. Here and elsewhere Hofmannsthal, who had no dramatic talent, can attain overpowering dramatic effects with the irresistible seduction of his lyricism.

In the first row of the stalls sat the former Crown Prince and his wife. He has gone quite grey, almost white; the Crown Princess is a fat, elderly woman. Nevertheless, he has retained all his junior officer mannerisms, standing among the audience in the intervals with a cigarette hanging from his mouth, or prancing up and down and fawningly holding open doors for fat old Jews to pass in and out. For all his grey hairs, he continues to play the youthful prince who, in his character of a hussar, longed for a 'brisk, gay war', stood in his pyjamas at a window in Stenay and waved to the troops retiring raggedly from Verdun, and lugged along his French whores on campaign. The hereditary Hohenzollern lack of taste reaches in him almost monumental proportions.

Sunday, 12 October 1930   *Berlin*

In the evening saw Reinhardt's new production of *A Midsummer Night's Dream* at the Deutsche Theatre. Sheer enchantment. The dreamlike setting is divided between a festive chamber and a forest lit by stars. The entire cast is composed of very young players, all movement dissolves into the airiness of ballet. A sense of stateliness. Deliberate artificiality and yet vibrant with imaginative insight. The loveliest performance of the *Dream*, and the nearest in spirit to Shakespeare, that I have ever seen.

Monday, 13 October 1930   *Berlin*

Reichstag opening. The whole afternoon and evening mass demonstrations by the Nazis. During the afternoon they smashed the windows of Wertheim,

Grünfeld, and other department stores in the Leipzigerstrasse. In the evening they assembled in the Potsdamer Platz, shouting 'Germany awake!' 'Death to Judah', 'Heil Hitler.' Their ranks were continually dispersed by the police, in lorries and on horseback. At half past eleven I went down Leipziger Strasse to Friedrichstrasse and stood outside the Fürstenhof for three quarters of an hour. In the main the Nazis consisted of adolescent riff-raff which made off yelling as soon as the police began to use rubber truncheons. I have never witnessed so much rabble in these parts.

Nazis marching (Grosz)

In front of the Fürstenhof I watched some of these youngsters, unem-ployed[13] getting an extra dole, perform regular patrol duty. From time to time a pack of adolescents, pursued by the police, would rush by in wild disorder. Poor devils who had received two or three marks from the Thyssen money-box for proving their 'patriotic' frame of mind. These disorders reminded me of the days just before the revolution, with the same mass meetings and the same Catilinian figures lounging about and demonstrating.

If the Government does not take matters firmly in hand, we shall slide into civil war. In any case today's rioting will, I estimate, cost us between five hundred million and a milliard marks in stock exchange losses and the withdrawal of foreign assets. The destruction in Leipziger Strasse as well as the patrols between Prinz-Albrecht-Strasse and Potsdamer Platz confirm that the mischief was organized. Only businesses with Jewish names suffered. Christian ones (like Herpich, the Porcelain Manufactory, and the Goethe Bookshop) were ostentatiously left untouched. Nazis invaded the Palast-Hotel and in the hall roared 'Germany awake!' and 'Death to Judah.' The vomit rises at so much pig-headed stupidity and spite.

Saturday, 15 November 1930   *Berlin*

A visit to Reinhardt to recommend Nabokov as composer for the accompanying music to Savoir's play. We went on to talk about *Hard To Please* and *A*

Max Reinhardt (Gossmann)

Midsummer Night's Dream. When I especially praised the young dancer in the latter, Reinhardt said that he would much like to keep and save him from going on the music halls. 'How,' I asked, 'would it be if you produced *Josephslegende* and let Svend dance the part of Joseph, which has never been properly done yet?' The idea seemed greatly to appeal to Reinhardt. He suggested that it might be produced at Salzburg. We agreed to discuss the matter again in December on my return from London.

    Hard To Please, he told me, is a totally unexpected triumph. He staged it purely as an act of piety, expecting to take it off after a few performances.

Instead it plays to full houses every evening. The tragedy is that Hofmannsthal should not have lived to witness this. After the original first night, when the Berlin Press tore it to pieces, he wept. He had wanted to write more works on similar gossamer lines, but was too discouraged.

A strange thing is that Reinhardt has seen neither *Elga*, which is running in his own Kammerspiel theatre, nor Bruckner's *Elizabeth of England*. He finds it intolerable to watch a play as an ordinary spectator. He would like to make a talkie: it is something new and gives opportunity to do things that are impossible on the stage.

1931

Luncheon at the Princess Bassiano's in Versailles with André Gide and others. Gide recalled my balloon flight to Russia sundry decades back. (I forgot most of the details long ago.) He was highly indignant about the dispersal of the Pacifist Congress in the Trocadero on Friday and believes that the police grossly neglected their responsibilities. The outcome was that those ambassadors who attended the meeting (including Hoesch and Tyrrell) *avaient manqué d'être passés à tabac.*

I mentioned the dire poverty which exists in Germany. Doubtless the poverty of the broad masses is great, Gide commented, but it is difficult to convince the sceptics here. Frenchmen returning from Berlin are full of the incredible extravagance and manifest luxury which exist there and many German visitors to France simply throw their money about.

At table Gide remarked that he could never read *Thus Spake Zarathustra.* '*Je crois que j'ai tout lu de Nietzsche ; mais le* Zarathustra *non, je n'ai jamais pu.*' He also told the story of how Thomas Mann and Kayser (of the *Neue Rundschau*) argued with him that Goethe definitely never wrote any *Prometheus.* Both of them only knew *Pandora* and always mixed up the two. I dropped Gide in Paris at the Cinema des Miracles where, at my suggestion, he went to see *The Congress Dances*, starring Lilian Harvey.

I invited for tea Caffi, an Italian tutor in Princess Bassiano's household. She praised his scholastic qualities (specialist in Greek and a historian, pupil of Mommsen) in the highest terms. An interesting and fascinating man. For four years he was *Corriere della Sera* correspondent in Bolshevik Russia and afterwards worked at the Italian Embassy. He was in Cheka prisons twice, once for six weeks. The food was dreadful – a hundred grammes of black bread a day and a stinking fish soup, dished out by a Latvian female riddled with syphilis and heavily armed, *le fusil en bandoulière.* Every Saturday prisoners were shot in the cellar beneath his cell, a sound like that of doors being slammed. He was on quite good terms with Djerjinski because they had been students together. Apart from being a pathological case, he was, in Caffi's view, perfectly honest and wholly incapable of committing murder with his own hands. Herein he was just the opposite of Peters, the executioner, who later went mad. This was the fate of all Bolshevik executioners, none of whom could stand the job for more than two years at the most. Every lunatic asylum has its quota and the sanatoria on the Crimean coast are stuffed with insane executioners.

Saturday, 5 December 1931   *Frankfurt*

Lunch with Heinrich Simon and afterwards a talk with him about my memoirs. I told him that I would need a year to write them.

He spoke frankly about the 'legends', which he presumed to be not unfamiliar to me, relating to my origins. I am generally thought to be a Hohenzollern, son of the Emperor William I, and therefore 'uncle' to William II. This is why right-wing circles have always taken my support for the Republic so amiss. The matter can very easily be pinned down for the nonsense that it is, I replied. My poor mother was not introduced to the old Emperor until after my birth. True, he agreed, but she was in fact the old gentleman's last love. Maybe, I countered, but in the same way as Marianne was the last love of Goethe in his old age. Anyway, he went on, I did originate in this old and conservative environment. Consequently it will be interesting to read how I came to abandon this staunchly monarchic orbit for a path leading to opposition against William II and to republicanism.

William II's downright perverse bad taste, I said, was more responsible than anything else. Bad taste in the selection of his friends and advisers; bad taste in art, literature, politics and his style of living; bad taste revealed by every word he uttered. Yes, Simon agreed, William II's bad taste nurtured the German's bad instincts when the main need had been to personify and to establish for this culturally outstanding nation firm criteria which all could understand. William II, I commented, was the personification of a man without criteria (except that of bad taste). That made him the direct opposite to a German or English gentleman, either of whom has, if anything, too many rather than too few criteria. A crowned barbarian who gave the whole German nation a reputation for barbarity.

After this discussion with Simon, it is at any rate clear that the first chapter of my memoirs must be called 'My Mother' and once and for all do away with this idiotic gossip about my origins. To that degree the memoirs have become an essential act of piety.

Tuesday, 8 December 1931   *Berlin*

Today I was told that in Neukölln the Communist and the Reichsbanner have lined up together against the Nazis. The leaders continue at logger-heads, but the workers are united.[1] In the evening, at nine, Brüning spoke on the wireless about the new emergency decree and against Hitler. He struck a

Cartoon by Olaf Gulbransson, 1931. A comment on the Depression and on Hitler's attempts to come to power legally. Hitler and his temporary ally, the Nationalist Hugenberg, are outside the door of the Chancellery in search of employment

calm, slightly academic note. His voice has a light timbre, notably free of regional characteristics, positively antiseptic. Only when he came to deal with the Nazis did he sound a little fiercer, evidently a deliberate effort.

Wednesday, 9 December 1931   *Berlin*

Lunched with Eduard von der Heydt at the Esplanade. He asked me whether I know François-Poncet and what sort of a man he is. The point is of interest to him at this juncture, he continued, because evidently Poncet is looking for a go-between with the Nazis and there seems to be an idea of using himself as a link on account of his relations with the Thyssen Bank and the Hohenzollerns. He is no Nazi, he declared, and certainly no anti-Semite, having far too many Jewish friends for that. All the same, he sees no alternative to Nazi participation in the Government or a Reichswehr dictatorship. In that case he prefers the Nazis. They realize that they cannot do without experts (Schacht, for instance, who is completely their man). The generals remain generals and, while being just as green as the Nazis, would insist on knowing everything better. The Nazis are not nearly so bad as their programmes and manifestoes make them appear, nor would they behave stupidly in foreign affairs. They are seeking private contacts with France, a move encouraged by the major industrialists who appreciate that they must reach an understanding with French industry.

Very soon after the war, I told him, François-Poncet discussed plans of this kind with me. As far as I recalled, though he never spelled out the thought, Poncet's suggestion was that German heavy industry could rely on French military power for support in reducing the living standard of the workers and being enabled to produce more cheaply. Presumably he still has these or similar notions in mind. They are fundamentally unpalatable to me and I could never lend my hand to anything designed to reduce still further the standard of living of the broad masses in Germany.

Heydt requested that I treat the matter as strictly confidential. The initiative for this contact plainly emanates from the Nazis and probably Hitler himself. The French (Roland de Margerie, Poncet) have merely contented themselves with not saying 'no' so far.

Thursday, 31 December 1931   *Paris*

A melancholy New Year's Eve, the end of one catastrophic year and probably the beginning of an even more catastrophic one. Dinner at Wilma's, but to bed before midnight in the most dismal state of depression.

1932

During the morning I went over to 52 Avenue Kléber where Briand died and has been laid out. Anyone can go in. A small, four-roomed apartment on the second floor. Petit bourgeois, almost seedy furnishings, an interior appropriate to a lower-middle-grade civil servant, few books, trivial prints on the

Aristide Briand. Detail from a cartoon by Karl Arnold

walls. No sign of anything to satisfy intellectual or artistic needs, let alone a touch of luxury. Extraordinary! Did he really demand nothing over and above the average? I still see him sitting next to me, his eyes half closed as though he were dropping off to sleep, and listening while I tried to sound him out on what position he would concede Germany in the League of Nations. Suddenly he opened his eyes wide and gave an answer that clinched the matter: it would be ridiculous for Germany not to have a permanent seat on the Council, that is a foregone conclusion. The impression I had of him at that moment was of a highly intelligent, indeed crafty petit bourgeois. Perhaps it was this background which formed the bond of mutual understanding between Briand and Stresemann, innkeepers' sons, both of them.

Sunday, 13 March 1932   *Paris*

To wait for the election results, I went with Wilma and Christian to the
Russian film *Mongolian Express* and then at midnight to the *Matin* offices.
Half an hour later the last provisional result appeared. Hindenburg does not
as yet have an absolute majority, so that probably a second ballot will be
necessary, but he is so much ahead as to ensure his election on 10 April.
Hindenburg, 18,500,000 votes; Hitler, 11,324,000; Duesterberg, about two
million.[1] Hindenburg will lack a few hundred thousand votes for an absolute
majority. There were several hundred people in front of the *Matin* office,
though admittedly they were in part Germans.

Wednesday, 23 March 1932   *Berlin*

I hear some very strange reports[2] which leave no doubt but that both sides,
left and right, are making comprehensive preparations for civil war. One
story, which would be tragically grotesque if it were true, is that Communist
shock-troops, who have passed themselves off as 'Black' Reichswehr, are
to be trained in Silesia this spring under the direction and at the cost of
Ehrhardt, the old Kapp putsch leader, because he is under the delusion that
young right-wing extremists will be receiving instruction! That is almost
too funny to be plausible. The Communists apparently anticipate a Hitler
putsch in August and are supposed to be preparing, as a counter-move and
defensive measure, an armed workers' uprising under the leadership of the
Iron Front and the Red Front, which will align itself with the former.

Wednesday, 6 April 1932   *Berlin*

Lunched with Georg Bernhard. He thinks the Hitler movement has passed
its peak and is already on the way down. The material seized and published
by the Prussian police will do it much harm.[3]

Thursday, 7 April 1932   *Berlin*

In the late afternoon a discussion with Georg Bernhard about disposal of my
memoirs. He reviewed for me the financial state of the three major left-wing
newspaper publishing houses, Mosse, Ullstein, and *Frankfurter Zeitung*.
Mosse affairs are inscrutable, with Lachmann-Mosse not paying liabilities.
Ullstein derives a surplus from its *Illustrierte* while the *Vossische Zeitung*
probably makes a big loss; but the key point is that thirteen different
families are living on the proceeds of the business. Simon has no capital,

but conducts his concern prudently and still maintains a high standard. This last factor is no longer as true of Mosse and Ullstein as it used to be. He advises me to deal with Simon about the memoirs and, at a later stage, with Brahn (*Verlag für Kulturpolitik*) and to exploit them journalistically as well.

Friday, 8 April 1932   *Berlin*

Iron Front demonstration for Hindenburg in the Lustgarten. A mass of people and a forest of red flags, putting the black-red-gold colours in a distinct minority. Odd, this Red demonstration on Hindenburg's behalf. I had to think of what he said to me in 1917 at Kreuznach when David and a few other Social Democrats congratulated him on his birthday – that he was quite popular with the comrades and would soon have to acquire a red beret.

Sunday, 10 April 1932   *Weimar*

Second presidential election ballot. Hindenburg's victory over Hitler finally confirmed.

Wednesday, 13 April 1932   *Weimar*

In the evening, towards eight, official announcement on the radio of a decree signed by Hindenburg at the unanimous request of the Government, which dissolves the National Socialist military SA and SS formations. Result of Hindenburg's great election success on the tenth.

Saturday, 16 April 1932   *Weimar*

General demobilization and disarmament of the various civil war armies. It is a radical liquidation of the situation which, on my return to Germany, so surprised and disquieted me. At that time, a month ago, we really stood on the edge of a civil war between perfectly drilled, organized, armed, and fully equipped armies of several hundred thousand men on each side, simply waiting for the signal to attack one another. That this situation has been resolved by a stroke of the pen, that the SA and the SS (reputedly four hundred thousand men) allowed themselves with such lamblike patience to be disarmed and broken up (nowhere did they put up any resistance worth mentioning) seems almost suspicious.

If the operation has indeed been carried out seriously and thoroughly, it signifies the greatest change in public affairs since the defeat of the Spartacus uprising in March 1919. The behaviour of Hitler and his followers seems

'Let us build monuments' 1932 (Karl Arnold)

pretty chicken-hearted in comparison, but may well be consistent with the
infirm, strongly feminine character of Hitler and his entourage. Therein too
they resemble William II, loud-mouthed and nothing behind it when it
comes to the point. A fully equipped army of four hundred thousand men
(so Hitler maintains, and he probably believes it) and then, without the
slightest resistance, unconditional surrender! One doesn't know whether to
laugh or cry! Is this the 'German desire for military preparedness' which
Hitler ostensibly wants to re-awaken and invigorate? Pitiable!

Lunched with the Heinz Simons. He declared himself to be more or less at a loss what to make of the outcome of the elections. The German nation, he added, will always remain a riddle to him, with its depth of feeling and delicacy, as evinced in its poetry and medieval works of art, going hand in hand with barbarity. For my part, I said, I have through the years come to recognize two characteristics as being absolutely and inalterably basic to all Germans, but especially the younger generation, whether they belong to left or right, the Communists, the Nazis, the Social Democrats or the middle class: escape into metaphysics, into some sort of 'faith', and the desire for discipline, for standing to attention and receiving orders or issuing them. The German, because of some feeling or other of insecurity, is through and through a militarist and through and through an escapist into some kind of beyond or Utopia, and the awful part is that he mixes them together! – Simon's young nephew, who is a fifth former in a secondary school here, told me that all his class-mates are without exception Nazis.

In the late afternoon I had a visit from Fritz von Unruh. Our conversation veered of course towards the success of the Nazis and the collapse of the middle-class and republican parties. Seeing that he was the founder of the 'Iron Front', which tried at the last hour to prevent this breakdown, it was particularly interesting to hear what he had to say. The principal reason, he thinks, is that these parties completely failed to appreciate the role of youth and of heroism in politics. He preached their vital importance in the early days of the Republic (that is perfectly true), but met with nothing but lack of comprehension and rejection of his ideas. These two factors were pooh-poohed and therefore their weight tilted the scales in favour of the other side, the reactionaries. They proved the main contribution to the victory of the Hitler lot who knew how to secure for themselves an exclusive ascendancy over the young and their (mystic) longing for sacrifice. Even now, when he founded the Iron Front and his speech at the inaugural meeting was wildly cheered, he earned nothing but derision and contempt even in the *Frankfurter Zeitung*. The same held good for the SPD party bosses. These people failed because they see material welfare as the sole object of political activity and make no allowance whatever for idealism and a faith worth sacrifices. The Nazis put out feelers towards him, after his success at the Iron Front meeting. It crossed his mind for a moment whether it might not be expedient to join them in order to draw the movement over to the left, but of course the question never seriously arose for him.

All in all, his remarks conveyed the impression that he regards the situation of the Republic as pretty desperate. Should Hitler attain power, he argued, he will be finished in no time because it will be impossible for him to fulfil any of his promises. Then the Communists will take over. He seems to believe this course of events to be almost inevitable.

Thursday, 12 May 1932   *Berlin*

Wieland Herzfelde and Theodor Plivier came to lunch. Plivier is writing a book about the time immediately after 9 November 1918. I was surprised at his grey hair; I imagined him to be younger. He wants information and material from me about the revolutionary period. He and Herzfelde, talking about the distress prevailing in the working quarters of Berlin, mentioned a fact of which I was unaware. Some twenty to thirty thousand waifs, aged between eleven and fifteen, live there in packs of fully organized small gangs to which admission is possible only after very complicated induction ceremonies, in part of a sadistic sort. The head of the gang is called 'The Bull', if he is a boy, or 'The Cow', if a girl. They are utterly amoral, prepared to commit any crime whatever, and are to a considerable extent syphilitic and cocaine addicts.

We were still sitting at table when we heard of an unprecedented commotion in the Reichstag. A number of Nazis attacked a journalist with chairs and fists for having published the homosexual correspondence of Captain Röhm. Löbe summoned the police and had four Nazi deputies, including the political assassin Heine, arrested – an unparalleled event. The excitement in the Reichstag appears to be enormous.

In the evening a special edition of *Tempo* announced Groener's resignation. His downfall is supposed to have been engineered by the generals subordinate to him. A highly dubious proceeding which, together with the violence committed by the Nazis inside the Reichstag, is symptomatic of the distinctly revolutionary state of affairs prevailing in Germany.

To round off the picture, it should be recorded that a few days ago the Municipal Council of Frankfurt am Main, with the aid of a Nazi and right-wing radical majority, helter-skelter resolved that Fritz von Unruh's play *Zero* shall be discarded from the municipal theatre's repertoire. This is an obvious act of revenge for his foundation of the Iron Front. I cabled him and wrote to Heinz Simon, asking what the next step is. This slap in the face cannot be tamely accepted! An effort should be made to ensure the play's propagation on the widest scale. One way would be to obtain Iron Front subscriptions for its performance in the largest possible number of places.

Whit Monday, 16 May 1932   *Berlin*

Visited Wieland Herzfelde at Wannsee. He told me of last night's news on the radio that Japanese officers have assassinated the Prime Minister

Inukai and thrown bombs all over Tokyo. It is a conspiracy on the part of extreme nationalists who want to force a war with China and Russia. We are approaching the point where a catastrophic explosion is bound to occur unless political tensions are damped down. But how?

Herzfelde does not believe that the economic crisis can be alleviated within any foreseeable time. It would require a miracle to bring us safely through the next few months. I said that the title of Plivier's book, *The Emperor Went, The Generals Stayed*, becomes more topical from day to day. We are almost back where we were fourteen years ago under Ludendorff and, oddly enough, the same man stands at the head of affairs – Hindenburg.

Sunday, 22 May 1932   *Berlin*

To the Avus races. Two hundred thousand people are reported to have been present. What was interesting to watch was how a totally unknown young man suddenly becomes the darling of a gigantic crowd. It happened to young Brauchitsch when, in a German Mercedes car, he won over Carraciola, today driving an Italian car, who has been the German favourite so far. Suddenly Brauchitsch's name was on everyone's lips. The closer the race between him and Carraciola became, the more he was cheered. And when, at the last moment, he streaked ahead and won, the crowd went mad. The reasons were that he was driving a German car, but still more that he is a youngster, a handsome one at that, and an outsider. So the surprise factor entered into it too.

Saturday, 28 May 1932   *Berlin*

André Gide is here. Jenny de Margerie telephoned and asked whether I would go to Pichelswerder with her and Gide to see Erich Mendelsohn's villa. When I met Gide, he greeted me with open arms. We drove by the new housing estate at Uncle Tom's Cabin, which Mme de Margerie calls '*la cité magique*' and wanted to show Gide. He was obviously very impressed by this new aspect of German architecture and lamented French backwardness. Why should the French have entirely lost their feeling for architecture, whereas in Germany it has suddenly blossomed forth? To look on this architecture simply as architecture, art for art's sake, so to speak, is to miss its point, I commented. It has to be understood as a new way of living, a new assessment of what life is for and how it should be lived. That holds good for architecture at any particular period and explains the hideous, fussy and ostentatious building at the turn of the century, reflecting precisely the vulgar ideals of the time.

Later Knickerbocker, the American journalist, wanted to hear my view of the world crisis. He is writing a book on the subject which sets out to examine whether the difference between this and former economic crises is merely one of size or also of kind. I reminded him of the aphorism that there comes a moment when quantity becomes a matter of quality. My fear is that in the current crisis this moment has already arrived because the sheer dimension of it makes it different in kind from previous occasions.

Monday, 30 May 1932   *Berlin*

Brüning has resigned. More properly speaking, Hindenburg has dismissed him. Backstairs influence has had its way, just as in the days of Eulenburg and Holstein. That means a distinct aggravation of the world crisis. Strange to say, the Berlin stock exchange, presumably in expectation of the blessings of the Third Reich, has partly reacted with a sharp boom, shares rising and fixed income investments falling. Inflation prospects. Today sees the end, provisionally of the Republic's parliamentary rule.

Tuesday, 31 May 1932   *Berlin*

Street rioting. Several thousand Nazis, singing their songs and yelling *Heil* tried to escort the Marine Guard on its way through the streets to the Presidential Palace. Goebbels made a speech from a lorry in the Wilhelm-strasse. When the police tried to hold back the crowd and shut off the Bendlerstrasse, a shower of stones was flung at them. They then used their rubber truncheons and eventually employed their fire-arms. A woman received a shot in the shoulder and was carried away. People ran past my window. My manservant Friedrich was downstairs and came back very excited because the concierge, a fanatical Nazi, said that the Nazis will 'deal' with the policeman who shot the woman.

   In the evening the radio announced that Hindenburg has offered the Chancellorship to the former deputy Papen.

Friday, 3 June 1932   *Berlin*

The Reichstag has been dissolved. After the disastrous reception given to his Government by the Press and the blunt rejection of his overtures by the SPD and the Centre, Papen has not dared to face the Reichstag before its dissolution.

Saturday, 4 June 1932   *Berlin*

Papen's policy declaration. This almost incredible document is a rottenly phrased distillation of darkest reaction in comparison with which the declarations of Imperial Governments would strike a reader as specimens of dazzling enlightenment. Social insurance is to be scrapped, 'cultural Bolshevism' resisted, the German nation steeled for a foreign policy struggle through re-Christianization (i.e., cant) and 'concentrated' on the basis of extreme right-wing *Junker* ideas. All other orientations of thought and party, social democracy, bourgeois liberalism, Centre sympathies, are pilloried as being not 'national' and morally undermining. Not since the Polignac Government of 1830 has there been published an official document of such clumsiness and ineptitude. In its psychological blindness it clearly bears the imprint of the General Staff.

Saturday, 11 June 1932   *Berlin*

Weyhe, the New York German-American art dealer, paid me a visit. He painted the situation in the United States in the gloomiest colours. He has lost all his clients. Not a soul buys an expensive book any more. Rockefeller and Ford are in the process of losing their fortunes. Kuhn Loeb have been badly hit. He himself has perhaps made his last European trip. He always used to travel first class on board ship, but this time he sailed second. And so on, and so on.

Papen has made his first speech and spoke, like Bethmann-Hollweg, of 'divinely-ordained' organic evolution. The papers publish his photograph, *8-Uhr-Blatt* over the caption 'The New Look in Chancellors'. He has the air of an irritable billy goat trying to adopt dignity and wears for the occasion a silk-lined black jacket, Sunday best. A character from *Alice in Wonderland*.

Monday, 13 June 1932   *Berlin*

Visited Theodor Wolff. Yesterday he sat behind Papen at the Red-White Club tournament and watched his behaviour. He basked in the glory of his new position in the most ridiculous way, fussing around, kissing the hand of this lady here and that lady there, complacent and conceited. The fact is that Schleicher[4] needed a petty adventurer, vain and stupid, a man lacking both importance and background, but whom he could drop at a moment's notice. That does not take into account the whole of Schleicher's calculation, I commented, for he reckoned on Papen's bringing over a part of the Centre. Wolff admitted the force of this. Schleicher, he continued, talks to too many and too much about how he proposes to settle Hitler. The latter gets to know this of course, and the question is what may be Schleicher's precise purpose in being so indiscreet. To soothe Hitler that this is what he *has* to say in order to ensure smooth sailing for himself, or what?

Friday, 24 June 1932   *Berlin*

Tenth anniversary of Rathenau's assassination. In the morning a Government (Papen–Hitler!)[5] memorial service in the Rathenau House. Gerhard Mutius made the official speech and did his best to claim Rathenau on the 'national movement's' behalf. The rather poor attendance included Löbe, Severing, and Meissner[6] (as representing Hindenburg).

Saturday, 25 June 1932   *Berlin*

The country is coming apart. The repeal of the veto on uniforms has resulted in open Bavarian revolt against the Government. The Bavarian Government refuses to obey. Bismarck's achievement, the unity of the Reich, is being jeopardized because a few thousand silly youngsters want to take delight in wearing uniforms. Were it not so tragic, it would be grotesque.

Monday, 27 June 1932   *Berlin*

The struggles between the radical movements (Communists and Nazis) have much more affinity with the wars of religion during the sixteenth and seventeenth centuries in Germany, France and Britain than they have with the political struggles belonging to the eighteenth and nineteenth centuries. They are bitter armed disputes between two ideologies which exclude compromise, whereas in the case of political struggles compromise is the objective. This explains the bitterness and hatred.

Tuesday, 28 June 1932   *Berlin*

This afternoon Frau von Ossietzky[7] telephoned Guseck to say that Nazis are constantly patrolling up and down in front of her house in a quiet street in Friedenau. Gradually they are establishing a proper reign of terror in the streets of West Berlin.

Friday, 1 July 1932   *Berlin*

In the evening François-Poncet fetched me in his car and we drove for dinner to Wannsee. We ate alone and our conversation lasted from eight until shortly before midnight. Here a few notes:

Papen is finished. At Lausanne he committed not merely one *gaffe* (the

Cartoon by Karl Arnold, 1932. 'If this goes on any longer the only army we will have left will be the Salvation Army.' A comment on the battles of the Nazis, the Communists and the regular army

Matin interview) but two, and the second was more catastrophic than the first. To his statement that Germany can only pay if certain *political* clauses of the Versailles Treaty are revised, Herriot at once retorted, 'Aha! So you fail to pay not because you cannot, but because you don't want to!'

Schleicher. Very charming, but what lies behind his politeness remains impenetrable. Nevertheless he (Poncet) must admit that Schleicher is the only German statesman who has ever told him the *whole* truth.

Neurath. Narrow-minded and not very intelligent.

'*Le plus sérieux*' is Bülow. Rather uncommunicative, but very intelligent. For some time now he has shown proper appreciation of his (Poncet's) European reconstruction plan which foresees a control and quota system of production manipulated according to requirements by European cartels.

Brüning. Obviously Poncet does not have much time for him. He described him as having the cramped outlook of a Catholic priest and being in his heart of hearts 'a wild chauvinist'. Brüning has always looked towards Britain and America and has never wanted to exchange frank talks with France.

Reparations, according to Poncet, are dead. Germany has gained an enormous, unanticipated advantage. The main point now is European reconstruction. The Franco–German Economic Commission has been summoned to discuss the fifty-page memorandum prepared by him on the subject. Although nothing practical has been achieved so far, he is continuing his efforts. But here in Berlin he has encountered nothing but distrust and dislike, for all that he has put his whole energy into close Franco–German cooperation. Some sort of fate has brought him back to Germany, over and over again, since his fourteenth year. In Germany he awakened to the life of the mind. Germany is the country which always attracted him most. Destiny, he feels, selected him to crown his life's work here. I formulated it as '*Vous avez plus qu'une ambassade, vous avez une mission,*' and this clearly caused him great satisfaction. A Franco–German alliance (he expressly used the word *alliance*) must be the corner-stone on which a new Europe will be built.

Monday, 4 July 1932   *Berlin*

To tea in Helene Nostitz's garden. Other guests were Gerhard Mutius, Herbert von Hindenburg, a Princess Trubetzkoy, and so on. *Ancien régime*. From there to the Iron Front demonstration in the Lustgarten. A striking contrast between the dainty tea party in a summery garden and the ocean of red flags stretching far beyond the precincts of the Lustgarten itself. There must have been more than a hundred thousand people and it was by far the biggest demonstration there I have ever seen. Of great political significance and importance is that Communist contingents, with Soviet hammer-and-sickle banners, also joined in and that the new united front insignia, the two red flags on a silver background, was much in evidence. The new battle-cry, 'Freedom!', accompanied by the raising of a clenched fist, exercised a galvanizing effect. There were also great numbers of young people present. Which proves that the youngsters are not all on the Nazi side!

Friday, 8 July 1932   *Berlin*

Today at Lausanne reparations have been finally buried. Papen himself made the announcement on the radio in a boastful but pretty shabby speech which contained not a word of thanks to his predecessors Rathenau, Stresemann, and Brüning or even to MacDonald, who was the agreement's principal architect.

Tuesday, 12 July 1932   *Berlin*

While we spent Sunday driving through the lovely countryside, the unbridled, organized Nazi terror has again claimed seventeen dead and nearly two hundred wounded as its victims. It is a continuous St Bartholomew's Massacre, day after day, Sunday after Sunday.

Thursday, 14 July 1932   *Berlin*

In the evening at Nostitz's in Zehlendorf. The atmosphere there reeks of Nazism. Helene told me that her sister-in-law, Marie von Hindenburg, an Englishwoman by birth, has become a zealous National Socialist and eager Party worker. Criticism of the Nazis is met by an embarrassed silence.

Monday, 18 July 1932   *Berlin*

Yesterday there were again fifteen dead and numerous wounded all over the country, twelve of the fatalities occurring in Altona[8] alone. The Nazis, several thousand strong and doubtless meaning to provoke an incident, marched in their spick and span uniforms through the poorest quarters of Altona. The predictable result occurred. The unemployed and the loafers, probably criminal elements too, attacked them. But the guilt rests upon those who provided the provocation. There is great and general distress about this fresh Sunday bloodshed.

At one o'clock the Government announced over the radio a general veto on demonstrations throughout the country. But it took good care not to deal with the real cause of the bloodshed, the provocative Nazi uniform.

Wednesday, 20 July 1932   *Berlin*

At ten o'clock visited Abegg in the Ministry. He informed me that Papen has appointed himself Reich Commissioner[9] and has called in Bracht, the Lord Mayor of Essen, to act as Commissioner for Prussia. Severing and Hirtsiefer were in conference with Papen and therefore Abegg did not as yet know what the attitude of the Prussian Government would be. He had no doubt however that Papen's move is unconstitutional (making it a *coup d'état*).

At lunch-time the radio broadcast the Government declaration and the news that a military state of emergency has been proclaimed in Berlin and Brandenburg, that executive power has been put in the hands of a General von Rundstedt, and that the Prussian Prime Minister Braun, Severing and Grzesinski have been dismissed by the new Reich Commissioner Papen. Severing's answer was that he did not accept his dismissal and would only yield to force.

The guard at the entrance to the Defence Ministry has been doubled and is armed with rifles. Machine-guns are said to have been mounted in the courtyard. The Prussian Ministry of State, at 63 Wilhelmstrasse, has been occupied by the military since noon.

At five o'clock a Herr Krone, belonging to the Prussian Ministry of the Interior, came to me on Abegg's instructions. Abegg, he told me, has been dismissed by Papen, but regards his dismissal as invalid and is carrying on. Krone added that there are fears of a general strike tonight. Krone quite rightly described the manner in which Severing, Braun, Abegg, and others have been dismissed as the rudest and most inept imaginable. Abegg, for instance, received simply a telephone call: 'Reich Government speaking. You are herewith dismissed from office.' Badt, arriving at the airfield to fly to Leipzig and represent Prussia in front of the Supreme Court, was advised that the aeroplane permanently at the Prussian Government's disposal had been requisitioned by the Central Government. The Prussian Government was not even notified.

Friday, 22 July 1932   *Berlin*

At four o'clock this morning the Berlin Police Commandant was hauled out of bed by the Reichswehr and arrested for the second time. Also the local chairman of the Reichsbanner in Charlottenburg.

At lunch-time the radio announced forthcoming personnel changes at Berlin Police Headquarters. They are meant to ensure that those responsible for deciding cultural matters 'take their stand on the basis of the Christian way of life and culture' and that those who deal with left-wing radical matters strictly disassociate themselves from left-wing radical trends. In other words, we are sailing full steam ahead into a reactionary epoch on a Metternich[10] scale.

Sunday, 31 July 1932   *Berlin*

Reichstag polling day, day of destiny! Sultry weather, cloudy in the morning, but it cleared somewhat towards lunch-time. At eleven o'clock cast my vote in the Kaiserin-Augusta-Strasse next to the Defence Ministry. During the morning a telephone call from Helene Nostitz, rather anxious and depressed. In the afternoon drove to Altenhof via Lanke, Finow, Bernau, and so on. A good many flags had been put out in the northern part of the city and it seemed as though the Socialists and Communists together had a slight preponderance over the swastikas. In the villages very few flags, the proportion between left and Nazis about fifty-fifty, and an atmosphere of complete calm.

In the evening at the Hilferdings. Listened to election results until half past two. The sensation was the uprush in the Communist vote, the expansion of the Centre, and the utter collapse of the Government party. Although forecast, the stagnation in the Nazi vote, which even went down in some constituencies, is still surprising. The SPD has maintained its strength by a hair's breadth and has distinctly fallen behind the KPD. The radio, between issuing results, played disgracefully bad music, circus tent quality, which at its best attained the level of a second-class spa concert.

Monday, 1 August 1932   *Berlin*

The right lacks a majority in the new Reichstag. As against its 230 Nazi seats, 37 Nationalists, 7 People's Party, and 6 others, totalling 280 in all, there are 327 seats belonging to the Centre and left-wing parties. The Communists, with their 89 seats as against 78 formerly, are again the third strongest party. The National Socialists, most of whom expected a fifty to sixty per cent majority, are bitterly disappointed.

This morning Nazis in Königsberg attacked the former East Prussian administrative governor (People's Party) in his home, using firearms, murdered two Communist workers in their homes, and attacked the buildings where the SPD and the Hartung (Government leanings) newspapers are published. In short, they launched an operation which demonstrates in miniature what they proposed to do all over the country, on a bigger and far more thorough scale, if they had won the election.

Last night the latent civil war claimed another fifteen dead and many wounded.

Friday, 5 August 1932   *Berlin*

Assaults, bomb-throwings, and murders continue in East Prussia, Bavaria, and Holstein. It has now been officially established that the cases of arson and bomb-throwing at Königsberg were committed by Nazis. The Government held a Cabinet meeting on the subject yesterday, but confined itself to threatening vigorous action. It obviously hesitates about getting on the wrong side of the Nazis.

In the afternoon visited Frau Foerster-Nietzsche. The Nietzsche Archives are now, as she herself put it, 'right in the centre of politics'. Emge, a Nazi professor of legal philosophy at Jena and a prospective Nazi Minister in the Thuringian Government, has been appointed chairman. Inside the Archive everyone, from the door-keeper to the head, is a Nazi. Only she herself remains a Nationalist.

She recounted how Hitler came to see her after the first night of Mussolini's play at the Weimar National Theatre. He had himself announced while she was talking to a number of Italian newspaper correspondents and, carrying an enormous bouquet, entered her box accompanied by his staff. Hitler, in the presence of the Italians, began a lively political discussion, expressing himself, in her view, rather incautiously about Austria and an *Anschluss*. He emphasized that he has no desire for this because Vienna is not a purely German city. She did not think it right that he should have said that in front of foreigners.

I asked her what impression Hitler made on her as a man. Is his a personality of any stature? Chiefly, she said, she noticed his eyes, which are fascinating and stare right through one. But he struck her as a religious rather than political leader and she did not feel him to be an outstanding politician.

Winifred Wagner, she told me, is a keen Nazi sympathizer. In fact this whole section of German intellectuals, whose background is really Goethe and the Romantic Movement, is Nazi-contaminated without knowing why. The Nietzsche Archives have at least derived material advantage from their Fascism: Mussolini sent them twenty thousand lire at the end of last year. 'Empress' Hermine has announced her attendance at an 'Authors' Tea' which Frau Foerster-Nietzsche gives next Thursday. Börries Münchhausen will read poems and Walter Bloem honour the occasion with his presence. It is enough to make one weep to see what has become of Nietzsche and the Nietzsche Archives!

As for the wife of the former Emperor paying court to this eighty-six year-old woman, the notion is almost grotesque when His Majesty's attitude towards Nietzsche in pre-1914 days is recalled! She added that the officers of the Reichswehr divisional staff headquarters include her in their official calls when they are posted here. What happened in my youth at Potsdam when Bernhard Stolberg, I, and our friends read Nietzsche? Stolberg was removed by his father and locked up with a priest for six months. At that time Nietzsche was reckoned as a revolutionary and almost as unpatriotic a fellow as the Socialists.

We talked in the small parlour on the first floor. Through the connecting door I had a view of the sofa where Nietzsche sat, looking like an ailing eagle, the last time I saw him; our conversation made a deep impression on me. Mysterious, incomprehensible Germany.

Sunday, 14 August 1932   *Théoule near Cannes*

In the morning at Marseilles read the news that Hindenburg, during yesterday afternoon's interview with Hitler, declined to make him Chancellor and that hereupon the negotiations between the Nazis and the Government were broken off. The crucial talk between Hindenburg and Hitler lasted only thirteen minutes. What now? Civil war or the inglorious crumbling of the Nazi movement? The one thing certain is that we are heading for darkest reaction. It is difficult to say which of the two competing parties, the Nazis or the Schleicher clique, is the more reactionary. The only hope is for these two lots of bigots to exterminate each other, now that they have fallen out.

Thursday, 18 August 1932   *Théoule*

With Géraud in his motor boat to the Îles de Lérins. On the way back, about five hundred yards from shore, I jumped into the water and struck out for land. I soon noticed that, perhaps because I had been too hot, I was unable to go on. I managed, though, to signal Géraud. He dived after me and skilfully took me in tow, else I would presumably have drowned.

Tuesday, 23 August 1932   *Théoule*

According to the newspapers here, the death sentence passed on five Nazi murderers by a court at Beuthen has caused terrific excitement throughout the Nazi Party. It evidently thought itself above the law while committing the vilest crimes. Hitler has sent the murderers a personally signed telegram, assuring them of his sympathy and declaring it 'a point of honour' that they shall be pardoned. And these are the sort of people who are now to enter the Government!

Friday, 26 August 1932   *Paris*

German internal politics, particularly the duel between Schleicher and Hitler, are the focus of interest in the French Press. This applies to both the Parisian and such provincial newspapers like *Éclaireur de Nice* and *Petit Marseillais*. Every day they carry two to three columns about Hitler, Papen, Schleicher. French politics and politicians recede wholly into the background.

   Le Français moyen is today better and more vividly informed about

German home affairs than about his own. The French clearly feel that a volcano has appeared in their immediate neighbourhood and that its eruption may at any moment turn their fields and cities into a wilderness. They therefore observe the slightest stir with awe and trepidation. A natural phenomenon against which they are almost helpless. Today, as during the war, Germany is (alas!) once more the international star whose antics the masses watch, in the papers and in the cinema, with a mixture of fright, incomprehension, and reluctant admiration laced with quite an amount of glee at the trouble we are in. We are the huge and tragic, sinister and dangerous character which has played even Russia off the world stage, something like France's role during the Dreyfus Affair. All eyes are riveted on us in fearful expectation of what will happen.

Murky factors like bathing in the buff ('le nudisme'), dives where pretty boys substitute for girls, and the reassessment of moral values among German youth have their part in the almost pathological interest taken in Germany. And, as already indicated, *Schadenfreude*, last refuge of the cowed and powerless. The French sense the birth of a new world which could involve even more immediate danger for them than Bolshevism and they vaguely hope that it will die before it is born.

Films like *Mädchen in Uniform* and *Emil und die Detektive*, in the original German, run here for weeks to packed houses. *Mädchen in Uniform* has, I believe, already been performed for nineteen weeks.

Sunday, 28 August 1932   *Paris*

In the afternoon I visited Maillol at Marly. I found him reading in a shady spot of his garden, radiant with contentment and, as it seemed to me, health. The reasons for his contentment were various. In the first place, his wife is away with Lucien in Chamonix. '*Je suis bien tranquille ici maintenant ; ma femme est à Chamonix! Malheureusement elle revient dans huit jours. Quand elle est ici, elle m'injurie toute la journée. Elle est folle ; je ne comprends même pas ce qu'elle me dit.*'

He is also very happy about the war memorial which he has erected on the island facing Banyuls. A low, mausoleum-like structure of a blueish grey stone, it stands at the tip of the rocky islet. There are three figures in relief. In the centre is that of the dead warrior which I possess in miniature and which has here been enlarged to life-size. He brought me photos of the memorial and also of the celebration that Banyuls, of which he is a native, organized in April in his honour. This caused him especial pleasure. The photographs show him in the company of girls and fishermen, and dancing as well as four sheep being roasted on a spit in the forest and girls performing a round dance. '*C'est tout à fait grec,*' he commented, the highest praise he can give.

I asked him whether he has been to the Manet Exhibition. No, he answered, not yet, but he proposes to go, although he has already seen several Manet Memorial Exhibitions. He first loved his work, later hated it. . . . *Maintenant* . . .? I said something about finding the women in Manet's paintings, apart from their colouring, uninteresting, no spur to the imagination. '*Ce n'est que de la peinture! Pour avoir un Gauguin de Tahiti je ferais n'importe quel sacrifice, je vendrais ma dernière chemise; pour avoir un Manet, je ne vendrais même pas mes vieux souliers.*'

We talked of course about the depression. For his part, he admitted, he cannot complain. A few days ago he sold a big statue to America and recently Druet made a similar sale for him. But artists in general are having a bad time. Lucien has been unable to sell anything. '*Le monde est tombé dans un trou. Ce que je ne comprends pas, c'est que le génie de l'homme ne suffise pas à le sortir de ce trou.*' His spirit dwells in a more profound reality than any that our phantasmagoric daily squabbles can claim.

Yesterday evening, he told me beamingly, Mlle Passavant (now Mme Nicolas) paid him a visit with her husband. She arrived somewhat ahead of her husband and cried when she saw the studio again. Her husband is a very nice young man and she is happy with him, much to Maillol's satisfaction. I asked about Bonnard. Nobody ever sees him, he replied. Marthe Bonnard, his wife, allows him no visitors and throws everyone out who comes, even his oldest friends. '*Sa femme est encore plus folle que la mienne.*'

Thursday, 1 September 1932

Guest of the American copper-king Guggenheim at Hiller's.

Next to me sat Wanda Prittwitz (now Frau von der Marwitz). I last met her in her mother's drawing-room thirty years ago. She told me, with great delight, that all her relations are Nazis and what a good thing it is about the 'Movement' that all these young people, whatever their social status, feel themselves to be comrades. The spirit of *camaraderie* among them is wonderful. She herself is not a Nazi, but, though remaining a Nationalist, she is of course an anti-Semite. So, presumably, am I? No, I retorted, else I would not tonight be the guest of a Jew. She is so dotty that she did not even feel the thrust, but went gushing calmly on. Baroness Rebay (a painter, responsible for arranging the party), whose father was a general during the war, lived in Strasbourg until 1918 and still feels herself to be an Alsatian. She too has strong Nazi leanings, though holding it against them that they have closed the Bauhaus at Dessau. The splendid thing about the 'Movement' is, according to her, that it is teaching ordinary folk that they too must make sacrifices, whereas during the war it was only 'our sort' who did that. All the same, I remarked, several million ordinary folk were killed and several hundred thousand starved to death; none of my acquaintances died of hunger.

Mrs Guggenheim, who is reputed to have an extremely fine collection of primitives and modern abstract paintings, said that she loves both sorts, 'though of course you cannot compare the two, a point which is obvious from the fact that the Primitives are so much more expensive'.

Monday, 12 September 1932   *Weimar*

Worked with Max at the press on *Daphne and Chloe*.

Today Papen, head over heels and without even having held his previously announced major policy speech, dissolved the Reichstag at the very moment when, at the beginning of the session, a vote was to be taken on the lack of confidence motion and repeal of the emergency decree. Indeed the division was already in process. A shyster's trick which amounts to plain violation of the popular assembly!

At half past seven Papen spoke on the radio, alleging that he was appealing to the German people because in the Reichstag he had, unconstitutionally, been refused any opportunity to speak. What followed was an emotional, bungling, lying speech which, with its impudent claim that he has all decent Germans behind him, bordered on fraud and humbug. The mixture of hollow pathos and lack of restraint was really revolting. The thick coating of unctuous Christianity, in crass contrast to the excited, brusque tone of command, added to the nauseous impression. What factually emerged was that this bell-wether wants to load us back past Bismarck and Stein, into the Enlightened Absolutism of the eighteenth century.

Monday, 19 September 1932   *Berlin*

Today the British answer to the German Government's demand for 'equality of status' has been made public. Like that of the French, it is almost entirely negative and contains a very severe criticism of the German Government for imperilling a successful solution to the global economic crisis by putting forward its claims at this moment.

Tuesday, 20 September 1932   *Berlin*

The shattering impression made by the British Note is even stronger today. In the Wilhelmstrasse it appears to have caused stupefied surprise and dismay. A government which within a week has twice sustained overwhelming defeat, first in home affairs (513 against 32 votes) and then in what it terms the vital question of foreign policy, yet still sticks to power, is surely a novelty in history. Papen nonetheless continues to have himself photographed, by the Press, day after day, as he attends smiling and self-satisfied every theatre first night, tennis tournament, fashion show, and racecourse occasion. *Un inconscient* is what the French call such a windbag and coxcomb. He strongly gives the impression of a German Gramont, the man of 1870 who light-heartedly manoeuvred his country into catastrophe. Baccarat players and gentlemen jockeys are probably after all not the right stuff for foreign ministers.

Wednesday, 21 September 1932   *Berlin*

Partridge for dinner at the Georg Bernhards'. The guests were the former Prussian Finance Minister Klepper, who was dismissed on 20 July, Heinrich Mann, the Hugo Simons, Misch, of the *Voss*, Privy Councillor Demuth, and Herr Manasse. I expressed my surprise to Frau Klepper, my neighbour at table, that Severing[11] should have submitted on 20 July without more ado instead of alarming the police and cordoning off Unter den Linden. She said that this coincides precisely with her husband's point of view and I should talk to him about it. So, when we left table, I approached Klepper and told him how I imagined things should have proceeded.

His reply was not merely very interesting but amounted to a sensational revelation. It showed matters up in an even more humiliating light. According to Klepper, he had secured for himself a source of information in the Defence Ministry and was advised two weeks beforehand of what was in the wind. He drove at once, with the individual concerned, to Hirtsiefer and discussed counter-measures. He proposed, should the Central Government attempt a *coup d'état* against Prussia, to alarm the police and arrest the members of the Government or at least to place the Prussian Ministry of the Interior, with police assistance, on a defensive footing. Hirtsiefer agreed and they went to talk to Severing. He however declared that he also had his sources of information and their reports were entirely different: the question of an arbitrary act of the sort that Klepper feared did not arise. What would he do, Klepper asked, if nevertheless the Central Government did commit such an act? He would react appropriately, Severing replied, but he was not in the habit of making decisions about occasions that had not arisen. Klepper and Hirtsiefer accepted this answer because at that time they still had a high opinion of Severing's character.

When, on 20 July, Papen at a conference with Schleicher, Severing, Hirtsiefer and Klepper told the last three that he proposed to dismiss them, Klepper suggested that, as Prussian Ministers, they should confer among themselves before giving any answer. Hirtsiefer supported him, but, to his surprise, Severing rejected the suggestion and contented himself with making some innocuous rejoinder. Papen and Schleicher accepted this with visible relief. It was quite obvious that both of them felt very unsure of their ground and had anticipated something quite different. Severing's histrionic statement about 'bowing to force alone' was simply a case of playing to the gallery. What in fact happened was that he asked Bracht not to apply the force at six in the evening, when he had a conference, but to postpone it until half past seven. This resulted in the classic story about Bracht having inquired, 'At what time, Minister, do you instruct force to be applied to yourself?'

Severing's conduct, Klepper thinks, is only explicable in terms of his being a 'little man' who continues to feel enormous respect for his 'betters' and believes that, for heaven's sake, nothing should be done to infringe the ruling-class's conventions. He (Klepper) has since asked himself whether he could not have saved the situation by organizing resistance on his own initiative. The police force, on which this depended, was however outside his control as Minister of Finance. Had Severing cordoned off Unter den Linden and made a serious effort at defence, nothing would have happened and the Central Government would immediately have entered into negotiations. (Herewith Klepper confirms what I have always maintained.)

Heinrich Mann, who listened in silence to this account, later gave it as his opinion that the Socialists owed their downfall to their contempt for intellect. Their rebuff of the intellectuals and the predominance of the trade unions had taken its toll. Severing lacked the intellect to offer resistance.

Later in the evening a larger group discussed Hitler's historic reception by Hindenburg on 13 August. It is untrue, Misch said, that the whole interview took place with the parties standing. It started with all those present being seated. Schleicher and Hindenburg arranged with each other, Klepper put in, that as soon as Hitler uttered the word 'leadership', Hindenburg would interrupt, 'Oh, so you claim the sole leadership in the state. But that is something which I cannot transfer to you!' and therewith dismiss him. At that moment, Misch continued, Hindenburg did rise and stood there leaning on his stick while Hitler tried, in great embarrassment, to explain that he was not planning any putsch. Hereupon Hindenburg made a threatening gesture, pointing his finger at him, and exclaimed, 'Herr Hitler, I'll shoot!' That ended the interview. At any rate a nice anecdote for later reference works. It may even be true.

Monday, 31 October 1932   *Berlin*

Gide lunched with me. He is entirely preoccupied with the idea of Europe and a Franco–German reconciliation, but he is also very pessimistic. Herriot's disarmament plan is not to be taken seriously. He is playing to the gallery and relies on it being rejected. Nevertheless, an understanding between the two *peoples*, the Germans and the French, is perfectly possible.

(This was in answer to doubts I expressed and which have for some time now grown ever stronger inside me.) Germany is thirty years ahead of France (in respect of architecture, public health, sport, outlook on life), just as Berlin is ahead of Paris as regards the theatre, metropolitan living, and so on.

André Gide (Colin Spencer)

He showed me an article in the *Journal des Débats* which predicts a monarchist restoration in Germany. Presumably it is a piece of propaganda, he commented, meant to scare the French middle classes and render them pliable for the imposition of new armament outlays. What do I think of it? I do not believe in any restoration within a short space, I replied, and it also seems to me improbable at a later date. Even if it occurred, it would not last long. Monarchy could not maintain itself in Germany because the great mass of the nation is of a thoroughly revolutionary and anti-capitalist frame of mind. The prevailing crisis is less of a political than of a religious and ethical nature, and it goes much farther and is more dangerous than a political or even social crisis. It is more like the birth of a new religion and a new type of man than that of a new kind of polity. Gide listened with interest to my analysis and agreed with me.

Sunday, 6 November 1932   *Berlin*

Reichstag election. The fifth big election in eight months. During the morning went to the polling booth and voted SPD. In the afternoon drove through various parts of the city. Everywhere the same picture of more or less sleepy Sunday afternoon quiet to the accompaniment of damp, cold, overcast weather. Very sparse show of flags in the western and central parts, but those to be seen were almost exclusively swastikas. In Neukölln and Moabit (Wedding) the display was greater and here the preponderance lay with the 'three arrows'[12] and hammer and sickle banners.

The traffic strike continues, but is noticeable only in a negative way in so far as there are hardly any trams and no buses at all. What makes this strike so odd is that the Nazis and Communists support it while the Social Democrat trade unions disapprove and disassociate themselves from it. At any rate it has improved the Nazis' electoral chances and impaired those of the SPD and Papen adherents (Nationalists).

Monday, 7 November 1932   *Berlin*

The outstanding features of the election results are that the Nazis have lost thirty-five seats (nearly two million votes) and the Communists made strong gains. Ninety per cent of the electors voted against the Government, and the Nazis and Centre together do not have a majority but need the Nationalists.

In the evening I went with Jenny de Margerie to a lecture by the young French author Drieu La Rochelle who has written a book called *L'Europe contre les parties*. The lecture, which dilated in great detail on subsidiary manifestations like Dadaism, André Breton and Aragon, was pretty thin. François-Poncet was cutting and fault-finding about it. Afterwards supper and reception at the Margeries'. The whole staff of the French Embassy, Roger Martin du Gard, Alexandro Shaw, Philippe Barrès (son of Maurice and now *Matin* correspondent in Berlin), Helene Nostitz, and others. Martin du Gard is enchanted with Berlin. It is his first visit and what fascinates him most is the life in the streets, '*la Rue de Berlin*'. The people he sees there seem to him quite different from those in Paris; the future is reflected in their looks. The new man, the man of the future, is being created in Germany. The Russian is too far from Europe and too little individualist. In the West, in France, Britain and America, the idealism, the inner impetus essential to fresh creation, is lacking. Germany is where the type of man will arise who will embody the synthesis between past and future, individualism and socialism.

He is ignoring the social round, he said, and concentrating entirely on life in the city's streets, particularly those in the northern and eastern districts. Gide (with whom he is on terms of close friendship) is now also quite preoccupied by his interest in Germany and Russia, but he is mistaken about Russia; Germany is the country of the future. Martin du Gard is much impressed with the fine appearance of the German race. The handsome boys and beautiful young girls are, to him, a reincarnation of ancient Greece. Afterwards the four of us, Martin du Gard, François-Poncet, Shaw and myself had a long talk together.

Shaw lunched today with Papen. He has not as yet made up his mind whether Papen is simply frivolous or in some degree qualified for office. So far his feeling is that frivolity predominates and that Papen is no more than a clubman who has always been well off and is totally unfamiliar with real difficulties. He professed himself satisfied with the outcome of the election and asked Shaw what *his* impression of Germany is. Shaw answered that Germany seems to him like a splendidly organized laboratory furnished with the most modern equipment, but also fitted with two or three small retorts which he would be reluctant to handle because of their capacity to blow the whole building sky-high. Papen merely laughed. Brüning, whom Shaw also saw, was very worried. While not afraid of a putsch on a national scale, he does anticipate very serious local uprisings.

Poncet complained about the idle talk of war that prevails in France. It is nonsense, but derives from the logical mentality of the French. They remain Cartesians and cannot believe that the same effects must not always follow upon the same causes. Because today the men of 1914 are in power in Germany, their logical deduction is that the same events as in 1914 must recur. But history does not repeat itself.

Tuesday, 15 November 1932   *Berlin*

In the afternoon with Max Reinhardt. Discussed my play with him and my wish that Helene Thimig should accept the part of the Grand Duchess because she is the only actress capable of presenting convincingly the combination of radiant purity of heart and great lady. He was very taken with the theme, saying that the downfall of Tsarism is a subject that calls out for a Shakespeare and one that is also most tempting from a production point of view. He suggested that I should read the completed scenes to him and Frau Thimig on Friday at six. There is a young actor named Clausen whom he regards as predestined for the role of Kaliajeff; I ought to see him in Kleist's *The Prince of Homburg*. I asked him to invite Clausen to the reading as well. A promising start, especially as Reinhardt added that what the Berlin theatre lacks is authors and audiences. It is, in itself, a wonderful instrument of a perfection that has hitherto perhaps never existed, but there is no one prepared to take advantage of it.

In the evening attended the festival performance of *Gabriel Schillings Flucht* at the National Theatre, for which invitations were issued by the Government. Hauptmann sat with Bracht and Grete Hauptmann in the dress circle proscenium box. All the ambassadors (the Rumbolds, Poncets, and the rest) were seated with Gayl, Minister of the Interior, and his fat wife in the former Imperial box. The luminaries of politics, art and literature had their places in the dress circle, upper circle, and stalls. Mine was in the second row of stalls behind the Einsteins, Kardorffs, and Heinrich Mann. I was flanked on the one side by Hugo Simon and on the other by Fulda and Seeckt, while in the row behind me were the Nostitzes.

The play made an outdated impression, its problem no longer of any concern to us. Einstein's remark, when after the first act Hugo Simon leaned forward and asked him what he thought, was the pithiest definition of the feeling it engenders: 'Well, so what!' Even Lady Rumbold, who has Edwardian leanings, afterwards said to me that the play seemed old-fashioned to her and that we have 'other sorrows' now. It was an excellent performance, though, apart from Werner Krauss who was a failure in the main part, slimy and superficial. I thought Elisabeth Bergner, playing the Russian vamp Hannah Elias, on this occasion a really great artist, comparable with Duse. I have never before liked her acting.

The truly major tragicomedy, the squabble between the lawful and the provisional Prussian Governments as to which of them was entitled to hand Hauptmann the official medal today, took place offstage and on this side of the footlights. In the morning the lawful Government had the accompanying deed handed over to him at the Hotel Adlon, but the document lacked the official seal because this is in the custody of the provisional Government. This evening a very restricted number of people were invited after the performance to watch the provisional Government handing him the medal and a second deed with seal attached. The natural thing would of course have been for the event to take place on the stage in front of all the guests. Instead, clearly out of fear of disturbances, the strange ceremony was performed by Bracht in the presence of this doubly hand-picked selection of spectators who cannot have amounted to more than thirty to forty in all. I stood next to the Schillings and Helene Nostitz. A little farther away were Sam Fischer, his wife and family. Not one of the truly distinguished personalities who graced the auditorium was, as far as I could see, among those present.

Bracht, while cocking one eye down at the long-winded speech which he read from a typed piece of paper lying on the table before him, rubbed his hands as though he were washing them. The stance of semi-submissive devotion adopted by him was a very lowly posture for a gentleman laying a claim, however ephemeral, to dictatorial powers. Deportment and tone were proper to a village headman greeting his sovereign. Every movement of his shoulders and hands was eloquent of his embarrassment and somewhat uneasy conscience. To make certain that the elements of a satyr play should not be missing, Bracht, the man next to Papen chiefly responsible for the chaos and scandalous schism in Prussia, closed with the quotation from Hauptmann '*Der deutschen Zwietracht mitten ins Herz!*'[13] In the auditorium this could not have failed to stir among the assembly of illustrious guests a certain perceptible reaction and therefore it was quite wise of Bracht to limit his audience to the tiniest circle. Hauptmann replied tactfully and diplomatically.

Afterwards a supper party and unofficial celebration at the Adlon with Max Reinhardt, Theodor Wolff, Jessner and others. Hauptmann attended prior to a late-night performance of *Michael Kramer*[14] and did not return to the party until after one o'clock. I said goodbye at half past two when everything was still in full swing.

Thursday, 17 November 1932   *Berlin*

To lunch with Hugo Simon. Ivo Hauptmann, who was also there, said that Badt, the permanent under-secretary of state in the Prussian Ministry of the Interior, had been to see his father this morning and in a rather importunate way implored him to take sides openly on behalf of the lawful Prussian Government. Gerhart Hauptmann declined because on principle he does not want to intervene in day-to-day politics.

In the evening I went to the performance of *The Prince of Homburg*[15] at the Deutsche Theater. Reinhardt sent me tickets to let me form an estimate of Clausen. He gave a lively rendering of the part of the Prince, all flashing blue eyes and golden locks but with neither shades of characterization nor charm. The dream-like, ethereal quality of the figure receded utterly behind uncreative outbursts. Ham of the old school. I cannot yet envisage him as Kaliajeff.

Friday, 18 November 1932   *Berlin*

Last night Papen and the entire Cabinet resigned. At last! In six months this smiling, frivolous dilettante did more harm than any preceding Chancellor ever accomplished within so short a time. The worst perhaps is that he hopelessly compromised old Hindenburg.

In the evening towards six I went with Max to Reinhardt's office at the Kammerspiele and read him and Helene Thimig the first act and the beginning of the second act of my play. Reinhardt accepted it with the proviso that he must submit it to his two directors. He does not doubt their acceptance on his recommendation. There is room enough in the spring production programme, for which only one or two plays have so far been fixed. He thinks the second scene in the first act excellent. His only criticism is of Kaliajeff's language in the first scene: what the character says is right, but not the way he says it. The manner is too rhetorical and the sentences are too rounded. That is how revolutionaries talked in the French Revolution, but nowadays their utterances are briefer, more to the point, less oratorical. I protested that this is precisely the way Kaliajeff actually spoke, but inwardly

I was at once convinced that Reinhardt is perfectly right from a dramatic and production point of view. I must revise the scene.

I promised Reinhardt to complete the play by about the end of January. Frau Thimig seemed much taken with her part. In answer to my direct question, she said that she would much like to do it. After listening to the first scene, Reinhardt of his own accord expressed doubts about Clausen's suitability. Frau Thimig commented that he altogether lacks aura (which is indispensable to the role of Kaliajeff). Reinhardt stuck however to his opinion that Clausen is one of the few among the younger actors who has the prospect of a big theatrical career ahead of him.

Friday, 2 December 1932 *Berlin*

Today Hindenburg entrusted Schleicher with the formation of a government. That spook Papen, who to the last continued to hover around, has finally been banished. To the distress of Hindenburg, the German nation's nausea has finally spewed him out.

Friday, 23 December 1932 *Berlin*

I went to Ullsteins' and talked to Krell. He and Schaeffer have read the first hundred pages of my manuscript;[16] he expressed himself 'delighted', Schaeffer sent me a telephone message on the same lines, and Krell said that Ullsteins in principle agree to accept the work for publication. When he wanted to make me an offer, I interrupted and told him that I do not like negotiating about money matters. I shall send him someone on my behalf. I added that I thought the material would need two volumes. He agreed to that too.

1933

Dinner-party at Hilferding's. Brüning made a quite different impression on me than what I expected from photos and caricatures of him. Much younger and more sprightly, in fact almost jovial. His eyes are *pleins de malice*. He was plainly at pains to please me and was very charming. We talked for a long time about the days of the 1918 revolution. He was stationed with a railway transport section in the Aix-la-Chapelle-Eupen border area and gave a very lively description of conditions there. Taking me home in his car afterwards, he said that he will ring up in the course of the week as he would enjoy another meeting between us.

After the meal talked to Schaeffer about my memoirs. He is very keen for Ullstein to publish them. Hertz is slowly recovering from the proposal that there should be *two* volumes and, after the initial shock, is weakening in his resistance to the idea. Ullsteins would be very generous in their terms, more so than with anyone else, Bülow and Stresemann excepted. In Stresemann's case other than commercial considerations (support for the family) prevailed.

Apropos of Bülow,[1] the State Secretary, Schaeffer told me, is demanding that Ullsteins publish in their entirety the passages cut, these being assembled in a supplementary volume to be sent gratis to all subscribers. They include such aphorisms as that it is ridiculous to dispute Germany's war-guilt, the Emperor is 'a liar and cheat', and similar matter. I warned Schaeffer that if it included utterances of that sort about certain British people (Lonsdale, for instance), publication could turn out to be costly, involving amounts which even Ullsteins will not regard as a trifle. He should make sure of reinsurance from the Bülow tribe.

Schaeffer replied that he would like to send me all the omitted passages for comment. He has drawn Bülow's attention to the fact that, as State Secretary, it can hardly be a point of indifference to him for his uncle to corroborate Germany's responsibility for the World War and that it may seriously affect his position in the Ministry of Foreign Affairs. Bülow answered that he does not care a jot; he insists on publication of every word cut.

Schleicher has fallen and Papen is to form a new government. He now plays unequivocally the part of presidential minion, for he lacks all other support and has almost the whole nation against him. I feel physically sick at the thought of this mutton-head and gambler ruling us again and apparently acting as Foreign Minister as well. In that capacity he will smash all our

Cartoon by Karl Arnold. Hitler, watched by the other political parties, promises to assist the Chancellor, von Papen, when called upon. In fact Hitler is soon to become Chancellor himself

carefully restored relations. The gravest aspect is the background to this intrigue which has resulted in a totally superfluous swop of Chancellors. The Eastern Aid[2] scandal was about to become public and for the Elbe grandees' taste Schleicher was too slack in hushing up their corrupt practices. So the

Old Man had to be served up quickly again with his favourite, who will have no scruples about proceeding more vigorously in such a cause. The business is a mixture of corruption, backstairs' intrigue, and nepotism reminiscent of the worst days of absolute monarchy. The only unfamiliar feature is the speed with which these poisonous weeds have spread in the growing shade of dictatorship. What can be foreseen is that when the next Cabinet, whether Papen's, Hitler's, or Schacht's, falls, it will drag down the President with it.

Monday, 30 January 1933   *Berlin*

At two o'clock Max came to lunch and brought with him the news of *Hitler's appointment as Chancellor*. I was astounded. I did not anticipate this turn of events, and so quickly at that. Downstairs our Nazi concierge inaugurated exuberant celebrations.

In the evening dinner at the Kaiserhof followed by Coudenhove's lecture on 'Germany's European Mission', which he of course interprets as fulfilment of his Pan-European idea. What I dislike is that he wants to see it established as a preventive against Soviet Russia and thereby plays into the hands of those imperialists and propagandists who want a war of annihilation against the Bolsheviks. He expressly quoted Churchill and Amery as supporting his Pan-European concept.

In the discussion which followed, Hoetzsch very properly told him that the notion of playing off western Europe against Russia is one to appeal only to the generation aged over fifty: European youth as a whole (including right-wingers) is already far too imbued with collectivist and socialist theories to go along with him. Coudenhove's trains of thought are logically cogent but remain unconvincing because they derive from far too narrow and biased a selection of facts. All the same, he speaks clearly and has a humanely appealing approach; *un homme de coeur*.

I sat at a small table between Coudenhove and the celebrated Herr von Strauss, formerly of the Deutsche Bank, who talked very big about his intimate association with Hitler. The latter, he claimed, has promised to fulfil whatever wish he may acquaint him with. I permitted myself to chaff him wickedly by saying that a few days ago I was pleased to learn, from someone who ought to know, that Otto Wolff has paid Hitler's debts for him.[3] Strauss, very red in the face, was extremely cross and growlingly denied my story. Simons, the former Supreme Court president, was at our table. So was Seeckt, who invited me to attend one of his wife's regular Monday afternoon at-homes. Gossip included the titbit that the first Cabinet meeting this morning already saw a row between Hugenberg and Hitler.

Tonight Berlin is in a really festive mood. SA and SS troops as well as uniformed Stahlhelm units are marching through the streets while spectators crowd the pavements. In and around the Kaiserhof there was a proper to-do, with SS drawn up in double line outside the main door and inside the hall. When we left after Coudenhove's address, some secondary celebrities (Hitler himself was in the Chancellery) were taking the salute, Fascist style, at an endless SA goose-stepping parade.

I drove with S.[4] to the Fürstenberg beer hall. SA troops were also marching back and forth across the Potsdamer Platz, but the peak of the festive mood was reached inside the hall. Five of us were sitting with S. at a table when a couple of blonde tarts appeared on the scene. They promptly accepted his invitation to sit down and we spent the rest of the evening, until two o'clock in the morning, in their company. At first I was under the impression that the pair were old acquaintances of S. This turned out to be a mistake. He became more and more embarrassed as time moved on but they did not. They swallowed down with hearty appetite whatever was offered them, suggested that he *tutoyer* them, and called him 'grandad'. It was a worthy ending to, and appropriate to the general temper of, this 'historic' day.

Thursday, 2 February 1933   *Berlin*

The Reichstag has been dissolved and fresh elections, to take place on 5 March, have been proclaimed. The Government has forbidden the Communist demonstration on Friday and the SPD demonstration in the Lustgarten on Sunday, but has sanctioned a state funeral for Maikowski, the SA leader shot in a street brawl! Carcass propaganda.

Sunday, 5 February 1933   *Berlin*

The 'state funeral' for the SA butcher Maikowski in the Berlin Cathedral (the last lying-in-state there was for the old Emperor) was attended by the former Crown Prince, Chancellor Hitler, et cetera. The grotesque occasion passed off quietly.

Monday, 6 February 1933   *Berlin*

At lunch-time discussion with deaf old Sam Fischer about my memoirs. He has read the first chapter and greeted me unctuously with the words, 'I congratulate you. You are a poet'. But he declines to negotiate as long as I am bargaining with Ullsteins.

Wednesday, 8 February 1933   *Berlin-Weimar*

This morning Frau Fischer rang me up about the memoirs. She 'wept bitterly' on reaching the last part (of the first chapter, Mama's death) and the whole, she assured me, is a self-contained piece of artistry which her husband would much like to print on its own in his *Rundschau*. She had barely finished when Hugo Simon telephoned on the same topic, pleading for Sam Fischer.

Sunday, 19 February 1933   *Berlin*

Freedom of Speech Congress in the big Kroll festival hall, which was packed. Yesterday the preparatory committee elected me, without forewarning, to the main committee. I sat therefore, under the chairmanship of Police Super-intendent Lange, between old Tönnies and Georg Bernhard. The meeting began quietly enough, but gathered momentum when Grimme, Prussian Minister for Religious Affairs, appeared on the rostrum, an event not fore-seen in the programme. The police, he announced, had thwarted the Cultural League rally at the Volksbühne by Levetzow licensing an SA open-air concert for the same hour and cordoning off Bülowplatz for this purpose, thereby cutting off public entry to the Volksbühne. His statement was received with loud cries of 'Shame!'

'German autumn' (Heine)

Grimme then read a message from Thomas Mann sent to the League rally. While warmly supporting the Republic, it did not spare it the reproach of being responsible for the current situation on account of its easy-going nature. This passage was the one which earned most applause from the audience. Hereafter old Tönnies spouted a political retrospect into his beard, lulling listeners to sleep again, although, speaking to me in private, he had attacked Hitler with the utmost vehemence. He always refers to Hitler as HW. These, he explained to me, are the initials of 'Hans Wurst'.[5] HW is the most ignorant young man he has ever encountered in the course of his career.

The next speaker was Heine. He immediately launched a fierce attack compounded of biting scorn and caustic irony. Now, I told Bernhard, the meeting would be dissolved. Quite right. When Heine reached the point of suggesting that possibly the new Nazi conversion to Christianity is to be ascribed to the recent find in Palestine of a swastika in a two-thousand-year-old grave, a police officer approached Lange and declared the meeting dissolved. Loud cries of 'Carry on! Carry on!', but Lange amid much noise dissolved the meeting. On all sides there were shouts of 'Freedom!' and, in various quarters, 'Red Front!' A large part of the assembly joined in singing the *Internationale* and *Brüder, zur Freiheit*.

During the singing the hall gradually emptied. The situation was very moving. Many, I am certain, had the same feeling as I did that for a long time to come this would prove the last occasion in Berlin when intellectuals would be able publicly to demonstrate on behalf of freedom. On news of the meeting's dissolution becoming known in my house, the wife of the concierge Schlöttke (he is a member of the SA) came out into the courtyard, shook her fist threateningly upwards, and shrieked, almost hysterically, 'That serves them right! There's a lot of other things coming to that pack of criminals up there!'

Monday, 20 February 1933   *Berlin*

Wieland Herzfelde asked to see me on a matter of great urgency. He has absolutely reliable information, he said, that the Nazis plan a fake attempt on Hitler's life which is to be the signal for a general massacre. The sources of his information are the SA in Dortmund and a tapped telephone conversation between Hitler and Röhm. The only hope of stopping this crime is to publicize the intention as widely as possible in the foreign Press, this being impossible at home. Perhaps that will scare them off.

Wednesday, 22 February 1933   *Berlin*

Abegg to lunch. He re-affirmed his prediction of a massacre, a St Bartholomew's Eve. Not even Hitler can prevent its occurrence, for he has nothing else to offer his followers. He is in the position of a lion-tamer locked in a cage with ten hungry lions. If he has no meat for them, he will be torn apart himself. He is terrified and never moves without a bodyguard of twelve roughs. Göring and Levetzow, representing the extremist elements, are hostile and, in case of a palace revolution, will not protect him. Levetzow has said that he would even arrest old Hindenburg if he opposed him. Papen and Hugenberg are thoroughly frightened of these extremist elements. They have arranged an invitation by the Bavarian People's Party during the days of the election so as to keep the Old Man out of Berlin, where he is no longer safe.

Abegg confirmed the news about the Nazi plan for a sham attempt on Hitler's life. Löbe proposes to reveal this plot in a speech in a few days' time. Not that that will help. Fortunately the horrible state of affairs cannot last much longer because the Nazis and the Papen–Hugenberg lot must come to blows. That, he estimates, will be in about six weeks and at latest by July. Then there will be a settlement of accounts, and very different it will be from 1918! Once again he emphatically warned me to take myself off before the elections: the one essential now is to survive the next few weeks.

My manservant Friedrich corroborated, indirectly and unawares, Abegg's warning. Yesterday he came to me and asked for a holiday: his father, a pensioned civil servant and Nazi living in Pankow, needs him urgently. Today he came and said that he must leave my employ. His father insists on this because there will shortly be 'unpleasantness' in my household and he does not want his son to be involved. The lad was pale as a sheet. I told him that he can go if he wishes; I have no desire to imperil anyone, but perhaps later he may regret having left his master at a critical moment. He finally said that he would like to think things over and let me know tomorrow.

Thursday, 23 February 1933   *Berlin*

Completed the revision of the French translation of my Rathenau book and sent it to Paris. Thank goodness, under the circumstances! Ten pages have been written entirely anew and many parts, like that dealing with the Genoa Conference, condensed.

The Münchhausens gave a tea for the Prince de Rohan, who was accompanied by his brother Karl Anton. The Margeries and Nostitzes were among the guests. Alfred Nostitz told me, basing himself on inquiries he has made in Nazi circles, that it will be better if I do not stay in Berlin at election time; something might happen. Karl Anton re-emphasized the view which he expressed to me recently that after the elections Hitler will move completely over to the left and in ten years there will not be a Marxist remaining in Germany. I took leave to doubt the latter point.

Dined with the Hugo Simons. They are sending their daughter away, but will stay themselves because Simon does not want to leave his employees in the lurch. At lunch-time I went to Sam Fischer and, after vainly trying yesterday and today to reach Hertz by telephone, completed the contract with him. The old Fischers are going to Rapallo. Bermann[6] is still uncertain of his plans.

Monday, 27 February 1933

A historic day of prime importance. The planned assault has taken place, though not on Hitler but the Reichstag building. Towards ten o'clock this evening, as I was sitting with Max in Lauer's on the Kurfürstendamm, old Lauer came to our table and said he had just received news that the Reichstag is in flames! What follows from this remains to be seen. During the afternoon I visited Hilferding. He told me in strict confidence and 'not for onward transmission' that Schleicher, who continues to have his quarters in the Defence Ministry, is very active against the Government. Hilferding knows of the planned massacre and said that he, Gerlach and Braun are among the first five names on the proscription list. He is going to Munich since he sees no point in waiting to be slaughtered in Berlin.

Tuesday, 28 February 1933   *Berlin*

Marinus van der Lubbe, a poor wretch of an alleged Dutch Communist, has been arrested as the incendiary responsible for the Reichstag fire. He promptly confessed that he was suborned by Communist deputies to perform the deed and that he was also in touch with the SPD. This twenty-year-old youth is supposed to have stowed inflammable material at thirty different spots in the Reichstag and to have kindled it without either his presence, his activity, or his bestowal of this enormous quantity of material being observed by anyone. And finally he ran straight into the arms of the police, having carefully taken off all his clothes except for his trousers and depositing them in the Reichstag so as to ensure that no sort of mistake could fail to result in his identification. He is even supposed to have waved with a torch from a window.

Göring has immediately declared the entire Communist Party guilty of the crime and the SPD as being at least suspect. He has seized this heaven-sent, uniquely favourable opportunity to have the whole Communist Reichstag party membership as well as hundreds or even thousands of Communists all over Germany arrested and to prohibit publication of the entire Communist Press for four weeks and of the Social Democratic Press for a fortnight. There appear to be no limits set to the continuation of arrests, prohibitions, house searches, and closure of Party offices. The operation proceeds to the tune of blood-thirsty speeches by Göring which savour strongly of 'Stop, thief!'

Everything suggests that this all too convenient transgression, with the concomitant arrests and so on, is the outcome of a compromise between the two trains of ideas in the Nazi Party. The extremists relinquished the projected 'assault' on Hitler and the subsequent massacre for the arson in the Reichstag, less dangerous for Hitler and therefore more appealing to him, followed by neutralization of the KPD and SPD leadership through imprisonment. This solution was not only acceptable to both wings of the Party, but indeed a more advisable one in view of the fact that the previous plans had become generally known. Not one person to whom I have spoken believes in 'Communist arson'. Incidentally, and apart from any political purposes whatever, destruction of the hated Reichstag could not but make a warm appeal to the NSDAP crew.

In the afternoon, as I was about to leave for Weimar for a day, I had a call from a young man who urgently requested to see me on behalf of Plivier. He brought a letter from him in which the latter asked me to hear what he had to say. The young man, deathly pale, told me that at six o'clock this morning Storm Troopers arrived to fetch Plivier from the apartment he shares with him. They mistook another young man lying in bed for their prey and beat him up terribly. On discovering their error, they smashed the apartment amid yells that they will yet avenge themselves on that swine Plivier, who is now hiding somewhere or other with not a penny in his pocket and unable to get away. Later, when the young man who was talking to me returned to the apartment to see what could be saved from the ruins, he watched how a close friend was knocked down in front of his door by Nazis and brutally manhandled.

Left for Weimar by the evening train to negotiate about the mortgage. The old porter on Weimar station met me with an utterly scared look on his face. Things are terrible in Weimar, he told me, with 'auxiliary police' (SA) everywhere and nobody daring to speak a word.

Monday, 6 March 1933   *Frankfurt am Main*

The Nazis have won 288 seats and 43.9 per cent of the Reichstag vote (as against 196 and 33.1 per cent on 6 November and 230 and 37.3 per cent on 31 July). The Social Democrats, regardless of the scandalous pressure exercised against them and the complete paralysis of their propaganda, have lost only a hundred thousand votes, the KPD only a million. That is astounding and a wonderful tribute to the imperturbability of the 'Marxist front'. The Nazis and the Nationalists now have constitutionally complete freedom of action for the next four years, though lacking a two-thirds majority to introduce constitutional changes.

Wednesday, 8 March 1933   *Frankfurt–Paris*

In the afternoon left for Paris via Saarbrücken, where the train stopped for an hour. I went into the town and in a local paper read an article, reprinted from a Nazi Palatinate newspaper, on Nazi policy towards the workers. The pith of it is that Germany is to become a real home for German workers, a land fit for heroes to live in. A new trap for dunces is all that this can amount to, a revival of the patriarchal principle whereby the boss looks after his employees, these being pampered to a greater or lesser degree but remaining like minors without any right of self-determination. In other words, not a vestige of 'leftist' policy, the essence of which lies in each man's right to self-determination and not stall-feeding. The struggle against 'Marxism', as far as Hitler is concerned, is simply the struggle against the worker's right to self-determination and against personal liberty, a struggle against the freedom of man. The state is to become a snug stable where all obedient domestic animals will feel happy and, as necessity requires, allow themselves to be tamely led to slaughter. I cannot think of any idea which would seem to me more degrading and revolting.

Saturday, 18 March 1933   *Paris*

Until now I had hoped to be able to return to Berlin. Today I have had through diplomatic courier a letter from Roland de Margerie which puts an end to these hopes. Goertz called on him and informs me, via de Margerie, that he learned from an SS company commander of something being afoot against me. He consulted Mutius. The latter was told at the Ministry of Foreign Affairs that my arrest was not planned, '*mais que, pour éviter des violences possibles de jeunes gens irresponsables, l'on envisagerait de vous appliquer, si vous reveniez en Allemagne, le régime de la "Schutzhaft". Dans ces conditions, il semble à M. Goertz comme à M. Mutius (et comme à moi-même, s'il m'est permis d'émettre un avis) absolument nécessaire que vous prolongiez, pour un certain temps, votre séjour à Paris.*' In the evening I received a telephone call from ex-Ambassador de Margerie to emphasize the urgent nature of his son's letter.

Sunday, 19 March 1933   *Paris*

A visit from André Gide. I showed him de Margerie's letter; he was deeply shocked. He wants to write a preface, rather a long one, to my Rathenau book, but is not feeling quite well. He is also somewhat puzzled how to frame a preface which will do justice to the weightiness of the book. He thinks *what* he will do is to write me an open letter which can then be printed as a preface. He told me that he and Stravinsky are writing a ballet, *Persephone*, for Ida Rubinstein. Later we drove to a Stravinsky concert in the Salle Pleyel and met there Ida Rubinstein and Guy de Pourtalès. I had not seen her since 1914. She has become an old woman, strangely shrivelled.

Friday, 24 March 1933   *Paris*

Called on Ambassador de Margerie to thank him for his telephone call. He
asked me, with an expression of utmost astonishment, just why I, who of
recent years have kept wholly in the political background, should find myself
in danger in Germany. It seems totally incomprehensible to him. On political
conditions in general, Stresemann in his view was far more dangerous to
France than Hitler is. The whole world is becoming irritated by Hitler,
whereas Stresemann *'grignotait petit à petit'* at the Treaty of Versailles. He
mentioned, almost triumphantly, the swing in public opinion in Britain. He
has a very low opinion of Hitler. He listened on the radio to his speech and
thought it, though very verbose, utterly devoid of content. There was not
one fresh idea in it. It amounted to nothing but a jumble of familiar mass
meeting garrulity. (This is my opinion too.) Margerie believes in an early
outbreak of war as little as I do.

'That'll learn 'em.' Cartoon by Grosz commenting on the persecution of the Jews

Saturday, 1 April 1933   *Paris*

The abominable Jewish boycott has begun. This criminal piece of lunacy has
destroyed everything that during the past fourteen years had been achieved
to restore faith in, and respect for, Germany. It is difficult to say which
feeling is stronger, loathing or pity, for these brainless, malevolent creatures.

Wednesday, 5 April 1933   *Paris*

Hugo Simon is here. He had to leave Germany because he was no longer safe. At first friends who have connections to Papen and Hitler told him that he could stay. Papen, and possibly even Hitler, would see that he came to no harm. Then these same friends came and said that they urgently advised him to depart because they could no longer guarantee his safety. So a week ago he visited his children at Villefranche and intends to go to Amsterdam tomorrow to meet friends from Berlin and hear exactly what the position is. He has had to give up his chairmanship of the S. Fischer board. He is not sure whether the firm will be able to carry on in Berlin.

Thursday, 6 April 1933   *Paris*

Quidde came to lunch. He is not a refugee and proposes to return to Germany. He gave me the details of Gerlach's pretty adventurous escape from Berlin to Munich and then without a passport to Switzerland. He thinks that probably an Army putsch is alone capable of freeing us from the Brownshirt plague, adding that it is indeed a strange reversal of situation when he, as an old pacifist, is forced to pin his hopes on the military.

Saturday, 8 April 1933   *Paris*

Arrival of a small suitcase with papers and letters. Also a letter from Goertz, telling me that it is my manservant Friedrich who has been stealing my things and betraying me to the Nazis. 'Three days ago, at Friedrich's instigation, three Nazis came and hauled your banner[7] out of the attic and tore it to pieces in the courtyard. Friedrich was not ashamed to express his special satisfaction at this occurrence. It was Friedrich (I have proof of what I say) who supplied the Nazis with the wildest information about you. It was he who betrayed the whereabouts of your safe and all those with whom you have been in contact.'

Sometimes I seem to be going through an evil dream from which I shall suddenly awake. These last few days have been grim. Yet life somehow continues. I work, I can concentrate on work, I talk to people, and I read. But all the time I am aware of a muffled pain throbbing like a double-bass.

Sunday, 16 April 1933   *Paris*

A meal with the Georg Bernhards, who have recently arrived as refugees, and Annette Kolb at Vilma's in the Avenue Kléber. Bernhard told the story of his fairly hazardous escape via the Franciscan Hospital, a Mecklenburg forester's house, Warnemünde and Copenhagen. He said he never wants to return to 'that country' (Germany) and no longer regards himself as a German. He spoke with the utmost bitterness.

Sunday, 23 April 1933   *Paris*

With Nolef visited Mme Homberg. Discussed the outlook for establishing a German-speaking theatre in Paris. Agreed on a plan to arrange for Klemperer to come to Paris and conduct a German opera season at the Théâtre des Champs-Elysées: Weill's *Silbersee* and Berg's *Wozzeck*. Her advice was to have Mme Charles de Noailles (*née* Bischoffsheim) as head of the initiating committee. As Mme Homberg leaves for Florence tonight, the matter cannot be got under way until her return in June. Heinz Simon was here briefly. At lunch he discussed, in confidence, a project to found a German school and university in Barcelona for Germans living abroad.

Tuesday, 25 April 1933   *Paris*

Voigt, the *Manchester Guardian* correspondent who ten days ago returned from Germany, told me the splendid retort made by a Berlin working woman to the Nazis. They demanded entry into her home to arrest her husband, who was away at that moment. One of the Nazis held a pistol against her breast. Instead of losing her composure, she asked quite calmly, 'Why do you threaten me with your pistol? I am not proposing to do anything to you.' The Nazis are continuing to arrest and maltreat working people in a dreadful manner. They abduct a man from his home, keep him for a week to a fortnight, thrash him over and over again, and constantly threaten him with death. When he returns home, he is a physical and mental wreck.

Friday, 5 May 1933   *London*

During the morning saw Hoesch for an hour and a half. He is more diplomatic and cold-blooded than Bernstorff, but what he says amounts to the same as the latter told me. A fortnight sufficed to swing British public opinion into the diametrically opposite direction to what it had previously been. Before Hitler it was distinctly pro-German and ready to make all kinds of concessions, both in the field of disarmament measures and border revisions. Today it is without exception pro-French and there is not a concession to be wrung out of it. The swing occurred during the time when MacDonald and John Simon were in Rome. One of them told him, 'I left an England which was pro-German, and when I came back, I found an England which was unanimously pro-French.'

Hoesch gave me a long, extremely clear, intelligent analysis, almost in legal terms, which makes it perfectly obvious that *all* trends of British public opinion (he counted them up, one after the other), omitting only a few wholly uninfluential circles, are now anti-German or, properly speaking, anti-Nazi. And, what is more, the British are fiercer about this than the French because in their case it is the upshot of a sort of disappointed love affair.

Hoesch's sober, dispassionate assessment is more crushing than Bernstorff's subjective one. For all his reservations, having listened to it, the only possible comment is '*Lasciate ogni speranza.*' This is the most horrible suicide a great nation has ever committed. Hoesch does not know how much longer he will be retained here. His British friends, he said, are perhaps still nicer to him personally than they were before and write him countless letters. But let a man of the type of Rosenberg be appointed in his stead and he will suffer the fate of Maiski, the Soviet ambassador, who sits at home and is completely ignored by society.

Thursday, 18 May 1933   Paris

At the Grasset office to autograph, at Grasset's own wish, two hundred copies of the French edition of my Rathenau book. Henry de Montherlant sat at the next table doing precisely the same thing for one of his own books. We exchanged copies. Physically he is a peasant type – thick-set, sturdy, with strikingly fine, lively blue eyes.

Saturday, 20 May 1933   Paris

In the afternoon to Charles du Bos' small Saturday-reception on the Île St Louis. The du Bos' flat on the fifth floor is tiny, with barely room to move but a lovely view of the Seine, the Panthéon cupola, and so on. Naturally Germany and the Nazis were the focal point of conversation.

Du Bos propounded as a fundamental difference between France and Germany the fact that in France '*l'idée du Droit*' is vividly imprinted on the mind of the nation, but in Germany it is not.[8] This concept automatically acts as a brake on French behaviour, but plays absolutely no part in stemming the dynamic thrust of the Germans.

Tuesday, 23 May 1933   Paris

My birthday. In the evening with Wilma and Jacques to the Théâtre des Champs-Elysées to see the dancer Argentina. Met there Keyserling, who is giving a series of lectures here, and in the interval sat with him and his wife, née Bismarck.

Keyserling, with his headlong manner of speech, overwhelmed me with the most horrifying description of conditions in Germany that I have yet heard. The last three months have been the most oppressive of his life, he says, including his experiences during the Russian Revolution. The latter was 'as a flea to an elephant' compared with what is happening in Germany. The Nazi revolution is 'total revolution', a complete levelling down, the real extinction of all class differences. The Bolsheviks substituted for the old ruling class a new one, the proletariat. The Nazis are radically eliminating all classes.

Cartoon drawing of Keyserling by Arnold

This is however contradicted by what Keyserling went on to say about farmers and small shopkeepers, vendors of cheese and 'sour gherkins', being the only people who count any more. It is the rule of the lower middle class and the dictatorship of the non-intellectuals. Artists, authors, intellectuals of every kind have ceased to be of importance. That is however what the Philistine always wanted and regarded as the ideal state of affairs. Consequently seventy per cent of the German nation is delighted with what is happening and stands solid behind Hitler. Therefore this regime has come to *stay*. Only during the past three days, that is since he has been in Paris, has he been able to sleep quietly again.

When I expressed my surprise that his brother-in-law, Gottfried Bismarck, who is a prominent Nazi, should not be able to protect him, he replied that connections of that sort don't play any part at all any more, ha ha ha! Countess Keyserling said nothing, but her sad look seemed to confirm his assertion. He, his wife and children, he continued, constantly received threats until one day he picked up the telephone, which was being tapped, and told a friend that he would wring the neck of the first Nazi who entered his house. That did the trick. Since then he has not been bothered any more, ha ha ha!

Wednesday, 24 May 1933 *Paris*

Again spent hours at Grasset's, dedicating copies. After lunch I went to Pierre Viénot where a small company of German refugees was assembled. Annette Kolb Hilferding, Kracauer (I cannot get used to his hideous ugliness), a young writer by the name of Helmer who had to flee all of a sudden and still looks thoroughly haggard. He and Hilferding described the icily coldblooded process of Nazi maltreatment. It is applied to workers and intellectuals on an entirely individual pattern. For days and weeks they are mentally tortured and thrashed some three times a day, morning, noon, and night. But what gets the victims down more than anything, said Helmer, is that they are forced to watch the ill-usage of their fellows. That induces complete breakdown.

Hilferding described the filthy torments to which Sollmann was subjected. Clearly sadism, a hysterical pleasure at flow of blood and suffering, plays an important part, a pathological feeling of power in the imposition of torture, cruelty of a decadent category which history shows constantly recurring among peoples at the end of their nervous tether, a final titillation among the impotent, the sick soul of the sexual murderer (Jack the Ripper) suddenly active among hundreds of thousands.

In the evening I went to Keyserling's lecture in the enormous, but nearly empty, Salle Pleyel. He spoke in French (with a Russian accent) on '*Les bas-fonds de la nature humaine*'. Outstanding, in content and presentation. He delineated how at certain periods the lowest sediments of the soul, the primal instincts of fear and hunger operative among the pre-mammalian creatures, rise to the surface again and for a time flood the whole super-structure of civilization. Intellect counts for nothing among these movements and ideologies which derive their impetus from primeval instincts. Never-theless he promised in his next lecture to indicate what resistance the intellect can put up against them. Without ever mentioning Germany or Hitler, his address was nothing less than a devastating criticism of the Nazi revolution. It attested to great, almost foolhardy courage, seeing that Keyserling proposes to return to Germany.

Sunday, 11 June 1933 *Paris*

The Georg Bernhards, Valeriu Marcu and Anton Kuh were my guests for lunch. Kuh loosed off a brilliant cascade of jokes and anecdotes. One story had a nearly Shakespearian touch. On 31 July 1914, when the whole world was waiting for the Serb reply to the Austrian ultimatum, he saw Berchtold[9] in the fun-fair part of the Vienna Prater standing by a merry-go-round notorious as a meeting-place for male prostitutes. An extremely pretty youth, in white trousers and white pullover, winked broadly every time the merry-go-round carried him past a very smartly-dressed man whose eyes never left him. When the merry-go-round halted, the youth stepped down and went up to the gentleman, who greeted him and took him along. The gentleman was Berchtold. At the moment that the two were leaving, newspaper sellers rushed on the scene with shouts of 'Serb Answer to the Ultimatum! War with Serbia! Austrian Invasion of Serbia!' The start of the World War which Berchtold had precipitated.

Monday, 12 June 1933 *Paris*

In the evening met Wieland Herzfelde, who is here in transit, at the Café de la Paix. He has reopened his Malik publishing-house in Prague and plans the establishment, with a capital of a hundred thousand marks which have been placed at his disposal, of another, non-Communist, one for the works of banned German authors. He leaves tomorrow for a discussion of this plan in Amsterdam. Underground activity in Germany, he told me, is under way. The *Rote Fahne* is appearing again, regularly though illegally, and meetings of functionaries also take place. A very favourite venue are buses, where three or four (never more) functionaries 'happen' to meet. A bus ride lasting three quarters of an hour is time enough and offers some guarantee against being watched and having lines tapped.

Tuesday, 13 June 1933 *Paris*

In the afternoon a reception by the Comtesse Jean de Pange, *née* Broglie, in honour of the co-option of her brother, the great physicist Louis de Broglie, into the Academy of Sciences. He has a handsome, scholarly face, with a serious expression and a dark mop of hair, not unlike Einstein. He looked completely out of place and embarrassed in the mixed crowd of society people and academics which swirled around and pinned him against the wall. An extremely vivacious personality, on the other hand, is his brother, the Duke. In spite of his white hair, he raced the lift (into which he thrust me) up the five floors to his sister's apartment.

The Countess (a great-granddaughter of Mme de Staël, about whose 'discovery' of Germany she has written a small book) introduced me to a heap of people, including the Duc de Lévis-Mirepoix, a long detachment of Countesses who surged around me, and the very nice and intelligent Mme Paul Morand, all of them smothering me with compliments. Suddenly a woman, whom at the moment I did not recognize because she had her back to the light, broke through the circle. '*Vous ne me reconnaissez pas, j'ai lu votre livre, votre admirable livre. Non, non, je le vois que vous ne me reconnaissez pas.*' Out of politeness I lied that I did recognize her until, to my no mean annoyance, I really did recognize the Duchess de Clermont-Tonnerre who so insulted me in her book. Now it was too late. She drew me into a corner by the window, said that we must see each other, and so on, and so on.

I made the acquaintance of our ambassador, Köster, and his very charming, elegant wife. I explained to him why I had not called on him. He replied that the Nazis' opinion of me is a matter of complete indifference to him and he looks forward to my visit. Frau Köster also said that she would welcome it if I came.

Thursday, 15 June 1933   *Paris*

In the afternoon to the rehearsal of Nabokov's *Hiob* in the Théâtre des Champs-Elysées. Serious music of major dimension. Afterwards to Misia Sert. Serge Lifar, Nabokov, Nathaniel Wolff were also there. Lifar criticized Wolff's ballet libretto, but so skilfully and tactfully that even Wolff agreed with him. Of the *Ballets 1933* in general and Kurt Weill's *Seven Deadly Sins* in particular, Lifar said '*C'est de la pourriture de ballet.*' Weill's ballet has been a disappointment to most people here.

Friday, 16 June 1933   *Paris*

Thirty-five years ago today I started this diary.

In the afternoon visited Guy de Pourtalès in his studio at Passy. Large and well-lit, antique furniture, East Asian miscellanea, a large collection of books on tall shelves. What is called 'cultivated surroundings', though, rather like his books, lacking much originality. He told me that during the war he had both Lenin and Trotsky as tenants on his Swiss estate, but without knowing who Lenin, passing himself off under the name of Ulianov, really was. He drove them into town and talked to them. Trotsky seemed to him the more outstanding of the pair, but Lenin had more heart. He looked through the books they left behind after their departure. Those read by Lenin had masses of pencilled remarks, all of them dissentient and constituting a sort of running dispute with the author. Nietzsche and Maupassant were Lenin's favourites and the contempt of the latter for humanity, his pessimism, clearly made a strong impression on Lenin.

In the evening the first performance of Nabokov's *Hiob* oratory within the framework of the *Ballets 1933* programme at the Théâtre des Champs-Elysées. Unfortunately an unsuccessful event, partly because so serious a work is wholly unsuited to inclusion within the framework of a ballet season, boring and irritating the balletomane audience, partly because the chorus and soloists were mediocre. There were whistles and a part of the audience left demonstratively before the end. A major contribution to the failure was provided by the confusing and ridiculous-seeming magic lantern projections taken from Blake's illustrations of the Book of Job.

Saturday, 17 June 1933   *Paris*

In the evening with Jacques to the Théâtre des Champs-Elysées to see Kurt Weill's pantomimic *Seven Deadly Sins*, performed as part of the *Ballets 1933* programme. It has had a bad reception both from the Press and the public, despite Weill's popularity here. I thought the music attractive and individualistic, though not much different from *Dreigroschenoper*. Lotte Lenya, whose voice has only small range but considerable appeal, sang (in German) Brecht's ballads and Tilly Losch danced and mimed both gracefully and fascinatingly. Obviously too much has been expected of Weill, snobbery dictating that he should be put right away on the same level as Wagner and Richard Strauss.

Sunday, 18 June 1933   *Paris*

In the afternoon at the Clemenceaus'. More German than French to be heard there, with even the maid receiving guests in German. I saw Antonina Vallentin (Mme Luchaire), with whom Paul Clemenceau declines to speak, Fräulein Köster, Mme Sautreau, Chocarnes, Frau von Porada, Toch, Alfred Kerr and his wife (both very 'stuck up', although they are pretty badly off), Casella, and Marya Freund.

Thursday, 22 June 1933   *Paris*

Lunched with Bermanns and Tagger (Bruckner)[10] at Calvet. Beforehand talked to Bermann about the negotiations with Plon and Faber, which are just about to be concluded. Bermann maintained that the Fischer publishing-house has not been molested in any way and that there is no Nazi cell inside it. He has even, in spite of being a Jew, been nominated to the 'Obscenity and Trash' supervisory committee. Provided I obtain from the Consulate in Paris a re-exit visa, he sees no objection to my temporary return. He does not think that I would meet with trouble. The regime is gradually softening up. It has implored some individuals (Jews) whom it had thrown out, especially in the film world, to come back; it cannot do without them. On the other hand the economic situation is hopeless and becomes increasingly so. All the same, he believes that the regime will last a long time. Tagger takes just the opposite view, asserting that it will break down through its incompetence.

In the evening I was delighted to get a telephone call from Max at Weimar. The garden, he said, is indescribably lovely, the roses have shot up to an astounding degree and are in magnificent bloom, the magnolias were weighed down with blossoms, and it is all like a fairy-tale. I was deeply moved.

Friday, 23 June 1933   *Paris*

In the evening with Bermanns to a cinema on the Champs-Elysées. Afterwards we ran into Franz Osborn, Frau Schnitzler, and others. The whole of the Kurfürstendamm is descending on Paris. Bermann sticks to his theory that the Nazis will remain in power a long while although their ultimate downfall is certain. I explained why I disagree with him.

Wednesday, 28 June 1933   *Paris*

Hugenberg has resigned and the Nationalists have 'dissolved' their party organization. They are paying the bill for their shameful betrayal of the German nation. Papen's turn will come too. At present he is in Rome, obviously to pacify the Pope who is becoming more and more indignant about the growingly severe persecution of Roman Catholics in Germany.

At ten o'clock I had a discussion with Bermann. He was in a very bad state, close to a nervous breakdown. On arrival from Germany, he took quite a rosy view of the situation. Now, as he himself puts it, a week abroad has been enough to turn his ideas inside out and he fears sequestration of property belonging to Jews, banks, and estate owners, Bolshevism, and so on. He wonders whether it would not be better to emigrate from Germany as quickly as possible. I calmed him down, telling him that he merely has a dose of the émigré sickness which, like measles or 'flu, everyone has to go through at one stage or another. He will feel better in a week, and so on, and so on.

In fact I too see matters gloomily. Undoubtedly a sort of Bolshevism lies ahead. Eventually it will be countered by a revolt among the preponderant part of the German nation – Socialists, Communists, conservatives, farmers, Catholics, Protestants, industrialists, and the merchant communities of the Hansa cities – which Hitler will be unable to handle. So far the Communists have proved the most active element, even though Hitler is fulfilling their object. But the others will also be galvanized into greater self-defence. And once the first spark of revolt has been struck, the whole ramshackle Hitler structure will go up in flames. The Vienna *Reichspost* claims that the *Rote Fahne* has once again an illegal distribution of three hundred thousand copies(!?).

Thursday, 6 July 1933   *Paris*

To the Gare de l'Est, Countess Keyserling's point of departure for Germany: Hermann Keyserling stays until tomorrow. After she left, we sat down together on the terrace and drank a couple of bottles of champagne while Keyserling held forth most interestingly about the Nazis and Hitler. He repeated that the Nazis have a much more radical revolution in mind than that of the Bolsheviks. They want to alter fundamentally the intellectual as well as the political and social structure of the German nation. It is really a religious upheaval, like Mohammed's, though of strictly local character. They are in the process of abolishing Protestantism and Roman Catholicism, indeed Christianity altogether, in order to effect a return to what they regard as the Old Teutonic faith. They therefore have neither interest in nor time for foreign policy and make concessions that no earlier Government would have made. They may be found saying to other nations, like Trotsky did at Brest-Litovsk, 'Why so little? Don't you want this, and that too?' According to his handwriting and physiognomy, Hitler (whom he has studied in detail) clearly falls into the potential suicide category, a man looking for death. He embodies a fundamental trait of the German nation, which has always been in love with death and to whom the tribulation of the Nibelungs is a constantly recurrent basic experience. Germans only feel integrally German when this situation is given; they admire and they desire purposeless death in the shape of self-sacrifice. And they sense that through Hitler they are once more being led towards grandiose destruction, a tribulation of the Nibelungs. That is what fascinates them about him. He is fulfilling their deepest longing. The French or the British want victory; Germans always only want to die.

Keyserling seems to me profoundly perceptive and right in this point. He does not believe that at present anything can be undertaken against the Nazis. But in about two years they will come to grief. That will be the time for free spirits, such as his, to step into the breach. Meanwhile he proposes to stay silent, preparing himself for the task to come. The Nazis' unprecedented oppression is producing an unprecedented intellectual elite. We are back in the sixteenth century, in the age of the Reformation. The Jews will again be powerful in Germany, more powerful than they have ever been. In ten years they will dominate Germany because they alone will be allowed to carry on commerce, a monopoly acquired on the basis of some sort of minority statute. Germans will be degraded to the status of peasants and mujiks headed by a small group of intellectuals. Hitler is nothing, simply a medium for the Nazi movement. But, Keyserling added, Hitler is the sole restraining factor. If anything happens to him, should he die or disappear, we shall witness something truly dreadful, the most frightful of pogroms in which tens of thousands will be killed.

Monday, 10 July 1933   *Paris*

In the afternoon visited Frau von Porada. She is just back from Berlin, where she saw Gottfried Benn. He has become a fanatical Nazi and maintains that the Nazi 'revolution' is a historic event of the first order, a total rebirth of the German nation, and the salvation of Europe. All that, laced with metaphysics of every kind.

Tuesday, 11 July 1933   *Paris*

With Jenny de Margerie and Mme de Courcel to the Louvre and called on the Director of the Egyptian Department, Borreu. It gave me a chance to see how, under the influence of Berlin's Pergamon Museum, the *Victory of Samothrace* has been freshly positioned. The result restores to the work all its ravishing romanticism and sublimity. *Paris-Soir* is the only one of the evening papers to publish as a last-minute item the news that, according to an ordinance of the German Ministry of the Interior, the 'German Revolution' has today 'ended'. What that is supposed to mean nobody knows!

Saturday, 15 July 1933   *Paris*

Talked to Albert Flechtheim. He told me what is happening in the Berlin art world. Diametrically opposed trends exist among the Nazis. One supports modern art, including Barlach and Nolde; the other, under the leadership of Schultze-Naumburg, wants to exterminate it. He gave me details about the exhibition planned by National Socialist students and then prohibited. He thinks that there is a bitter running fight between antagonistic trends and personalities inside the Party. Göring and Goebbels, for instance. These internal quarrels and the inevitable dreadful economic emergency will destroy them. The crash, in his view, will come in the autumn.

Saturday, 14 October 1933   *Paris*

The afternoon papers report the German Government's announcement of
its withdrawal from the League of Nations and the Disarmament Conference
as well as its dissolution of the Reichstag and proclamation of fresh elections
on 12 November. The effect here, and in London too it seems, is that of a
bomb-shell. '*Coup de tonnerre*' write the papers. It is the most momentous
European event since the occupation of the Ruhr. Within a short time it
can lead to the blockade of Germany and possibly war.

Thursday, 19 October 1933   *Paris*

In the morning visited Hermann Keyserling. He has been taking part here
in a congress of the '*Coopération Européenne*' and was in a state of the most
exuberant excitement. He and Paul Valéry conducted the entire congress, he
had to make speeches the whole time, and everything went off splendidly.
He has hopes of the alliance between a few hundred European intellectuals
proving the salvation of European civilization. Lack of intellectuality is the
most terrible thing about the Hitler regime. For the time being, though,
there is nothing to be done about it other than creating a haven where the
intellectuals can take refuge.

Friday, 20 October 1933   *Paris*

Saw Keyserling off at the station. First had dinner with him. He was in a
state of almost alarming excitement. The German nation, he said, is composed of sixty per cent cowardice and forty per cent jealousy. Not a soul has
courage any more. Even leading Nazis are nauseated by the spectacle of the
prevailing shallowness. Hitler, when some former Nationalist bigwig
appeared before him with the Nazi badge in his buttonhole, simply said, 'I
thought that you had more character', and turned his back on him. Keyserling
asserts that he has not yet met a single person over thirty in Germany who
is a Nazi; but they all behave as though they are. If he had to choose between
Nazis and Bolsheviks, he whispered in my ear, he would choose the Bolsheviks. A similar sort of remark was quoted to me recently by Bernstorff:
Winston Churchill told his niece Claire Sheridan that against Hitler he
would even enter into an alliance with the Bolsheviks.

Monday, 23 October 1933   *Paris*

In the afternoon saw Madariaga at the Spanish Embassy to obtain my visa
and to ask for an introduction to the Governor of Mallorca.

Friday, 27 October 1933 *Basle*

In the morning from Zurich to Basle. Saw my Maillols in the Kunsthalle. Painful!

Wednesday, 15 November 1933 *Palma*

Have at last found the right house. Plaza Iglesia 3, in the Bona Nova quarter, on the hill overlooking Palma and with a magnificent view out to sea, of the bay of Palma and the town. A pretty, one-storied modern house, pleasantly furnished, with large terraces and flower-beds facing south. At once decided to rent it.

Friday, 1 December 1933 *Palma*

Completely clear skies and a hot day as in summer. Sat in the garden and again started work on my memoirs. Leipzig, 1890–91.

Friday, 22 December 1933 *Palma*

In the evening at eight, while I was sitting quite quietly with a newspaper in front of the fire, I suddenly felt queer and had a severe haemorrhage. Within a few minutes I lost well over a litre of blood. I called to Max and Uschi, who were on the terrace, while blood poured in streams from my mouth. Max at once summoned a doctor (César Banolas) by telephone. He arrived very quickly and gave me an injection which stopped the flow. Otherwise I would really have bled to death. The doctor said that the blood came from the right lobe of the lungs.

Sunday, New Year's Eve 1933 *Palma*

A quiet New Year's Eve because I am still weak. Before midnight in bed. Thus ends this tragic year.

1935

Read Hitler's great speech, which he held Tuesday in the Reichstag, in the original. One may think of him what one chooses, but this speech is an eminent piece of statesmanship. Its thirteen points offer a basis which, honestly consolidated, could ensure European peace for decades ahead. For other states not to examine these proposals carefully and to turn into reality everything that is feasible about them would be a crime against Europe and against humanity. It must also be recognized that this speech was only rendered possible by the re-introduction of compulsory military service. That alone has transformed Germany into a negotiating party which has to be taken very seriously and whose offers and proposals have to be heard with respect.

Again studied Hitler's speech. I would like to know how much of it is Ministry of Foreign Affairs and how much genuine Hitler. The spirit of Stresemann and Rathenau continues to be a more potent force in the Ministry than Hitler's. Major portions of the speech could just as well have been made by Rathenau or Stresemann. Regrettably, the most amateurish and dubious part, the philippic against Russia, is authentic Hitler. Taken as a whole, the speech looks like a compromise between Hitler, who was conceded his ranting against Russia, and Gaus and Bülow, especially Gaus. This makes it possible to assess to some degree how honestly the proposals are meant. The constructive portions represent the continuous and consistent policy of the Ministry since Rathenau's time until today. Having successfully carried it with Hitler, the Ministry will probably have the strength to continue to insist on its implementation. Hitler's contribution, apart from the stupid attack on Russia, has been the tone and phraseology of the speech.

Young Kusche says that there are now in Germany not only 'Honorary Aryans', like Francesco Mendelssohn, but also 'Temporary Aryans' (Aryans *pro. tem.*, Aryans on recall). He quotes the case of Lewald who has been appointed an Aryan for the period of the Olympic Games because he is President of the German Olympic Committee. Other Olympic Committees, in Britain, France, and elsewhere, have declared that his deposition would place conditions in Germany in such a light that they would be unable to assume responsibility for sending their sportsmen to the Games in Berlin. Faced with the threat of this disgrace, the Nazis have for the time being, though on recall, put up with the fact of Lewald's Jewish blood. After the Games he becomes irrevocably non-Aryan.

Sunday, 14 July 1935   *Paris*

The last few days have witnessed here a great deal of nervousness (which I did not share) about the two major demonstrations by the 'Front Populaire' and 'Front National' (Croix de Feu) respectively. Under torrid conditions, I watched both of them, that of the Radical-Social Democratic-Communist unitary front on the Place de Bastille and that of the Croix de Feu at the Arc de Triomphe. They passed off perfectly quietly. The left-wing one made a rather sleepy, decently middle-class impression, as of a big family party suffering somewhat from the heat, with the demonstrators crawling rather than marching along, many of them holding their children by the hand, though all this did not prevent them yelling bloodthirsty slogans: '*La Roque poteau*' and '*Les Soviets partout.*' The procession is supposed to have taken five hours. That of the Nationalists, which I attended from start to finish, lasted precisely an hour, from six until seven. The demonstrators 'marched', meaning that they moved more or less in step and with a certain amount of *élan*. The spectators roared enthusiastically '*Vive La Roque*' and '*La France aux Français*'. The mood was just a little revolutionary here as there. No comparison with the Berlin processions in 1932–3 of the Reichsbanner, Nazis, and Red Front!

Saturday, 20 July 1935   *Paris*

Today my poor domestic furnishings in Weimar are being auctioned. That closes the main chapter of my life and is the end of a home built up with great love.

During the morning I ran into Annette Kolb in the company of former Chancellor Brüning. He is here incognito and gave me an impression of distinct wariness, almost anxiety. He did however ask Annette whether we could not have a meal together tonight.

This evening the three of us ate in her small, attractive attic, 21 Rue Casimir-Périer, and chatted until midnight. The reason for Brüning's marked caution soon appeared. This is his first overnight stay in Paris and he is hiding himself because on no account does he want to have anything to do with any émigré clique. He was especially severe about Georg Bernhard here and Olden in London. Their exaggerated fuss at the outset, and their dissemination of stories which turned out to be untrue, did great harm. The result is that wide circles in Britain no longer believe a word stated by émigrés.

Surprising and new to me was that immediately after the 1932 presidential election Brüning, as he frankly admitted, tried to contrive a monarchic restoration. 'Germany needs a uniform at its head.' That is why he has always been a convinced monarchist. The monarch's identity is pretty well a matter of indifference. In 1932 his own choice was Prince Louis Ferdinand who is rather more open-minded than most of his fellow-princes, and he tried to arrange a discussion on the subject with the Crown Prince. The talk should have taken place in the home of General von Willisen, but Schleicher got wind of the matter, prevented the Crown Prince's acceptance of the invitation, and instead arranged a lunch in his own apartments at which Brüning and the Crown Prince met. The encounter was meant to remain secret; the very next day Schleicher disclosed its occurrence at a Press conference. The whole operation thereupon petered out. Old Hindenburg made difficulties too. Before the presidential election, Brüning's task was to win over and hold the Social Democrats. Immediately afterwards, though, he undertook these restoration steps(!).

He is very scathing about Hindenburg. It has always been typical of him, even during the war, to shirk responsibility at the last moment and to let himself be swayed by all kinds of side-issues, innuendoes of friends (Oldenburg–Januschau),[1] sentimental recollections of his youth, and feelings of resentment deriving from an inferiority complex. In 1915 (or maybe 1914), for example, Ludendorff wanted to lure the Russians into Silesia as far as the Riesengebirge in order to cut them off and annihilate them. At the last minute Hindenburg said no because of his memories of Wahlstatt (where he had been a cadet), the estates of friends, and so on.

Brüning's slogan 'Stick out the last hundred yards!' was coined with the President specifically in mind. Both he and Oskar Hindenburg were very strongly swayed by inferiority complex, as exemplified in the acquisition of Neudeck. Oskar moreover lacks capacity in every respect, including the military field. He slithered into all sorts of murky stock exchange dealings and consequently found himself in a position where he was constantly afraid of 'revelations'. The same applied to Meissner. Hence the two of them fell right into the hands of Papen and the Nazis. Oskar also terrorized his father and, if the Old Man did not want to join in something, shouted at him so loudly that it could be heard in the Wilhelmstrasse. Finally, under his son's pressure, the Old Man became panicky and in that condition summoned Hitler to power.

The Nazis discredited Schleicher in Hindenburg's eyes by breaking into a legal record-office, obtaining documents relating to the divorce proceedings brought by Frau von Schleicher, and arranging for Hindenburg to see them.

The Centre Party never took Papen seriously as a political factor, but he had been a protégé of Kaas, who had a weakness for aristocrats. When I referred to Papen's activities in the United States, Brüning commented that this was by no means Papen's worst effort. In spite of the American fiasco,[2] he was entrusted on his return with the establishment of a spy organization in Belgium. Subsequently it turned out that all his 'agents' belonged to the British Secret Service. Consequently German General Staff plans were constantly passed to the British, every projected offensive was known to the enemy long beforehand, and hundreds of thousands of unnecessary losses were sustained on the German side. Von Rintelen, a former Papen agent in America who was sacrificed by him, set out the facts in a book which contained such hair-raising details that Brüning called on the American anbassador in Berlin and managed to have the most appalling of them eliminated. Certain things would have been intolerable for Germany's reputation.

This is how Brüning describes the murder of Papen's secretary, Jung: he (Brüning) warned Jung that he was on the Nazis' Black List for 'elimination'. Jung went into hiding, but returned to his flat for a letter which he had forgotten. The Gestapo was already at the door, arrested him, and shot him on the same day, 29 June. The principal reason for his murder was that Jung was one of the few who knew all about a piece of treason committed in 1932 by Hitler, an 'eyewitness'(?), if I understood correctly.[3] Now only Brüning and one other person know the minutiae of this treason.

Hitler is cowardly and just the opposite to a *Führer*, being indecisive, dithering, and easily influenced, so that he is always changing his mind according to whom he has last spoken to. On the other hand he has a peasant's craftiness and is cruel as only weak people can be. Murderers are always weak men and Hitler is no exception to the rule. On taking possession of the Chancellery, nothing less would of course content him than to sleep in Bismarck's bedroom. In addition, the eleven preceding apartments were reserved for his use. In the first of them sleeps his ADC Brückner; the other ten are occupied by his personal body-guard, big, strapping youngsters who let no one by. For all that, Hitler at night never dares pass beyond the third apartment. He suffers from frightful fits of nerves and then screams for Brückner. But the latter occasionally goes across to the Kaiserhof for a glass of beer and is missing at the crucial moment, so that Hitler snarls at the body-guard, demanding why they have let him go.

Once one of them went to the Kaiserhof to fetch him. Brückner, instead of budging, simply said, 'Man alive, have you *still* not noticed that the Führer is nuts?' Hitler always allows the murder of people with whom he is on friendly terms to be 'wrested' from him. He tears his hair like a Wagnerian hero, makes a show of despair ('I really *cannot* permit that'), and finally 'concedes' what he decided on a week ago. 'Richard III,' I commented. 'Much worse,' replied Brüning, because the theatrical, sentimentally romantic, Wagnerian element enters into it.

Göring is a mass murderer, brutal and bloodthirsty, but only when he has had a morphia injection. At other times he tends to be pliant and fairly sensible.

Of Goebbels's intellectual capacities, Brüning has a high opinion. He is diabolically clever and his oratorical gifts are quite exceptional, far greater than Hitler's. In the 30 June tragedy he played a truly devilish part. By wire-tapping he overheard the conversations between Göring and Hitler when Göring incited Hitler to the 'execution' of Röhm and his friends. Goebbels, seeing that matters were becoming critical and dangerous for himself, promptly flew down to visit Hitler, outdid Göring in description of the 'plot', and with Hitler took the lead in the Munich blood bath. It was only after Röhm and Heines were shot that a murdered youth was put in their room. (Probably a Goebbels propaganda trick.) Göring and Hitler, not Goebbels, whose life he once saved, were responsible for placing Brüning's name on the list of those to be 'eliminated'.

In regard to the state of mind inside Germany and the duration of the Nazi regime, Brüning (he doubtless garners very precise information from a thousand different sources) said as follows: at least sixty per cent of students are anti-Hitler. So are most of the younger Reichswehr officers. The catastrophe for which the regime is heading can be postponed for perhaps a year to eighteen months. Armaments can go on being manufactured for another year. But when all the arsenals are full and the financial cupboards empty, the armaments industry will suffer retrenchment and hundreds of thousands of workers will be thrown on the streets. For another six months (winter 1936–7) the Nazis may be able to keep their hold by daily 'eliminating' an indefinite number of individuals. Then the explosion must come either way (through war or revolution).

The regime's downfall right at the start was prevented by Daladier. Pilsudski sent him a message that he was ready to march into Germany. Daladier first hesitated, finally said no (probably because the popular mood in France was not prepared to support a war). Since then Poland has turned away from France, realizing that it cannot depend on the French.

The Vatican and the concordat. The terms of the concordat are so elastically framed that in the present situation the Vatican derives little advantage from it. Papen bamboozled Pacelli. Even at the very last moment, when everything was laid down and he had been awarded a high papal decoration, Papen fraudulently smuggled in a paragraph which was never discussed. However, when it came to signing, the Vatican bureaucracy discovered the deception and the paragraph was of course cut. His status with the Vatican has since been simply that of a small-time confidence trickster and cheat. The arrangement with Hitler should not be ascribed to the Pope, but to the Vatican bureaucracy and its policy-maker, Pacelli. What he has in mind is a perpetual alliance between an authoritarian secular state and an authoritarian Church ruled by the Vatican bureaucracy. This is why Catholic parliamentary parties, like the Centre Party in Germany, are a source of inconvenience to Pacelli and his friends and will be dropped by them without regret. The Pope does not share these views. On the contrary, he has an encyclical ready which will completely reorganize the Vatican bureaucracy and the government of the Church.

Brüning gave no clear answer to my question why the Pope does not publish this encyclical. He merely said that he is now not *persona grata* in the Vatican, the Pope would not receive him, and as Chancellor he had the most vehement altercations with Pacelli because he would not allow him to tender advice on German internal matters. 'As Chancellor I am alone responsible for internal German affairs. I therefore deprecate your excellent counsels.' At these words Pacelli wept. Brüning frankly granted the elegant, lady-like quality of Pacelli's appearance. Pacelli, *c'est la Duse*, as Annette put it.

My impression is that Brüning wants and hopes to attain power again. I observed that to bring down the Nazis will require a superior ideology, not merely the wholly negative criticism practised by the refugees. Perhaps not an ideology, he replied, but more effective slogans. At a later stage he hinted that he has a constructive counter-programme. He gave me an address in London and asked me to look him up when I am next there. I assume his programme to be restoration of the monarchy in one form or another, with the identity of the monarch an immaterial detail. All the same, omelettes cannot be made without eggs.

Tuesday, 30 July 1935   *Paris*

Spent the afternoon at Annette Kolb's with Jacques and a young Russian, a Prince Bagration, connected with the Russian Imperial Family (his aunt is a daughter of the Grand Duke Constantine), who, as a traveller for a brush factory, leads an indigent and yet half 'society' existence.

In the evening I went with him and Jacques to a popular (cheap) performance of a Russian ballet in the very large hall of the Trocadéro (most expensive seat, fifteen francs). The whole of the Russian *ancien régime* was present, including the Grand Duke Andrew in a box with his wife, the dancer Kshesinskaya, in whose Petrograd palace (she used to be the mistress of Tsar Nicholas II) Lenin set up his quarters. Was introduced to her son, Prince Kshesinsky, a very ordinary looking and badly dressed young man who certainly does not give the impression that the blood of Great Catherine and Frederick William III runs in his veins.

All these Russian aristocrats have gone downhill so much that they were indistinguishable from the remainder of the petit bourgeois audience. A Count Loris-Melikov, grandson of Alexander II's Imperial Chancellor, is a taxi driver and laboriously earns twenty francs a day. The company, apart from Voigikovsky, was mediocre but performed Diaghilev's famous old ballets, *Spectres de la Rose*, *Sylphides*, the *Prince Igor* dances, and the rest. The setting, the stage, the performers, and the audience had something macabre about them, like seeing the ghosts of a long past age.

Thursday, 15 August 1935   Paris

Today completed the revision of that portion (ending with the Ascot school chapter) of the French translation of my memoirs which has been submitted to me. The translator (Blaise Briod), an official of the *Coopération Intellectuelle*, has utterly failed to appreciate either their literary form or what is to be read between the lines. His rendering of my work is as though he had been dealing with a League of Nations statement or legal treatise. Its relationship to the original is like that of a colour print to a painting. I have had to redraft nearly every sentence, shaping it afresh, adapting it to the exigencies of the French language, and breathing fresh life into it, so that the French 'translation' stands alongside the German like an original piece of writing. And the labour involved! In six weeks I have nearly worked myself to death. I have now got it right and I hope that it will convey something of what I wanted to say. But how may things stand in regard to French (or German) translations of Tolstoy, Dostoevsky or Pushkin? What and how much may have been ignored there? Probably the decisive factor – the tone.

Thursday, 22 August 1935   London

The outcome of today's Cabinet meeting, dealing with the Italo–Abyssinian conflict, is awaited with intense excitement.

Visited Brüning at the home of a Mrs Mona Anderson who inhabits one floor, charmingly adapted on something like Pre-Raphaelite lines, of a palatial apartment house in Portman Square. Brüning described this as his permanent address. Tomorrow he leaves for two months for America. I brought the conversation around to the subject of the most difficult problem after the downfall of the Nazis, the regeneration of German youth. For with the Nazis will disappear the only faith they possess and their spiritual carpet will be torn from under their feet.

This is a view which he entirely shares, Brüning replied, but which is completely unfamiliar to the military men. They fancy that with the dropping of certain impossible individuals like Göring, Goebbels, Streicher, and so on, the job will be done. They think of Hitler in terms of a 'regent', a sort of honorary chairman, whom it will be possible to retain in that capacity. Their plans go no farther. Such a solution is not however feasible. For his part, he is certainly not going to sit in a Cabinet with a murderer like Hitler. The toleration extended by the Reichswehr to the numerous murders committed, in particular those of 30 June, is a unique occurrence in the Prussian Army which so far has always strictly insisted on its own code of honour. This contravention of its own internal morality is bound to have a detrimental effect on the Reichswehr. The junior officers laugh at Hitler and hold him in contempt, but are themselves sceptics and opportunists.

The same holds good for many sections of German youth and those in opposition to the Nazis. Having tried everything, without anything proving durable and worth while, they believe in nothing any more. Opposition to the Nazis derives in great part from the fact that the various forms of service demanded complicate and prolong the time required to complete studies essential to earning a living. He doubts very much whether the Catholic Church will have the strength morally to regenerate its youthful members. Scepticism against everybody and everything has gained ground in much the same way as in the years of the Roman Empire before Diocletian. The similarity between conditions prevailing then and now is startling. The degree to which moral values have gone off the rails amongst youngsters in the labour camps is shocking. The cases of fifteen- and sixteen-year-old girls becoming pregnant there run into hundreds and thousands. Young people are being perverted downright systematically. How is youth in those circumstances to be regenerated? It is crumbling away inside and it finds no support anywhere. Neither theories nor sermons can in this instance be of help. Only great personalities will be able to effect any transformation and to call forth a new idealism, personalities who will inspire the conviction that they are ready to stake their lives for their ideals. The two Churches have become too much of a bureaucracy and the parson is now simply an official with an adequate income, pension, and other amenities. This is not the stuff to produce conviction. Possibly persecution, reducing many parsons to extreme poverty and need, will bring a reawakening, but meanwhile neo-heathen notions are making progress not only in Germany, but in Britain and Holland too. Lord Redesdale's daughter has come back from Germany entranced by these ideas. She attended the midsummer's night festival at Göring's place and participated in the rites the whole night through.

1936

Monday, 6 July 1936   *Pontanevaux*

Today I have sold my beloved Weimar house. How many memories and how much of my life vanish with it.

Sunday, 19 July 1936   *Pontanevaux*

News of a military rising in Spain under the leadership of Generals Franco and Godet.

Friday, 30 October 1936   *Paris*

Lunched at Mme van Rysselberghe with André Gide and Jean Schlumberger. Gide seems to have returned deeply disappointed from Russia. He is aghast at the Trial of the Sixteen. Freedom of intellect seems to him to be undergoing an even more horrible suppression in Russia than in Germany; he found its harassment intolerable. He fears the likelihood of a second trial which will be conducted as disgracefully as the initial one and involve Radek, Bukharin, and their confrères. The Trial of the Sixteen[1] has severely shaken Stalin's prestige among the Russian masses and, to refurbish his popularity, he will at all costs support the Spanish Government with arms and technical specialists. Nothing will deter him. '*Il ira jusqu'au bout.*' The best Soviet pilots are already in Spain.

Soviet aviation is in Gide's view far superior to anything Germany can offer. German fighter machines fly at two hundred kilometres per hour, Russian 'planes at four hundred. The offensive begun the day before yesterday by the Madrid forces against the rebels appears to rely already on Russian supplies and Russian fighter 'planes. What, I asked, will happen if a Russian ship is torpedoed in the Mediterranean? War, replied Gide. I do not believe that France will in that case hurry to Russia's support, I commented, because it will prove impossible to mobilize in France for that purpose. What then? Civil War in France, said Gide. He clearly thinks that both will happen.

I asked him when he is to publish his impressions of his Russian trip. Within a very few days, he answered, regardless of the fact that many of his friends advise him not to do so and are trying to influence him not to bring the book out at all. (Evidently his Communist friends, who are aware that his book will be unfavourable to Stalinist Russia.) Gide mentioned, as a symptom of how far bourgeois reaction has progressed in Russia, that Church bells are again being cast in the foundries. A completely hierarchic order of society is in process of evolution, with a new aristocracy, a new middle class, and so on down the ladder. This imposes increased intransigence on Stalin in the Spanish affair in order to throw a sop to the masses. This Spanish business is genuine Trotskyism (world revolution).

Sunday, 1 November 1936   *Paris*

At lunch-time to Marly to visit Maillol. I was pleased to see him again and the whole family, assembled in the kitchen, seemed very pleased to see me. He showed me the big statue (much larger than life-size) which he has been officially commissioned to do for the World Exhibition. It is a variation in theme on my *Crouching Woman*, very powerful and in the best sense monumental. His name for it is *La Montagne*. I also saw the figure of a *Woman Standing*, which is intended for an open-air site in Paris (probably the courtyard of the Louvre) as well as other works I did not know. A *Pomona* in marble, and a group of three young girls, life-size, holding hands and blending into a sort of round dance, which he calls '*les Nymphes de la prairie fleurie*'.

Spanish events excite him deeply. His sympathies seem to lie wholly with the rebels. He grumbles about the Blum Government, '*un gouvernement idiot*', but admits that he knows nothing about politics and only exceptionally (now, for example, on account of Spain) scans newspapers. He has read my book and appears particularly impressed by the first part ('*Mémé*'). He was delighted with the pages about Sarah Bernhardt because he fully shares Mama's devastating opinion of her. His house, the garden and the studio put me in a pretty sadly reminiscent frame of mind.

Thursday, 5 November 1936   *Paris*

Maillol lunched with me at Marius. Afterwards I accompanied him to the Luxembourg to see the statue which has been recently set up there. He complained about his wife. She is in a constant bad temper and creates scenes with him all the time about absolutely nothing. This has gone on now for nearly forty years.

His statue in the Luxembourg stands proud as a queen amidst a collection of insignificant, pretentious, and ugly figures. Most of the pictures too, especially the 'fresh acquisitions', are improbably poor. Only the two Toulouse-Lautrec paintings, done for la Goulue, loom overwhelmingly above the rest on the score of their grandiose composition, monumentality, and humour. Maillol stood in front of them for a very long time and appeared unable to see his fill of them.

Wednesday, 11 November 1936   *Paris*

In the afternoon to the Julien Cains in the National Library: *Porte six à huit*. Cains said very pleasant things to me about my book. Berenson, whom I had not seen for more than twenty years, has also read it. Oddly enough, he asked me why I did not write it in French. Because I am German, I retorted, and German is my language. He has changed but little, remains cutting and witty, and says that his villa in Florence is strictly watched by the Fascists. They have thrown a sort of *cordon sanitaire* around him, warning his American compatriots against him and suggesting that he is old and imbecile.

Friday, 13 November 1936   *Paris*

Visited Cocteau, who was run down a few days ago. He lay in bed with several days' growth of beard. We talked about his voyage round the world. The ideal place to stay, he claimed, is Pekin. It is possible to live there in an old palace for nothing; five hundred francs a month makes a man a bigwig. But, for all that he is anything but a nationalist or chauvinist, he finds it impossible to feel really happy anywhere else than in France. Is it not equally my experience with regard to Germany? I told him that he is right. and I am indeed beginning to feel mighty homesick.

Friday, 11 December 1936   *Pontanevaux*

At ten o'clock this evening I listened on the BBC to Edward VIII's farewell speech to his peoples and his homeland. He spoke for barely five minutes, but the simplicity, dignity, and genuine humanity of the statement were profoundly moving, like a speech from one of Shakespeare's royal dramas.

Tuesday, 15 December 1936   *Pontanevaux*

To the Spanish Consulate in Lyon to obtain a visa for Palma. The secretary told me that, according to latest instructions, visas may no longer be issued to Germans and Italians. But I should not worry and sail for Palma. As it is in rebel hands,[2] things will be just the other way around there and nobody will refuse me, as a German, permission to land.

Wednesday, 23 December 1936   *Pontanevaux*

In the evening George Heywood and his wife arrived unexpectedly, on their way through Cap Ferrat, and had dinner with me. He is now brigade commander at Aldershot. Inevitably talk turned to the Abdication. What worries him most, said Heywood, is that this enforced abdication has undoubtedly done severe harm to the monarchic concept in Britain. If a Prime Minister can compel a king to abdicate without his having done anything unconstitutional, then a republic with a president may possibly be preferable.

Thursday, 31 December 1936   *Pontanevaux*

In the evening listened on the radio with Wilma to the New Year's Eve celebrations in Berlin. To be abroad and hear at midnight, Berlin time, the ringing of the church bells was a very moving experience. At midnight, French time, the bells of Paris answered. At the same moment Biederle, who had been sleeping in front of the fire jumped on my lap as though to present me with his New Year wishes.

1936 has been a cheerless, unhappy year full of worry. The prospects for 1937, contrary to Léon Blum's optimistic broadcast in a slightly quavering, indistinct voice, are not rosy.

1937

Sunday, 10 January 1937   *Paris*

At nine o'clock in the morning an outbreak of nose-bleeding which gradually developed into such a haemorrhage that I almost choked in my own blood. The doctor came and slowly the bleeding stopped. I had to lie completely still on my back all day.

Monday, 11 January 1937   *Paris*

This afternoon Cocteau and Picasso suddenly entered my room and were just as suddenly gone again. Afterwards Cocteau apologized for having mixed up the rooms. He also remonstrated with me for not having him called yesterday.

Wednesday, 13 January 1937   *Paris*

In the afternoon visited Misia Sert. She suggested giving me an introduction to Quiñones de Leon so that he can facilitate my journey to Mallorca and the forwarding of my papers from Palma. He seems to be the semi-official representative in Paris of the rebel Government at Burgos. She also said some extremely pleasing things about my book. She has remained as young and charming as twenty years ago. In her opinion I must, in the second volume, definitely mention and rebut the slanders spread about me here at the beginning of the war. She regards it as essential. Why, I objected, bring up these old, distressing matters again? But she insisted.

About Sert's second wife, *née* Mdivani, who became half crazed as a result of her brother's death, Misia said that in her madness she refused for a long time to meet face to face with Misia, but would frequently ring her up in the middle of the night because she felt Misia to be the one person who could help her. Oddly enough, Misia added that this woman, who supplanted her, is the one person in the world whom she really loves, loves above everything. She and I are '*pour ainsi dire la même personne*'. That is, subjectively, probably profoundly true and helps Misia emotionally to bridge the false situation.

Thursday, 14 January 1937   *Paris*

The guests at Misia Sert's big luncheon-party included Marcel Achard, 'young' Porel (son of Réjane), and a number of people I had not met before. One of them, Anatole Mühlstein, son-in-law of Robert de Rothschild and a Minister in the Polish diplomatic service, is writing a book about Pilsudski, whom he declared to be 'greater than Napoleon'. He said that he has always wished to make my acquaintance, to write to me or ask for a discussion between us, so as to learn certain details about Pilsudski's liberation and the explanation for certain points that have always remained a mystery to him. He wanted to know, among other things, whether Pilsudski gave me a signed declaration that he would not undertake any action hostile to Germany. I confirmed that Pilsudski's word of honour was the sole declaration I received from him because I told General Hoffmann that I refused to request the assurance in writing. As early as 1915 Pilsudski assured me that he did not desire an inch of German territory although he would be unable to reject an Allied offer of, for instance, West Prussia. That, exclaimed Mühlstein, throws light for him on Pilsudski's behaviour at the peace negotiations. He has always been puzzled why Pilsudski should have briskly declined to participate in the debates about Poland's western border, leaving Dmowski to handle these, while he confined his attentions to points concerning the eastern border. He obviously felt that his word of honour to me, about not demanding an inch of German soil, precluded him from taking part in the annexation negotiations and he stayed away from them.

Mühlstein added (and repeated several times) that Filippovicz, the Deputy Minister of Foreign Affairs who served on me the demand to leave Warsaw, was '*un fou*' and acted without instructions.

Friday, 15 January 1937   *Paris*

Visited Maillol at Marly in the studio put at his disposal by van Dongen's brother and, although it was nearly dark, found him hard at work on his big statue for the World Exhibition.

He cannot disengage himself from the statue. For months now he has been toiling away in order to bring the masses into ever more harmonious and convincing proportions to one another. He proceeds from minor correction to minor correction, slowly feeling his way, until he has at last achieved complete consonance of form. The patience and diligence he displays is infinite. Not that this stops him from reviling his *metteur au point* as an '*imbécile*' who has failed to set the masses right through not heeding the precise details of the clay model. For the past thirty years he has abused each of his *metteurs au point* for letting him down and causing superfluous labour. In fact it is this continual elaboration of his figures which gives him greatest pleasure.

Arriving at his house, we found the doors locked because Mme Maillol had taken the keys with her. Had not by chance his studio been open, he would have had to wait in the dark, damp and cold. The way that Maillol is neglected and ill-treated by his wife is strangely analogous to the story, for which Maillol quotes Judith Cladel as his authority, of Rodin dying of cold in his house at Meudon because the city of Paris refused to repair his central heating.

To tea at Annette Kolb's and met there Dumaine, head of the British Department at the Quai d'Orsay. I induced him to talk about the panic caused on Sunday by the false reports, on the radio and elsewhere, of German troop landings at Melila. The Quai d'Orsay, he explained, did not have any news of German troop landings, but it did possess information that far-reaching preparations for such landings existed. From this information about preparations there germinated, by a sort of '*génération spontanée*', the reports of landings having actually occurred. It may however have proved '*un mal pour un bien*'. The false news occasioned Hitler's statement to Poncet and in any case frustrated, if it ever existed, a plan whose implementation would have brought a danger of war with it.

Saturday, 16 January 1937   *Paris*

At lunch-time ran into Gordon Craig in the Café de la Paix. He is quite white-haired now and this white mane is well suited to his fine, impressive features. He sat down at my table and told me that he has recently not only been to Moscow but also had twenty minutes' private talk with Mussolini. He was astounded by the doltishness and vacuity of the latter's facial expression: 'Quite the Italian waiter! "What can I do for you, Sir?" ' In Moscow he visited the Jewish State Theatre and thought the company and production the best that he has ever seen. The performance of *King Lear* is exalted and shattering. One day he would like to bring it to Europe.

Monday, 18 January 1937   *Paris*

Went to the Hotel Maurice to see Count Molina, secretary to the former ambassador Quiñones de Leon who now semi-officially represents the Burgos Government here and to whom Misia Sert spoke on my behalf. In default of a visa, I wanted a letter of recommendation from him to the authorities in Mallorca. But I never caught a glimpse of him. Molina expounded to me that Quiñones is in no position to issue an official document and knows nobody in Mallorca to whom he could write.

I noticed that Molina was in a state of considerable irascibility. '*Nous vivons ici en pays ennemi, car vous vous rendez bien compte que la France est pour nous un pays ennemi!*' He asked whether I am a Frenchman. When I said no, a German, he became friendlier. '*Alors c'est différent, si vous êtes*

Allemand. Nous faisons tout ce que nous pouvons pour les Allemands. Ils nous aident, alors nous les aidons, c'est juste.' All the same, he would be unable to give me any sort of document from Quiñones. I should set out for Mallorca and not worry. As a German, nobody will refuse me permission to land.

Tuesday, 19 January 1937   Paris

Invited Gordon Craig for lunch to the Café de la Paix. He told me about Moscow. The Russians regard themselves as the happiest and best-off people in the world whereas all other peoples exist in complete indigence and slavery. The manager of the Hotel Metropol in Moscow asked him whether his hotel is not the best that can be found anywhere. Whereupon Craig replied, 'No, Sir! It is the very worst I have ever been in!' There was neither salt nor pepper to be had in its restaurant unless 'you clamoured for it'. Some spy or other dogged his every step. An intellectual whom he knew from the olden days is living with his family, five souls in all, in a single room. Meyerhold on the other hand inhabits a luxurious villa, but when he appears on the stage always wears a shabby old overcoat.

Thursday, 21 January 1937   Paris

Lost the whole day through difficulties at the Préfecture de Police over my visa. The Préfecture refused to give me one without production of the *carte d'identité* which I do not have in my possession, but which a letter from the Quai d'Orsay informed the Préfecture is lying for me in the prefecture of Mende in Lozère. The Quai d'Orsay emphatically demanded that the Préfecture should nonetheless provide me with the visa. Especially Comert and his secretary de Nerciat rallied to my support. De Nerciat is Lozèrien, or half Lozèrien, his mother being a Morangiès, and out of a sort of local patriotism was especially staunch in his assistance. After a great deal of to and fro and journeyings between the Quai d'Orsay and the Préfecture, the tenacity of the Quai d'Orsay finally won the day and I was promised the visa for tomorrow.

Friday, 22 January 1937   Paris

In the afternoon to the Préfecture and at last obtained my visa. In the evening with Jacques to Hugo Simon, where we met Schickele, whom I had not seen for years, his wife, Marchese Farinolla and his (second) wife, Annette Kolb, and Hans Siemsen. The latter caused an unpleasant incident by saying to Marchesa Farinolla, 'Mussolini can kiss my arse.' Farinolla, sitting beside his wife, stood up in protest and left the room. Schickele gazed at Siemsen wide-eyed as if at a lunatic. Finally Siemsen departed, and then telephoned an apology. Both the Farinollas were furious and made no bones about it. My projected Palma trip met with protests on the part of all present. Farinolla implored me not to go.

Saturday, 20 February 1937   *Zurich*

Lunched with the Brentanos at Küssnacht. A small country house, in a small garden and with small rooms, but furnished in a simple, modern style and with a cosy library and a large, comfortable writing-table. After moving so long among impersonal hotel rooms it gave me a strange feeling to find myself once more in a proper, well-furnished study. Two plump, fair-haired boys, three and a half years and eighteen months old respectively, completed the picture of happy, solid domesticity.

Afterwards I visited Thomas Mann, living only a few hundred yards farther on in a handsome villa. Very large and light study with a fine view of the lake. He talked about my memoirs, which greatly appealed to him and from which he quoted certain passages. Then he spoke about Hofmannsthal. To his mind *Der Rosenkavalier* will prove immortal, a completely successful work, like *Figaro*, the *Barber*, and *Carmen*. I told him of my share in the scenario.

Later Frau Mann arrived and the conversation rather levelled off. Mann told me that he is working on a major Goethe theme, a visit by the sixty-year-old Lotte Buff to Goethe in Weimar. Once, in earlier years, he wanted to use Goethe as a character in a piece of fiction, but then lacked the courage to attempt the venture. Instead he wrote his *Death in Venice*, transforming the Goethe–Marianne von Willemer situation into that of an author (a figure based more or less on himself) in love with a boy.

Wednesday, 10 March 1937   *Paris*

Woke up with a temperature. Remained in bed.

Saturday, 13 March 1937   *Paris*

Taken to a nursing home. I have incipient pneumonia and an intestinal haemorrhage.

Tuesday, 13 April 1937   *Paris*

After repeated blood transfusions and constantly recurrent intestinal haemorrhages, I have been operated on. I suffered a great deal because, for fear of heart complications, I could not be properly anaesthetized.

Tuesday, 25 May 1937   *Paris*

At last, after two and a half months, left the nursing home.

Mussolini and Hitler. An unholy alliance

Monday, 31 May 1937   *Paris*

Yesterday Spanish Government aircraft bombarded the *Deutschland* in the harbour of Ibiza, killing twenty-three of the crew and wounding eighty others. An extremely serious incident which warrants the utmost anxiety. German warships have bombarded Almeria in reprisal and have flung a few score dead into the balance against the unfortunate German lads. Let us hope that Hitler's prestige requirement is thereby satiated.

Monday, 21 June 1937   *Pontanevaux*

The *Leipzig* is alleged to have been attacked by a Spanish Government submarine, though no damage was done and nobody saw any torpedoes.

Germany is demanding common measures by the four Control Powers against the Spanish Government.

Thursday, 24 June 1937   *Pontanevaux*

France and Britain have rejected Germany's demand. Hereupon Germany has declared that it will no longer participate in the watch on the Spanish coasts, but will strengthen its naval forces in the Mediterranean. Italy is cementing its front with Germany.

Saturday, 11 September 1937   *Fournels*

This morning it snowed for a quarter of an hour. The weather is distinctly cold. This evening Jacques returned to Paris. Saw him off to the station at Saint Chély. On the way he did his best to dissuade me from going to Mallorca. It is mainly in the hands of the Germans, meaning Nazis, and I might just as well travel to Berlin, he argued. At Paris he has been in touch with Bernanos, who was in Mallorca until a short while ago. Although he is a Franco supporter, he could not stand it any longer and through Jacques urgently advises me not to go there unless I am on good terms with the Nazi Government. Conditions are dreadful, and so on.

Thursday, 30 September 1937   *Fournels*

With Christian to Marvejols to have my heart X-rayed. A pleasant young doctor, Dr de Fleury, has at his disposal in the municipal *dispensaire* an apparatus which has been donated with American money by the Marquise de Chambrun, the wife of the senator, who is American by birth. The little town, old-fashioned and picturesque, is reminiscent in style and atmosphere of Weimar, but is of a much more southern character.

Notes

1918

1. Jozef Pilsudski, a Polish-Lithuanian noble, Polish nationalist leader. Aged forty-seven in 1914, with a stormy career of conspiracy behind him, Pilsudski recruited a small Polish force with the aid of the Austrian authorities to fight the Russians, his hatred of whom dominated his career. When the Polish-populated areas were cleared of Russian occupation in 1916, the German High Command announced their future intention of establishing a limited Polish State in order to secure the loyalty of the Poles, who had become numerous enough to be called a Legion. Pilsudski quarrelled, however, with the Austro-Germans during the collapse of the Russian armies in 1917, and was interned in the fortress of Magdeburg, where he was treated honourably by the Germans in case they needed him again. This moment came at the armistice when Count Kessler, who had met Pilsudski at the Front during the war, was set to free him, return him to Poland, and engage him not to turn on the Germans. The written undertaking required by the two generals, Groener and Hoffmann (respectively Quartermaster General of the Imperial General Staff and Chief of Staff to Army Group East), was disliked by Kessler who feared that Pilsudski would be offended by a demand for a formal undertaking; it was finally dropped in favour of a personal promise by Pilsudski, as we read much later in the Diaries.
2. Friedrich Ebert (1871–1925) was elected to the Reichstag in 1912, became the Chairman of the SPD and was elected President of Germany in 1919, until his death in 1925. He was moderate and dignified, an anti-revolutionary who was not even sure whether he wanted a Republic until after it was declared.
3. Phillip Scheidemann (1865–1939), an SPD deputy, who announced the Republic from a window of the Reichstag to the crowds outside on 9 November 1918, when Ebert was only thinking of the abdication of the Emperor, not of getting rid of the Hohenzollern altogether. Ebert is said to have been very angry, fearing a Bolshevik revolution if the Socialists moved too fast.
4. No 'Imperial coronation' ever took place. What Kessler has in mind is the acclamation of William I, King of Prussia, as 'German Emperor' in the Hall of Mirrors at the Palace of Versailles on 18 January 1871.
5. Adolf Joffe, or Yoffe, a member of the Brest-Litovsk peace delegation, went to Berlin as Soviet Ambassador after the peace with Germany. He was a member of the delegation to Genoa in 1922, which, incidentally, travelled via Berlin. Later he went to China, again as negotiator. He committed suicide in 1927, after Trotsky was formally expelled from the CPUSSR.
6. Karl Liebknecht (1871–1919), leader of the radical left wing of the Socialist movement, was a lawyer then in his forties, the son of a friend of Karl Marx, Wilhelm Liebknecht. He was an excitable, unstable but gifted demagogue

who could always arouse the masses with his fiery speeches. He spent eighteen months in prison for an anti-militarist pamphlet written in 1907 and after his release was idolized by the pacifist left wing. Elected to the Reichstag in 1912, he did vote for the war credits of 1914, but shortly afterwards reverted to un-compromising pacifism. During the revolutionary period of 1918–19 he advocated immediate Bolshevik revolution against the advice of, among others, such radical leaders as Rosa Luxemburg (1875–1919), who shared his fate of being assassinated by right-wing fanatics. There was little doubt that the fear and hatred he aroused in all but a tiny section of the Berlin population was the cause of the double murder of the two leaders.

7. Prince Max of Baden (1867–1929), the last appointee of the Kaiser.

8. Magdeburg was a tenth-century fortress. The citadel was only once stormed, by Tilly in the Thirty Years' War (1631) and was the bishopric from which a Christianization mission went to what later became Poland, so that it was thought an appropriate place of honourable confinement for Pilsudski. By 1918 it was a largish industrial town; it is now in East Germany.

9. Paul Cassirer (1871–1926) was a well known Berlin art dealer and publisher, an enthusiast for modern art.

10. Hugo Haase, the chairman in the Reichstag of the SPD, was the leader of the Independent Socialists who left the SPD (Majority Socialists) in 1916 for pacifist reasons. Karl Kautsky and Eduard Bernstein, the two intellectual theorists of the Party, joined him. So did Liebknecht, but he was jailed for protesting against the war publicly at meetings.

11. Friedrichstrasse was a popular amusement area.

12. Karl Friedrich Schinkel (1781–1841), architect, town planner, had great in-fluence over Berlin architecture during his lifetime. Kessler writes here of the Imperial Palace which was completely demolished during the 1950s.

13. The Constituent Assembly was elected on 19 January 1919, women voting for the first time. As this entry makes clear, it was already planned in the previous November. Its purposes were: to form an elected government to replace the caretaker government formed from the largest parties in the Reichstag and partially formed and supported by the Soldiers' and Workers' Councils; to negotiate (as the Germans still believed) and sign a peace treaty to end the war; and to write and pass into law a Republican Constitution. The Assembly met in the State theatre at Weimar in February 1918 and its meeting place became the name of the Weimar Constitution. Weimar was chosen partly for these cultural reasons and partly because it was com-paratively easy to defend against rioters; it was also outside the area of Prussian tradition.

14. In the German language the word *Bürgerlich* means middle class as well as the quality of citizenship, and has a third meaning in civil law as being data officially registered about any person. Thus, '*bürgerliche Name*' means lawful name. Context has therefore an important meaning for the word and the editors have throughout used the word 'bourgeois' to mean 'of the property-owning middle classes' to distinguish its meaning from 'citizens'.

15. The first mention of a noble family provides an occasion for a general note on names and titles. Courtesy titles in most European aristocracies consist of the repetition of the family title, such as Count or Countess. Thus if Harry

Kessler, who inherited his father's title, had had a younger brother, he also would have been Count Kessler. To distinguish members of the families the Christian name is usually added, as in this reference. Kessler assumes that anyone will understand his reference to the princely Hohenlohe family and only needs to say which member of it he means. Where a noble family possessed a *ruling* function, the actual ruler and head of the family was distinguished by a separate title.

16. Two diplomats stationed in Warsaw as part of the war-time civil administration, the High Commission. Its chief, Beseler, had already left.

17. The republican colours, as distinct from the Hohenzollern and Prussian colours of black-white-red. These latter were re-adopted when the National Socialists came to power and the republican black-red-gold was once again assumed when the two German republics were formed in 1949.

18. The Bolshevik left wing immediately after the German revolution took its name from the leader of the slave revolt in ancient Rome. It became the Communist Party of Germany on 1 January 1919, this name gradually superseding the original one after the murders of Liebknecht and Luxemburg when the Revolutionary Shop Stewards and the Executive Council of the Workers' and Soldiers' Councils were without effective leadership.

19. This was one of the Armistice conditions, but it only later became clear to either side that any effective Allied intervention was out of the question.

20. The Fourteen Points frequently referred to were expounded by President Wilson in a speech on 9 January 1918 about the Russo–German Peace Treaty of Brest-Litovsk. In Point 13 Wilson advocated the establishment of an independent Polish state with guaranteed access to the sea.

   The conditions for peace were announced as applying to both parties in the conflict. It was the acceptance of them by the Germans which led directly to the Armistice. They were enumerated without prior consultation with Britain, France or the other Allies and differed at important points not only with established international laws and customs, but with various secret treaties made between allies during the war.

21. This is a veiled reference not only to Pilsudski's anti-Jewish views, but also to the fact that for historical reasons almost all leading Russians, Polish and German Bolsheviks at that time were of Jewish origin.

22. Rawicki was a Socialist lawyer with good connections with the Polish Socialists, attached to Kessler by the German cabinet. Dr Hans Meyer, a diplomat, and Rittmeister (cavalry captain) Gülpen, who knew Sosnkowski, were chosen personally by Kessler as friends he could rely on in difficult situations. Strahl and Fürstner were professional diplomats.

23. In Polish, Lwow, capital of Austrian Poland. The name is left as Lemberg since no German speaker would refer to it as Lwow. A good example of the recurring Polish imbroglio; they took it from the Ukraine when they possessed a large empire and it was ever after coveted by the Russians.

24. To understand these frequent hints by Polish officials it is necessary to recall that there was a rival, Entente-backed Polish 'government' still in Paris; and, too, that in such chaotic situations rumours and conspiracies always flourish.

25. After the Battle of Tannenberg the Germans rolled the Russians back across Russian Poland and remained in occupation of this north-eastern part of

Poland for the rest of the war. This event was the beginning of misgivings in Russia about the capacity of the government and the High Command and was also the foundation of the military reputations of (later) Field-Marshal Hindenburg and his Chief of Staff Ludendorff.

26. Poznan in Polish. Like most towns in what is now Western Poland it was German-built and settled for hundreds of years, trade and industry being entirely German; but as industry and population increased, large numbers of Poles drifted to the towns here, as elsewhere, to work, and the balance of population began to tend towards the Poles in the late nineteenth century. They thus claimed it as a Polish town.

27. The date is mistaken; so was the then widespread assumption in both countries and through all parties that the German rump of Austria-Hungary would be joined with Germany. This *Anschluss* was achieved by force in 1938 when the Austrians no longer universally agreed about it, and lasted until 1945, when the second Austrian Republic was established.

28. The point of all these Polish–German negotiations, the strategic facts having been decided by the victorious Allies, was the immense equipment of the German armies and their administrative installations. These were desperately needed by the Poles, who had plenty of men but no equipment, transport, communications, etc. The eastern, Russian, part of Poland, besides being naturally very poor, had always been kept in a quasi-desert state by Russian policy for political reasons.

29. The German ambassador to the Communist government in Russia after the peace of Brest-Litovsk, who was assassinated on 6 July 1918.

30. *BZ (Berliner Zeitung)* and *Voss (Vossische Zeitung)* were the familiar abbreviations of two Berlin newspapers.

31. Not a member of the noble family, but one of the ringleaders of the original naval mutiny.

32. *Vorwärts* ('Forward'), the newspaper of the Socialist Party, in the control of the majority, or Government, faction.

33. This is certainly an exaggeration but not so ridiculous as it looks at first sight; the old city of Berlin, built in the seventeenth and eighteenth centuries, was a very handsome town, well proportioned and sparely elegant. It is now, of course, in East Berlin. Hardly any of its buildings have survived the last war and subsequent re-building.

34. Gustav Noske (1868–1946), a Socialist, first defence minister of the Republic, organized the defence of Berlin against the Spartacist uprisings, but left politics in 1920 after the Kapp putsch fiasco.

1919

1. Reference is to the efforts of the government to remove the Spartacist sympathizer, Police Chief Emil Eichhorn, from his office. This was the first Spartacus uprising in Berlin and, in spite of its lack of organization, it resulted in considerable fighting before the hasty measures of Noske to collect various bodies of troops still not demobilized could restore the precarious authority of the caretaker government.

2. The revolutionaries took to the roof-tops, from which they could see a clear line of fire. Berlin being mainly a nineteenth-century city, it lacks the warrens of cellar-passages and alleys which are so useful to rioters in very old towns. It was not easy to hide in the wide streets, and in any case it is a confirmed German custom to lock doors, even inside houses.

3. Considering that the contemporary Berlin newspapers showed a startling variety of reports, and that the truth was not established for some months, this version is almost correct. Rosa Luxemburg's body was not recovered until 31 May and this disappearance gave rise to rumours, some of which persisted until recent years. However, the course of events has in fact been clear since 1919. The two conspirators were detected in their hiding place by a patrol and taken to its Command Post in the Eden Hotel for interrogation, where one by one they were clubbed over the head while going out through the door to transport which was to deliver them to gaol. Liebknecht was shot in the Tiergarten part and a second car, carrying Luxemburg, stopped near the Liechtenstein Bridge over the Landwehr canal, and her body, dead or alive, was thrown in the water.

4. This is a reference to the tardy attempt late in 1917 to put through the reform of the Prussian voting system, up to then based on property ownership, to conform with the universal suffrage of the Reich. The reactionaries in the Reichstag blocked this reform, which had been promised as earnest of future democratization. The importance of the Prussian suffrage was that, while all sections of the Reich had considerable local autonomy, Prussia was the largest and, as it were, the central kingdom of the Empire. It supplied the main part of government and high administrations and the senior army officers, the King–Emperor being Prussian.

5. George Grosz (1893–1961), the famous caricaturist. He was the object, then and later, of particular hatred by the reactionaries because he made them ridiculous. He went into exile in the United States after Hitler came to power.

6. Alfred and Helene Wallwitz Nostitz were lifelong friends of Kessler. He was a Minister of the King of Saxony, she was connected with the Hindenburg family, among others, and with Russo-Germans. They were posted as diplomats in Vienna during the war, and knew Hofmannsthal well.

7. This is a contemporary misunderstanding. In fact, this was precisely what Luxemburg *did* understand, and she had opposed immediate attempts at revolution.

8. Gisbert von Romberg, wartime German Minister in Berne. Kessler served in the Legation there during the negotiations between the Germans and Lenin.

9. Rudolf Nadolny, a diplomat, involved in the wartime intrigues with the Russian Bolsheviks. He was Ambassador to Moscow 1933–4.

10. Karl Radek (1885–?) was a Polish-Jewish socialist, once a close friend of Rosa Luxemburg's until he quarrelled with her. He was sent to Berlin to encourage the revolutionaries by the Russian Bolsheviks who then believed that they could only establish Marxism with the help of Germany. This project earned him the renewed hatred of Luxemburg and they had a violent dispute. Radek tried hard to influence the Revolutionary Shop Stewards

and the Councils' Executive Committee towards armed rebellion, and an alliance with Bolshevik Russia. After the collapse of the Spartacus revolt, which he opposed as premature, and Luxemburg's murder, Radek went into hiding. He was gaoled for a short time in Berlin, and last reported seen in 1939 in a Soviet labour camp.

11. Richard von Kühlmann was State Secretary (senior civil servant) at the Foreign Ministry from August 1917 to July 1918, and therefore responsible for the period immediately leading up to the defeat of Germany as far as diplomacy had any real responsibility at that time. Power, in reality, then resided with the General Staff.

12. Walther Rathenau (1867–1922) was a founder member of the Democratic Party, like Kessler, and for a short time Foreign Minister. He was assassinated in Berlin on 24 June 1922. Kessler wrote a biography of him which is a standard work in German. The son of Emil Rathenau, who bought the patent rights of the great American technician Edison for Europe, and developed mass production of such items as the electric light bulb, which revolutionized domestic and commercial life. His factories later became the huge AEG concern, which dominated the European electricity market.

13. Kurt Eisner, the leader of the Bavarian Communist government from November 1918 until his assassination in 1919, published excerpts from secret Bavarian government papers which suggested that the Prussian government was entirely responsible for the war. These were said, then and later, to be inventions. In fact they were genuine, but carefully edited and rearranged, quotations.

14. Gustav Stresemann (1878–1929), leader of the People's Party, conservative but not extremist. His political life went well back into the pre-war period. From 1923 until his death he was Foreign Minister and one of the few first-class political talents produced by Germany between the wars.

15. Ulrich, Count Brockdorff-Rantzau (1869–1928), former German ambassador to Copenhagen, was the leader of the German delegation to the Versailles Peace Conference, and therefore an important person to Kessler's hopes of a pacifist League of Nations. Rantzau was a controversial personality but certainly an accomplished diplomat and a sincere patriot; he said on his death bed that his experiences at Versailles, where he was personally humiliated in a quite uncivilized fashion, broke his heart. He came of a very old land-owning family.

16. Elisabeth Foerster-Nietzsche, the sister of the philosopher and administrator of his property. Foerster was her former husband's name. Before his death they lived in Paraguay.

17. Hugo Preuss (1860–1925), was Interior Minister in the caretaker government. A professor of political science and an authority on constitutional law, he composed the Weimar Constitution.

18. A card game, rather like bridge, much played in Germany.

19. Which Kessler founded.

20. Matthias Erzberger (1875–1921), a leading figure in the Centre Party, who 'knew everybody' and had good connections with the Pope and his Nuncio in Bavaria, Pacelli (later Pope Pius XII), and who had travelled to most of the fronts. He made a speech on 19 July 1917 to the Reichstag Naval Com-

mittee demanding a negotiated peace and backed the demand with much evidence. In spite of the Emperor's and Government's refusal, an inter-party committee was set up to examine the chances of ending the war with the aid of the Pope who had been working hard for some time in this direction (the Austrian Emperor was separately and privately in touch with the Pope as well). This was the first occasion on which the Reichstag defied the Emperor's government and therefore a turning-point in parliamentary history in Germany. To prove that Erzberger had advocated the annexation of this mining district *after* this speech would therefore demonstrate his disingenuity. He was murdered by right-wing extremists for his anti-war record.

21. Johannes R. Becher. Although he was careful at this time not to take sides clearly, he was at any rate later a Communist, and after the Second World War became prominent in the cultural life of the GDR.

22. It was already known that the proposed new Constitution was to abolish the Soldiers' and Workers' Councils; that is, that the Republic was to be a parliamentary and not a Soviet dictatorship of the proletariat.

23. Rantzau, Foreign Minister of the caretaker government, was discussing the need to persuade the left-wing Independents to return to the government. Without them, the militant working class was outside the government and therefore irresponsible, while the existence of the Councils, just abolished, offered the possibility of organized resistance to the government. This could lead to a counter-government and thus to civil war, which is what had happened in the autumn of 1917 in Russia.

24. The Austrians and the Rhinelanders are almost entirely Catholic, and to shut their party out of the coalition would make all Catholics apprehensive of North German Protestant domination. The French were known to be trying to set up separate republics on the Rhine and in south Germany (Bavaria with Austria), detached from the Reich.

25. Literally, bankruptcy, but idiomatically meaning 'The Mess' or moral bankruptcy.

26. Wilhelm Reinhardt, one of the first collectors of troops loyal to the government, which about this time began to be called Free Corps.

27. Kessler means the Prussian tradition of service to the state and King; he does not mean the 'decadent' form of Prussianism typified by the former Emperor, which he hated.

28. 'Fort Eichhorn' was the working-class name for Police Headquarters during its Spartacus-Chief's time (Emil Eichhorn). After his removal by force, the Communists occupied the brewery referred to as their headquarters. Frankfurterallee in East Berlin was renamed after 1948 Stalinallee, and was the first part of East Berlin to be rebuilt in the Stalinist Russian style. It was the scene of the uprising in East Germany in 1953 when the building workers went on strike.

29. Max Reinhardt (1873–1943), the well known theatrical producer. He was noted for his spectacular productions, and for introducing the Expressionist playwrights to the public. He used two theatres in Berlin and built a third, finding traditional buildings not large enough for his ideas, some of which he adapted from Gordon Craig. Also co-founder with Hugo von

Hofmannsthal of the Salzburg Festivals. He went to the United States in 1933 and later worked in Hollywood as well as in the theatre there.

30. Albert Einstein (1879–1955), the great physicist. We have found no confirmation of this.

31. This is an example of the way opinions swung to and fro from hour to hour. If someone as politically able as Kessler was in such confusion little could be expected of those who had no idea of what was happening.

32. This was the short-lived Soviet republic of Béla Kun, a Bolshevik leader who held control in Hungary for 133 days from March to August 1919.

33. Count Michael Karolyi became Minister President of a separate Hungarian government on 1 November 1918 and was elected President of the first Hungarian Republic the following January. He was an idealistic socialist although a member of the high aristocracy; an unlucky politician, almost the same thing happened to him after the Second World War, but on that occasion he was forced to flee by the Red Army.

34. Walter Gropius (1883–1969), well-known architect, who directed the Bauhaus after 1918 and moved it to Dessau from Weimar in 1925. He was a leader of the functional style. Went to London in 1934 and to America in 1937.

35. Correspondent of the *Daily Mail*.

36. A tantalizing remark. Did Hutten-Czapski, a Polish-born diplomat, mean Kühlmann's part in the return of the Bolshevik leaders to Russia? Or the failure of the Foreign Office under his State Secretaryship to end the war in 1917?

37. The summons was to receive the conditions of peace, not for negotiation but for signature. This was news to all Germans. Up to this moment it was assumed that traditional diplomatic treaty negotiations would follow the issue of an Entente draft. Rantzau replied that he would send 'a Privy Councillor of the Foreign Ministry' to collect the terms; this was instantly refused and a deputation empowered to sign the terms was demanded. Rantzau with his colleagues then left for Paris.

38. Ignace Jan Paderewski (1860–1941), a Polish pianist who briefly became head of the new Polish independent government in 1919 and again (in exile) in 1941. His great fame and popularity as an artist gave him also great influence with the Peace Conference, as this reference shows.

39. Sign the Peace Treaty, that is. The ubiquitous Erzberger was a member of the German Delegation to Versailles.

40. Erzberger had claimed to have good contacts with the French and British at Paris and particularly with an American Intelligence Officer then in Berlin, and to be able to influence the terms of the Peace Treaty. His self-importance landed him in serious difficulties, for people now believed his claims. He was murdered in 1921.

41. Dietrich Bethmann was a German diplomat in Vienna in 1914 when 'his cousin Theobald' was German Chancellor.

42. Count Czernin (1872–1932), the Austro-Hungarian foreign minister, was then suspected of having informed the German Emperor of the secret attempts at negotiated peace being made by the Austrian Court during 1917 through his indiscretion. This was probably a contemporary misjudgement, however. The occasion of this reference was the controversy about the declar-

ation of unrestricted submarine warfare, which Czernin among many others had no confidence in.

43. Cardinal Pacelli (later Pope Pius XII) tried desperately to end the war.
44. Presumably Kessler's account of travels to Mexico.
45. This parenthesis is the only indication we have that Kessler knew something of Helphand before he met him; if Helphand Parvus (the second half of the name was the pen-name under which Helphand contributed for years to revolutionary newspapers, etc.) really said this, it was a good indication of his increasing association with Ebert.

1920

1. Ferrucio Benvenuto Busoni (1866–1924), of half-German, half-Italian parentage, was internationally renowned as a pianist (début aged eight), teacher (Moscow, Berlin, Boston, etc.), arranger of music, opera composer (including *Doktor Faust*). Settled in Berlin in 1894, but during the First World War was director of the Bologna and, later, Zurich Conservatories. He died in Berlin.
2. Jacques was Kessler's elder nephew, the son of his sister Wilhelma and the Marquis de Brion; Kessler's heir.
3. Dr Wolfgang Kapp (1868–1922), an agricultural civil servant in East Prussia and a fanatic nationalist. As Kessler says, the putsch was a farce. Much of the international uproar was caused by the activity among the foreign Press of a Hungarian adventurer named Trebitsch-Lincoln, who had lived in England and been in trouble with the police there. Among many other wild rumours he began the story that the British were in favour of the putsch (entry for 16 March). This was the occasion on which General Seeckt made his famous remark: 'Soldier does not fire on soldier' when asked to meet the putschists with armed force. Seeckt was not anxious to precipitate civil war and wanted to keep the army out of civil disorders.
4. General Ludendorff, in fact, managed to keep out of responsibility at this time; his try at a putsch was to come later, in 1923, with Adolf Hitler in Munich. Lüttwitz, another General, did openly back Kapp; but it was not only reactionary soldiers who seized what at the time looked like an opportunity to grasp local power. At least two Social Democrats and a number of varied minor political figures became entangled in the crossed loyalties.
5. Alfred Kerr was a well known Berlin critic. Hölderlin was, of course, a famous poet. The song title means 'Ah! Did I But Know the Way Back.'
6. Riots in the Ruhr had induced the German government to move troops there. But it was a stupid move, for the French occupation troops retaliated by occupying Frankfurt am Main which was not strictly part of the occupied area. This was the first time that French attitudes were publicly criticized by their allies.
7. Without approving of profiteers it is only fair to point out that the Peace Treaty forbade import restrictions and Germany was well supplied with foreign luxuries while millions were starving.
8. *Femebund* was an underground group which 'condemned' people to death in

secret and committed a number of murders. The origin of the word seems to have meant tribal courts of honour in the Dark Ages. The modern victims were politicians who advocated the fulfilment of the Peace Treaty. The *Feme* groups showed strong, irrational anti-Semitic feelings.

9. Ferdinand Lassalle (1825–64), founder of the German Workers' Movement and enemy of Bismarck. His party joined together with the Social-Democratic Party of Germany led by August Bebel (1840–1913) and Wilhelm Liebknecht in 1875.

10. General Hans von Seeckt (1866–1936) was Chief of Staff, although legally the post could not exist under the Versailles Treaty, to the German Army from 1919 to his retirement in 1926. The organization of the Black Reichswehr is generally supposed to have been his work, but by definition this was and is hard to establish. It was Seeckt who as Military Governor after the Hitler–Ludendorff putsch, banned the NSDAP and the KPD; an uncompromising supporter both of the old Army tradition and of the lawful organization of the nation, he accepted the Republic without much personal enthusiasm. His real loyalty was, like most professional soldiers, to the Army and he looked upon the preservation and continuity of the Army as his life-work.

11. Berger was a senior civil servant in the Prussian Interior Ministry. It is not clear in the original at what date Brussilov made his prediction about the Polish–Russian war of 1920. Brussilov was Russian Commander in Chief under Kerensky in 1917 and volunteered to serve in the newly formed Red Army under the Soviet government, when the Poles attacked in the Ukraine. The Poles won the war, but their victory brought them little fortune.

12. Maximilian Harden was a well-known journalist who is discussed in a later note to the entry of 27 March 1927.

13. Fritz von Holstein (1837–1909), assistant under-secretary at the Foreign Ministry for many years, who had an influence on German foreign policy in the nineteenth century out of proportion to his position, but probably not as great as his many enemies alleged. He was a recluse and a constant intriguer.

14. Kessler was supposed to be cultural attaché in Berne but his main job was to sound out French attitudes to peace feelers; he also negotiated there with the Russian revolutionaries. Unfortunately these years of the diaries are not available.

1921

1. Tilla Durieux, one of the most famous actresses of the German-speaking world, whose career spanned this century. The present editor saw her play only a year or so ago in Berlin.

2. The Vatican still existed at this time on the basis of a guarantee of protection by the Italian State. This proved unworkable under the Fascist government and the Vatican City became a neutral City State, its head the Pope, in 1929.

3. Kessler was bi-lingual and people would not know he was a German.

4. Caillaux was a pre-war French politician who was accused of corruption. His wife shot a newspaper editor who attacked her husband.

5. The great dancer was the original choice for the part of Joseph in *The Legend of Joseph*. He briefly rehearsed the role during the Russian Ballet's tour of South America in August 1913. Owing to his quarrel with Diaghilev, the company's famous impresario, he was replaced by the very young, wholly unknown Miässin who was subsequently to become known all over the world as the dancer and choreographer Leonide Massine. In March 1914 Nijinsky performed in London with a company of his own and this must have been the occasion of Hoesch's efforts on Kessler's behalf. (See also note on entry for 1 February 1930.)

1922

1. The Pope in question was Benedict XV. Kessler's incisive pen-picture is perhaps somewhat less than fair to the Pontiff, who in August 1917 appealed to the warring powers for a cessation of hostilities and in May 1920 published an encyclical admonishing the world to resist the perpetuation of old hatreds by the addition of false accusations.

2. Rathenau was appointed Foreign Minister on 1 January 1922. He was the object of hatred by the extreme right wing who considered him a traitor for trying to fulfil the Versailles Treaty, an attitude compounded by his Jewishness. In fact, Rathenau was an idealistic nationalist, passionately devoted to Germany.

3. At a meeting at Boulogne Raymond Poincaré, the French Prime Minister, tried to force on Lloyd George a defence treaty specifically directed against Germany. Lloyd George diplomatically accepted the idea of a treaty, but not directed against any one country and with many reservations. It was believed at the time, however, that he agreed with Poincaré.

4. Josef Wirth was appointed Chancellor in 1921. But he was also for a time Finance Minister.

5. Emil Ludwig enjoyed a great vogue during the twenties as the author of popular biographies. In the English-speaking world *Napoleon* was his best-known work, but in Germany he ensured his reputation with *Bismarck*. This is the point of the anecdote recounted in the entry for 5 October 1928.

6. Snobbish joke. 'Wirt' is German for host or innkeeper.

7. Play by Gerhart Hauptmann (1862–1946), based on a theme similar to Christopher Sly in *The Taming of the Shrew*.

8. Contacts with the Russians were, of course, not begun here. The first agent who tried to form economic bonds to post-war Germany was Karl Radek, and while he was actually imprisoned in Berlin he was visited not only by several generals, but by Rathenau. The British proposal for aid to Russia contained controls as to how the aid was to be used and was therefore unacceptable to the Soviet government.

9. Dr Giannini, a former financial counsellor at the Italian Embassy in London. He played a large part in the preparations for the Genoa Conference.

10. Sanctions against Germany, for making a unilateral treaty with the Russians.

11. Alexander Moissi (1879–1935), a famous actor with a controversial reputation, the favourite of Max Reinhardt in classical parts. Joanna Terwin was his wife.

12. These sentences were added later.

13. Helfferich, a speaker for the Nationalist Party on foreign affairs, and a pathological chauvinist, attacked Rathenau scurrilously; he was not an anti-Semite, in fact, but used any weapon that could damage his opponent Rathenau, whom he saw as destroying Germany. His speeches were taken as literal suggestions by the thugs who killed the Foreign Minister.

14. Organization E may be a mistake in reading the original, because Erhardt's organization was 'Organization Consul', or C. The Berlin police quickly found the murderers, one of whom was killed upon arrest. Others received various sentences, but on this and other occasions the real criminals went unpunished, the actual killers being ignorant and stupid young men. This misuse of the Law for political reasons was a potent factor in the undermining of Weimar. The public prosecutor of a vigorous government of whatever colour would have rejected the often derisory sentences for such crimes; but the governments of Weimar were all impotent.

15. Ernst Toller, an Expressionist playwright who had considerable success in the twenties. He was a member of the Soviet 'Government' of Bavaria, but saw that the attempt was ridiculous or perhaps that he was no politician, and resigned before the collapse of the Councils and the military overthrow of the communists. All his plays were revolutionary in context.

16. Edward Gordon Craig (1872–1966), the son of Ellen Terry, was a notoriously difficult man to work with. Kessler had tried to engage him for Max Reinhardt but the project failed over Craig's immoderate financial demands.

17. Konrad Adenauer (1876–1967), then Mayor of Cologne, later the first Chancellor of the Federal Republic of Germany.

18. Gerhard Hauptmann's sixtieth birthday. He was one of the new 'realist' playwrights of the Ibsen school and then the most famous German in the literary world. His plays are still constantly staged in Central Europe but he is almost unknown in the English-speaking world.

19. Samuel Fischer (1859–1934), the famous publisher. As his publisher, he organized the celebration for the 'Republican' Hauptmann and apparently was accepted by the reactionary members of the University although he was Jewish as well as Republican. He was one of the most beloved men of his time.

20. Count Stürghk (1847–1916), Minister President of Austria, murdered in 1916 by the Austrian Socialist politician Friedrich Adler.

21. Techow drove the car in which Rathenau's murderers went to the assassination.

1923

1. Erik Satie (1866–1925), son of a French father and Scotch mother, both composers, abandoned his studies at the Paris Conservatory after only a year,

became a café pianist and composer for a Montmartre song-writer and music-hall singer, and was a friend of Debussy. At thirty-one he returned for three years to the serious study of music. *Socrate*, first performed in 1920, was a symphonic drama with texts translated from Plato's *Dialogues*, but was not intended for stage performance.

2. François Poulenc (1899–1963), was influenced by Satie and orchestrated some of his piano works. He, Georges Auric and Darius Milhaud (born 1899 and 1892 respectively; see entry for 1 June 1926), and Arthur Honegger (1892–1925) were the outstanding members of *Les Six*, the name given to a temporary association of composers said to be inspired in part by the ideas of Jean Cocteau.

3. Misia Sert was of Polish–Russian origin, a patron of the arts and a woman of great personal charm. Her life was ruled by personal passions, her own and others for her. She left her first husband for what would now be called a tycoon, Alfred Edwards, who, in spite of being British, founded the newspaper *Le Matin* and owned a Paris theatre. He in his turn was abandoned for Jose-Maria Sert, a Spanish sculptor. Sert dominated her life for many years and then left Misia for a much younger Georgian, Roussandana Mdivani; all changes being accompanied by extravagant dramas.

4. The remark by Thomson has a legal significance not immediately obvious to civilians. A soldier is lawfully entitled to disagree with an order and even to say so. He commits a military offence if he conspires with other soldiers to do so in unison. That is mutiny. The events referred to are usually known as the Curragh Affair.

5. Count Albrecht Bernstorff was at the German Embassy in London from 1922 until 1933, when he was forced to retire from the German Foreign Service. He was murdered by the Nazis in 1945.

6. Cuno was the latest Chancellor, from September 1922 to August 1923. From December 1922 to the next year the international crisis over reparations went from bad to worse. The French and British could not agree, but Belgium and Italy backed France in demanding measures to ensure the deliveries of goods-reparations. Poincaré, perhaps not seriously, demanded that business funds of German companies should be sequestrated by the Reich government to pay reparations; this was a suggestion of far-reaching danger to business everywhere in the world, an unheard-of precedent. If anything was needed to finish the German mark, Poincaré then thought of it. He would send a team of investigators to the Ruhr to find out why coal deliveries were late, on the perfectly true excuse that timber deliveries were overdue, in breach of the Peace treaty. Of course, the coal owners promptly removed themselves and their files out of the area, to Hamburg. At the same time everyone agreed that the German government could both keep up deliveries and stop the Inflation if it wished. This was a fallacy; first the government was too unstable to make a decision on reform of the currency; second, it would not have worked in the state of public insecurity; third, nobody in Germany could see any sense in plunging themselves into yet greater trouble to please their foreign tormentors. Two Anglo-French conferences were held with their other allies, excepting America, and failed even to examine their various suggestions; that of Germany was not looked at. During the summer the

French decided to work the Ruhr mines by force. There was instant and complete non-co-operation by the workers and for a few days all Germany was united in opposition to France. The mark ceased to have any measurable value. Historians agree that Germany could have delivered the missing wood and coal, but they also agree that Poincaré would have found some other reason for entering the Ruhr. In London the Prime Minister, Bonar Law, was too vague and inexperienced to grasp the nettle and everyone in ruling positions who was not weak or helpless was at the time practically mentally unsound.

Money reparations were also in default to France and the other Allies, so they could not pay their debts to Britain and Britain could not pay the United States. The British Government then fell, and elections brought Labour to office but not to power. The Americans introduced a little common sense into the insane situation and a financier named Dawes was appointed to devise a compromise. He separated the German State Bank from the Government, set up an industrial consortium as mortgage for the first stage of reparations payments, privatized the railways and appointed them and certain customs dues as guarantors of future payments. For the first time reparations payments were definitely fixed and so were procedures to be followed in case of default (in order to prevent the French again acting unilaterally). Finally, a large loan was offered to Germany to re-establish the currency on the gold standard and this was done in November 1923. This set the pattern for the next two years. Germany was loaned nearly as much money as she paid in reparations, but the moral and psychological damage was done, and the structure of ownership of every kind was hopelessly disrupted.

7. Sir John Simon, of the Liberal Party, then in opposition.

8. This refers to the Senate of Hamburg, a city noted rather for stolidity than flare.

9. The first mention of Adolf Hitler (1889–1945); the foregoing analysis shows better than anything the chaotic state of the country and the impossibility of the government's enforcing order.

1924

1. A former Imperial officer in control of a 'working Company' (that is, part of the Black Reichswehr) staged an attempt to capture the garrisons at Küstrin and Spandau, just outside Berlin. From this time, at the latest, the Army High Command and Government must have known that parts of the Army were basically disloyal. Certainly the police knew; the illicit army organizers were at daggers drawn with the Prussian and other North German police forces. Otto Gessler, who took over the Defence Ministry from Noske in 1920 and was in office until 1928, maintains in his memoirs that he knew nothing.

1925

1. Eric Gill (1882–1940), sculptor, typographer and engraver. He collaborated with Kessler on several books. Now chiefly remembered by the public for his high-relief statuary of Ariel for Broadcasting House, London, and the Stations of the Cross in Westminster Cathedral.
2. He became the Mayor of East Berlin after the Second World War. The Reichsbanner was the defence force of the SPD.
3. August Wilhelm was a younger son of the ex-Emperor, who later became a Nazi; but in any case Kessler was a firm Republican.
4. Regina Deutsch was an old friend of Walther Rathenau's. Kessler was pursuing his researches for the biography of Rathenau.
5. Brigadier-General J. H. Morgan, of the Inspection Commission, author of *Assize at Arms*.
6. Kessler's claim that Hudson procured him a seat inside the strict precincts of the Chamber is remarkable and is difficult to reconcile with the rules and traditions of the House of Commons. The phrase should in any case be 'below the gangway', an illustration of Kessler's fluent but not always impeccable use of English.
7. The Rhineland, it will be recalled, was occupied by French and British forces, the latter being centred on Cologne. The US Senate had refused to ratify the Versailles Treaty without modifications, one of which concerned the occupation of the Rhineland, so that no American troops were stationed there. The British contingent was a token force.
8. The proposal was for all the borders of the contracting countries to be guaranteed; this would include Germany's eastern borders and nobody was inclined to guarantee them since they were in effect wide open and the Reichswehr – even with its secret reserves – was quite inadequate to protect them. There had been general movement all over these borders since 1914 and although they were then to remain as they were until 1938, nobody knew that at the time.
9. Instead of his correct title, 'Herr Reichtagspräsident', that is, Chairman of the House, or Speaker of the House of Commons or House of Representatives.

1926

1. The Conference of Locarno, September–October 1925, was the result of long quiet negotiations in previous years and settled frontiers in the west. It was a triumph for the steady, unspectacular opposition of the London Foreign Office towards French and German intransigence. Both Poland and Czechoslovakia were included in the arrangements. This was a moment of hope which gave Europe a breathing space. The results were excellent and if they had been given time might have proved lasting. The World Economic Crisis beginning in 1929 cut the progress short.

2. The great actress was Cassirer's wife. They had separated shortly before.

3. Georg Büchner (1813–37), wrote *Woyzeck* in 1836. He was one of the naturalist school, reacting against the classic declamatory theatre. Both this and another play of his, *Death of Danton*, have been made into operas. *Woyzeck* was produced as *Wozzeck* in Berlin in 1925, the music by Alban Berg, and *Danton* was composed later by Gottfried von Einem.

4. *Les Poseuses.*

5. Karl Gustav Volmoeller was at that time a very well known and successful playwright. His pantomime or spectacle, *The Miracle*, was a 'smash hit' in England and the United States as well as Germany. Diana Duff-Cooper (Lady Norwich) took part in it for years as the Virgin Mary. The original production was by Max Reinhardt. It was called *Achtes Wunder der Jungfrau Maria* in German.

6. The highest of German orders, having military and civil sections.

7. Elsa Brändström was the daughter of the Swedish Ambassador to (Tsarist) Petrograd. She devoted herself to the relief of suffering among the thousands of German and Austrian prisoners of war who were abandoned and cut off from their homelands, and often from every kind of supply, by the Russian revolution and by the consequences of defeat in their own countries. She enjoyed a reputation in central and northern Europe similar to that in nineteenth-century England of Florence Nightingale.

8. Paul von Schwabach was a banker. One of his daughters was married to Edvard von der Heydt, also a well-known banker and art collector (see entries for 19 May 1926 and 9 December 1931).

9. Germany's entrance into the League of Nations.

10. Otto Dix (1891–1969) painted with a ruthless realism deriving from his experiences during the First World War and the subsequent turbulent events. Less extravagant in manner than George Grosz, he was very close to the *Neue Sachlichkeit* ('new objectivity') movement and a natural subject of hostility to the Nazis.

11. Carl Fürstenberg was a banker known for his *bons mots*. (See entry for 23 October 1927.)

12. Dr Hans Luther, Chancellor from January 1925–May 1926.

13. 'A hair in the soup' is a German idiom for anything socially out of order.

14. The Italian princess after whom this ship was named suffered a horrible fate. She was married to Prince Philip of Hesse, a Nazi, who was used on diplomatic missions in Italy by Hitler. After Mussolini's fall (July 1943) they were both arrested as a preventive measure against treachery such as that against his fellow-dictator. She was killed in an Allied air-raid on Buchenwald where she is reported to have been imprisoned in the camp brothel.

15. Ramon Lull, a Catalan philosopher 1234–1316, the writer of a number of didactic novels as well as other works; philosophically he inspired Leibniz. Some of his books were printed by Caxton.

16. In December 1925 General Primo de Rivera's military dictatorship was, after two years, formally brought to an end by his appointment as Prime Minister. Catalonia's desire for autonomy and the radical sympathies of its industrial population were two of the principal issues of the day.

17. Hugo von Hofmannsthal (1874–1929) was one of the finest writers in

the German language of his time. The disappearance of the whole society and its ruling class, in Austria, of which he wrote, has removed his influence. He is known to English-speaking readers as the librettist of Richard Strauss's operas, notably *Der Rosenkavalier*. This, though not his most important writing, is quite able to stand by itself, either as poetry or as a play; there are even critics who maintain that Strauss's music vulgarized the work of Hofmannsthal. It was Harry Kessler who lent Hofmannsthal a French eighteenth-century romance from which a light opera had already been taken and while they were staying at Weimar, where Kessler wished Hoffmannsthal to become director of the theatre, they worked out the story of *Rosenkavalier* together. They had already been through 'coolnesses' before, notably in disagreeing about Gordon Craig, and when the opera was written a disagreement over the acknowledgements on the title page caused a serious estrangement. An open breach was avoided but they never recovered the spontaneity of real friendship again. Helene von Nostitz first met Hofmannsthal before the war in Kessler's house and they were close friends during the time her husband was a diplomat in Vienna.

18. 'Successor States' was the term applied after 1918 to Czechoslovakia, Yugoslavia, Poland, and Rumania as heirs to territories of the former Austro-Hungarian Empire containing national minorities.

19. Constant Lambert (1905–51), who was still a student at the Royal College of Music when Diaghilev commissioned the ballet from him.

20. Nicolas (originally, Nicolai) Nabokov, the composer, born in 1913 in Russia, pupil of Busoni and a cousin of Vladimir Nabokov, the author.

21. Ignaz Seipel (1876–1932), a priest who became Chancellor of Austria for most of the twenties. He was passionately hated by the Socialists, and almost died in 1924 after being shot. His historical importance lies in his bringing the Church directly into Party politics, a major misfortune for his country.

22. Arnolt Bronnen, a playwright and poet of extreme nationalist views.

23. The reference is to a plebiscite organized by the SPD with the cooperation of the Communists which, if effective, would have dispossessed the former ruling princes with no compensation.

24. The Charité was the biggest hospital in Berlin – now in East Berlin.

1927

1. The gossip here is one of those politico-social scandals that shake capital cities from time to time. Prince Phillip zu Eulenburg was an admirer of Emperor Wilhelm II, and was attacked in print by an admirer of Bismarck's (who died in 1898). This was in 1907 and the journalist was Maximilian Harden, the stage name of the son of a silk merchant called Wittkowsky, who moved from acting to journalism and became one of the most feared and hated men of his time. In his own newspaper *Zukunft* ('Future') he inveighed against 'violet-scented courtiers' about the Emperor, who were undoing Bismarck's life work, foremost among them Eulenburg, a diplomat. The family of Moltke, the victor of the Franco–Prussian war, was dragged in and the member of the family named went through four lawsuits against Harden

who combined class feeling with loyalty to Bismarck and thoroughly enjoyed the whole affair. These lawsuits ensured a continuing publicity but the trial of Eulenburg came first when he was accused of perjury in that he denied homosexuality. But the trial never finished because the Prince collapsed and was counted unfit to plead. The other trials were civil actions for slander and libel. Harden spared nobody in his efforts to avenge Bismarck (he was, it was clear, in reality attacking the Emperor) and anyone who knew Eulenburg or his friends went in fear and trembling for months. The only one who knew nothing was the Emperor Wilhelm and when his heir explained what the whole matter was about he dropped his admirer instantly. Fifteen years later, Harden was beaten up by Nationalist hooligans as recounted in the entry of 4 July 1922.

2. The founding Monastery of the Benedictine Order, built by Benedict of Norcia in AD 529. It was self-sufficient and the monks no longer wandered about begging their bread. This stability was the beginning of the great influence of monastic orders in the medieval church. There was an international controversy when the monastery, in its later form, was destroyed in 1943 by Allied artillery.

3. Leipzig was the centre from the early Middle Ages of, among other trades, the German book trade. Today it is in East Germany. By 'me' Kessler means the Cranach Press.

4. *The Robbers*, Schiller's first play, was romantically revolutionary. *Clavigo* was by Goethe, and so was *Wilhelm Meister*.

5. Probably *Hamlet in Wittenberg* by Hauptmann.

6. Till Eulenspiegel is an archetypal figure in German, seen by Hauptmann as rejecting, rather than being rejected by, bourgeois society. The writer is repeating his social, even revolutionary, theme of *Before Sunrise*, *The Weavers*, etc. in a fresh form.

7. Gerhart Hauptmann was susceptible to young girls, and there were a number of 'affairs' which swung between wild emotion and middle-class concern for his public reputation. Of these perhaps his infatuation with the actress Ida Orloff is the best known 'secret'. His egocentricity makes these stories comical, which is not to say that Hauptmann was not a great playwright.

8. Alexander Humboldt was a naturalist and traveller. His brother Wilhelm founded Berlin University after the Napoleonic Wars. This is now in East Berlin and called Humboldt University to distinguish it from the Free University in West Berlin, built by American funds after the Second World War.

9. Conrad Ferdinand Meyer (1825–90) was one of the outstanding German-language Swiss novelists of the nineteenth century.

10. Two Italian anarchists condemned to death in the United States for murder and robbery in 1920. The delay in execution as well as the sentence created widespread disgust. Their guilt was strongly doubted and it was believed that the verdict was politically motivated: that is, that they were executed because of their belief in anarchy.

11. Another version of this anecdote declares that the dancer made the same proposal to George Bernard Shaw. 'But, my dear Isadora,' he retorted, 'suppose the child had my body and your brains.'

12. W. H. Hudson (1841–1922), and R. B. Cunninghame Graham (*sic*, Kessler's

spelling is mistaken) (1852–1936) were popular contemporary essayists and novelists, but represented very different outlooks. Hudson was more interested in the plant and animal life which formed the background to his works; Cunninghame Graham was a romantic and admirer of heroic action. What they had in common was their use of the South American scene and a love of nature.

13. A German prince, Wilhelm von Wied, was elected to the throne of Albania in 1914 after its freedom was won from Turkish rule.

14. Piscator (Erwin Fischer) was director of the Volksbühne (People's Stage) 1925–7. He believed in a proletarian theatre as a weapon in the class war, but, in spite of theories which do not go well with the theatre, was a producer of genius. He returned to Berlin many years later, still fighting the class war, and was the original producer of Rolf Hochhuth's *The Representative* among other successes.

15. Cf. entry for 5 May 1930, p. 385.

16. Kessler closed his Rathenau biography with the text of this letter: 'In my inexpressible grief I hold out my hand to you, most pitiable of women. Tell your son that, in the name and spirit of he who was murdered, I forgive him, and may God forgive him if he makes full and frank confession to the human tribunal and repents before the divine. Had he known my son, he would sooner have turned the fatal weapon on himself than on the noblest being that walked this earth. May these words bring peace to your soul. Mathilde Rathenau.'

1928

1. Wirth, then Finance Minister, took the two greatest industrialists in Germany, Stinnes and Rathenau, as advisers with him to the first conference with the Entente over reparations held at Spa in Belgium, July 1920. Stinnes, in suggesting 'Bolshevization', meant that the Entente should be allowed to invade Germany and reduce it to chaos rather than try to fulfil the demands of the Versailles Treaty.

2. The reference to the Russians makes it clear that it was the course of events at the Genoa Conference in 1922 that was under discussion. The passage also shows how close Kessler still was to the Foreign Ministry.

3. The Briand–Kellogg Pact, meant to outlaw war 'for ever', was signed on 27 August 1928 at Paris by Belgium, Czechoslovakia, France, Germany, Great Britain, Italy, Japan, Poland, and the United States. In Washington the Senate approved the Pact with the reservation that 'Should any signatory violate the terms . . . there is no obligation . . . upon the other signers . . . to engage in punitive or coercive measures.'

4. A battle between Germanic tribes in AD 451 during the breakdown of the Roman Empire and the Great Migrations which repopulated all Western Europe. Valmy was the site of the cannonade in 1792 which effectually ended the first Prussian and Austrian monarchies to help Louis XVI against the revolutionaries. Goethe witnessed this use of artillery tactics; it formed his entire later view of politics. At the Marne in 1914 the French Army stopped

the German advance on Paris, which began the static warfare that lasted until 1918.

5   Literally, 'Threepenny Opera', the German version of *The Beggar's Opera* which made Brecht's name. Some of the tunes by Kurt Weill, notably 'Mackie Messer', are still sung.

6. Otto Brahm, first critic and then theatre producer, introduced many of the realist playwrights to Berlin, including Hauptmann.

7. Lion Feuchtwanger's name was familiar abroad as author of the historical novels *The Ugly Duchess* and *Jew Süss*, but he also wrote a notable *roman-à-clef* about the chaos of contemporary political affairs in Germany.

8. Bertolt Brecht (1898–1956) was then not famous except for *Dreigroschenoper*. Arnold Bronnen was another controversial playwright of the twenties, like Brecht extreme in politics, but to the right. He is described in the entry of 16 June 1926.

9. The Empress Frederick was William II's mother and daughter of Queen Victoria. The ferocity of Kessler's hatred of the former Emperor is startling: after all, it was ten years since his downfall but perhaps the date of the entry has something to do with it.

10. Roland de Margerie was the son of the French ambassador to Berlin and later himself a distinguished French diplomat *en poste* in London and ultimately ambassador in Bonn.

1929

1. Victoria (Vita) Sackville-West, the poet.

2. Yehudi Menuhin was thirteen at this date. His Berlin début took place two years earlier.

3. Joseph Joachim (1831–1907), to whom Brahms dedicated his Violin Concerto, was the most famous violinist of his day.

4. Hans von Bülow was a great orchestral conductor of the end of the nineteenth century. His wife Cosima left him for Richard Wagner whom she eventually married. Bülow then married again. Johann Strauss was the composer of *Fledermaus*, one of the most enchanting light operas ever written.

5. A moving letter from Strauss, dated 16 July, to Gerty von Hofmannsthal explained that he was mentally too shattered and physically unwell to be able to attend the funeral.

6. Max Goertz, Kessler's colleague at the Cranach Press. The letter to him from Hofmannsthal reads almost as if the poet knew he was dying. A letter from Richard Strauss also exists, to Kessler, blaming Franz Hofmannsthal for dragging his sensitive father into death with him.

7. The re-written first act of *Arabella* is mentioned with grief in the above letter. The composer praises it and promises the opera as a memorial to the poet.

8. By Immanuel Kant (1724–1804), the great German philosopher, of fundamental importance for the ideas of the nineteenth century.

9. This novel of the First World War made its unknown author world famous, and its title, taken from a phrase used frequently in army communiqués, has passed into our own language, summarizing the terrible suffering of that war.

In German its title is *Im Westen Nichts Neues,* and it is still considered a great novel. Remarque later went to Hollywood.

10. Arnold Zweig was also a pacifist writer, hence his envy of the immediate success of 'the amateur'. Not to be confused with Stefan Zweig, an Austrian writer whose immense popularity was ended, like Remarque's by the Nazis four years later.

11. Philip Snowden was then Chancellor of the Exchequer in London. The reference is to the various negotiations about reparations during 1929 and 1930 in the League of Nations and at the two Hague conferences which issued in the Young Plan. This revised the Dawes Plan for reparations and in effect ended them, since 25 October 1929 was the day of the great Stock Exchange crash in New York. Julius Curtius was for a short time German Foreign Minister. The death of perhaps the greatest political talent in Germany at this time, Stresemann, was probably a major factor in the subsequent lack of drive and clear purpose in Berlin where politics degenerated into a tangle of intrigue, constant elections and violence during the mass unemployment period.

12. The future ownership of sequestrated German property abroad was part of the complicated reparations negotiations.

13. At the German Embassy.

14. Prince Lichnowsky was Imperial German ambassador in London in 1914. Sir Edward Grey was British Foreign Secretary. The reference is to Grey, as Shaw and Kessler believed, being dangerously one-sided in his pro-French views.

15. Brioni is a small island in the Northern Adriatic, once Austrian, later Italian, now Yugoslav and the summer home of President Tito.

16. An example of the intransigent attitudes often taken to Germany during this period.

17. Then at the British Embassy in Berlin. This is a strange little tale of intrigue. Why should Kessler have inspired a publication that was an insult to himself personally and a denial of the hopes held out to him by Snowden of further negotiations on a subject of great importance to public opinion in Germany? Nicolson did indeed go beyond his instructions, as he told Kessler a week later, but this reason for his doing so does not seem likely.

18. Hjamlar Schacht (1877–1970) was President of the State Bank and Hilferding the Finance Minister. The Reichsbank was worried about the huge government deficit, which already approached bankruptcy. Schacht resigned three months later, bringing the government, for the sixteenth time since 1919, down with him.

19. This was in October 1908. In the jockeying for position in the Balkans after the Austro–Hungarian annexation of Bosnia-Herzogovina, the Russians tried to induce the British to agree to an advance on their part towards the Bosphorus.

20. The reference is to Kessler's account of the Genoa Conference in *Rathenau.* Lloyd George evidently believed that it was the distrust felt by the French after Genoa that caused the Ruhr occupation. This is unlikely; the distrust was strongly present even before Genoa and the whole Ruhr quarrel was about non-delivery of reparations, and the efforts of the French to detach

the Rhineland from Germany, the Ruhr being immediately north of the Rhineland proper and of immense industrial importance.

1930

1. Lady Cunard and half the *haut monde* of London and Paris were involved for several years in interminable fascinating and, in the end, tragic quarrels over Diaghilev and Nijinsky. The reference here is to Nijinsky having been the original choice for the title part in *The Legend of Joseph*. He left the company just as rehearsals were beginning.

2. Princess Pauline Metternich (1836–1921), wife of the Austrian ambassador to the court of Napoleon III, intimate friend of the Empress Eugénie, and an ardent champion of Richard Wagner before this became the fashion, was well-known for her beauty and wit. Her life-long promotion of charitable causes earned her the nickname 'Our Dear Lady of Vienna'.

3. Lord Berners (1883–1950), composer of ballets, a comic opera, and songs, all with an ironic touch, was also an author, diplomat, and painter. *The Wedding Bouquet*, a ballet with words by Gertrude Stein, was produced at Sadler's Wells Theatre, London, in 1937, with settings designed by himself. The terms 'balletomane' and 'balletomania' are attributed to him.

4. The *British* Government of India, at that time.

5. A slip on Kessler's part. Maillol was born in 1861.

6. Saxony was a 'Red' area, because of the heavy industrialization, and Werewolves were a right-wing youth group. Both sides made a practice of demonstrating in areas where the other was strong.

7. Later Sir John Rothenstein, of the Tate Gallery in London.

8. Paul (called Tristan) Bernard (1866–1947) was a French playwright and novelist noted for his brilliant wit, and translator of George Bernard Shaw.

9. Alfred Hugenberg (1865–1951), a leader of the Nationalist Party (Deutschnationale), a former General Manager of Krupps, made a huge fortune in the inflation and used it to buy propaganda media. He owned a Berlin newspaper and controlled UFA, the largest German film company. His political importance lay in his steady opposition to the 'Treaty fulfilment' policies of successive governments. He joined forces, at first informally, with the Nazis and in 1931 made a formal alliance with them, thinking of this as a temporary expedient and believing that he could control his partners through his wealth.

10. His mother was the great actress, Ellen Terry. The letters were published in 1931.

11. The Prussian Government, like those of the other Provinces, or *Länder*, still existed. They were all abolished on 30 January 1934 in a Law for the New Construction of the Reich.

12. An example of how even the most intelligent can fall victim to flattering notions of themselves. First, Kessler could by no stretch of imagination be visualized as a Viennese. Second, Helene in Hofmannsthal's play is a virginal young girl who marries the central character, while any relationship other than friendship Kessler may conceivably have had with Helene Nostitz

would have had to be adulterous. Helene Thimig acted for many years in Max Reinhardt's productions and eventually married him as his second wife.

13. In December 1930 the official unemployment figure was 4.4 million. It later rose above six million in a population of sixty million.

1931

1. In December 1931 the unions and the various SPD organizations formed a joint *Reichsbanner*, hoping to create a more effective republican and Social Democratic alternative to the NSDAP and its SA (the SS was then only Hitler's personal guard). The Communists were forbidden by the Comintern to support the SPD in fights against the right-wing groups but in working-class districts like Neukölln this rule was increasingly broken.

1932

1. Duesterberg was the Stahlhelm (War Veterans) candidate and Thaelmann the Communist. The latter was later betrayed to the Gestapo by his own comrades and died in a concentration camp.

2. Newspaper reports of this kind of rumour were a daily occurrence at this time, which exacerbated the fears of normal people and the hopes of the extremists. Many of them were deliberately printed by the NSDAP paper, *Völkische Beobachter* (literally, 'People's Observer') in order to add to the confusion. There was no Hitler putsch planned; he meant to slip easily into the government. This he did, and this was the meaning of his various assurances that he would never use illegal methods; he knew he would not need to.

3. This resulted in the ban on party armies on 13 April 1932. Kessler's report of the analysis of this situation on 16 April was quite mistaken. Provincial Diet elections on 24 April showed increased Nazi votes, and in Prussia the SPD-led coalition, which had survived since 1925, fell, the NSDAP with the KPD (Communists) gaining an absolute majority in the Prussian Diet which they used together to bring down the strongest factor for order in the whole Reich, the stable government in Prussia.

General Kurt von Schleicher was a friend and adviser of President Hindenburg until 1932, and Chancellor from December 1932 to January 1933.

5. Hitler was not yet in the government, but this comment makes clear that his advent was expected at any moment. He refused the Vice Chancellorship in August. The Reichstag meanwhile had to be dissolved on a constitutional point and in the resulting elections on 6 November the Nazi vote dropped. Hitler then made up his mind that he must quickly take the next chance of entering the government before his support dropped further.

6. State Secretary to the Presidents from 1923 to 1945. His *Memoirs*, naturally an apologia, are of immense value for source detail, although not for judgements.

7. Wife of Carl von Ossietzky, a prominent pacifist publicist. He received the Nobel Prize after his imprisonment by the Nazis and was killed by them at the end of the war.

8. A working-class district of Hamburg.

9. The Prussian government referred to is the former cabinet, continuing in office until a new one can be found. The appointment of a High Commissioner instead of continuing the party conference to form a new cabinet was, of course, unconstitutional. The ban on party uniforms was lifted on 14 June. It is difficult at this date to decide from the conflicting contemporary accounts what Schleicher and von Papen intended. Both von Schleicher and von Papen were inexperienced in government.

10. Prince Metternich (1773–1859) was Chancellor of Austria from 1821 to 1848 when he was overthrown by the Revolution of 1848.

11. Severing, Klepper and Hirtsiefer were all ministers of the former Prussian government. Bracht, Mayor of Essen, was appointed by von Papen to the Prussian Interior Ministry.

12. The old Social Democratic symbol. Neukölln and Wedding are working-class districts.

13. 'A body-blow to German discord.' A famous line from *Florian Geyer*, the play by Gerhart Hauptmann.

14. *Michael Kramer*, produced in 1900, was one of Hauptmann's naturalistic dramas.

15. *The Prince of Homburg* by Heinrich von Kleist, which was written in 1811 under the influence of the liberation of Prussia from domination by Napoleon.

16. *Not* the play mentioned above; the first volume of Kessler's *Memoirs*, but they were not then published in Germany.

1933

1. Count Bernhard Bülow was publishing the papers of his uncle who was Chancellor to Emperor Wilhelm II from 1900 to 1909. He was himself a high official of the Foreign Ministry.

2. Eastern Aid (*Osthilfe*) was the name for state subsidies to the impoverished large estates of Prussia, which is reckoned as beginning roughly at the River Elbe. President Hindenburg's son and his friends and neighbours were involved in the administration of these funds and rumour had it that corruption in this administration was to be investigated.

3. Kessler's joke is that Wolff, a metal dealer, was Jewish.

4. The initial is in the original. It could be either Judge Simons or General Seeckt. Or some other guest at the dinner.

5. Old German expression for a fat, silly fellow, in carnival processions etc.

6. Samuel Fischer's son-in-law and partner. He too later left Germany.

7. It is not clear from the original whether this is a Republican flag (black-red-gold) or an old cavalry pennant, or even possibly some form of armorial bearing.

8. Modern Germans would not agree with this. It was at least partly the narrow legalistic attitudes of lawyers and politicians that allowed them to

continue in their positions under the Nazis. This now recognized error is called in German '*Rechtspositivismus*', which means the belief that what is law is right.

9. Then Austro-Hungarian Foreign Minister.

10. The playwright Ferdinand Bruckner, whose real name was Theodore Tagger. He was Jewish, a nuisance for the Nazis for his best-known play, a hostile portrait of Queen Elizabeth I, would otherwise have been welcome to them.

1935

1. Oldenburg-Januschau was one of the large East Prussian landowners. He and Hindenburg, like most country gentry, were no politicians, although they thought they were.

2. Papen was at the German Embassy in Washington until America entered the war in 1917. He was engaged in secret as well as purely diplomatic activities.

3. This, somewhat garbled, may refer to the odd little story of Hitler acquiring legal German citizenship in 1932 since he could not, it was tardily realized, hold office without establishing this point. Hitler was, it will be remembered, born in Austria and served in the First World War with the Bavarian Army.

1936

1. The show trials of Stalin's rivals began in 1935 and 1936. The Trial of the Sixteen was a contemporary expression for the first of these trials and Gide's fears of further purges were only too justified. The book in which Gide recounted his impressions of Russia became famous as *Return from the USSR*.

2. That is, in Franco's and therefore in pro-German hands.

Index